Models at Work

Global Financial Markets series

Global Financial Markets is a series of practical guides to the latest financial market tools, techniques and strategies. Written for practitioners across a range of disciplines it provides comprehensive but practical coverage of key topics in finance covering strategy, markets, financial products, tools and techniques and their implementation. This series will appeal to a broad readership, from new entrants to experienced practitioners across the financial services industry, including areas such as institutional investment; financial derivatives; investment strategy; private banking; risk management; corporate finance and M&A; financial accounting and governance; and many more.

Titles include:

Daniel Capocci
THE COMPLETE GUIDE TO HEDGE FUNDS AND HEDGE FUND STRATEGIES

Frances Cowell
RISK-BASED INVESTMENT MANAGEMENT IN PRACTICE (*2nd Edition*)
Practitioner's Guide to the Active Management of Credit Risks

Jawwad Ahmed Farid
MODELS AT WORK
A Practitioner's Guide to Risk Management

Guy Fraser-Sampson
INTELLIGENT INVESTING
A Guide to the Practical and Behavioural Aspects of Investment Strategy

Michael Hünseler
CREDIT PORTFOLIO MANAGEMENT
A Practitioner's Guide to the Active Management of Credit Risks

Ross K. McGill
US WITHHOLDING TAX
Practical Implications of QI and FATCA

David Murphy
OTC DERIVATIVES, BILATERAL TRADING AND CENTRAL CLEARING
An Introduction to Regulatory Policy, Trading Impact and Systemic Risk

Gianluca Oricchio
PRIVATE COMPANY VALUATION
How Credit Risk Reshaped Equity Markets and Corporate Finance Valuation Tools

Andrew Sutherland and Jason Court
THE FRONT OFFICE MANUAL
The Definitive Guide to Trading, Structuring and Sales

Michael C. S. Wong and Wilson F. C. Chan (*editors*)
INVESTING IN ASIAN OFFSHORE CURRENCY MARKETS
The Shift from Dollars to Renminbi

Global Financial Markets series
Standing Order ISBN: 978–1137–32734–5

You can receive future titles in this series as they are published by placing a standing order. Please contact your bookseller or, in case of difficulty, write to us at the address below with your name and address, the title of the series and the ISBN quoted above.

Customer Services Department, Macmillan Distribution Ltd, Houndmills, Basingstoke, Hampshire RG21 6XS, England

---

Models at Work

A Practitioner's Guide to Risk Management

Jawwad Ahmed Farid

First published 2014 by
PALGRAVE MACMILLAN

Palgrave Macmillan in the UK is an imprint of Macmillan Publishers limited, registered in England, company number 785998, of Houndmills, Basingstoke, Hampshire RG21 6XS.

Palgrave Macmillan in the US is a division of St Martin's Press LLC, 175 Fifth Avenue, New York, NY 10010.

Palgrave Macmillan is the global academic imprint of the above companies and has companies and representatives throughout the world.

Palgrave® and Macmillan® are registered trademarks in the United States, the United Kingdom, Europe and other countries

ISBN: 978–1–137–37163–8

This book is printed on paper suitable for recycling and made from fully managed and sustained forest sources. Logging, pulping and manufacturing processes are expected to conform to the environmental regulations of the country of origin.

A catalogue record for this book is available from the British Library.

A catalog record for this book is available from the Library of Congress.

To Ammi, Aba & Fawzia.
For all the times when you should have said no, but said yes

Contents

Part II   Monte Carlo Simulation

List of Figures

Preface

Models at Work

I am not a Quant.

I always wanted to be one but it took a single meeting with Goldman's Firmwide risk team in London to clear any delusions I may have harbored. All remaining reservations were removed in the one PhD finance elective that I took with Maria Vassalou at Columbia. Despite Maria's kindness and dedication, it was obvious in April 1999 that I was just an ordinary mortal and not a Quant.

In 1999, the realization wasn't heart breaking. Even if one couldn't live in the exotic world of high finance, the less exalted levels in the banking and trading world offered enough to keep you engaged and happy as a professional.

But that was then. The last six years have shown that the impact of quantitative models travels beyond the inner circle of the more mathematically inclined amongst us. Imagine being a board member at a large bank or a financial institution; imagine the board meeting dossier filled with numbers and graphs that come with no cheat sheet or Rosetta Stone and then envisage the need for you, as a board member, to initial and certify it all with your name and reputation.

The challenge is that armed without a PhD in the subject or years of experience on the trading desk we are hopelessly lost when it comes to dissecting models at work. Even if one wants to learn there is little material available in a language that mortals can understand. The foundation of the field of risk management is based on well-aged sciences of mathematics and statistics. It is but natural that books heavy on mathematical and statistical treatment of the subject are common and abundant, while those relying on simple layperson language and do-it-yourself modeling in EXCEL are not.

Ideally, a book should introduce a framework for managing risk and follow it through with a number of real-world illustrative examples with numbers and data. If you are interested, it should allow you to build and test simple models that you can then use to strengthen your understanding of the conditions under which models can break down or predict where things can go wrong. A great text should educate you enough to not only ask the right questions but also evaluate and digest the answers provided.

Over the last decade, as we put together teaching notes for participants in our workshops for bankers, traders, treasurers and executive MBA students, we found that the above design on teaching risk management worked well. The challenge most professionals face is not with theoretical derivations but with practical applications in the real world.

What is this book about?

The book uses four sections to present frameworks, tools, cases and context around risk management. Here is a quick review of each section:

Part I   Risk

A framework for thinking about risk begins with an evaluation of complexity in analysis versus complexity in models. The chapters in this section start with an introduction to dealing with volatility, measuring risk using Value at Risk, managing risk using target accounts and ends with two short chapters on risk policy and risk regulation.

Part II   Monte Carlo Simulation

A multi-chapter crash course in Monte Carlo Simulation using a simplified approach in EXCEL. We begin with simple simulation models for generating prices for equities, currencies and commodities. The simple models are then used to build a second layer that evaluates the impact of changes in simulated prices on business and performance metrics. Building up on the complexity in analysis themes, while the models used are simple, the objective is to understand relationships that drive the risk distribution.

Part III   Fixed Income & Commodity Markets – Dissecting Pricing Models

Armed with frameworks and simple tools, the third section presents an opportunity to apply them. Rather than build models we focus on identifying relationships, drivers and data across commodity markets. Four cases are presented from the point of view of a research analyst. They include:
1.   Rolling volatility and correlations in commodity markets
2.   Drivers of crude oil and gold pricing
3.   The relationship between crude oil price shocks and inflation rates in emerging markets
4.   Real interest rates in India and Pakistan
To get the most out of the frameworks and tools presented in the first two sections, each case can be used as the foundation of a more detailed modeling exercise. For example in the two cases that cover drivers behind

crude oil and gold price changes we identify price drivers that are left as black boxes in the case. If you are interested, there is enough data in this section for you to replace the black boxes with your own models.

Part IV   Derivative Securities

A text on risk management cannot be complete without a review of the product universe, pricing and valuation models. While a more detailed treatment is available in Hull, Wilmott, Tuckman and Fabozzi, we attempt a short introduction to the product and pricing world to ensure the book remains self-contained for our audience. The decision to add the section was taken once we included the section on Monte Carlo Simulation, since many of the simulations exercises would remain incomplete without product and pricing context.

Who is this book for?

If you are looking for detailed mathematical derivations, differential equations or easy answers, you will be disappointed.

The book is about building intuition around risk and using simple tools to test that intuition against the real world. Taleb calls it "playing with the generator function". My mentors in the field have called it the "Build, Test, Dissect, Decode" mode of learning. Until you figure out how to break it, you won't really learn how it works.

The book shows you how to build models, shares the framework that you can use to test and stretch them and in some instances gives you the data to extend them. But it stops short of putting it all together. It will show you the way and partially unlock the door, but you have to make the effort to open it and walk inside.

This book is for you if you ever wondered about risk and its implications in the real world; if you wanted to model risk but felt awed by the terminology; if you like to question assumptions and test them; if your board is a "What if" board and you want to put a better process around their troubling questions; and if you wanted to be a quant, but like me, are not.

Happy reading.

Acknowledgments

The material for this book has been in a mental jar for about a decade and change. Without the contribution and support of a number of individuals it would still be there. I would like to thank:

Agnes Paul, Fellow of the Society of Actuaries and model builder, for having built, tested and validated almost all of the models presented in this book. The cases and the mathematical analysis in the commodity section also owe their existence to her commitment to data, models and analysis. If there is one person who should claim this book as much as I can, it would be Agnes.

Uzma Salahuddin, dedicated perfectionist, for being the editor at large during the last nine years of everything Agnes and I have written, printed or shared. She has seen this book grow from a few thousand words to its current form.

Paul Petty, a mentor and Executive Director at Goldman's Prime Brokerage desk showed me why, when it came to risk, it was important to write simply without numbers, formulas and complex equations. Without Paul, I would have not had an affair with risk, with models or the path that ultimately led to Alchemy.

Mark Broadie and Howard Corb, at Columbia Business School, for teaching us how much we didn't know about security pricing and Excel despite twenty odd cover-to-cover readings of John C. Hull and a decade of building complex Excel spreadsheets.

Maria Vassalou, for letting me be part of her PhD course on Continuous Time Finance at Columbia in my first term and laying the foundation that made it possible for me to teach and build risk models that worked for the next ten years.

Nassim Taleb and John C. Hull, for the twenty cover-to-cover readings and teaching us the importance of asking questions and building generator functions.

Sir Aziz Ullah, at BVS Parsi High School, for introducing us to the magic behind numbers, the art of teaching young children and inspiring us to become teachers ourselves.

And finally, my students, for asking difficult and awkward questions in Dubai, Abu Dhabi, Riyadh, Singapore, Kuala Lumpur, Bangkok, Bahrain, New York, Seattle and Karachi that made me go back to my models to dig up satisfactory answers. Without your questions and curiosity, there wouldn't be a book.

Any mistakes and errors remain mine.

About the Author

Jawwad Ahmed Farid has been building, selling and implementing risk models since 1999. Working with clients on four continents he has helped bankers, boards and regulators take a more practical approach to risk management.

He runs Alchemy Technologies, a risk consulting practice and writes about risk and treasury products at FinanceTrainingCourse.com. When he is not travelling for work he teaches risk and derivative pricing at the SP Jain School of Global management in Dubai and Singapore. Jawwad has an undergraduate degree in Computer Science from FAST ICS, an MBA from Columbia Business School and is a Fellow of the Society of Actuaries.

Part I
Risk

- Working with volatility
- Measuring risk
- Target accounts
- Building risk systems
- Why doesn't bank regulation work?

1
What Is Risk?

Risk is uncertainty. Risk is opportunity. Risk is misunderstood.

An uncertain outcome requires planning to manage the downside. Risk management is the field that specializes in managing the downside of uncertain outcomes.

Just like any other business process, risk management requires a combination of intuition and common sense, mixed with the right processes and controls. Intuition and common sense come with experience, while processes and controls are organizational design problems. How the above four elements are balanced determines the effectiveness of risk management. With the right mix the recipe works; take one element out of alignment and it stops functioning.

Is risk limited to just the financial services industry? Or are there broader applications that cross over beyond boundaries of markets and prices? If you are not a large bank or a hedge fund manager, do you still need to think about risk?

The truth is that we are tuned to think about risk at an intuitive level. We just have to look around ourselves to see that thinking at work.

Think about an important desired outcome such as attending a business meeting on time. To ensure you are not late (*negative outcome*), you will look up directions (*preparation*) and leave a little early (*prevention*) so that you can reach the appointment on time (*desired outcome*) or a little early (*preferred outcome*).

A few more examples on how we think about risk are given below:

(a) If you are stuck in traffic (uncertainty), you will look at alternate routes (management) or call ahead (hedging) to let your client know (managing expectations). The next time you head in the same direction you will adjust your behavior (learning and adaptability) based on how long it took you to finally get to your destination. If you make the same trip on a daily basis, your behavioral adjustments will fine-tune

3

themselves using average, likely and unlikely conditions (data set and probabilities). If there are powerful incentives (large business deal or a promotion) or penalties the game will change again depending on how you read and interpret them.

(b) What if you are a manufacturer, trader and supplier of goods? Apply the same principles to lock in costs before input prices rise to ensure that your margins are protected and remain within an acceptable range (*desired outcome*). If you run the sales function, how do you ensure revenues and profitability meet the year-end quota even if the average unit sale price falls?

(c) Think like a project manager for a large construction site. How do you ensure that you deliver on time and under budget (*desired outcome*)? What are the biggest challenges to these two desired outcomes? How do you track them? What are the possible causes of uncertainty that can derail your plans? How do you address them?

These are all applications of risk management. Some occur at an intuitive level, others involve tools and frameworks. The science is just an extension of the same.

Price volatility

Let's begin with a simple example: prices.

As traders[1], manufacturers of goods, construction site project managers or the heads of proprietary desks for banks, we all care about the movement of prices as well as their timing.

Price risk is not the only risk we are exposed to. It is, however, one that is easily quantifiable, using objective data (historical prices) and statistical models and tools (volatility and distribution). For that one reason it provides a great canvass for showcasing our risk management framework.

What do we know about price movement? Prices go up and down, as well as sideways. Once upon a time they used to move within reasonable ranges; occasionally you could factor in seasonality, and predict the direction and size of the movement. The modeled price ranges were factored in when you drew your budget.

Today prices move abruptly and without notice, ignoring budgets, quotas, reasonable historical behavior, profitability or economic impact. You can model supply and demand as well as market sentiment, but your model price will fail to track the actual market price on days that count.

Do price changes impact all of us the same way? If you trade on a daily basis and bring your investments down to zero when markets close, you care about price changes that occur during trading hours (intraday price movements). However, if you buy steel and concrete mix every week and are planning on buying it for the next two hundred weeks, do intraday price changes matter? They don't.

Unfortunately, if you are a non-trader married to price volatility as a buyer, seller or inventory holder, when it comes to managing price risk your reaction time is simply not fast enough.

Price changes are measured through volatility, an alternate term for standard deviation. Volatility tracks historical price movements and does a reasonable job of indicating the range of prices we are likely to see over a given period. Every now and then it misbehaves and breaks down. But for most applications standard deviation is a good first indicator of risk and price behavior.

In the field of risk management volatility is the beginning and the end. It has many names, some more fashionable than others, but the most common you are likely to see is volatility or vol. (a common trade short form). As with the many names, there are just as many variations when it comes to calculating volatility. The reason why volatility is important is because it is one of the four elements that define the distribution of returns. The other three are the location or center defined by the mean; skewness, a measure of symmetry that could be positive or negative, indicating which direction the distribution leans toward; and kurtosis, which on a relative basis represents how tall the distribution is and how fat its tails are.

Take one statistical measure, sprinkle a few crude assumptions, apply some presentation lessons and you can take a rough shot at estimating risk. Sophistication in models gets added across all three dimensions – measurement, assumptions and presentation. More sophisticated models have a higher breakage frequency since a better fit (read: more parameters, higher accuracy) for one data set is no assurance for the future fit on untested data sets. Adjustments and tweaks only add value when they improve explanatory power[2].

1. Price volatility: a first look – Methods 1 and 2

Are markets today more volatile? It certainly feels that way. This is possibly because of the speed with which markets now move and the reaction time of traders to news. Do we have any objective evidence that supports this assertion? Let's try out a few approaches that give us an indication of how volatility has moved across time and markets.

Figure 1 shows one way of viewing price volatility for three commodities, gold, crude oil and cotton, by using a plot of daily price changes (*daily returns*)[3].

A daily returns plot tracks the percentage change in prices on a daily basis. The changes are first order changes, since we are only looking at relative price change from one period to the next. The plot can be used to

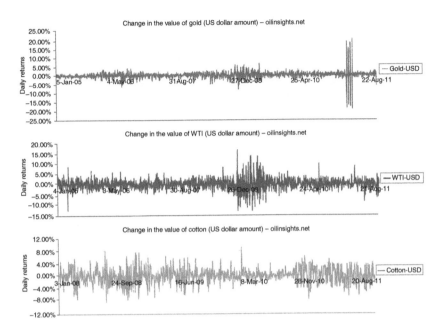

Figure 1 Daily return plot for gold, oil and cotton – January 2008 to August 2011

eyeball the average price change (the benchmark) as well as time intervals where prices became more volatile. For instance:

(a) For oil we can see that there was a period of volatile price changes between mid 2008 and mid 2009, see-sawing as much as +15 percent in one day and –12 percent on others.
(b) For cotton, price volatility died down in the period immediately following the fall in crude oil volatility in mid 2009 (the result of the global recession and its impact on textiles manufacturers' demand for cotton).
(c) While gold has generated significant returns during this time frame, on a relative basis its price volatility has been the lowest when compared with the volatilities of the other two commodities.

Eyeballing the chart above serves us well for basic insight. It gives us an initial sense of the range within which price changes are likely to move for the three commodities.

We can take the same daily returns data set and draw a histogram using EXCEL spreadsheet tools to get a better sense of the distribution of price changes.

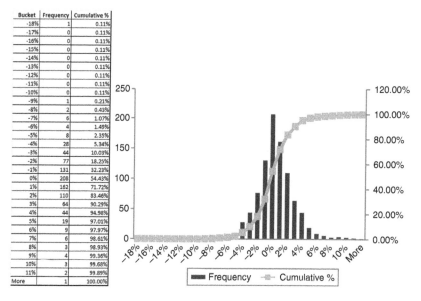

Bucket	Frequency	Cumulative %
-18%	1	0.11%
-17%	0	0.11%
-16%	0	0.11%
-15%	0	0.11%
-14%	0	0.11%
-13%	0	0.11%
-12%	0	0.11%
-11%	0	0.11%
-10%	0	0.11%
-9%	1	0.21%
-8%	2	0.43%
-7%	6	1.07%
-6%	4	1.49%
-5%	8	2.35%
-4%	28	5.34%
-3%	44	10.03%
-2%	77	18.25%
-1%	131	32.23%
0%	208	54.43%
1%	162	71.72%
2%	110	83.46%
3%	64	90.29%
4%	44	94.98%
5%	19	97.01%
6%	9	97.97%
7%	6	98.61%
8%	3	98.93%
9%	4	99.36%
10%	3	99.68%
11%	2	99.89%
More	1	100.00%

Figure 2   Daily return histogram for fuel oil – 2008 to 2011

For instance, Figure 2 uses a daily return series calculated for fuel oil prices from 2008 to 2011. But rather than plotting daily price changes we bucket price changes together and do a count of how many price changes fall in a given bucket. Once the results are tabulated we plot them in a chart. The chart output and the tabulation are shown side by side.

We have just built our first histogram of the distribution of fuel oil price changes.

A histogram uses the same data (relative price changes) but provides a different visual perspective (distribution of price changes).

The distribution plot provides a clear summarized view of the entire dataset. We can see that the most common percentage change lies between –1 percent and +1 percent. The average change is no change (0 percent). The two extreme price changes in a given day are a fall of 18 percent and a rise of 11 percent.

We have moved further with our attempts at understanding price volatility. Our initial plot was a simple dump of daily price movement; useful but limited in insights that could be gained from looking at it.

2. Ramping up sophistication – Method 3

Our next image presents a more sophisticated view of price volatility. Volatility, like prices, is not constant. Imagine the implications of this on models that work with the assumption of constant volatility.

In our third attempt at dissecting volatility, rather than looking at relative price changes we use 60 days of relative price movements to calculate volatility. This process, repeated for our entire data set, results in a moving average of volatility, which is then plotted as shown in Figure 3. We do this for gold, silver, two blends of crude oil (WTI and Brent) and the EUR–USD exchange rate. Our objective is to see how the moving average of volatility behaves when the shorter lens of price changes is intersected with a longer time horizon.

The approach gives us a trail or path that volatility has followed as it moves through time, adding a new day to the data set and dropping an old one, one day at a time.

Compared to our first approach, where we were limited to the dimension of relative price changes, we have moved up in terms of depth. A plot of second order changes (volatility is a second order function) cutting across time gives us a sense of how volatility is likely to behave. Figure 3 confirms that, just like prices, volatility goes up and down.

The moving average also adds different insights when viewed in context with our daily price change plot (Method 1).

(a) We have an objective measure of how much volatility jumped for crude oil in the 2008–9 period (from 2 percent to 7 percent for a sixty day moving average).

(b) How the volatility of gold compares to crude oil (for example, 1 percent versus 2 percent at the start of the period for which volatilities have been plotted above).

(c) The fact that the lowest volatility in the series belongs to the EUR–USD exchange rate, a confirmation that currencies experience lower

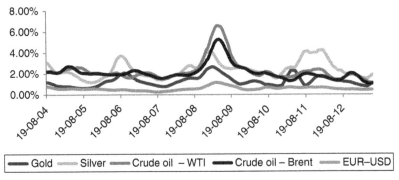

Figure 3 Rolling volatilities for gold, silver, oil and EUR–USD – August 2004 to June 2013

volatility than commodities. In turn, commodities are, in principle, exposed to higher volatility compared to equities, with the exception of gold.

3. A histogram of volatility distribution – Method 4

Our last variation on dissecting volatility brings the best of these two worlds together – calculating rolling volatilities to get a moving average and then graphing a distribution plot or histogram on them, as shown in Figure 4.

Why do we need this?

We already know that volatility is not constant; we know that it goes up and down from the preceding example. If you are building a price model that uses underlying volatility, which value should you pick? The most likely candidates lie within the 1.7 percent – 2.4 percent range. You can pick the number closest to the average and use 2 percent. Or you can stress your model and see what a spell of high volatility could do to prices and use 5 percent. In either instance it would be useful to know what the actual likelihood of either of these two events (a realized volatility of 2 percent vs. a realized volatility of 5 percent) is.

The volatility distribution given above already provides us with the actual likelihoods for the given volatility buckets plotted. With it we can easily map out the distribution. For fuel oil the most common volatility is 2 percent (with an actual likelihood in the given data set of almost 13 percent, that is, 13 days in every 100 days), and the midpoint of the distribution is 2.2 percent. The two extremes are a low of 1.1 percent and a high of 5.8 percent and upwards (with actual likelihoods in the given data set of 0.1 percent and 0.5 percent respectively).

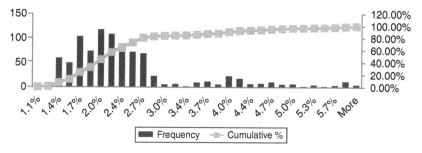

Figure 4   Distribution of fuel oil volatility – 2008 to 2011

What is risk?

Now compare all of the above iterations of evaluating price volatility to the simplest of tools used by ordinary mortals: a plot of absolute price levels depicting daily highs and lows – the one-dimensional price chart shown in Figure 5.

Which of the five approaches shared so far would you prefer?

1. The absolute price chart
2. The relative price return plot
3. The distribution/histogram of price changes
4. The rolling volatility plot
5. The distribution/histogram of volatility.

When I put this question in front of my students, a common pushback is with my earlier statement about model sophistication – Occam's razor. Do we really need this sophistication? Isn't a simpler model better? What is needed is sophistication in analysis, not complexity in models. These are two very different worlds. The volatility dissection process that we have followed is just one way of getting a better grip on the expected future behavior of prices.

Irrespective of the approach picked, you should notice one common trend. Risk, volatility and price movements are not constant. They range. They have seasons. They go through violent mood swings. Some years are better than others. Some years are disasters.

Each method has a place in the tool kit of a risk analyst. Rather than looking at a single dimension (absolute prices) we look at multiple dimensions. We plot relative price changes, we review distribution histograms, we track rolling volatility and we dissect the distribution of rolling volatility.

Figure 5   Daily price series of crude oil

The key word here is distribution. Price or volatility, an understanding of the distribution is an understanding of the risk involved. If you want to be comfortable with understanding risk, you must understand the distribution of risk.

As can be seen in Figure 6, if you traded in risk, 2008, 2009 and 2011 were great years based on their high volatility index. By contrast, 2012 was a terrible year for risk traders given the lowest levels of volatility in the eight year period plotted. There was uncertainty, but nothing like the levels of 2008. Traders like risk and uncertainty because uncertainty breeds opportunity and trades. Stability is great for grandmothers and Warren Buffett but toxic as cyanide for trading Profit & Loss (P&L) accounts.

As ordinary mortals, not traders, we tend to misread risk. We do a poor job of forecasting, estimating and assessing risk because we don't deal with it on a daily basis. We assume that our intelligence, our background and our experiences give us license to forecast the direction and magnitude of the next wave of risk, but we are often wrong. We overcompensate. We are cautious. We ignore history and trends in favor of our own biases. We play it safe.

A safe player, not raised on a strict diet of trading and risk, would never forecast a three-times jump in underlying volatility in the Euro-USD exchange rate. In fact, with the stability and strength in Euro seen in 2008 and early 2009, we would have been laughed out of most boardrooms for suggesting such an event. The prevalent school of thought in

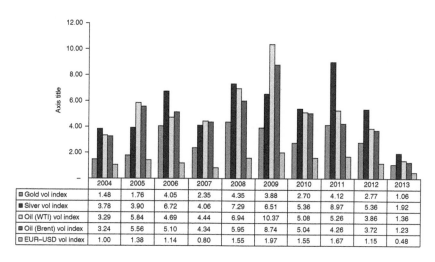

	2004	2005	2006	2007	2008	2009	2010	2011	2012	2013
▣ Gold vol index	1.48	1.76	4.05	2.35	4.35	3.88	2.70	4.12	2.77	1.06
■ Siver vol index	3.78	3.90	6.72	4.06	7.29	6.51	5.36	8.97	5.36	1.92
▢ Oil (WTI) vol index	3.29	5.84	4.69	4.44	6.94	10.37	5.08	5.26	3.86	1.36
▣ Oil (Brent) vol index	3.24	5.56	5.10	4.34	5.95	8.74	5.04	4.26	3.72	1.23
▢ EUR–USD vol index	1.00	1.38	1.14	0.80	1.55	1.97	1.55	1.67	1.15	0.48

Figure 6   Risk assessment: volatility index, ten years – 2004 to 2013
Source: FinanceTrainingCourse.com

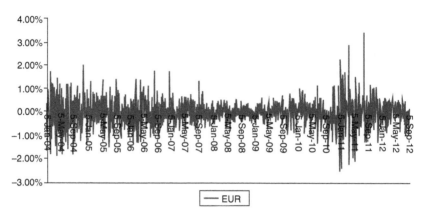

Figure 7 Risk assessment: EUR–USD exchange rate, daily rate changes, eight years –
2004 to 2012

early 2008 predicted the demise of the US dollar as a global reserve currency and its replacement by the European Union Standard, even more so after the 2008 asset backed security crisis in US markets.

Yet the Euro fell from its April 2008 exchange rate high of 1.595 USD to a low of 1.19 USD, and saw an even steeper intraday low with unheard of 2 percent negative moves in the first and second quarters of 2011 (see Figure 7).

1. How should one think about risk?

Risk is uncertainty. Risk is opportunity. Risk is misunderstood.

Here is a simple rule. Don't think in terms of absolutes and averages. Think in terms of levels, trends and scales.

The risk is not that you will get the average or the averaging period wrong. The risk is that you will misread the level and threshold of risk you are facing. You will misread the change and miss the transition to the next level of intensity.

Expect the unexpected to misbehave and surprise you. It will.

2. Thinking about risk – from exposure to impact

Before your family physician prescribes any medicine or procedure he has to diagnose what is wrong: an upcoming season for the influenza virus – a flu shot; a muscular injury – an anti-inflammatory painkiller; an infection – antibiotics; a fracture – a splint.

The same holds true for risk. Before we decide on our approach for managing risk we have to understand what are we exposed to. With financial risk management this translates into determining a numerical

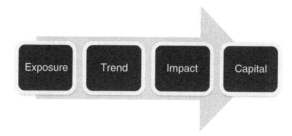

Figure 8   Risk management framework

value for your risk. We call this numerical value exposure. Exposure is a gross number that may indicate consumption, position, size or amount. While the actual risk is dependent on exposure, exposure is not risk.

If you drive a car, the chances of you making a claim on your insurance policy are directly linked to the number of miles you drive in a year and the neighborhoods you drive in. Within investments, portfolios and commodities, exposure is the analogous number to miles driven and the neighborhoods driven through. Its most common manifestation is the total investment value or the dollar sum of all of your positions. If you run a book of 200 million USD that 200 million USD is your exposure. Your risk will be measured in terms of that number.

The next step is to examine the trend of exposure to ensure that you adjust for seasonality and don't over or under estimate exposure. Armed with these two elements you are now ready to calculate the actual risk or the financial impact of uncertainty. We do this by tracking exposure and matching it with the relevant risk drivers or factors. The combination of these two elements (exposure and risk factors) creates a number, which is uncertain and volatile. We label it impact. Impact, unlike exposure, is measured on a net basis and represents the amount at risk of the un-hedged exposure.

This leads us to four questions that we need to answer before we can complete our diagnoses of risk.

1. What is the exposure?
2. What is the trend for the exposure?
3. What is the impact of the risk factors on exposure?
4. What is our risk appetite?

Let's look at how these numbers can be estimated.

Four examples follow. Four businesses exposed to either a rise in fuel prices or changes in exchange rates or movements in input (commodities) prices. The industries in question are airlines, trading houses, exporters and goods manufacturers, respectively.

BUSINESS	EXPOSURE	RISK FACTOR	IMPACT
Airlines	Jet fuel price volatility. Demand shifts on account of recession	Fuel prices move up. Limited ability to raise ticket prices	Dollar impact on fuel bill on account of jet fuel price changes
Importers of Audi 4 door sedans	Payment for imports in Euro due in 90 days	Appreciation of Euro against base currency	Change in the amount due in base currency on account of appreciation of Euro
Exporters of textile products to Japan	Payment for exports to be received in 120 days	Depreciation of Yen against base currency	Change in the amount received in base currency on account of depreciation of Yen
Auto part manufacturers	Fixed price contract. No room for changes on account of input cost	Rise in the price of input components	Impact of change in the price of the basket of inputs on profitability

Figure 9   Examples of exposure, risk factor and impact

Estimating exposure and impact – Emirates airline

Emirates is a leading Middle Eastern airline known for its commitment to redefining business travel and operating the largest business and first class transit lounges in the world, at Dubai Airport. Emirates flies 40 million passengers a year and its last reported financial year (2012–13) grossed just under 20 billion USD in annual revenues. It employs 50,000 employees spread across six continents and its fleet includes 200 aircraft.

As air travel has rebounded and jet fuel prices have climbed, Emirates has seen its profits erode despite rising revenues. Profit margins have plummeted from a high of 9.9 percent in 2010–11 to 3.1 percent in 2012–13. Margins have also impacted returns on shareholders' funds, which dropped from a high of 28 percent in 2010–11 to 10 percent in 2012–13[4].

Yet Emirates decided to leave its jet fuel exposure unhedged for the last two years. Why is that? To answer this question we have to dig a little deeper. We have to find out the actual amount at risk and then compare it with Emirates' internal outlook on fuel prices.

We will do that using the four questions we have just identified in the preceding section. Exposure. Trend. Impact. Risk Appetite.

1. What is Emirates' exposure?

As Emirates grows its network and passenger handling capacity, its fuel bill is also rising. Emirates consumed 7.2, 6.1 and 5.1 million tons of jet fuel in the last three financial years respectively (most recent to past). In dollar terms, Emirates' fuel bill was 7.5, 6.6 and 5.7 billion USD for the same time periods, shown in Figure 10.

Therefore, the most recent jet fuel *exposure* is 7.2 million tons. The same exposure in USD equivalent terms is 7.5 billion USD.

2. What is the trend for Emirates' exposure?

Emirates' fuel exposure is rising. While we assume that there is some seasonality in fuel consumption, we don't have enough data available through public disclosure to estimate that.

However, we do have price, rolling volatility and distribution data for jet fuel on a monthly basis, which is shared in Figures 11, 12 and 13 respectively.

We can see that while prices started rising in 2009, they have stayed at their high levels since 2010. Price volatility, on the other hand, has dropped to historical lows over the same period. Average monthly historical volatility is about 9 percent. Recent monthly volatility has hovered around 5 percent.

Financial Year	Fuel Expense For the year (AED Million)	Fuel Expense For the year (USD Million)	Fuel consumed Tonne ('000)	Price Per Tonne USD	Price Per Barrel USD
2012-13	27,855	7,580	7,171	946.1	119.3
2011-12	24,292	6,610	6,145	929.6	117.2
2010-11	20,864	5,677	5,149	907.0	114.4
	Emirates Airline Fuel Bill				

Figure 10   Fuel expense and consumption for Emirates

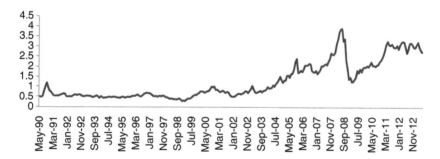

Figure 11   Jet fuel price series 1990–2013

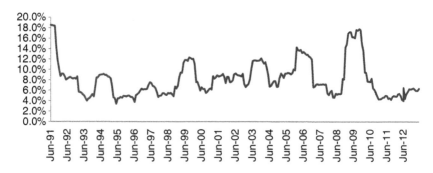

Figure 12 Jet fuel price volatility 1990–2013

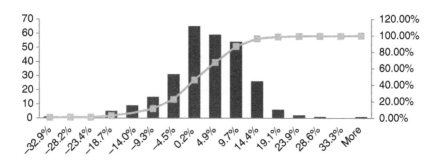

Figure 13 Distribution of jet fuel price changes – histogram plot

The historical distribution of monthly price changes is slightly skewed. Prices are more likely to rise than decline, as per the histogram in Figure 13.

3. What is the impact?

The frequency count of the histogram of monthly price changes given in Figure 14 has some interesting highlights. As of June 2013, jet fuel prices ranged between 880 and 920 USD per ton, depending on the geographic location where you took delivery of your fuel.

The question we want to ask is: "What price movement are we most likely to witness in the future?" While we are at it, we would also like to make an educated guess about the extreme price movements that we may see over our projection time horizon.

The historical distribution in the table below gives us a range of price movements and their historical likelihood. We conveniently assume (for now) that historical price changes are reasonable predictors of future price changes.

Bucket	Frequency	Cumulative %
−37.6%	1	0.36%
−32.9%	1	0.72%
−28.2%	1	1.08%
−23.4%	0	1.08%
−18.7%	**5**	**2.89%**
−14.0%	9	6.14%
−9.3%	15	11.55%
−4.5%	31	22.74%
0.2%	65	46.21%
4.9%	**59**	**67.51%**
9.7%	54	87.00%
14.4%	26	96.39%
19.1%	**6**	**98.56%**
23.9%	2	99.28%
28.6%	1	99.64%
33.3%	0	99.64%
More	1	100.00%

Figure 14 Distribution of jet fuel price changes – frequency table

Using the two tools (the histogram chart and the frequency table) we can see that the probability of a price rise is significantly higher than that of a price decline. Based on the cumulative probability table and plot the probability of a price decline is 22 percent. The probability of a price rise is 77 percent.

On the extreme movement front there is a 3.6 percent chance of seeing a price rise of greater than 9.7 percent in any given month. The odds translate to one such move every 25 months.

So if prices rise by over 10 percent in any given month, what amount will Emirates airline have to pay in excess of its usual fuel bill in that month? More importantly, if prices rise are they likely to immediately come down or will they stay up there in the stratosphere? If they rise, and Emirates can somehow pass the increase on to its consumers, how deeply will that action impact demand and capacity utilization? What about tickets that have been purchased months in advance and paid for by corporate customers? What proportion of Emirates business is advanced booking?

These are all important questions that need to be factored into our impact assessment model. But for now we only need to answer the first question. If prices rise by 10 percent and stay there, what will be the net impact on Emirates fuel bill?

Financial Year	Fuel Expense For the year (AED Million)	Fuel Expense For the year (USD Million)	Fuel consumed Tonne ('000)	Price Per Tonne USD	Price Per Barrel USD
2012-13	27,855	7,580	7,171	946.1	119.3
2011-12	24,292	6,610	6,145	929.6	117.2
2010-11	20,864	5,677	5,149	907.0	114.4
		Emirates Airline Fuel Bill			

Figure 15   Fuel expense and consumption for Emirates

Based on the 2012–13 Figures, Emirates would spend an additional 758 million USD on its fuel bill, assuming the price rise has no impact on passenger demand and capacity utilization.

We initially assume a linear relationship, which implies that if prices rise by 15 percent the fuel bill will also rise by 15 percent. Later on in our jet fuel hedging case study we build a non-linear model, which will take into consideration additional factors, some of which are identified in the questions above.

4. What is Emirates' risk appetite?

This question is a little tricky. If we work for a financial institution or a bank we evaluate market exposures in terms of capital adequacy and capital allocation. Banking boards and regulators are comfortable with these two measures, and no new context and background is required to appreciate the results presented.

But for non-banking boards, capital allocations and capital adequacy are meaningless measures. These two measures do not translate well at the senior management or board level of an airline. What works though are profitability, margin and probability of shortfall. While we won't touch on all three in this chapter, we will use profitability and margin to answer the question for Emirates airline.

Can Emirates afford a possible price shock of 750 million USD?

Financial Year	Profitability For the year (AED Million)	Profitability For the year (USD Million)	Profit Margin For the year
2012-13	2,283	621	3.10%
2011-12	1,502	409	2.40%
2010-11	5,375	1,463	9.90%
	Emirates Airline Profitability		

Figure 16   Emirates profitability and profit margins

With 621 million USD in profitability, a 750 million USD price shock would push Emirates' bottom line into the red zone. While a 10 percent price shock will only add 4.5 percent to the operating cost base of the airline, this additional increase will vaporize what little profitability Emirates has recorded.

A board member can easily come back and state that there is only a small chance of this event being realized. Historical data indicates that the likelihood of a 10 percent increase is 3.6 percent. Is there a need to counter this argument?

The same table that gives us a 3.6 percent probability for an increase larger than 10 percent, also shows us that the probability of a greater than 5 percent increase is around 32 percent. These are 1 in 3-month odds. A 5 percent increase adds 380 million USD in excess fuel charges, and keeping everything else constant accounts for over 61 percent of Emirates' 2012–13 profitability. Now the odds and the projected loss are much more real and immediate.

Yet, as per Emirates financial disclosure, we see that in their assessment they are still better off leaving the fuel purchase and the associated price risk unhedged.

Before you move forward, spend a little time thinking about the argument in favor as well as against fuel hedging. Emirates has been in the flying business for over two decades. They are not new to the fuel hedging game. If they see the same data we see and think hedging is not going to add value, what is it that we are missing in our analysis?

5. Conclusions from the Emirates example

A logistics business covers a wide range of services. From airlines that carry passengers, freight and cargo to bulk carriers that transport containers of finished goods, as well as raw ore and commodities. From small distributors that ensure delivery of your products to retail stores to large national fleets that are the backbones of just-in-time inventory systems. They are all reliant on one crucial, volatile commodity. Fuel.

Fuel expenses today represent between 35 and 40 percent of total operating expenses for the logistics industry. Fuel is a commodity, which is volatile and in many instances very difficult to hedge perfectly. If you were responsible for managing the risk in this business, where would you start? What kind of questions would your board ask? How would you go about answering them?

After reviewing the Emirates example, some of the answers should be derived by common sense. Consider the following factors:

- oil price volatility,
- exchange rate volatility,
- fuel price volatility,
- relationship between oil and fuel prices,
- total input price volatility – any additional correlations,
- demand forecasting and price elasticity,
- hedging transaction costs,
- purchase, payment and consumption lags.

These factors don't work in isolation or exact sequence. If they did we would have a simple linear model.

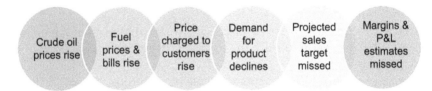

Figure 17   What is risk? The cascading waterfall impact of one risk factor on P&L

A reasonable model considers the impact of complex interactions between these factors. Some interactions cannot be modeled and are handled outside of the model, which implies that our results and conclusions are imperfect. They are qualified or subject to limitations.

As model builders we may have faith in our conclusions, but boards need to understand that our recommendations are based on imperfect assumptions and relationships that may not hold under times of stress.

So what does Emirates sees that we are not seeing? To answer this question we have to revisit the jet fuel price and volatility graphs presented earlier. The first graph in Figure 18 shows price plot, while the second shows rolling volatility.

Emirates has two concerns.

The first is that jet fuel prices are at historical highs. In their opinion, at these levels the likelihood of prices going up is low. There is a much higher chance that prices will decline. If Emirates hedges its jet fuel exposure at current prices, fuel cost will be locked in at these levels, which would be especially painful if fuel prices were to collapse.

Emirates is not the only airline to feel this way. After the collapse of crude oil price in 2008, a number of regional airlines took a bath when

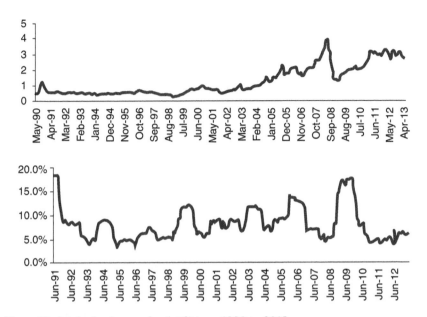

Figure 18 Jet fuel prices and volatilities – 1990 to 2013

their hedging strategies backfired by locking them in at peak price levels of 130 USD a barrel while the market tanked to 33 USD a barrel.

The second concern is volatility. While prices are at historical highs, volatility is at historical lows. The question is when (not if) volatility rises, will prices rise or decline? Emirates apparently feels that with the rise in volatility they are more likely to decline.

Given the above context, Emirates believes that until the picture about jet fuel clears up, they would be better off by partially passing on the cost increase to customers via fuel surcharges and adjustments. Such an approach is more flexible given the current context, and allows Emirates the option to hedge its exposure when prices can be locked at lower levels.

Hence Emirates' decision to leave their jet fuel exposure unhedged in 2012–13.

Parting words

Remember the four questions.

1. What is the exposure?
2. What is the trend for the exposure?
3. What is the impact of risk factors on exposure?
4. What is our risk appetite?

As with everything else, a misdiagnosis followed by an incorrect prescription does more damage than good. You don't want a flu shot when what you really need is a splint.

Annexure 1 – Building a histogram in EXCEL

The EXCEL Data Analysis Tool Pack comes with a powerful histogram tool that you can use to dissect distributions, prices and percentage returns.

A histogram is calculated on a series of daily price changes on a given financial security. Within risk terms we call daily price changes daily returns, and these returns could be positive or negative. The histogram in Figure 19 takes a daily return series, sorts the series and then slots each return in a given return bucket.

We will show how to build a simple histogram for the USD–EUR exchange rate.

Use the daily exchange rate series to calculate daily returns. Each return is calculated by the application of *LN(P1/P0)* where *LN* is the natural log function in EXCEL, P1 is the new exchange rate, P0 is the old exchange rate. This is approximately equal to the daily percentage price change in the underlying exchange rate.

We will take this return series and use it to calculate a histogram similar to the one in Figure 19.

You can find the histogram tool under the Data Analysis Tools tab in EXCEL. If for some reason you don't see a Data Analysis Tools tab in your version of EXCEL, go to EXCEL Options, chose Add-ins and then simply add the Data Analysis Add-in to enable this tab (see Figure 21).

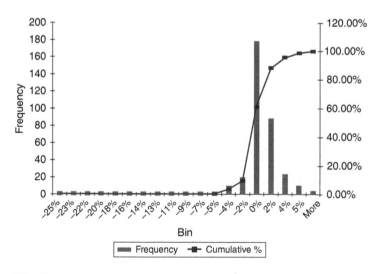

Figure 19   Histogram

Data	USD-EUR	Daily Returns
1/2/2010	1.4326	
1/4/2010	1.438	0.376%
1/5/2010	1.442751	0.330%
1/6/2010	1.4373	-0.379%
1/7/2010	1.4353	-0.139%
1/8/2010	1.432301	-0.209%
1/9/2010	1.44145	0.637%
1/11/2010	1.451401	0.688%
1/12/2010	1.448101	-0.228%
1/13/2010	1.45065	0.176%
1/14/2010	1.451749	0.076%

Figure 20 USD–EUR daily returns

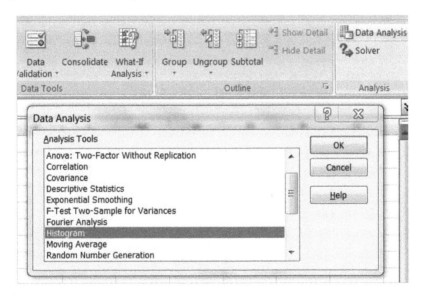

Figure 21 EXCEL's data analysis functionality

To generate the histogram, select the daily return series as your input range. Opt for *New Worksheet Ply, Cumulative Percentage* and *Chart Output* (see Figure 22) to see a graphical representation of the histogram as well as a supporting frequency count table.

When you press Ok, EXCEL will create a new tab for you and show the histogram.

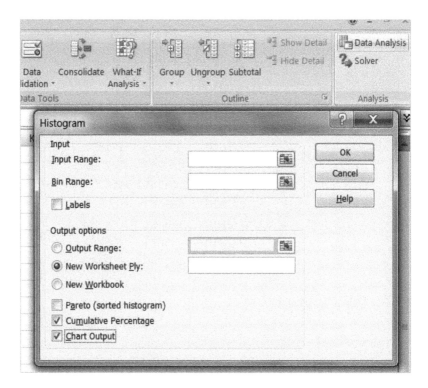

Figure 22   EXCEL's data analysis histogram functionality

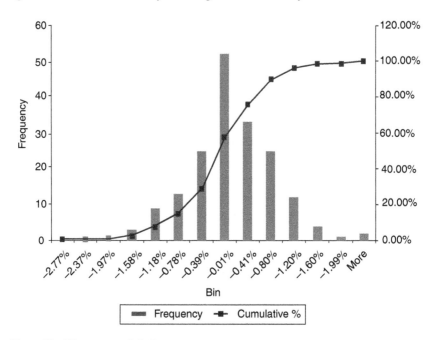

Figure 23   Histogram of daily returns

The histogram is a great summary of the entire distribution of prices. The worst-case daily price shock (the downside) in the histogram in Figure 23 is marked at –2.77 percent. The upside is about 1.99 percent

If I asked you what is the worst that can happen, you can easily tell me that my nightmarish scenario based on historical returns is a loss of over –2.77 percent (the extreme left corner on the bottom) if I am long (bought) Euro or a loss of over 1.99 percent if I am short (sold) Euro versus the US dollar.

My next two questions would be, over what time frame and with what odds?

The returns are calculated on a daily basis, hence the answer to the first question is over any given trading day.

The second answer requires a bit of work. There are approximately 181 days (frequency count) in the graph above (Figure 23). Your worst-case loss is a once in 181 days event. The probability of you seeing a loss greater than this number is 1/181 or 0.55 percent.

Luckily for us our EXCEL histogram output worksheet already includes a table with these probabilities and numbers in it, shown in Figure 24.

If you put all of the above material together, there is only a 0.55 percent chance that you will see a worst case loss of over –2.77 percent on any given trading day if you bought Euros, and a 1.1 percent chance that you will see a loss of over 1.99 percent if you sold Euros.

Bin	Frequency	Cumulative %
-2.77%	1	0.55%
-2.37%	0	0.55%
-1.97%	1	1.10%
-1.58%	3	2.76%
-1.18%	9	7.73%
-0.78%	13	14.92%
-0.39%	25	28.73%
0.01%	52	57.46%
0.41%	33	75.69%
0.80%	25	89.50%
1.20%	12	96.13%
1.60%	4	98.34%
1.99%	1	98.90%
More	2	100.00%
	181	

Figure 24 Frequency table output for histogram of daily returns

Annexure 2 – Trailing (rolling) correlations and volatilities

1. Rolling volatilities

Rolling or trailing volatilities analyze the trends in volatility over a period of time for a particular instrument or portfolio of instruments. They are graphical representations of how the riskiness of given instruments have changed over time, and depict the trend witnessed in risk levels. A rising trend indicates an increase in risk due to increased fluctuations in under-lying prices (level and/or frequency) over the period of study. A horizontal trend line indicates that average volatilities have remained stable over the period, whereas a declining trend line shows decreasing levels of risk.

It is calculated by obtaining price time series for the given instrument or portfolio. We have considered time series data for gold spot prices obtained from www.onlygold.com, silver spot prices (London PM fix in USD) from www.kitco.com, crude oil spot prices from www.eia.gov and the EUR–USD exchange rates from www.oanda.com for the period 1 January 2004 to 7 June 2013. See Figure 25 for an extract of this data set.

The daily return series is then calculated from the price data as the natural logarithm of the ratio of successive (consecutive) prices:

$$\ln = \left(\frac{\text{Price}_t}{\text{Price}_{t-1}} \right)$$

A series of daily volatilities for 90-day windows is determined on a roll forward basis, rolling forward a day at a time. The daily volatilities are cal-culated using EXCEL's STDEV() function applied to 90 consecutive return observations.

	A	B	C	D	E	F
3	Prices					
4		Gold	Silver	Crude Oil - WTI	Crude Oil - Brent	EUR USD
5	01/01/2004	416.25	5.97	32.51	30.30	1.2576
6	02/01/2004	417.25	5.97	32.51	29.55	1.2542
7	05/01/2004	420.60	5.98	33.71	32.30	1.2583
8	06/01/2004	424.40	6.28	33.54	31.20	1.2654
9	07/01/2004	421.75	6.22	33.57	30.99	1.2736
10	09/01/2004	423.35	6.25	34.38	31.91	1.2764
11	12/01/2004	425.25	6.65	34.92	31.41	1.2830
12	15/01/2004	419.50	6.32	33.61	31.43	1.2650
13	16/01/2004	408.40	6.21	35.16	31.26	1.2565
14	19/01/2004	406.60	6.34	35.16	31.67	1.2169
15	20/01/2004	409.25	6.39	36.21	32.26	1.2351
16	22/01/2004	409.25	6.26	35.12	31.42	1.2630

Figure 25   Extract of data set

PRICE		▼	⊙ ✕ ✓ *fx*	=LN(F6/F5)		

	F	G	H	I	J	K	L	M
3			**Returns**					
4	**EUR USD**			**Gold**	**Silver**	**Crude Oil - WTI**	**Crude Oil - Brent**	**EUR USD**
5	1.2576		02/01/2004	0.24%	0.00%	0.00%	-2.51%	=LN(F6/F5)
6	1.2542		05/01/2004	0.80%	0.17%	3.62%	8.90%	0.33%
7	1.2583		06/01/2004	0.90%	4.98%	-0.51%	-3.46%	0.56%
8	1.2654		07/01/2004	-0.63%	-1.04%	0.09%	-0.68%	0.65%
9	1.2736		09/01/2004	0.38%	0.48%	2.38%	2.93%	0.22%
10	1.2764		12/01/2004	0.45%	6.28%	1.56%	-1.58%	0.52%
11	1.2830		15/01/2004	-1.36%	-5.17%	-3.82%	0.06%	-1.41%
12	1.2650		16/01/2004	-2.68%	-1.76%	4.51%	-0.54%	-0.67%
13	1.2565		19/01/2004	-0.44%	2.07%	0.00%	1.30%	-3.20%
14	1.2169		20/01/2004	0.65%	0.86%	2.94%	1.85%	1.48%
15	1.2351		22/01/2004	0.00%	-2.06%	-3.06%	-2.64%	2.23%
16	1.2630		23/01/2004	-0.06%	1.35%	-0.51%	2.08%	0.62%
17	1.2709		26/01/2004	-0.20%	-1.59%	-1.53%	-2.94%	-1.02%

Figure 26   Calculation of daily returns

PRICE		▼	⊙ ✕ ✓ *fx*	=STDEV(I5:I94)				

	H	I	J	K	L	M	N	O	P	Q	R	S	T
3	**Returns**							**Rolling Volatilities (90 - day)**					
4		**Gold**	**Silver**	**Crude Oil - WTI**	**Crude Oil - Brent**	**EUR USD**			**Gold**	**Silver**	**Crude Oil - WTI**	**Crude Oil - Brent**	**EUR USD**
5	02/01/2004	0.24%	0.00%	0.00%	-2.51%	-0.27%		26/05/2004	=STDEV(I5:I94)		2.08%	2.28%	0.92%
6	05/01/2004	0.80%	0.17%	3.62%	8.90%	0.33%		27/05/2004	1.18%	3.31%	2.12%	2.29%	0.92%
7	06/01/2004	0.90%	4.98%	-0.51%	-3.46%	0.56%		28/05/2004	1.18%	3.31%	2.09%	2.09%	0.93%
8	07/01/2004	-0.63%	-1.04%	0.09%	-0.68%	0.65%		01/06/2004	1.18%	3.27%	2.18%	2.13%	0.93%
9	09/01/2004	0.38%	0.48%	2.38%	2.93%	0.22%		02/06/2004	1.18%	3.27%	2.27%	2.15%	0.93%
10	12/01/2004	0.45%	6.28%	1.56%	-1.58%	0.52%		03/06/2004	1.18%	3.30%	2.26%	2.19%	0.93%
11	15/01/2004	-1.36%	-5.17%	-3.82%	0.06%	-1.41%		04/06/2004	1.18%	3.23%	2.27%	2.19%	0.92%

Figure 27   Calculation of 90-day daily volatilities (part 1)

PRICE		▼	⊙ ✕ ✓ *fx*	=STDEV(I6:I95)				

	H	I	J	K	L	M	N	O	P	Q	R	S	T
3	**Returns**							**Rolling Volatilities (90 - day)**					
4		**Gold**	**Silver**	**Crude Oil - WTI**	**Crude Oil - Brent**	**EUR USD**			**Gold**	**Silver**	**Crude Oil - WTI**	**Crude Oil - Brent**	**EUR USD**
5	02/01/2004	0.24%	0.00%	0.00%	-2.51%	-0.27%		26/05/2004	1.18%	3.30%	2.08%	2.28%	0.92%
6	05/01/2004	0.80%	0.17%	3.62%	8.90%	0.33%		27/05/2004	=STDEV(I6:I95)		2.12%	2.29%	0.92%
7	06/01/2004	0.90%	4.98%	-0.51%	-3.46%	0.56%		28/05/2004	1.18%	3.31%	2.09%	2.09%	0.93%
8	07/01/2004	-0.63%	-1.04%	0.09%	-0.68%	0.65%		01/06/2004	1.18%	3.27%	2.18%	2.13%	0.93%
9	09/01/2004	0.38%	0.48%	2.38%	2.93%	0.22%		02/06/2004	1.18%	3.27%	2.27%	2.15%	0.93%
10	12/01/2004	0.45%	6.28%	1.56%	-1.58%	0.52%		03/06/2004	1.18%	3.30%	2.26%	2.19%	0.93%
11	15/01/2004	-1.36%	-5.17%	-3.82%	0.06%	-1.41%		04/06/2004	1.18%	3.23%	2.27%	2.19%	0.92%

Figure 28   Calculation of 90-day daily volatilities (part 2)

The resulting volatility series is graphed in Figure 29 for gold, silver, crude oil (Brent and WTI) and the EUR–USD exchange rate.

A given point on the graph represents the daily volatility calculated using the past 90 returns available. Another way of presenting the results is to calculate an average of consecutive volatilities, again on a roll forward basis, as shown in Figure 30.

The graph in Figure 31 depicts the volatility trend line for a series of 60 volatility averages.

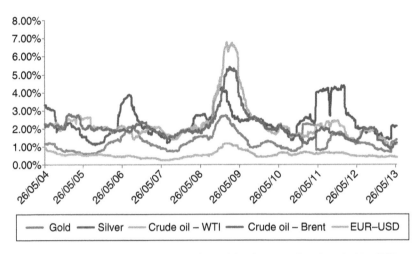

Figure 29 90-day rolling volatilities for gold, silver, crude oil and EUR–USD

	N	O	P	Q	R	S	T
			Gold	Silver	Crude Oil - WTI	Crude Oil - Brent	EUR USD
4			Gold	Silver	Crude Oil - WTI	Crude Oil - Brent	EUR USD
5		26/05/2004	1.18%	3.30%	2.08%	2.28%	0.92%
6		27/05/2004	1.18%	3.31%	2.12%	2.29%	0.92%
7		28/05/2004	1.18%	3.31%	2.09%	2.09%	0.93%
8		01/06/2004	1.18%	3.27%	2.18%	2.13%	0.93%
9		02/06/2004	1.18%	3.27%	2.27%	2.15%	0.93%
10		03/06/2004	1.18%	3.30%	2.26%	2.19%	0.93%
11		04/06/2004	1.18%	3.23%	2.27%	2.19%	0.92%
12		07/06/2004	1.19%	3.19%	2.23%	2.19%	0.92%
13		08/06/2004	1.15%	3.18%	2.23%	2.19%	0.91%
14		09/06/2004	1.16%	3.18%	2.23%	2.20%	0.85%
2246		07/06/2013	1.40%	2.13%	1.15%	1.21%	0.41%
2247							
2248		**Average Rolling Volatilities - 60 vols**					
2249			Gold	Silver	Crude Oil - WTI	Crude Oil - Brent	EUR USD
2250		19/08/2004	1.18%	3.12%	=AVERAGE(R5:R64)		0.80%
2251		20/08/2004	1.18%	3.11%	2.23%	2.21%	0.80%
2252		23/08/2004	1.18%	3.11%	2.24%	2.21%	0.79%
2253		24/08/2004	1.18%	3.10%	2.24%	2.20%	0.79%
2254		25/08/2004	1.18%	3.10%	2.24%	2.20%	0.79%
2255		26/08/2004	1.18%	3.09%	2.24%	2.20%	0.78%
2256		27/08/2004	1.18%	3.08%	2.24%	2.20%	0.78%

PRICE   X ✓ *fx* =AVERAGE(R5:R64)

Figure 30 Calculation of 60-vol average rolling volatilities

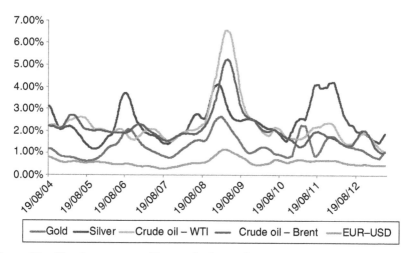

Figure 31 60-vol average rolling volatilities for gold, silver, crude oil and EUR–USD

A given point on the graph represents the average of the previous 60 volatilities at that particular date.

Rolling forward a day at a time means that the periods for consecutive daily volatilities overlap. A large return would continue to impact the results until it dropped out of the 90-day window range. When using historical volatilities in calculations, it is more appropriate to use rolling volatilities that are calculated for discrete non-overlapping intervals, to remove the bias of previous intervals.

To determine non-overlapping discrete intervals we define the window length (90 days in Cell AL1), and the start row and final row references in the sheet. The latter two entries are the start and end cells of the date column for the returns section of the sheet.

For the first interval the end row reference is calculated as start row reference + window length − 1. For the following intervals the start row reference will be the previous end row + 1, while the end row will be the

PRICE			▾	⊙ × ✓ ƒx	=ROW(H5)						
	H	I	J	K	L	M	AK	AL	AM	AN	AO	AP
1								window	90			
2									column	i		
3	Returns						final row	2335		j	k	l
4		Gold	Silver	Crude Oil - WTI	Crude Oil - Brent	EUR USD	start row	end row		Volatilities - non - overlapping		
										Gold	Silver	Crude Oil - WTI
5	02/01/2004	0.24%	0.00%	0.00%	-2.51%	-0.27%	=ROW(H5)		25/05/2004	1.18%	3.30%	2.08%
6	05/01/2004	0.80%	0.17%	3.62%	8.90%	0.33%	95	184	04/10/2004	0.89%	1.97%	2.20%
7	06/01/2004	0.90%	4.98%	-0.51%	-3.46%	0.56%	185	274	17/02/2005	0.78%	2.19%	2.47%
8	07/01/2004	-0.63%	-1.04%	0.09%	-0.68%	0.65%	275	364	29/06/2005	0.60%	1.38%	2.60%
9	09/01/2004	0.38%	0.48%	2.38%	2.93%	0.22%	365	454	04/11/2005	0.79%	1.22%	2.10%
10	12/01/2004	0.45%	6.28%	1.56%	-1.58%	0.52%	455	544	20/03/2006	1.34%	1.80%	1.92%
11	15/01/2004	-1.36%	-5.17%	-3.82%	0.06%	-1.41%	545	634	26/07/2006	2.10%	3.86%	1.80%
12	16/01/2004	-2.68%	-1.76%	4.51%	-0.54%	-0.67%	635	724	04/12/2006	1.32%	2.04%	1.88%

Figure 32 Defining the start row for determining non-overlapping intervals for rolling volatilities

Spreadsheet — formula bar: PRICE ▼ × ✓ *fx* =ROW(H2335)

Returns (columns H–M)

	Gold	Silver	Crude Oil - WTI	Crude Oil - Brent	EUR USD
02/01/2004	0.24%	0.00%	0.00%	-2.51%	-0.27%
05/01/2004	0.80%	0.17%	3.62%	8.90%	0.33%
06/01/2004	0.90%	4.98%	-0.51%	-3.46%	0.56%
07/01/2004	-0.63%	-1.04%	0.09%	-0.68%	0.65%
09/01/2004	0.38%	0.48%	2.38%	2.93%	0.22%
12/01/2004	0.45%	6.28%	1.56%	-1.58%	0.52%
15/01/2004	-1.36%	-5.17%	-3.82%	0.06%	-1.41%
16/01/2004	-2.68%	-1.76%	4.51%	-0.54%	-0.67%
14/05/2013	0.21%	-0.93%	-0.85%	0.52%	-0.09%
15/05/2013	-1.67%	-2.46%	-0.01%	-1.11%	0.05%
16/05/2013	-2.08%	-2.70%	0.95%	2.62%	-0.65%
17/05/2013	-0.89%	1.16%	0.91%	-0.42%	-0.12%
20/05/2013	-1.03%	-3.89%	0.59%	0.69%	-0.35%
21/05/2013	0.44%	3.54%	-0.77%	-1.40%	0.14%
22/05/2013	3.45%	0.80%	-1.66%	-0.94%	0.24%
23/05/2013	-2.01%	-0.67%	0.15%	-1.66%	0.18%
24/05/2013	0.70%	-0.40%	-0.30%	0.77%	-0.22%
27/05/2013	0.00%	0.00%	0.00%	0.00%	0.37%
28/05/2013	-0.99%	-0.09%	0.86%	2.47%	0.04%
29/05/2013	0.43%	0.00%	-1.62%	-1.58%	-0.23%
30/05/2013	2.22%	1.42%	0.47%	-0.34%	-0.06%
31/05/2013	-1.35%	-0.49%	-1.77%	-1.35%	0.71%
03/06/2013	0.71%	-0.62%	1.60%	1.19%	0.05%
04/06/2013	-0.36%	0.36%	-0.05%	0.40%	0.24%
05/06/2013	0.32%	-0.62%	0.00%	0.00%	0.35%
06/06/2013	-0.29%	1.11%	0.00%	0.00%	0.07%
07/06/2013	-1.01%	-0.09%	0.00%	0.00%	0.47%

window: 90   column: i   final row: =ROW(H2335)

Volatilities - non - over (columns AK–AO)

start row (j)	end row (k)		Gold	Silver
5	94	25/05/2004	1.18%	3.30%
95	184	04/10/2004	0.89%	1.97%
185	274	17/02/2005	0.78%	2.19%
275	364	29/06/2005	0.60%	1.38%
365	454	04/11/2005	0.79%	1.22%
455	544	20/03/2006	1.34%	1.80%
545	634	26/07/2006	2.10%	3.86%
635	724	04/12/2006	1.32%	2.04%

Figure 33 Defining the final row for determining non-overlapping intervals for rolling volatilities

Spreadsheet — formula bar: PRICE ▼ × ✓ *fx* =STDEV(INDIRECT(CONCATENATE(AN$2,$AK5,":",AN$2,$AL5)))

Returns (columns H–M)

	Gold	Silver	Crude Oil - WTI	Crude Oil - Brent	EUR USD
02/01/2004	0.24%	0.00%	0.00%	-2.51%	-0.27%
05/01/2004	0.80%	0.17%	3.62%	8.90%	0.33%
06/01/2004	0.90%	4.98%	-0.51%	-3.46%	0.56%
07/01/2004	-0.63%	-1.04%	0.09%	-0.68%	0.65%
09/01/2004	0.38%	0.48%	2.38%	2.93%	0.22%
12/01/2004	0.45%	6.28%	1.56%	-1.58%	0.52%
15/01/2004	-1.36%	-5.17%	-3.82%	0.06%	-1.41%
16/01/2004	-2.68%	-1.76%	4.51%	-0.54%	-0.67%

window: 90   column: i … l … m   final row: 2335

Volatilities - non - overlapping (columns AK–AR)

start row	end row		Gold	Silver	Crude Oil - WTI	Crude Oil	EUR USD
5	94	25/05/2004	=STDEV(INDIRECT(CONCATENATE(AN$2,$AK5,":",AN$2,$AL5)))	1.97%	2.20%	2.15%	0.62%
95	184	04/10/2004	0.89%	1.97%	2.47%	2.69%	0.57%
185	274	17/02/2005	0.78%	2.19%	2.60%	2.07%	0.52%
275	364	29/06/2005	0.60%	1.38%	2.10%	2.07%	0.59%
365	454	04/11/2005	0.79%	1.22%	1.92%	1.91%	0.44%
455	544	20/03/2006	1.34%	1.80%	1.80%	1.84%	0.50%
545	634	26/07/2006	2.10%	3.86%	1.88%	2.36%	0.37%
635	724	04/12/2006	1.32%	2.04%			

Figure 34 Calculating rolling volatilities for non-overlapping intervals

minimum of the start row reference for that interval + window length – 1 and the final row reference.

In row 2, columns AN to AR, we specify the columns where the return series are present, that is, I to M. This will be used in identifying the interval range to be used in the calculations. For example, the formula in cell AN5, identifies the range "I5:I94" and calculates the standard deviation of the returns in this range (see Figure 34).

The volatility trend line using this methodology is given in Figure 35.

Crude oil price daily volatilities peaked in early 2009, to over 6 percent for WTI and over 5 percent for Brent. They have fallen to around 1 percent since then. Silver currently has the highest volatility among the

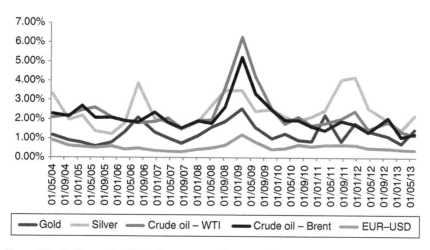

Figure 35 Rolling volatilities for non-overlapping discrete intervals

instruments considered here, while EUR–USD exchange rates have experienced a flat, slightly declining, trend for the past 2 to 2.5 years.

2. Rolling correlations

A similar analysis was done with respect to correlations with gold price returns. The trend lines show how correlations of gold with each instrument in turn, silver, crude oil, EUR–USD, have varied over time.

Using the return series and EXCEL's CORREL() function applied to the gold return series and another instrument's series, the 90-day rolling correlations have been calculated in Figure 36.

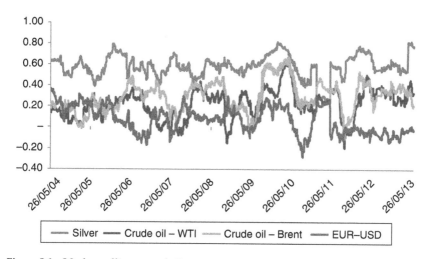

Figure 36 90-day rolling correlations

Taking an average of the previous 60 correlations, a series of average rolling correlations is also determined in Figure 37.

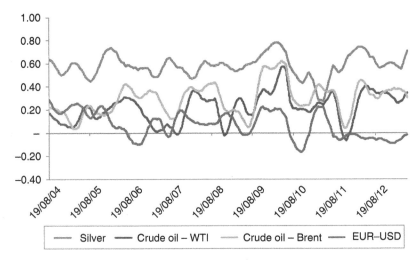

Figure 37   60-correlations average rolling correlations

To remove the bias of previous intervals on any given interval, a discrete non-overlapping interval rolling correlation series is also derived. A methodology similar to that for identifying discrete intervals for volatilities has been used. The formula at cell AU5 works out to "=CORREL($I5:$I94, $J5:$J94)", as shown in Figure 38.

A graphical representation of the non-overlapping interval rolling correlations is given in Figure 39.

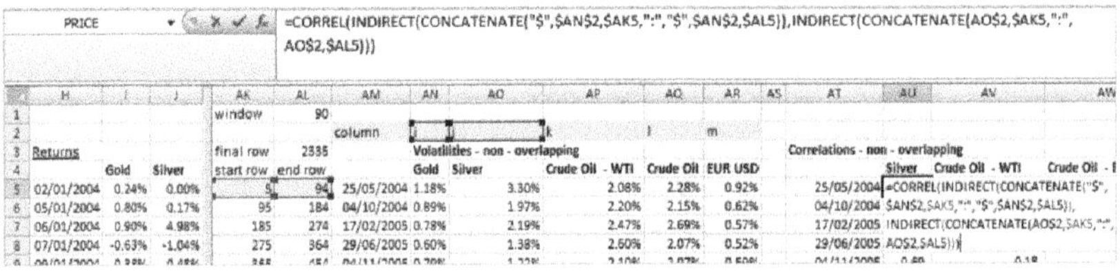

Figure 38   Calculating rolling correlations for non-overlapping intervals

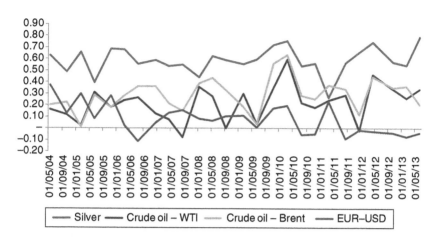

Figure 39 Rolling correlations for non-overlapping discrete intervals

2
Measuring Risk

In Chapter 1 we introduced a simple framework for estimating risk exposure when faced with uncertainty and volatility. In this chapter we will build up on that foundation and take a first step towards measuring risk.

While volatility and volatility distribution give us an indication of likely price movements, we need a measure that we can translate into language that can be understood across businesses. The same measure should be benchmarked, tracked and reported on a periodic basis, so that if exceptions occur they can be immediately identified and the appropriate corrective action can be taken.

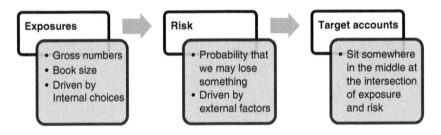

Figure 40 Exposure, risk and target accounts

Exploring target accounts

In some instances this number may be the same as the impact of price change. With others, it may be advisable to add more meaning and relevance to the analysis by taking a few additional steps.

For example, in the Emirates case we discussed the probability of a given price move and its dollar impact on net income. A next step would be to ask the questions: what is the probability that Emirates suffers a profit shortfall of a given size if we don't hedge our exposure? How does that probability change if we do hedge our exposure? Is there a process where we can change our hedging decisions and our hedging exposures based on changes in this probability?

From Emirates' point of view the trigger point for the decision to hedge could be the crossing of a probability threshold. If the likelihood of a 50 percent shortfall in profits is greater than 30 percent, jet fuel exposure will be hedged; if the probability stays below 30 percent, jet fuel exposure will be carried as is.

In this specific instance the probability of profit or margin shortfall would be a *target account*. Who sets the thresholds? While the board of directors approves the threshold as part of a policy document, the groundwork and recommendations to the board are made by finance and operations teams.

Probabilities and odds are a double-edged sword. They confuse audiences but, if presented correctly, turn absolute measures into language that the audience can relate to. For target accounts they come in handy, because they answer the board's favorite questions:

> What is the risk, the odds of this event happening? And if the event does happen what is our worst-case loss? What can we do to reduce that loss and the probability of its occurrence?

As a board member, which of the following statements comes down to actionable information to the above questions?

1. Our portfolio can suffer a price loss of US$ 500,000.
2. Our portfolio can suffer a loss of 5 percent of total assets invested.
3. Our portfolio could suffer a loss of 5 percent over any ten-day holding period.
4. A 5 percent price loss will reduce our declared year to date (YTD) return by 30 percent.
5. A 5 percent price loss will turn the YTD return into a negative return.
6. The probability of a YTD negative return is 12 percent at current risk levels. A 10 percent reduction in portfolio volatility will reduce this probability to 6 percent or less.

My choice would be (6). It's not the best possible option, but relative to the other choices I pick (6) because it focuses on:

(a) a desired outcome – positive return;
(b) the probability that the desired outcome may not be achieved;
(c) the action required to reduce the odds of the desired outcome not being achieved;
(d) it can be easily extended by a historical plot of negative return probabilities against portfolio volatility, allowing the audience to immediately place current values in the right context.

Admittedly, the underlying model and assumptions are questionable. Later on, when we build this model, we will see why it is broken, despite the exact and impressive numbers we generate from it. For now, ignoring the flaws in our model, if we look at the presentation of information we can see that there is some potential. In the case of (6) above the probability of a negative YTD return is a target account.

A target account is a measure that moves with the underlying risk and is reported in language that business can understand and relate to. It has acceptable value ranges, boundaries and thresholds that trigger corrective action if they are breached. The corrective action is referred to as management action, and the threshold that triggers the action is known as management action trigger.

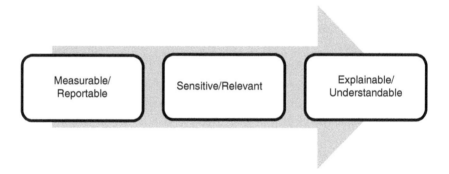

Figure 41   Target account characteristics

Ideally, a target account is benchmarked and calibrated to normal business conditions as well as to extreme scenarios. The objective is to get a sense for what would be considered acceptable values and what levels should trigger corrective action. We don't want intervention as part of routine business operations, but only when it is warranted.

Similarly to the Emirates example, reporting of the target account and triggers could be simple values or probabilities linked to a desired or undesired outcome. An effective presentation would plot historical target account levels with the trigger levels superimposed so that the audience can clearly see historical norms for the target account and the accepted number of breaches acceptable in a given reporting period.

While the shape and form of a target account is dependent on the underlying business as well as the risk being measured, common forms include:

- changes in income, P&L or earnings for a given risk factor,
- changes in shareholders' equity or value for a given risk factor,

- changes in portfolio and position profitability,
- changes in benchmark risk levels or risk to reward ratios.

In addition to the probability of shortfall measure discussed above, other examples of target accounts include:

1. impact of a unit change in interest rates on net interest income for a bank,
2. impact of a unit change in interest rates on shareholders' equity for a bank,
3. impact of a unit change in exchange rates on trading income for a foreign exchange (FX) trading position,
4. the number of accounts that slip into a higher risk days past due (DPD) category for a loan book,
5. the percentage of accounts/loans that shift to lower rated non-performing classifications for a loan book.

1. Target accounts and management action: value at risk and stop loss limits

Within the portfolio, investment and risk management world we use value at risk (VaR) as a measure of the risk inherent in a portfolio. VaR uses volatility or the underlying distribution to estimate the worst-case return over a given holding period with a certain confidence level.

For example, working with a portfolio invested only in gold, the VaR estimate would be a dollar value that the portfolio may drop over the next ten trading days. The actual number may vary depending on the confidence level picked. If we are interested in losses that may only be exceeded under the rarest of instances we will pick a confidence threshold of 99 percent, implying that the VaR estimate would only be exceeded in 1 percent of the scenarios.

If we use VaR as a target account, there are multiple management actions possible. Since VaR is a function of volatility, as volatility and VaR rise, for conservative investors it would make sense to cut or reduce their positions. When volatility and VaR fall, the size of the positions may be increased again. Alternatively, rather than reducing our exposure, we may allocate additional capital.

A third possibility is linked to stop loss limits. Stop loss limits are thresholds that when crossed require the underlying position to be cut immediately to ensure that trading-related losses on the position are limited to the original allocated capital.

Unlike VaR, stop loss is a limit, a threshold or a boundary condition. It doesn't just control capital, it also indicates the trading range a trader may utilize to run his positions. Larger stop loss limits create a bigger playground for traders, while smaller limits restrict them. When capital is short, rising volatility leads to tighter stop loss. Since VaR is a function of volatility, a rise in VaR may also lead to a reduction in stop loss limits.

If as a trading desk we use recent volatility (measured using historical data) and VaR to gauge our risk, they serve as target accounts. The management action in response to triggers (for example, higher vol. or VaR) is a change or review of stop loss limits.

The design problem is deciding the level at which the VaR threshold should be set to trigger the review of stop loss limits. Think about this while we move on to formally introduce VaR and its many variations.

Introducing value at risk

Value at risk has been around for over three decades. It is a measure that uses many simplifying assumptions to produce a crude but useful indicator of downside risk in a trading book. Its effectiveness has been the subject of persistent debate. From the long term capital management (LTCM) crises in August 1998 to the 2008–9 meltdown in financial markets, VaR has been in the news for all the wrong reasons.

VaR's most celebrated critic has been Nicholas Nassim Taleb, who dissected the risk measure for its flaws in his initial debate on this subject with Philippe Jorian in Derivative Strategy, followed by his two signature texts – *Fooled by Randomness* and *The Black Swan*. Taleb's analysis focused on allied human failings and biases that make a single precise sounding measure ineffective. His advice was to acknowledge our information translation challenges, focus on the process (the generator function) that originates risk, rather than risk numbers, and be wary of underlying assumptions wandering off to uncharted territory under times of stress.

Interestingly enough, Taleb's criticism wasn't really aimed at the model. It was aimed at its users and the models' many salesmen – which is where the bitterness in the VaR debate crept in.

Taleb's stance was vindicated when the Bank for International Settlements (BIS) committee started evaluating alternate and supplementary measures, in addition to VaR, for tracking capital adequacy in 2009–10.

Like all tools, VaR's efficacy depends on how the tool is put to use. The following are some of the key issues (first the bad news) raised in current literature about VaR.

- Is the one number sufficient by itself to completely capture the risk in a position?
- Do the users of VaR understand the limitations (of the tool) and the implications of those limitations, especially in view of the pseudo-precise nature of VaR's pronouncements?

- When calculating VaR for a portfolio we assume that volatility and correlations are stable and historical levels will track future results. However, under times of stress correlations malfunction and volatilities gyrate beyond their normal ranges. In such scenarios, when VaR is most needed, the underlying model breaks down.
- Risk management is concerned with extreme events or large deviations from what is expected. The most common tool used for measuring the above is variance, an average (of sorts) of all the deviations from the mean. Although it is the key tool used in calculating VaR, it is not the most appropriate. Higher order factors that measure symmetry or length and thickness of tails would be more accurate.
- VaR uses data from all events to evaluate the impact of extreme events. It is forced to do this because, by definition, extreme events do not occur frequently enough to generate sufficient data. The downside is that extreme events have much higher means and variances. This means that if VaR (somehow) did use extreme events, it would lead to a much higher VaR estimate.
- Given that the objective of risk management is to understand risk exposures and neutralize them, there is a strong emphasis on supplementing VaR with scenario analysis or sensitivity testing.

But despite all of the above issues, VaR usage is pervasive throughout the financial services industry. We don't just use it for measuring portfolio risk. We also use it for estimating client default probabilities, loss given default estimates on margin accounts, and pre-settlement risk limits on counterparty exposures, as well as for configuring our stop loss limits.

This happens because the measure is by now widely accepted (primarily due to the adoption by BIS as a recommended regulatory standard for risk). Till the industry finds a better alternative, VaR is here to stay.

1. What is value at risk?

Value at risk is a market risk measurement approach that uses historical market trends and volatilities to estimate the likelihood that a given portfolio's losses will exceed a certain amount.

In one sense it is an extension (or even a simplification, depending on who you ask) of the probability of shortfall calculations model used in the early 1980s by pension fund managers to estimate the probability that they would eat into surplus and the probability of ruin models used by insurance companies for the last 200 years.

Value at risk measures the largest loss likely to be suffered on a portfolio or a position over a holding period (usually one to ten days) with a

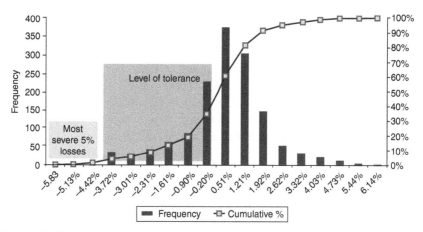

Figure 42   Distribution of returns

given probability (confidence level). As an example, assuming a 99 percent confidence level, a VaR of US$ 1 million means that there is only a 1
percent chance that losses will exceed the US$ 1 million figure over the
next ten days. It is also "fashionable" to refer to this loss as the one day
in 100 days loss.

2. Value at risk methods

There are three primary methods used for calculating VaR:

(a) variance/covariance method;
(b) historical simulation method;
(c) Monte Carlo simulation method.

All methods have a common base, but diverge in how they actually calculate VaR. They also have a common problem in assuming that the
future will follow the past. This shortcoming is normally addressed by
supplementing any VaR figures with appropriate sensitivity analysis and/
or stress testing. In general, the VaR calculation follows five steps:

- identification of positions;
- identification of risk factors affecting valuation of positions;
- assignment of probabilities (or statistical distribution) to possible risk
  factor values;
- creation of pricing functions for positions as a function of values of
  risk factors;
- calculation of VaR.

a. Variance/Covariance (VCV) approach

This method assumes that the daily returns follow a normal distribution. From the distribution of daily returns we estimate the standard deviation (σ). The daily VaR is simply a function of the standard deviation and the desired confidence level. In the variance/covariance method, the underlying volatility may be calculated either using a simple moving average (SMA) or an exponentially weighted moving average (EWMA). Mathematically, the difference lies in the method used to calculate the standard deviation (σ).

The SMA approach places equal importance on all returns in the series, whereas the EWMA approach places greater emphasis on returns of more recent durations.

The variance/covariance method makes a number of assumptions. The biggest of these is normal return – assuming that security price changes follow a normal distribution. The accuracy of the results depends on how valid and stable these assumptions are. The method gets its name from the variance/covariance matrix of securities that is used to calculate VaR.

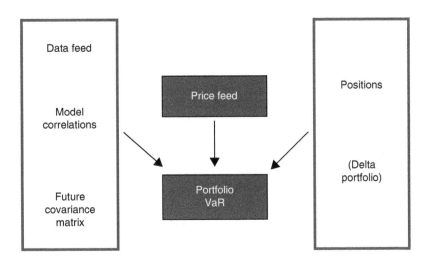

Figure 43   Variance/Covariance approach

The method starts by calculating the standard deviation and correlation for the risk factor, and then uses these values to calculate the standard deviations and correlation for the changes in the value of the individual securities that form the position. If price, variance and correlation data is available for individual securities then this information is used directly. The values are then used to calculate the standard deviation of the portfolio. Value at risk for a specific confidence level is then calculated by multiplying the standard deviation by the appropriate normal distribution factor.

In some cases, a method equivalent to the variance/covariance approach is used to calculate VaR. This method does not generate the variance/covariance matrix, and uses the following approach.

1. Separate the portfolio into a long side and a short side.
2. Calculate the return series for the long side and the short side.
3. Use the return series to calculate the correlation and variances for the long and short sides.
4. Use the results in (3) to calculate the VaR.

The modified approach can be used where, due to the nature of the institution's strategies, a number of positions would net close to zero on a portfolio basis, and also where the set of securities employed is so large that a variance/covariance approach would have significant resource/ time requirements.

b. Historical simulation method

This approach requires fewer statistical assumptions for the underlying market factors. It applies the historical (100 days) changes in price levels to current market prices in order to generate a hypothetical data set. The data set is then ordered by the size of gains/losses. Value at risk is the value that is equaled or exceeded the required percentage of times (1 percent, 5 percent, 10 percent).

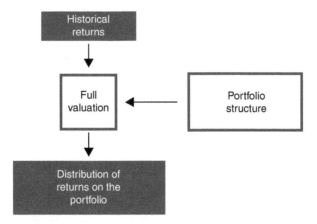

Figure 44 Historical simulation method

Historical simulation is a non-parametric approach of estimating VaR, that is, the returns are not subjected to any functional distribution. Value at risk is estimated directly from the data without deriving parameters or making assumptions about the entire distribution of the data. This methodology is based on the premise that the pattern of historical returns is indicative of future returns.

c. Monte Carlo simulation

The approach is similar to the historical simulation method described above except for one big difference. The hypothetical data set used is generated by a statistical distribution rather than historical price levels. The assumption is that the selected distribution captures or reasonably approximates price behavior of the modeled securities.

A Monte Carlo simulator uses random numbers to simulate the real world. A Monte Carlo VaR model uses the following sequence of steps:

- generate randomly simulated prices,
- calculate daily return series,
- repeat the steps in the historical simulation method described above.

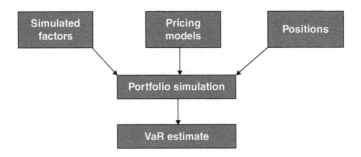

Figure 45 Monte Carlo simulation method

3. Caveats, qualifications, limitations and issues

- Value at risk is dependent on historical data and therefore may never fully capture severe shocks that exceed recent or historical norms. Also, if the time period used in the calculation is a relatively stable one then the computed VaR will tend to understate the risk. If the time period showed more volatile data, however, VaR could end up being too high.
- In evaluating risk and setting thresholds there is value in using a lower VaR threshold (95 percent instead of 99 percent) as an early warning tool.

As the low threshold is more likely to be crossed with greater frequency than the higher threshold VaR it could serve as a signal to management to make queries that could uncover anomalies and previously unrecognized risk.

- Multiple VaR methods may be used to assess risk from all available information and hence obtain challenging and different views of risk. Volatility estimates from the recent past (EWMA) could act as early warning signals of changes in current market conditions while estimates drawn from a longer historical interval (SMA or historical simulation) may be used to assess and identify stressful episodes in the past.

- Generally, the variance/covariance approach does a reasonable job of assessing, over very short time periods, the VaR for portfolios that do not include options. The historical simulation approach works best for a risk source that is stable and for which there is a good, reliable and substantial historical database. For options or portfolios with nonlinear portfolios, or where the data is volatile and unstable and the normality assumption underlying the Variance Covariance (VCV) cannot apply, the Monte Carlo simulation method is the best approach.

- Value at risk numbers should not be used in isolation. They must be back-tested against actual profit and loss numbers. Anomalies between P&L and VaR should alert management to query or probe them. This investigation could reveal areas for improvement in calculation/reporting. On the other hand it could reveal the possibility of previously unrecognized risks or emerging stress conditions. P&L reporting must be of sufficient granularity to be useful in assessing risk for a given business line/portfolio.

- Since the underlying return distributions for the variance/covariance and Monte Carlo simulation approaches are assumptions of what the actual distributions could be, a violation of these assumptions would result in incorrect estimates of the VaR measure. Even the historical simulation approach, which is a non-parametric approach, is based on the fact that we are assuming that the historical distribution of returns based on past data will be representative of the distribution going forward. If this is not the case, the VaR calculation would lead to inaccurate estimates.

- There is significant literature, which evidences that returns of various risk factors are not normally distributed and that events considered outliers based on the normal distribution occur more frequently in reality. This could result in companies/banks being underprepared for events considered to be extremely unlikely using a normal distribution.

- The VaR measure across risk factors also relies on, explicitly or implicitly, correlations between the risk factors. As we know, correlations tend to vary greatly over time and do not remain static. If future correlations were to change between factors relative to what was experienced in the past then VaR measures based on past data would result in incorrect estimates of the true risk.

- Value at risk should not be relied on as the sole measure of risk. By its definition, VaR only looks at risk from one angle – the maximum loss that could occur over a certain period with a certain degree of certainty. In doing so a great deal of valuable information on the risk distribution tends to be ignored. For example, the extent of loss in the extreme ranges remains unknown.

- When using VaR the user should not just stick to regulatory parameters such as the 95 percent or 99 percent confidence levels. This has been shown to lead to suboptimal risk management decisions as the focus is not on intermediate losses, which fall below the probability threshold. These managers tend to do worse than their counterparts, who also monitor the intermediate losses because they do not reign in their losses until the specified probability threshold or worst-case scenario is crossed.

- Value at risk measures have a tendency to be gamed by managers to meet the VaR risk constraint by selecting the approach or the look back period. For example, using the historical simulation approach, where the data set ignores a recent sudden upsurge in the volatility of commodity prices, would result in a low VaR number that would satisfy requirements but would fail one of the objectives of risk management, which is to alert the company to a possibly deteriorating situation that could be unfolding.

4. Risk or factor sensitivities

A common mistake is confusing risk with risk or factor sensitivities. Several examples follow.

(a) If you wanted to measure an equity security's movement with a broad based equity market index, you would use the measure Beta. Beta is a measure based on the covariance of a given equity security with the market based index. If the market moves up by 1 percent, Beta indicates how much the security in question is likely to move (up or down).

(b) If you wanted to measure the change in the price of a bond based on a change in the underlying interest rates, you would use the measure modified duration (Duration for short). Duration is based on the good old tangent (the slope equation in high school math) to the bond-pricing curve. It measures the change in price of a bond based on a unit change in the yield to maturity.

(c) If you were evaluating a portfolio of options, you would use delta. Delta estimates the change in the value of the option based on a change in the underlying spot price. Like Duration, it is a first order estimate that also uses tangents.

Beta, Duration and delta are factor sensitivities, but they do not represent risk. The first is a measure of covariance with the market, the next two are rates of change in the security of interest based on the rate of change in some underlying variable.

To translate these into risk you need to determine their likely, expected or unexpected moves and then calculate the price impact on the security in question.

Calculating value at risk – step by step walkthrough

1. Methodology

a. Setting the scene

Sample portfolio

Our sample portfolio consists of the following items:

- 5 shares of GOOG (Google Inc.);
- 15 barrels of crude oil (West Texas Intermediate, WTI);
- 1 foreign exchange denominated asset with market value of EUR 1000 on 17 June 2013;
- 50 units of 10-year US treasury bonds with issue date of 15 February 2013 and coupon rate of 2 percent; this means that the outstanding term of the bond is 9.67 years.

Revaluation date and value of the portfolio
We are calculating portfolio VaR on the June 17, 2013 at the end of the day.

b. Preliminary steps

The following steps are common to all the above mentioned VaR approaches.

Step P1: Determine look back period
Determine the period over which the risk is to be evaluated. For illustration purposes let us assume a look back period from December 31, 2012 to June 17, 2013. In practice, window lengths may cover a much wider duration, such as 1 year, 3 years, and so on.

Step P2: Obtain the daily time series data for each risk factor for the determined look back period

The risk factors related to the assets in our portfolio are equity prices (GOOG), commodity prices (WTI), foreign exchange rates (EUR–USD) and interest rates (US treasury daily yield curve rates particularly for years 7 and 10 respectively) as given in Figure 46.

DATE	GOOG	WTI	EUR–USD	US TREASURY 7 YEAR (%)	US TREASURY 10 YEAR (%)
31/12/2012	707.38	91.83	1.3215	1.18	1.78
02/01/2013	723.25	93.14	1.3196	1.25	1.86
03/01/2013	723.67	92.97	1.3234	1.31	1.92
.	.	.	.	.	.
.	.	.	.	.	.
.	.	.	.	.	.
13/06/2013	877.00	96.66	1.331	1.6	2.19
14/06/2013	875.04	97.83	1.334	1.53	2.14
17/06/2013	886.25	97.86	1.3342	1.57	2.19

Figure 46   Daily time series data

Step P3: Adjustments to original time series data

The interest rate risk factors, that is, the US treasury yield curve rates, need to be adjusted to take into account the portfolio's exact exposure to this risk factor. The rate series will first be interpolated based on the outstanding term to maturity of the bond, and then will be converted into a price series, which will be used in the actual VaR calculation.

The detailed steps to this process are given below.

Determine the outstanding term of the bond as of the calculation date (June 17, 2013):

$$\text{Outsiding Term in years} = \frac{(\text{Maturity Date-Revaluation Date})}{365} = 9.67 \text{ years.}$$

$$= 9.67 \text{ years.}$$

Calculate an interpolated rate series for this outstanding term. Interpolation will be done using the formula

$$\text{US Treasury}_{\text{interpolated}} = \frac{(T_2 - T) \times \text{US Treasury}_{7 \text{ years}} + (T - T_1) \times \text{US Treasury}_{10 \text{ years}}}{(T_2 - T_1)}$$

where

T = outstanding term = 9.67 years,

T_1 = rounded down value of the outstanding term to an available tenor
= 7 years,

T_2 = rounded up value of the outstanding term to an available tenor
= 10 years.

Using US Treasury Daily Yield Curve rates for June 17, 2013, the interpolated rate is calculated as

$$\textbf{US Treasury}_{interpolated} = \frac{(10 - 9.67) \times 1.57\% + (9.67 - 7) \times 2.19\%}{(10 - 7)} = 2.122\%.$$

The resulting interpolated US Treasury rate series works out to

	US Treasury_Interpolated
31/12/2012	1.714%
02/01/2013	1.793%
03/01/2013	1.853%
.	.
.	.
.	.
13/06/2013	2.125%
14/06/2013	2.073%
17/06/2013	2.122%

Figure 47   Interpolated interest rates

Calculate the price of the bond at each data point using:

- Settlement date = Revaluation date = June 17, 2013,
- Maturity Date = February 15, 2023,
- Coupon Rate = 2.00 percent,
- Yield = US Treasury interpolated rate applicable to that data point,
- Redemption value = 100,
- Coupon payment frequency = 2,
- Basis = Actual/365 (1 in EXCEL).

This may be done using EXCEL's Price formula or by discounting the cash flows using the formula

$$Price = \left[\frac{(Redemption\ Value)}{\left(1 + \dfrac{yield}{freqency}\right)^{N-1+\frac{t}{E}}} \right] + \left[\sum_{k=1}^{N} \frac{\dfrac{100 \times coupon\ rate}{frequency}}{\left(1 + \dfrac{yield}{freqency}\right)^{k-1+\frac{t}{E}}} \right] - \left(\frac{100 \times coupon\ rate}{frequency} \times \frac{A}{E} \right)$$

where

    t = number of days from settlement to next coupon date,

    E = number of days in coupon period in which the settlement date falls,

    N = number of coupons payable between settlement date and redemption date,

    A = number of days from beginning of coupon period to settlement date.

The resulting bond price series works out to:

	BOND PRICES
31/12/2012	102.5337
02/01/2013	101.8267
03/01/2013	101.2927
.	.
.	.
.	.
13/06/2013	98.90914
14/06/2013	99.36129
17/06/2013	98.93755

Figure 48   Derived bond price series

Step P4: Calculate a return series from the time series data

A return series is derived from the given time series data by taking the natural logarithm of the ratio of successive prices/rates, that is, $R_t = \ln\left(\dfrac{s_t}{s_{t-1}}\right)$, where s_t is the price/rate at time t. For example for GOOG, the return on January 2, 2013 = $\ln\left(\dfrac{723.25}{707.38}\right)$ = 2.2187 percent. The return series for the rest of the portfolio is given below in Figure 49.

	GOOG	WTI	EUR–USD	BOND PRICES
02/01/2013	2.2187%	1.4165%	−0.1439%	−0.6919%
03/01/2013	0.0581%	−0.1827%	0.2876%	−0.5258%
.	.	.	.	.
.	.	.	.	.
.	.	.	.	.
14/06/2013	−0.2237%	1.2032%	0.2251%	0.4561%
17/06/2013	1.2729%	0.0307%	0.0150%	−0.4274%

Figure 49   Daily returns series

Step P5: Calculate a return series for the portfolio

In order to evaluate the VaR for the portfolio, its return series will be required. This is derived by calculating a weighted average return series using the individual return series for each instrument in the portfolio. This is a short cut method to the lengthy and cumbersome variance/covariance matrix derivation method of determining portfolio returns. The proof of how this method yields the same results as the variance/covariance matrix methodology is given at the end of this section.

The portfolio return series will be determined as follows.

Calculate the weights of the respective instruments in the portfolio on the revaluation date, where *weight = value of the instrument ÷ total value of the portfolio*. The weights for the portfolio are given in Figure 50.

Derive a weighted average return series by calculating for each point in time in the data series the sum product of the weight and return across instruments/scripts in the portfolio. *The resulting weighted average return series will be correlation adjusted, that is, it will account for correlations between the various instruments.* For example, for the data point January 2, 2013 the portfolio return will be

$$36.38\% \times 2.2187\% + 12.05\% \times 1.4165\% + 10.95\% \times (-0.1439\%)$$
$$+ 40.61\% \times (-0.6919\%) = 0.6811\%.$$

The return series for the sample portfolio is as shown in Figure 51.

INSTRUMENT	UNITS	DETAILS	VALUE	WEIGHTS
GOOG	5	Shares	4,431.25	$\frac{4431.25}{12180.23} = 36.38\%$
Crude Oil (WTI)	15	Barrels	1,467.90	12.05%
EUR	1	Asset of EUR 1000	1,334.20	10.95%
10-year US treasury bond	50	Units	4,946.88	40.61%
Portfolio on 17th June 2013			12,180.23	100%

Figure 50 Calculation of portfolio weights

	Portfolio Return
02/01/2013	0.6811%
03/01/2013	−0.1829%
.	.
.	.
.	.
14/06/2013	0.2735%
17/06/2013	0.2949%

Figure 51 Portfolio daily return series

2. VaR approach specific steps

a. Variance/Covariance (VCV) VaR

Determining SMA volatility

Under the VCV–SMA VaR approach the returns calculated in steps P4 and P5 above are given equal weight when calculating the underlying volatility, as given by the formula

$$\sigma^2 = \frac{1}{n-1}\sum_{t=1}^{n}\left(R_t - E(R)\right)^2,$$

where R_t is the rate of return at time t and $E(R)$ is the mean of the return distribution, that is,

$$E(R) = \frac{1}{n}\sum_{t=1}^{n}R_t.$$

The number of return observations used in the calculations is represented by n.

In our look back period there were 116 observed rates/prices per instrument (using GOOG's quote dates). This resulted in 115 return observations, that is, $n = 115$ in the formulas above.

Detailed steps for SMA volatility are given below.

Step A1: Calculate the mean of the distribution
Sum the returns over the series and divide by the number of returns in the series. For the portfolio return series this is calculated as

$$\frac{\left(0.6811\% + (-0.1829\%) + \ldots + 0.2735\% + 0.2949\%\right)}{115} = 0.0663\%.$$

Alternatively, this may be arrived at by applying the EXCEL's "AVERAGE" to the return series.

Step A2: Calculate the variance of the distribution
At each point in the return series calculate the difference of the return from the mean calculated in step A1 above. Square the result and then sum over all squared differences. Divide the resulting sum by the number of returns in the series less one. For the portfolio return series this is as follows:

DATE	RETURNS (*R*)	(*R*−*E*(*R*))²
02/01/2013	0.6811%	0.0038%
03/01/2013	−0.1829%	0.0006%
.	.	.
.	.	.
.	.	.
14/06/2013	0.2735%	0.0004%
17/06/2013	0.2949%	0.0005%

Figure 52   Squared differences of the returns series

$$\text{SMA Variance,} \frac{(0.0038\% + 0.0006\% + \dots + 0.0004\% + 0.0005\%)}{(115 - 1)} = 0.0021\%.$$

Alternatively this may be arrived at by applying the EXCEL function "VAR" to the *return* series.

Step A3: Calculate the SMA volatility
The daily SMA volatility is equal to the square root of the variance calculated in step A2 above, that is, it is the standard deviation or σ. For the portfolio return series this is

$$\sigma = \sqrt{0.0021\%} = 0.4574\%.$$

Alternatively, this may be arrived at by applying the EXCEL function "STDEV" to the *return* series.

Determining EWMA volatility

The SMA approach gives equal importance to all observations used in the look back period and does not account for the fact that information tends to decay or become less relevant over time. The EWMA method on the other hand gives more importance to recent information and hence places greater weight on more recent returns. This is achieved by specifying a parameter, lambda (λ), ($0 < \lambda < 1$) and placing exponentially declining weights on historical data.

The EWMA variance formula is

$$\sigma^2 = \sum_{t=1}^{n}(1-\lambda) \times \lambda^{t-1} \times R_t^2 \, .$$

Step B1: Specifying λ
In general, the EWMA methodology places more emphasis on recent data as higher weights are assigned through the formula to more recent data. However, the λ value determines the weight-age of the data in the formula and the sample size actually considered. The smaller the value of λ the quicker the weight decays. If we expect volatility to be very unstable then we will apply a low decay factor (giving a lot of weight to recent observations and effectively considering a smaller sample as weights taper to zero more quickly). If we expect volatility to be constant we will apply a high decay factor (giving more equal weight to older observations).

We have used the industry standard of $\lambda = 0.94$ in our example.

Step B2: Determining weights
As given in the formula above, the weights are calculated at each data point as shown in Figure 53.

$\lambda = 0.94$	$t-1$	$1-\lambda$	λ^{t-1}	Weights (%) = $(1-\lambda) \times \lambda^{t-1}$
02/01/2013	114	0.06	0.000864	0.0052%
03/01/2013	113	0.06	0.000919	0.0055%
.	.	.	.	.
.	.	.	.	.
.	.	.	.	.
14/06/2013	1	0.06	0.94000	5.6400%
17/06/2013	0	0.06	1.00000	6.0000%

Figure 53 Calculation of weights under EWMA

Step B3: Scaling weights
One special property of the weights used in the EWMA formula is that their sum to infinity will always be equal to 1. However, it is not possible to have an infinite set of historical data, so if the sum of weights is not close to 1 then adjustments need to be made. These adjustments include expanding either the data set or the look back period to ensure that it is

large enough that this sum of weights is close to 1. Alternatively, weights have to be rescaled so that their sum equals 1. This rescaling is achieved by dividing the weights calculated in Step B2 by $1-\lambda^n$, where n is the number of return observations. This is illustrated in our example in Figure 54.

WEIGHTS		SCALED WEIGHTS = WEIGHTS $\div$ $(1 - \lambda^n)$
02/01/2013	0.0052%	0.0052%
03/01/2013	0.0055%	0.0055%
.	.	.
.	.	.
.	.	.
14/06/2013	5.6400%	5.6446%
17/06/2013	6.0000%	6.0049%
Sum of weights	99.919%	100.00%

Figure 54   Scaling of weights

Step B4: Calculating the EWMA variance

The first step in calculating the variance is to calculate the squares of the returns at each data point. Next multiply the squared series with the weights applicable to that data point and then sum the resulting weighted squared series. This is illustrated for the portfolio return series in Figure 55.

dd/mm/yyyy	SCALED WEIGHTS	RETURNS (R)	R^2	SCALED WEIGHTS $\times R^2$
02/01/2013	0.0052%	0.6811%	0.0046%	0.0000002%
03/01/2013	0.0055%	−0.1829%	0.0003%	0.0000000%
.	.	.	.	.
.	.	.	.	.
.	.	.	.	.
14/06/2013	5.6446%	0.2735%	0.0007%	0.0000422%
17/06/2013	6.0049%	0.2949%	0.0009%	0.0000522%
			Sum(Variance) =	0.00203%

Figure 55   Calculation of EWMA variance

Step B5: Calculating the EWMA volatility

The daily EWMA volatility is obtained by taking the square root of the result in Step B4 above:

$$\sigma = \sqrt{0.00203\%} = 0.4509\%.$$

Determining SMA and EWMA daily VaR

The daily VaR is simply a function of the standard deviation or volatility and the desired confidence level. Specifically, *σ × z-value of standard normal cumulative distribution corresponding with a specified confidence level.*

For example, for a confidence level of 99 percent the z-value is 2.326 (EXCEL's function "NORMSINV(.99)" may be used to determine the z-value) and the daily VaR = 2.326σ. For our sample portfolio the VCV VaRs at the 99 percent confidence level work out as shown in Figure 56.

	SMA		EWMA	
	σ	DAILY VAR = 2.326σ	σ	DAILY VAR = 2.326σ
GOOG	1.2554%	2.9206%	1.1244%	2.6157%
WTI	1.0932%	2.5431%	1.0555%	2.4555%
EUR–USD	0.4336%	1.0088%	0.3462%	0.8055%
Bond prices	0.3543%	0.8241%	0.4356%	1.0135%
Portfolio	0.4574%	1.0640%	0.4509%	1.0489%

Figure 56   SMA and EWMA daily VaRs

Determining historical simulation daily VaR

Step H1: Order return series derived in Steps P4 and P5
The first step is to order these daily returns in ascending order. Each ordered return corresponds to an index number. In our example this is illustrated as shown in Figure 57 for the portfolio return series.

INDEX NUMBER	R (SORTED IN ASCENDING ORDER)
1	−1.2042%
2	−0.8258%
.	.
.	.
.	.
114	1.5062%
115	1.8263%

Figure 57   Ordered portfolio return series

Step H2: Determine the index value corresponding to 1 – confidence level percent
This is given by the number of return observations × (1 – confidence level percent). The resulting number is truncated, or rounded down to an

integer. For a confidence level of 99 percent and 115 return observations, the resulting number is 1.15, so the index value will be equal to 1.

Step H3: Identify the daily historical VaR
The daily historical VaR is the absolute value of the return in the ordered series in Step H1 that corresponds to the index value derived in Step H2. For the portfolio return series this is the absolute value of the return at index number 1, that is, 1.2042 percent.

b. Scaling of the daily VaR

Step S1: Determine the holding period
The holding period is the time it would take to liquidate the asset/portfolio in the market. In Basel II, for most instances, a 10-day holding period is a standard requirement.

Step S2: Scaling the daily VaR
To determine the VaR for a J-day holding period the square root rule will be applied, that is, the J-day VaR $= \sqrt{J} \times$ (daily VaR). For the portfolio, the holding VaR for each approach is as shown in Figure 58.

APPROACH	DAILY VAR	10-DAY HOLDING VAR % = DAILY VAR ×√10	10-DAY HOLDING VAR AMOUNT = VAR% × PORTFOLIO VALUE
SMA	1.0640%	3.3647%	409.83
EWMA	1.0489%	3.3168%	404.00
Historical	1.2042%	3.8079%	463.81

Figure 58 Holding period VaR

The maximum loss that we could experience in our portfolio over a 10-day holding period with 99 percent probability is US$ 404.00 using a EWMA VaR approach. In other words there is a 1 percent chance the losses will exceed this amount in a 10-day holding period.

3. Proof of equivalence: short-cut method versus VCV matrix approaches to portfolio VaR

a. Theoretical overview

Portfolio VaR is a very important measure for assessing the market risk inherent in the entire portfolio of an entity. It is a measure whose calculation is often linked to heartburn because the risk manager envisions the very labor-intensive construction of the variance/covariance matrix. Above, we demonstrated a remedy that should provide the user with some level of comfort – a short cut approach to the matrix, first highlighted by Columbia University Business School's Professor Mark Broadie, using a weighted average series of portfolio returns.

However, it is human nature to question a doctor's prescription, to seek a second opinion, and we've had a number of people ask us for proof of whether the more efficient, practical and convenient weighted average return version of calculating portfolio VaR really does give the portfolio VaR derived using the traditional variance/covariance matrix approach. Or were the results simply coincidental, mathematical magic per se?

The proof follows:

$$\text{Variance } (aX + bY) = a^2 \text{ Variance } (X) + b^2 \text{ Variance } (Y)$$
$$+ 2ab \text{ Covariance } (X,Y).$$

The square root of variance is the standard deviation, which, as you know, in VaR terminology is volatility, the edifice of the Simple Moving Average Variance/Covariance (SMA VCV) approach to calculation of the metric.

The traditional VCV approach methodology employs the construction of the infamous variance/covariance matrix, which in statistical equation terms is denoted by the right hand side (RHS) of the above equation – a conglomeration of squared weights, individual asset return variances and covariances between pairs of variables.

Our short cut approach focuses on the oft-forgot left hand side (LHS) of the equation, that is, the variance of the weighted average sum of variables. If the weighted average sum of variables $aX + bY = Z$, then all we need is the variance of Z. In terms of the VaR calculation the variables are the daily return series for each asset in the portfolio; the weighted average sum of variables, that is, Z, is the weighted average sum of daily return series; Z is therefore the portfolio return series. And therefore by calculating the variance of Z, the weighted daily return series, square rooting the result and applying the appropriate multiplier factor representing the confidence level and holding period, we arrive at the SMA variance/covariance VaR result.

Low and behold the proof of our short cut approach ... it is truly equal to the SMA VCV VaR using the traditional variance/covariance methodology.

It should be noted however that if you are applying the EXCEL functions of VAR() and COVAR() to calculate the variance and covariance respectively, there will be a slight difference in results obtained from the traditional variance/covariance matrix method and efficient weighted average return short cut method. The error lies with the traditional approach, as there is an inconsistency between the variance and covariance formulas underlying the EXCEL functions. The COVAR() formula in EXCEL uses a sample size of n in the divisor whereas VAR() employs a sample size of $n-1$. A simple adjustment may be made to COVAR() prior to use in the RHS of the equation above to remove this discrepancy, specifically: Adjusted COVAR() = COVAR() $\times$ $n/(n-1)$.

Alternatively, instead of the RHS given above we could use

a^2 Variance (X) + b^2 Variance (Y)
  + $2ab$ Correlation (X,Y) Standard Deviation (X) Standard Deviation (Y).

[Recall statistically that Correlation(X,Y) = Covariance(X,Y)/ Standard Deviation(X) Standard Deviation(Y)]

In EXCEL, the CORREL() function is given as

$$\text{Correl}(X,Y) = \frac{\sum (x - \bar{x})(y - \bar{y})}{\sqrt{\sum (x - \bar{x})^2 \sum (y - y)^2}}.$$

This implicitly assumes consistency between the variance and covariance formulas, as the divisors of each cancel out. Using CORREL() instead of COVAR() removes the discrepancy between results obtained using the traditional approach to SMA VCV VaR and results derived using the short cut approach.

b. Calculating portfolio VaR with and without VCV matrix

Above we have presented the theoretical proof of how the portfolio VaR obtained using the short cut weighted average return method produces the same result as would have been obtained if a detailed VCV matrix derivation approach had been used. We now look at a specific example where daily VaR for the sample portfolio is first obtained using the short cut technique and then the same result is arrived at using the detailed matrix methodology.

The portfolio is assumed to consist of two equity instruments, two FX forward instruments and two bonds. The returns series have already been obtained from the historical series of prices for all securities (including bond prices).

We have also determined the weights of each instrument as the value of each instrument in the portfolio to the total portfolio value. Please note that in our illustrations here these values have been taken as given.

	A	B	C	D	E	F	G
7	**Return series**						
8	Dates	EQUITY 1	EQUITY 2	FX FORWARD 1	FX FORWARD 2	BOND 1	BOND 2
9	01/01/2009	-5.13%	-5.13%	0.00%	-5.11%	0.00%	-8.55%
10	02/01/2009	4.87%	-5.12%	-5.08%	4.85%	0.00%	-9.35%
11	05/01/2009	4.87%	-5.12%	-5.12%	4.87%	0.00%	-5.03%
12	06/01/2009	3.31%	-5.12%	-5.13%	3.00%	0.00%	-4.21%
13	09/01/2009	-1.65%	2.63%	-5.12%	-3.25%	0.00%	7.26%
14	12/01/2009	-0.42%	-5.12%	-5.13%	0.85%	0.00%	0.00%
15	13/01/2009	0.51%	-5.12%	-5.13%	0.15%	0.00%	0.00%
16	14/01/2009	-3.43%	-5.12%	-5.13%	-5.12%	0.00%	0.00%
17	15/01/2009	-4.14%	-5.13%	-5.13%	-5.13%	0.00%	0.00%
18	16/01/2009	-5.12%	-5.13%	0.00%	-5.12%	0.00%	0.00%
19	19/01/2009	-4.86%	-5.12%	0.00%	-5.10%	0.00%	0.00%
20	20/01/2009	-0.86%	-5.13%	0.65%	-5.03%	0.00%	0.00%
21	21/01/2009	0.18%	-5.12%	-4.32%	-5.13%	0.00%	0.00%

Figure 59 Return series of instruments in the sample portfolio

PRICE		X ✓ *fx*	=B5/$B$1			
	A	B	C	D	E	F	G
1	Portfolio	1,000,000.00					
4	Weights	=B5/$B$1	20.00%	20.00%	20.00%	25.00%	5.00%
5	Value	100,000.00	200,000.00	200,000.00	200,000.00	250,000.00	50,000.00

Figure 60 Weights of instruments in the sample portfolio

Calculating VaR without using the VCV matrix

Using the short cut technique we derive a weighted average return series for the portfolio. In EXCEL the portfolio weighted average return is determined for each date as SUMPRODUCT (array of returns for that date, array of instrument weights).

PRICE		X ✓ *fx*	=SUMPRODUCT(B9:G9,$B$4:$G$4)								
	A	B	C	D	E	F	G	H	I	J	K
1	Portfolio	1,000,000.00									
2									Confidence level	95%	
3									z-score	1.64	
4	Weights	10.00%	20.00%	20.00%	20.00%	25.00%	5.00%				
5	Value	100,000.00	200,000.00	200,000.00	200,000.00	250,000.00	50,000.00		Daily VAR	3.445%	
6									Daily volatility	2.094%	
7	Return series										
8	Dates	EQUITY 1	EQUITY 2	FX FORWARD 1	FX FORWARD 2	BOND 1	BOND 2		Portfolio return		
9	01/01/2009	-5.13%	-5.13%	0.00%	-5.11%	0.00%	-8.55%		01/01/2009	=SUMPRODUCT(B9:G9,$B$4:	
10	02/01/2009	4.87%	-5.12%	-5.08%	4.85%	0.00%	-9.35%		02/01/2009 =$G$4)		
11	05/01/2009	4.87%	-5.12%	-5.12%	4.87%	0.00%	-5.03%		05/01/2009	-0.84%	
12	06/01/2009	3.31%	-5.12%	-5.13%	3.00%	0.00%	-4.21%		06/01/2009	-1.33%	
13	09/01/2009	-1.65%	2.63%	-5.12%	-3.25%	0.00%	7.26%		09/01/2009	-0.95%	
14	12/01/2009	-0.42%	-5.12%	-5.13%	0.85%	0.00%	0.00%		12/01/2009	-1.92%	

Figure 61 Weighted average return for the portfolio

The daily volatility for the portfolio then equals STDEV (array of portfolio returns). Note that in EXCEL the STDEV formula is calculated as $\sqrt{\dfrac{\sum(x - \bar{x})^2}{(n - 1)}}$ using the "*n*–1 method" (as sample mean, $\bar{x}$, is being calculated from the data), where *n* is the sample size (= 70 in our illustration).

	I	J
1		
2	Confidence level	95%
3	z-score	1.64
4		
5	Daily VAR	3.445%
6	Daily volatility	=STDEV(J9:J78)
7		
8		Portfolio return
9	01/01/2009	-2.99%
10	02/01/2009	-1.05%
11	05/01/2009	-0.84%
12	06/01/2009	-1.33%
13	09/01/2009	-0.95%
14	12/01/2009	-1.92%
15	13/01/2009	-1.97%

Figure 62   Daily SMA volatility of the portfolio

J5		f_x =J3*J6
H	I	J
1		
2	Confidence level	95%
3	z-score	1.64
4		
5	Daily VaR	3.445%
6	Daily volatility	2.094%
7		
8		Portfolio return
9	01/01/2009	-2.99%
10	02/01/2009	-1.05%
11	05/01/2009	-0.84%
12	06/01/2009	-1.33%

Figure 63   Daily SMA VaR of the portfolio

The daily VaR of the portfolio is daily volatility times the *z*-value of standard normal cumulative distribution corresponding with a specified confidence level. Using a 95 percent confidence level the *z*-score = 1.64. The resulting daily VaR is 3.445 percent.

Calculating VaR using the VCV Matrix

For the detailed VCV matrix method we need to first define a six by six (based on the number of instruments in the portfolio) variance/covariance matrix as shown in Figure 64.

	L	M	N	O	P	Q	R
7	Variance Covariance Matrix						
8		EQUITY 1	EQUITY 2	FX FORWARD 1	FX FORWARD 2	BOND 1	BOND 2
9	EQUITY 1	0.09%	0.05%	0.02%	0.06%	-0.01%	-0.02%
10	EQUITY 2	0.05%	0.21%	0.08%	0.10%	-0.02%	0.03%
11	FX FORWARD 1	0.02%	0.08%	0.11%	0.05%	-0.01%	0.03%
12	FX FORWARD 2	0.06%	0.10%	0.05%	0.18%	-0.01%	-0.02%
13	BOND 1	-0.01%	-0.02%	-0.01%	-0.01%	0.04%	0.00%
14	BOND 2	-0.02%	0.03%	0.03%	-0.02%	0.00%	0.26%

Figure 64 Variance/Covariance matrix

Each element in the grid is a covariance between the returns of the instruments in the intersecting row and column. For example, cell M10 is the covariance between the returns of Equity 2 and Equity 1. The covariance between the returns of an instrument with the returns of itself is by definition the variance. In EXCEL however there will be a difference between COVAR (array of returns of Equity 1, array of returns of Equity 1) and VAR (array of returns of Equity 1) (*VAR as in variance*). This is because the former is calculated using the "*n*" method while the latter is calculated using the "*n*–1" method:

$$\mathbf{Cov}(X,Y) = \sum \frac{(\mathbf{x} - \bar{\mathbf{x}})(\mathbf{y} - \bar{\mathbf{y}})}{\mathbf{n}}$$

$$\mathbf{VaR}(X) = \sum \frac{(\mathbf{x} - \bar{\mathbf{x}})^2}{(\mathbf{n}-1)}$$

As the short cut method uses the function STDEV for calculating the portfolio's daily volatility, which also employs the "*n*–1" method, EXCEL's COVAR function has to be adjusted by multiplying it with a factor of [*n*/(*n*–1)] to make it consistent with the STDEV() function. Hence, covariance elements in the matrix grid are calculated as given in Figure 65.

PRICE		▼ × ✓ *fx*	=COVAR($B$9:$B$78,B$9:B$78)*$M$4/$M$5				
	L	M	N	O	P	Q	R
4	n	70					
5	n-1	69					
6							
7	Variance Covariance Matrix						
8		EQUITY 1	EQUITY 2	FX FORWARD 1	FX FORWARD 2	BOND 1	BOND 2
9	EQUITY 1	=COVAR($B$9:$B$78,B$9:B$78)*$M$4/$M$5				-0.01%	-0.02%
10	EQUITY 2	0.05%	0.21%	0.08%	0.10%	-0.02%	0.03%
11	FX FORWARD 1	0.02%	0.08%	0.11%	0.05%	-0.01%	0.03%
12	FX FORWARD 2	0.06%	0.10%	0.05%	0.18%	-0.01%	-0.02%
13	BOND 1	-0.01%	-0.02%	-0.01%	-0.01%	0.04%	0.00%
14	BOND 2	-0.02%	0.03%	0.03%	-0.02%	0.00%	0.26%

Figure 65 Adjustment made to EXCEL's covariance

The next step is to present the weights of the instruments calculated earlier in two ways. A six by one vertical matrix, W, and its one by six transpose, W^T.

	L	M	N	O	P	Q	R
16	**Weights Matrix (W)**						
17							
18	EQUITY 1	10.0%					
19	EQUITY 2	20.0%					
20	FX FORWARD 1	20.0%					
21	FX FORWARD 2	20.0%					
22	BOND 1	25.0%					
23	BOND 2	5.0%					
24							
25	**Weights Matrix - Transposed (W^T)**	EQUITY 1	EQUITY 2	FX FORWARD 1	FX FORWARD 2	BOND 1	BOND 2
26		10.0%	20.0%	20.0%	20.0%	25.0%	5.0%

Figure 66   Weights matrix and its transpose

M29		f_x	=SQRT(MMULT(M26:R26,MMULT(M9:R14,M18:M23)))			
	L	M	N	O	P	Q	R
7	**Variance Covariance Matrix**						
8		EQUITY 1	EQUITY 2	FX FORWARD 1	FX FORWARD 2	BOND 1	BOND 2
9	EQUITY 1	0.09%	0.05%	0.02%	0.06%	-0.01%	-0.02%
10	EQUITY 2	0.05%	0.21%	0.08%	0.10%	-0.02%	0.03%
11	FX FORWARD 1	0.02%	0.08%	0.11%	0.05%	-0.01%	0.03%
12	FX FORWARD 2	0.06%	0.10%	0.05%	0.18%	-0.01%	-0.02%
13	BOND 1	-0.01%	-0.02%	-0.01%	-0.01%	0.04%	0.00%
14	BOND 2	-0.02%	0.03%	0.03%	-0.02%	0.00%	0.26%
15							
16	**Weights Matrix (W)**						
17							
18	EQUITY 1	10.0%					
19	EQUITY 2	20.0%					
20	FX FORWARD 1	20.0%					
21	FX FORWARD 2	20.0%					
22	BOND 1	25.0%					
23	BOND 2	5.0%					
24							
25	**Weights Matrix - Transposed (W^T)**	EQUITY 1	EQUITY 2	FX FORWARD 1	FX FORWARD 2	BOND 1	BOND 2
26		10.0%	20.0%	20.0%	20.0%	25.0%	5.0%
27							
28			Difference				
29	Daily volatility	2.094%	-				
30	Daily VaR	3.445%	-				

Figure 67   Daily SMA volatility determined using the VCV matrix approach

Daily volatility is then determined in three stages, as follows, using EXCEL's matrix multiplication function, MMULT(), and square root function, SQRT():

Stage 1: Matrix 1 = MMULT(Variance/covariance Matrix, W);
Stage 2: Matrix 2 = MMULT(W^T, Matrix 1);
Stage 3: Daily Volatility = SQRT(Matrix 2).

Putting all three stages together we have daily volatility determined as in the screen shot in Figure 67.

As you can see, the result is the same as that calculated earlier using the short cut technique. Daily VaR is calculated as mentioned before, that is, daily volatility times z-score corresponding to the confidence level = 2.094% × 1.64 = 3.445%.

VaR using the VCV matrix and correlations
As mentioned earlier, another way of calculating the VCV matrix that will not require you to make the adjustment for the difference in EXCEL methods for COVAR and VAR (STDEV) is to first calculate CORREL (EXCEL's correlation function).

U10		f_x =CORREL($C$9:$C$78,B$9:B$78)					
T	U	V	W	X	Y	Z
8 Correlation	EQUITY 1	EQUITY 2	FX FORWARD 1	FX FORWARD 2	BOND 1	BOND 2
9 EQUITY 1	1.00	0.38	0.20	0.45	- 0.17	- 0.12
10 EQUITY 2	0.38	1.00	0.54	0.51	- 0.20	- 0.12
11 FX FORWARD 1	0.20	0.54	1.00	0.35	- 0.14	0.16
12 FX FORWARD 2	0.45	0.51	0.35	1.00	- 0.11	- 0.09
13 BOND 1	- 0.17	- 0.20	- 0.14	- 0.11	1.00	0.03
14 BOND 2	- 0.12	0.12	0.16	- 0.09	0.03	1.00

Figure 68   Correlations matrix

Then multiply the resulting number with the STDEV()s of the corresponding instruments in the intersecting row and column of the matrix grid to arrive at covariance. STDEV (array of returns of a given instrument) is the daily volatility of the instrument determined from its return time series (see Figure 69).

You can see that this grid is similar to the VCV matrix determined earlier. The added benefit, though, is that we now have the grid of correlations, which we can utilize to give us further insights. Correlations may be changed to see the impact on VaR numbers. *Note: implicit in this manipulation of the correlation matrix though is that the underlying series of returns and volatilities, as well as the correlations of those instruments with others in the portfolio, remain unchanged. This is counterintuitive as CORRELs and volatilities are determined from the same returns series.* However, despite these limitations useful insights may still be obtained and the methodology may be used for stress testing the portfolio.

For example, what would be the impact on the VaR number if the all instruments were to become perfectly correlated with each other due to certain market conditions?

PRICE	▾	=U10*U$17*$S20

	S	T	U	V	W	X	Y	Z
8		Correlation	EQUITY 1	EQUITY 2	FX FORWARD 1	FX FORWARD 2	BOND 1	BOND 2
9		EQUITY 1	1.00	0.38	0.20	0.45	- 0.17	- 0.12
10		EQUITY 2	0.38	1.00	0.54	0.51	- 0.20	0.12
11		FX FORWARD 1	0.20	0.54	1.00	0.35	- 0.14	0.16
12		FX FORWARD 2	0.45	0.51	0.35	1.00	- 0.11	- 0.09
13		BOND 1	- 0.17	- 0.20	- 0.14	0.11	1.00	0.03
14		BOND 2	- 0.12	0.12	0.16	0.09	0.03	1.00
15								
16								
17	daily volatility		2.98%	4.54%	3.35%	4.22%	2.04%	5.11%
18		Covariance	EQUITY 1	EQUITY 2	FX FORWARD 1	FX FORWARD 2	BOND 1	BOND 2
19	2.98%	EQUITY 1	0.09%	0.05%	0.02%	0.06%	-0.01%	-0.02%
20	4.54%	EQUITY 2	=U10*U$17*$S20		0.08%	0.10%	-0.02%	0.03%
21	3.35%	FX FORWARD 1	0.02%	0.08%	0.11%	0.05%	-0.01%	0.03%
22	4.22%	FX FORWARD 2	0.06%	0.10%	0.05%	0.18%	-0.01%	-0.02%
23	2.04%	BOND 1	-0.01%	-0.02%	-0.01%	-0.01%	0.04%	0.00%
24	5.11%	BOND 2	-0.02%	0.03%	0.03%	-0.02%	0.00%	0.26%

Figure 69   Using correlations and standard deviations (volatilities) to determine covariance

	S	T	U	V	W	X	Y	Z
8		Correlation	EQUITY 1	EQUITY 2	FX FORWARD 1	FX FORWARD 2	BOND 1	BOND 2
9		EQUITY 1	1.00	1.00	1.00	1.00	1.00	1.00
10		EQUITY 2	1.00	1.00	1.00	1.00	1.00	1.00
11		FX FORWARD 1	1.00	1.00	1.00	1.00	1.00	1.00
12		FX FORWARD 2	1.00	1.00	1.00	1.00	1.00	1.00
13		BOND 1	1.00	1.00	1.00	1.00	1.00	1.00
14		BOND 2	1.00	1.00	1.00	1.00	1.00	1.00
15								
16								
17	daily volatility		2.98%	4.54%	3.35%	4.22%	2.04%	5.11%
18		Covariance	EQUITY 1	EQUITY 2	FX FORWARD 1	FX FORWARD 2	BOND 1	BOND 2
19	2.98%	EQUITY 1	0.09%	0.14%	0.10%	0.13%	0.06%	0.15%
20	4.54%	EQUITY 2	0.14%	0.21%	0.15%	0.19%	0.09%	0.23%
21	3.35%	FX FORWARD 1	0.10%	0.15%	0.11%	0.14%	0.07%	0.17%
22	4.22%	FX FORWARD 2	0.13%	0.19%	0.14%	0.18%	0.09%	0.22%
23	2.04%	BOND 1	0.06%	0.09%	0.07%	0.09%	0.04%	0.10%
24	5.11%	BOND 2	0.15%	0.23%	0.17%	0.22%	0.10%	0.26%
25								
26								
27								
28			Difference	% change				
29	Daily volatility	3.486%	1.39140%	66.44%				
30	Daily VaR	5.733%	2.28865%	66.44%				

Figure 70   Stress test – instruments are perfectly correlated

The portfolio daily VaR increases from 3.445 percent to 5.733 percent under this stressed condition – an increase of more than 66 percent.

Value at risk for bonds

1. Calculating VaR for bonds

Here are two common challenges that come up when we apply risk management concepts to individual bonds and bond portfolios.

(a) How do you measure the risk of a newly issued bond that has no history of trading prices?
(b) How do you integrate the risk of a bond issued in a foreign currency into your default base currency?

Both questions have simple solutions that will be illustrated in this two-part case study. In the first part we will focus on calculating risk for a newly issued bond. In the second part, we will review calculating risk for a bond that trades in a foreign currency.

a. Bond risk management – background

When it comes to bond risk management, the primary measure used by portfolio and investment managers is modified duration – a measure of interest rate sensitivity that tracks changes in bond prices on account of changes in interest rates. Value at risk is a relatively new arrival to the scene and brings price volatility into the picture. However, a newly issued bond, as well as an illiquid bond, may have limited, thin or no trading data. In the absence of trade related price data we look at other options.

One possible option is to identify the relevant interest rates for the bond in question. For example, to price a 10 year bond with no price history we can pick up the history of applicable 10 year rates and then use them to price the bond, assuming that future rates and price behavior will be similar to that witnessed in the past. When we apply historical rates, we

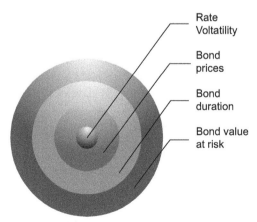

Rate
Voltatility

Bond
prices

Bond
duration

Bond value
at risk

Figure 71   Value at risk for bonds

also assume constant maturity so that changes witnessed in the price of the bond are only on account of changes in interest rates and not because of a change in days to maturity of the bond. We use the above concept to calculate the risk inherent in a single bond or a portfolio of bonds. If you have calculated VaR before for equities and currencies, here is a quick question on calculating bonds and fixed income instrument VaR. Should you calculate VaR using interest rates (rate VaR) or bond prices (price VaR)? Think about it. If bonds don't trade or are illiquid, which one of the above two (rate vs. price VaR) is a better choice, is more representative of the risk inherent in your fixed income positions – interest rates or prices?

The answer should be clear.

The relevant risk measure is price VaR, because it reflects actual changes in prices. Rate VaR only reflects changes in interest rates or interest rate volatility but is not an accurate measure of value changes.

A 10 year bond reacts very differently to a 1 percent change in rates when compared to a 3 month treasury bill. If that doesn't convince your audience, here is another argument. In general, overnight rates have the highest volatility. What should be the likely change in the price of a treasury bill that only has one day to go? If you use rate VaR you will have an unreasonably high number. Even if rates double, the impact of the new rates on one day of interest accrual would be minimal. Hence, price VaR is the right choice as it factors the relative insensitivity of near maturity bonds to interest rate changes into the calculation.

The question of which measure, rate VaR or price VaR, is better rarely comes up, but has been asked once or twice by board members. Risk committees, given all the attention bestowed on them after the London Whale crisis, are now more curious about the relationship between rate and price VaR, and it is best to be prepared with easy to understand logic that can clear their confusion.

b. VaR for bonds and fixed income instruments model walkthrough

For our base case we use a hypothetical 10 year maturity newly issued bond (issued on January 1, 2013).

The coupon is paid on a semi-annual basis. The yield to maturity mentioned in Figure 72 is the bond yield on the date of settlement.

Inputs	
Date of Settlement	01/01/2013
Date of Maturity	30/12/2022
Coupon	9.00%
Yield to Maturity (%) on settlement	8.36

Figure 72 Inputs

To calculate modified duration we use EXCEL's MDURATION function with settlement date, maturity date, coupon rate, yield rate as defined above. Frequency is set to 2. This denotes semi-annual payments of coupon. Day count basis for accrual is Actual by Actual, denoted by 1 in the EXCEL formula.

B11		f_x =MDURATION(B7,B8,B9,B10%,2,1)/100		
	A	B	C	D
6	Inputs			
7	Date of Settlement	01/01/2013		
8	Date of Maturity	30/12/2022		Delta
9	Coupon	9.00%		VaR
10	Yield to Maturity (%) on settlement	8.36		Vol
11	Duration	6.59%		

Figure 73 Calculation of duration

We will now calculate the rate VaR and price VaR, as well as the delta normal approximation to price VaR, which translates rate VaR into price VaR using the modified duration calculated above.

Note that in the calculation of volatility and VaR we first need to obtain a historical time series of rates applicable to the outstanding term of the bond on the settlement date. We have obtained this for the period Febraury 2, 2012 to January 1, 2013. The two columns below (*columns B and C*) show the historical yields for 10 year bonds as well as the change in those yields (return series) on a daily basis. The return series is calculated by taking the natural logarithm (*LN*) of the ratio of two consecutive yield to maturities (YTMs) (that is, $LN(P_t/P_{t-1})$, where P_i is the rate/price at time *i*).

	A	B	C	D	E	F
15	Date	Rates (%)	Returns		Price	Returns
16	02-Feb-12	6.45			118.57204	
17	03-Feb-12	6.45	0.00%		118.57204	0.00%
18	04-Feb-12	6.45	0.00%		118.57204	0.00%
19	05-Feb-12	6.46	0.15%		118.49075	-0.07%
20	06-Feb-12	6.46	0.00%		118.49075	0.00%
21	07-Feb-12	6.46	0.00%		118.49075	0.00%
22	08-Feb-12	6.45	-0.15%		118.57204	0.07%

Figure 74 Historical rates and their return series

Calculating rate VaR

Let us assume that we are calculating VaR using the variance/covariance methodology. We use a confidence level of 99 percent and holding period of 10 days.

C14		f_x	=STDEV(C17:C350)	
	A		B	C
14	**Historical Data**		**Rates Vol**	1.179%
15	**Date**		**Rates (%)**	**Returns**
16	**02-Feb-12**		6.45	
17	03-Feb-12		6.45	0.00%
18	04-Feb-12		6.45	0.00%
19	05-Feb-12		6.46	0.15%
20	06-Feb-12		6.46	0.00%
21	07-Feb-12		6.46	0.00%
22	08-Feb-12		6.45	-0.15%
23	09-Feb-12		6.45	0.00%
24	10-Feb-12		6.45	0.00%
25	11-Feb-12		6.45	0.00%
26	12-Feb-12		6.49	0.62%

Figure 75 Rate standard deviation

C13		f_x	=C14*$B$4*SQRT($B$3)	
	A		B	C
1	**VaR Parameters**			
2	**Confidence Level**		99%	
3	**Holding period**		10	
4	**z-factor**		2.326	
5				
6	**Inputs**			
7	**Date of Settlement**		01/01/2013	
8	**Date of Maturity**		30/12/2022	
9	**Coupon**		9.00%	
10	**Yield to Maturity (%) on settlement**		8.36	
11	**Duration**		6.59%	
12				
13			**Rates VaR**	8.674%
14	**Historical Data**		**Rates Vol**	1.179%
15	**Date**		**Rates (%)**	**Returns**
16	**02-Feb-12**		6.45	
17	03-Feb-12		6.45	0.00%

Figure 76 Rate VaR

Using the return series for interest rates, the EXCEL standard deviation (STDEV) function is applied to this series to calculate the volatility of rate returns.

The rate VaR is then calculated as the product of the volatility, square root of the holding period and inverse of the cumulative standard normal distribution at the specified confidence level.

Calculating price VaR

For calculating price VaR, the full valuation approach to calculating VaR for bonds, the process is similar to rate VaR with a few additional steps. In order to calculate price VaR we need to first have a price return series. This series is derived from a price series. To calculate the price series we assume the same settlement date, maturity date, and coupon rate as in EXCEL's price formula, but assume that the interest rate at each data point in turn is the yield in the formula.

	E16			f_x =PRICE($B$7,$B$8,$B$9,B16%,100,2,1)		
	A		B	C	D	E
5						
6	Inputs					
7	Date of Settlement		01/01/2013			
8	Date of Maturity		30/12/2022			Delta Normal
9	Coupon		9.00%			VaR
10	Yield to Maturity (%) on settlement		8.36			Vol
11	Duration		6.59%			
12						Full Valuation
13			Rates VaR	8.674%		Price VaR
14	Historical Data		Rates Vol	1.179%		Price Vol
15	Date		Rates (%)	Returns		Price
16	02-Feb-12		6.45			118.57204
17	03-Feb-12		6.45	0.00%		118.57204
18	04-Feb-12		6.45	0.00%		118.57204
19	05-Feb-12		6.46	0.15%		118.49075
20	06-Feb-12		6.46	0.00%		118.49075

Figure 77 Obtaining the price series

Again, we apply the natural log to the ratio of consecutive prices to obtain the price return series and then calculate the standard deviation on this return series to determine the price volatility. Price VaR is calculated by multiplying the price volatility with the square root of the holding period and inverse of the cumulative standard normal distribution at the specified confidence level.

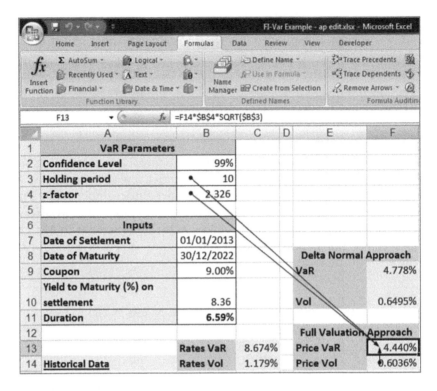

Figure 78   Price VaR

Comparing rate VaR and price VaR

Now that we have both rate VaR and price VaR, let's do a quick comparison of the results of the two methods.

For the 10 year bond, rate VaR shows almost double the VaR estimate as compared to price VaR. What happens when maturity drops from 10 years to 3 years while keeping volatility constant? The screenshot in Figure 79 shows the revised calculations for a 3 year bond (*we have assumed that the historical series of rates for a 10 year bond and a 3 year bond are the same, which may not be the case in the real world. However, it is still a useful exercise in seeing the impact that the bond's own characteristics, such as time to maturity, have on the two VaR numbers*).

While rate VaR doesn't change, price VaR immediately reflects the impact of the reduced term to maturity.

	A	B	C	D	E	F
6	Inputs					
7	Date of Settlement	01/01/2013				
8	Date of Maturity	01/01/2016			Delta Normal Approach	
9	Coupon	9.00%			VaR	1.878%
10	Yield to Maturity (%) on settlement	8.36			Vol	0.2553%
11	Duration	2.59%				
12					Full Valuation Approach	
13		Rates VaR	8.674%		Price VaR	1.727%
14	Historical Data	Rates Vol	1.179%		Price Vol	0.2348%
15	Date	Rates (%)	Returns		Price	Returns
16	02-Feb-12	6.45			106.85571	
17	03-Feb-12	6.45	0.00%		106.85571	0.00%
18	04-Feb-12	6.45	0.00%		106.85571	0.00%
19	05-Feb-12	6.46	0.15%		106.82769	-0.03%
20	06-Feb-12	6.46	0.00%		106.82769	0.00%
21	07-Feb-12	6.46	0.00%		106.82769	0.00%
22	08-Feb-12	6.45	-0.15%		106.85571	0.03%
23	09-Feb-12	6.45	0.00%		106.85571	0.00%
24	10-Feb-12	6.45	0.00%		106.85571	0.00%
25	11-Feb-12	6.45	0.00%		106.85571	0.00%

Figure 79 Comparison between rate and price VaR

An alternative approach to calculating price VaR from rate VaR: the delta normal method

The delta normal method can be used to find an approximate value for price VaR. Given that historical interest rates may be more easily available than the price series, and calculating the bond price series may be time consuming, particularly if we are dealing with multi-position portfolios, the delta normal approximation may provide a quick (though crude) solution to this dilemma.

The delta normal volatility is calculated as the product of the rate volatility, the modified duration calculated earlier and the YTM on the settlement date.

Multiplying the z-factor and square root of the holding period by this volatility result yields delta normal VaR.

Alternatively, the delta normal VaR = rate VaR × YTM × modified duration.

While the fit is not perfect on account of the convexity of the bond, it is a much better result than the original rate VaR estimate.

	F10	▾	*fx* =C14*B11*B10				
	A	B	C	D	E	F
6	Inputs					
7	Date of Settlement	01/01/2013				
8	Date of Maturity	01/01/2016			Delta Normal Approach	
9	Coupon	9.00%			VaR	1.878%
10	Yield to Maturity (%) on settlement	8.36			Vol	0.2553%
11	Duration	2.59%				
12					Full Valuation Approach	
13		Rates VaR	8.674%		Price VaR	1.727%
14	Historical Data	Rates Vol	1.179%		Price Vol	0.2348%
15	Date	Rates (%)	Returns		Price	Returns
16	02-Feb-12	6.45			106.85571	
17	03-Feb-12	6.45	0.00%		106.85571	0.00%
18	04-Feb-12	6.45	0.00%		106.85571	0.00%
19	05-Feb-12	6.46	0.15%		106.82769	-0.03%
20	06-Feb-12	6.46	0.00%		106.82769	0.00%
21	07-Feb-12	6.46	0.00%		106.82769	0.00%
22	08-Feb-12	6.45	-0.15%		106.85571	0.03%
23	09-Feb-12	6.45	0.00%		106.85571	0.00%
24	10-Feb-12	6.45	0.00%		106.85571	0.00%
25	11-Feb-12	6.45	0.00%		106.85571	0.00%

Figure 80   Delta normal volatility

	F9	▾	*fx* =F10*SQRT(B3)*B4				
	A	B	C	D	E	F
1	VaR Parameters					
2	Confidence Level	99%				
3	Holding period	10				
4	z-factor	2.326				
5						
6	Inputs					
7	Date of Settlement	01/01/2013				
8	Date of Maturity	01/01/2016			Delta Normal Approach	
9	Coupon	9.00%			VaR	1.878%
10	Yield to Maturity (%) on settlement	8.36			Vol	0.2553%
11	Duration	2.59%				
12					Full Valuation Approach	
13		Rates VaR	8.674%		Price VaR	1.727%
14	Historical Data	Rates Vol	1.179%		Price Vol	0.2348%
15	Date	Rates (%)	Returns		Price	Returns
16	02-Feb-12	6.45			106.85571	
17	03-Feb-12	6.45	0.00%		106.85571	0.00%
18	04-Feb-12	6.45	0.00%		106.85571	0.00%

Figure 81   Delta normal vaR

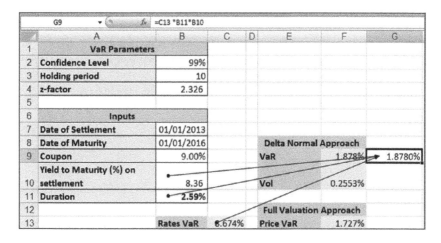

Figure 82 Delta normal VaR – alternate calculation methodology

Annexure 1 – Calculating value at risk: a study of VaR flavors

To better understand VaR, it would help if we took a sample portfolio and calculated VaR figures using the three approaches using a simple EXCEL spreadsheet:

- variance/covariance approach;
- historical simulation approach;
- Monte Carlo simulation approach.

In addition, we calculate VaR related risk measures, the flavors, including:

- *incremental VaR*, which measures the impact of small changes in individual positions on the overall VaR;
- *marginal VaR*, which measures how the overall VaR would change if one position was completely removed from the portfolio;
- *conditional VaR*, which measures the mean excess loss or expected shortfall beyond VaR at a given confidence level;
- *probability of shortfall*, which measures the probability that investment returns will not reach a given goal or alternatively the probability that investment returns will fall below a given goal.

There is some overlap with earlier material presented in the main body of this chapter, especially with respect to traditional VaR calculations, but the numbers are needed to perform a comparison across flavors.

For our sample portfolio consider the positions shown in Figure 83.

Base Portfolio as at 30-09-2012				
	Crude Oil	EUR-USD	Gold	Silver
Price	92.18	1.2855	1,776.00	34.65
Quantity	100	1000	10	100
Amount	9,218.00	1,285.50	17,760.00	3,465.00
Weights	29.05%	4.05%	55.97%	10.92%

Figure 83   Investment portfolio

For this exercise we have obtained data for WTI, EUR–USD exchange rate, gold and silver for the period January 2004–September 2012 from EIA, OANDA, onlygold.com and kitco.com, respectively.

Before we move on to the specifics of each approach we will determine the return time series for each position. This is obtained by taking the natural logarithm of successive prices. This return series is the foundation for all the methods (except Monte Carlo simulation) and metrics mentioned above.

	C5			f_x	=LN(B5/B4)
	A	B	C	D	E
1			2.49%		
2	Date	Cushing, OK WTI Spot Price FOB (Dollars per Barrel)	Returns	EIA	End Da
3	05/01/2004	33.71			01/01,
4	06/01/2004	33.54	-0.51%		02/01,
5	07/01/2004	33.57	0.09%		03/01,
6	08/01/2004	34.27	2.06%		04/01,
7	09/01/2004	34.38	0.32%		05/01,
8	12/01/2004	34.92	1.56%		06/01,
9	13/01/2004	34.26	-1.91%		07/01,

Figure 84   Calculating return series for each position

We will also determine the portfolio return series. As you may recall, this return series is a correlation adjusted series, that is, a series that takes into account the correlation between the various positions in the portfolio. Using the weights of each position with respect to the portfolio, we calculated a weighted average sum of the returns for each point in time.

F23			f_x	=SUMPRODUCT($B$20:$E$20,B23:E23)	
	A	B	C	D	E	F
20	Weights (origi	29.05%	4.05%	55.97%	10.92%	100%
21						
22		Crude Oil	EUR-USD	Gold	Silver	Portfolio
23	02/01/2004	-0.51%	-0.27%	0.24%	0.00%	-0.02%
24	03/01/2004	-0.51%	0.38%	0.24%	0.00%	0.00%
25	04/01/2004	-0.51%	-0.08%	0.24%	0.00%	-0.02%
26	05/01/2004	-0.51%	0.02%	0.80%	0.17%	0.32%
27	06/01/2004	-0.51%	0.56%	0.90%	4.98%	0.92%
28	07/01/2004	0.09%	0.65%	-0.63%	-1.04%	-0.41%

Figure 85 Calculating portfolio return series

1. Variance/Covariance (VCV) approach

This method assumes that the daily returns follow a normal distribution. The daily VaR is simply a function of the standard deviation of the positions return series and the desired confidence level.

Within the approach, sigma may be calculated in two ways.

- Using an SMA approach. This places equal importance on all returns in the series. Using EXCEL, sigma can be determined by using the STDEV function on the array of return series.

F19			f_x	=STDEV(F23:F3217)	
	A	B	C	D	E	F
19	SMA daily volatility	2.44%	0.48%	1.56%	2.64%	1.34%
20	Weights (original)	29.05%	4.05%	55.97%	10.92%	100%
21						
22		Crude Oil	EUR-USD	Gold	Silver	Portfolio
23	02/01/2004	-0.51%	-0.27%	0.24%	0.00%	-0.02%
24	03/01/2004	-0.51%	0.38%	0.24%	0.00%	0.00%
25	04/01/2004	-0.51%	-0.08%	0.24%	0.00%	-0.02%
26	05/01/2004	-0.51%	0.02%	0.80%	0.17%	0.32%
27	06/01/2004	-0.51%	0.56%	0.90%	4.98%	0.92%
28	07/01/2004	0.09%	0.65%	-0.63%	-1.04%	-0.41%
29	08/01/2004	2.06%	-0.79%	-0.63%	-0.24%	0.19%
30	09/01/2004	0.32%	1.01%	0.38%	0.72%	0.42%
31	10/01/2004	0.32%	0.48%	0.38%	0.72%	0.40%
32	11/01/2004	0.32%	0.00%	0.38%	0.72%	0.38%
33	12/01/2004	1.56%	0.04%	0.45%	6.28%	1.39%
34	13/01/2004	-1.91%	-0.68%	0.45%	-0.53%	-0.39%

Figure 86 Calculating daily SMA volatility

- Using an EWMA approach, where sigma is determined as

$$\sigma^2 = \sum_{t=1}^{n} (1 - \lambda) \times \lambda^{t-1} \times R_t^2$$

Depending on the lambda chosen, greater emphasis may be placed on more recent durations as compared to the SMA approach.

- We start by specifying a value for lambda. The smaller the value of lambda, the greater the weight that is applied to more recent observations. We have used a lambda of 0.5.
- Next we determine the weights $(1 - \lambda) \times \lambda^{t-1}$. Depending on the sample size used, the weights may need to be scaled (by dividing each weight by $1-\lambda^n$) so that the sum of weights equals one.

	K23			f_x	=J23/(1-$B$3^COUNT($I$23:$I$3217))		
	A	B	G	H	I	J	K
1	Confidence Level	99%					
2	α	2.33					
3	lambda	0.5					
21					sumofweights	100.00%	100.00%
22		Crude Oil			T-1	Weights	Scaled Weights
23	02/01/2004	-0.51%		02/01/2004	3194	0.00%	0.00%
24	03/01/2004	-0.51%		03/01/2004	3193	0.00%	0.00%
25	04/01/2004	-0.51%		04/01/2004	3192	0.00%	0.00%
26	05/01/2004	-0.51%		05/01/2004	3191	0.00%	0.00%
27	06/01/2004	-0.51%		06/01/2004	3190	0.00%	0.00%
28	07/01/2004	0.09%		07/01/2004	3189	0.00%	0.00%
29	08/01/2004	2.06%		08/01/2004	3188	0.00%	0.00%
30	09/01/2004	0.32%		09/01/2004	3187	0.00%	0.00%
31	10/01/2004	0.32%		10/01/2004	3186	0.00%	0.00%

Figure 87 Calculating weights for determining EWMA volatility

	M23			f_x	=B23^2			
	B	G	H	I	J	K	L	M
22	Crude Oil			T-1	Weights	Scaled Weights	R2	Crude Oil
23	-0.51%		02/01/2004	3194	0.00%	0.00%		0.00%
24	-0.51%		03/01/2004	3193	0.00%	0.00%		0.00%
25	-0.51%		04/01/2004	3192	0.00%	0.00%		0.00%
26	-0.51%		05/01/2004	3191	0.00%	0.00%		0.00%
27	-0.51%		06/01/2004	3190	0.00%	0.00%		0.00%
28	0.09%		07/01/2004	3189	0.00%	0.00%		0.00%
29	2.06%		08/01/2004	3188	0.00%	0.00%		0.04%

Figure 88 Calculating squared returns

- Determine the EWMA variance by taking the weighted average sum of the weights and the squared returns as given in the formula above.
- Determine the EWMA volatility by taking the square root of the resulting variance.

	M20	▼	f_x =SUMPRODUCT($K$23:$K$3217,M23:M3217)				
	J	K	L	M	N	O	P	Q
20			EWMA Variance	0.00%	0.00%	0.01%	0.04%	0.01%
21	100.00%	100.00%	Weights	29%	4%	56%	11%	100%
22	**Weights**	**Scaled Weights**	**R2**	**Crude Oil**	**EUR-USD**	**Gold**	**Silver**	**Portfolio**
23	0.00%	0.00%		0.00%	0.00%	0.00%	0.00%	0.00%
24	0.00%	0.00%		0.00%	0.00%	0.00%	0.00%	0.00%
25	0.00%	0.00%		0.00%	0.00%	0.00%	0.00%	0.00%
26	0.00%	0.00%		0.00%	0.00%	0.01%	0.00%	0.00%
27	0.00%	0.00%		0.00%	0.00%	0.01%	0.25%	0.01%
28	0.00%	0.00%		0.00%	0.00%	0.00%	0.01%	0.00%
29	0.00%	0.00%		0.04%	0.01%	0.00%	0.00%	0.00%
30	0.00%	0.00%		0.00%	0.01%	0.00%	0.01%	0.00%
31	0.00%	0.00%		0.00%	0.00%	0.00%	0.01%	0.00%

Figure 89   Calculating EWMA variance

	M19	▼	f_x =SQRT(M20)			
	L	M	N	O	P	Q
19	**EWMA Volatility**	0.67%	0.33%	0.80%	1.93%	0.79%
20	EWMA Variance	0.00%	0.00%	0.01%	0.04%	0.01%
21	Weights	29%	4%	56%	11%	100%
22	**R2**	**Crude Oil**	**EUR-USD**	**Gold**	**Silver**	**Portfolio**
23		0.00%	0.00%	0.00%	0.00%	0.00%
24		0.00%	0.00%	0.00%	0.00%	0.00%
25		0.00%	0.00%	0.00%	0.00%	0.00%
26		0.00%	0.00%	0.01%	0.00%	0.00%

Figure 90   Calculating EWMA volatility

Once we have obtained daily volatility, we determine the daily VaR. This is the product of the volatility and the inverse of the standard normal cumulative distribution for a specific confidence level. For a confidence level of 99 percent, the inverse z-score works out to 2.33. The results for the VCV SMA and VCV EWMA approaches are given in Figure 91.

	Crude Oil	EUR-USD	Gold	Silver	Portfolio
SMA VAR	5.68%	1.11%	3.62%	6.15%	3.12%
EWMA VAR	1.56%	0.76%	1.87%	4.50%	1.83%

Figure 91   SMA and EWMA VaR

2. Historical simulation approach

Historical simulation is a non-parametric approach for estimating VaR, that is, the returns are not subjected to any functional distribution. VaR is estimated directly from the data without deriving parameters or making assumptions about the entire distribution of the data. This methodology is based on the premise that the pattern of historical returns is indicative of future returns.

We use the histogram of returns to determine daily VaR. The EXCEL data analysis histogram function may be used directly on the return series calculated or you may in turn derive the histogram yourself as follows.

- Calculate a minimum and maximum return of the return series.
- Calculate the width of each bin for the histogram. This will be the difference between the minimum and maximum divided by the number of bins or buckets that you want to use. We have used 60 buckets.
- Calculate the bin range values as: bin(1) = minimum value of return, bin(t) = bin(t–1) + bin width.
- Determine the cumulative frequency, that is, the number of returns that fall within the specified bucket. Using the COUNTIF EXCEL function we determine the number of returns that are less than or equal to the bin value.
- Determine frequency for bin (t) as cumulative frequency (t) less cumulative frequency (t – 1).
- Determine cumulative percent as cumulative frequency/ total number of return observations.
- Determine confidence level as 1 – cumulative frequency.
- Determine the VaR value that corresponds to the specified confidence level. For example, for a confidence level of 99 percent the VaR will be the interpolated value between –6.98 percent and –6.49 percent, that is, 6.565 percent.

B3219	▼	*fx*	=B3218+B$3215		
	A	B	C	D	E	F
3211	min	-12.83%	-2.53%	-19.33%	-18.69%	-10.76%
3212	max	16.41%	3.46%	19.02%	18.28%	10.57%
3213						
3214	Number of buckets	60	60	60	60	60
3215	Bin width	0.0048734	0.00099908	0.00639101	0.006162	0.00355511
3216						
3217	bin Range	Crude Oil	EUR-USD	Gold	Silver	Portfolio
3218	1	-12.34%	-2.43%	-18.69%	-18.08%	-10.41%
3219	2	-11.85%	-2.33%	-18.05%	-17.46%	-10.05%
3220	3	-11.36%	-2.23%	-17.41%	-16.84%	-9.69%
3221	4	-10.88%	-2.13%	-16.77%	-16.23%	-9.34%
3222	5	-10.39%	-2.03%	-16.13%	-15.61%	-8.98%
3223	6	-9.90%	-1.93%	-15.49%	-15.00%	-8.63%
3224	7	-9.42%	-1.83%	-14.85%	-14.38%	-8.27%

Figure 92 Determining bin range values for histograms

14		Crude Oil				
15	02/01/2004	-0.51%			▓Frequency ━━Cumulative	
16	03/01/2004	-0.51%	Crude Oil			
17	04/01/2004	-0.51%	Bin	Cumulative Frequency	Frequency	Cumulative%	C
18	05/01/2004	-0.51%	-12.34%	=COUNTIF($B$15:$B$3208,CONCATENATE("<=",H18))		
19	06/01/2004	-0.51%	-11.85%	3	-	0.09%

Figure 93 Calculating cumulative frequency

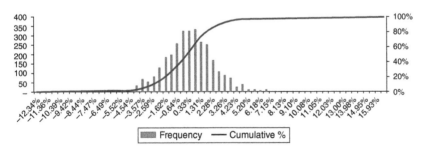

Figure 94 Histogram of historical crude oil price return series

Crude Oil

Bin	Cumulative Frequency	Frequency	Cumulative%	Confidence Level
-12.34%	3	3	0.09%	99.91%
-11.85%	3	·	0.09%	99.91%
-11.36%	3	·	0.09%	99.91%
-10.88%	8	5	0.25%	99.75%
-10.39%	8	·	0.25%	99.75%
-9.90%	12	4	0.38%	99.62%
-9.42%	14	2	0.44%	99.56%
-8.93%	16	2	0.50%	99.50%
-8.44%	18	2	0.56%	99.44%
-7.95%	18	·	0.56%	99.44%
-7.47%	21	3	0.66%	99.34%
-6.98%	26	5	0.81%	99.19%
-6.49%	33	7	1.03%	98.97%
-6.00%	39	9	1.22%	98.78%

B4			f_x	=ABS((($B$1-B6)*B9+(B8-$B$1)*B7)/(B8-B6))	
	A	B	C	D	E	F
1	Confidence Level	99%				
2	Investment	Crude Oil	EUR-USD	Gold	Silver	Portfolio
3	Probability of Shortfall	44.36%	40.01%	36.82%	43.49%	41.14%
4	Daily VaR	6.565%	1.316%	4.140%	8.018%	4.008%
5						
6	Confidence Level	98.97%	98.50%	98.90%	98.873%	98.998%
7	Return	-6.49%	-1.2316%	-3.9897%	-7.6013%	-4.0059%
8	Confidence Level	99.19%	99.09%	99.31%	99.061%	99.343%
9	Return	-6.98%	-1.33%	-4.63%	-8.22%	-4.36%

Figure 95   Daily historical simulation VaR

3. Monte Carlo simulation approach

The approach is similar to the historical simulation method described above except for one big difference. A hypothetical data set is generated by a statistical distribution rather than historical price levels. The assumption is that the selected distribution captures or reasonably approximates price behavior of the modeled securities. For illustration purposes only we have used the Black Scholes terminal price formula $S_t = S_0 e^{\left(\mu - \frac{1}{2}\sigma^2\right)t + \sigma\sqrt{t}z_t}$ as our Monte Carlo simulator.

We have replaced μ by r, the risk-free rate of 1 percent, used the annualized scaled daily SMA volatility as our estimate of sigma and taken the initial spot price to be the price available at the end of the period of analysis.

However, for this method to be applied in practice we need to select a model that is able to explain the behavior of that position's price over time, so that the simulated distribution of values converges to the true distribution of values of the positions and portfolio.

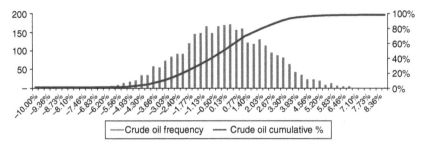

Figure 96 Histogram of simulated crude oil price return series

The Monte Carlo VaR model is created using the following steps.

1. Generate randomly simulated prices.
2. Calculate the daily return series including the portfolio return series.
3. Determine daily VaR as per the historical simulation histogram approach.
4. Repeat the above three steps a large number of times. EXCEL's data table functionality may be utilized to generate a table of results for each simulated run.
5. Calculate the average VaR across all simulated runs.

BC1		f_x	=AVERAGE(BC6:BC8)		
	BB	BC	BD	BE	BF	BG
1	Average	5.628%	1.094%	3.555%	5.996%	2.670%
2						
3	VaR - Simulated Runs					
4		Crude Oil	EUR-USD	Gold	Silver	Portfolio
5		5.619%	1.115%	3.471%	6.231%	2.615%
6	1	5.747%	1.093%	3.510%	5.942%	2.671%
7	2	5.570%	1.073%	3.599%	5.915%	2.572%

Figure 97 Average MC simulated daily VaR across all simulated runs

Figure 98 shows the summary of results from all the approaches:

Confidence Level	99%				
	Crude Oil	EUR-USD	Gold	Silver	Portfolio
SMA VaR	5.68%	1.11%	3.62%	6.15%	3.12%
EWMA VaR (lamda=0.5)	1.56%	0.76%	1.87%	4.50%	1.83%
Historical Simulation VaR	6.57%	1.32%	4.14%	8.02%	4.01%
Monte Carlo Simulation VaR	5.61%	1.07%	3.56%	6.19%	2.77%

Figure 98   Summary of results from all approaches

4. Incremental VaR

Incremental VaR (IVaR) measures the impact of small changes in individual positions on the overall VaR. There are two different approaches to calculating incremental VaR:

1. full valuation approach;
2. approximate solution to IVaR, or the short cut approach.

a. Full valuation approach

In the full valuation approach, the entire process for VaR is repeated based on the revised positions of the portfolio. This means that we are calculating the VaR value twice. Incremental VaR will be the difference between the original VaR calculation and the revised VaR calculation.

Let us review our portfolio once again.

Base Portfolio as at 30-09-2012				
	Crude Oil	EUR-USD	Gold	Silver
Price	92.18	1.2855	1,776.00	34.65
Quantity	100	1000	10	100
Amount	9,218.00	1,285.50	17,760.00	3,465.00
Weights	29.05%	4.05%	55.97%	10.92%

Figure 99   Investment portfolio

The total portfolio value works out to 31,728.50. The SMA daily VaR was calculated as 3.12 percent. The portfolio VaR amount worked out as $31,728.50 \times 3.12$ percent $= 991.23$

Assuming a 1 percent increase in all positions with respect to the total portfolio value, the revised portfolio (all positions increase by 317.285) will be as follows.

	Crude Oil	EUR-USD	Gold	Silver	Portfolio
Positions	9,535.29	1,602.79	18,077.29	3,782.29	32,997.64
Weights (original)	29.05%	4.05%	55.97%	10.92%	100%
Weights (revised)	28.90%	4.86%	54.78%	11.46%	100%
SMA daily volatility	2.44%	0.48%	1.56%	2.64%	1.33%
VAR	5.68%	1.11%	3.62%	6.15%	3.10%

Figure 100 Revised portfolio values, weights, volatility and VaR

The revised portfolio VaR works out to 32,997.64 × 3.10 percent = 1,023.89

The incremental VaR therefore is 32.66.

This process may not seem too tedious with just four positions, but a financial institute may have a portfolio comprising of hundreds of different positions, which could make the full valuation process a time consuming one.

There is however a short cut solution to IVaR that does not require two separate VaR valuations.

b. Approximation to IVaR

The incremental VaR using the short cut method is approximately equal to

Absolute value of (Change in position relative to original portfolio value × Original portfolio value) × inverse z-score of selected confidence level × Covariance between original position returns and original portfolio returns/ Original portfolio volatility.

PRICE =ABS(B13)*$B$2*IF(OR(AND(B13>=0,B16>=0),AND(B13<=0,B16<=0)),1,-1)*B17/$F$19

	A	B	C	D	E	F	G	H
1	Confidence Level	99%	INPUT Cells					
2	α	2.33						
3	lambda	0.5						
4	**Portfolio Value (original)**	31,728.50						
5	**Portfolio Value (new)**	32,997.64						
6	**Portfolio VaR (original)**	991.23						
7	**Incremental VaR**	32.58	Incremental VaR measures the impact of small changes in individual component pos					
8	**New Portfolio VaR (using IVaR)**	1,023.808						
9	**New Portfolio VaR (using full-valuation)**	1,023.895	32.664					
10	**Difference**	- 0.09	- 0.09					
11		Crude Oil	EUR-USD	Gold	Silver	Portfolio		
12	Approx. Incremental VaR (SMA)	=ABS(B13)*$B$2*IF(OR(AND(B13>=0,B16>=0),AND(B13<=0,B16<=0)),1,-1)*B17/$F$19						
13	Increase/ Decrease in positions	317.29	317.29	317.29	317.29	1,269.14		
14	change in position relative to old portfolio	1%	1%	1%	1%			
15	Absolute positions	9,218.00	1,285.50	17,760.00	3,465.00	31,728.50		
16	Positions	9,218.00	1,285.50	17,760.00	3,465.00	31,728.50		
17	Covariance	0.02%	0.00%	0.02%	0.02%	0.02%		
18	SMA VAR	5.68%	1.11%	3.62%	6.15%	3.12%		
19	SMA daily volatility	2.44%	0.48%	1.56%	2.64%	1.34%		
20	Weights (original)	29.05%	4.05%	55.97%	10.92%	100%		

Figure 101 Calculation of IVaR using the approximate method

If you look at the above formula you will notice that we have attached a condition on the calculated covariance. If we are long on the original position and the incremental position is an increase in the position or if we are short of the original position and incremental position increases the short position then we take the covariance as is. However, if we are long on the original position and the incremental position is a decrease in the position or if we are short of the original position and incremental position decreases the short position then we take the covariance as $-1 \times$ covariance.

Using the approximate method we arrive at an incremental VaR of 32.58, which is 0.09 less than the IVaR figure, derived using the full valuation approach.

Note: *The covariance for the EWMA VaR approach is calculated as the sum product of the following series: the return series of a given position, the return series of the original portfolio and the scaled weights.*

5. Marginal VaR

Marginal VaR measures how the overall VaR would change if one position was completely removed from the portfolio.

As a first step in this process we determine the weights of the portfolio assuming all four positions are present, and then again if one position (at a time) were to be eliminated as shown in Figure 102.

Next we recalculate the portfolio return series using the revised weights as in Figure 103.

We then recalculate the volatility, VaR percent and VaR amount based on the revised return series.

The marginal VaR if crude oil was removed from the existing portfolio is 226.51, that is, the VaR amount will reduce by this figure. Note that in percentage terms, portfolio VaR has increased but the portfolio value to

	Crude Oil	EUR-USD	Gold	Silver	Portfolio
Weights - Base Case	29.05%	4.05%	55.97%	10.92%	100.00%
Weights (excl. Crude Oil)	0.00%	5.71%	78.90%	15.39%	100.00%
Weights (excl. EUR-USD)	30.28%	0.00%	58.34%	11.38%	100.00%
Weights (excl. Gold)	65.99%	9.20%	0.00%	24.81%	100.00%
Weights (excl. Silver)	32.61%	4.55%	62.84%	0.00%	100.00%

Figure 102 Portfolio weights – original and revised positions

	Portfolio - all 4 positions - Base Case	Portfolio - sans crude oil	Portfolio - sans EUR-USD	Portfolio - sans Gold	Portfolio - sans Silver
13					
14	-0.02%	0.17%	-0.01%	-0.36%	-0.03%
15	0.00%	0.21%	-0.01%	-0.30%	0.00%
16	-0.02%	0.18%	-0.01%	-0.34%	-0.02%
17	0.32%	0.66%	0.33%	-0.29%	0.34%
18	0.92%	1.51%	0.94%	0.95%	0.43%
19	-0.41%	-0.62%	-0.46%	-0.14%	-0.34%
20	0.19%	-0.58%	0.23%	1.23%	0.24%
21	0.42%	0.47%	0.40%	0.48%	0.39%
22	0.40%	0.44%	0.40%	0.43%	0.36%
23	0.38%	0.41%	0.40%	0.39%	0.34%
24	1.39%	1.32%	1.45%	2.59%	0.79%
25	-0.39%	0.23%	-0.38%	-1.45%	-0.37%
26	0.44%	0.20%	0.46%	0.44%	0.63%
27	-2.05%	-1.68%	-2.10%	-2.92%	-1.86%
28	-0.41%	-2.42%	-0.40%	2.48%	-0.25%
29	-0.38%	-2.39%	-0.40%	2.54%	-0.21%
30	-0.44%	-2.46%	-0.40%	2.41%	-0.28%
31	1.22%	-0.13%	1.34%	3.32%	1.11%
32	1.37%	0.73%	1.37%	2.29%	1.44%
33	-0.27%	0.40%	-0.36%	-1.44%	-0.13%
34	-0.39%	-0.07%	-0.42%	-0.89%	-0.26%

Figure 103   Portfolio returns – original and revised series

Marginal VaR		Total VaR reduced by			
	-	- 226.51	- 1.80	- 404.81	- 102.26
Confidence Level	99%				
Portfolio Value	31,728.50	22,510.50	30,443.00	13,968.50	28,263.50
Daily VaR Amount	991.23	764.73	989.43	586.42	888.97
Daily VaR %	3.12%	3.40%	3.25%	4.20%	3.15%
Daily SMA volatilty	1.34%	1.46%	1.40%	1.80%	1.35%
	Portfolio - all 4 positions - Base Case	Portfolio - sans crude oil	Portfolio - sans EUR-USD	Portfolio - sans Gold	Portfolio - sans Silver
	-0.02%	0.17%	-0.01%	-0.36%	-0.03%

Figure 104   VaR – original and revised values

which the VaR percent applied has reduced, hence there is a reduction in the overall VaR amount.

6. Conditional VaR

Conditional VaR measures the mean excess loss or expected shortfall beyond VaR at a given confidence level.

For our illustration purposes we assume that VaR percent has been calculated using the historical simulation approach. The VaR amount is calculated as VaR percent × portfolio or position value.

For each data point we first calculate the amount of loss, which is the portfolio or position value × return. If the return is negative it will be taken as a loss, whereas if it is positive then zero losses will be recorded.

	PRICE	▾ × ✓ fx	=ABS(IF(A10<0,A10*$B$1,0))
	A		B
1	Crude Oil		9,218.00
2	Confidence Level		99%
3	Daily VaR		6.565%
4	VaR Amount		605.17
5	Conditional VaR %		8.948%
6	Conditional VaR Amount		824.83
7			
8	Sum		242,044.27
9	Returns	▾	Losses ▾
10		-0.51%	=ABS(IF(A10<0,A10*$B$1,0))
11		-0.51%	46.60
12		-0.51%	46.60
13		-0.51%	46.60
14		-0.51%	46.60
15		0.09%	-
16		2.06%	-
17		0.32%	-

Figure 105   Loss amounts

We next determine the conditional losses. In effect this is the loss amount already calculated above but subject to a restricting condition, that is, only those losses than exceed the VaR amount will be considered.

We next determine the conditional VaR amount. This is the average of the conditional losses. EXCEL's AVERAGEIF function is used to calculate this value so that only losses greater than zero will be considered. The conditional VaR percent is the conditional VaR amount/position value.

This conditional VaR percent may also be determined independently of the position value by simply applying the AVERAGEIF function to the returns column, so that only returns less than the negative of the

	A	B	C
	PRICE ▼ × ✓ *fx* =IF(B10>$B$4,B10,0)		
1	Crude Oil	9,218.00	
2	Confidence Level	99%	
3	Daily VaR	6.565%	
4	VaR Amount	605.17	
5	Conditional VaR %	8.948%	8.948%
6	Conditional VaR Amount	824.83	
7			
8	Sum	242,044.27	27,219.31
9	Returns ▼	Losses ▼	Conditional Losses ▼
10	-0.51%	46.60	=IF(B10>$B$4,B10,0)
11	-0.51%	46.60	-
12	-0.51%	46.60	-
13	-0.51%	46.60	-
14	-0.51%	46.60	-
15	0.09%	-	-
16	2.06%	-	-

Figure 106   Conditional loss amounts

	A	B	C
	PRICE ▼ × ✓ *fx* =AVERAGEIF(C10:C3203,">0")		
1	Crude Oil	9,218.00	
2	Confidence Level	99%	
3	Daily VaR	6.565%	
4	VaR Amount	605.17	
5	Conditional VaR %	8.948%	8.948%
6	Conditional VaR Amount	=AVERAGEIF(C10:C3203,">0")	
7			
8	Sum	242,044.27	27,219.31
9	Returns ▼	Losses ▼	Conditional Losses ▼
10	-0.51%	46.60	-
11	-0.51%	46.60	-
12	-0.51%	46.60	-
13	-0.51%	46.60	-
14	-0.51%	46.60	-
15	0.09%	-	-
16	2.06%	-	-
17	0.32%	-	-
18	0.32%	-	-
19	0.32%	-	-
20	1.56%	-	-
21	-1.91%	175.89	-
22	1.05%	-	-
23	-2.96%	272.93	-
24	4.51%	-	-
25	4.51%	-	-

|◄ ◄ ► ►| ╱ Historical Simulation ╱ Monte Carlo Simulation ╱ Marginal VaR ╲ **Conditional VaR** ╱

Figure 107   Conditional VaR

daily VaR percent may be considered, that is, –AVERAGEIF(Returns array, CONCATENATE("<",–Daily VaR percent)).

7. Probability of shortfall

Probability of shortfall measures the probability that investment returns will not reach a given goal or alternatively the probability that investment returns will fall below a given goal. For illustration purposes we assume that our goal is that position or portfolio returns should never be negative, in other words they should be greater than zero.

Given our distribution of returns, what is the probability that returns will be negative?

Using the histogram methodology of the historical simulation approach we have already determined the cumulative frequency of returns being less than or equal to a particular value. We just need to identify this cumulative frequency for returns less than or equal to 0 percent.

Crude Oil				
Bin	Cumulative Frequency	Frequency	Cumulative%	Confidence Level
-12.34%	3	3	0.09%	99.91%
-11.85%	3	-	0.09%	99.91%
-11.36%	3	-	0.09%	99.91%
-10.88%	8	5	0.25%	99.75%
-10.39%	8	-	0.25%	99.75%
-9.90%	12	4	0.38%	99.62%
-9.42%	14	2	0.44%	99.56%
-8.93%	16	2	0.50%	99.50%
-8.44%	18	2	0.56%	99.44%
-7.95%	18	-	0.56%	99.44%
-7.47%	21	3	0.66%	99.34%
-6.98%	26	5	0.81%	99.19%
-6.49%	33	7	1.03%	98.97%
-6.00%	39	6	1.22%	98.78%
-5.52%	54	15	1.69%	98.31%
-5.03%	66	12	2.07%	97.93%
-4.54%	75	9	2.35%	97.65%
-4.05%	109	34	3.41%	96.59%
-3.57%	181	72	5.67%	94.33%
-3.08%	236	55	7.39%	92.61%
-2.59%	319	83	9.99%	90.01%
-2.11%	447	128	13.99%	86.01%
-1.62%	634	187	19.85%	80.15%
-1.13%	831	197	26.02%	73.98%
-0.64%	1091	260	34.16%	65.84%
-0.16%	1417	326	44.36%	55.64%
0.33%	1747	330	54.70%	45.30%
0.82%	2084	337	65.25%	34.75%

Figure 108 Evaluating the probability of shortfall for crude oil from the histogram table

Investment	Crude Oil	EUR-USD	Gold	Silver	Portfolio
Probability of Shortfall	44.36%	40.01%	36.82%	43.49%	41.14%

Figure 109 Probability of shortfall

For crude oil we can see that the probability that returns will be negative is 44.36 percent.

For the other positions the probability of shortfall is given as shown in Figure 109.

Annexure 2 – Value at risk application: margin lending case study

You head Risk Management for the Prime Brokerage desk at an investment bank on Wall Street. Three of your top customers are *Hedge Fund Manager A, Hedge Fund Manager B and Hedge Fund Manager C*, who all specialize in large, leveraged (margin financed) commodity trades.

The Prime Brokerage desk lends money on margin to hedge fund customers. As the Head of Risk Management it is your responsibility to decide and recommend a suitable margin requirement for all margin lending transactions. As part of your customer lending agreement, the amount is lent against the security value of the account (the value of the commodity position) and will be liquidated if the margin falls below a certain threshold and is not replenished. Your employer is reputed on the street as "the" bank that hates writing off capital (it is a capital offence) and since you report directly to the Board Risk Management Committee, your primary objective is to reduce the probability of capital loss.

Given recent volatility in commodity market prices, the board is concerned that the margin calculation process should be reviewed. The objective of the margin is to secure the interest of the desk and protect it against adverse price movement if the desk is forced to liquidate the position of the hedge fund.

Ideally the margin should be sufficient to cover the impact of price volatility over a typical holding period. It should also cover the time required to liquidate the position and any liquidation losses if a default occurs.

The loss given default (LGD) is based on the worst-case price that you would realize when you sell a client's commodity portfolio if they failed to meet a margin call. Your holding period as the bank is based on the period required to liquidate the portfolio subjecting you to inventory losses on account of volatility. Your loss should be partially (or completely) offset by your customer's margin deposit.

The board believes that margin requirements should now be set in such a fashion that the probability of default (PD) measure as per your PD model should not exceed *2 percent* for any client. In addition, LGD after taking the margin under account should not exceed *5 percent* of net exposure.

The table below shows the portfolio weights for three of your largest hedge fund clients.

RISK PARAMETERS	HEDGE FUND MANAGER A	HEDGE FUND MANAGER B	HEDGE FUND MANAGER C
Commodities traded with portfolio weights	Oil (50%), Gold (50%)	Gold (100%)	Gold (80%), Oil (20%)
Holding period of trades	20 days	3 months	6 months
Equity in trades	10%	5%	5%
Liquidation days (based on size of position as a percentage of market volume)	30 days	90 days	270 days
Size of position	500 million US$	1.5 billion US$	5 billion US$

Figure 110   Risk parameters for Hedge Fund Managers A, B & C

1. Designing a solution

Let's think about the design of our solution before we break the ground on numbers. What do we need to do?

(a) We need to identify a conservative basis for margin calculation that is workable for both risk and business (competitive).
(b) We need to link this basis to a measure that estimates PD by a client.
(c) We have been given an acceptable range for the PD measure by the board.

One approach would be to estimate volatility and VaR figures based on the portfolio exposure of each hedge fund and then use these as a basis for estimating the PD. We can then change margin amounts and see how they impact our PD estimates, and zero in to the PD range specified by the board members.

Rather than use an average number for volatility, we would also recommend that we look at the volatility distribution to ensure that we understand how quickly volatility can move and its historical highs and lows.

To calculate these values we will use the concept of rolling volatility and VaR calculations covered earlier. The focus of our discussion will be values and their implications, not calculation methods.

Step One – Oil and gold volatility

What is the volatility experienced in oil and gold prices over the complete period of the data set? While it would have been enough to simply quote SMA daily volatility of 2.686 percent for WTI and 1.35 percent for gold, it would be better to also calculate trailing volatility for 2, 4 or 6 weeks for later use.

	WTI	Gold
Volatility	2.686%	1.350%

Figure 111   Volatility for case study data set – WTI & gold spot prices

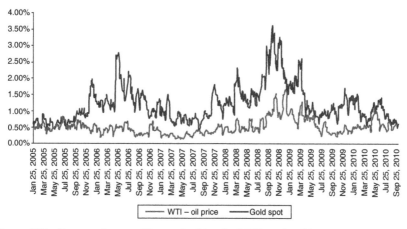

Figure 112   Case study – trailing volatility for WTI and gold spot prices using a two-week moving window

Step Two – Portfolio volatility for the three hedge funds

What is the portfolio volatility for each hedge fund? The fastest way of answering this question is through a simple data table and a color code representing each hedge fund manager.

Header rows and columns represent the quantities of the two respective commodities. We obviously can't scale this approach to more than two instruments, but for this specific case an EXCEL data table is the way to go. We have used the weighted average return shortcut approach to calculate portfolio variance/covariance VaR. The results below show the average portfolio volatility over the entire look back period.

Port. Vol			Hedge Fund A
Avg	Gold		Hedge Fund B
			Hedge Fund C
Oil			
1.623%	100%	50%	80%
0.0%	1.35%	0.67%	1.08%
20.0%	1.55%	0.95%	1.30%
50.0%	2.09%	1.62%	1.89%

Figure 113   Portfolio volatility – oil & gold

However, a better and preferred solution would be to also work with maximum and minimum volatility thresholds calculated from the series of trailing volatilities.

Port. Vol			
Max	Gold		
Oil			
4.69%	100%	50%	80%
0.0%	3.52%	1.76%	2.82%
20.0%	4.20%	2.71%	3.60%
50.0%	6.07%	4.69%	5.50%

Port. Vol			
Min	Gold		
Oil			
0.33%	100%	50%	80%
0.0%	0.37%	0.18%	0.30%
20.0%	0.42%	0.24%	0.35%
50.0%	0.52%	0.33%	0.43%

Figure 114   Portfolio volatility – oil & gold: min and max volatility levels

Step Three – Volatility distribution
Take this one step further and generate a histogram of trailing volatility which gives us a better and more complete picture than a simple minimum, maximum or average volatility pick. The histogram in Figure 115 shows you clearly that *median volatility is between 1 percent and 1.3 percent,*

that you are likely to see *jumps to 2.5 percent to 3.3 percent quite frequently* and that there is a possibility of seeing *daily volatility levels of 4.6 percent and higher.*

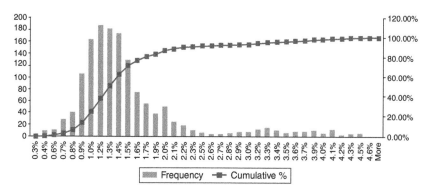

Figure 115 Portfolio volatility – histogram – tracing median volatility and the long tail effect

If you didn't make the jump to trailing volatility earlier, in particular plotting the histogram of trailing volatilities, you will never reach the perfect solution for determining the margin deposit to be made for each hedge fund. Suggesting margins based on maximum volatility levels will get you skewered by your board for suggesting impractical thresholds that could potentially kill the underlying business. The trailing volatility histogram on the other hand will enable you to more clearly see the impact of your suggested margin numbers on inventory losses and LGD ratios, and help in recommending a more practical solution for setting margins.

Step Four – Margin requirement for hedge funds

We use VaR as a proxy for margin requirements since they indicate the maximum likely portfolio loss based on historical returns. We have used 99 percent here as an illustrative confidence threshold. In real life we are more likely to use 95 percent.

The right approach in calculating VaR is to use the estimated liquidation period based on trading volume or turnover and estimated impact costs rather than the given holding periods of different trade classifications. To stress test the requirement we have used both maximum volatility and average volatility levels. The recommended margins based on the volatility level we have picked up are given in the last column, titled VaR.

This is where the median volatility levels calculated above (take another look at the histogram) come to your aid and allow you to suggest usage of average volatility levels rather than maximum trailing historical volatility.

	Max Trail Vol	Hold. Period	Confd. Int	Z-Factor	VaR
Hedge Fund A	4.69%	20	99%	2.33	32%
Hedge Fund B	3.52%	90	99%	2.33	51%
Hedge Fund C	3.60%	180	99%	2.33	74%

	FinanceTrainingCourse.com				
	Avg Trail Vol	Hold. Period	Confd. Int	Z-Factor	VaR
Hedge Fund A	1.62%	20	99%	2.33	11%
Hedge Fund B	1.35%	90	99%	2.33	20%
Hedge Fund C	1.30%	180	99%	2.33	27%

Figure 116 Value at risk and suggested margin requirements for margin lending

	Avg Trail Vol	Liqd. Period	Confd. Int	Z-Factor	VaR
Hedge Fund A	1.62%	30	99%	2.33	14%
Hedge Fund B	1.35%	90	99%	2.33	20%
Hedge Fund C	1.30%	270	99%	2.33	33%

Figure 117 VaR lending margin requirements – suggested using average or median volatility

Alternate solutions – Margin requirements
You can go ahead and suggest margin thresholds or margin lending using maximum volatility levels, but you will get laughed out of the board room based on your impractical suggestion. It may be an acceptable academic solution, but it is a suicidal real life suggestion because it will kill the underlying business.

	Max Trail Vol	Liqd. Period	Confd. Int	Z-Factor	VaR
Hedge Fund A	4.69%	30	99%	2.33	39%
Hedge Fund B	3.52%	90	99%	2.33	51%
Hedge Fund C	3.60%	270	99%	2.33	90%

Figure 118 VaR based margin requirements – using maximum trailing volatility

If you are thoroughly confused and not sure, the safest solution would be to simply put the ranges from your model out there for the board to discuss.

Your technology and operations team suggests that in order to reduce the systems overhead, only one margin requirement should be charged across all customers and commodities. Your sales team agrees. Is this a good or bad idea?

The simple, clear and concise answer is no, it is not a good idea to use one margin threshold across all products and customers, as it would be statistically incorrect. The correct practical answer is that while you can get away with different margin requirements across different products, doing the same across different customers may bring its own challenges.

	Holding Period			Recommended	Liquidation Period	
Recommended Range for Margin Requirements						
		Min	Max		Min	Max
Hedge Fund A		11%	32%	20%	14%	39%
Hedge Fund B		20%	51%	30%	20%	51%
Hedge Fund C		27%	74%	40%	33%	90%

Figure 119 Alternate solution – margin requirements for margin lending using VaR

Step Five – PD for hedge fund clients

The PD using the Black Scholes Merton structured approach is given by $N(-d_2)$ where $N(.)$ is the standard normal cumulative distribution and d_2 is calculated as given below.

$$V_E = V_A N(d_1) - e^{-rT} X N(d_2)$$

where

V_E is the market value of the firm's equity r

$$d_1 = \frac{\ln\left(\frac{V_A}{X}\right) + \left(r + \frac{\sigma_A^2}{2}\right)T}{\sigma_A \sqrt{T}},$$

$$d_2 = d_1 - \sigma_A \sqrt{T}, \text{ and } \sigma_E = \frac{V_A}{V_E}\Delta\sigma_A$$

r is the risk free interest rate.

Figure 120 Merton structured approach – using Black Scholes to calculate PD

		Asset (VA)	Equity (BVE)	Strike	Avg Asset_Vol	Annual Asset. Vol	MVE	d1	d2	N(d1)	N(d2)	N(-d2)
PVF	99%											
Time	1											
RiskFree	1%											
	Hedge Fund A	500	210	290	1.62%	26%	213	2.2635661	2.003566	98.8%	97.7%	2.256%
	Hedge Fund B	1,500	600	900	1.35%	22%	610	2.4773892	2.257389	99.3%	98.8%	1.199%
	Hedge Fund C	5,000	2,000	3,000	1.30%	21%	2,032	2.585122	2.375122	99.5%	99.1%	0.877%

Figure 121 Calculating PD for margin lending customers

For background on using the Merton structured approach for calculating PD, see Annexure 3.

Equity is calculated as the margin requirements (42 percent of asset value for Hedge Fund A and 40 percent of asset value for Hedge Funds B and C). The strike is the difference between the asset position and the margin deposits. The trick here is to acknowledge that the volatilities you are calculating are actually asset volatilities, so there is no need to do the iterative asset volatility to equity volatility calculation typically required for the Merton approach. You could go directly to the solution to arrive at PD.

Position		Position Delta	Margin	PD	LGD	Margin Required
500	Hedge Fund A	1	210	2.256%	14	42.0%
1,500	Hedge Fund B	1	600	1.199%	(164)	40.0%
5,000	Hedge Fund C	1	2,000	0.877%	(2,513)	40.0%

Figure 122 Margin requirements, LGD and position delta

Step Six – Presenting results to the board

With your new margin requirements, do all hedge fund managers now represent equal risk? Or are there differences between them? Which one of these funds would you like to lend more to? Against which one of these funds should exposure be reduced?

To arrive at solutions to these questions, we plot the probabilities of default in the form of a graph against rising and declining volatility. We use EXCEL's data table functionality to arrive at results for different volatilities for each hedge fund.

Despite the higher LGD and the size of the exposure, from a PD point of view customer C (Hedge Fund C) is the preferred customer.

	PD_FundA	PD_FundB	PD_FundC
	2.256%	1.199%	0.877%
5%	0.0%	0.0%	0.0%
10%	0.0%	0.0%	0.0%
15%	0.4%	0.1%	0.0%
20%	1.8%	0.9%	0.6%
25%	4.5%	3.1%	2.5%
30%	7.9%	6.4%	5.6%
35%	11.8%	10.3%	9.5%
40%	15.7%	14.3%	13.5%
45%	19.5%	18.3%	17.6%
50%	23.2%	22.2%	21.4%

Figure 123 PD across volatility levels

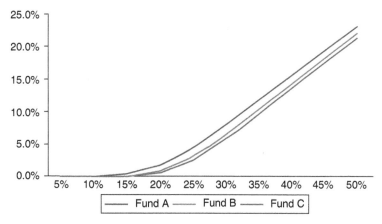

Figure 124 PD across volatility levels plotted

Annexure 3 – Probability of default modeling using Merton's structured approach

The essence of the Merton structured model is simple. The market knows best and knows it first, before any of the analysts' reports cover it. If you have a liquid publicly listed security, the price behavior of that security will be the first to indicate that something has gone wrong or is expected to go wrong. A valid, credible trade data signal is superior to an analyst research report.

But how do you best use market based signals? The Merton model is actually a variation of the Black Scholes model (discussed further in the Derivative Pricing section of this book). Let us take a quick look at its intuition.

1. The valuation of firm equity as a call option on firms assets

We assume that the value of firm or shareholders equity is just like any other option. It becomes more valuable as the firm grows and becomes less valuable as the firm declines. On one side of our balance sheet the value of the firm is represented by its assets, which serve as a great proxy for how valuable the firm is. As long as firm assets exceed firm liabilities we are in good shape.

Equity is like a call option on those assets. As long as the value of liabilities of the firm is less than the value of its assets, firm equity has value. The minute the value of liabilities exceeds the value of assets there is no incentive for the owner of firm equity to exercise the option. Rationally speaking, the owner is better off simply handing over the firm to the bankers and walking away.

The Merton model for calculating PD uses the Black Scholes equation to estimate the value of this option. The model specifications are mapped as shown below.

Figure 125   Merton structured approach for calculating PD using equity prices

So Spot = V = Market value of firm assets, Strike = X = Book value of firm liabilities, Time = Term of liabilities. However, which volatility do you need? Firm assets or owner's equity? The right answer is firm assets. However, we have a challenge. The observable volatility from market data is actually equity volatility – so we need to transform or convert it into firm assets volatility. Once that is done we have almost everything we need to calculate the PD. To make the transformation we need to estimate the market value of firm equity, using the equation

$$E = V \times N(d_1) - X \times \text{PVF} \times N(d_2) \tag{1}$$

where

E	= market value of equity (option value);
X	= book value of liabilities (strike price);
V	= market value of assets;
T	= time horizon;
$N(.)$	= cumulative normal distribution function whose value is calculated at d_1 and d_2, where
d_1	= $[\ln(V/X) + (r + 1/2\ \text{sigma}_a^2) \times T]/[\text{sigma}_a \times (\text{squareroot}(T)]$
d_2	= $d_1 - \text{sigma}_a \times \text{squareroot}(T)$
r	= risk-free borrowing and lending rate;
Sigma_a	= percentage standard deviation (volatility) of asset value;

In equation (1) there are two unknowns: the market value of assets (V) and volatility of asset value (sigma_a). In order to solve for these unknowns we need another equation. It is possible to derive this other equation from equation (1), by taking its mathematical expectation after differentiating both sides of the equations. We obtain the following expression:

$$\text{sigma}_e = [N(d_1) \times V \times \text{sigma}_a]/E. \tag{2}$$

In equations (1) and (2), the known variables are the market value of equity (E), volatility of equity (sigma_e that is estimated from historical data), book value of liabilities (X), and the time horizon (T). The two unknowns are the market value of the assets (V) and the volatility of the assets (sigma_a). Because there are two equations with two unknowns, a solution can be found.

What is our estimate of PD? In the analysis of the Black Scholes formula (discussed in our Derivative Pricing chapter) the probability that the terminal price on exercise will exceed the strike price is given by $N(d_2)$. However, in the case of PD, the default will occur when the terminal price (S_T) is less than the strike price (X). What is the probability that $S_T < X$? It is $N(-d_2)$. This is your estimate for PD.

3
Managing Risks

A framework for risk management

Any effort to create a framework for managing risk should start by asking the following questions:

- What is the metric that we use for measuring risk?
- How frequently do we monitor it?
- How sensitive is this measure to changing prices and market conditions?
- How is this sensitivity benchmarked or calibrated?
- Do we use our realized historical experience in this calibration exercise?
- What models do we use to predict the range of values for this measure in the future?
- How stable are these models?
- Under what conditions will these models fail or break down?
- What are the assumptions behind these models?
- What is included in the data set used to run these models?
- Do we have a pre-defined tolerance for movement in this measure on account of prices and market conditions?
- How is this tolerance calculated? Who reviews and approves it? How frequently?
- How does this tolerance relate to expected loss? How does expected loss relate to actual capital that needs to be set aside to support this tolerance?
- Are there any policies and processes in place that document the answers to these questions?
- How frequently are these policies and processes reviewed?
- How do we measure the effectiveness of these policies in controlling the risk metric that we are tracking?

A first look through the above questions allows us to classify them in the following categories:

- policy,
- data,
- models,
- metrics and sensitivities,
- limits and tolerance levels,
- process and control.

A good risk framework examines the interaction of each of these categories with each other as well as the categories in isolation. As the figure below shows, risk capacity, preference and appetite drive the policy, which sets the limits for risk and risk sensitivities. The limits are enforced, monitored and tracked through operational and control processes, and the effectiveness of this framework determines the realized returns. Here the word return is used in a generic sense. Where risk minimization is the objective, the absolute scale of returns (or even the sign) is immaterial; what is relevant is that in the end results are within pre-defined limits, loss tolerances and risk appetite.

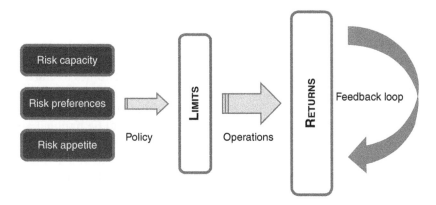

Figure 126   Risk framework

We start by taking a look at each of these elements individually.

1. Risk policy

A policy document identifies roles, responsibilities and occasionally the outline of a process to review, set and evaluate limits. It is the source document that drives the behavior of the other seven components of a risk management framework and is generally approved by the Board of Directors (BOD) and is implemented by a lower layer responsible for execution.

By the definition and nature of our businesses we put capital at risk every day. Here capital is defined differently from the conventional regulatory reporting sense. Within the context of risk policy, capital means that a transaction we execute may lead to the realization of financial loss. Given the nature of our positions and our business, this loss can only be offset by retained earnings or by the capital entrusted to us by our shareholders.

The primary objective of this risk policy is to ensure that while we go ahead and take reasonable risks that are required to generate reasonable returns, whenever we put capital at risk we do it in an objective, documented and transparent fashion. That these risks are taken within pre-approved limits and, when these limits are breached, the exceptions are reported and addressed. The objective of risk policy is not to eliminate capital loss, it is to ensure that such losses are put to good use by allowing us to learn from earlier mistakes and improve the chances of avoiding them in the future.

How a risk policy is put together is a question that leads to enormous contention between advisors, consultants and clients. As an inanimate object one would think that a risk policy document would not lead to such intense, passionate discussion at the drafting stage. A policy document is just a policy document; where are these extreme reactions coming from?

Apparently there are two schools of thought when it comes to crafting policy. The *less is more* school of thought believes that a policy document should be philosophical in nature and, rather than describing all risks in great detail, it should focus more on how risk would be handled and treated at a (you guessed it) policy level. For this school a policy document focuses more on the logistics of approvals, exceptions and mandates rather than actual limits or categorization of risk. The risk identification, limit setting, evaluation and reporting component is left to the supporting process document that accompanies the policy everywhere.

In their defense, the less is more school believes that boards do not have sufficient time to do justice to risk policy. An involved, multi-chapter risk policy document would only get a superficial review at the board level and would most likely get stamped for approval on account of the shortage of time and the competition for attention within the number of items on the board's agendas these days. So it is better to keep the policy short, sweet and relevant and shift the details to the process document that may or may not require direct approval from the board. As long as the process document is in alignment with the policy, the board has discharged its primary obligation by reviewing and approving the policy document without creating unnecessary delays in the approval process. Thereafter the board can be pulled in and involved on an as-needed basis on risk issues without spending too much time on the approval of minor or process oriented changes to the policy or process documents.

On the other side is the *descriptive and prescriptive* school of policy thought. Under this approach the policy document is a far more comprehensive write-up that does not only include the types and categories of risks addressed, but also the suggested and proposed limits. These policies include everything that the less is more school suggests and then some.

Both schools have their place in a risk group. Which one is right depends on how involved your board is in the risk management process, the frequency with which it meets, its composition, its accessibility and the amount of time it can honestly devote to risk items on its agenda. Where a board's risk review group includes members whose availability and time is limited, where risk committee meetings are held once every quarter and where even ordinary risk items often get covered over multiple board meetings, the less is more school is a better bet. Where the boards are more actively involved and board members are easily accessible, and where risk agenda items are covered in the same meeting, the second school may be more appropriate.

In the end, what really matters is that both the process and policy documents support the reality that unfortunately exists regarding demands on BOD's time, at least here in this region. In the absence of SOX like regulation in large parts of the Middle East and Asia Pacific it means that your policy documents shouldn't turn the BOD meeting into a recurring bottleneck when it comes to implementing risk policy.

2. Good data and a first look at models

The second element in our list deals with data and models. While it is not directly visible in the risk mindset diagram, when it comes to calculation of exposures, estimation of capital losses and allocation of capital, and using these to define risk preferences, capacity and risk appetite, data and models have central stage.

Risk and transaction systems differ in many ways. But they both suffer from a common ailment – absence of good data and market relevant models. On a risk platform the integrity of the data set is dependent on the underlying transaction platform and the quality of data feeds. Keeping the incoming stream of information clean and ensuring that the historical data set remains pure is a full time job. The resources allocated to this problem show how committed and reliant an organization is to its risk systems.

In organizations still ruled by the compliance driven checklist mindset, you will find that it is sufficient to simply generate risk reports. It is sufficient because no one really looks at the results and, when they do, in most cases they may not have any idea about how to interpret them. Or, even worse, how to work with the numbers to understand the challenges they represent for that organization's future.

The same problem haunts the modeling domain. It is not sufficient to have a model in place. It is just as important to understand how it works and how it will fail. But, once again, as long as a model exists and as long as it produces something on a periodic basis, most boards in the region feel they have met the necessary and sufficient condition for risk management.

Is there anything that we can do to change this mindset and fix this problem?

One could start with the confusion at the board level between risk and the underlying transaction. A market risk platform is a very different animal from the underlying treasury transaction. The common ground, however, is the pricing model and market behavior; the uncommon factor is the trader's instinct and his gut. Where risk and the transaction systems clash is on the uncommon ground. Instincts versus statistics!

The instinct and gut effect is far more prominent within business lines where prices and decisions are not just determined by market forces. Relationships and strategic imperatives drive the domain driven business. The credit and lending equation in the banking system is a great example. Analytics and models drive the credit risk side. The credit business is "name" based, dominated by subjective factors that assess relationships, one at a time. There is some weight assigned to sector exposure and concentration limits at the portfolio level, but the primary "lend," "no lend" call is still relationship based. The credit risk side on the other hand is scoring, behavior and portfolio based. A payment delay is a payment delay, a default is a default. While the softer side can protect the underlying relationship and possibly increase the chances of recovery and help attain "current" status more quickly, the job of a risk system is to document and highlight exceptions and project their impact on the portfolio. A risk system focuses on the trend. While it is interested in the cause of the underlying event, the interest is purely mathematical; there is no human side.

I asked earlier if there is anything we can do to change the board's mindset. To begin with, boards need to spend more time and allocate more resources to the risk debate. Data, models and reports are not enough. They need to be poked, challenged, stressed, understood, grown and invested in. Two hours once a quarter for a Board Risk Committee meeting is not sufficient time to dissect the effectiveness of your risk function. You may as well close your eyes and ignore it.

But before you do that, remember: hell hath no fury like a risk scorned.

3. Models and tools

The first question that needs to be addressed is the level of application of limits. Value at risk (VaR) based limits may be set anywhere in the hierarchical structure, from limits on individual traders, desks, business units or across the organization. The primary consideration here is the level of risk overlap between different risk centers. Once these limits are set, the control and monitoring process takes over (covered in the "Limits and controls" section below).

Breaches in VaR limits may occur due to an increase in volatility, which results in an increase in the VaR numbers. This situation may be dealt with in two ways. The more conservative approach would be to adjust the limit immediately when a breach occurs. The other approach is to recognize that increases in volatility may be temporary, and set an acceptable band to accommodate temporary increases in volatilities before any changes to the limits are made. Of course, the approach used to calculate volatilities can play a significant role. Volatilities calculated using simple moving averages tend to remain high till the observation that caused the spike does not drop out of the look back period. This problem may be addressed by moving to exponentially weighted moving averages, where the weight of the observation decreases exponentially as we move forward. Irrespective of the model used to calculate volatilities, temporary breaches in VaR limits due to a sudden increase in volatilities may still occur and must be addressed.

It is important to highlight the fact that, like most quantitative finance and risk management models, VaR has its limitations. VaR is not the maximum possible loss. VaR is simply an estimate to better understand the risk

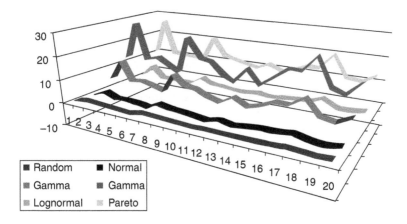

Figure 127 Various distributions

we are taking. In addition, this estimate is based on observed volatilities and correlations. The volatility over the next ten trading days may differ significantly, and correlations may not hold. Finally, two of the three VaR calculation models assume an underlying normal distribution as the distribution behind price behavior. The world (as shown in Figure 127) is a bit more complicated than that.

While VaR used to be sufficient to quantify the required regulatory capital for trading portfolios, there is now literature questioning the effectiveness of this approach. The original critique of these models came through Nicholas Nassim Taleb (NNT) in a three part series in Derivative Strategies at the turn of the century, where Taleb raised questions on the rationale behind using one number to describe the distribution. He took issue with the sense of false security provided by VaR based risk approaches, the breakdown of correlations under times of stress, the compliance driven mindset that led people to check off risk management once they had implemented an analytics and reporting system and the absurdity of assuming a normal distribution for returns when we know the world is not normal. This was followed by even more serious questions regarding the impact of VaR platforms on overall market volatility and the increase in systematic risk rather than the expected decrease[1].

Taleb's message focused on using risk profiles and price distributions over a period of time to better understand the underlying risk distribution. This would only be possible if prices and volatilities were tracked through time, if models were back tested, the right percentiles (lower) were used and expectations and incentives were set clearly and appropriately at the board level and between risk takers and risk managers.

4. Metrics and sensitivities

A VaR based model can be extended to frame a number of questions for commodity consumers concerned about extreme price changes. For any change in price levels of a given commodity or a change in market level risk factors you can test for a change in P&L, a change in margins and a net change in the balance sheet. We use a simple case study using crude oil to illustrate the approach.

Crude price changes impact two primary types of crude consumers. The first group includes users who use crude oil as an input and produce derivative refined petrochemical products as an output. The risk profile of this group originates from three drivers. Volatile input cost, fixed output prices (for a short or long period) and a lag between the time input products are purchased and consumed and the time it takes for the output produced to reach downstream customers.

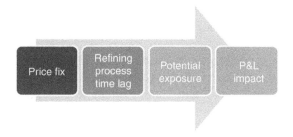

Figure 128 Time line – from changes in input prices to P&L impact

The second group includes downstream users who consume refined petrochemical products and use them to produce electricity and other derivative products such as PVC, resin, synthetic fibers and fertilizer.

A dollar movement in the price of crude oil has two impacts. As prices move, prices of downstream products also move accordingly. These downstream price changes impact inventory, storage and product in the pipeline. Interestingly enough for this group, the primary risk is not rising prices but declining prices. As crude prices rise, the inventory and product in storage gets marked up, adding inventory gains to the P&L statement. As prices decline, the booked gains get marked down as losses change the direction and sign of the P&L. While inventory losses have an impact on the balance sheet as well as the P&L, the same approach can also be used to do a more detailed gross refining margin analysis. The margin analysis focuses on the impact of dollar changes in crude input on output margins and can be used to project worst-case margin changes and expected margin changes, as well as the probability of margin shortfall.

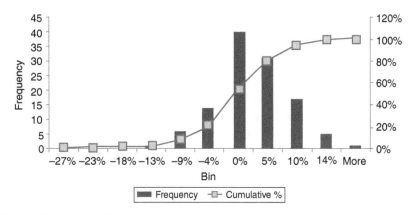

Figure 129 Crude oil price change distribution

Margin shortfall analysis is a three-step process. It also produces inventory loss estimate as a by-product. The three steps are:

1. estimate the crude input price variation distribution,
2. estimate the crude output price variation distribution,
3. project the impact of 1 and 2 and estimate the margin variation distribution.

The first step is to calculate and produce the crude oil price distribution histogram you see above. It shows most likely, unlikely and extremely unlikely month on month changes in crude oil prices.

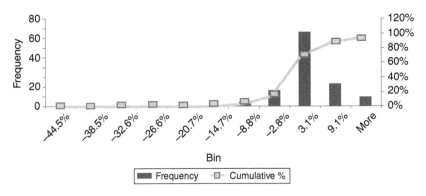

Figure 130 Output product price change distribution

The second step is to calculate and produce the output product price distribution histogram you see in Figure 130. It shows most likely, unlikely, and extremely unlikely month on month changes in output product prices.

The third and final step is to extend the input and output product price change model to create a margin shortfall model. Similar to prices, a margin shortfall model tracks changes in gross refining margins and can be used to answer questions such as:

• What is the probability that margins will decrease in any month over the next quarter, the next half-year, or the next full year?
• What is the range of these projected reductions?
• What is the worst-case reduction in any month over the next 12 months?
• What is the likely reduction in any month over the next 12 months?
• What is the probability that gross margins will shrink below the minimum profitability threshold?
• What is the probability that gross margins will turn negative?
• What is the likely expected gross margin number at current price volatility levels?

- How will this number change if volatility moves by a percentage point?
- By how much does a dollar change in crude prices change the expected margin number?

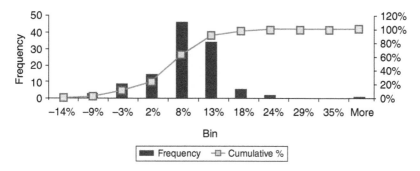

Figure 131 Margin change distribution

All of this would not be possible without understanding the volatility distribution model and its relationship with crude oil prices, a fairly deep understanding of the refinery industry and the composition of its margin formulae. Taleb calls this being one with the distribution.

Figure 132 WTI prices and volatilities

Once the four models are ready you are now in a position to tackle questions related to inventory losses or margin shortfall as illustrated in the next two figures.

Odds	Percentile	Input Price Shock – Low	Input Price Shock – High	Inventory Losses – Low	Inventory Losses – High
1%	99%	145.0	363.8	25.0%	63.4%
11%	90%	79.9	200.4	13.6%	34.7%
18%	85%	64.6	162.1	11.0%	28.0%
25%	80%	52.5	131.6	8.8%	22.7%
33%	75%	42.0	105.5	7.0%	18.1%
43%	70%	32.7	82.0	5.4%	14.0%
52%	66%	25.7	64.5	4.2%	10.9%
67%	60%	15.8	39.6	2.4%	6.6%
82%	55%	7.8	19.7	1.0%	3.1%
96%	51%	1.6	3.9	−0.1%	0.3%

Figure 133   Expected input price and margin shortfall ranges at different odds of occurrence

Margin shortfall analysis looks at both current and extreme volatility scenarios to calculate expected margin shortfall at different odds of occurrence. As confidence levels are lowered the odds of occurrence increase. Rather than looking at extreme cases with very low odds, it is more instructive and useful to calibrate the margin shortfall distribution to actual historical realized experience.

The same mechanics and process works for inventory losses projections below.

Odds	Percentile	Input Price Shock-low	Input Price Shock-high	Margin Shortfall Low	Margin Shortfall High
1%	99%	145	364	79,287,743	198,916,085
11%	90%	80	200	43,678,476	109,580,009
18%	85%	65	162	35,324,237	88,620,999
25%	80%	52	132	28,684,553	71,963,442
33%	75%	42	105	22,988,294	57,672,742
43%	70%	33	82	17,872,878	44,839,251
52%	66%	26	64	14,057,773	35,267,963
67%	60%	16	40	8,634,702	21,662,630
82%	55%	8	20	4,282,852	10,744,766
96%	51%	2	4	854,411	2,143,535

Figure 134   Expected input price and inventory losses ranges at different odds of occurrence

5. Limits and control process

Risk models only have value if they are used effectively in combination with a limit management and control process. While a control function requires and relies on reports, the key is not generation of quantitative numbers, formatted in ten different variations and cuts; it is the interpretation and application of that analysis that matters. The objective of a risk function is not just to gather data, run reports, submit and analyze them; it is to ensure that unpleasant surprises and their impacts are limited.

While you can't control the timing and magnitude of such surprises, a well-managed and well-run risk function can help manage expectations as well as plan ahead for unexpected shocks.

Limits play a major role in achieving that objective. But where do you start when you first review limits? How do you decide what is acceptable and what is not?

Ideally the limit setting process should be based on the following core principles:

- Before limit setting, a review of what is considered prudent risk and a review of normal business thresholds for key risk measures should be completed. This sets the baseline level for limit calculations.
- Limits should be risk based, that is, the measurement of limit utilization should be directly proportional to the amount of risk taken.
- Limits should be fungible at lower levels. The trader should be allowed to take risks to exploit the best opportunities available without being too tightly bound by a complex rigid multi-layered limit system. Similarly a senior trader should be allowed to move limits from one subordinate desk to another.
- Both hard and soft limits need to be set. If the limit is hard then traders know that they will be disciplined or fired for violating the limit. If the limit is soft a violation simply leads to documentation, exception reporting and a conversation where the trader is advised to reduce the position.
- If a portfolio is to be managed within a given set of limits, it should not be possible for changes in another portfolio to cause the limits for the former portfolio to be broken.

The limit framework relies on both operational (stop loss, action trigger) and transactional (position, dealer, desk, product) limits. We take a look at both.

a. Operational (exception or management action) limits

Operational limits are generally exception limits that require immediate management action or intervention when the limit is breached and generally lead to a partial reduction or a closeout of the offending transaction.

b. Capital loss and stop loss limits

Stop loss limits act as a safety valve in case something starts to go wrong. Stop loss limits state that specified action must take place if the loss exceeds a threshold amount. Tight stop loss limits reduce the maximum possible loss and therefore reduce the capital required for the business. However, if the limits are too tight they reduce the trader's ability to make a profit.

The first step in setting stop loss limits is to determine the appetite of the company regarding its risk tolerance. This translates into specifying the amount of capital that the company can afford to lose.

c. Inventory age limits

Inventory age limits set the time for which any security is held without being sold. This is to prevent traders from sitting on illiquid positions or positions with an unrecognized loss. The time allowed will depend on the overall purpose of the desk. If the desk is expected to trade in and out of the position quickly, the limits will be in the order of days. If the desk is expected to use long-term strategies then the limit can be in the order of weeks or months.

d. Concentration limits

Concentration limits prevent traders from putting all their eggs in one basket. They ensure that the trader's risk is not concentrated in one instrument or market. For example the equity desk may be limited to a maximum of 3 percent in any one company. This may also be subject to a limit on the total percentage of that company's equity that may be held.

e. Transaction limits

While it is common to raise and approve exceptions to a transaction limit, a high frequency of such exceptions implies that the risk process and limit setting threshold need to be re-calibrated. The calibration is required because either the market has moved to a different level of volatility and volume or the limits framework is out of touch or has broken down and is no longer being taken seriously.

f. Exposure and sensitivity limits

Exposure limits are control limits that restrict the dollar amount that can be booked in a given day in any dealer, product, desk, tenor or risk combination.

g. Pre-settlement risk (PSR) and potential future exposure (PFE) limits

PSR and PFE limits are product based counterparty limits that measure the worst-case loss that is likely to occur if counterparties default prior to the settlement of a transaction. The worst-case loss calculation assumes an unfavorable price movement, a client default and the cost of recovering or squaring the transaction again from the open market.

For instruments that trade and are repriced on a daily basis PSR and PFE consider the interaction of credit risk (a counterparty default) and price risk (the risk that the market has moved against us).

For example, what happens if a counterparty defaults on settlement when:

(a) They have to deliver a bond that the bank has purchased and
  • bond prices have moved downwards?
  • bond prices have moved upwards?
(b) They have to take delivery of a bond that the bank has sold and
  • bond prices have moved downwards?
  • bond prices have moved upwards?
(c) They have to deliver Euros that the bank has purchased and
  • US$/Euro exchange rate has appreciated in favor of Euro?
  • US$/Euro exchange rate has appreciated in favor of US$?

h. Hierarchy of limits

For monitoring market risk, the company will need to segment the overall investment portfolio. They may for instance segment the portfolio by product, then trading desk, then trades. For each segment of the portfolio, limits will be defined. Generally, limits increase as you move up in the hierarchy. A risk metric is selected (duration, VaR, and so on) and risk limits are specified for each component of the hierarchy based on this metric.

Once limits are set, the reporting and exception review process kicks in. It gets triggered every time market conditions change or a limit is breached on a target indicator or a pre-defined review period starts or ends.

The next two diagrams do a quick walkthrough of the process.

For the process to monitor and track target limits the reporting process needs to be set in such a fashion that early warning indicators, exception reports and management action triggers all get tracked and reported on a daily, weekly or monthly basis. Within these reports it is important that exceptions are highlighted whenever they occur.

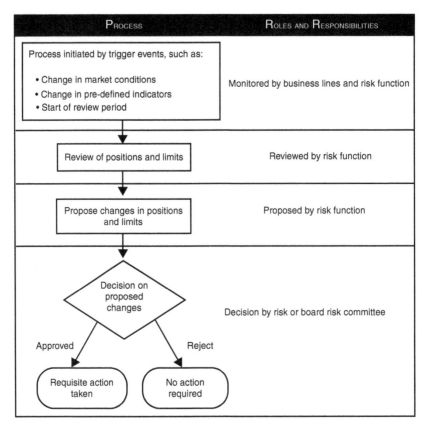

Figure 135   Limit monitoring and review process

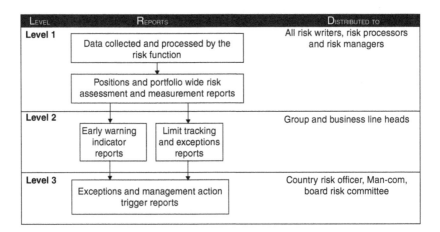

Figure 136   Risk reporting process

What are these exceptions? There are three primary categories.

- A range breach, where a metric being tracked suddenly jumps above or below a historical range or a barrier. These breaches can occur at single or multiple points.
- Volatility breach, where there is a sudden increase or decrease in underlying volatility.
- A systemic degradation, where values for the metric being monitored fall below historical thresholds and stay there.

Good reporting systems make it easier to highlight exceptions when they occur rather than hide them in the volume of data and reports that are being produced.

6. Conclusion

It is time to revisit the first image we presented when we started.

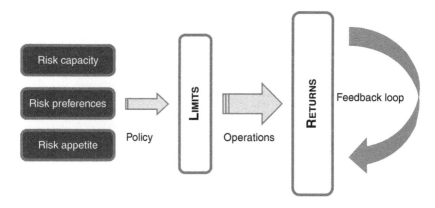

Figure 137   Risk framework revisited

The right risk management mindset is not driven by a single moving part. As we have seen above, it is driven by eight inter-related elements. For it to work, they all need to come together and work. If you get just one of these elements right (data or model or policy or process or limits or control) and miss the others, the approach will fail.

Setting limits

1. Capital loss and stop loss limits

Stop loss limits act as a safety valve in case something starts to go wrong. Stop loss limits state that specified action must take place if the loss exceeds a threshold amount. Tight stop loss limits reduce the maximum possible loss and therefore reduce the capital required for the business. However, if the limits are too tight they reduce the trader's ability to make a profit.

The first step in setting stop loss limits is to determine the appetite of the company regarding its risk tolerance. This translates into specifying the amount of capital that the company can afford to lose.

The following elements would need to be considered when determining the capital loss amount.

- The expected rate of return that will be earned on the capital within the next twelve-month period.
- The minimum acceptable rate of return that will be required to satisfy shareholders.

In no situation should the capital loss amount eat into the principal capital amount or in other words the rate of return required should never be negative. This is elaborated in the following example.

Capital	AED 1,000,000,000
Rate of return expected	6% p.a.
Expected return	AED 60,000,000
Minimum acceptable rate of return	1% p.a.
Return required	AED 10,000,000
Capital loss amount	AED 50,000,000

Figure 138   Capital loss calculation example

The next step in this process is to specify a target stop loss limit. The stop loss limit gives us the amount of money that a portfolio's single-period market loss should not exceed.

This limit, together with the capital loss amount, will be used in determining the book size of the company. Using the example above the target stop loss limit is set at 10 percent. This implies that the capital loss amount is equal to 10 percent of the book size or alternatively the book size is the capital loss amount divided by 10 percent. This would mean that the book size will be 50,000,000 ÷ 0.10 or AED 500,000,000. It may be noted that this assumes that the company has perfect ability to liquidate assets at the optimal level if the stop loss limit is activated.

After the target stop loss limit has been defined, and the book size determined, the amount will be allocated to individual investment lines and the stop loss limits will be set at the individual asset level.

These actual stop loss limits implemented at individual levels will have to be lower than the target stop loss limit to account for slippage, in other words, instances when the company would not be able to liquidate the position at a price for which the stop loss limit is exactly met. We recommend actual stop loss limits 1 to 2 percent less than the target stop loss limit depending on the daily movement in a specific market.

This is illustrated in Figure 139. We assume that a book size of AED 500,000,000 is allocated among ten lines of investment (positions) equally and that the entire allocated amount is utilized so that the allocated amount is equal to the book value of the investment. While the internal stop loss limit is set at 10 percent, the actual hard stop loss limit is set at 8 percent to provide room for 2 percent of slippage and is supported by AED 40,000,000 of stop loss capital.

Expected Capital Loss @ Stop Loss = AED 40,000,000.

Rate of return adjusted for expected capital loss
  = 6 percent – (40,000,000 ÷ 1,000,000,000) = 2 percent.

Slippage, or the reason for having the actual stop loss limit at a level lower than the target, is illustrated in Figure 140. The example assumes that all MTM prices are lower than 10 percent from those given above. If the actual stop loss limit is breached then the investment can only be liquidated at MTM (revised) = MTM × (1–10 percent).

Capital Loss = AED 30,460,661.

Rate of return adjusted for capital loss
  = 6 percent – (30,460,661 ÷ 1,000,000,000) = 2.34 percent

In summary the portfolio unit would need to:

- specify the target stop loss limit,
- specify the period of time over which this limit is applicable (daily, weekly, monthly, and so on),
- determine the book size of the portfolio using the target stop loss limit, the capital amount and the return required for the period,
- allocate the book size across various segments of the portfolio,
- specify the actual stop loss limits for the various segments of the portfolio,
- specify the period of time over which these actual limits would be applicable (daily, weekly, monthly, and so on).

Lines of Investment	Allocated/Book Amount	Purchase Price	Quantity	Stop Loss	Stop Loss Amount	MTM	Market Value	Gain/Loss	Stop Loss Decision
1	50,000,000	110	454,545.45	8%	4,000,000	112	50,909,091	909,091	Within Limit
2	50,000,000	201	248,756.22	8%	4,000,000	200	49,751,244	−248,756	Within Limit
3	50,000,000	150	333,333.33	8%	4,000,000	151	50,333,333	333,333	Within Limit
4	50,000,000	95	526,315.79	8%	4,000,000	100	52,631,579	2,631,579	Within Limit
5	50,000,000	35	1,428,571.43	8%	4,000,000	34	48,571,429	−1,428,571	Within Limit
6	50,000,000	348	143,678.16	8%	4,000,000	350	50,287,356	287,356	Within Limit
7	50,000,000	42	1,190,476.19	8%	4,000,000	45	53,571,429	3,571,429	Within Limit
8	50,000,000	549	91,074.68	8%	4,000,000	545	49,635,701	−364,299	Within Limit
9	50,000,000	250	200,000.00	8%	4,000,000	265	53,000,000	3,000,000	Within Limit
10	50,000,000	100	500,000.00	8%	4,000,000	150	75,000,000	25,000,000	Within Limit

Figure 139   Allocation of actual stop loss limits by lines of investment

Lines of Investment	MTM (Revised)	Market Value	Gain/Loss	Stop Loss Decision	Loss if Exceeding Stop Loss	% of BV	Slippage/ Excess Loss
1	100.8	45,818,182	-4,181,818	Liquidate	4,181,818	8.36%	181,818
2	180	44,776,119	-5,223,881	Liquidate	5,223,881	10.45%	1,223,881
3	135.9	45,300,000	-4,700,000	Liquidate	4,700,000	9.40%	700,000
4	90	47,368,421	-2,631,579	Within Limit			–
5	30.6	43,714,286	-6,285,714	Liquidate	6,285,714	12.57%	2,285,714
6	315	45,258,621	-4,741,379	Liquidate	4,741,379	9.48%	741,379
7	40.5	48,214,286	-1,785,714	Within Limit	–		–
8	490.5	44,672,131	-5,327,869	Liquidate	5,327,869	10.66%	1,327,869
9	238.5	47,700,000	-2,300,000	Within Limit	–		–
10	135	67,500,000	17,500,000	Within Limit	–		–

Figure 140 Example of slippage

2. Value at risk limits

The company would need to decide on the level of VaR based on the risk appetite of the company.

They would also need to decide on how much liquidity would need to be incorporated into the VaR measure, that is the time that would generally be taken to liquidate the portfolio/sub portfolio.

We recommend 1:3 VaR, that is VaR calculated at a confidence level of 75 percent for a 10-day holding period, as this represents a fairly high likelihood of loss event. In other words there is a possibility that losses will exceed the maximum loss amount one day in four days, that is the 1:3 odds. This will be subject to an upper bound equal to the capital loss amount specified earlier.

Odds	VaR Limits
1:99	99%
1:9	90%
1:4	80%
1:3	75%
1:2	66%
2:3	60%

Figure 141   Odds, confidence levels and limits

Alternatively, an appropriate level of odds may be set such that the VaR percent × book size is approximately equal to the capital loss amount.

For example if the VaR limit works out to 15.5 percent for the entire portfolio then the limit will be the minimum of the upper bound and the VaR amount, i.e. min (15.5 percent × 500,000,000, 50,000,000) = AED 50 million.

Once they decide on the level of confidence and the liquidity factor to use, the VaR limit will be determined for the entire portfolio and then for the sub portfolios within that portfolio. This may be done as follows.

For the portfolio as a whole, the limits could be set by starting with the total capital available to the trading operation and relating that to the maximum amount of VaR that can be supported by that capital, that is, Available capital = y × 10-day holding VaR. In other words, the VaR limit for the total portfolio = Available capital/y × (sqrt(10)), where y is a multiple of the 10-day holding VaR. An industry standard for required capital for market risk is 3 × VaR (99 percent confidence level, 10-day holding), that is, $y = 3$.

Y=			3		
Available capital=			AED 1,000.00		
Liquidity factor=			Sqrt (10) = 3.16227766		
VaR limit (total)=			AED 105.41		
VaR limit % of available capital=		10.54%			
SUB PORTFOLIO			REVENUE PER UNIT OF STANDALONE VAR		
1			1.5		
2			1.3		
Average correlation of the two portfolios=			0.3		
VaR LIMIT 1	VaR LIMIT 2	REVENUE 1	REVENUE 2	TOTAL	
105	–	157.50	–	157.50	
100	14	150.00	18.04	168.04	
95	25	142.50	31.89	174.39	
90	33	135.00	43.48	178.48	
85	41	127.50	53.57	181.07	
80	48	120.00	62.55	182.55	
75	54	112.50	70.66	183.16	
70	60	105.00	78.04	183.04	
65	65	97.50	84.81	182.31	
60	70	90.00	91.04	181.04	
55	74	82.50	96.79	179.29	
50	79	75.00	102.10	177.10	
45	82	67.50	107.02	174.52	
40	86	60.00	111.57	171.57	
35	89	52.50	115.77	168.27	
30	92	45.00	119.63	164.63	
25	95	37.50	123.18	160.68	
20	97	30.00	126.43	156.43	
15	100	22.50	129.38	151.88	
10	102	15.00	132.04	147.04	
5	103	7.50	134.41	141.91	
–	105	–	136.50	136.50	

Figure 142   Example – setting VaR limits for sub portfolios

For sub portfolios VaR will be determined as follows.

Method 1: VaR limits specify the maximum amount of VaR that each desk can cause. The practical starting point for setting VaR limits is to measure the current standalone VaR for each desk and set the VaR limits to be a little higher or lower depending on whether management wants the given desk to grow or shrink. This method does not account for correlations between portfolios and does not consider the overall VaR limit.

Method 2: VaR limits for the sub portfolio are defined by using the VaR limit defined for the total portfolio and then accounting for average correlations between sub portfolios. The optimal amount to be allocated to each portfolio depends on the expected revenue per unit of standalone VaR. This is illustrated in the numerical example below assuming the portfolio comprises of two sub portfolios and amounts are in millions.

Using the quadratic equation we get,

$$\text{VaR Limit 2} = \frac{-2 \times \text{Correlation} \times \text{VaR Limit 1} + \sqrt{(2 \times \text{Correlation} \times \text{VaR Limit 1})^2 - 4(\text{VaR Limit 1}^2 - \text{VaR Limit total}^2)}}{2}$$

Based on the maximum revenue, the optimal VaR limits for the sub portfolios are AED 75 for sub portfolio 1 and AED 54 for sub portfolio 2.

3. Regulatory approach limits

Under Basel II's IMA approach, VaR is set at a 99 percent confidence level over a 10-day holding period. This will be subject to an upper bound equal to a multiple of the capital loss amount.

The multiple will be determined as follows:

MULTIPLE	UPPER BOUND ON VAR LIMIT
Normsinv (99%) – Normsinv (75%) = 2.326 – 0.674 = 1.65	1.65 × 50000000 = 82,592,906
Normsinv (99%) – Normsinv (60%) = 2.326 – 0.253 = 2.07	2.07 × 50000000 = 103,650,039

Figure 143   Determination of multiple for setting an upper bound on VaR limit

Normsinv (.) = inverse of the standard normal distribution.

For example, if the VaR limit is based on a 75 percent confidence level and if the regulatory approach VaR works out to 15.5 percent of the entire portfolio then the limit will be the minimum of the upper bound (based on ratio) and the VaR amount, that is, min (15.5 percent × 500,000,000, 82,592,906) = AED 77.5 million.

4. Other market risk limits

a. Duration limits

Duration measures the sensitivity of the price of the product/value of the portfolio to changes in the interest rate. In order to limit the sensitivity the company needs to decide what the acceptable level of duration for the product/portfolio should be. For example, it may want the portfolio duration to be not more than 2 years. In other words it would like to limit its exposure to interest rate changes so that an increase in interest rates of 1 percent would not result in a decline in the portfolio value of greater than 2 percent. For example, if the portfolio value was AED 1 million then the limit would be breached if the portfolio's value fell below AED 980,000.

b. Convexity limits

Duration does not account accurately for large changes in the interest rates. So in order to assess sensitivity more accurately the convexity measure may also be included in the calculation. The duration and convexity metric will then be used in setting the exposure limits. This metric is calculated as follows for duration and convexity[2]:

A 1 percent increase in interest rates leads to an x percent decrease in price where x = absolute value of $\{-1 \times \text{Duration} \times (0.01) \times 100 + \text{Convexity} \times (0.01)^2 \times 100\}$.

This is illustrated in the following example for 3-year bond issues. The duration limit is set at 2.3 percent whereas the duration and convexity limit is set at 2.2 percent.

3-YEAR BOND	P0	P–	P+	DURATION METRIC (%)	DURATION & CONVEXITY METRIC (%)	DURATION LIMIT	DURATION & CONVEXITY LIMIT
Issue 1	97.51	99.95	95.14	2.46	2.42	Breach	Breach
Issue 2	97.56	99.93	95.27	2.39	2.35	Breach	Breach
Issue 3	97.67	99.92	95.47	2.28	2.24	Safe	Breach
Issue 4	98.02	99.94	96.15	1.93	1.91	Safe	Safe

Figure 144 Setting duration and convexity limits

c. PVBP limits

PVBP is the change in present value of an instrument brought about by a 1 basis point change in interest rates. PVBP limits may be set separately for each maturity bucket or may be evaluated across all buckets. The PVBP metric is calculated to determine the change in present value by increasing the underlying interest rates by 0.01 percent. If the PVBP metric calculated for the portfolio exceeds this limit, a limit violation occurs. This is illustrated below.

INTEREST RATE	6%	MATURITY BUCKET				
	Total Across Buckets	0–1	1–2	2–3	3–4	4–5
Amount	125,000	25,000	25,000	25,000	25,000	25,000
PV @ time zero	105,309	23,585	22,250	20,990	19,802	18,681
PVBP metric	29	2.22	4.20	5.94	7.47	8.81
Limit as a % of PV	0.02%	0.01%	0.02%	0.03%	0.03%	0.04%
PVBP limit	27	2.17	3.53	6.38	6.93	7.52
Limit status	Breach	Breach	Breach	Safe	Breach	Breach

Figure 145 Setting PVBP limits

5. Credit risk limits

a. Pre-settlement risk (PSR) limits

Pre-settlement risk (PSR) is the risk that a counterparty to a transaction, such as a forward contract, will not settle or honor their end of the deal.

PSR limits are based on the worst-case loss that is likely to occur if the counterparty defaults prior to the settlement of the transaction. The worst-case loss assumes an adverse movement in the price/rate, a client default and the subsequent cost of recovering the transaction from the open market. Therefore, in setting a limit all three of these factors need to be considered, that is, the credit worthiness of the counterparty in the same way as is done for traditional credit lines, the likelihood of an adverse market movement and the cost of covering the transaction from the market.

As the limit is based on the worst-case scenario, a VaR based approach has been used in calculating the PSR limits[3].

For example, let us assume that Tom anticipates that the price of crude is likely to increase past US$ 83 in the next ten days. To benefit from this position, he enters into a forward contract with Bill to purchase 1000 barrels of WTI crude oil 10 days from now for US$ 83 per barrel, that is, for US$ 83,000. Currently the price of the crude is US$ 81.45 per barrel. If Bill were to default on the deal, Tom would have to cover the position by purchasing 1000 barrels of crude from the market, possibly at a price much higher than the current price. The difference between this higher price and the contract value is the loss that he would suffer on the deal.

Over the past year crude oil price has experienced an average daily volatility of 1.94 percent. This daily volatility has been calculated using the simple moving average (SMA) approach. The volatility over the pre-settlement period therefore is 6.12 percent (= 1.94 percent × $\sqrt{10}$). Given this volatility, the pre-settlement period price impact would be US$ 4.98 (= 81.45 × 6.12 percent), that is, the price impact is a function of the current price and pre-settlement period volatility. This pre-settlement period price impact may also be denoted as the 1-sigma price impact, as the pre-settlement volatility is considered as is and is not enhanced by any factor. This means that given the volatility, the price of crude is expected to move by around US$ 4.98 in the next ten days.

However, when determining the PSR limit we are not merely concerned in determining what the price impact is for a 1-sigma move in prices. What we are really interested in the worst-case loss over this period. This worst-case loss incorporates a multiple of the volatility into the calculation. The multiple is based on a confidence level or the probability that such an event is likely to occur and is usually taken as 99 percent. Based on this confidence level the multiple is 2.33 (= the inverse of the standard normal cumulative distribution function at 99 percent probability) times the volatility or 2.33-sigma.

Recall that VaR, in particular for SMA (or EWMA) VaR, is a function of the SMA (or EWMA) volatility and the inverse of the standard normal cumulative distribution. Hence the PSR limit in this case is based on the 10-day holding VaR at the 99 percent confidence level.

The total worst-case shock to the current price therefore will be set as the worst-case price shock times the number of barrels of crude that would be purchased. This works out to US$ 11,595 (= 11.595 × 1000). The market value based on the worst-case shock will be US$ 93,045 = [(81.45 + 11.595) × 1000].

The PSR loss or the PSR limit that will be set will be the market value of gold based on the worst-case shock less the contract value. This works out to US$ 10,345 (=93,045−83,000). This is 12 percent of the contract value at inception (=10,345/83,000).

Let us consider another example. Sally enters a forward contract with Harry to exchange EUR 100,000 for US$ 141,000 after ten days. Sally anticipates that the EUR–USD rate will fall in the near future and she enters the contract to protect her dollar position. If Harry were to default before the contract was to be settled, Sally would have to go to the market to cover her position, in this case to obtain US dollars. If the EUR–USD rate were to decline as she had anticipated she would lose on the transaction, as she would get fewer dollars for every Euro. In order to limit her potential losses she calculates the PSR limit applicable to this transaction so that she can take appropriate action if the limit is breached. This she does as follows.

The current EUR–USD rate is 1.395. The rate has experienced an average daily volatility of 0.50 percent over the last year. This daily volatility has been calculated using the SMA approach. The other values are calculated as follows.

1. Pre-settlement volatility over the ten day period = 0.50 percent × $\sqrt{10}$ = 1.59 percent.
2. Pre-settlement FX rate impact works out to = 1.59 percent × 1.395 = 0.022.
3. Worst-case FX rate shock (at 99 percent confidence interval) = 0.022 × 2.33 = 0.05145, that is, the EUR–USD rate falls by US$ 0.05145.
4. Total worst-case FX shock (in US$) = 0.05145 × 100000 = 5,145.
5. Market value based on worst-case shock (US$) = (1.345 + 0.05145) × 100,000 = 144,665.
6. PSR Loss or Limit (US$) = 144,665−141,000 = 3,665.
7. PSR Limit (percent of contract value) = 3 percent.

The final PSR limit to be determined would also consider the credit worthiness of the counterparty involved in line with how the credit worthiness is assessed for traditional credit lines. For example if Sally had also entered into a similar contract with Larry and Larry also defaulted on the contract, but Larry's credit worthiness is worse as compared to Harry's, then Larry's final PSR limit would ideally be higher than that of Harry's.

In addition to this limit, the credit exposure arising from PSR should be aggregated with all other credit exposures for that counterparty and be compared with the overall credit limit for that counterparty to ensure that the credit exposure lies within acceptable bounds.

b. Settlement risk limits

Settlement risk exists only when the principal cash flows have been exchanged but the delivery of the instrument/asset has not occurred as yet. It is therefore short term in nature. However, as the risk involves the exchange of the total notional value of the instrument or the principal cash flow, the total dollar value of the settlement risk exposure tends to be larger in most cases than the credit exposure due to PSR.

Settlement risk limits should reflect the credit quality of the counterparty to the transactions, the company's own capital adequacy, operations efficiency, credit expertise, the efficiency and reliability of the settlement systems and the period of time for which the exposure will be outstanding. The limits would restrict the maximum value of contracts with the same counterparty on the same settlement date.

c. Financial institution (FI)/counterparty limits

The company's Financial Institution (FI) limit setting process should be aligned to its approved FI process and policy. The same process with a few minor changes will also be applicable for the company's other counterparties and brokers.

Generally the FI limit setting process depends on the following.

- The FI's credit rating (the limits will be set based on the credit rating of the issuer of the debt).
- An analysis of the FI's financial health and strength, including capital adequacy, asset quality, earnings/profitability, liquidity position, cash flow generation capacity, primarily through the measurement of financial, NPL, liquidity, and so on ratios (the limits are set based on acceptable levels for financial ratios). Examples of these financial ratios are given below.
- The institution's profile, such as its history, nature of business, types of business, product offerings, branch network and compliance with know-your-customer (KYC) procedures (the limits are set based on acceptable benchmarks for each characteristic).

The limit will be based on the *overall* risk/exposure that the company is willing to accept with any given counterparty (FI, broker, and so on). These limits should be reviewed and revised regularly.

d. FI – Financial analysis ratios

A combination of any of the following ratios may be used to set FI limits depending on the company's own FI policy. The limit may be subject to maximums specified by the regulatory authority to which the company is subject.

Capital adequacy
- Times Interest Earned: Earnings before Interest and Tax/Interest Expense.
- Capital Adequacy Ratio: (Tier 1 + Tier 2 Capital)/Risk Weighted Assets.

- Equity to Assets: Total Equity/Total Assets.
- Debt to Debt and Equity: Debt/Debt + Equity.

Asset quality
- Loan Loss Ratio: Amount Written Off/Average Loans Outstanding.
- Loan Loss Reserve to NPLs (Coverage Ratio): Loan Loss Reserve/Non-performing Loans.
- Percentage of NPLs to Advances: NPLs/Total Advances × 100.
- Percentage of Earning Assets to Total Assets: Earning Assets/Total Assets.

Earnings/Profitability
- Return on Assets (ROA): Profit after Tax/Total Assets.
- Return on Equity (ROE): Profit after Tax/Total Equity.
- Net Interest/Profit Margin Ratio: Profit after Tax/Interest Earned.
- Return on Earning Assets: Net Income/Earning Assets.
- Earnings per Share (EPS): Net Income/Total Shares Outstanding.
- Cost Income Ratio: Cost/Income.
- Interest Income to Earning Assets: Interest Income/Earning Assets.
- Net Interest Income to Earning Assets: (Interest Income–Interest Expense)/Earning Assets.

Liquidity
- Current Ratio: Current Assets/Current Liabilities.
- Current Assets to Total Assets: Current Assets/Total Assets.
- Earning Assets to Total Assets: Earning Assets/Total Assets.
- Working Capital to Total Assets: (Current Assets–Current Liabilities)/Total Assets.
- Operating Cash Flow to Total Assets: Cash Flow from Operating Activities/Total Assets.

e. Regulatory limits

Regulatory limits are limits that are imposed by the regulatory authority that may include limits on the total outstanding exposure to any single person or group.

f. Internal/concentration limits

1. Geographical region limits.
2. Economy/industry sector limits.
3. Days Past Due (DPD) limits.
4. Credit portfolio risk limits (based on scoring distribution).
5. Infection ratio limits and so on.

6. Application to products

a. Money market

INSTRUMENT	LIMITS
Repo/Reverse Repo	Credit risk limits including Financial Institute (FI) limits will apply
Call/Clean	Credit risk limits including FI limits will apply
Outright purchase/sale	Market risk limits will apply, such as: • Stop loss limits • VAR limit, i.e. 1:3 VaR • Regulatory limit, i.e. 99% VaR • Inventory age limits • Concentration limits • Duration limits • Convexity limits • PVBP limits

Figure 146 Limits applicable to money market products

b. Capital market

INSTRUMENT	LIMITS
Outright purchase/ sale	Market risk limits will apply, such as • Stop loss limits • VAR limit, i.e. 1:3 VaR • Regulatory limit, i.e. 99% VaR • Inventory age limits • Concentration limits

Figure 147 Limits applicable to capital market products

c. Foreign exchange

INSTRUMENT	LIMITS
Forward sell/purchase	Credit risk limits including FI limits will apply
Swaps	Credit risk limits including FI limits will apply
Outright purchase/sale	Market risk limits will apply, such as • Stop loss limits • VAR limit, i.e. 1:3 VaR • Regulatory limit, i.e. 99% VaR • Inventory age limits • Concentration limits

Figure 148 Limits applicable to foreign exchange products

7. Setting limits for liquidity risk

In general, liquidity limits have to be assessed for "normal" business operation conditions as well as for stressed scenarios to ensure that there is sufficient liquidity at all times. The following should be considered when determining liquidity risk limits.

- The company's risk appetite.
- The level of the company's capital.
- The level of the company's earnings.
- The perceived likelihood of an unusual funding need.
- The level of confidence in measures of current and projected liquidity.
- The company's level of immediately available liquidity.
- The ability to quickly and reliably convert standby liquidity sources into cash.
- The relationship between the potential risk and the potential reward.
- The other risk exposures to which the bank is currently exposed.
- The time periods, scenarios and stress levels that the limits will be calculated for.

The following limits may be determined.

a. Cash flow mismatch or gap limits

Limits on discrete (or individual) and cumulative cash flow mismatches or gaps over specified short- and long-term horizons under both expected and adverse business conditions need to be set. These could be in the form of cash flow or liquidity coverage ratios or specified aggregate amounts based on historical averages or desired targets.

b. Maturity limits

Maturity limits are useful for liquidity risk control. These limits control exposure by controlling the volume or amount of securities that mature in a given time period. By staggering the maturities of the securities, the company can reduce the volatility as well as control the liquidity position of the company at any given time period.

c. Target liquid reserves

Set targets for unpledged liquid asset reserves. These are usually expressed as aggregate amounts or as ratios.

d. Concentration limits

- *Asset concentration limits* need to be set in particular with respect to more complex exposures that are illiquid or more difficult to value.
- *Funding concentration limits* that address diversification issues relating to the nature of the deposits or the sources of borrowed funds.

Concentration limits have to be assessed in terms of the maturity patterns/nature of liabilities.

e. Contingent liability limit

These limits are set so that the amounts of unfunded loan commitments and lines of credit remain reasonable relative to available funding.

f. Review

Limits should be reviewed at least annually to account for changes in

- risk tolerance levels,
- strategies,
- the size and composition of the company's balance sheet and off-balance sheet positions,
- market conditions,
- regulatory guidance.

8. Setting limits for interest rate risk

a. Repricing limits

Repricing limits are set for interest rate management. These limits control exposure by controlling the volume or amount of securities that are repriced in a given time period. By staggering the repricing of the securities the company can reduce the volatility as well as control the degrees of sensitivity in the asset and liability portfolios.

Limits are often expressed as the ratio of rate sensitive assets (RSA) to rate sensitive liabilities (RSL) in a given time period. A ratio greater than one suggests that the company is asset sensitive and has more assets than liabilities subject to repricing. All factors remaining constant, the earnings for the company will be reduced by falling interest rates. An RSA/RSL ratio less than one on the other hand suggests that the company is liability sensitive and its earnings may be reduced by increasing interest rates.

Other gap limits to control exposure include gap to asset ratios, gap to equity ratios and absolute limits on the net gap.

9. Limit breach, exception processing, action plan for trigger zones

a. Exception handling

Limits will usually be set at two levels:

- A few "hard" limits set for cumulative buckets or set at higher levels that are approved by a higher authority in the company such as the BOD, and

- Many guidance or threshold limits set for individual buckets or set at secondary or sub levels.

In general the violation of hard limits will lead to immediate corrective actions to improve the situation (for example, the breach of a stop loss limit for an investment would lead to its immediate liquidation) or will require the approval of a higher authority such as the BOD if the situation is to be treated as an exception. On the other hand, violations to guidance or threshold levels would lead to closer monitoring, more frequent reporting and/or additional analysis.

b. Example of an action plan for trigger zones

The limits will be used to determine a triggering system for various degrees of action. The metric on which the limits are based may fall into one of three zones: Comfort zone, Warning zone and Stress zone. These zones will be defined as follows:

- Comfort zone: no early warning indicators.
- Warning zone: trigger of early warning indicator.
- Stress zone: trigger of early warning indicator and limit approaching.

The action plan that the company will take, depending on where the metric lies, could be as follows.

Stress zone:
- Treat the case as an exception and allow the exposure.
- Define steps to reduce exposure within a given time frame to bring the exposure back within the defined limit.
- Review the limit before a specified annual review date.
- Increase the base, and so on.
- Initiate an exit strategy.

Warning zone:
- No further action taken but stricter monitoring for further signs of deterioration/increasing concentration.
- Define steps to reduce the exposure within a given time frame to bring the exposure back within acceptable levels.

Comfort zone:
- Provided that at this exposure level no early warning signals have been raised no further action would be required.
- If the current exposure lies below targeted levels, steps will be defined to increase exposure.

Annexure 1 – Setting stop loss limits

1. A guide to setting stop loss limits

One of the biggest advantages of working as a risk consultant and risk advisor is that you get to see a lot of dirty laundry. By working with clients across the world you get a sense of what works and what doesn't, especially in financial markets. If you are lucky sometimes you get to see stuff that had worked for years stop working.

While implementing risk management solutions it is common to see confusion at the implementation (translation) level. Theoretical models suggest a direction but market data and practicality recommends another. If a risk consultant doesn't come from a trading background or is not exposed to risk practices and ends up working with a client who is just as unfamiliar, together they can do a lot of damage. Given the inherent tension in the relationship between front office (traders) and middle office (risk managers) teams, it is very common to end up with a bipolar schizophrenic relationship. It just multiplies the miscommunication risk by an order of magnitude.

The biggest damage I have seen in my two decades in the field occurred on account of incorrect stop loss limits and misinterpretation of what the stop loss process was supposed to accomplish. It led to a well-capitalized and respected financial institution relegated to the sidelines of financial markets from its position of strength and leadership. The tragedy didn't lie in their fall from grace. It lay in their continued reliance on incompetent consultants, incorrect misconceptions and equally bad advice.

2. Stop loss limits example and case study

a. Context and background

You run a proprietary commodity trading desk for a large un-named investment bank in London. As part of your risk audit, your stop loss limits are being reviewed to judge their effectiveness. The three commodities your group deals with on a daily basis are WTI crude oil, gold and silver future contracts. You have been tasked to identify stop loss limits for the desk for both long and short positions in the three commodities, as well as justify the level and the thresholds based on a review of historical data. You have also been asked to identify market-based triggers that should lead to an immediate review of stop loss limits based on changes in market conditions.

Here is what we plan to do in the next few pages.

(a) Walk through the process of setting up stop loss limits for the three commodities (oil, gold, silver).
(b) Evaluate (back test) stop loss limits based on market data.
(c) Evaluate the impact of correlations on portfolio risk limits.

To review VaR, histograms, volatility and correlation, refer to Chapter 2 before moving ahead.

b. Data requirements

What you need to ensure is that the stop loss limits set by you will keep the bank safe. If they fail, what is the magnitude of failure you are likely to see? Before answering this question you would need to get some basic data. The data you would need includes:

(a) Histogram of prices for the three commodities. You will use these histograms to identify likely as well as extreme price movements for the commodities under consideration.
(b) A distribution of volatility for the three commodities. You will use the distribution to stress test your stop loss limits as well as your estimates of maximum or worst-case loss.
(c) Amount of capital that can be risked by a trader on a trade or a position in a given day.
(d) Amount of total risk capital allocated to the proprietary trading desk.

c. Setting stop loss limits – first pass

Let's start first with the histogram for the three commodities (oil, silver and gold, in that order). The three histograms give you a range of worst-case maximum losses on a given trading day using just under 8 years of

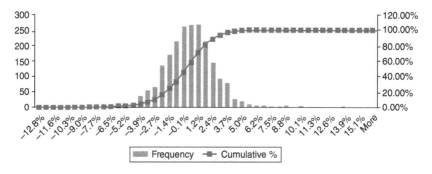

Figure 149   WTI – histogram of daily returns

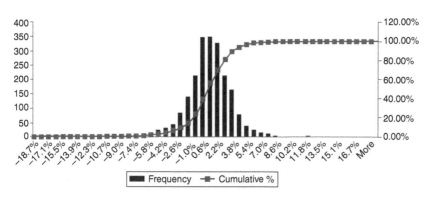

Figure 150 Silver – histogram of daily returns

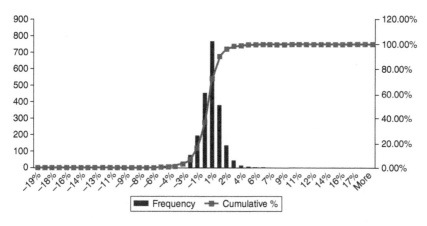

Figure 151 Gold – histogram of daily returns

data (2,157 observations). For gold and silver the range of daily returns is between *–19 percent to +17 percent,* whereas for oil the range of daily returns is between *–13 percent to 15.1 percent.*

However, what you are really interested in is the central section of the three distributions, the so-called stop loss zones. (We will come back to the extreme values later). Your primary interest is in the range of likely losses, losses you are likely to see daily or at most once in every two to three days. We term this the *every other day loss.*

Remember the idea behind stop loss is capital conservation. The minute you hit a threshold of losses you want to cut your position and retreat. "Where should this threshold be?" is the question you are trying to answer. Ideally you would like to set the threshold not at the end of the daily returns range but somewhere in the middle.

Bin	Frequency	Cumulative %	Cumulative Total
-12.8%	1	0.05%	1
-12.2%	2	0.14%	3
-11.6%	0	0.14%	3
-10.9%	3	0.28%	6
-10.3%	1	0.32%	7
-9.6%	2	0.42%	9
-9.0%	2	0.51%	11
-8.4%	3	0.65%	14
-7.7%	2	0.74%	16
-7.1%	5	0.97%	21
-6.5%	6	1.25%	27
-5.8%	10	1.72%	37
-5.2%	13	2.32%	50
-4.6%	13	2.92%	63
-3.9%	37	4.64%	100
-3.3%	55	7.19%	155
-2.7%	66	10.25%	221
-2.0%	125	16.05%	346
-1.4%	170	23.93%	516
-0.7%	213	33.81%	729
-0.1%	263	46.01%	992
0.5%	267	58.40%	1259
1.2%	270	70.92%	1529
1.8%	214	80.84%	1743
2.4%	146	87.62%	1889
3.1%	92	91.88%	1981
3.7%	80	95.59%	2061
4.3%	28	96.89%	2089
5.0%	21	97.87%	2110
5.6%	11	98.38%	2121
6.2%	7	98.70%	2128

Figure 152 Setting thresholds for stop loss limits for crude oil

To pick your values, you look at the *cumulative probability distribution percentage*. These numbers are given in column 3 above. You start off with the numbers between 24 percent and 71 percent, which together represent about 47 percent of the cumulative probability distribution shared in the highlighted portion of the graph above. The range of gains and losses is between –1.4 percent and +1.2 percent.

You further trim away a loss of 0.7 percent and a gain of 1.2 percent for crude oil prices. Why and how? A 33.8 percent percentile rank in the above distribution corresponds to a 1 in 9 (or a 1 in 10 depending on if you round up or round down) trading day loss. There are a total of 2157 observations, of which 213 fell in the range between *–1.4 percent and –0.7 percent*. For a long position, the soft stop loss limit is set at –0.7 percent with a hard limit set at –1.4 percent. The soft limit triggers a sale and a reduction in exposure. The hard limits results in an immediate unwinding of the position.

The reason for picking this range for oil is that you want your traders to have the flexibility to run the position for a few days. If oil is at US$ 90 a barrel, a 1.5 percent move (loss) would lead to a US$ 1.35 loss per barrel.

The *every other day loss* sets two thresholds for you.

The stop loss limit has to be set higher than the every other day loss limit. A long position in oil is likely to touch a 0.7 percent loss every week or at best every alternate week. Similarly, a short position is going to experience a positive jump of 1.2 percent at best every alternate week. The *–0.7 percent to 1.2 percent* range is the amount that the bank will lose when your limit is hit and the position is sold if you decide to trade oil and strictly follow your stop loss limits.

The histogram of daily returns also represents how the market slices value and prices on a weekly basis and how fine your own stop loss grid needs to be. Your allocated trade capital per trade in oil has to weigh in at higher than 1.2 percent per week per trade. Any lower and you will get wiped out much sooner, sometimes even with a single trade.

So for crude oil, giving traders the ability to run a position for a week requires a stop loss capital allocation maybe 1.5 percent of notional under normal (average) market conditions. The stop loss capital requirement is different from the market risk capital requirement which, based on the above data, may be as high as 8 to 14 percent of notional exposure.

If you want to run a tighter ship and only approve positions to run for intraday, the stop loss limit is going to be even tighter (small band and range). If you approve positions to be run for a month, you would be working with wider limits (longer band and ranges).

The every other day loss figure for silver is slightly different at *–1 percent to +1.4 percent.* Compared to oil you can clearly see that the distribution is much more compact and compressed and the tails are wider.

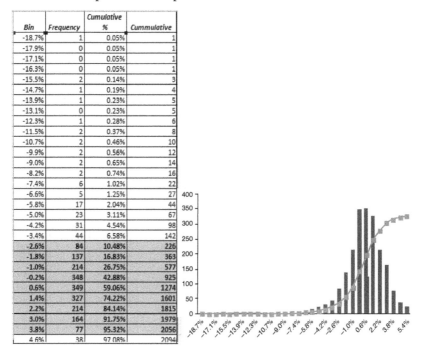

Bin	Frequency	Cumulative %	Cummulative
-18.7%	1	0.05%	1
-17.9%	0	0.05%	1
-17.1%	0	0.05%	1
-16.3%	0	0.05%	1
-15.5%	2	0.14%	3
-14.7%	1	0.19%	4
-13.9%	1	0.23%	5
-13.1%	0	0.23%	5
-12.3%	1	0.28%	6
-11.5%	2	0.37%	8
-10.7%	2	0.46%	10
-9.9%	2	0.56%	12
-9.0%	2	0.65%	14
-8.2%	2	0.74%	16
-7.4%	6	1.02%	22
-6.6%	5	1.25%	27
-5.8%	17	2.04%	44
-5.0%	23	3.11%	67
-4.2%	31	4.54%	98
-3.4%	44	6.58%	142
-2.6%	84	10.48%	226
-1.8%	137	16.83%	363
-1.0%	214	26.75%	577
-0.2%	348	42.88%	925
0.6%	349	59.06%	1274
1.4%	327	74.22%	1601
2.2%	214	84.14%	1815
3.0%	164	91.75%	1979
3.8%	77	95.32%	2056
4.6%	38	97.08%	2094

Figure 153 Setting thresholds for stop loss limits for silver

Bin	Frequency	Cumulative %	Cummulative
-19%	1	0.05%	1
-18%	0	0.05%	1
-18%	0	0.05%	1
-17%	0	0.05%	1
-16%	0	0.05%	1
-15%	0	0.05%	1
-14%	1	0.09%	2
-13%	1	0.14%	3
-13%	0	0.14%	3
-12%	0	0.14%	3
-11%	0	0.14%	3
-10%	0	0.14%	3
-9%	0	0.14%	3
-8%	0	0.14%	3
-8%	1	0.19%	4
-7%	0	0.19%	4
-6%	2	0.28%	6
-5%	5	0.51%	11
-4%	9	0.93%	20
-3%	11	1.44%	31
-3%	33	2.97%	64
-2%	80	6.68%	144
-1%	197	15.81%	341
0%	457	37.00%	798
1%	768	72.60%	1566
2%	378	90.13%	1944
2%	136	96.43%	2080
3%	44	98.47%	2124
4%	15	99.17%	2139
5%	10	99.63%	2149

Figure 154   Setting thresholds for stop loss limits for gold

For gold the same ratio comes in at *–1 percent to 0.7 percent.*

Once again the idea is to set a stop loss limits based on the number of days you want your traders to run a position and the shape and form of the underlying price distribution. You don't want the traders to get hit by limit breaches and be required to approve extensions or exceptions to the limit every day, but you also don't want them to risk more capital than you can afford to burn.

3. Setting stop loss limits – limit review triggers and back testing

In our case study on setting stop loss limits we reviewed stop loss limit estimates for oil, gold and silver futures trading. We now take a look at market-based triggers that should lead to a review of stop loss limits:

- Changing volatility,
- Frequency of breaches,
- Capital levels,
- Profitability targets,
- Market Liquidity.

The original stop loss thresholds that were initially calculated were linked to volatility levels. As volatility levels rise or decline, the range of price swings also adjusts. Volatility levels also have an impact on the market's view of price direction. A change in volatility levels should trigger a review of stop loss limits to see if a tightening or widening of the stop loss band should be recommended. If you don't track volatility or are not focused on the right moving average, a proxy indicator is the actual limit breaches compared with anticipated limit breaches. When reported limit breaches cross expected limit breaches you should review stop loss limits to better understand the rise in limit exceptions. Is it because the original limits were set incorrectly or because volatility levels and thresholds have changed?

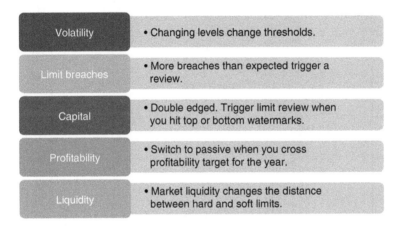

Volatility	• Changing levels change thresholds.
Limit breaches	• More breaches than expected trigger a review.
Capital	• Double edged. Trigger limit review when you hit top or bottom watermarks.
Profitability	• Switch to passive when you cross profitability target for the year.
Liquidity	• Market liquidity changes the distance between hard and soft limits.

Figure 155   Limit review triggers

Capital and profitability are two additional triggers that have double touch (top and bottom) thresholds. If you hit your profitability target, switch to passive mood and book your profits. If you hit your capital contribution target (also linked to profitability) once again do the same. Counter intuitive but safe.

Finally, liquidity and trading volumes in the underlying market determine the amount of time and price impact you will have to book before your position is sold off. Like volatility, a drop in market liquidity should trigger an immediate review and should lead to a tighter stop loss band.

How frequently and widely does price volatility move? As you can see below for gold and oil prices, daily return volatility ranges from 0.5 percent to 8 percent in the last 8 years. A half percent move when oil is trading at US$ 50 is worth US$ 2.5. An 8 percent move when oil is trading at US$ 150 is worth US$ 12. Hence the argument for reviewing stop loss limits on account of changes in volatility and liquidity levels.

Back testing stop loss limits is a little bit more involved.

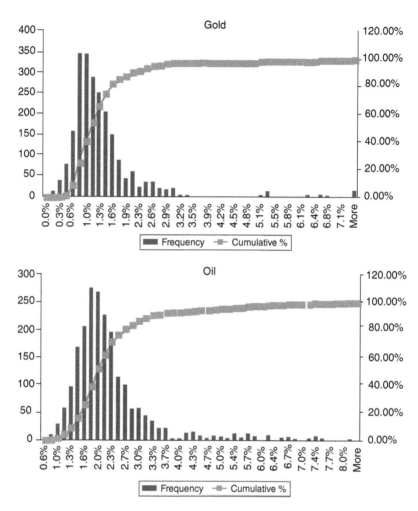

Figure 156 Daily return volatility ranges for gold and oil

Once a threshold has been decided, you need to simulate, using historical data, the entire sequence of events triggered by a stop loss limit breach. When the trigger is hit, the position is sold, the stop loss related hit booked against the available pool of stop loss capital. The question you want to answer is "How long will it take before the capital pool runs out?" To do this correctly and accurately you need market trade data with volumes. Once the limit is breached you sell the entire inventory at market prices, using market volume data if available. If the data is not available you need to build a simple impact cost model that forecasts or simulates market prices based on the size of the sell order and market direction.

The final tweaking in stop loss limits can be made after the back testing exercise has been completed and you have tested the sufficiency of the capital pool.

Annexure 2 – Risk metrics

1. Holding period return

The holding period return represents the return earned by the instrument over the period of analysis. It is calculated as follows:

$$\text{Holding period return} = \left(\frac{\text{Final price}}{\text{Initial price}} - 1 \right).$$

For the calculation of the Sharpe and Treynor ratios (see below) the holding period return derived above is scaled to a year, that is, to 252 trading days if the holding period exceeds the number of trading days in a year.

2. Standard deviation/volatility (Vol)/σ

Risk arises because prices tend to move with a degree of uncertainty and an entity is exposed to this uncertainty now or in the future. Prices may turn out to be different from what one has expected given past information. Mathematically, this expected value is represented by the average number one would calculate from a given set of values. This is known as the mean of that set and is represented by the Greek symbol, μ.

The differences between this mean and the actual values in the data set are the deviations from the mean. The adjusted average of these deviations represents uncertainty, otherwise known as volatility. Mathematically, risk, uncertainty or volatility in the prices is calculated by determining the standard deviation of the given data set. The standard deviation is represented by the Greek symbol, σ. The standard deviation is calculated by the following formula:

$$\sigma = \sqrt{\frac{1}{n-1} \sum_{i=1}^{n} (X_i - \mu)^2},$$

where X_i is the ith price/rate, μ is the mean (average) of the data set, that is,

$$\mu = \frac{1}{n} \sum_{i=1}^{n} X_i,$$

and "n" represents the number of values in the data set.

3. Annualized return

The annualized return is calculated by compounding the daily return over 252 trading days:

$$\text{Annualized Return} = (1 + \text{daily return})^{252} - 1.$$

4. Annualized volatility

The annualized volatility is calculated by multiplying the daily volatility with the square root of 252 trading days:

Annualized Volatility = daily volatility $\times \sqrt{252}$.

5. Duration

Duration is a measure of how rapidly the prices of interest sensitive securities change as the rate of interest changes. For example, if the duration of a security works out to 2, this means that for a 1 percent increase in interest rates the price of the instrument will decrease by 2 percent. Similarly, if the interest rates were to decrease by 1 percent the price of the security would increase by 2 percent.

Assuming a 100 basis point (1 percent) change in interest rates, duration is calculated as follows:

$$\text{Duration} = \frac{\begin{array}{c}\text{Price if interest rates are decreased by 1\%}\\ -\text{ Price if interest rates are increased by 1\%}\end{array}}{2 \times \text{Inital Price} \times 0.01}$$

Initial price can be taken as the price on the revaluation date, prior to applying the interest rate changes. The other two prices used in the numerator will also be calculated on this date.

6. Convexity

Duration approximates the change in price of an instrument due to changes in the yield. However, this approximation tends to work only for small changes in yield. For larger changes there will be a significant error term between the actual price change and that estimated using duration. Convexity improves on this approximation as it explains the change in price that is not explained by duration.

Convexity is given by

$$\text{Convexity} = \frac{P_+ + P_- - 2P_0}{2P_0 (\Delta i)^2}$$

where,

Δi = change in yield (in decimals),

P_0 = initial price,

P_+ = price if yields increase by Δi,

P_- = price if yields decline by Δi.

Another important aspect of convexity is that it takes into account the curvature of the price/yield relationship. The duration measure assumes that the size of approximated change in price (in percentage terms) would be the same if yields were to either increase or decrease by the same amount. Convexity, depending on the sign, accounts for the direction of the change in yield and the curvature of the price/yield relationship. A positive convexity measure indicates a greater price increase when interest rates fall by a given percentage relative to the price decline if interest rates were to rise by that same percentage. A negative convexity measure indicates that the price decline will be greater than the price gain for the same percentage change in yield.

Approximate price change
The approximate price change using both the duration and convexity measures will be as follows:

Total estimated percentage price change = –Duration × Δi × 100
+ Convexity × $(\Delta i)^2$ × 100.

Terminology: modified and effective
The term modified is used with duration and convexity when the changes in yield are assumed not to affect the expected cash flows of the security (for example, for option free instruments). The term effective is used with duration and convexity when changes in yield are also assumed to impact the expected cash flows of the security (for example, for derivatives).

7. Sharpe ratio

The Sharpe Ratio measures risk adjusted performance. It is calculated by subtracting the risk free rate from the rate of return and dividing the result by the standard deviation of the return:

$$\text{Sharpe Ratio} = \frac{R_I - R_f}{\sigma_I},$$

where R_I is the holding period return of investment I (if the number of days in the holding period exceeds the number of trading days in the year, the holding period return is proportionately adjusted to arrive at the holding period return for a year), R_f is the annualized risk free rate of return and σ_I is the annualized standard deviation of rates of return of investment I.

The measurement is useful in determining which investments yield high returns without adding too much extra risk. The greater the ratio the better the risk adjusted performance and the better the return relative to the risk involved.

The annualized volatility has been obtained by multiplying the daily SMA volatility with the square root of 252, (the number of trading days). The risk free rate is the average rate on a risk free instrument during the period being analyzed.

8. Put premium

The put premium calculates the premium value using Black Scholes formula of a put option, using downside price change in stock as the strike price. It essentially measures the extent of the worst-case loss, that is, the loss that occurs 1 percent of the time under the VaR approach. It answers the question "How much would you pay for protection against the possibility that the loss exceeded the worst case loss?"

The Black Scholes formula for the put premium, p, on the equity is given below:

$$p = Ee^{-rt}N(-d_2) - SN(-d_1),$$

where

$$d_1 = \frac{\ln(S/E) + (r + \sigma^2/2)t}{\sigma\sqrt{t}}$$

$$d_2 = d_1 - \sigma\sqrt{t}$$

- S = the most recent price/rate of the underlying stock/rate in the period of study;
- E = the strike price/rate = downside price/rate change after application of SMA 10-day holding VaR = $S \times (1 - \text{SMA 10-day holding VaR})$;
- r = the continuously compounded risk free interest rate = $\ln(1 + R_f)$ where R_f is the risk free rate as mentioned for the Sharpe Ratio above;
- t = the time in years until the expiration of the option;
- σ = the implied volatility for the underlying stock/rate = SMA daily volatility × $\sqrt{252}$;
- $N(.)$ = the standard normal cumulative distribution function.

The put premium percentage is given as the put premium divided by the price/rate of the underlying stock/rate: $(p/S) \times 100$.

9. Beta with respect to market indices

Beta is a quantitative measure of the volatility, or systematic risk of a given equity to the overall market. The formula for the beta of an asset within a portfolio is

$$\beta_a = \frac{\text{Cov}(r_a, r_p)}{\text{Var}(r_p)},$$

where

r_a measures the rate of return of the asset,

r_p measures the rate of return of the portfolio of which the asset is a part

$Cov(r_a, r_p)$ is the covariance between the rates of return.

In the capital asset pricing model (CAPM) formulation, the portfolio is the market portfolio that contains all risky assets, and so the r_p terms in the formula are replaced by r_m, the rate of return of the market. Rate of return of the broad market index is used as a proxy to the rate of return of the market.

A beta of 1 indicates that the security's price will move with the market. A beta of less than 1 means that the security will be less volatile than the market. A beta of greater than 1 indicates that the security's price will be more volatile than the market. For example, if a stock's beta is 1.2, it is theoretically 20 percent more volatile than the market.

10. Treynor ratio

The Treynor ratio is a risk adjusted performance metric that measures the returns earned in excess of the return on a risk free security per unit of market or systematic risk as measured by the investment's beta. It is given by

$$\text{Treynor ratio} = \frac{R_I - R_f}{\beta_I},$$

where R_I is the holding period return of investment I (if the number of days in the holding period exceeds the number of trading days in the year the holding period return is proportionately adjusted to arrive at the holding period return for a year), R_f is the annualized risk free rate of return (the risk free rate is the average rate on a risk free instrument during the period being analyzed) and β_I is the beta of investment I with respect to a market benchmark. The market benchmark is usually taken as a broad market index.

11. Jensen's Alpha

Jensen's Alpha is the risk adjusted performance metric that measures a portfolio manager's returns against those of a benchmark. The market benchmark is usually taken as a broad market index. Using the time-series data for the daily returns of equities and the market index the following equation is estimated by regression analysis:

$$R_{It} = \alpha_I + R_f + \beta_I [R_{Mt} - R_f],$$

Annualized $\alpha_I = (1 + \alpha_I)^{252} - 1,$

where

 R_{It} = the daily return of investment I at time t,

 R_f = the daily risk free rate of return = $(1 + \text{annual risk free rate})^{1/252} - 1$,

 R_{Mt} = the daily returns of the market index at time t,

 β_I = the beta of the equities with respect to the market index.

The alpha estimated through this regression analysis (by minimizing the sum of squared differences between the actual equity return and the estimated equity return) is a measure of the equity's performance relative to the respective indices and represents the unique return of the investment. If the alpha is not statistically different from zero there is no unique return. A statistically positive alpha means that the equity outperformed the market index while a negative value means that the equity underperformed the relevant market index.

12. Correlation coefficient, *r*

The correlation coefficient is given by

$$ r = \frac{1}{n-1} \sum_i \left(\frac{x_i - \bar{x}}{\sigma_x} \right) \left(\frac{y_i - \bar{y}}{\sigma_y} \right), $$

where

 n is the sample size,

 x_i is the measurement for the ith observation of asset x,

 $\bar{x}$ is the mean of all the observations of asset x,

 σ_x is the standard deviation of the observations of asset x,

 y_i is the measurement for the ith observation of asset y,

 $\bar{y}$ is the mean of all the observations of asset y,

 σ_y is the standard deviation of the observations of asset y.

The correlation coefficient is a measure of the strength and direction of a linear relationship between two variables. It can range from -1 to $+1$ inclusive. The strength is gauged from the absolute magnitude of r; the greater the absolute value of r the greater the relationship between the two variables. The direction informs us of the way one variable moves in relation to the other. A positive correlation means that as one variable increases the other is also likely to increase. A negative correlation indicates that as one variable increases the other is likely to decrease. An r of -1 or $+1$ signifies perfectly negative or positive linear correlation, respectively. A correlation of zero indicates that the two variables are not related.

 The correlation coefficient assumes that the underlying variables have a linear relationship with each other. When the relationship is non-linear then the correlation coefficient could lead to false and misleading results.

Correlation could also lead to misleading results when there are outliers in the dataset, when data groups are combined inappropriately or when the data is too homogeneous.

Another important point to note is that a correlation between two variables does not imply causation, that is, it is not necessarily the case that one variable is causing a response in the other variable. There are other possible interpretations to the observed relationship that must be kept in mind when analyzing results, such as the fact that both variables could be affected by other variables and there may be no direct causation factor between the two variables being analyzed, and so on.

It is possible to evaluate the magnitude of the correlation numbers using five "Rules of Thumb" as follows.

Range	Interpretation
$0 < r < 0.2$	no or negligible correlation
$0.2 < r < 0.4$	low degree of correlation
$0.4 < r < 0.6$	moderate degree of correlation
$0.6 < r < 0.8$	marked degree of correlation
$0.8 < r < 1$	high correlation

Figure 157 Rules of thumb for interpreting correlations

In order to test whether the correlation is in fact significant rather than a chance occurrence we have used hypothesis testing. Specifically, we are testing the mutually exclusive hypotheses.

Null Hypothesis:	$r = 0$
Alternative Hypothesis:	$r <> 0$

Using a significance level of 5 percent, a two tailed test and $n - 2$ degrees of freedom (df) (n is the number of observations), a critical value is determined from the table below. If the exact degrees of freedom is not available in the table then the critical value at the next lower degrees of freedom will be used. For example if there are 328 observations, degrees of freedom works out to 326. This value is not present in the table and so we will use the critical value at the next lower degrees of freedom, that is, the critical value at degrees of freedom of 300.

If the calculated correlation is greater than the critical value or less than $-1 \times$ critical value, it can be concluded that the calculated correlation is not a chance finding but is statistically significant. As a result we reject the null hypothesis and accept the alternative. On the other hand, if the

	CRITICAL VALUES			
DEGREES OF FREEDOM	LEVEL OF SIGNIFICANCE FOR A TWO-TAILED TEST			
(N – 2)	10%	5%	2%	1%
1	0.988	0.997	0.9995	0.9999
2	0.9	0.95	0.98	0.99
3	0.805	0.878	0.934	0.959
4	0.729	0.811	0.882	0.917
5	0.669	0.754	0.833	0.874
6	0.622	0.707	0.789	0.834
7	0.582	0.666	0.75	0.798
8	0.549	0.632	0.716	0.765
9	0.521	0.602	0.685	0.735
10	0.497	0.576	0.658	0.708
11	0.476	0.553	0.634	0.684
12	0.458	0.532	0.612	0.661
13	0.441	0.514	0.592	0.641
14	0.426	0.497	0.574	0.623
15	0.412	0.482	0.558	0.606
16	0.4	0.468	0.542	0.59
17	0.389	0.456	0.528	0.575
18	0.378	0.444	0.516	0.561
19	0.369	0.433	0.503	0.549
20	0.36	0.423	0.492	0.537
21	0.352	0.413	0.482	0.526
22	0.344	0.404	0.472	0.515
23	0.337	0.396	0.462	0.505
24	0.33	0.388	0.453	0.496
25	0.323	0.381	0.445	0.487
26	0.317	0.374	0.437	0.479
27	0.311	0.367	0.43	0.471
28	0.306	0.361	0.423	0.463
29	0.301	0.355	0.416	0.456
30	0.296	0.349	0.409	0.449
35	0.275	0.325	0.381	0.418
40	0.257	0.304	0.358	0.393
45	0.243	0.288	0.338	0.372
50	0.231	0.273	0.322	0.354
60	0.211	0.25	0.295	0.325
70	0.195	0.232	0.274	0.303
80	0.183	0.217	0.256	0.283
90	0.173	0.205	0.242	0.267
100	0.164	0.195	0.23	0.254
125		0.174		
150		0.159		
200		0.138		
300		0.113		
400		0.098		
500		0.088		
1000		0.062		

Figure 158 Table of critical values for a two tailed test of significance

calculated correlation is less than the critical value or greater than $-1 \times$ critical value, then we will conclude that there is no proof of correlation given the dataset and parameters used.

It is important to note that the size of the sample used affects whether a specific observed result attains statistical significance. With very large sample sizes, low correlation values which are demonstrative of a weak relationship between the assets can turn out to be statistically significant. This doesn't interpret to a significant relationship between the assets but simply illustrates that the correlation is not zero. Practical significance of the result should be gauged by the observed strength of the relationship, that is, by its magnitude.

13. Portfolio volatility taking into account correlations

The portfolio's daily volatility taking into account correlations has been calculated using the formula:

$$\text{Portfolio volatility} = \sqrt{\text{Variance}(aX + bY + cZ)},$$

where

$$\begin{aligned} \text{Variance}(aX + bY + cZ) = {} & a^2\,\text{Variance}(X) + b^2\,\text{Variance}(Y) \\ & + c^2\,\text{Variance}(Z) + 2ab\rho_{xy}\sigma_x\sigma_y \\ & + 2bc\rho_{yz}\sigma_y\sigma_z + 2ac\rho_{xz}\sigma_x\sigma_z \end{aligned}$$

a, b and c are the weights of the respective asset in the portfolio, and X, Y and Z are the assets in the portfolio;

Variance (X) is the variance in X price/rate returns, that is, it is X's returns volatility squared (S_x^2);

Variance (Y) is the variance in Y price/rate returns, that is, it is Y's returns volatility squared (S_y^2);

Variance (Z) is the variance in Z price/rate returns, that is, it is Z's returns volatility squared (S_z^2);

ρ_{xy} is the correlation between X and Y returns;

ρ_{yz} is the correlation between Y and Z returns;

ρ_{xz} is the correlation between X and Z returns.

(*Note*: This formula is for a portfolio that consists of three assets. However it can easily be extended to account for more assets).

If it is assumed that there is independence between the assets, the correlation terms are set equal to zero in the equation above. If it is assumed that the assets are perfectly correlated then the volatility of the portfolio is equal to the weighted average sum of the asset volatilities.

14. Volatility trend analysis

Volatility trend analysis is carried out by calculating sixty day moving averages of daily SMA volatilities in the given look back period. The daily SMA volatility is calculated based on the prior sixty return observations. The graphical depiction of the trend line shows the average volatility of the next sixty volatilities at a given point in time. An upward sloping trend line indicates that the average volatilities are increasing, a horizontal line shows stable volatility levels, whereas a downward sloping trend line shows declining volatilities.

4

Building Risk Systems

The old days of handling risk through an EXCEL spreadsheet are gone. Given the data portfolios generate and the speed with which markets move, risk functions need to react at the same speed as traders. Manual processes and interventions raise credibility issues and test the competence and survival of a risk manager.

If the arguments of size, credibility, competence and speed aren't sufficient, the last nail in the EXCEL model coffin was hammered in by the JP Morgan Chase London whale crisis in 2012. A simple formula copying error resulted in a significant understatement of the value at risk (VAR) figures[1]. In JP Morgan's case the error was unintentional, but if you are committed it is just as easy to hijack and manipulate a manual spreadsheet that reports risk numbers. Then there is the issue of productivity versus effort. Would you rather focus on analyzing risks and recommending corrective action or on collecting and collating data and debugging your EXCEL formula?

The objective of a risk function is not just to gather data, run reports, submit and present them at board meetings; it is to ensure that unpleasant surprises and their impact is limited. While you can't control the timing and magnitude of such surprises, a well-managed risk function can help manage expectations, as well as plan ahead for unexpected shocks. Practiced, trained, well thought out responses versus bungled and knee jerk reactions can limit the impact of disagreeable shocks.

We know that all models are wrong (by definition they are approximations to the real world) but some are more useful than others[2]. The usefulness comes not from accurate modeling, but from the process that allows a bank to think through exposures, chalk out and test an exit strategy before a crisis hits. Part of this is understanding the distribution, but a much more important part is getting comfortable with our reactions to the distribution.

We also need to remember that there is a human element to the risk function, an incentives issue with controls and an agency problem with management. If you have got the models right but missed the human element, your function will still fail. If you get models and the human element right but are married to rigidity, not flexibility, your function will still fall short. It doesn't mean that the models failed, it means that either your organizational design was flawed or you didn't use the models to explore the distribution of risk.

The right time to manage risk is not when a full blown risk related crisis is brewing. It is when there is still time to think through reactions and pick the most suitable options available. Sometimes the best reactions are counterintuitive because they seek survival via flexibility of thought. But the muse for counterintuitive reactions is discussion, debate and an open mind. Counter intuition is very much like our subconscious; you can't find it when you seek it, it has to find you. Unfortunately, when you are on fire, counter intuition is the last thing on your mind.

A good risk management plan takes into consideration possible scenarios and appropriate reactions and then gets a mandate from the board to execute on those reactions if such a need ever arises. A great risk management plan goes one step further and validates and tests all assumptions and fall backs if assumptions break down during a crisis.

Risk models only have value if they are used in combination with active limit management and efficient control process. The key is not generation of quantitative numbers, formatted in ten different cuts; it is the interpretation and application of analysis behind reports that matters.

Buying expensive systems and platforms doesn't deliver on this objective. Educated users, managers, team leaders and board members are the ones who really make it work. While we don't recommend that you skimp out on your technology budget and go back to an EXCEL spreadsheet, we do recommend that you need to spend just as much on the people side

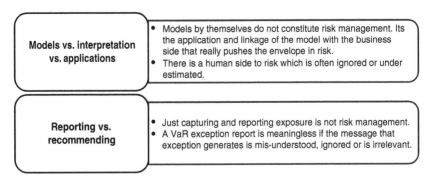

Figure 159   Risk management systems – what it is and what it is not

of the equation as you do on technology. A US$ 20 million risk platform is not going to help you much if the person operating it is clueless, rigid, ignorant or inexperienced.

Within financial services and banking, risk takes two forms:

(a) Price or market risk: The risk linked to changing prices and interaction of these changes with value. The market risk function provides oversight to trading, portfolio and investment management functions.
(b) Credit or underwriting risk: The risk linked with default on credit and lending products. One part of this risk is making bad lending decisions (underwriting) while the other is the inability to track a portfolio of loans through their natural life cycle (credit risk management).

While there are other risk flavors – including operational, concentration, execution, liquidity, regulatory reporting, compliance and strategy, resources – reporting and exposure is concentrated within credit and market risk.

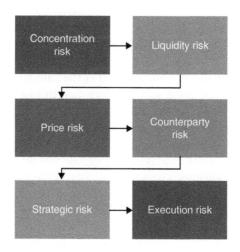

Figure 160 Flavors of risk

How does risk differ across these two functions?

Treasury and market risk

Market risk deals with questions of value and changes in value. Investment management is a modeling, trading and valuation business and price risk is a function of all three.

The risk function (Risk)'s value to the trading desk is in direct relationship to the accuracy of models and the ability of these models to predict and forecast swings in market prices before they occur. Risk can increase that value significantly by walking away from EXCEL models and focusing more on deal flow, but that requires a different skill set and a very different mandate. Alternatively, it can also take the voice of reason or play the devil's advocate role, helping identify gaps and challenges in trades and structures before they become black holes for bank capital.

The challenge in market risk is that in most cases Risk is wrong. This is because the models relied on are wrong – they are inaccurate by definition and design. They represent approximations to the real world. Not Risk's fault, but this is how the game is structured.

As long as boards and business understand this and the fact that Risk's value rests not with models but with the questions they ask and the answers they seek, the risk function will survive and may even do well. A boss who understands that prices move outside of models, that models break, that crises arrive without warning, is just as important for the survival of the risk function. If bosses do not understand this (also quite common) then one fine morning the model will blow up and try to kill the bank and Risk will be the team held responsible for that failure.

The person responsible for Risk's well being, who decides if they deserve to live, is the treasurer, the individual responsible for the portfolio management function, the head of investments. His title may vary but for Risk he represents the business function and is the one who signs Risk's paycheck. He gets risk. He plays with it every day. But he hates unqualified, armchair amateurs telling him how to do his job.

The holy grail for a treasury risk team member is to think like a trader but act like a risk manager in such a fashion that treasury teams ask for input not because you are a risk manager but because you add real value by your analysis. The trick however is to remember that there is a fine line that cannot be crossed between being a risk advisor and being a risk taker.

Because of this conflict of interest between risk advisor and taker, the person you would probably get along best with, who would understand what you do and why it is important, sits on the other side of the table.

While you report to the head of risk or the head of risk policy, and while these individuals are very qualified, educated and experienced, they are not traders. The treasury or investment management function for them is the closest thing to black magic or voodoo that a bank can have. Money comes in, money goes out; sometimes much more comes out than goes in; sometimes what goes in disappears and sucks the rest of the bank with it.

1. The challenge with treasury risk management

Treasury risk management, today more than at any time in the recent past, suffers from a serious credibility challenge. While the push to Basel II and now Basel III created all sorts of expectations, roles, divisions and budgetary allocations, the reality still remains that most treasurers have a real problem with respect when it comes to middle office teams.

Boards are worse. If you hit turbulence in markets and the bank books a loss on account of that turmoil the common questions board members and shareholders will ask are "What was Risk doing?" "Where was it when we needed it?" "Why are we paying you so much money?"

This challenge in credibility exists because:

Figure 161   Treasury risk challenges

Treasury Risk teams fail to link models to market prices and market behavior – when it comes to data we are forced to work with implied or indicative prices rather than real trade transactions. More often than not we divorce ourselves from the impact of a trade on markets or ignore the real reason why model prices diverge or converge to market prices. For example, why do FX swap points converge at higher maturity to model prices but diverge at shorter maturities? In the graph below, the two thick lines show the market price and the model price. It shows great convergence for the 1 year swap point curve between the market and the model.

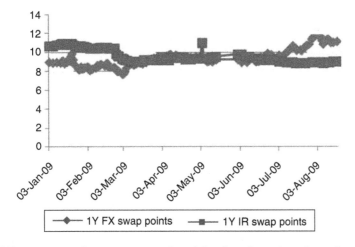

Figure 162   Treasury risk – convergence of model and market price – the real reasons

The answer is liquidity and the difference between binding trade quotes and indicative quotes. At lower maturities the market is liquid and trade data is widely available. The trade data forms the market. At higher maturity there is no volume and in order to fill the quote sheet, the market quotes the model without a willingness to support those quotes.

Treasury Risk teams are reliant on models that work with historical data and don't have the bandwidth, the resources or the mindset to incorporate forward looking price projections or properly dissect the data using the frameworks presented in earlier chapters. Even if they could, they cannot drive the treasury bus by sitting in the back seat or looking out of the rearview mirror.

Treasury Risk teams face a serious disconnect from daily trading activity. In one way this disconnect is necessary to stay emotionally uninvolved from a trade. But in a different perspective it furthers the divide between traders and risk managers. A trader will not respect you till he respects you either as a trader or because of your ability to forecast price movements and act on them.

The best talent comes from the business side. Sometimes in order to survive you have to look beyond the numbers and look at the context. Business trains you to think that way. Models don't.

The credit risk function

Unlike market risk and treasury, credit risk is entertaining, it is engaging, and it has people rather than models. The function is trusted and is not treated as an extension of witchcraft.

If the models break down you can always blame it on the customer, on the economy, or on bad data. The central bank and regulators give you space and leeway in provisions and recoveries because you are essential to the health of the financial system. If you need any additional support, boards expect you to drop some cash on some customers because it is part of the business model. There is no lending without default.

Compared to the treasury function where a small loss with leverage can wipe out a large part of your capital base, in credit you lend in syndicates and some losses are always expected. Treasury on the other hand is absolute and time dependent. A trade is a call on direction – sometimes you are right; sometimes you are wrong. When you make money on a trade you are golden (within reasonable limits), but if you start bleeding capital heads can easily roll.

A single deal and the ensuing relationship can feed you in credit for years. In treasury you have to identify, hunt and kill your game every alternate day. In credit you hunt together as part of a team, in treasury you go it alone, in competition with other hunters outside the bank.

Treasury is absolute and unforgiving, credit is not. Because board members do not understand what you do, as a treasurer you are generally not trusted. Maybe trust is too strong a word. You are viewed as a speculator, a wild one who is only looking for the right opportunity to bet the bank and their capital, a fair weather friend who will first crack the hull on a reef and then dump the sinking ship as soon as capital runs out. Because with a flick of a finger you can kill a bank, there are many more controls and checks and balances on what you can or cannot do as part of the treasury team, compared to the credit function.

1. What does credit management involve?

How does the credit management function work at a bank? What are the different layers and sub functions involved in credit management?

Let's assume that we are helping a large investment bank set up their brand new credit risk management function in Asia. As part of their big move they are looking for someone to head and design their credit risk platform. You are a leading candidate for the role and they have asked you a simple question highlighting your vision for the function. Where would you start?

Figure 163 Credit management lifecycle

You have to begin with how risk is booked on the bank balance sheet and how it flows through the different layers of the credit management function over its life cycle. This means you have to consider everyone, from the relationship managers (RMs) who bring and book assets to the bank balance sheet to credit admin, if the loan performs, or special assets, if it does not.

a. Credit proposal

What do RMs look at? If Tom wanted to borrow US$ 1 million and Sam was his relationship manager, where would he start? What would Sam look at? What information would he need and how would he convince the lending function at the bank to approve Tom's request? Let's make a list of relevant data that he would need to evaluate such a request.

(a) Tom's credit history as a borrower as an individual or an entity in the past with this bank or other banks.
(b) The nature of his business and the industry segment.

(c) The outlook for that segment as well as the entire economy/region.

(d) The reason why Tom needs to borrow money.

(e) Tom's plans for usage of the proceeds from the loan and the impact of that plan on his ability to repay.

(f) His sources of loan repayment and ability to pay.

(g) Any security or collateral that he can pledge to the bank to secure the loan.

As a relationship manager Sam would look at all of this and more and prepare a document called a credit proposal. A credit proposal documents all of the above and makes a recommendation in alignment with the credit policy of the bank to lend or not lend, approve or not approve the credit proposal. While the universal name is Credit Proposal or CP, we also recognize it by the following monikers, Application for Limits (AFL), Limit Approval or Credit Application.

b. Credit policy

When a credit application is received by the bank, it cannot just walk in through the door. It generally has a sponsor (the relationship manager) or a champion and it must make its way past a gate keeper called the negative list. A negative list is a list of attributes, the presence of which will guarantee the kiss of death for a credit application. At any given point in time banks will decide that a given sector or segment is too risky because of their prior experience or the banking industry's experience, capital requirements for such loans or products, security or collateral which is not acceptable for securing a loan or attributes of owners, shareholders or sponsors that the bank has decided to not take a risk on.

This negative list plus a number of additional credit selection/underwriting decisions are documented in the credit policy document of the bank. The credit policy document defines acceptable credit for the bank; the

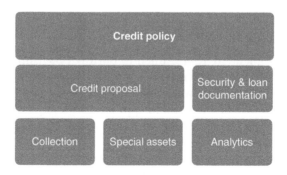

Figure 164 Credit management and credit policy

information requirement for a CP; the format of a borrower fact sheet; the reporting requirement for the credit risk management function; and much more. Credit policy documents also come in two flavors. The lean and mean policy version that only focuses on policy decisions as well as the thick brick manuals that also detail policy implementation procedures and processes. There would generally be separate credit policy documents for commercial, SME, retail and consumer businesses, while product specific credit policy issues may get addressed as part of the program or product guides.

A credit policy is also influenced by central bank policy with respect to specific segments and products. For example, in developing, emerging and frontier markets a credit policy document is generally in close alignment with the national economic policy of the government and the central bank. However, the ownership of the credit policy document rests with the head of credit but it is approved by the board of directors and reviewed and audited by the central bank supervision team every year.

As a relationship manager it is required for Sam to be familiar with credit policy requirements of his bank so that he doesn't waste time in preparing proposals that will not make it pass the initial filtering list.

c. The underwriting and approval decision

So Tom is lucky enough to make it pass the initial filters and the requirements specified in the credit policy. His proposal is now safely sitting on the desk of the credit portfolio analyst who is going to review it and make his recommendation. The analyst will review the recommendations made by the relationship manager as well as the branch, and if the proposal meets all the requirements needed to approve the loan, the credit analyst will make a positive recommendation and forward the proposal to the next level in the chain of approval. If the proposal is deficient on account of a specific factor, in most cases the proposal won't be declined outright but sent back to the RM with feedback on the deficiency. Once the deficiency is fixed, the cycle would restart at the credit portfolio analyst desk.

A large part of the analysis is based on the original need for the loan, the product being used to finance it, sources of value creation, sources of repayment, security and collateral, margin, documentation and guarantees by sponsors, shareholders and directors. The analysts also look at the capacity of Tom's balance sheet, as well as his P&L, to bear the loan and debt servicing capacity.

d. Post approval life cycle of a loan

Once the loan is approved, the CP moves through the next stages in the life cycle. The first post approval step is loan documentation. This is the step where the loan offer or term sheet is shared with the client and is returned with his acceptance. The term sheet specifies the loan terms and conditions (loan covenants), the specification of collateral, the nature of the pledge, pledge documentation, loan servicing requirements, late payment penalties, arbitration, collection and repossession clauses. It also includes the legal documents required for registering a charge against the asset of the entity being financed with the regional or national charge registration authority (Corporate Law Authority, the Registration of companies or the Securities and Exchange Commission).

Figure 165   Post loan approval credit life cycle

Once these two steps are completed the loan is ready to be disbursed and the consumption and repayment cycle of the loan starts. Throughout the life cycle the relationship manager for the client plays a central part, since in addition to the bank he has the most data about the relationship and its prospects at any given point in time.

Figure 166   The role of a relationship manager

However, while the credit management function can use that insight, it cannot solely rely on the relationship manager to control the risk inherent in a given credit relationship because there is an inherent conflict of interest. Therefore the credit management function relies on a mix of

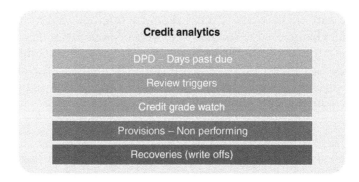

Figure 167   Credit management – credit analytics

branch level data as well as its own analytics to manage, control and run the function.

These analytics include:

(a) A breakdown by product, region, branches and segments of the days a payment is overdue (days past due or DPD analysis) across the entire banking franchise and how it compares with the overall industry average.
(b) Relationship review triggers that serve as leading indicators of blood in the water, such as issues with margins, deposits, transactions, industry slowdown, credit downgrades, client specific chatter on the banking system grapevine and defaults on other banking relationships.
(c) Client or industry specific credit downgrade by internal or external credit rating systems.
(d) Changes in sector, segment, region provisions or loan classifications.
(e) Changes in recoveries and write offs.
(f) Bank exposure concentrations across sectors, segments, products, markets and clients.

The DPD tracking piece is the most crucial analytic generated by the credit management function. It is used not just in collections tracking and client management but also in provisions projections and capital management. But the source and control of DPD data is crucial. If the credit management function relies on branches to generate and compile DPD data they are just asking for trouble. For DPD data to be reliable and effective it should be generated automatically without manual intervention by any concerned or related party.

e. The 10,000 meters view

From policy to proposal, from proposal to approval, from approval to disbursement, from disbursement to analytics, the credit management function seems to have its fingers everywhere. If you run the credit management function you need to be comfortable with all the dimensions of the function. The challenge in credit risk however is the inherent conflict built in the nature of these dimensions. Proposals and approvals are market driven. Documentation and charges are legal. Analytics are performance and behavior driven. Provisions, recoveries and special assets use a completely different language and rely on negotiations, positions, and give and take. Hence, the requirement for a head of credit risk is to have experience in business development and corporate banking as well as special assets and credit administration, and technology and analytics too.

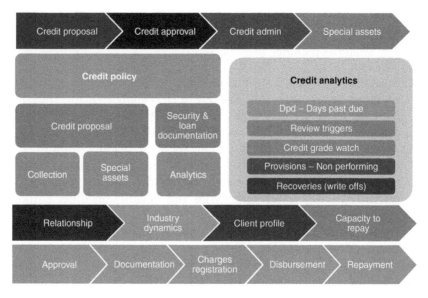

Figure 168   The credit management function – 10,000 meters view

The survival of risk

Risk functions and roles that do well have a common set of characteristics:

(a) Either they are part of an *embedded risk function* reporting directly to the head of trading/business and not the head of risk.
(b) Or, they are part of a *risk function that is led by a risk head who originally came from business* and is in effect the second most powerful person in the bank. He has direct access to the board, has a track record, a mile long whip and is not afraid to use it.
(c) Or, they are part of a team where the *risk reporting unit is created and sponsored by the business side* – not by corporate governance, compliance or regulatory reporting teams – where the risk team works hand in hand with the business team.

Assessment framework

Running a risk function at a bank is a fine balancing act between the following dimensions:

Figure 169   Dimensions of running a bank's risk function

Risk functions in an organization with a compliance driven mindset tend to stop at the first three dimensions (identification, measurement, reporting). In mature and risk driven organizations, on the other hand, the full cycle is successfully balanced. These risk teams with super survival odds because of their mandates and their sponsors have a different design for information and process flow.

1. Measurement: Automated Exception Tracking and Reporting. For instance, automated weekly tracking and reporting of DPD analysis; movement in DPD classification by branch and area office; and changes in exposure to negative sectors by branch and area office.

2. Review: Risk Audits & Stress Testing – Regular Analysis and Dissection of Risk Exposures. Risk management function dissects exposure across industry sectors, branches, regions and products for performance and actual profitability in order to identify and fix deviations from allocated risk budgets immediately.

The analysis needed is done every six months to build an internal benchmark of historical levels, track deviations, and educate risk takers and risk managers about the behavioral nature of the bank's exposure. The review is also an important step in *accountability and validation of assumptions* made in the original business, product and strategic plan. It ensures that the right expectations are set and reduces the chances of unpleasant surprises.

Once this view has been developed it is stress tested at the bank level at the same frequency to evaluate impact on growth, earning capacity, capital shortfall and internal capital adequacy targets.

1. The risk survival information flow design

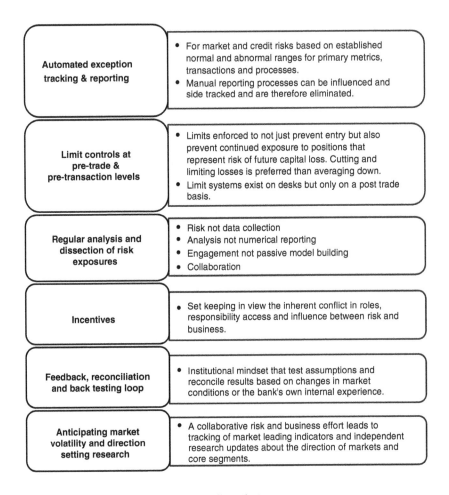

Figure 170   Risk survival information flow design

2. Risk systems for central banks

If you were tasked to build an ideal risk management system for a central bank using the above design principles, what would you look for? To answer this question you have to ask a different question first.

If you are a central bank in Europe, the Middle East, the Far East, or Central Asia, which of the following is your biggest challenge?

(a) Issuing guidelines to regulated banks on regulatory reporting and risk management?
(b) Making policy decisions that have long term economic and market impact?
(c) Collating market data and creating an economic profile of the nation that creates visibility, sets benchmarks for investors and stakeholders, allows policy decisions to be measured and evaluated objectively?
(d) Taking corrective action on items that impact and change behavior of banks and their customers in the country to ensure that key metrics such as the liquidity, private sector credit, inflation, savings, income mobility and velocity of money remain within their pre-determined ranges?
(e) Implementing banking regulation guidelines and best practices based on BIS recommendations and guidelines?

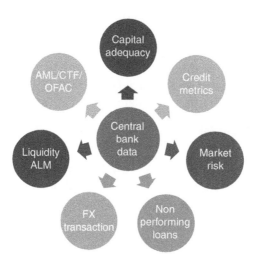

Figure 171   Risk management – risk software – central banks

The right answer would be a mix of all of the above. But the mix of all of the above relies on one crucial element that central banks all over the world collect by the megabytes, but can't do much with.

One word. *Data*. One Application. *Meaningful Metrics*.

a. Risk management for central banks – ideal end state

Here are some queries that arise on a regular basis if you are a central bank regulator in any part of the world that you can answer (with ease) if you have data and meaningful metrics.

If you don't have data and meaningful metrics, each of the answers could take a few months of allocated resources, bandwidth and time and an EXCEL spreadsheet crafted manually.

(a) What is the sector specific default rate for an SME customer? A middle market customer? A corporate or commercial customer? How much bank capital should be allocated against this rate? How does this rate vary across regions, business sectors and segments?

(b) Against the default rates identified above what is the average loss given default? The average recovery rate? What is the transition rate between non performing loan classifications?

(c) What is the distribution of collateral and guarantees? If a wave of defaults, foreclosures and forced sales flows through the banking system, which asset class will suffer the most? What would be the impact of depressed values on the national economy? On credit growth?

(d) What kind of sector or segment specific incentives can you create to ease the pain and rekindle growth?

(e) If you raise or lower the policy interest rates by 50 basis points, what will be the impact on banks' balance sheets? On P&L? On recovery rates and non performing loan classification?

(f) If you increase or reduce the forced sale value (FSV) benefit, how much flexibility can you give to regulated banks in the banking system?

b. Risk management for central banks – context

The list of questions is infinite, but the cost of a system that answers many of these questions is not. A centralized analytics driven data warehouse for central banks has been the holy grail of reporting for over two decades now, but the dream remains unrealized.

The reason is simple. You need to think like a central banker and then integrate at least 7, possibly 9, different themes and systems to get to the final warehouse design. You need to marry business, technology, banking, risk, analytics, usability and data together to get to the right reports. There are about 200 people in the world that can do this and they are all well placed and compensated enough not to get their hands dirty with selling such technology solutions or, even worse, implementing them.

The right mix of resources required to deliver on the promise of this solution includes a selling team comfortable with institutional selling, an implementation partner with influence, patience and resources, a technology team that gets the domain, and an architectural design that realizes the amounts of data a central bank receives and needs to analyze.

Getting all of them together at the same time and getting them to agree on an request for proposal (RFP) issued by a central bank is an impossible task. If you can crack it, it is a problem worth solving.

5
Stress Testing, Bank Regulation and Risk

Stress testing

In the world that we live in, operating conditions get categorized as normal, abnormal and extreme. When we spend too much in the normal state, our ability to predict, handle and react to extreme events is degraded[1]. Stress testing refers to a process through which we try and assess the impact of abnormal and extreme conditions on our processes, control systems, organization and capital.

Within financial services, stress testing takes a second dimension where the focus shifts from assessing impact to identifying breaking points; the maximum amount of stress a financial institution would be able to bear before it breaks down and fails. Think of it as breakeven analysis with a twist. Rather than looking for the point where you turn cash flow positive, look for the transition in risk levels that break the bank.

Many of the processes and controls in a financial institution are dependent on models based on assumptions. Stress testing provides a framework for testing these assumptions, as well as conditions under which assumptions will no longer hold.

The level of interconnectivity between financial markets and institutions has made this threshold of failure more important, since the failure of a single institution can trigger a deep and painful system-wide crisis that can easily turn into a regional or global contagion. Contagions are not just driven by the correlation between markets and institutions, but also by the complex interaction of changes in sentiments that trigger mass panics.

Regulators, shareholders and boards are very interested in the margin of safety an organization should maintain. While shareholders focus on incremental demands on capital, regulators use stress tests to identify weak institutions and situations where early intervention can make a difference.

Boards are also aware that the right time to develop and test a strategy for managing and handling a crisis is when operating conditions are normal and everyone can think clearly. Therefore, in addition to identifying the threshold of failure, stress testing also serves as a tool for testing reactions and responses to the crisis before it occurs.

The approach marks a move away from the old school expected value models to the new school distribution testing and fat tail models. Old school models were constrained by computational power and the complexity of account level modeling. Average risk or expectations were considered an improvement over flying blindly without any insights on risk. The growth in computational and modeling tools improved our capacity to model complexity at higher levels of detail at significantly faster speed. This increased capacity made it possible to build, store and simulate bank wide models that stand behind the new distribution testing approach.

1. A stress testing framework

To create a viable stress testing framework we need the following elements:

1. pool of metrics – elements or items that need to be measured or tracked (target accounts);
2. benchmark value for metrics – ranges and thresholds for metrics being measured (normal, critical and extreme values);
3. set of extreme scenarios or an extreme dataset – a collection of scenarios that will be used to test (based on historical crisis or simulations);
4. tests for stability – a definition of stability as well as tests (capital sufficiency);
5. tests for probability of survival (shortfall or ruin);
6. a list of core risk factors;
7. an initial crisis management plan for each of the core risk factors;
8. a criteria for evaluating the crisis management plan;
9. testing, modifying and approving the crisis management plan.

Let's start with the first step – metrics and measures that we use or are likely to focus on in our stress test.

Within banking, insurance institutions and with regulators, the original focus was on stress testing capital. Then we added liquidity, provisions, changes in collateral values and market signals. Starting off with minimum acceptable capital thresholds applicable to all players, capital guidelines slowly moved to risk-based models – models that zeroed in to risk specific to an individual institution and the amount of capital required to carry that risk. However, the question was, risk as well as capital by which definition?

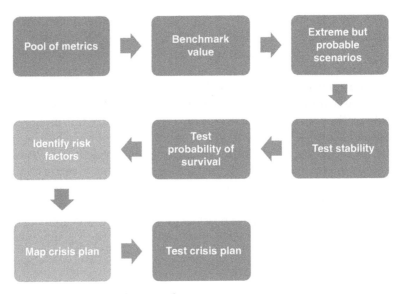

Figure 172   Stress testing framework

Thinking around capital evolved over time from the original capital sufficiency and adequacy framework to the probability of shortfall or probability of ruin framework. The shortfall framework is not a new approach.
Insurance companies and portfolio managers have been using it for the
last four decades and the idea itself originated four hundred years ago in
the late 17th century with Christiaan Huygens[2].

What is the difference between the two approaches?

The first approach (capital sufficiency) focuses on identifying the likely
ranges of value expected to be seen in the market under current and
future conditions. The objective is to create or predict an extreme set of
prices and then test the business and the underlying model. We tend to
use value at risk (VaR) measures calculated with the historical simulation
approach to identify and create a set of extreme value for prices, rates and
rolling correlations.

The second approach (shortfall) starts with capital and then assesses
the magnitude of shock that a given level of capital can comfortably bear.
Variations link the size of the shock or threshold to probabilities giving an
indicative likelihood of failure. Flipped on its head, the approach allows
us to create probability of shortfall models that display level of capital and
probability of failure side by side.

Once again we can use a VaR based model to estimate the likelihood
that a shock of a given magnitude can occur. A sophisticated board can

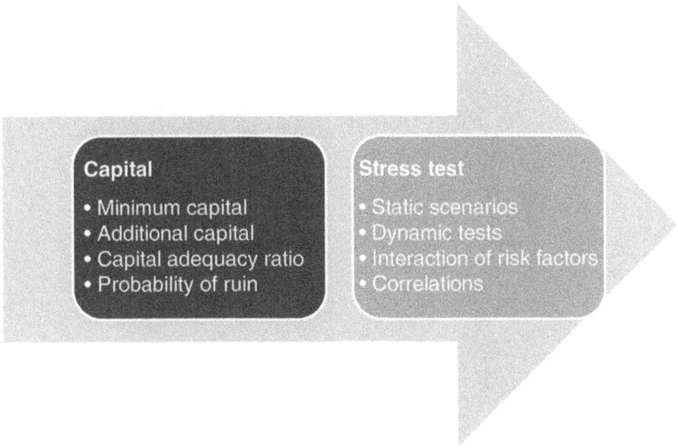

Figure 173 Capital and stress tests

then create a limit structure linked to the probability of failure of the bank. Within the insurance industry, a variation of this approach is used to calculate probability of ruin and test product pricing models.

Given the role that bank and insurance failures have played in the two great depressions our world has seen in the last 100 years, both regulators and shareholders are interested in the right amount of capital.

The right amount to do what?

(a) Operate under normal conditions – aka operating capital.
(b) Operate under stressed conditions – aka risk capital.
(c) Operate under extreme conditions – aka signaling capital[3].

There is a fine line between (b) and (c), and banking regulation and capital requirements are an ongoing battle between shareholders' interpretation of how much capital is needed to survive the occasional hiccups and the regulatory understanding of the amount of capital a bank should carry on its balance sheet before it should be allowed to solicit deposits from customers. Over the last two decades each group, regulators and shareholders, has created a model for optimal capital. Unfortunately, what is optimal from a shareholders' point-of-view is sub-optimal from a regulatory point-of-view, and vice versa.

For instance, there is a big ongoing debate about the actual category of capital on which this analysis should be focused.

1. Economic capital – the actual capital required to run a business including provisions for expected extreme conditions.

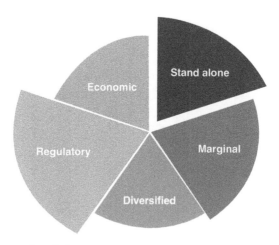

Figure 174   Types of capital

2. *Regulatory capital* – the regulatory capital required to operate a business. In most instances this should be significantly higher than economic capital.
3. *Marginal capital* – the capital required by a given business line or product assuming it operates in isolation.
4. *Diversified capital* – the capital adjusted for the benefits of synergies and correlation between business lines.

Before you decide your stance in this debate, think about a region where required regulatory capital is less than economic capital. As a regulator, would you prefer regulating in such a market?

The official speed limit on the six lane Dubai – Abu Dhabi Shaikh Zayed road is 140 km per hour. But you will find drivers driving anywhere between 100 and 200 km per hour. The actual speed a driver opts for is a function of personal risk preferences, traffic conditions, the state of the road, the vehicle being driven, the presence of mobile radar traps, the size of speeding fines and the points on your license.

Regulatory capital requirements are like speed limits. Unless aggressively enforced (radar and traffic fines) they are viewed as broad guidelines with some indiscretion tolerated as long as you don't become a threat to larger society and are not caught by a speed trap or capital inspection. Individual indiscretion when it comes to traffic fines or banking capital is a function of risk appetite (between strict compliance and desperation), market conditions (everyone else is doing it) and regulatory vigilance (resources and resolve).

Besides reviewing the basic and static capital adequacy framework, regulators are also keen on testing capital adequacy under a range of scenarios.

Some static, some a replay of historical crisis and others that are a simulation of complex interaction between all the market factors that impact the balance sheet of a bank.

Should you build a separate stress testing process for each of these capital types or build one that stress tests the variation on an incremental basis? When you report stress testing results to regulators and shareholders do you report separate results based on a specific type of capital and depending on the intended audience?

Given the myriad exposures of banks and insurance companies, this stress testing process needs to be applied on:

(a) all investment positions across bonds, currencies, equities and commodities – covered under stress testing market risk;
(b) all funding and financing choices – covered under interest rate mismatch or gap risk;
(c) all liquidity structure choices – covered by liquidity gap;
(d) all credit positions – covered by stress testing credit risk;
(e) operational elements – covered by operation risk models;
(f) correlation effects within the first four.

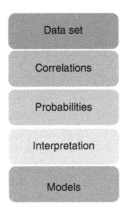

Figure 175   From data to models

This brings up a number of challenges.

• How do you maintain a dataset that cuts across the entire back office of a financial institution?
• Who is responsible?
• How do you measure and track risk correlations between your investment portfolio, your funding choices and your credit decisions?
• We know that there is a relationship, but how do we measure it?

- Even if you could measure it, how do you translate all of this in a framework that allows you to calculate probabilities?

From what we have seen so far, the above process is anything but simple. How do you create a robust and stable model that gives consistent results across normal as well as extreme conditions? How do we report it in a simplified manner to shareholders and board members who may not necessarily have the inclination or the background to understand complex statistical and computational finance concepts?

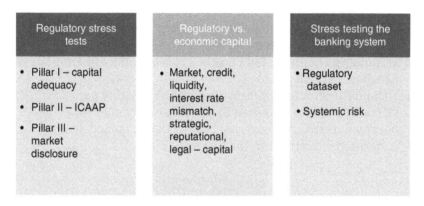

Figure 176   Bank regulatory capital and stress tests

Within the banking sector, there has been work done in creating simple as well as complex stress tests, from using data sets from extreme and turbulent events to sophisticated Monte Carlo simulators that dry run the entire bank in EXCEL spreadsheets. Twenty years ago we could only think and do static tests linked to static shocks. Today our understanding of bank capital and the challenges it faces is much more sophisticated. Events linked to the financial crises in 1987, 1998, 2001 and 2008 have made it possible to build and invest in tools not just because of regulatory pressure. There is money to be made in the tidal waves triggered by the fall of a large bank.

Evolution of banking regulation

1. The great depression and Regulation Q

The great depression circa 1929 was a watershed event for bank regulators because it showed, though not for the first time, how bank failures impact society. A number of lessons came out of that event; the two most relevant to our topic are the following.

(a) The critical role that the banking sector played in providing credit and access to capital at regional, national and global levels, and its effect on economic growth.
(b) The scale of human misery when the banking system failed and was no longer in a position to play that role.

The first attempt post depression to regulate banks came from the liability side. If there was a cap on the maximum rate a bank could pay to its depositors there was no longer an incentive for it to invest in increasingly risky assets. As long as an investment earned a reasonable spread over the cost of bank funds, a bank would stick to safer products and solutions. The culprit, in the thinking of that time, was rate-based competition for deposits – leading to increasingly risky behavior on the part of banks. If you could control cost of deposits, you could control rate-based competition and risky behavior. The thinking stayed in vogue for more than 50 years after it first came into being as Regulation Q – a part of the Banking Act, 1933 – that authorized the Federal Reserve to impose ceilings on the interest rates paid on time and savings deposits by member banks. It was in the high-inflation, high-yield 1980s that this thinking was first challenged by emerging non-banking deposit products. Why earn a miserly 2 to 4 percent before taxes when your money-market account could easily credit three to five times that amount? Challenged by non-banking sector products that changed the dynamics of the deposit market, banks could no longer compete as long as they were held back by Regulation Q. One side effect was non-price competition for deposits including over supply of branches, automated teller machines, additional banking hours, free toasters, and subsidized cash and exchange management services. The other, better-known side effect was the growth and development of the offshore Euro Dollar market. The time was now ripe for a more risk sensitive regulatory standard.

2. Basel I and amendments to the capital accord

Basel I marked the shift towards linking capital with risk taking behavior when it introduced minimum capital requirements dependent on the risk profile of a bank's credit portfolio. Introduced in 1988 as the Basel I capital accord or BIS 88, the regulatory framework took the first step towards supporting risk-based pricing and creating a level playing field as far as capital was concerned in member countries. Once the capital accord was rolled out, it became evident that credit was not the only source of risk on the balance sheet of a bank. Proprietary trading profits represented another source of volatility that banks could use to exploit risk-based gaps in the capital accord and sidestep the intent of the regulatory framework. Amendments to the capital accord followed in 1996, and became the basis for BIS 98. The revised standard now provided for calculation of market risk capital based on the profile of the trading book and a total capital adequacy ratio that factored both credit and price risk.

3. Basel II

The Basel I accord had a number of well-documented shortcomings. It ignored portfolio effects across a large, well-diversified banking book, it ignored relative credit worthiness between and across corporate and Organization for Economic Corporation & Development (OECD) borrowers, it created a regulatory loophole supporting 364 day revolving facilities with no capital charge, it did not allow for netting or provide any incentives for credit risk mitigation. It employed a simplified flat risk charge based approach so that the methodology could be applied across the industry with the least resistance and complication. However, this simplification meant that items carrying different risks were subjected to the same risk charge. These problems led to suggestions that the banking industry should be allowed to develop their own internal models to calculate the minimum capital requirements. This would serve as the credit risk equivalent of the BIS 98 standard for market risk capital requirements and allow well-diversified banks to report numbers that were more reflective of the risks carried on their balance sheets. The Basel II accord addressed some of these concerns, introduced the concept of operational risk capital and provided capital requirements for new products that were not handled in the original capital accord. It took what is now regarded as the third and final step towards capital requirements that were reflective of credit, market and operational risk.

a. Pillars of Basel II

The three pillars of Basel II merit a second, deeper look. Even though the standard lost a great deal of good will during the financial crisis, and was universally maligned, it did bring a different, more invasive approach to banking regulation.

In recent years, banking supervisory bodies have all issued their own frameworks defining how Basel II is to be implemented in their respected domains. Let's take a quick look.

The Basel II accord itself is composed of three pillars:

- minimum capital requirements,
- supervisory review,
- market discipline.

1. Minimum capital requirements

This is the first pillar, where banks would need to maintain a minimum regulatory capital amount that covers the three main risks, that is, credit, market and operational risks, that the banks face. The credit risk component can be calculated using one of a standardized approach, a foundation internal ratings-based approach or an advanced internal ratings-based approach. In the standardized approach, the risk weights are applied on the basis of the rating of the counterparty and the maturity profile of the exposure. In the internal ratings-based approaches the values of probability of default, loss given default, exposure at default and maturity are used in the computation for capital charge. The values are estimated using historical data of the bank's credit portfolio. The market risk component relies on VaR approaches to compute the risk of the exposure. For a selected portfolio, VaR shows how much you stand to lose, over a certain period and with a certain probability.

The operational risk component can be calculated using one of a basic indicator approach, a standardized approach or an advanced measurement approach. In the basic indicator approach, the average of the positive annual gross income figures is used to calculate the charge. In the standardized approach, the banks' activities are divided into eight business lines and the capital for operational risk for each of these lines is computed as a percentage of the bank's gross income from that particular line of business. In the advanced measurement approach, the institutions employ their own empirical models to calculate the required capital for operational risk.

2. Supervisory review

This is the second pillar, and it deals with the regulatory response to the first pillar and provides a framework for dealing with the residual risks such as systemic risk, pension risk, concentration risk, strategic risk, reputation risk, liquidity risk and legal risk that are not covered in the minimum capital requirements. The supervisory review process ensures that the banks have considered all material risks in the business and encourages banks to develop and use better risk management techniques in monitoring and managing their risks.

All risks that are material to the bank need to be quantified and stress tested, and the relevant procedures for carrying out this assessment, the results and additional or target capital requirements that are commensurate with the bank's risk profile and control environment would need to be communicated through an Internal Capital Adequacy Assessment Process (ICAAP) document, first to the board of directors and then to the supervisor and the market.

Supervisors evaluate the ICAAP report to see how well banks are assessing their capital needs in relation to their risks. They would expect banks to operate above, and hold more than, the minimum capital requirements. If there are deficiencies identified in the process/capital, the supervisors would intervene, and prompt, decisive action would be taken to reduce the risk or restore the capital.

3. Market discipline

This is the third pillar, and it details the obligations of the bank to disclose information to all stakeholders. The clients and shareholders should have sufficient understanding to comprehend how the bank manages its risks. The purpose is to allow more transparency and let the market have a better idea of the banks risk positions so that they can deal with the bank in a better way.

b. ICAAP requirement

Under Pillar 2, a bank must have an ICAAP in place. ICAAP consists of internal procedures and systems that ensure that the bank will possess adequate capital resources in the long term to cover all of its material risks. It involves the determination of economic capital as opposed to regulatory capital, and is a process that is run in parallel to the regulatory capital requirement determination process. Economic capital is the capital required to cover all risks, and is estimated using internal risk models of the bank. ICAAP should be an integral part of the bank's processes and must be embedded within the organization. Senior management and the board of directors (BOD) should be supportive and fully engaged in the process.

The main purpose of ICAAP is to ensure that the bank's overall capital is adequate in relation to the level of risk it takes or is subject to. The risk profile must be understood. There should be systems in place to quantify and monitor these risks. The extent and depth of the process should be proportional to the nature, size and complexity of the bank's business processes.

A pre-requisite for an effective ICAAP is, therefore, a sound risk management framework within the bank. What this entails is that the bank should be subject to strong and effective levels of BOD and senior management oversight, an effective risk monitoring and review process, where the policies and procedures that are used to identify, assess and report all material risks are credible, and a system or process of regular and independent review of ICAAP and its review process.

Within the ICAAP framework, the BOD and senior management have the following responsibilities.

- They must set the level of risk appetite/risk tolerance of the bank.
- They must ensure that the bank operates within the set level of risk tolerance.
- They must task the bank's management to establish a framework for ICAAP. This includes:
  - identifying risks through a thorough analysis of the bank's activities, its business units, the market environment, historical scenarios, and so on;
  - assessing the materiality of the risks identified based on pre-specified levels of materiality;
  - quantifying material risks – the models used to quantify the risks should be appropriate based on the level of materiality of the risk being assessed;
  - assessing capital requirements in relation to risks;
  - assessing additional capital requirements for stressed scenarios and capital planning for this additional capital;
  - reconciling ICAAP's economic capital with Pillar 1 capital;
  - reporting and monitoring compliance of the actual processes with those outlined through internal policies and limits.

The purpose of documenting ICAAP is as follows.

- Inform the bank's BOD of the ongoing assessment of all of the firm's risks. This includes:
  - risks that are not fully captured during the Pillar 1 process, such as concentration risks, residual risks that arise from credit risk mitigation, and so on;
  - risks that are not taken into account in the Pillar 1 process, such as liquidity risk, interest rate risk, strategic risk, reputation risk, concentration risk, securitization risk, pension obligation risk, insurance risk, and so on;
  - risk factors which are external to the bank, such as risk arising due to regulatory, economic, business, and so on, situations.
- Inform the BOD and senior management of the key results of the risk assessments, how the firm intends to mitigate those risks, how much current and future capital is necessary, and any issues that could arise
- Explain its ICAAP to the supervisor.

The ICAAP report must be approved by the BOD or senior management. Therefore, the report must be in a format that is easily understood at this level, and must contain all necessary information so that the BOD, and in turn the supervisor, may be able to make informed judgments and decisions regarding the appropriate level of capital to be maintained and the risk management approach used by the bank.

In the assessment of risk, ICAAP must employ a consistent, sound and comprehensive approach for deriving risk measures for all the risks that are material to the bank. By consistent, we mean that the assessment must be in line with the bank's level of risk tolerance and must be calibrated to be not less than the risk tolerance levels assumed for Pillar 1 assessment. However, it may not be possible to arrive at a quantitative assessment for some risks, which are more difficult to quantify. In such cases, a qualitative assessment and management judgment must be employed in arriving at reasonable risk estimates. In addition, it is important that for all capital and risk models employed, a degree of qualitative assessment and management judgment with regard to the inputs and outputs of the model must be undertaken. The bottom line is that ICAAP should include all material risks, regardless of whether such risks are easily quantifiable or not.

An ICAAP framework should be forward looking. It must account for factors such as changes in the bank's strategic plan and a range of different business conditions at varying points in the business cycle that could impact the bank's capital adequacy. Stress tests should be performed to identify plausible severe loss events and adverse changes in market conditions. Stress scenarios should be based on historical movements during times of crisis or based on expert judgment, and must include supervisory, historical, bank-specific and hypothetical scenarios. The current and future capital requirements must be considered in relation to the bank's near and longer-term capital needs, capital expenditures required for the foreseeable future, target capital levels and external capital sources.

ICAAP should distinguish between the bank's regulatory (that is, minimum) capital requirements, the actual capital that it holds and the amount of internal capital that it would need to hold for business purposes based on the capital adequacy assessment process. Banks not only have to compute the economic capital under ICAAP, they also need to reconcile this capital with regulatory capital. This involves comparing the internal model and assumptions with the regulatory model and assumptions and then attributing the differences in results to specific factors.

ICAAP should incorporate an adequate risk monitoring and report process. This process should be able to identify how changes in the bank's profile would impact the bank's capital requirements. The system employed should allow management and BOD to receive regular reports or updates of the bank's risk profile and capital needs which would allow them to:

- evaluate the level and trend of the material risks and the effect on capital;
- evaluate the sensitivity and reasonableness of the assumptions used in assessments;
- determine the sufficiency of capital against various risks;
- determine whether the bank is meeting its internal capital adequacy goals;
- determine whether future capital requirements based on forward looking factors are in line with the banks risk profile.

ICAAP should be reviewed on a regular, dynamic basis to ensure that it continues to assess all material risks and that the capital coverage is adequate and reflects the risk profile of the bank. The process would need to be reviewed if there are changes in the strategic focus, business plan, operating environment and other factors that could materially affect its assumptions and methodologies.

ICAAP and its review process should be subject to an independent internal review to ensure the integrity, reasonableness and accuracy of the process. It should also be subject to internal and external audits to ensure that:

- it remains appropriate with regard to the nature, size and complexity of the bank's operations;
- the data inputs used are complete and accurate;
- the severe loss scenarios that are considered are reasonable and valid;
- the methodology, assumptions and inputs of stress tests are adequately analyzed and appropriate.

4. Basel III

Subsequent to the financial crisis of 2008, amendments were suggested to the capital accord to address some of the loopholes and deficiencies in Basel II. The changes in Basel III over Basel II include:

1. higher risk weights for risky (trading and securitization) assets;
2. more assets and exposures brought into the RWA calculations;
3. less reliance on external rating agencies;
4. CVA capital charge to account for the market risk of counterparty credit risk on over-the-counter (OTC) derivatives;
5. counterparty credit risk will be based on stressed parameters;

6. correlations with financial institutions will be assessed a higher risk weight/multiplier to account for systemic risk between institutions;
7. additional margin requirements for illiquid derivative exposures;
8. higher regulatory capital requirement and much better quality of capital with greater loss absorbing capacity:
   (a) increase in Tier 1 Capital from 4 percent to 6 percent (cannot include hybrid instruments that have incentives to redeem before maturity);
   (b) increase in common equity in Tier 1 Capital from 2 percent to 4.5 percent;
   (c) eliminate Tier 3 Capital;
   (d) regulatory adjustments will be deducted from common equity (that is, only the net amount of common equity is counted towards minimum required Tier 1 common equity);
   (e) capital conservation buffer (distribution of earnings is restricted if the buffer is not met, a cushion to absorb losses in times of financial and economic stress);
   (f) counter cyclical capital buffer (capital is built up in times of increased aggregate asset (credit) growth and may be reduced when there is a down turn);
   (g) absolute non-risk weighted leverage ratio of Tier 1 Capital to total exposures;
   (h) systemically important financial institutions will be required to have loss absorbing capacity in excess of the other financial institutions subject to BASEL III;
9. requirements for effective management of liquidity risk:
   (a) liquidity coverage ratio (LCR);
   (b) net stable funding ratio (NSFR);
   (c) metrics for monitoring liquidity risk;
10. enhanced supervisory review and disclosures.

a. Basel III liquidity reforms

1. Global liquidity ratio adjustments

Another reaction to the crisis was the liquidity ratio updates to the Basel II standard, also known as Basel III adjustments.

The Basel Committee has published the liquidity portion of the Basel III reforms[4] to the capital and liquidity framework. These reforms cover the supervisory framework for liquidity risk measurement via two minimum funding liquidity standards.

According to the reforms to the capital and liquidity framework, Basel III would require the banking sector to maintain and monitor two key minimum funding liquidity standards as part of the supervisory/regulatory approach to managing liquidity risk. This would be in addition to the supervisory assessments that regulators would be required to undertake to review whether liquidity risk management frameworks set up by the banks are consistent and in line with the seventeen basic principles of liquidity risk management as set out in the Basel Committee's published document "Principles for Sound Liquidity Risk Management and Supervision[5]".

The two standards are LCR and NSFR.

The former is a measure of the strength of the short-term liquidity position of the banks. It implies that banks should hold, on a continuous basis, sufficient unencumbered, high-quality assets that can easily be converted into cash to meet liquidity needs that could arise during a 30-calendar day period of significantly severe liquidity stress. The stress scenario is specified by the supervising authority through various parameters applicable to elements of the ratio and in general considers and incorporates most of the shocks to liquidity experienced during the recent financial and liquidity crisis. It is given by the following ratio:

LCR = Value of stock of high-quality liquid assets in
stressed conditions/Total net cash outflows.

The value of this ratio should be greater than or equal to 100 percent. It will come into effect in 2015.

The NSFR is a measure of the bank's longer-term liquidity risk profile. It covers a horizon of one year, under conditions of extended firm-specific stress, and aims to dissuade banks from relying on short-term funding of their longer-term assets. Rather, they should rely on more stable sources of funding on an ongoing basis. In essence, it is hoped that the ratio will ensure that any short-term structural funding liquidity mismatches are effectively captured, which can then ensure that they are addressed and removed and that the bank can move to more stable longer-term funding. The NSFR is given by the following ratio:

NSFR = Available amount of stable funding/
Required amount of stable funding

The value of this ratio should be greater than or equal to 100 percent. It will come into effect in 2018.

The calculations of these ratios rely on parameters applicable to various elements of the detailed formulation of these ratios. Most of these parameters are prescribed by the Committee and are said to be internationally calibrated. However, there are some parameters that would be specific to the jurisdictions in which the bank operates. In these instances, national supervisors would be responsible for determining the parameters. In addition, national supervisors may also subject individual banks to stricter standards or parameters based on the assessment of how that bank's liquidity risk management shapes up against the Committee's published basic liquidity risk management principles. Both ratios will be subject to an observation period prior to their implementation deadlines, during which time their calibration and designs will be monitored and assessed to ensure that there are no unintended consequences to the banking sector and financial system because of their introduction.

2. Metrics for monitoring liquidity risk

Besides the two supervisory standards proposed in the Basel III liquidity reforms, the liquidity framework also presents five metrics that would be used by banks to monitor their liquidity positions on a consistent basis. National supervisory authorities have the discretion of suggesting additional measures that could be used to monitor liquidity, as well as acting as early warning indicators of liquidity stress.

The measures mentioned in the Basel III document are as follows.

a. Contractual maturity mismatch

This presents the contractual cash and security inflows and outflows from all on- and off-balance sheet items for each defined maturity time band. It is used to identify the maturity gaps and mismatches for each maturity time band defined.

b. Concentration of funding

There are three metrics measured within this tool, one each for assessing wholesale funding concentrations by counterparty, product/instrument and currency. They are used to identify significant sources of funding that, if withdrawn, could lead to a liquidity crisis for the bank. Significant funding sources, by counterparty or product, are assumed to be those having a value greater than 1 percent of the bank's total balance sheet, whereas by currency, it is assumed to be those with aggregate liabilities denominated in that currency over 5 percent of the bank's total liabilities. The specific metrics are calculated as follows.

(a) By counterparty: Funding Liabilities sourced from each significant counterparty/Balance Sheet Total.
(b) By product: Funding Liabilities sourced from each significant product/Balance Sheet Total.
(c) By currency: Asset and Liability amounts/significant currency.

c. Available unencumbered assets

This is a report of the amount, currency, type and location of, and estimated haircuts applicable to, available unencumbered assets, which can be used as collateral in the secondary markets and/or are central bank eligible.

d. LCR by significant currency

This metric allows banks and supervisors to track potential currency mismatches under a stress scenario. It is given by the following ratio:

Foreign Currency LCR = Value of stock of high-quality liquid assets in each significant currency/Total net cash outflow over the next 30 day period in each significant currency.

e. Market-related monitoring tools

This involves the use of high frequency market data, having little or no time lag, to identify signs of potential liquidity stress. This data is to be monitored at the following levels.

Market-wide

- Equity prices
- Debt markets
- Foreign exchange markets
- Commodities markets
- Product indices

Financial sector

- Equity prices
- Debt markets
- Product indices

Bank-specific

- Equity prices
- Credit Default Swap (CDS)/credit spreads
- Money-market trading prices
- Rollovers and prices by funding length
- Yield on bank-issued debt

5. Comprehensive capital analysis and review (CCAR) – the US response

The 2008 financial crisis and the eventual failure of Lehman Brother triggered a review of banking supervision practices in the US. The biggest benefit of the crisis and the troubled asset relief program (TARP) were the dreaded stress tests, namely the comprehensive capital analysis and review (CCAR) exercise.

Large bank holding companies in the US are required to submit on an annual basis a BOD approved comprehensive capital plan to the Federal

Reserve. The plan is a long run (2 year/9 quarter) forward looking quantitative and qualitative review of the firm's ICAAPs and capital resource management strategies.

Key components of the plan include:

- description of regulatory capital base, key contractual terms of capital instruments and management plans to retire, refinance or replace the instruments over the planning period;
- description of capital distribution plan over the 2 year horizon, including actions taken to reduce distributions in adverse environments;
- description of processes and policies used to determine the size of the dividend and stock repurchases under different operating conditions;
- an assessment of the potential losses, earnings and other resources that may be used to absorb losses in stressful environments and how these losses may impact the firm's capital adequacy and capital needs, that is, the sensitivity of the bank's projected capital ratios was tested for changes to loss and earnings estimates;
- an assessment of the post-stress test capital requirement for a firm to ensure that it continues operating and meeting its obligations and functioning as a credit intermediary.

If economic or financial conditions deteriorate as compared to those assumed when drawing up the original plan, or if there is a change in the firm's risk profile, business strategy or corporate structure, then the firm is required to submit a revised comprehensive capital plan with revised capital distribution proposals.

Currently the Federal Reserve assesses these plans in five areas on a firm specific as well as horizontal (industry wide) perspective. These include the following.

(a) Quantitative and qualitative reviews of the robustness of the firm's capital adequacy assessments, planning and allocation of capital resources processes, including firm wide risk measurement and management practices. This consists of whether the firm is able to calibrate and maintain an internal target level of capital over time and the effectiveness of implementation risk policies and procedures, governance over internal capital adequacy assessments, comprehensiveness of capital plans and planning processes.

(b) The acceptability and appropriateness of the capital distribution policy over the planning horizon. This is done to ensure that capital actions are well supported by capital resources and are consistent with the firm's capital plan under a number of financial and economic scenarios, its internal capital adequacy processes and corporate governance as well as Federal Reserve expectations.

(c) An assessment of the plans for repaying any US government investment made, before increasing or renewing capital distributions to shareholders.

(d) Stress testing to assess the firm's ability to absorb losses for a range of economic, financial market and operational events. This includes the ability of the plan to capture all material risks under stressed conditions by way of translating risk exposures into potential loss estimates. The outputs assessed are quarterly projections of a firm's regulatory capital ratio over a 9 quarter planning horizon under three scenarios (a firm generated baseline most likely scenario, a firm generated stress scenario and an adverse supervisory stress scenario generated by the Federal Reserve). The latter scenario covers an additional four quarters. In addition, the largest firms are also required to estimate losses under a very conservative global market shock scenario.

(e) An assessment of the plans for meeting the enhanced capital requirements in Basel III and the Dodd-Frank Act. To assess the impact of Basel III requirements, the firms needed to provide forecasts of regulatory and capital ratios using the fully-phased in target capital levels for at least a two year period. The firms were also required to provide their strategies for taking account of certain provisions of Basel III and the Dodd-Frank Act such as strategies for restricting or precluding certain capital instruments, improving risk modeling, changing business focus or operations that impacted risk weighted assets, leverage ratio assets or capital.

Areas (c) and (e) are relevant for the firms as long as these issues continue to impact the firms' capital adequacy, planning and management processes. In the future, the Federal Reserve may identify and evaluate other areas of assessment. Also, assessments of areas (a), (b) and (d) will continue to evolve as financial and economic conditions change and new ways of measuring and managing risk evolve over time.

Firms are required to submit a significant amount of support analysis and data to help in the evaluation of their plans.

Why doesn't bank regulation work?

The relevant history of bank regulation for our generation actually starts with the great depression and ends with the 2008 financial crisis. Regulation is not static, generally consensus driven, debated through years of exposure drafts and comment periods and, as we have seen, is quite sophisticated.

Given these complex models, tools and requirements, it is difficult to understand why regulation doesn't work. It is one thing for a given bank to fail in a decade; it is another when the entire system collapses across the world. This is the common question asked by everyone – students, academics, consumers, politicians and activists.

Figure 177   Evolution of banking regulation

Why doesn't banking regulation really work?

(a) If you look at the evolution and history of what we call banking today, you will realize that banks have been around much longer than bank regulation. This means that banks have a lot more experience in dealing with regulators and regulation than regulators themselves, and is the reason why big banks are so successful in short circuiting efforts that they see as harmful to the long-term interests of the financial services industry.

(b) Much like the field of medicine, banking regulation has been an experimental science, not driven by research or needs but by crisis and calls for actions. Given its reactive nature, it is driven by people who understand banking best – bankers. Banking regulation partly doesn't work because bankers have too much say in deciding the shape and form of regulation.

(c) Models and technology are only small pieces of the puzzle. A much larger piece is incentives and organizational design. While regulators have tried to model the impact of both elements, like all attempts to tame complex systems, their designs have often fallen short. If that isn't bad enough, employees and management at regulated businesses are more driven and aware of identifying short circuits and arbitrage opportunities within the regulatory framework.

(d) On the incentive front, there is a design problem in how the risk function is structured and managed within financial institutions. By the law of unintended consequences, matters became much worse by segregating the risk function from business. While the conflict of interest argument made sense when separation was originally debated, its implementation was a failure. There are exceptions, and some organizations did get it right. But in general risk functions suffer chronically from staffing challenges, the influences they exert on the actual risk taking behavior, their understanding of risk and its interaction with business, as well as their bite and teeth when faced with non-compliance. While the grand design was impressive and textbooks paint a majestic picture, the risk animal in real life is a sorry portrait. It would be generous to describe it as a lame duck.

But does this mean we should give up on regulation and risk? Allow the market to self regulate and determine for itself the right doses of risk? Did that work well in the 1920s and 1930s? Did it work during the last decade?

Regulators have not taken this lying down. There has been a response, and the risk function and risk reporting landscapes are slowly changing. CCAR, ICAAP and the liquidity adjustments to the Basel II frameworks are all big wins.

Annexure 1 – Capital estimation for liquidity risk management

Capital estimation for liquidity risk management is a difficult exercise. It comes up as part of the internal liquidity risk management process, as well as the ICAAP. By definition, banks take a small return on asset (1 to 1.5 percent) and use leverage and turnover to scale it to a 12 to 18 percent return on equity. When market conditions change and a bank becomes the subject of a name crisis and a subsequent liquidity run, the same process becomes the basis for a death chant for the bank. We try to de-lever the bank by selling assets and paying down liabilities, and the process quickly turns into a fire sale driven by the speed at which word gets out about the crisis.

Reducing leverage by distressed asset sales to generate cash is one of the primary defense mechanisms used by the operating teams responsible for shoring up cash reserves.

Unfortunately, every slice of value lost to the distressed sale process is a slice out of the equity pool or capital base of the bank. An alternate

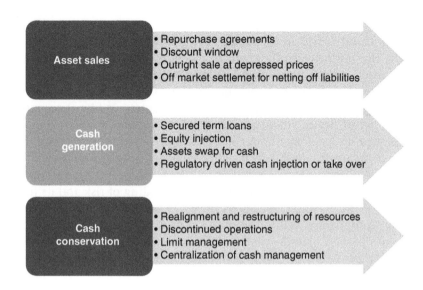

Figure 178   Increasing cash reserves

mechanism that can protect capital is to use the Interbank Repurchase (Repo) contract with liquid or acceptable assets as collateral, but that too is dependent on the availability of unencumbered liquid securities on the balance sheet as well as availability of counterparty limits. Both can quickly disappear in times of crisis. The last and final option is the central bank discount window, the use of which may provide temporary relief but serves as a double-edged sword by further feeding the name and reputational crisis. While a literature review on the topic also suggests cash conservation approaches by a re-alignment of businesses and a restructuring of resources, these last two solutions assume that the bank in question would actually survive the crisis to see the end stage benefits of re-alignment and restructuring.

1. Liquidity reserves: real or a mirage

A questionable assumption that often comes up when we review liquidity contingency plans is the availability or usage of statutory liquidity (SLR) and cash reserves (CRR) held for our account with the central bank. You can only touch those assets when your franchise and license is gone and the bank has been shut down. This means that if you want to survive the crisis with your banking license intact, there is a very good chance that the 6 percent core liquidity you had factored into your liquidation analysis would NOT be available to you as a going concern in times of

Figure 179   Liquidity risk and liquidity run crisis

crisis. That liquidity layer has been reserved by the central bank as the last defense for depositor protection, and no central bank is likely to grant abuse of that layer to a going concern bank.

As the Bear Stearns case study (see Annexure 2) illustrates, the typical liquidity crisis begins with a negative event that can take many shapes and forms. The resulting coverage and publicity leads to pressure on not just the share price, but also the asset portfolio carried on the bank's balance sheet, as market players take defensive cover by selling their own inventory or aggressive bets by short selling the securities in question. Somewhere in this entire process, ratings agencies finally wake up and downgrade the issuer across the board, leading to a reduction or cancellation of counterparty lines. Even when lines are not cancelled given the write down in value witnessed in the market, calls for margin and collateral start coming in and further feed liquidity pressures.

What triggers a name crisis that leads to a vicious cycle that can destroy the inherent value in a 90-year old franchise in less than three months? Typically, a name crisis is triggered by a change in market conditions that impacts a fundamental business driver for the bank. The change in market conditions triggers either a large operational loss or a series of operational losses, at times related to a correction in asset prices, at other times resulting in a permanent reduction in margins and spreads. What happens next depends on when this is declared and becomes public knowledge, and what the bank does to restore confidence. One approach used by management teams is to defer the news for as long as possible by creative accounting or accounting hand waving, which simply changes the nature of the crisis from an asset price or margin related crisis to a much more serious regulatory or accounting scandal with similar end results.

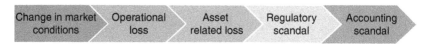

Figure 180   What triggers a name crisis?

The problem, however, is that market players have a very well established defensive response to a name crisis after four decades of bank failures. This implies that once you hit a crisis, the speed with which you generate cash, lock in a deal with a buyer and get rid of questionable assets determines how much value you will lose to the market driven liquidation process. The only failsafe here is the ability of the local regulator and lender of last resort to keep the lifeline of counterparty and interbank credit lines open. As was observed at the peak of the crisis in North America, UK and a number of Middle Eastern markets, this ability to keep markets open determines how low prices will go, the magnitude of the fire sale, the length of the correction cycle and the number of banks that actually go under.

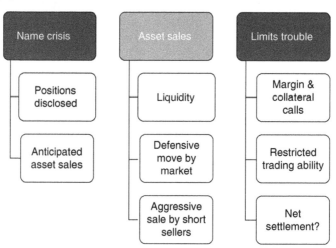

Figure 181   Market response to a name crisis and the liquidity run cycle

The above context provides a clear roadmap for building a framework for liquidity risk management. The ending position or the end game is a liquidity driven asset sale. A successful framework would simply jump the gun and get to the asset sale before the market does. The only reason why you would not jump the gun is if you have cash, a secured contractually bound commitment for cash, a white knight or any other acceptable buyer for your franchise and an agreement on the sale price and shareholders' approval for that sale in place. If you are missing any of the above, your only defense is to get to the asset sale before the market does.

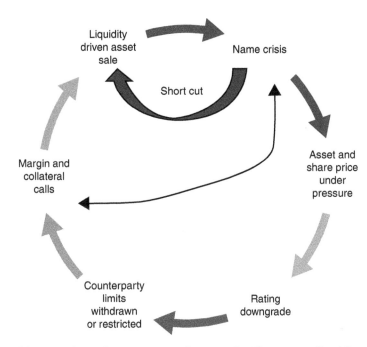

Figure 182   Liquidity risk management framework – Short cut to liquidity driven asset sale

The problem with the above assertion is the responsiveness of the BOD and the senior executive team to the seriousness of the name crisis. The most common response by both is a combination of the following.

1. The crisis is temporary and will pass. If there is a need we will sell later.
2. We cannot accept these fire sale prices.
3. There must be another option. Please investigate and report back.

This happens especially when the liquidity policy process is run as a compliance checklist and does not run its full course at the board and executive management level. If instead a full-blown liquidity simulation is run for the board and the senior management team, and they see for themselves the consequences of the speed of a liquidity crisis, as well as delay in response, that is, asset sale, their reactions would be different. The time for debate is before the crisis hits, not during a meltdown. The board and the senior management team must understand that illiquid assets are equivalent to high explosives, and a delay in asset sales is analogous to a short fuse. When you combine the two with a name crisis you will blow up the bank irrespective of its history or the power of its franchise. When the likes of Bear, Lehman, Merrill, AIG and Morgan failed, your bank and board are not likely to see a different or more pleasant fate through the crisis.

2. Estimating capital for liquidity risk: the framework

If we agree on the above, then from a liquidity risk capital estimation point-of-view you have to answer the following questions.

1. What would a liquidity driven disruption of normal business cost your bank in terms of opportunity and real costs? The primary focus of this question is the loss of future business and loss of spread on that business.
2. What is the expected contraction in balance sheet size and spread income that your bank will suffer in case of a liquidity crisis within its existing books of business? (Not future but current.)
3. What is the expected loss that will be realized due to a fire sale of liquid and illiquid assets to shore up cash reserves?
4. What is the additional interest expense that your bank will book in case of tightening of credit markets?

The actual estimated liquidity risk capital would be a weighted combination of the above four elements. How do we actually go about determining this capital estimate for liquidity risk?

Start with a valuation model and do a full valuation for the business on an as is-going-concern basis. If you like you can calibrate the model with the current market price of your institution. Let's call this Base Case A. Now reduce the growth rate to zero. This revised price is Base Case B. Now turn the growth negative by the estimated reduction in your book size. This is Base Case C. The difference between Base Case B and Base Case A is your capital estimate for (1) above. The difference between Base Case C and Base Case B gives you the capital estimate for (2).

The third piece (liquidation cost) is more complex and would require an asset by asset estimate of liquidity haircuts (VaR driven) but is a purely mechanical exercise. The last and final piece is simpler and is your current liquidity gap (or your expected liquidity gap) multiplied by the worst case (a VaR estimate) incremental interest rate cost you are likely to experience in a liquidity crisis.

Combine the four pieces and you have an initial estimate for liquidity risk capital, which can be fine tuned in later iterations.

Annexure 2 – Liquidity driven bank failures and near misses[6]

1. Case study: Bear Stearns

When property values began to plummet in 2006–7, subprime mortgage payers in the US defaulted on their payments, which initiated a chain reaction whereby there was a significant drop in the cash inflows from these mortgages, which would have been used to pay off the obligations on the derivate instruments. With the decline in property value and the subsequent impact on mortgage payments, the values of the mortgage-backed derivative instruments also fell as investors tried to liquidate their positions in these instruments in a relatively illiquid market.

a. The beginning of the name crisis

On June 14, 2007 Bears Stearns reported a decline of 10 percent in profits for the second quarter over the previous quarter's profits to US$ 486 million. On June 18, 2007 Merrill Lynch seized US$ 850 million of collateral comprising of thinly traded collateralized debt obligations (CDOs) from one of Bear's hedge funds that were heavily invested in subprime mortgages. The seizure was due to increased margin calls as well as failures of payment of debt obligations by the hedge fund because of the depressed values and illiquid markets for its assets. When Merrill Lynch went to liquidate these derivatives, they were only able to do so fractionally (only US$ 100 million worth could be auctioned) and that too at marked-down values because of the lack of market liquidity for these instruments.

This led to Bear Stearns pledging US$ 3.2 billion in secured loans to bail out one of its subprime hedge funds, Bear Stearns High-Grade Structured Credit Fund, on June 22, 2007. It also began negotiating loans with other banks against its collateral to bail out another hedge fund, Bear Stearns High-Grade Structured Credit Enhanced Leveraged Fund. This was done in order to counter what the failure of these hedge funds could do to its reputation as well as how the asset values would be impacted if the collateral continued to be sold in the illiquid and depressed market.

On July 17, 2007, as a result of the continually declining value of subprime mortgages and the resulting fall in asset values of the derivative securities, Bear Stearns revealed to its clients that the hedge funds had lost all or almost all of their value. Investors in the two hedge funds sued Bear Stearns for the collapse of the funds and sought arbitration claims saying that the bank had misled them about its exposure to these funds. In response the funds filed for bankruptcy protection on August 1, 2007 and the company froze the assets of a third fund. The amount lost was around US$ 1.6 billion.

The co-president and the person responsible for the management of these funds, Warren Spector, who was much touted to succeed Bear Stearns' chief executive James Cayne, resigned on August 5, 2007 following the collapse of the funds. On August 6, 2007, the bank reassured clients by letter that the company was financially sound with the necessary experience and expertise to deal with challenging markets. On August 17, 2007 Bear Stearns cut 240 jobs from the loan origination units of the bank.

On September 20, 2007, the bank reported a drop of 61 percent in profits for the quarter to US$ 171 million. In early October 2007, Bear Stearns' CEO and president informed the public that most of its businesses were beginning to recover. It cut an additional 300 jobs. On October 22, 2007, it received an injection into its funding when it entered a share-swap deal with CITIC, China's largest state-owned securities firm. Under the deal CITIC would pay Bear Stearns US$ 1 billion for a 6 percent share in the bank, with an option to buy a further 3.9 percent of the investment bank, and in return Bear Stearns would eventually pay a similar amount for a 2 percent share in CITIC.

On November 14, 2007, Bear Stearns' CFO, Molinaro, reported that it would write down its assets and book a fourth quarter loss. This resulted in a ratings downgraded by S&P 500 from A+ to A, stating that the outlook was negative. At the end of November 2007, Bear Stearns released news that it planned to further reduce its global workforce by 4 percent, or 650 jobs. In early December 2007 Joe Lewis, an influential shareholder, increased his share in Bear Stearns on grounds that he believed the bank's shares to be undervalued and that the bank was on its way to recovery.

The bank registered its first loss in its 85-year history in the fourth quarter of 2007, amounting to US$ 854 million due to a write down of US$ 1.9 billion of the value of its holdings of mortgage assets. Barclays bank sued Bear Stearns for allegedly misleading them about the performance of the two collapsed hedge funds, which were pledged as collateral against a US$ 400 million loan granted to Bear's asset management division.

Top employees of the company said they'd skip their bonuses, but they, including the CEO, Cayne, sold their company's stock, together worth over US$ 20 million, in December 2007. James Cayne resigned as CEO in early January 2008, though remained as the bank's non-executive chairman with a remaining 5 percent share in the bank. Moody's Investors Service downgraded the ratings of 46 tranches issued by Bear Stearns in 2006 (including 24 to junk status) and an additional eleven tranches of Alt-A deals issued in 2007 were also placed under review for possible downgrade based on higher than expected rates of default and foreclosure.

Due to the news of the quarter's losses, sales of stock by the top employees and downgrades of its derivative securities, including a more general concern that the US economy would slip into a recession, Bears Stearns' share price fell drastically by more than 20 percent. As a result of this fall, it was reported in mid-February 2008 that CITIC, the Chinese state-owned lender, had begun to renegotiate their share-swap agreement with the bank.

On March 7, 2008, Carlyle Capital Corporation, a hedge fund that had suffered because of the subprime crisis, had received substantial margin calls and default notices from its lenders. Due to this it had its shares suspended in Amsterdam. As the Carlyle Group was founded by Bear Stearns, which also had a 15 percent shareholding in the Carlyle Capital Corporation, many investors and clients viewed Bear Stearns as being heavily exposed to it. This fuelled concerns regarding whether or not the investment bank had sufficient cash/funds to do business. The cost of insuring US$ 10 million worth of Bear Stearns credit default swap debt went from US$ 350,000 to over US$ 1 million. Borrowing costs for Bear Stearns began to rise sharply.

In response to this, Bear issued a press release on March 10, 2008 stating that there were no grounds for any rumors regarding their lack of liquidity, saying that it has US$ 17 billion in cash. However, the fact that a public announcement was made was read as a signal by many Wall Street experts that the bank was in trouble. There were also reports that a major bank had refused to lend to Bear via a repo transaction a short-term loan of $2 billion and therefore rumors persisted that the bank was losing confidence among its creditors.

On March 11, 2008 Bear continued to reassure its customers and investors that nothing was wrong with its liquidity position, with CFO Molinaro announcing on CNBC that the rumors were false. However, on the same day Goldman Sach's credit derivatives group told its clients via email that it would no longer step in on their behalf to execute derivative deals with Bear Stearns. Other banks also refused to provide further credit protection against Bear Stearns debt.

On March 12, 2008, the CEO Alan Schwartz gave a televised assurance to investors that there was no liquidity crisis and that the first quarter of 2008 would likely turn a profit for the bank. However, when the news regarding the Gold Sach's email leaked into the market many more hedge funds and clients began withdrawing their funds from the bank. Banks were backing out of providing credit and Bear Stearns credit lines were dramatically reduced. Hedge funds, mutual funds and capital management companies stopped using Bear Stearns' brokerage service for executing their trades.

On March 13, 2008, Carlyle Capital Corporation hedge fund collapsed, which resulted in a fall in the Bear Stearns share price of 17 percent.

The CEO publicly continued to maintain that all was well and that the collapse of the hedge fund and subsequent fall in share value had not weakened the bank's balance sheet. However, liquidity had now dropped to US$ 2 billion. Schwartz approached JP Morgan to negotiate a rescue package. In the meantime the bank contacted a major client to encourage them to publicly express their confidence in Bear. The client declined.

On March 14, 2008 Bear Stearns confirmed the news that they had secured short-term funding amounting to US$ 30 billion from JP Morgan, the clearing agent for its collateral, in order to stabilize its position, strengthen its liquidity and meet the demands of its lenders. The collateral pledged would be backed by the Federal Reserve Bank of New York against the risk of its decline. However, this funding was not sufficient to quell fears by investors regarding Bear Stearns' financial stability, and share prices fell by more than 40 percent on the news. S&P and Moody's slashed ratings on the bank to just above junk status with a warning that further downgrades were possible.

On March 16, 2008, JP Morgan announced that it had acquired Bear Stearns for US$ 2 per share. By March 24, 2008, the offer was raised to US$ 10 per share in order to appease Bear Stearns shareholders. This was eventually approved by them.

b. Timelines

December 20, 2007: BS records fourth quarter loss, writes down mortgage assets of US$ 1.9 billion. Is sued by Barclays for misleading hedge fund performance.

December 28, 2007: Employees sell BS stock worth US$ 20 million.

Early January 2008: CEO James Cayne resigns. Moody's downgrade of MBS tranches issued by BS.

Mid-January 2008: Over 20 percent fall in BS share price.

March 7, 2008: Shares of Carlyle Capital Corporation (CCC), to which BS has significant exposure, suspended because of margin calls and defaults notices by lenders. Triggers concerns regarding liquidity.

March 10, 2008: BS press release to reassure investors that liquidity concerns are false. Rumors of loss of confidence and cancellation of credit facilities.

March 11, 2008: CFO says rumors are false. Goldman Sachs says it will not stand in for clients if they wish to undertake derivative deals with BS.

March 12, 2008: CEO says no liquidity crisis on CNBC and that quarter will show profit. Banks withdraw credit lines and clients stop using BS brokerage.

March 13, 2008: CCC hedge fund collapses. BS share price falls 17 percent. CEO announces all is well. Liquidity falls from US$ 17 billion to US$ 2 billion.

CEO approaches JP Morgan for rescue package and clients to express confidence in BS publicly. Latter declined.

March 14, 2008: BS says JP Morgan with Fed Reserve has agreed to provide funding. Share price falls 40 percent. S&P and Moody's cut BS ratings.

March 16, 2008: JP Morgan announces that they have acquired BS for US$2 per share.

2. Case study: Lehman Brothers

Between 2003 and 2004 Lehman Brothers acquired five mortgage lenders, including the subprime originator BNC Mortgage LLC and Alt-A mortgage originator Aurora Loan Services. During the house price bubble these acquisitions contributed to Lehman achieving record revenues and becoming the fastest growing investment bank or asset management company by revenue. In 2007 it surpassed Bear Stearns in becoming the largest underwriter for mortgage-backed securities. It retained a significant portion of these securities on its books, amounting to US$ 85 billion or around four times its equity. Due to this growth its share price reached an all-time high of US$ 86 in February 2007.

On March 13, 2007 the stock market suffered its largest one-day drop in five years amidst fears that the growing number of defaults in the subprime mortgage market, to which Lehman was significantly exposed, would affect its profitability. However, on March 14, 2007, Lehman reported a record in revenue generation and profits for its first fiscal quarter, claiming that the growing defaults would not significantly impact its earnings as losses were being effectively controlled.

However, as delinquencies in the subprime market continued, which also led to the collapse of two Bears Stearns hedge funds and a sharp decline in Lehman's share value, the bank announced on August 22, 2007 that it would be closing down its subprime mortgage originator BNC Mortgage, which eliminated 1200 jobs. It also closed down its Alt-A originator offices in a number of states. However, as the subprime crisis continued it continued to actively generate mortgages through its other mortgage lending acquisitions, as well as continuing to underwrite and issue mortgage-backed securities.

On December 13, 2007, Lehman reported record net income for the year of US$ 4.2 billion and revenue of US$ 19.3 billion due to a temporary recovery in the fixed income market and what appeared to be promising gains in global equity markets. However, it remained highly leveraged with a leverage ratio (Assets/Equity) of 31 to 1, making it very vulnerable to a deteriorating market situation. Lehman failed to avail the opportunity to cut down its large positions in risky assets at this time on the premise that financial markets would eventually recover.

On January 17, 2008, as defaults continued to rise and house prices continued to decline, Lehman announced that it would stop originating mortgages through its wholesale channels.

March 17, 2008 saw Lehman's share price decline sharply by more than 48 percent following the collapse of Bear Stearns and the Federal government backed takeover by JP Morgan Chase & Co. on March 16, 2008, which raised concerns in the market about whether other investment banks, in particular Lehman, would meet the same fate. There were reports that on that day South Asian Bank DBS Group Holding Limited instructed its traders not to work with Lehman. These instructions were later withdrawn.

Better than expected reported profits for the first fiscal quarter on March 18, 2008 caused Lehman share prices to rise, regaining the value lost the previous day. On April 1, 2008 it also announced that it had raised US$ 4 billion in preferred stock, which could be converted to common stock at a 32 percent premium to its current value. These events helped to restore investors' confidence to an extent.

On April 15, 2008 Lehman's CEO Richard Fuld told investors that he believed that the worst of the crisis had passed but that the financial environment would remain challenging for some time to come.

In May 2008, Lehman's share price continued to fall on reports that its hedge fund managers questioned the first quarter results on the belief that mortgage assets had not been valued correctly. On May 16, 2008 it trimmed an additional 5 percent of its work force: 1400 jobs cuts.

On June 9, 2008, Lehman announced its first quarterly loss of US$ 3 billion since becoming a public company after its spin-off from American Express, as a result of losing around 73 percent of its value due to the worsening credit crisis. To counter this loss, Lehman announced that it had sold US$ 6 billion in stock to strengthen its capital position, increased its liquidity to US$ 45 billion, and reduced its assets by US$ 147 billion, decreasing its exposure to residential and commercial mortgages by 20 percent. All of this had resulted in a lower leverage ratio of 25 to 1. In addition, on June 12, 2008 its CFO, Erin Callan, was removed and the president and COO, Joseph Gregory, stepped down and was replaced by Herbert McDade.

On August 19, 2008, Lehman's share price fell by around 13 percent due to reports that third quarter results would reveal significant write downs in its assets and that it was looking for buyers for its investment management business.

On August 22, 2008, its stock price recovered some of its value on news that the state-controlled Korean Development Bank (KDB) was considering buying it. Further, on August 29, 2008, reports also indicated that Lehman planned to cut an additional 6 percent of its work force, amounting to 1500 jobs, prior to the deadline of its third-quarter results. On September 2, 2008, news reports suggested that KDB would purchase a 25 percent stake in Lehman.

On September 8, 2008 the share price for Lehman fell sharply on reports that the talks with KDB had been put on hold due to rapidly declining values of global equity markets, lack of backing from KDBs regulators and difficulty in finding partners for the deal. Also, Lehman itself had difficulty attracting new investors and therefore struggled to raise new capital.

When news reports on September 9, 2008 indicated that the talks had ended, the 45 percent fall in Lehman's stock price pushed the S&P 500 and Dow Jones down. This was exacerbated when the US government announced that it would not bail out Lehman as it had done Bear Stearns if the situation became critical. Credit default swaps, default insurance for Lehman's debt, increased significantly, a reverse indicator of how the markets perceived Lehman's financial strength. This resulted in a run on the bank, with hedge fund clients pulling out, lines of credit being withdrawn, greater margin/collateral calls and trades being cancelled.

On September 10, 2008, in its third quarter results, Lehman reported a loss of US$ 3.2 billion as a result of asset write downs amounting to US$ 5.6 billion. In order to build up investor confidence it also announced that it planned to spin off its commercial real estate assets and a major stake of its asset management unit, Neuberger Berman. However, as a result of the announcement its stock price declined a further 7 percent. Moody's also announced that it would review Lehman's ratings and that it would have to down grade the entity if it could not find a strong buyer.

On September 11/12, 2008, Lehman's stock declined a further 42 percent as it struggled to find a buyer. Through the efforts of the US Treasury and Federal Reserve, who urged the Wall Street CEOs to come up with a solution for Lehman, Bank of America and Barclays came forward as potential buyers. By the week's end Lehman had only US$ 1 billion in cash. In the event that a deal did not materialize there was therefore the possibility that this could lead to an emergency liquidation of its assets.

On September 13/14, 2008, Wall Street leaders continued to meet with regulators over the weekend to come up with possible solutions. The two potential buyers wanted the government to provide a back stop guarantee as it had done for JP Morgan in the case of Bear Stearns. However, the government insisted that it would not provide assistance this time.

Barclays bank ended its bid when the US regulators assistance was not forthcoming and when its deal was vetoed by the Bank of England and the UK's Financial Services Authority. Bank of America also withdrew its bid. The latter diverted its focus to acquisition negotiations with another investment bank, Merrill Lynch, which it subsequently acquired in an emergency deal the following day.

On September 15, 2008, due to the failure of negotiations and no change in the US government's position regarding the possibility of a bail out, Lehman filed for bankruptcy protection. With US$ 639 billion in assets it was the largest bankruptcy filing in US history, causing the Dow Jones to suffer its largest drop in a single day since September 11, 2001. The bankruptcy led to a loss of over US$ 46 billion of Lehman's market value.

On September 22/23, 2008, the bankruptcy court approved the sale of Lehman's brokerage holding to Barclays and its Asian pacific franchise to Nomura Holdings Inc. The latter also announced plans to acquire Lehman holdings in Europe and the Middle East, which it completed in October 2008.

a. Timelines

February 2007: Lehman share price reaches all-time high of US$ 86.

March 13, 2007: Stock market suffers largest one-day drop in five years on reports that Lehman's profitability would be significantly impacted because of rising subprime mortgage delinquencies.

March 14, 2007: Lehman reports record revenues and profits for its first fiscal quarter.

August 2007: Announces closing of subprime mortgage originator BNC Mortgage cutting 1200 jobs. Also closes down offices of Alt-A originator offices in a number of states. It continues to write business through its other mortgage lenders.

December 13, 2007: Reports record net income for the year of US$ 4.2 billion and revenue of US$ 19.3 billion.

January 17, 2008: Stops originating mortgages through its wholesale channels.

March 17, 2008: Share price declines sharply by more than 48 percent following the collapse of Bear Stearns and the Federal government backed takeover by JP Morgan Chase & Co. on March 16, 2008.

March 18, 2008: Reports better than expected profits for the first fiscal quarter. Share prices rise to recover value lost the previous day.

April 1, 2008: Announces that it has raised US$ 4 billion in preferred stock.

April 15, 2008: Lehman's CEO Richard Fuld tells investors that the worst of the credit crisis is over but financial environment would remain challenging.

May 2008: Lehman's share price falls on reports of hedge fund managers questioning first quarter mortgage asset valuation results. Lehman cuts an additional 5 percent of its work force.

June 9, 2008: Lehman announces first quarterly loss of US$ 3 billion since becoming a public company. Also announces sale of US$ 6 billion in stock to raise capital, an increased liquidity position of US$ 45 billion, a 20 percent reduction in residential and commercial mortgage exposure and a reduced leverage ratio of 25 to 1.

June 12, 2008: Removes CFO, Erin Callan, and COO, Joseph Gregory.

August 19, 2008: Lehman's share price falls by around 13 percent on reports that third quarter results would be impacted by significant asset write downs and rumors that the bank was looking for buyers for its investment management business.

August 22, 2008: Stock price recovers on news that it had entered negotiations with state-controlled KDB.

August 29, 2008: News reports indicate that Lehman plans to cut an additional 6 percent of its work force.

September 2, 2008: News reports indicate that KDB would purchase a 25 percent stake in Lehman.

September 8, 2008: Lehman's share price falls sharply on reports that KDB talks are on hold due to falling global equity markets and no backing of investors and KDB regulators.

September 9, 2008: News reports indicate talks with KDB have ended. Lehman's share price falls by 45 percent. US government announces that it will not provide assistance or bail out Lehman. Credit Default Swaps rates increase indicates negative market perception regarding Lehman's survival. Liquidity begins to dry up as hedge fund clients start pulling out, lines of credit are withdrawn, calls for more margin/collateral increase and trades with Lehman are cancelled.

September 10, 2008: Lehman reports third quarter results, a loss of US$ 3.2 billion, as a result of asset write downs amounting to US$ 5.6 billion. It announces plans to spin off its commercial real estate assets and a major stake of its asset management unit, Neuberger Berman. Its stock price declines by 7 percent. Moody's announces potential credit ratings downgrade.

September 12, 2008: Lehman's stock declines a further 42 percent as it struggles to find a buyer. Bank of America and Barclays come forward as potential buyers.

September 14, 2008: Bids by both parties end as US government insists that it will not provide assistance.

September 15, 2008: Lehman files for bankruptcy protection. Dow Jones suffers its largest drop in a single day since September 11, 2001.

September 22/23, 2008: US Bankruptcy Court approves the sale of Lehman's brokerage holding to Barclays and its Asian pacific franchise to Nomura Holdings Inc.

October 2008: Nomura Holdings completes deal of acquired Lehman holdings in Europe and Middle East.

3. Case study: American International Group (AIG)

AIG Financial Productions Corporation (AIG FP), a subsidiary of AIG, issued and traded credit default swaps. These non-traditional insurance instruments insured the counterparty in the event of default on collateralized debt obligation payments. The company believed that the risk was very small because they primarily insured AAA-rated tranches, which, they presumed, would be close to risk-free. However, what they failed to factor in was the significant risk factor that as per contractual agreement they were required to post collateral with the counterparties in the event that values on the underlying CDOs declined; also that in the eventuality of a down grade in their credit ratings they would be required to post additional collateral with their counterparties. During the years prior to the financial crisis, and even during the crisis, AIG was confident that the risks that they were exposed to, in terms of declining values of CDOs and down grades, were negligible because they believed that the market would eventually recover and that they were too big an entity to fail.

In August 2007, subsequent to growing delinquencies in the subprime market and falling values of mortgage-backed instruments, Goldman Sachs demanded that AIG post collateral to cover its exposure to the fall in market value of its CDO portfolio. In October 2007, Goldman insisted on yet more collateral from AIG. In total AIG ended up posting around US$ 2 billion in collateral with them up to the end of October 2007.

In November 2007, AIG reported US$ 352 million in unrealized losses on its CDS portfolio. However, AIG also reported that they would most likely not realize these losses as they believed that the market would recover. What they also reported was that there were disagreements between counterparties and AIG regarding the amount needed as collateral. This suggested that there were differences in the valuations given to the underlying CDO portfolio by the insurance company and their counterparties. Further, AIG's external auditor PricewaterhouseCoopers privately warned the CEO that there were material weaknesses in the way

AIG managed the risk of its CDS portfolio, in particular with the risk models that they used to value the portfolio and assess its risk.

In December 2007, AIG reported a further US$ 1.15 billion in unrealized losses on its CDS portfolio. Despite this substantial increase in losses, AIG continued to tell investors that based on their risk models they believed that there was a very negligible possibility that any of these losses would actually be realized.

On February 11, 2008, the company disclosed the concerns of their auditor regarding the material weakness of their valuation and risk models used for the CDS portfolio. In light of these concerns the company revised November's unrealized losses estimates upwards to US$ 5.96 billion, and on February 28, 2008, they disclosed revised year-end unrealized losses of US$ 11.5 billion. They also reported that they had been required to post a total of US$ 5.3 billion as collateral to date. AIG again tried to assuage investors' fears by emphasizing that these losses were not expected to be realized, as the unrealized value would be reduced as the market recovered. They also informed that the chief of AIGFP, Joe Cassano, the unit responsible for this swap portfolio, had resigned.

On March 8, 2008, AIG reported additional unrealized losses for the first quarter of US$ 9.1 billion, also revealing that the total collateral that it had been required to post had risen to US$ 9.7 billion. On March 20, 2009, in order to strengthen its capital position, it was able to raise US$ 20 billion in private capital.

In June–August 2008 it reported US$ 5.6 billion unrealized losses for the second quarter of 2008 and that total collateral posted now stood at US$ 16.5 billion. The CEO of AIG, Martin Sullivan, resigned and was replaced by Robert Willumstad.

On September 9, 2008, AIG's share price fell sharply by 19 percent, the biggest drop since it became a public company in 1969, in response to investors' fears regarding the potential collapse of Lehman Brothers and its systemic impact on AIG's ability to meet its own commitments as well as the fact that AIG was finding it difficult to raise capital.

Following the bankruptcy filing of Lehman Brothers after the government's refusal to provide it with a bailout and the unexpected systemic impacts that the announcement had had on the financial markets, the Federal Reserve began to have concerns regarding the potential collapse of AIG if it was allowed to fail. In view of this, on September 14, 2008 the Federal Reserve asked private entities to provide AIG with short-term bridge loans to help AIG meet its liquidity demands. In addition, the FDIC relaxed rules to allow AIG to access around US$ 20 billion from its subsidiaries.

Despite these efforts from the regulators, on September 15, 2008 credit rating companies down graded AIG's credit rating below AA-levels because of its increasing inability to meet collateral demands, as well as because of its growing residential mortgage-backed losses. Following the down grading, counterparties demanded US$ 14.5 billion to be posted as additional collateral. In addition to this, investors discovered that AIG's subprime and Alt-A mortgages were valued significantly higher compared to similar assets on Lehman's balance sheet. In light of these developments AIG's share price declined sharply by 61 percent.

On September 16, 2008, with AIG's share price still headed downwards, the Federal Reserve Bank announced a bailout package for the insurer. It provided an US$ 85 billion credit-liquidity facility, backed by collateral consisting of assets of AIG and its subsidiaries, payable at an interest rate of 8.5 percent over the 3-month LIBOR, in exchange for warrants for a 79.9 percent equity share in the company. These terms were accepted by AIG's board. This turned out to be the first of a number of bailouts provided by the government to AIG to keep it from failing.

On September 17, 2008, the CEO, Willumstad, was forced to resign and was replaced by Edward Liddy.

In early October 2008, the Fed provided an additional US$ 37.8 billion to AIG, the second bailout, as it struggled to meet demands of cash from its clients withdrawing from its securities lending program. In the case of the latter, AIG had lent clients securities in return for cash which it had in turn invested in other securities. Due to the loss in value of these other securities AIG could not honor the demands of its clients. With the new bailout facility the Fed agreed to borrow these other securities in return for cash so that AIG could in turn close the outstanding deals with its clients.

The government also imposed bonus and pay restrictions on AIG employees and executives. AIG continued to use the loan to pay off its obligations on credit default swaps purchased to hedge against defaults of Lehman and other bankrupted entities. It also announced plans to sell off its life insurance operations in various countries. However, AIG's credit default spreads continued to widen during this period, an indicator that the company was headed for default. In light of this the government announced a third bailout on November 10, 2008. As part of this bailout, the terms and conditions of AIG's original bailout loan were modified, including lowering the interest rate and extending the term of the loan. In addition the government agreed to purchase US$ 40 billion of senior preferred stock as well, as it created two entities that would purchase over US$ 50 billion worth of residential mortgage-backed securities that were owned by AIG and CDOs owned by counterparties and guaranteed by AIG's CDS.

By February 2009, AIG had raised only US$ 2.4 billion in divestures and asset sales. However, news reports indicated that the CEO was not going ahead with plans to fund bailout loan repayments through the sales of

AIG assets because of the difficulty in finding strong potential buyers and because of the declining valuation of its insurance assets. Following reported losses of US$ 61.7 billion, the government enhanced the rescue package to AIG on March 2, 2009 by providing more favorable terms such as lower, non-cumulative, dividend payments on the preferred stock already purchased by the government, purchasing an additional US$ 30 million worth of preferred stock and restructuring of the company, including putting two life insurance subsidiaries into separate trusts of which the Federal Reserve would purchase up to US$ 26 billion in preferred stock.

In early August 2009, CEO Liddy was replaced by former MetLife CEO Robert Benmosche as president and CEO of AIG.

Since receiving its first bailout AIG has continued to sell its assets, including its asset management businesses and major insurance subsidiaries, using the proceeds to pay off its loan to the government. In September 2010 it announced a plan to repay the government loan off early by allowing the US Treasury to swap the preferred stock that it held for common stock, a 92 percent stake in AIG, which could then be sold in the market. In addition, it would pay off the Federal Reserve loan through earnings and asset sales. AIG is expected to sell US$ 10–30 million of shares to the public in a re-IPO of the company, with the US Treasury being the primary seller to the deal, in April–May 2011.

a. Timelines

August 2007–October 2007: Goldman Sachs asks AIG to post additional collateral in view of the falling market value of CDO assets. The insurer posted around US$ 2 billion in collateral up to the end of October 2007.

November 2007: AIG reports US$ 352 million in unrealized losses on its CDS portfolio. It also reports that there are differences between AIG and counterparties valuations of CDO portfolio. AIG's external auditor PricewaterhouseCoopers privately warns of material weaknesses in valuation methodology.

December 2007: AIG reports a further US$ 1.15 billion in unrealized losses on its CDS portfolio.

February 11, 2008: AIG discloses the concerns of the external auditor. It revises its unrealized loss figures upwards. It also reports that they have posted a total of US$ 5.3 billion as collateral to date. CEO of AIG Financial Products, Joe Cassano, the unit responsible for the CDS portfolio, resigns.

March 8, 2008: AIG reports additional unrealized losses for the first quarter of US$ 9.1 billion and total collateral posted of US$ 9.7 billion.

March 20, 2009: Raises US$ 20 billion in private capital.

June–August 2008: Reports US$ 5.6 billion unrealized losses for the second quarter of 2008 and total collateral posted of US$ 16.5 billion. The CEO of AIG, Martin Sullivan, resigns and is replaced by Robert Willumstad.

September 9, 2008: AIG's share price falls sharply by 19 percent in response to investors' fears regarding the potential collapse of Lehman Brothers and its systemic impact on AIG.

September 14, 2008: Federal Reserve asks private entities to provide AIG with short-term bridge loans to help meet liquidity demands. FDIC relaxes rules to allow AIG to borrow around US$ 20 billion from its subsidiaries.

September 15, 2008: Credit rating companies downgrade AIG's credit rating below AA-levels because of its increasing inability to meet collateral demands as well as because of its growing residential mortgage-backed losses. Counterparties demand additional US$ 14.5 billion in collateral. There are reports of major differences in the values of AIG's subprime and Alt-A mortgages versus that of Lehman Brothers. AIG's share price declines sharply by 61 percent.

September 16, 2008: Federal Reserve Bank announces a bailout package for the insurer of an US$ 85 billion credit-liquidity facility in exchange for warrants for a 79.9 percent equity share in the company. AIG's board accepts terms of bailout.

September 17, 2008: AIG CEO Willumstad is forced to resign and is replaced by Edward Liddy.

Early October 2008: The Fed provides an additional US$ 37.8 billion to AIG in order to help the insurer meet demands of cash from its clients withdrawing from its securities lending program.

November 10, 2008: Government announces a third bailout. The terms and conditions of AIG's original bailout loan are modified, including lowering the interest rate and extending the term of the loan. In addition the government agrees to purchase US$ 40 billion of senior preferred stock as well as creating two entities to purchase over US$ 50 billion worth of RMBS.

September 2008–February 2009: AIG has raised only US$ 2.4 billion in divestures and asset sales and faces difficulty in finding strong potential buyers in light of falling asset values.

March 2, 2009: Following reported losses of US$ 61.7 billion, the government enhances the rescue package to AIG, providing more favorable terms, purchasing an additional US$ 30 million worth of preferred stock and putting two life insurance subsidiaries into separate trusts of which the Federal Reserve would purchase up to US$ 26 billion in preferred stock.

Early August 2009: CEO Liddy is replaced by former MetLife CEO Robert Benmosche.

September 2010: Announces plan of an early repayment of the government loan in April–May 2011 by converting government's share of preferred stock to common stock, which would ultimately be sold to the public in the market, and through earnings and asset sales.

October 2010: Sells subsidiary AIA shares in US$ 20.5 billion IPO

November 2010: Metlife acquires ALICO for US$ 16.2 billion

January 14, 2011: The Federal Reserve Bank of New York announces that it is closing the recapitalization of AIG and that AIG had fully repaid its loans. Further it transfers the remaining AIA/ALICO preferred interests and AIG common stock to the Treasury. Undrawn TARP commitments and asset sales used to complete this settlement.

February 2011: Sells subsidiary Star/Edison to Prudential Financial Insurance for US$ 4.8 billion

May 2011: Treasury sells US$ 200 million AIG shares and cancels undrawn TARP commitment of US$ 2 billion

August 2011: Sells subsidiary Nan Shan for US$ 2.2 billion

February 2012: Sale of AIG related securities in Maiden Lane II nets a gain of US$ 2.8 billion for the Federal Reserve

March 2012: Sells US$ 6 billion in AIA shares and repays Treasury preferred interests. Treasury in turn sells US$ 6 billion of AIG common stock.

May 2012: Treasury sells US$ 5.75 billion worth of AIG common stock.

August 2012: Treasury sells US$ 5.75 billion worth of AIG common stock. The remaining mortgage related assets acquired by the Federal Reserve from AIG are also liquidated or sold.

September 2012: Treasury underwrites a public offering to sell US$ 20.7 billion worth of AIG common stock. At this point US$ 182 billion committed to AIG during the financial crisis was fully recovered by the Treasury & Federal Reserve with a combined positive return of US$ 15 billion. After the close of this public offering Treasury only has a stake of 16 percent in AIG common stock.

December 2012: Treasury sells all of the remaining AIG common stock for approximately US$ 7.6 billion, in the sixth and final public offering over a 19-month period.

Sources

1. http://www.treasury.gov/connect/blog/Pages/aig-182-billion.aspx (INFOGRAPHIC)
2. libraryguides.law.pace.edu/financial crisis
3. http://www.insurancejournal.com/news/national/2012/12/10/273418.htm
4. http://www.usatoday.com/story/money/business/2012/12/11/treasury-sells-aig-stake/1760625/

Part II
Monte Carlo Simulation

- Building a simple simulator
- Using the true distribution

6
Monte Carlo Simulators in EXCEL

Building Monte Carlo Simulators in EXCEL

1. Introduction

Pricing a financial instrument is not an exact science. There, it's out there, now you can go ahead and lynch me for blasphemy.

While the formulas, the mathematics, the derivation, the proofs and the exact models would like us to believe otherwise, in essence pricing financial securities in these markets is more along the lines of a science of approximation. It's a guessing game.

How do we approximate something for which we do not have a clearly defined underlying model? Sometimes we focus on behavior and build a symptomatic model – a model that under most conditions will approximate behavior and (we hope) pricing. In other instances we build models with their foundations in economic theory – a game of supply and demand that theoretically indicates where a security would trade, if the real world took its inspiration from a classical economic textbook.

Both approaches demand an understanding of core price driving processes. The best approaches are a hybrid and then some. All approaches after a certain point in time need to dry run the model to see how it would behave under sets of assumptions, input factors and historical data sets.

Enter simulation!

A simulation is an experiment. How will people react when you ring their doorbell and run? Short of actually ringing the doorbell and running do you have any other options? But sometimes ringing doorbells and running is not possible in an academic or professional setting.

An easy compromise is a coin toss. In case of heads they will open the door, in case of tails they won't. In case of heads they will scream and shout and curse, in case of tails they will quietly shake their heads and close the door. In case of heads the wrath of God will strike you down, in the case of tails clouds will part, angels will sing and you will receive manna from heaven.

Over the last two centuries, the science around coin tossing has been refined to mathematical poetry. All coin tosses are not created equal. Some lead to symmetry and are treated as fair. Others are clearly biased and are treated as skewed. Some come with memory (your result is dependent on the history of coin tosses), while others start afresh with each toss (as pure as driven snow).

So toss a coin a hundred times and if it is fair, you will travel the distance from the binomial distribution all the way up to the normal distribution. Toss it without memory and you can throw in the waiting game along with the Poisson analysis. Want a bit of a skew? Introduce the Lognormal, the Gamma and the Beta. The choice is yours, but the results are very different.

The graph that follows shows the result from a short simulation using some of the above-mentioned distributions. While not all distributions are equal, you can clearly see that some are more equal than others.

The art of using a coin toss to simulate the results of an experiment is one form of simulation. Inspired by the ancient tradition of counting tosses and the close relationship between coin tosses, cards and gambling, the science is called Monte Carlo simulation.

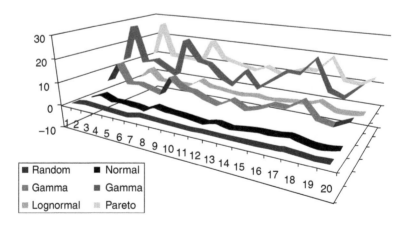

Figure 183 Simulated results using various distributions

2. What is a Monte Carlo simulator?

A Monte Carlo simulator at its heart is a simple coin tossing machine. Depending on the tool used to build the machine (the choice of distribution) the simulator will behave in a certain fashion (symmetric, asymmetric, normal and skewed, with thin tails or long fat tails).

MS EXCEL comes with its own built-in Monte Carlo (MC) simulator. The simplest and easiest is the function called RAND(). The graph above was generated using the RAND() function embedded within function calls to the normal, Lognormal, Beta and Gamma distributions in MS EXCEL.

The choice of the underlying distribution is one of the primary factors in the model. The other driver is the model itself.

3. The process or generator function[1, 2]

Each MC simulation model comes with certain behavioral assumptions. These assumptions are based on process or what Nicholas Nassim Taleb (NNT) calls the generator function[3]. One of the objectives of the simulation is to understand how the model interacts with the assumptions and how that interaction changes the distribution of simulated results.

For instance, let's look at a simple function that calculates the rate of change in the price of a zero coupon bond on a continuously compounded basis. The generator function for bond prices will simply give you the change in bond prices every time you call it. The bond price you get would be based on three key factors:

(a) The principle invested in the bond
(b) The interest rate at which interest is being accrued
(c) The unit of time over which interest is being calculated.

How would you write this in the world of Monte Carlo simulators? Don't go into shock as yet, there is a simple key for this equation:

$dB = rBdt.$

In the equation above:

dB = the rate of change in bond price,
r = the rate at which interest is being accrued,
B = the principal invested in the bond at inception or time zero,
dt = the unit change in time.

If you solve this equation for the rate of change in bond price, you can actually calculate the bond price at any given point in time:

$B_t = B_0 e^{rt}.$

How do you read this? The value of a bond B at time t (B_t) is equal to the initial principal invested at time zero (B_0) continuously compounded at the interest rate, r, for time, t; e^{rt} represents the *continuous compounding at interest rate r for time period t* function. Since all the drivers in this case are known and not volatile, there is no uncertainty or volatility in prices. The only change is on account of passage of time.

If you were to plot this it would look something like the graph that follows.

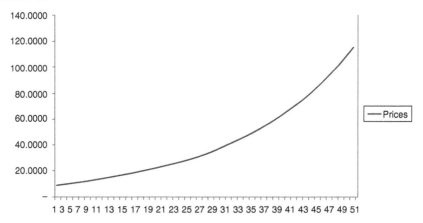

Figure 184   Bond pricing curve, B_t

Congratulations! You have just deciphered your first generator function. If you were to go back you would see that the function had three primary components.

1. An equation that described the change in bond prices from one node in time to the next (the *dB* equation).
2. An equation that described the full price at any given point in time (the B_t equation).
3. A graphical simulation of the model that shows how bond prices change over a period of time for a given yield to maturity (YTM).

4. Building your first MC simulator model

The first price generating function we have built above has one basic element missing. There is no uncertainty. Prices will change when you change rates or maturity but other than that there is really nothing to simulate. It is a great model for introducing us to the terminology of Monte Carlo simulators, but it is not really a simulator. It's a static pricing function.

So how do we build on what we have to create a Monte Carlo simulator? A model with a bit more dynamism and volatility?

Here is a slightly revised model for calculating the change in price of an equity security:

$$dS = \mu Sdt + \sigma Sdz.$$

While the equation looks a little bit more complex than the rate of change in bond price equation above (and below) the form of the factors is similar. Rather than the risk free rate, r, we have μ (*the expected return*); rather than B we have S (*the spot price*).

In addition to the single static factor that this model has in common with bond pricing, there is one more change:

$$dB = rBdt.$$

There is a new factor, which at first glance looks similar but requires a more detailed review.

Let's take another look:

$$dS = \mu Sdt + \sigma Sdz.$$

In the new factor, rather than r or μ we have *sigma* (σ) and rather than dt we have dz.

Before we try and understand what these changes represent let's take a look at the graphical model output, side by side with the bond pricing model. As you can see below, the clean, smooth bond pricing curve has been replaced by a jagged, volatile (some would say violent) trend. And since the shape and form of the first factor is similar to the bond pricing equation, this must be the work of the second factor.

The dz term that we have added above represents uncertainty. It is a random sample from a normally distributed simulator that is then scaled by the size of volatility or sigma.

Here is what that means within the context of the above equation. The change in the stock price is comprised of two factors:

1. A static return in proportion to the price of the equity security as well as the expected return (also known as drift)
2. A scaled return in proportion to the price, volatility and a normally distributed uncertainty factor.

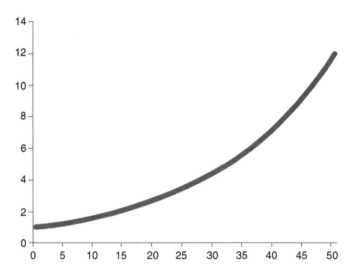

Figure 185   Bond pricing curve – single static factor

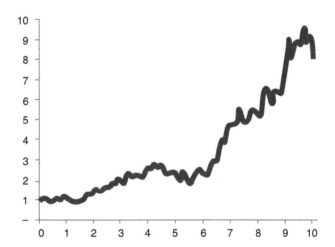

Figure 186   Equity pricing curve – with additional uncertain factor

When we solve this we get the following equation:

$$S_t = S_0 e^{\left(\mu - \frac{1}{2}\sigma^2\right)t + \sigma\sqrt{t}z_t}.$$

As with the bond pricing solution, this solution comes with a similar interpretation. The change in price from one period to the next is proportional to the original price times a factor. The factor is based on the expected return (adjusted for volatility drag – the half sigma square term) and the scaled volatility times an uncertain component.

This simple two-factor base line model is the heart of Monte Carlo simulators and rate generators for equities, currencies, commodities and other non-interest bearing securities – drift and diffusion, expected return and volatility, mu (μ) and sigma (σ):

$$dS = \mu S dt + \sigma S dz.$$

In the risk neutral Black Scholes world, we replace mu (μ) by the risk free rate. We do this because in the risk free world all assets earn the risk free rate and all investors are content with receiving the risk free rate.

Here is a simple EXCEL worksheet that implements this MC simulation model. The first table shares the numerical result from the MC simulation. The second exposes the underlying formula behind the calculations required for the MC simulation. For these results we have assumed that:

Spot price at time zero = S_0 = 30
Constant Volatility = σ = 50 percent
Time-step = t = 1 year
Risk free discount rate = r = 1 percent
Dividends = 0.0 percent.

Parameters	Inputs
S_0	30
μ	1%
σ	50%
t	1

Simulated Run	Random Number	Normally Scale Random Number (z_t)	Fixed Piece; ($\mu-0.5\sigma^2$)t	Random Piece; $\sigma\sqrt{t}z_t$	Change; Exp(Fixed+Random)	Simulated Stock Price; Previous Price*Change = S_t
1	0.49740	(0.00652)	(0.11500)	(0.00326)	0.88846	26.65
2	0.95382	1.68308	(0.11500)	0.84154	2.06791	55.12
3	0.96424	1.80219	(0.11500)	0.90110	2.19481	120.97
4	0.21113	(0.80251)	(0.11500)	(0.40125)	0.59675	72.19
5	0.45196	(0.12072)	(0.11500)	(0.06036)	0.83915	60.58
6	0.22019	(0.77155)	(0.11500)	(0.38577)	0.60606	36.71
7	0.67435	0.45196	(0.11500)	0.22598	1.11737	41.02
8	0.40415	(0.24263)	(0.11500)	(0.12131)	0.78953	32.39
9	0.48915	(0.02721)	(0.11500)	(0.01361)	0.87932	28.48
10	0.44316	(0.14296)	(0.11500)	(0.07148)	0.82988	23.64

Figure 187 MC simulation – numerical results

	A	B	C	D	E	F	G
1	Parameters	Inputs					
2	S₀	30					
3	μ	0.01					
4	σ	0.5					
5	t	1					
6	Simulated Run	Random Number	Normally Scale Random Number (z₁)	Fixed Piece; (μ-0.5σ²)t	Random Piece; σ√tz₁	Change; Exp(Fixed+Random)	Simulated Stock Price; Previous Price*Change = Sₜ
7	1	=RAND()	=NORMSINV(B7)	=($B$3-($B$4^2)/2)*$B$5	=$B$4*SQRT($B$5)*C7	=EXP(D7+E7)	=$B$2*F7
8	=A7+1	=RAND()	=NORMSINV(B8)	=($B$3-($B$4^2)/2)*$B$5	=$B$4*SQRT($B$5)*C8	=EXP(D8+E8)	=G7*F8
9	=A8+1	=RAND()	=NORMSINV(B9)	=($B$3-($B$4^2)/2)*$B$5	=$B$4*SQRT($B$5)*C9	=EXP(D9+E9)	=G8*F9
10	=A9+1	=RAND()	=NORMSINV(B10)	=($B$3-($B$4^2)/2)*$B$5	=$B$4*SQRT($B$5)*C10	=EXP(D10+E10)	=G9*F10
11	=A10+1	=RAND()	=NORMSINV(B11)	=($B$3-($B$4^2)/2)*$B$5	=$B$4*SQRT($B$5)*C11	=EXP(D11+E11)	=G10*F11
12	=A11+1	=RAND()	=NORMSINV(B12)	=($B$3-($B$4^2)/2)*$B$5	=$B$4*SQRT($B$5)*C12	=EXP(D12+E12)	=G11*F12
13	=A12+1	=RAND()	=NORMSINV(B13)	=($B$3-($B$4^2)/2)*$B$5	=$B$4*SQRT($B$5)*C13	=EXP(D13+E13)	=G12*F13
14	=A13+1	=RAND()	=NORMSINV(B14)	=($B$3-($B$4^2)/2)*$B$5	=$B$4*SQRT($B$5)*C14	=EXP(D14+E14)	=G13*F14
15	=A14+1	=RAND()	=NORMSINV(B15)	=($B$3-($B$4^2)/2)*$B$5	=$B$4*SQRT($B$5)*C15	=EXP(D15+E15)	=G14*F15
16	=A15+1	=RAND()	=NORMSINV(B16)	=($B$3-($B$4^2)/2)*$B$5	=$B$4*SQRT($B$5)*C16	=EXP(D16+E16)	=G15*F16

Figure 188   MC simulation – EXCEL formula

5. Extending MC simulation models to currencies and commodities

Extending the original MC simulator for equities to currencies and commodities requires a few simple changes. Rather than using just *r*, we now use an adjusted *r* for the model: the interest rate differential between domestic and foreign currencies for currencies, risk free rate net of the convenience yield of the commodity for commodities. An adjusted *r* (risk free return net of dividend yield) may also be used in the case of simulating prices for equities where a dividend yield percentage is payable on the underlying stock.

6. MC simulations models – understanding drift, diffusion and volatility drag

Let's take another look at our standard rate of change equation for a financial security:

$$dS = \mu S dt + \sigma S dz.$$

We have introduced mu (μ) as drift and sigma (σ) as diffusion (or standard deviation or volatility or vol.). We have also gone out and built a simple EXCEL based Monte Carlo simulation model for generating stock prices. While the process is focused on equity securities, the same underlying structure, with some tweaks, can be used to generate rates for currencies, commodities and interest bearing securities.

When we solve the equation above our solution looks something like this in discrete form:

$$S_t = S_0 e^{\left(\mu - \frac{1}{2}\sigma^2\right)t + \sigma\sqrt{t}z_t}.$$

In a risk neutral world, the risk free rate r takes over from mu (μ).

Let's do a simple experiment. We have two variables and four possible variations:

	MEAN (MU, DRIFT, RISK FREE RATE R)	SD (SIGMA, DIFFUSION, VOL)
Zero drift, Zero vol	0%	0%
Unit (%) drift, Zero vol	1%	0%
Zero drift, Unit (%) vol	0%	1%
Unit (%) drift, Unit (%) vol	1%	1%

Figure 189   Variations for model input-mu and sigma

Here are the graphical results from the same Monte Carlo simulator we had built earlier. The simulated values have been plotted to give a more visual idea of the direction and trend of simulation results. The starting or initial spot price for the simulated security is 10.

a. The zero drift, zero diffusion case

The first case is zero drift and zero volatility. The simulation plot is a flat line going nowhere.

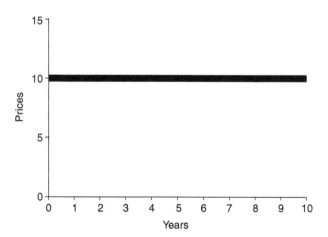

Figure 190   Simulated stock price – zero drift, zero volatility

b. The unit drift, zero diffusion case

The second case is unit drift and zero volatility. The simulation plot is a flat line going upwards. The unit drift grows the trend in a 45 percent angle line per unit of time and there is no uncertainty.

In some ways this is the same case as the exponential curve we saw earlier for bond pricing on a continuously compounded basis. There is a clear upward trend with no uncertainty or volatility.

However, the exponential curve that we would expect to see, in the absence of volatility, is missing. That is simply because our simulation time-step, as well as our unit of return for that time-step, is very small. If we increase either we will see the exponential curve come into focus.

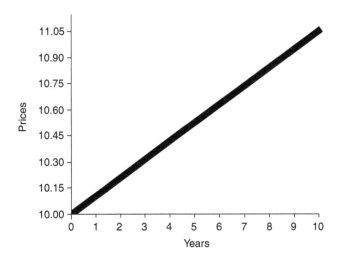

Figure 191   Simulated stock price – unit drift, zero volatility

c. The zero drift, unit diffusion case

The third case is zero drift and unit volatility. And we can see that while the overall trend is flat, there is now some uncertainty in results.

Within our EXCEL Monte Carlo simulator, every time we press F9 the chart below will change, and while there will be instances of directional trends (both upwards and downwards) a large majority of cases will have a flat trend with volatility.

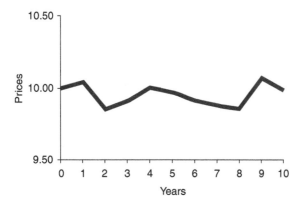

Figure 192 Simulated stock price – zero drift, unit volatility, scenario 1

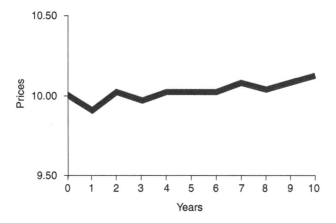

Figure 193 Simulated stock price – zero drift, unit volatility, scenario 2

d. The unit drift, unit diffusion case

The final case is unit drift and unit volatility. A clear up trend is visible now. Once again, while there may be some instances of downward and flat trends for these values, in a majority of cases the price trend will be upwards and positive.

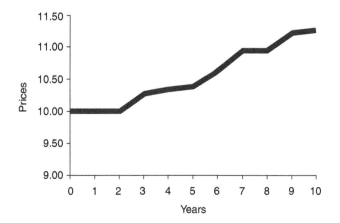

Figure 194 Simulated stock price – unit drift, unit volatility

e. Understanding volatility drag or ½σ²

What happens if we increase the drift to five units from the original one? You will see that the uptrend is now consistent across all iterations of your Monte Carlo simulation model. And the reason is that in our two-factor model, drift now dominates over diffusion.

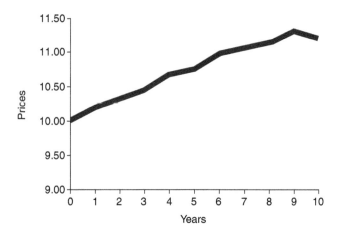

Figure 195 Simulated stock price – increased drift

If you increase volatility in the same proportion to five units, you will still see a consistent up trend but every once in a while a high enough *dz* value will drag returns down as in the simulation results shown below.

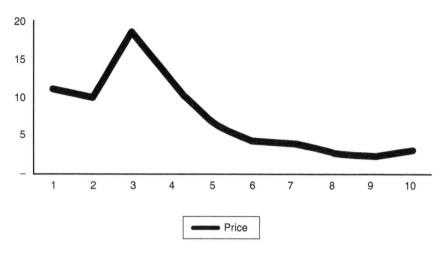

Figure 196   Simulated stock price – increased drift, increased volatility

As you carry on increasing volatility (to 10 units and then 25 units) in proportion to drift, the frequency of flatter and downward returns will increase. This happens because $-1/2 \times \sigma^2$ now dominates drift.

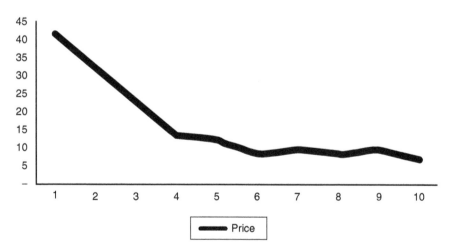

Figure 197   Simulated stock price – increased volatility drag

Within the option pricing world an alternate way of looking at the same data and the volatility drag term, is comparing the probability of prices rising higher than a given point ($N(d_1)$ and $N(d_2)$) to the maximum price attained within a simulation path.

As volatility rises we would expect to see deeper and longer swings in prices. The range of prices with rising volatility will increase. But will the probability of a certain price being crossed also increase? Or will it decrease? The graph that follows answers that question. With rising volatility, while option prices go up, both probabilities, $N(d_1)$ and $N(d_2)$ dip and decline.

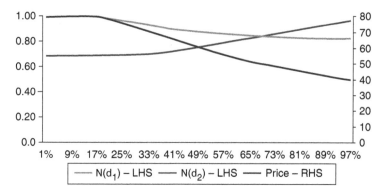

Figure 198   Impact of volatility drag on Black Scholes probabilities and option prices

7. Linking Monte Carlo simulation with binomial trees and the Black Scholes model

How are the following three equations related?

- From the Black Scholes model for the price of a European call option:

$$d_2 = \frac{\ln\left(\dfrac{S}{X}\right) + \left(r - \dfrac{1}{2}\sigma^2\right)(T - t)}{\sigma\sqrt{(T - t)}},$$

$$d_1 = \frac{\ln\left(\dfrac{S}{X}\right) + \left(r + \dfrac{1}{2}\sigma^2\right)(T - t)}{\sigma\sqrt{(T - t)}}.$$

- From the binomial trees model determining the size of the up-jump and the down-jump in a binomial tree:

$$u = e^{\sigma\sqrt{\Delta t}},$$

$$d = \frac{1}{u}.$$

- And from the Monte Carlo Simulation model:

$$S_t = S_0 e^{\left(\mu - \frac{1}{2}\sigma^2\right)t + \sigma\sqrt{t}z_t}.$$

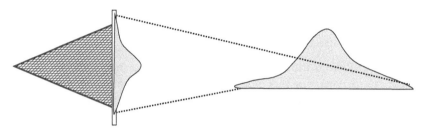

Figure 199 Underlying distribution linking Monte Carlo simulation with binomial trees and Black Scholes model

The common theme in all three is the underlying distribution and the assumption with respect to the mean return and the standard deviation.

The return and standard deviation in all three equations is given by

$$\text{Return} = \left(r - \frac{1}{2}\sigma^2\right),$$

$$\text{Standard Deviation} = \sigma\sqrt{(T - t)}.$$

A binomial tree uses the same process to generate a path that the Monte Carlo simulation model uses, which is also the same model that the Black Scholes solution integrates over an infinitely small interval.

From node zero to the terminal node in a binomial tree is a single Monte Carlo simulation path. The more steps in a tree, the larger the base of paths that can be used to price an instrument. The average value across all paths adjusted for probabilities and interest rate is the value of the instrument in binomial trees as well as Monte Carlo simulation.

The Black Scholes equation provides an elegant closed form solution to the entire process that also serves as an exact answer for certain but not all types of derivative instruments.

Build a large enough tree, run 50,000 simulations or solve the Black Scholes equation for the price of a European call and chances are that the three results will converge to the same value.

8. Simulating interest rates using CIR (Cox Ingersoll Ross) and HJM (Heath, Jarrow & Merton)

While we can club equity, commodity and currency simulators in one category, interest rate simulators are a completely different animal.

First, because there is more than one way of modeling interest rates.

Equilibrium models and arbitrage free models

- An equilibrium model is based on a simplified macro model of interest rate drivers. For instance the CIR model assumes a mean reverting process (if rates go up, they must come down, if they come down they must go up) that makes assumptions about a long term average rate and an adjustment process that pulls interest rates back to the long term mean.
- An arbitrage free model is a model that calibrates the output of the model on day one to the existing interest rate environment so that there are no opportunities for mis-pricing or arbitrage on day one between the real world and the interest rate model. For example, the Black Derman and Toy (BDT) model calibrates the existing interest rate environment as represented by zero curves and the volatility at each point in the term structure with the model to project the entire forward rate term structure.

Second, because unlike a price tree there are a number of additional questions that need to be answered for an interest rate tree.

- Are you going to simulate one rate or the entire term structure? A single short rate projection model is built very differently than a multi-factor forward rate projection model.
- What are the drivers that will drive interest rate movement in your model? Economic, statistical or data set/model specific?
- How are you going to model these drivers? Assumptions, data sets, fit?
- Will your model be a theoretically correct model driven by fundamentals of economic theory?
- Or will it be a model that matches model prices at inception with market prices?
- If you do match market price, what is the process used to resolve differences between model prices and market prices? How do you calibrate your model to match market prices?
- How will you translate simulated interest rates into bond prices within your model? In addition to a rate lattice (tree) or simulator you will also need a linked bond pricing lattice or simulator.

Compared to a price generating tree or Monte Carlo simulator for equities, currencies and commodities, the same engine for an interest rate simulator also faces another interesting challenge. A conventional binomial tree assumes a constant risk free interest rate to hold throughout the length of the tree. The same assumption holds for a Monte Carlo simulator. When forecasting interest rates, how can you simulate and then use the same rate in the same model at the same time. The short answer is you can't.

9. Monte Carlo simulation using historical returns

The traditional Monte Carlo simulation model generates future prices using the Black Scholes terminal price formula:

$$S_t = S_0 e^{\left(\mu - \frac{1}{2}\sigma^2\right)t + \sigma\sqrt{t}z_t},$$

where z_t is a random sample from a normal distribution with mean zero and standard deviation of 1. In EXCEL, z_t is obtained by normally scaling the random numbers generated using the RAND() function, NORMSINV(RAND()).

The traditional Monte Carlo simulation model assumes that the underlying return distribution is normal.

However, the question arises "Does the normal distribution truly reflect how price returns actually evolve over time?" Let us consider the price return series for gold. We have the following information and parameters available to us.

Commodity	🔲🔲 🔲🔲		
Parameters	Explanation	Inputs	
	🔲🔲🔲🔲🔲🔲🔲 🔲🔲		
S_0	🔲🔲 🔲 🔲	🔲🔲🔲🔲🔲🔲🔲🔲	🔲🔲🔲🔲🔲🔲🔲🔲🔲
r	🔲🔲🔲🔲🔲🔲 🔲🔲🔲🔲	🔲🔲🔲🔲🔲	
	🔲🔲🔲🔲🔲🔲🔲🔲🔲🔲		
q	🔲🔲🔲🔲	🔲🔲🔲🔲🔲	
	🔲🔲🔲🔲🔲🔲🔲🔲		
	🔲🔲🔲🔲🔲🔲 🔲🔲🔲🔲🔲🔲🔲🔲		
σ	🔲🔲🔲🔲🔲	🔲🔲🔲	
	🔲🔲🔲🔲🔲🔲🔲 🔲🔲		
	🔲🔲🔲🔲 🔲🔲🔲🔲 🔲🔲		
t	🔲🔲🔲🔲🔲🔲	🔲🔲🔲🔲🔲🔲🔲🔲🔲🔲🔲	

Figure 200 Parameters and inputs for the Monte Carlo simulation model

The spot price for gold on March 14, 2011 was 1,422.25. The one year US Treasury Yield curve rate on this date was 0.22 percent, which we have taken as a proxy to the risk free rate. We have assumed a convenience yield of 0 percent. The average annualized volatility of actual price returns over the 365 trading day period from March 15, 2011 to September 28, 2012 was 25 percent.

Using the Monte Carlo simulation model with the Black Scholes terminal price formula we simulate prices for the next 365 trading days. Note that μ is replaced in the formula above by the risk free rate less the convenience yield. The total period being considered is 365 days (= N) and the time-step, t, is a daily time-step, that is, 1/365 expressed in years.

The actual price series against one scenario of the resulting simulated price series is given in the graph below.

In this scenario, at first glance, the simulated price series seems to be fairly consistent with the actual gold spot price series. However, consider the histograms of price return series below. The histograms plot the frequency distribution of the return series.

Actual returns show a much wider dispersion of returns and much longer tails than their normally simulated counterparts.

In another scenario, the prices series are themselves very divergent.

Figure 201 Actual gold spot price series versus one scenario of Monte Carlo simulated price series using the original approach

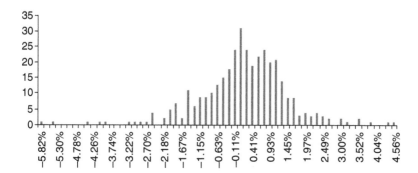

Figure 202 Actual gold spot price return series histogram

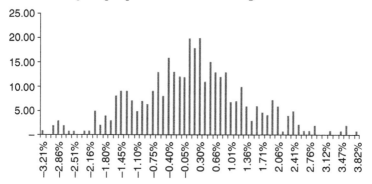

Figure 203 Simulated gold spot price return series histogram using the original Monte Carlo approach under one scenario

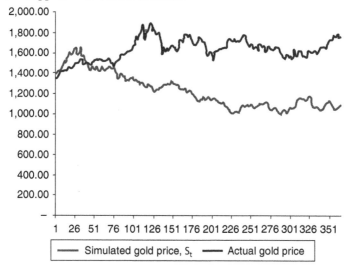

Figure 204 Actual gold spot price series versus another scenario of Monte Carlo simulated price series using the original approach

There is nearly a US$ 700 difference between the actual and simulated price on day 365. And once again the normally simulated series do not capture the actual extreme tail events, as can be seen in the figure below.

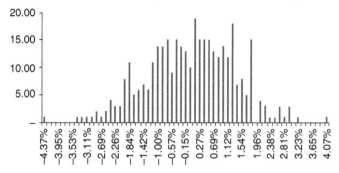

Figure 205   Simulated gold spot price return series histogram using the original Monte Carlo approach under another scenario

Scenario	Terminal price
1	1,674.38
2	1,604.03
3	1,373.40
4	1,302.63
5	1,952.19
6	1,323.04
7	1,163.05
8	2,432.34
9	2,246.90
10	1,077.96
11	913.60
12	2,364.31
13	1,329.86
14	1,335.39
15	1,358.59
16	1,443.24
17	1,513.25
18	1,262.80
19	2,040.76
20	1,443.77
21	1,303.30
22	1,077.78
23	1,077.42
24	1,291.67
25	788.14

Figure 206   Data table of terminal prices simulated for 25 scenarios using the original Monte Carlo simulation approach

Average Terminal Price	1,467.75
Actual Terminal Price	1,776.00
Difference	−308.25

Figure 207 Average terminal prices across 25 scenarios using the original Monte Carlo simulation approach

Average terminal price at day 365 over the following 25 scenarios show a difference of US$ 300 between the actual price and the simulated price.

In this section, we present an alternative method for simulating the price series to reconcile some of the differences that we see between actual historical and simulated returns. However, the important point to note here is that this method is a form of calibration of simulated results to historical returns. In reality there is no guarantee that the future will pan out in a similar manner as the past. This is a necessary caveat or qualification that needs to be made if this model is used. If the future turns out differently from what has actually happened over the historical period of study being considered, results and decisions made on those results may not retain their validity.

In the alternate method, the z-scores are determined from the actual historical return series, rather than by applying the inverse of the standard normal distribution function in EXCEL to the random numbers generated using the RAND() function, NORMSINV(RAND()).

To see how this is done, let us once again look at the terminal price formula:

$$S_t = S_0 e^{\left(\mu - \frac{1}{2}\sigma^2\right)t + \sigma\sqrt{t}z_t}.$$

By rearranging the equation we have $z_t = (\ln(S_t/S_{t-1}) - (r - q - 0.5\sigma^2)t)/\sigma\sqrt{t}$.

Note that we have replaced μ with the risk free rate less the convenience yield, $r-q$, and S_0 with S_{t-1}. The latter has been done because the simulated price path is determined using an iterative process where prices for that day, t, are derived using the previous day's ($t - 1$) simulated price.

The natural log of the ratio of successive prices, $\ln(S_t/S_{t-1})$ is the daily price return at time t. If we replace this price return with the actual daily historical return, then z_t will in effect be a derived z-score applicable to that historical return.

Each derived z_t will be assigned an index number. This index number will be a multiple of 1/number of time-steps, in this instance, 1/365. Why 1 in the numerator? Because the range between the minimum and maximum numbers in the uniform random series is 1. The first z_t will be assigned 1/365, the second 2/365, the third 3/365 and so on.

In a variation to this method, the actual return series may first be put in ascending order, smallest to largest, and then the derived z_t's are assigned index numbers as above.

Random numbers are generated as in the original Monte Carlo simulation construction as discussed earlier, using EXCEL's RAND() function. However, instead of normally scaling the random number, the random number is taken to stand for a particular index number. Using EXCEL's VLOOKUP functionality the corresponding derived z_t is then selected.

The rest of the model works in a similar manner to the traditional MC simulator:

- It calculates a path of prices, S_t, for each time-step up to and including the terminal price at the end of the specified duration, T.
- It uses N time-steps, in this instance 365.
- It uses EXCEL's DATA Table functionality to generate terminal prices for 25 different scenarios.
- It calculates an average terminal price from the results generated for the 25 scenarios.
- It plots the path of prices and a histogram of the distribution of returns for each scenario. By pressing the function key, F9, new scenarios are graphically displayed.

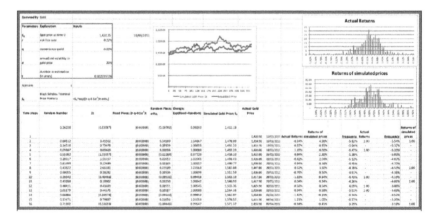

Figure 208 Monte Carlo simulation model using historical returns

The scenarios generated under this alternative approach produce results that are more in line with the actual historical returns, as can be seen from the price graph as well as the return histograms below.

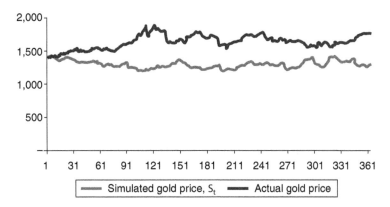

Figure 209   Actual gold spot price series versus one scenario of Monte Carlo simulated price series using the historical returns approach

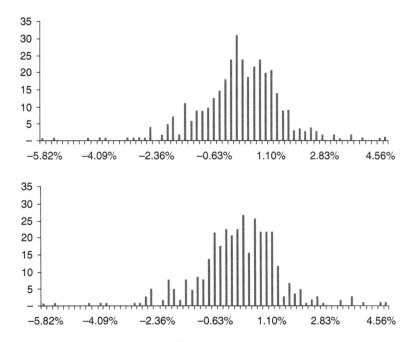

Figure 210   Actual versus simulated gold spot price return series histograms using the Monte Carlo simulation with historical returns approach

Though there is variation in results from one scenario to the next, the deviations from the true value on average are much less pronounced as compared to the original Monte Carlo simulation model. In our model, across the 25 scenarios captured in the data table, the average of terminal prices converges more closely to the actual spot price of gold on September 28, 2012.

Average terminal price	1,797.49
Actual terminal price	1,776.00
Difference	21.49

Figure 211 Average terminal prices across 25 scenarios using the Monte Carlo simulation with historical returns approach

10. Option pricing using Monte Carlo simulation

1. Terminology

An option is a contract between the buyer/holder of the option and the seller/writer of the option that grants the buyer the *right* to purchase from, or sell to, the option seller a designated asset at a specified price (*exercise/strike price*) within a specified period of time. The buyer of the option pays the contract seller an option price or *option premium* for this right. Options are used for:

1. Speculation or investment
2. Hedging or risk management.

The *maturity date*, or *expiration date*, is the date after which the option is no longer valid. *American options* are options that can be exercised at any time up to and including the expiration date. *European options* are options that can only be exercised on the maturity date.

A *call* option is one that gives the buyer the right to buy the instrument from the option seller at a specified price within a specified period of time. A *put* option is one that gives the buyer the right to sell the instrument to the option seller at a specified price within a specified period of time.

While the buyer has the right to exercise the option, the seller of the option has the *obligation* to perform on the contract. This characteristic means that the buyer will only exercise the option when it is advantageous to him, and will let it expire if conditions are not in his favor. However, the seller must deliver or receive the asset, whenever the option is exercised, even if this means he will make a substantial loss. This makes the risk/reward relationship one sided or asymmetrical where the payoff in the contract tends to favor the option buyer.

In other words, the most the option buyer (the *long position*) can lose is the option premium in the event that he never exercises the option. However, if price of the underlying instrument moves in his favor, he has all the upside potential where his gains will only be reduced by the premium that he paid when he purchased the contract.

On the other hand, the maximum amount that the contract seller (the *short position*) can realize is the price he receives for the option contract.

However, he is exposed to substantial downside risk as the option will only be exercised to the advantage of the option buyer or conversely the disadvantage of the contract seller.

This is illustrated below for a call option:

- Designated asset: 100 shares of XYZ Company
- Exercise price: 50 per share
- Option price: 2 per share.

If the price of the shares rises to 55 and the buyer exercises his right, he will realize a profit of 300 [=(55 − 50 − 2) × 100]. The seller of the option will only receive 5,000 for shares worth 5,500 in the market. His total loss will be 300 [= (50 − 55 + 2) × 100].

On the other hand, if the share price falls to 46, the buyer of the option will not exercise the option. The most that he will lose is 200, the option price. The seller of the option will only realize 200.

Per share payoff to the buyer and seller of the call option is depicted below.

Figure 212   Payoff to the buyer and seller of a call option

Payoffs for the put option are illustrated below:

- Designated asset: 100 shares of ABC Company
- Exercise price: 50 per share
- Option price: 2 per share.

If the price of the shares falls to 45 and the buyer exercises his right, he will realize a profit of 300 [= (50 − 45 − 2) × 100]. The seller of the option will be purchasing shares for 5,000 whereas if he were to go to the market for them he would have only to pay 4,500. Therefore his total loss will be 300 [= (45 − 50 + 2) × 100].

On the other hand if the share price rises to 56, the buyer of the option will not exercise the option. The most that he will lose is 200 (the option price). The seller of the option will only realize 200.

Per share payoff to the buyer and seller of the put option is depicted below:

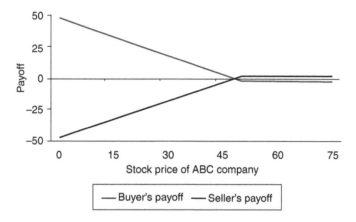

Figure 213   Payoff to the buyer and seller of a put option

Option contracts have two values that we have to consider.

One is the option price already mentioned above and elaborated in more detail below. The other is the *intrinsic value* of the option. This can be thought of as the price an investor would pay if the option were to be exercised immediately. Using the call example given above, when the price of XYZ share fell to 46, the option becomes worthless to the contract buyer as he could get a better deal by buying the shares directly from the market. The intrinsic value is therefore 0. However, when the share price rose to 55, the shares are more expensive in the market by comparison. The intrinsic value is 5 (= 55 − 50).

When the intrinsic value is positive the option is said to be *in-the-money,* when it is zero it is said to be *out-of-the-money.* When the market price of the designated asset is equal to the exercise price of the option, the option is said to be *at-the-money.*

a. Elements of the option price

The price of the option depends on the following:

(a) *Asset Price*: For an American or European call option, the higher the asset price the higher will be the option price, all other things unchanged. On the other hand, for a put option the lower the asset price the higher will be the option price, all other things being held constant.

(b) *Exercise Price*: For an American or European call option, the higher the exercise price the lower will be the value of the option, all other things being held constant. The opposite is true for the put option, where the higher the value of the exercise price, the higher will be the value of the option, all other things unchanged.

(c) *Interest Rates*: Increases in interest rates decrease the present value of the exercise price. For an American or European call option this means that the cash outflow is lower in discounted terms, which in turn makes the option more valuable to the buyer of the option, other things being equal. The opposite is true for a put option as the cash inflow is lower in discounted terms when interest rates increase, making the option less valuable to the buyer of the option, other things remaining unchanged.

(d) *Volatility of the Asset Price*: Volatility is a friend for option contracts. When expected volatility is high there is a greater likelihood that the option price will rise (or fall) in relation to the exercise price, hence increasing the value of the American or European call (or put) option, other things kept constant.

(e) *Time to Expiration*: When the time to maturity is farther away in the future the American or European option prices will be higher in general. This is because:

- There is greater likelihood that the prices will move sufficiently to breach the exercise price and provide value to the option buyer.
- For call options, the cash outflows (from the exercise price) are discounted over a longer time, making them lower and thus more valuable to the buyer. For American put options, even though this means lower cash inflows in discounted terms, the benefit from (a) usually tends to outweigh the disadvantage of discounting, and if this is not the case then contract holders have the option of exercising the option earlier than the maturity date.
- For European put options a longer time to maturity can go either way, depending on whether volatility or discounting has a greater impact.

(f) *Cash Distributions*: This is relevant if the asset is a common stock that pays cash dividends. When a cash dividend is paid, the stock price falls. For a call option this means that the value of the option will decline, all other things being equal. For a put option the opposite is true.

b. European option price

The option prices calculated using Black Scholes formulas are as follows:

Call option price (c)

$$c = S_0\, e^{-qT}\, N(d_1) - K e^{-rT}\, N(d_2),$$

Put option price (p)

$$p = K e^{-rT} N(-d_2) - S_0 e^{-qT} N(-d_1),$$

where

$N(x)$ is the cumulative probability distribution function (pdf) for a standardized normal distribution,

S_0 is the price of the underlying asset at time zero,

K is the strike or exercise price,

r is the continuously compounded risk free rate,

σ is the volatility of the asset price,

T is the time to maturity of the option,

q is the yield rate on the underlying asset.

Alternatively, if the asset provides cash income instead of a yield, q will be set to zero in the formula and the present value of the cash income during the life of the option will be subtracted from S_0:

$$d_1 = \frac{\ln(S_0/K) + (r - q + \sigma^2/2)\, T}{\sigma\sqrt{T}}$$

$$d_2 = \frac{\ln(S_0/K) + \left(r - q - \sigma^2/2\right)T}{\sigma\sqrt{T}} = d_1 - \sigma\sqrt{T}\,.$$

2. Option pricing in EXCEL – Model framework
a. Model framework

We walk through a simple modeling framework used for pricing vanilla options in EXCEL.

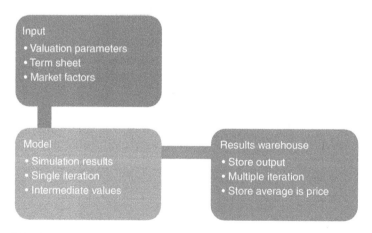

Figure 214   Option pricing framework

Let's start with a look at a desired end state snapshot when it comes to building an option pricing model in a spreadsheet.

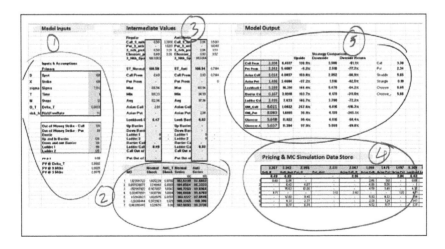

Figure 215   Option pricing model snapshot

Our EXCEL option pricing model (shown below) has the following key pieces (highlighted and marked up).

- A section for model inputs driven by market factors and term sheet variables (Section 1).
- A simulator that simulates the underlying variable and uses simulation results to produce a range of intermediate values (Sections 2 and 3).
- A pricing and Monte Carlo simulation results store where we store the results from our desired number of simulations (Section 4).
- A model output section where we summarize and present our model output (Section 5).

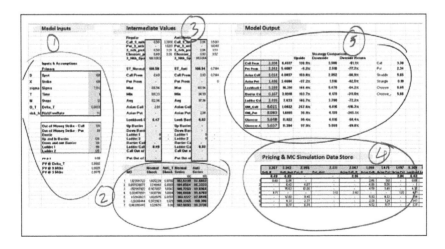

Figure 216   Option pricing model snapshot – labeled

b. Model focus

Of the above components, in general, model input, the underlying price simulator, model output and Monte Carlo simulation data store remain the same (structurally speaking) from one option pricing exercise to the next. While model values and parameters would certainly change, there is not a lot of tweaking or remodeling required. The only thing that does change from one pricing exercise to the next is the intermediate values section (Section 3), which we use to price the product in question.

Sometimes model parameters and input values (Section 1) also change based on the option product family being priced. For example, for exotic options you would need to add a variable to define barriers, averages, path functions and thresholds.

Section 3, however, is also broken down into four steps, and within that set of steps our focus will remain on step 2, which calculates option payout for a given simulation run.

For example pricing of a vanilla call option, option payout will be Max $(S_T - X, 0)$. For a put option this will change to Max$(X - S_T, 0)$. For both instances, S_T is the terminal value of the underlying option being simulated, while X is the strike price. The value of the option for that iteration will be simply the discounted present value (PV) of the payout. We will store PV of payout in our simulation results warehouse and move on to

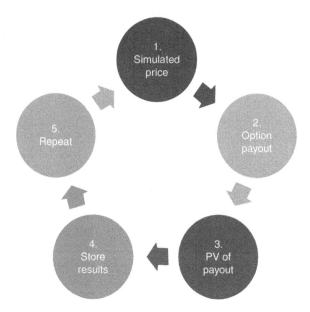

Figure 217   Monte Carlo simulator process

the next iteration. When the desired number of iterations (simulation runs) are completed we will take the average of the stored results and use that as an estimate of the actual option price.

3. Using Monte Carlo simulation to explain Black Scholes risk adjusted probabilities

Lars Tyge Nielsen[4] provides an interpretation of $N(d_1)$ and $N(d_2)$ and an explanation behind the difference between these risk adjusted probabilities of the Black Scholes equations. He does this by considering the value of a European call option on a stock which pays no dividends prior to the expiry date of the option as given by the following formula:

$$C = SN(d_1) - Xe^{-rt}N(d_2),$$

where

> C is the value of the European call option,
> S is the current value of the stock price,
> X is the exercise price,
> t is the remaining time to expiry,
> r is the risk free rate of interest,
> $N(.)$ is the cumulative standard normal distribution, the risk adjusted probabilities.

To understand this process, the payoff of the call option is divided into two components: the payment of exercise price and the receipt of stock. Both of these are dependent on the option being exercised, which will only occur if the option is in-the-money or alternatively when the stock price on the exercise date, S_T, rises above the exercise price, X, that is, $P(S_T > X)$ (probability that terminal price exceeds strike price).

The expected value and PV of each component is then calculated as given below.

a. Payment of exercise price and $N(d_2)$

The expected value of payment of the exercise price is exercise price times probability of stock price exceeding exercise price (probability of exercise): $-X \times P(S_T > X)$.

The PV of the expected value of payment of the exercise price is determined by discounting this expected value using the risk free interest rate over the time remaining to expiry of the option:

$$-X \times P(S_T > X) \times e^{-rt}.$$

Hence, comparing this with the second portion of the call option value equation above,

$$-X \times P(S_T > X) \times e^{-rt} = -Xe^{-rt}N(d_2),$$

we see that $N(d_2) = P(S_T > X)$, that is, $N(d_2)$ is the risk adjusted probability that the option will be exercised.

b. Receipt of stock and $N(d_1)$

Explanation of $N(d_1)$ is a bit more complex. We begin with the expected value of the contingent receipt of stock.

The expected value of the receipt of stock is contingent on exercise of the option. It is therefore the product of the conditional expected value of the receipt of S_T given that exercise has occurred times the probability of exercise.

Statistically this is written as

$$E(S_T \mid S_T > X) \times P(S_T > X).$$

This equation can also be written as follows:

$$E(S_T \mid S_T > X) \times N(d_2).$$

Note that the first term in this equation is a conditional expectation. It is the expected value of S_T given that we are now only considering those future values of S_T which exceed the exercise price X. If this constraint were not added we would have $E(S_T) = Se^{rt}$, the unconditional expectation of S_T. Given the conditionality, therefore, $E(S_T \mid S_T > X)$ will always be greater than $E(S_T)$. We may understand this concept through the following simple probability example.

A six sided fair die is rolled. The probability of rolling 4 is 1/6. Now suppose we have additional information that tells us that the number rolled is greater than 3. In this instance what is the probability of a 4 having being rolled given that the number rolled is greater than 3? The conditional probability works out to 1/3 > 1/6. The conditional probability is higher because we are only considering those outcomes that exceed the number 3 in our calculation.

In a similar fashion, $E(S_T \mid S_T > X) > E(S_T)$ because the expected value will only consider those stock prices which exceed the exercise price in the calculation of the expectation. Hence $E(S_T \mid S_T > X) \times N(d_2) > E(S_T) \times N(d_2) = Se^{rt} \times N(d_2)$.

Let us now consider the PV of this expected value by discounting it with the risk free rate over the time remaining to option expiry. We have:

$$E(S_T | S_T > X) \times N(d_2) \times e^{-rt} > E(S_T) \times e^{-rt} \times N(d_2) = S \times N(d_2).$$

Comparing the left hand side of this inequality with first portion of the Black Scholes equation for the call option, $SN(d_1)$, we have:

$$SN(d_1) = E(S_T | S_T > X) \times N(d_2) \times e^{-rt} > E(S_T) \times e^{-rt} \times N(d_2) = S \times N(d_2).$$

UNDERSTANDING RISK ADJUSTED PROBABILITIES THROUGH THE VALUE OF A CALL OPTION		
	PAYMENT OF EXERCISE PRICE	**RECEIPT OF STOCK**
Payment/Receipt amount: Exercise Not exercised	$-X$ 0	S_T 0
Payment/Receipt type on exercise	Deterministic – can only take one value	Probabilistic – Must therefore consider expected value of S_T. Values of S_T must be $> X$
Expectation of amount on exercise	$-X$	$= E[S_T	S_T > X]$ $> $ $= E[S_T]$
Probability: Of exercise Of not being exercised	$P(S_T > X)$ $P(S_T <= X)$	$P(S_T > X)$ $P(S_T <= X)$
Discount factor	e^{-rt}	e^{-rt}
Present Value = Expectation* Discount Factor* Probability	$-X e^{-rt} P(S_T > X)$	$E[S_T | S_T > X] e^{-rt} P(S_T > X) > E[S_T] e^{-rt} P(S_T > X) = SP(S_T > X)$
Comparison with Black Scholes call option value formula components	$-X e^{-rt} N(d_2)$	$SN(d_1)$
RESULTS	$P(S_T > X) = N(d_2)$	$N(d_1) > N(d_2)$

Figure 218 Black Scholes risk adjusted probabilities explained

In other words, $N(d_1)$ ensures that the discounted expected value of the contingent stock price received on exercise will be greater than this current value of stock.

c. Difference between N(d₁) and N(d₂)

Given $SN(d_1) > SN(d_2)$, we have $N(d_1) > N(d_2)$.

As mentioned above, $N(d_2)$ is simply the risk adjusted probability that the option will be exercised. Its linkage to X suggests that it only depends on when the event $S_T > X$ occurs.

On the other hand, $N(d_1)$ will always be greater than $N(d_2)$ because in linking it with the contingent receipt of stock in the Black Scholes equation, $N(d_1)$ must not only account for the probability of exercise as given by $N(d_2)$ but must also account for the fact that exercise, or rather receipt of stock on exercise, is dependent on the *conditional* future values that the stock price takes on the expiry date. In particular, this means stock price being greater than the exercise price is taken as a given condition when calculating the expected future value of stock on the expiry date.

4. Black Scholes – an intuitive derivation of N(d₂)

Of all the intimidating equations and formulas out there, the derivation of the Black Scholes formula for a European option easily takes first prize for the most unapproachable of topics for new arrivals in this field. For many of us it is literally a one-way conversation with Greco Roman symbols. If the terminology doesn't kill you, Itto's Lemma will.

I have now been teaching executive MBA students and treasury professionals for a decade and have searched in vain for a treatment that is less shocking to the system at 9 pm in the evening.

I couldn't escape the equations or the mathematics involved completely, but have tried to keep it basic and concise. The objective is not to derive the equation but simply to get more comfortable with the intuition behind it.

The objective of this note is to answer some very basic questions:

- What is the setting and context for the Black Scholes formula?
- What is the easiest and simplest way for deriving $N(d_2)$ that does not require half a textbook on the mathematics of computational finance?

The following treatment is based on material presented in Lars Nielson's excellent and highly recommended textbook on the subject and Maria Vassalou's teaching notes from her days at Columbia Business School.

a. Underlying assumptions

Within the Black Scholes world we will assume that there is an available price series for a non-dividend paying financial security given by $S(t)$. We assume that $S(t)$ is distributed log normally, which simply means that if Y represents the price series and X represents a normally distributed random variable then:

$$Y = e^X,$$

and

$$\ln(Y) = \ln(e^X) = X.$$

The take away from the above equations is that while $S(t)$ is log normally distributed, $\ln(S(t))$ is normally distributed. We also assume that the standard deviation and expected return for $\ln(S(t))$ is given by:

Expected return $= \ln(S_0) + (r - 1/2\sigma^2)(T - t)$

and

standard deviation $= \sigma\sqrt{(T - t)}$,

and $\ln(S(t)/S_0)$ is normally distributed with:

Expected return $= (r - 1/2\sigma^2)(T - t)$

and

standard deviation $= \sigma\sqrt{(T - t)}$.

Why have we used the risk free rate? Because in the risk neutral world, investors are content with earning the risk free rate and all assets earn the risk free rate; $(T - t)$ will get simplified to just t in our illustrations.

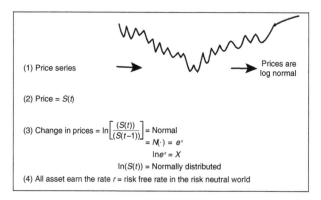

Figure 219 Derivation of $N(d_2)$ – the underlying assumptions

b. Estimating the jump

For a European call option we know that the option will only be exercised if the terminal price $S(t)$ is greater than the strike price X. Therefore, the first probability that we are interested in is the probability that $S(t) > X$ or $N(d_2)$. But to calculate the probability for our series, (remember we are dealing with $\ln(S(t))$ and not $S(t)$), we first need to convert our series to a standard normal distribution and estimate a z-score.

$$\text{Standard normal random variable} = \frac{X_i - \overline{X}}{\sigma}$$

where

X_i is a normally distributed random variable,
$\overline{X}$ is the mean of the random variable,
σ is the standard deviation of the random variable.

The z-score is basic statistics. As long as we have the value that needs to be compared as well as the mean and the standard deviation of the distribution we can simply plug them into the equation above. Mean and standard deviation we already have (see above discussion), the value that needs to be compared, X_i, is the jump. How high does $\ln(S(t))$ need to jump for the option to be in-the-money? $\ln(S(t))$ must be at least as high as the natural log of the strike, $\ln(X)$.

So in the standard normal variable formula, $\frac{X_i - \overline{X}}{\sigma}$:

$$\overline{X} = \ln(S_0) + (r - 1/2\,\sigma^2)(t)$$
$$\sigma = \sigma\sqrt{(t)}$$
$$X_i = \ln(X).$$

Once we have the standard normal variable or z-score then calculating the probability is a simple call to the normal distribution function in EXCEL.

c. Plugging in the values

We now take the jump and our estimates of expected return and standard deviation and plug them into the standard normal variable equation. We get the following results:

Standard normal variable or z-score,

$$y = \frac{X_i - \overline{X}}{\sigma} = [\ln(X) - (\ln(S_0) + (r - 1/2\sigma^2)(t))]/\sigma\sqrt{(t)}$$
$$= [\ln(X/S_0) - (r - 1/2\sigma^2)(t)]/\sigma\sqrt{(t)}.$$

But there is a small tweak that needs to be made before our work is complete for determining $N(d_2)$.

$N(y)$, the cumulative probability distribution for a standardized normal distribution, is the probability that the variable will be less than y, that is, $\Pr(Y \leq y) = N(y)$. This is graphically depicted below.

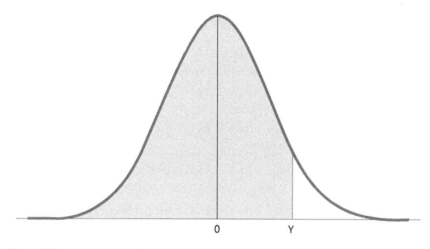

0   Y

Figure 220   Derivation of $N(d_2)$ – the underlying assumptions

For $N(d_2)$, however, we are interested in $P(Y > y) = 1 - N(y)$, that is, the probability that the terminal price will exceed the strike. This is not a big hurdle to d_2 from our derived value of y above. Rather than using the z-score y, all we need to do is use $-y$ (as $1 - N(y) = N(-y)$) and our job is done. We multiply our result, y, above with (-1) and simplify the result to the now very familiar Black Scholes value of d_2:

$$-y = -1 \times [\ln(X) - (\ln(S_0) + (r - 1/2\sigma^2)(t))]/\ \sigma\sqrt(t)$$

$$= [\ln(S_0/X) + (r - 1/2\sigma^2)(t)]/\ \sigma\sqrt(t) = d_2,$$

and
Probability $(S_t \geq X) = N(d_2)$

5. Pricing a European call option using Monte Carlo simulation

The price of the European call option may be derived using the closed form Black Scholes formula above. However, for the purpose of understanding the difference between results derived using Monte Carlo simulations and Black Scholes and the convergence to actual results, we present a step by step procedure for constructing a Monte Carlo simulator in order to derive the value of a European call option.

Using the Black Scholes call option price formula the call premium works out to US\$ 61.80.

PARAMETERS	EXPLANATION	INPUTS
Equity	Google	
S_0	Spot price at time 0	677.14
K	Strike or exercise price	650.00
R	Risk free rate	0.14%
Q	Dividend yield rate	0.00%
Σ	Annualized volatility in stock price	25.00%
T	T/N = Time-step (in years)	0.05
e^{-rT}	Discount factor	1.00
N	Number of time-steps	10.00
T	Tenor (year)	0.50

Figure 221 Inputs for determining a European call option

Step 1: Construct a Monte Carlo simulator for prices of the underlying security

Using the methodology already described earlier, construct a Monte Carlo simulator for determining the terminal price of the underlying security, in this case Google stock. We have used the terminal price formula,

$$S_t = S_0 e^{\left(\mu - \frac{1}{2}\sigma^2\right) t + \sigma\sqrt{t} z_t}$$

to derive the values below.

G26 =G25

	A	B	C	D	E	F	G
1	Parameters	Explanation	Inputs				
2	Equity	Google					
3	S_0	Spot price at time 0	677.14				
4	X	Strike or exercise price	650.00				
5	r	Risk free rate	0.14%				
6	q	Dividend yield rate	0.00%				
7	σ	Annualized volatility in stock price	25.00%				
8	t	T/N = Time step (in years)	0.05				
9	e^{-rT}	Discount Factor	1.00				
10	N	Number of time steps	10.00				
11	T	Tenor (year)	0.50				
15	Time Step	Random Number	Normally Scale Random Number (z_t)	Fixed Piece; $(r-q-0.5\sigma^2)t$	Random Piece; $\sigma\sqrt{t}z_t$	Change; Exp(Fixed+Random)	Simulated Stock Price; S_t
16	1	0.81757	0.90614	(0.00149)	0.05065	1.05039	711.26
17	2	0.85770	1.07005	(0.00149)	0.05982	1.06006	753.98
18	3	0.71462	0.56693	(0.00149)	0.03169	1.03066	777.10
19	4	0.79115	0.81042	(0.00149)	0.04530	1.04479	811.90
20	5	0.82565	0.93710	(0.00149)	0.05239	1.05221	854.29
21	6	0.95721	1.71922	(0.00149)	0.09611	1.09924	939.07
22	7	0.81540	0.89796	(0.00149)	0.05020	1.04991	985.93
23	8	0.51963	0.04923	(0.00149)	0.00275	1.00126	987.18
24	9	0.25988	(0.64373)	(0.00149)	(0.03599)	0.96322	950.86
25	10	0.28254	(0.57531)	(0.00149)	(0.03216)	0.96691	919.40
26						Terminal Price (S_T)	919.40

Figure 222 Generation of terminal prices using the Monte Carlo simulation

Step 2: Run scenarios

Next, run a number of scenarios and store the resulting terminal prices using EXCEL's data table functionality. This is shown for 25 simulated runs below.

Scenario	Terminal Price ($_T$)
1	846.51
2	682.64
3	655.83
4	461.79
5	517.08
6	653.98
7	644.33
8	771.71
9	631.30
10	667.40
11	511.25
12	765.34
13	597.17
14	530.64
15	525.84
16	662.50
17	591.02
18	739.25
19	648.14
20	856.94
21	797.46
22	697.14
23	527.25
24	829.51
25	893.20

Figure 223 Terminal prices from 25 simulated runs

Step 3: Calculate the intrinsic value or payoffs

For each of the simulated runs calculate the payoff of the European call option using the terminal price and the strike value: Payoff = Maximum of (Terminal Price – Strike, 0). The payoffs corresponding to the 25 terminal prices are given below.

Scenario	Terminal Price ($_T$)	Payoff
1	846.51	196.51
2	682.64	32.64
3	655.83	5.83
4	461.79	–
5	517.08	–
6	653.98	3.98
7	644.33	–
8	771.71	121.71
9	631.3	–
10	667.4	17.40
11	511.25	–
12	765.34	115.34
13	597.17	–
14	530.64	–
15	525.84	–
16	662.5	12.50
17	591.02	–
18	739.25	89.25
19	648.14	-
20	856.94	206.94
21	797.46	147.46
22	697.14	47.14
23	527.25	–
24	829.51	179.51
25	893.2	243.20

Figure 224   Payoffs for 25 simulated runs

Step 4: Calculate discount values of payoffs (prices)

For each simulated run calculate the discounted values of the payoff as follows:

Payoff $\times$ e^{-rT},

where r is the risk free rate and T is the tenor of the option, that is, 0.5 years.

The results are shown below.

Scenario	Payoff	Discount Value
1	196.51	196.37
2	32.64	32.62
3	5.83	5.83
4	–	–
5	–	–
6	3.98	3.98
7	–	–
8	121.71	121.62
9	–	–
10	17.40	17.39
11	–	–
12	115.34	115.26
13	–	–
14	–	–
15	–	–
16	12.50	12.49
17	–	–
18	89.25	89.19
19	–	–
20	206.94	206.80
21	147.46	147.36
22	47.14	47.11
23	–	–
24	179.51	179.38
25	243.20	243.03

Figure 225   Discount value of payoffs for 25 simulated runs

Step 5: Determine the call premium
Finally, take the average of the discounted payoffs across all simulated runs to determine the call premium. Alternatively, take the average of all the payoffs across simulated runs and discount this average payoff using the discount factor, e^{-rT}, to determine the value of the European call option. In our example and for the 25 simulated runs illustrated above, the result is US$ 56.74.

There is a difference of around US$ 5 between the result obtained using the Black Scholes formula and that obtained using the Monte Carlo simulator.

11. Convergence and variance reduction techniques for option pricing models

1. Introduction

Monte Carlo simulation techniques are a useful tool in finance for pricing options, especially when there are a large number of sources of uncertainty (in modeling terms: state variables) involved. For derivatives having three or more state variables, closed form solutions like the Black Scholes formula for call option price may not exist. Also, numerical methods like binomial option pricing models become impractical when the sources of uncertainty increase. In such instances, Monte Carlo simulation techniques may produce convergent solutions.

The solution's accuracy however is dependent on the number of trials, N, that are used. Specifically, the uncertainty surrounding a possible solution is inversely related to the square root of N. This relationship of accuracy to number of trials is derived as follows.

The mean of the discounted payoff, μ, is the average of the discounted value of payoff across all trials, that is, the estimate of the value of the instrument. The standard deviation of these discounted payoff values is denoted by σ.

The standard error of the estimate is given by $\sigma/\sqrt{N}$.

A 95 percent confidence interval around the estimate is given by

$$\mu - 1.96\ \sigma/\sqrt{N} < \text{estimate} < \mu + 1.96\ \sigma/\sqrt{N}.$$

This shows that as the value of N increases, the range around the estimate reduces, that is, the accuracy of the estimate or the solution from the Monte Carlo methodology increases as the number of trials increase. Specifically, in order to increase the accuracy by a factor of x, the number of trials that should be used would need to be increased by a factor of x^2. For example, to double the accuracy of the estimate, the number of trials that should be used to ensure this level of accuracy would need to be quadrupled.

As the number of trials increases, the Monte Carlo simulation technique becomes more and more time consuming, as well as computationally intensive. In order to save on computational time there are a number of variance reduction techniques that may be used. These include:

- Antithetic Variable Technique,
- Control Variate Technique,
- Importance Sampling,

- Stratified Sampling,
- Moment Matching,
- Quasi-Random Sequences.

2. Antithetic variable technique and quasi-random sequences

So far, we have only referred in passing to the methods that may be used to improve the results obtained from Monte Carlo simulation. These variance reduction procedures decrease the standard error between the simulated result and the true value, as well as converging to the true result at a faster rate. In this section we will further elaborate on these methods. In particular we will be looking at the antithetic variable technique and the quasi-random Monte Carlo method.

First, however, we need to set the stage. We consider a European call option on a stock whose current spot price is 50. The strike price is also 50. The annual risk free rate is 5 percent, there are no dividends payable and the annual volatility in the underlying price series is 30 percent. The option will expire in 0.5 years.

Using the Black Scholes call option pricing formula we determine that the price of the European call option is 4.8174.

We now use a one time-step or single path Monte Carlo simulation model to simulate the option price. We execute the calculation for 100, 200, 300, ..., 1000 runs respectively. We then calculate the average value across the number of simulated runs to determine the estimated value of the option.

In the figure below we have plotted the results against the true Black Scholes result. You can see the variation of the results from the Monte Carlo methodology. This variation is also demonstrated in the magnitude of the standard error terms, where standard error is calculated as the standard deviation of the simulated results (the sample) divided by the square root of the number of runs.

One way of improving the results is to increase the number of simulated runs considered. We can see this from the graph and table above. The accuracy for 500 hundred runs is greater than that for 100, runs while the result obtained after 1000 runs has a smaller standard error than the result after 500 runs. As the number of simulated runs increases, in general the Monte Carlo simulated value converges towards the true value. Note, however, that as the number of simulated runs increases the computational time also increases. The other alternative is to use variance reduction techniques mentioned earlier, where for the same number of runs the estimated value converges to the true value of the option at a faster rate and with a greater degree of accuracy.

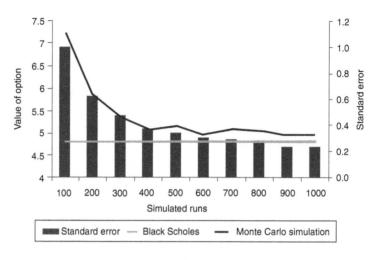

SIMULATED RUNS	BLACK SCHOLES	MONTE CARLO SIMULATION	STANDARD ERROR
100	4.8174	7.2358	1.0081
200	4.8174	5.8928	0.6397
300	4.8174	5.3798	0.4796
400	4.8174	5.0921	0.3966
500	4.8174	5.1697	0.3536
600	4.8174	5.0011	0.3166
700	4.8174	5.1071	0.2997
800	4.8174	5.0598	0.2749
900	4.8174	4.9729	0.2546
1000	4.8174	4.9995	0.2440

Figure 226   Black Scholes vs. Monte Carlo simulation

a. Antithetic variable technique

Using this method we have actually doubled the sample being considered for the same amount of simulated runs. For each run we use the original Monte Carlo simulation result along with its negatively correlated result. These are averaged to obtain the result for a given simulated run under the antithetic approach. This average series of results converges towards the true value of the option at a faster rate than the results from the original Monte Carlo simulation.

If the random numbers are generated from a uniform distribution ($X \sim U(0, 1)$ or RAND()), as is the case in our example, then the negatively correlated value is $1-X$, which is also uniformly distributed, ($1 - X \sim$

$U(0, 1)$ or $1-\text{RAND}()$). Alternatively, if the normally scaled number from the original Monte Carlo simulation is Y, the normally scaled number from the second stream will be $-Y$.

We now have two parallel streams of random numbers that result in two sets of simulated prices, intrinsic values and values of options. For each simulated run take the average of the two options values to obtain the result for that run. The results for the antithetic variable method are given in the figure below.

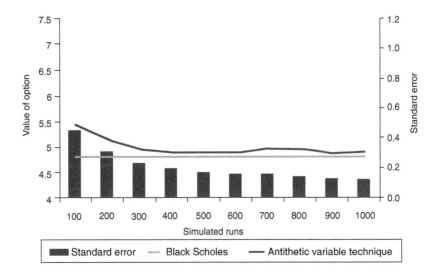

SIMULATED RUNS	BLACK SCHOLES	ANITHETIC VARIABLE TECHNIQUE	STANDARD ERROR
100	4.8174	5.4442	0.4585
200	4.8174	5.1461	0.3186
300	4.8174	4.9798	0.2410
400	4.8174	4.9013	0.2022
500	4.8174	4.8962	0.1788
600	4.8174	4.8678	0.1630
700	4.8174	4.9631	0.1563
800	4.8174	4.9634	0.1435
900	4.8174	4.8912	0.1340
1000	4.8174	4.9113	0.1280

Figure 227   Black Scholes vs. antithetic variable technique

If you compare the standard error terms above (calculated as mentioned earlier, that is, standard deviation of the simulated results divided by the square root of the number of runs) with the error terms from the original Monte Carlo simulation method, you will see that they are much lower and that the convergence to the true value is much faster.

b. Quasi-random sequences

Finally, we use the quasi-random Monte Carlo method to simulate the results for the value of the call option. Under this approach the random number series generated is actually not random at all, but deterministic. We have used the Halton sequence, which is a low discrepancy sequence, which means that the sample points are more evenly distributed in the sample space.

Unlike a random number series, where the data points tend to cluster together, the data points in the Halton sequence are more uniformly distributed in the sample space, as can be seen in the figure below.

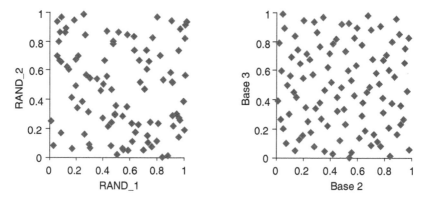

Figure 228   Random and quasi-random sequences

As we have only used a single time-step, that is, one time interval in the sample path in our simulation, the dimension for the Halton sequence is one. Note that the Halton sequence has a different prime base for each dimension. For example, for dimension one the prime base is two; for dimension two it is three; for dimension three it is five, and so on. In our calculations, because we have used only one dimension, the Halton sequence with prime base two will be used.

After normally scaling the values in this deterministic series we calculate the simulated prices, intrinsic values and values of option for each simulated run, as we have done before for the Monte Carlo simulation and the antithetic variable technique. The results from the quasi-random method are depicted below:

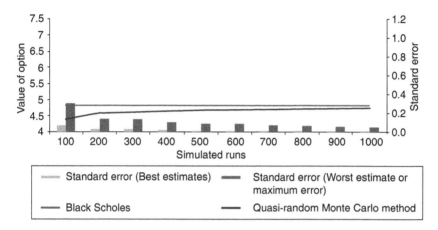

Figure 229 Black Scholes vs. quasi-random Monte Carlo method – graphical representation

Note that we have purposely kept the axis scales for all the graphs the same so that you can see the extent of the improvement in results. Compare the graph above to the earlier two. You can see that there is a significant improvement in the convergence rate of the results, in particular in comparison with the original Monte Carlo simulation results.

The data points drawn from the quasi-random sequence for each simulated run are not independent of each other, as is the case for the Monte Carlo simulation and the antithetic method, but are selected so as to more uniformly cover the entire sample space. Each subsequent number in the sequence is dependent upon the numbers that came before. Because of this dependency, the standard error term cannot be calculated as was done earlier for the original Monte Carlo simulation method and the antithetic variable technique.

For a quasi-random sequence method, the best estimate for the standard error is the standard deviation of the sample divided by the number of simulated runs in that sample. The worst case or maximum error is the standard deviation of the sample times (ln(number of simulated runs)^dimension) divided by the number of simulated runs.

The results are given in the table below.

SIMULATED RUNS	BLACK SCHOLES	QUASI-RANDOM MONTE CARLO METHOD	STANDARD ERROR (BEST ESTIMATE)	STANDARD ERROR (WORST ESTIMATE OR MAXIMUM ERROR)
100	4.8174	4.4134	0.0667	0.3072
200	4.8174	4.5911	0.0347	0.1841
300	4.8174	4.6280	0.0235	0.1338
400	4.8174	4.6922	0.0178	0.1068
500	4.8174	4.7005	0.0143	0.0886
600	4.8174	4.7124	0.0120	0.0766
700	4.8174	4.7151	0.0102	0.0671
800	4.8174	4.7489	0.0091	0.0606
900	4.8174	4.7527	0.0081	0.0549
1000	4.8174	4.7539	0.0072	0.0501

Figure 230   Black Scholes vs. quasi-random Monte Carlo method

To conclude, let us see the results from all the methods together.

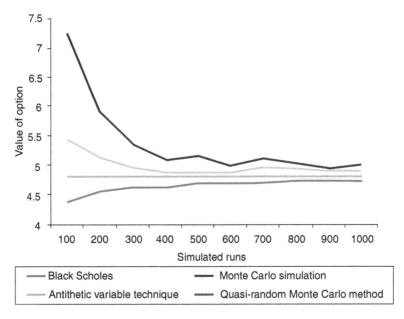

Figure 231   Value of a call option – Black Scholes vs. Monte Carlo vs. variance reduction techniques

As is apparent in the graph above, the results from the variance reduction procedures do in fact converge to the true value at a faster rate using a smaller number of simulated runs and show much smaller deviations from the actual result as compared to the original Monte Carlo simulation method.

7

Simulation Applications

1. Monte Carlo simulation VaR using historical returns

1. Monte Carlo simulation – early days

In 2004 we wrote the risk management engine for a derivatives portfolio. The client was a large emerging market bank. The portfolio included FX options, FX participating forwards, long dated interest rate swaps and cross currency swaps.

It wasn't supposed to be a big deal till we started factoring emerging market drivers, absence of secondary market trades, public quote data, trading volumes, market crises, crashes and biases. We had been working with Monte Carlo simulations for the last four years and, for someone deeply taken up with the algorithm, the simulation model was a natural choice.

Since this was a risk platform, the objective was to forecast a value at risk (VaR) number that the bank could use for internal capital allocation. None of the positions traded publicly, however data on the underlying currencies and rates was publicly available and quoted. The simulation model would simulate the underlying rates, mark to market the portfolio using the simulated rates, calculate the daily simulated price change and repeat the simulation exercise for the next 12 months. We would pick through the wreckage of simulated crises and crashes and identify the VaR estimate.

The implementation was elegant, a bit complex but an overall success, till the traders on the market making desk saw the results and threw them in a trash bin. I was heartbroken and disappointed but I knew that the traders were right. We had looked at the results and, despite our calibration and tweaks, knew that we were under estimating the true exposure.

We lost the client, killed the model and moved on to other alternate solutions.

2. Monte Carlo simulation revisited – fixing the distribution

Over the years we played with many different alternates. I became a big fan of the historical simulation model for calculating VaR, but wondered what would happen if I could bring the two approaches together. Run a simulation using the Monte Carlo method, but use the true distribution rather than the default normal distribution.

In 2009, working on another simulation exercise, we did exactly that. This time the portfolio was a collection of cross currency swaps. The question once again was capital allocation for the position, while the issue was estimating VaR. We calculated historical rates, ran a simulation to pick the returns, marked-to-market the portfolio, calculated returns based on this simulation and calculated VaR.

The original Monte Carlo simulation model uses the following process.

Figure 232   Original Monte Carlo simulation model process

The revised hybrid approach tweaked it to the following variant.

Figure 233   Monte Carlo simulation/historical simulation hybrid model process

The results were very interesting – much more real, and certainly a lot more acceptable to the traders. The approach made sense specifically for valuing exotic, illiquid, non-traded securities and positions that were dependent on traded, quoted underlying securities, currencies, rates or commodities. It was even more useful for emerging market exposures where simple simulation models would break down because they couldn't factor in the volatility of the underlying emerging market variables.

3. Monte Carlo simulation and historical returns – calculating VaR

A natural question that should come up after the above discussion is how does the hybrid Monte Carlo simulation model using historical returns fare in terms of VaR measurement compared to the traditional Monte Carlo simulation (based on the normally scaled random numbers) as well as the original historical simulation approaches?

We answer this question by estimating VaR numbers obtained using each of these three methods for gold, silver, crude spot prices and the EUR–USD exchange rates.

The traditional Monte Carlo simulation model (here also called the MC-Normal approach) for simulating prices, and the one derived using z_t's that are derived from historical returns (here also called the MC-Historical approach), have been discussed earlier in this text.

Once the price streams have been simulated, the returns series are determined by taking the natural log of the ratio of successive prices. In our example we have projected daily prices for a 365-day period to obtain 364 daily returns. For the historical simulation approach we have used a window of 365 days of the most recent actual prices available to us.

For the MC model using historical returns we have indexed rates for the years January 2004 to December 2012. This has been done by dividing the width of the random number space (1) into equal intervals for the total number of return observations. Eight years of data was used, specifically to improve and increase the number of actual "outliers" and provide a more complete true distribution for the simulation model.

We may then use EXCEL's data analysis histogram functionality to plot a histogram of returns for each of these methods and determine the daily VaR number from the histogram values and chart output. In our example, we have actually created the histogram ourselves so that it automatically updates as scenarios change.

The results of our analysis are given below.

The histogram of returns for the Monte Carlo simulation model that uses the normally scaled random numbers has a much narrower dispersion of values around the mean and does not capture the level of extreme events seen in the gold price series over the past years. VaR from the Monte Carlo simulation using historical returns reflects these extreme events in its tails. Across the 25 scenarios shown above, the daily VaR number using the MC-Historical approach is more in line with the daily VaR number obtained using the historical simulation approach relative to the daily VaR number from the MC-Normal approach.

Gold prices

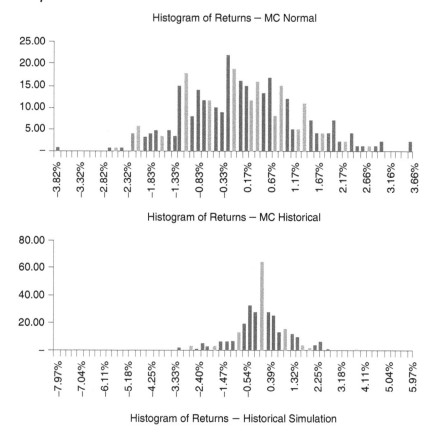

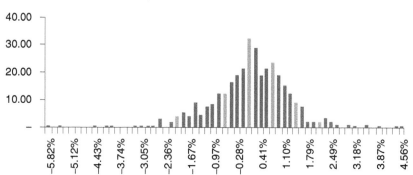

Figure 234 Comparing histogram of returns and VaR from Monte Carlo/historical simulation models – gold

Scenario	Daily VaR		
	MC Normal	**MC Historical**	**Historical Simulation**
1	2.3798%	4.3301%	4.1489%
2	2.7150%	4.1311%	4.1489%
3	2.3398%	2.6978%	4.1489%
4	2.5943%	4.0855%	4.1489%
5	2.7277%	3.9751%	4.1489%
6	2.3091%	3.2299%	4.1489%
7	2.4955%	3.4747%	4.1489%
8	2.6046%	3.8362%	4.1489%
9	2.6563%	3.1512%	4.1489%
10	2.7178%	4.7049%	4.1489%
11	2.5142%	3.2972%	4.1489%
12	2.1633%	5.0906%	4.1489%
13	2.5042%	4.6059%	4.1489%
14	2.6574%	4.4746%	4.1489%
15	2.4334%	3.8289%	4.1489%
16	2.6997%	4.3543%	4.1489%
17	2.5488%	4.3485%	4.1489%
18	2.3864%	4.5701%	4.1489%
19	2.7764%	4.4405%	4.1489%
20	2.7660%	5.3448%	4.1489%
21	2.7519%	4.5859%	4.1489%
22	2.3876%	2.9473%	4.1489%
23	2.1934%	4.8346%	4.1489%
24	2.6221%	3.3328%	4.1489%
25	2.3031%	4.5596%	4.1489%
Average	**2.5299%**	**4.0893%**	**4.1489%**

Figure 234   Continued

Note: For the gold MC model we have assumed an initial spot price of US$ 1,657.50 (as at December 28, 2012), an annualized volatility of 20.90 percent (for 2012 daily price returns), a risk free rate of 0.16 percent (1 year US Treasury yield curve rates as at December 31, 2012) and a convenience yield of 0 percent.

Silver prices

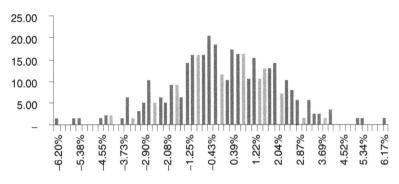

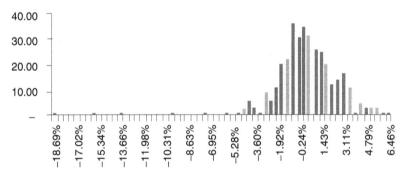

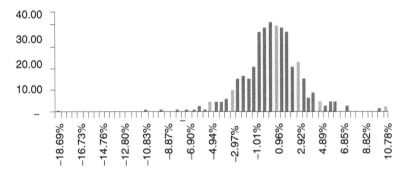

Figure 235   Comparing histogram of returns and VaR from Monte Carlo/historical simulation models – silver

Scenario	MC Normal	Daily VaR MC Historical	Historical Simulation
1	3.9767%	6.9382%	8.0621%
2	3.5909%	7.4120%	8.0621%
3	4.4343%	5.7782%	8.0621%
4	4.4723%	7.9538%	8.0621%
5	4.5543%	6.4649%	8.0621%
6	4.3744%	5.7541%	8.0621%
7	4.2804%	5.1403%	8.0621%
8	3.7117%	7.7446%	8.0621%
9	4.8962%	7.5248%	8.0621%
10	3.8130%	6.4446%	8.0621%
11	4.0149%	10.0670%	8.0621%
12	4.3983%	8.6216%	8.0621%
13	4.0405%	7.5504%	8.0621%
14	4.2691%	7.2518%	8.0621%
15	3.8993%	6.2657%	8.0621%
16	5.0175%	5.8274%	8.0621%
17	4.2185%	8.8950%	8.0621%
18	4.2830%	6.9418%	8.0621%
19	3.9255%	6.4852%	8.0621%
20	4.7337%	7.4909%	8.0621%
21	3.9862%	6.0455%	8.0621%
22	4.4915%	6.9707%	8.0621%
23	4.3411%	6.9382%	8.0621%
24	3.9054%	5.3512%	8.0621%
25	4.3867%	6.0118%	8.0621%
Average	**4.2407%**	**6.9548%**	**8.0621%**

Figure 235   Continued

Note: For the silver MC model we have assumed an initial spot price of US\$ 30.15 (as at December 28, 2012), an annualized volatility of 34.83 percent (for 2012 daily price returns), a risk free rate of 0.16 percent (1 year US Treasury yield curve rates as at December 31, 2012) and a convenience yield of 0 percent.

Crude oil prices

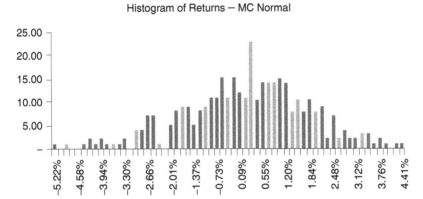

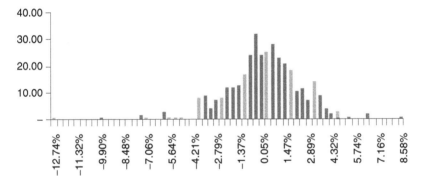

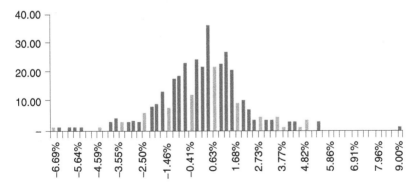

Figure 236 Comparing histogram of returns and VaR from Monte Carlo/historical simulation models – crude oil

Scenario	Daily VaR		
	MC Normal	MC Historical	Historical Simulation
1	4.0753%	8.3426%	5.7349%
2	4.2040%	7.3800%	5.7349%
3	3.8721%	7.6947%	5.7349%
4	3.7387%	7.5621%	5.7349%
5	4.0222%	6.3221%	5.7349%
6	3.5749%	7.8913%	5.7349%
7	3.6743%	5.7129%	5.7349%
8	3.7042%	7.2247%	5.7349%
9	3.3939%	6.5027%	5.7349%
10	3.4273%	7.6759%	5.7349%
11	4.0515%	6.8122%	5.7349%
12	4.4389%	6.3427%	5.7349%
13	3.7050%	6.1251%	5.7349%
14	3.5050%	6.1914%	5.7349%
15	3.5393%	6.2184%	5.7349%
16	4.1927%	8.6615%	5.7349%
17	3.4930%	6.6186%	5.7349%
18	3.7520%	6.7732%	5.7349%
19	4.3923%	6.0730%	5.7349%
20	3.2065%	6.4163%	5.7349%
21	4.5441%	9.4729%	5.7349%
22	3.8852%	6.7083%	5.7349%
23	3.4052%	6.4522%	5.7349%
24	3.8286%	7.5878%	5.7349%
25	3.5215%	7.3888%	5.7349%
Average	**3.8059%**	**7.0460%**	**5.7349%**

Figure 236   Continued

Note: For the crude MC model we have assumed an initial spot price of US$ 90.91 (as at December 27, 2012), an annualized volatility of 31.37 percent (for 2012 daily price returns), a risk free rate of 0.16 percent (1 year US Treasury yield curve rates as at December 31, 2012) and a convenience yield of 0 percent.

EUR–USD exchange rate

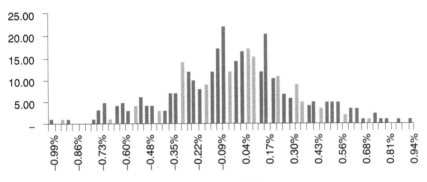

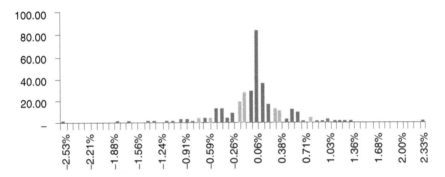

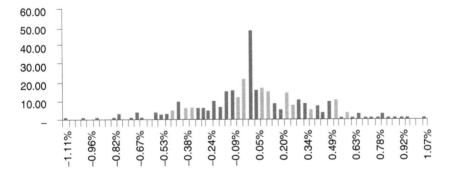

Figure 237 Comparing histogram of returns and VaR from Monte Carlo/historical simulation models – EUR–USD

Scenario	Daily VaR		
	MC Normal	MC Historical	Historical Simulation
1	0.8614%	1.0832%	0.9411%
2	0.7709%	1.2894%	0.9411%
3	0.7867%	1.2773%	0.9411%
4	0.7395%	1.2455%	0.9411%
5	0.8793%	1.3604%	0.9411%
6	0.7717%	1.3017%	0.9411%
7	0.9222%	1.2023%	0.9411%
8	0.8044%	1.2633%	0.9411%
9	0.8001%	1.1649%	0.9411%
10	0.7970%	1.2491%	0.9411%
11	0.9266%	1.2538%	0.9411%
12	0.8012%	1.2589%	0.9411%
13	0.8282%	1.4138%	0.9411%
14	0.7442%	1.3468%	0.9411%
15	0.8761%	1.7770%	0.9411%
16	0.8037%	1.3455%	0.9411%
17	0.8896%	1.3104%	0.9411%
18	0.8588%	1.2617%	0.9411%
19	0.8880%	1.4436%	0.9411%
20	0.8351%	1.3628%	0.9411%
21	0.8369%	1.3028%	0.9411%
22	0.8386%	1.3025%	0.9411%
23	0.7734%	1.0167%	0.9411%
24	0.7134%	1.0941%	0.9411%
25	0.9348%	1.4418%	0.9411%
Average	**0.8273%**	**1.2948%**	**0.9411%**

Figure 237 Continued

Note: For the EUR–USD MC model we have assumed an initial spot EUR–USD exchange rate of 1.3215 (as at December 31, 2012), an annualized volatility of 6.73 percent (for 2012 daily price returns), a USD risk free rate of 0.16 percent (1 year US Treasury yield curve rates as at December 31, 2012) and a EUR risk free rate of 0.44 percent (1 year Euro Libor rate as at December 31, 2012).

In general, the VaR calculated using the MC-Historical approach is more in line with the VaR derived using the historical simulation method, sometimes producing even more conservative results. The latter happens because of the wider window used for determining indexed rates (which in turn are used for determining the uncertain components, z_t, of the

MC-Historical model) in relation to the 1-year window used for the historical simulation approach.

2. Monte Carlo simulation: fuel hedging problem

1. Case context and background

In Part I, in our discussion on risk management, we introduced Emirates airline and their fuel hedging challenges. We will now revisit the problem and see how it could be modeled using Monte Carlo simulation.

Within the airline industry, the largest contribution to variable cost is fuel expense. Airlines use fuel hedges, fuel surcharges or a combination of both to manage the risk of changing oil prices on their bottom line. Our objective is to prepare a presentation for the board of directors advising them on two primary questions:

(a) Should the airline move forward with a fuel hedging program?
(b) If yes, what should be the correct hedge ratio? The hedge ratio represents the percentage of fuel expenses hedged by the airline.

One caveat on the data front. There are two relevant time series. One is the WTI crude oil data set while the other is the fuel oil data set. Even though fuel oil is not jet or aviation fuel, it has long been used as a proxy

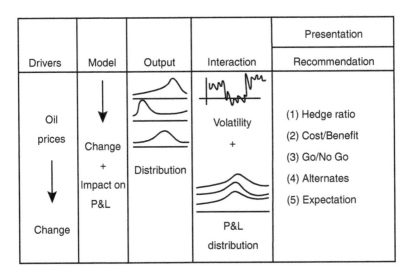

Figure 238 Fuel hedging problem – Monte Carlo simulation model framework

for jet fuel. From a hedging point of view, airlines had generally used a mix of crude, fuel oil and aviation fuel contracts to hedge their exposure. That is till the events in Libya happened and the rate of increase in fuel oil diverged dramatically from the rate of increase in aviation fuels.

The recommended reading list at the end of this section provides coverage of two points of view when it comes to fuel oil hedging.

There is the US Air point of view, which says that, like FedEx and UPS, it is best to simply pass on the increase in fuel costs to the consumer through fuel surcharges; that such an approach is far superior and more rational than the costly and sometimes deadly fuel cost hedging programs. The alternate point of view is the Southwest and Delta perspective, which is that hedging programs, when executed and timed correctly, create tremendous value for the airline and can actually become a source of competitive advantage.

For the purpose of the case discussion, there are four primary questions that need to be addressed:

(a) Should we recommend fuel hedging or not? If yes, what are the risk exposure of the airline and the resultant impact of the exposure on profitability?
(b) How is that exposure managed and reduced with the fuel hedging program?
(c) What is the correlation between fuel oil and crude oil prices? Which one should we use to hedge our client's jet fuel exposures?
(d) What is the probability that the airline profitability and margins will turn negative due to a rise in fuel oil prices in the absence of the hedging program?

a. Initial analysis and requirements

Our initial analysis suggests that the airline is exposed to oil, currency and interest rate risk. However, both volatility and impact on P&L are greatest for unanticipated changes in fuel expenses. This risk is aggravated further by aggressive fuel hedging strategies used by the competition which, if successful, will leave our client at a significant disadvantage. Compared to oil price risk, the impacts of currency and interest rate risks are a small fraction of simulated P&L.

The objective of our model is to therefore:

(a) Simulate crude oil prices
(b) Use changes in crude oil prices to model demand for fuel as well as total fuel expense for a given period
(c) Use Monte Carlo simulation to generate a distribution for operating margin

(d) Understand the interaction between model parameters – volatility, ticket demand, hedge ratio, operating margin and probability of shortfall

(e) Make recommendations to the board based on the analysis performed above.

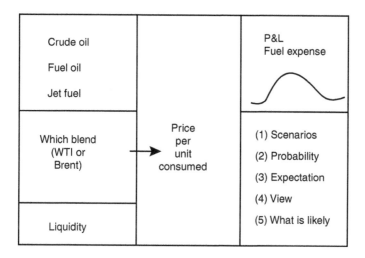

Figure 239   Fuel hedging problem – model building process

b. Two black boxes

The primary model output required for the above goals are simulating price per unit consumed and units of fuel consumed. We have decided to use WTI as our primary blend for forecasting crude oil prices. Since the airline purchases fuel in tons, rather than simulating price per barrel of oil, our model simulates price per ton.

There is a strong correlation between crude oil, fuel oil and jet fuel prices. An initial black box is created for the correlation between these three products. The initial black box would serve as a crude approxima- tion and would be refined later as the model is calibrated to market prices. Initial analysis indicates that while the average correlation is strong, it is not stable and experiences significant instability under times of market stress and volatility.

In addition to fuel expenses, we also link ticket demand (and in turn gross reveneus) to changes in fuel oil prices. The assumption here is that higher oil prices beyond a certain acceptable threshold ultimately lead to global recession and lower demand for air travel, and vice versa. Also, in addition to fuel, other items linked to the volume of flights and passenger miles flown are linked to the demand model. The original demand model is a simple black box which can be upgraded in a later iteration.

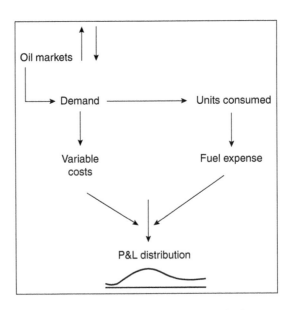

Figure 240 Fuel hedging problem – the two black boxes – fuel expense correlation and ticket demand

c. Identifying relationships to be examined

We are also very interested in examining the impact of volatility and correlation on hedge effectiveness as well as the P&L distribution. From a model output point of view this is a "must have" requirement without which meaningful and practical recommendations to the board of directors would not be possible.

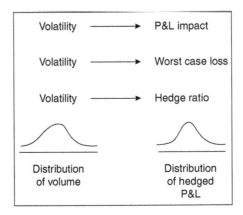

Figure 241 Fuel hedging problem – impact of volatility and correlation on hedge effectiveness and P&L

d. Board requirement and recommendations

Finally, whatever output the model produces has to meet the requirements for a board of director presentation. The presentation should put forward final recommendations backed by analysis that is generated by the Monte Carlo simulation model and must:

(a) Factor in the instability in correlation between different drivers in the model
(b) Focus equally on hedged as well as non-hedged scenarios in a neutral, unbiased fashion
(c) Give a range of values for likely, extreme and worst-case scenarios based on historical oil price volatility.

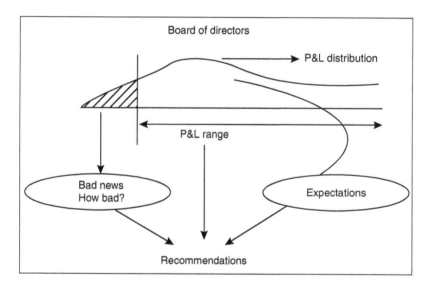

Figure 242   Fuel hedging problem – board of Directors' recommendations

2. Simulating crude oil prices

To simulate crude oil prices we will follow a multi-step process. We first present the input required and output produced from the simulation model and then follow with a step-by-step review of the model building process.

a. Model specification

To begin we need values for the following parameters.

The target output is a monthly series of simulated crude oil prices per ton.

We use expected return as a fundamental driver of value and add simulated noise to model random movements in prices. Return is constant as per the original model specification, while noise is random and changes from one simulation to the next. The last shaded column provides the final model output, which is also plotted using a line graph.

Model Inputs	
Gallons per Barrel	42
Barrels per Tonne	7.14
Spot Price per Tonne	678.3
Volatility	30%
Time	1
Steps	12
Delta_T	0.0833
RiskFree	1%
Conv. Yield	0%

Figure 243   Model parameters

	Rand() - Uniform	Normal Random (Zt)	Expected Return	Noise	Change	Spot Price 678
1	0.481	(0.048)	-0.29%	0%	99%	674
2	0.930	1.478	-0.29%	13%	113%	763
3	0.587	0.221	-0.29%	2%	102%	776
4	0.921	1.415	-0.29%	12%	113%	874
5	0.664	0.422	-0.29%	4%	103%	904
6	0.502	0.006	-0.29%	0%	100%	902
7	0.236	(0.720)	-0.29%	-6%	94%	845
8	0.551	0.129	-0.29%	1%	101%	852
9	0.193	(0.867)	-0.29%	-8%	93%	788
10	0.645	0.373	-0.29%	3%	103%	812
11	0.408	(0.232)	-0.29%	-2%	98%	793
12	0.812	0.884	-0.29%	8%	108%	854

Figure 244   Model for oil spot price

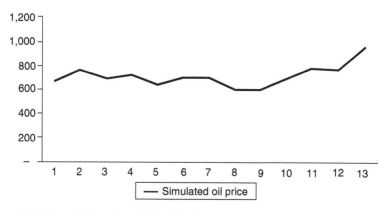

Figure 245 Simulated path of oil spot price

b. Simulating normally distributed random numbers

We can use EXCEL's *RAND() function* to generate a uniformly distributed random number between 0 and 1. Column D (the first column) in our model below does just that. However, for simulating a financial security, commodity, equity or currency we need a normally distributed random number. We can calculate that by calling the *NORMSINV function*. The input to the function is a number between 0 and 1, which is provided by our first call to the RAND() function in Column D. The input signifies probability and the output is a normally distributed random number from a normal distribution with mean zero and standard deviation one.

The normally distributed random number, Column E, will be used later in simulating noise/error/uncertainty in the model. A quick note, your numbers will not match these numbers since our laptops will use a different seed for the random number generator.

	A	B	C		D	E	F	G
15								
16					Rand() - Uniform	Normal Random (Zt)	Expected Return	Noise
17				1	0.481	=NORMSINV(D17)		0%
18				2	0.930	1.478	-0.29%	13%
19				3	0.587	0.221	-0.29%	2%
20				4	0.921	1.415	-0.29%	12%
21				5	0.664	0.422	-0.29%	4%
22				6	0.502	0.006	-0.29%	0%

Figure 246 Normally distributed random numbers

c. Calculating expected return

Column F calculates expected return by using the risk free rate, volatility and the time-step (small *t* or Delta_T). Since all three parameters are constant, the value will remain the same across all iterations.

LEFT		▾ × ✓ *fx*	=(riskfree_rate-0.5*sigma^2)*Delta_t					
A B	C	D	E	F	G	H	I	
8	Volatility	30%						
9	Time	1						
10	Steps	12				Max	962.15	
11	Delta_T	0.0833				Min	606.45	
12	RiskFree	1%				Avg Price	724.61	
13	Conv. Yield	0%						
14								
15							Spot Price	
16			Rand() - Uniform	Normal Random (Zt)	Expected Return	Noise	Change	678
17	1	0.925	1.442	=(riskfree_rate-0.5*sigma^2)*Delta_t			
18	2	0.136	(1.099)	-0.29%	-10%	91%	695
19	3	0.701	0.528	-0.29%	5%	104%	725
20	4	0.100	(1.283)	-0.29%	-11%	89%	647
21	5	0.863	1.094	-0.29%	9%	110%	709

Figure 247   Expected return

d. Calculating random noise

The original model specification uses a constant expected return (formula displayed in the figure above) and a simulated error (or uncertainty)

LEFT		▾ × ✓ *fx*	=sigma*SQRT(Delta_t)*E17					
A B	C	D	E	F	G	H	I	
8	Volatility	30%						
9	Time	1						
10	Steps	12				Max	962.15	
11	Delta_T	0.0833				Min	606.45	
12	RiskFree	1%				Avg Price	724.61	
13	Conv. Yield	0%						
14								
15							Spot Price	
16			Rand() - Uniform	Normal Random (Zt)	Expected Return	Noise	Change	678
17	1	0.925	1.442	-0.29%	=sigma*SQRT(Delta_t)*E17		
18	2	0.136	(1.099)	-0.29%	-10%	91%	695
19	3	0.701	0.528	-0.29%	5%	104%	725
20	4	0.100	(1.283)	-0.29%	-11%	89%	647

Figure 248   Random noise

term (formula displayed in the figure below) to estimate the change in the value of the simulated security from one time-step to the next.

In *Column G*, we multiply standard deviation for the period, *sigma* × *sqrt (delta_t)*, with the normally distributed random number, z_t, to get the uncertain element in our equation.

e. Estimating change in simulated prices

Our last step is estimating the change, Column H, and using that change to calculate the simulated price, Column I, for the period. Once we have completed this exercise for the first row, all we have to do is copy and paste the relevant cells all the way to the 12th row and the first pass on the model is complete.

			Rand() - Uniform	Normal Random (Zt)	Expected Return	Noise	Change	Spot Price 678
17		1	0.925	1.442	-0.29%	12%	=EXP(F17+G17)	
18		2	0.136	(1.099)	-0.29%	-10%	91%	695
19		3	0.701	0.528	-0.29%	5%	104%	725
20		4	0.100	(1.283)	-0.29%	-11%	89%	647
21		5	0.863	1.094	-0.29%	9%	110%	709
22		6	0.472	(0.070)	-0.29%	-1%	99%	703

Figure 249 Estimating change in simulated price

			Rand() - Uniform	Normal Random (Zt)	Expected Return	Noise	Change	Spot Price 678
17		1	0.925	1.442	-0.29%	12%	113%	766
18		2	0.136	(1.099)	-0.29%	-10%	91%	695
19		3	0.701	0.528	-0.29%	5%	104%	725
20		4	0.100	(1.283)	-0.29%	-11%	89%	647
21		5	0.863	1.094	-0.29%	9%	110%	709
22		6	0.472	(0.070)	-0.29%	-1%	99%	703
23		7	0.048	(1.669)	-0.29%	-14%	86%	606
24		8	0.555	0.138	-0.29%	1%	101%	612
25		9	0.946	1.611	-0.29%	14%	115%	=I24*H25
26		10	0.912	1.354	-0.29%	12%	112%	786
27		11	0.486	(0.035)	-0.29%	0%	99%	782
28		12	0.992	2.430	-0.29%	21%	123%	962

Figure 250 Simulated price

The last cell at *Column I, Row 28 (962)* has the number that we need, which is the simulated price of crude oil per ton.

The challenge, however, is that this value by itself is of limited use as it changes from one iteration to the next. To complete our simulation exercise we must store this result in a data table and average it out over 500 to 5,000 simulations. But rather than doing this here, we will build our data table and results warehouse when we have a few more items to store.

3. Linking financial model to the simulation

Since we have a model for simulating oil prices, we are now ready to link our oil price model to projected financial statements for the airline.

To do this we need to figure out how to link simulated crude oil prices to jet fuel expense on the P&L statement. This means we need to determine:

(a) The correct correlation model between crude oil prices and jet fuel prices. If we don't have a model we can start with a black box that we can refine later. This black-box-now-refine-later approach will be used whenever there is a need to reduce complexity and move forward with the modeling process.
(b) The relationship between oil prices and demand or economic outlook. If a relationship exists that is great, if it doesn't then we would need to build an independent model for economic outlook.
(c) A demand model for ticket sales (a combination of prices and volumes based on oil price shocks).

Since we want to stay focused on modeling the process, we take a simplistic and direct demand model that will use oil prices to directly forecast ticket and cargo sales. This is not an accurate approach, but it will allow us to quickly test our model end to end. We also assume a perfect correlation between crude oil and jet fuel prices for our first pass.

a. Building the demand model

Our simplistic demand model looks at the changes in oil prices and assumes growth or shrinkage in demand based on how high or low oil prices have moved as shown below. All the numbers below and the relationship between them have been picked out of thin air. In real life we would do a more robust job.

In the Oil Prices per Ton versus Impact on Ticket Sales section of the model, the two cells in bold (Oil Prices per Ton = 50 and 3000 respectively) serve as placeholders for the EXCEL *VLOOKUP()* function, which is used to pick the applicable change in ticket demand based on where oil prices land in a given iteration.

Demand Model	
1 year price	**390**
Average Oil Price - 1 year	**530**
Oil Prices per Tonne	**Impact on Ticket Sales**
50	25%
300	25%
450	20%
550	10%
700	0%
825	-15%
950	-20%
1100	-30%
3000	-30%
Demand Model Output	
Demand Impact - 1 year price	**25%**
Demand Impact - Average price	**20%**

Figure 251   Ticket demand model

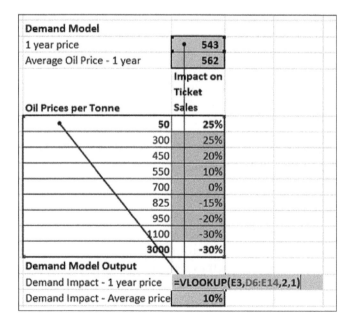

Figure 252   Demand impact output

b. Simulating fuel expense

To simulate fuel expense a two-step process is used. First, using the simulated price, the cost of fuel consumed is estimated by using the new price and the old fuel consumption. In the second step, the number of units consumed is adjusted based on the projected change in demand. The two calculations are linked together to estimate the revised fuel expense as shown below.

			LEFT		✕ ✓ ƒₓ	=D6*D5/1000000	

	A	B	C	D	E
3				Historical	Projected
4			Fuel Oil Consumption (USD)	350,000,000	Consumption
5			Fuel Consumption in Tonnes	6,000,000	1,500,000
6			Price per Tonne - 1 year Forecast	820.45	=D6*D5/1000000
7			Price per Tonne - Average 1 year	766.87	4,601

Figure 253   Revised fuel expense

			LEFT		✕ ✓ ƒₓ	=D18*(1+E15)	

	A	B	C	D	E
12			Drivers	History	Projection
13			Fuel Oil Tonnes - Consumed	1,500,000	1,650,000
14			Revised Fuel Expense		939
15			Demand Change		10.00%
16					
17			P&L Model Line Items	Historical	Projected
18			Ticket Sales & Cargo	2,845	=D18*(1+E15)
19			Other Income	181	181
20			Total Income	3,026	3,311

Figure 254   Impact on ticket sales and cargo

The revised fuel expense is then plugged into variable expenses. Any additional variable expenses are linked to the demand (revenue growth) model and move accordingly. The same process is used for Ticket Sales and Cargo as well as for Food and Beverage and Ticket Sale Commissions.

The final result is a simple simulation that allows us to model operating margin for the airline.

Drivers	History	Projection
Fuel Oil Tonnes - Consumed	1,500,000	1,650,000
Revised Fuel Expense		939
Demand Change		10.00%
P&L Model Line Items	Historical	Projected
Ticket Sales & Cargo	2,845	3,130
Other Income	181	181
Total Income	3,026	3,311
Operating Expenses		
Variable Expenses		
Food, beverages & supplies	77	85
Commissions	72	79
Fuel Expenses	733	939
Total Variable	882	1,103
Fixed Expenses	1,817	1,817
Total Operating Expenses	2,699	2,920
Operating Margin	327	391

Figure 255   Impact on operating margin

c. *Storing the results*

However, as mentioned earlier, a single iteration of the model is meaningless. We need to use our old data table trick to store the results of the simulation in a data store which can then be used to calculate the average of our modeled variables over 500 – 5,000 simulations.

More importantly, the resulting data set can then be used to plot and generate a first pass for distribution of P&L (operating margin) for the airline.

Average Results	4,087	4,104	3,000	1,194	170
	Fuel Expense - 12 mth Forecast	Fuel Expense - 1 year Average	Gross Revenue	Fuel Expense - Quaterly Model	Operating Margin - Model
	5,227	5,321	2,418	1,237	(455)
1	3,793	3,749	3,130	1,207	287
2	3,222	3,873	3,414	1,145	633
3	3,563	3,987	3,130	1,144	350
4	3,848	4,148	3,130	1,222	271
5	3,849	4,245	3,130	1,222	271
6	4,815	3,933	2,845	1,353	(144)
7	2,895	3,462	3,414	1,047	731
8	6,280	4,600	2,276	1,375	(735)
9	4,074	3,634	3,130	1,284	209
10	6,123	5,123	2,276	1,344	(704)
11	4,537	4,875	2,845	1,283	(74)
12	3,359	4,023	3,130	1,088	406

Figure 256   Data table of stored results

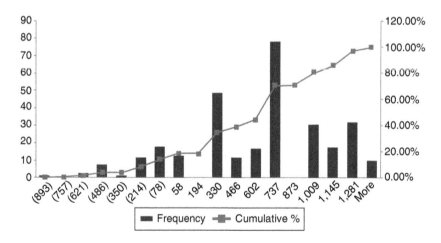

Figure 257   Operating margin distribution

d. Presenting the results

This model is by no means perfect. However, a first pass can be put together in under an hour and as more data and analysis comes in, each of the black boxes (correlation, demand, ticket sales, and so on) can be replaced by a more authentic and robust model. The most powerful output from the model is the P&L distribution. The distribution answers many common questions, from maximum loss and worst-case outlook to the probability that such scenarios will come to pass. It can also be used to evaluate hedge effectiveness across a range of possibilities; from testing the interaction of volatility and correlations to testing the demand model and the search for the right hedge ratio. Used correctly it can help us engage the board productively as well as help the board make a more informed decision.

4. Tweaking the model and making it more real

Let's start with correlations. We calculate the return series from daily price movements for fuel oil and WTI. We use that to calculate trailing correlations on a 10-day basis. The result is the following trend. If you were thinking about using WTI to hedge fuel oil exposure, the graph below is not encouraging. Not encouraging not only because correlations are all over the place, but also because they tend to be clearly negative.

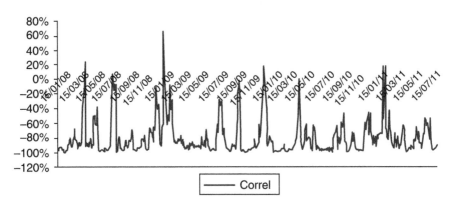

Figure 258   10-day trailing correlations between fuel oil and crude oil

But part of this problem is the time horizon used. If you use average monthly aviation fuel to WTI correlations, the picture changes dramatically. Which one of these two images is accurate and correct and which view of correlation is the right view – the 10-day trailing correlation (above) or the end of the month average correlation (below)? One of the objectives of this case study is to solve this riddle.

| | Correlation Matrix | | | |
	Fuel Oil	WTI	Gold	Jet Fuel
Fuel Oil	1.0000	0.8969	0.1690	0.9681
WTI	0.8969	1.0000	0.1307	0.8816
Gold	0.1690	0.1307	1.0000	0.1205
Jet Fuel	0.9681	0.8816	0.1205	1.0000

Figure 259 Monthly average correlations

To answer the above questions, we rely on a quick visual eye-balling of the return series for the three candidates – fuel oil, WTI and jet fuel. It will allow us to get a better understanding of the three distributions, as well as their similarities. Our data set as far as this case discussion is concerned goes back three years with monthly data points, resulting in a data set of 36 points of information. The distributions are given below.

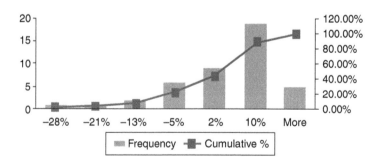

Figure 260 Distribution of fuel oil returns

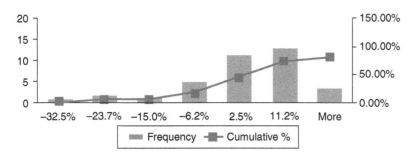

Figure 261 Distribution of crude oil returns

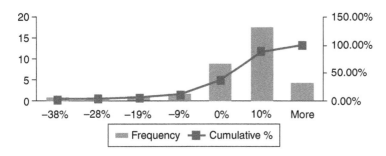

Figure 262 Distribution of jet fuel returns

The histograms also yield the minimum and maximum monthly price shocks documented for the three hedging candidates, fuel oil, WTI and jet fuel. The minimum and maximum changes correspond to a one in 36 point probability, corresponding to 2.78 percent or a 97 percent confidence level using the historical distribution.

	Fuel Oil	WTI	Jet Fuel
Stdev	9.79%	11.32%	11.05%
Min monthly shock	-28%	-32%	-38%
Max monthly shock	18%	20%	19%

Figure 263 Minimum and maximum monthly price shocks and volatility (Stdev) of price returns

5. Jet fuel price shock estimation

To keep things simple let's assume that we like the correlation and the fit between jet fuel and fuel oil and decide to use the fuel oil series as a hedge for our purposes. We also use VaR (the variance/covariance (VCV) approach) to calculate the maximum change in prices that we expect to see on a monthly basis and get the following numbers.

		Current Price Level	2.952			
		Vol	2.56%		22	
				Daily	Monthly	Monthly
	Probability		Norm	Price Shock	Price Shock	$ Price Shock
Confidence Level	of Loss		Factor	%		
66%	34.00%		0.41246313	1.06%	5.0%	0.15
75%	25.00%		0.67448975	1.73%	8.1%	0.24
90%	10.00%		1.28155157	3.28%	15.4%	0.45
99%	1.00%		2.32634787	5.96%	28.0%	0.83
99.99%	0.01%		3.71901649	9.53%	44.7%	1.32

Figure 264   Monthly price shocks using the VCV VaR approach

These price shocks, however, all assume a standard average volatility world. From a risk point of view we would like to use the maximum volatility level we have seen in times of stress, and use that as a basis for our calculation. The tool that we use is probability of shortfall, which is a variation of the break-even method you may be familiar with from your microeconomic days. However, in shortfall, rather than focusing on what volume or numbers it would take for one to break even, we focus on what price shock it would take to push profit margins into negative territory.

For now let us assume that a 40 percent increase in jet fuel prices, without an ability to pass the same to consumers in the form of fuel surcharges, would prove catastrophic for the airline. It would eat away all of its profit margin and a large part of its free cash generation capacity. The catastrophic impact would occur because a change in ticket prices would reduce air travel and volumes, budgeted revenues and impact the ability of the airline to service its debt obligations, leading to yet another round of bankruptcy and restructuring.

6. Shortfall using Monte Carlo implementation

In this section we will analyze the sensitivity of profit margins, that is, the relationship between profit margins and changes in crude oil prices as well as aviation fuel prices, and interpret what the VaR shock actually means. Board members have specifically asked for help in understanding how to interpret the data presented, as well as an explanation of the process used to complete the analysis.

The sequence followed for building a simplistic fuel hedging and margin simulation model is given below:

1. Build a simple crude oil Monte Carlo simulator
2. Link the crude oil model with the gross revenue generation model of the airline
3. Create a simple growth and contraction model using levels of crude oil prices. Higher crude oil prices lead to lower traffic volumes and revenues while lower crude oil prices lead to higher traffic and revenues
4. Hook up with the airline's P&L, with P&L summarized in two line items, gross revenues and profit margin
5. Translate the output into two output graphs which present both the results for crude oil prices and the simulated profit margin of the airline without any hedging in place.

Note that the above is initially carried out based on the most simplistic assumptions. This is done to test the model building process as well as to get immediate feedback from the board on the presentation format that it is most comfortable with. Once the model and reporting formats are finalized there will be time available to replace the crude assumptions made in the prototype shortfall model with more realistic and sophisticated choices.

The output from the model is given below.

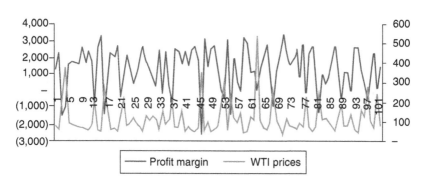

Figure 265   Simulated profit margins – version 1

Figure 266   Simulated profit margins – version 2

Both charts show the same results but using different formats. The idea is to test readability and preference at the board level for a given presentation format for the fuel oil hedging case.

The results are summarized using a histogram, where the final simulated margin numbers are as presented in the table below.

Bin	Frequency	Cumulative %
(2,072)	1	0.99%
(1,503)	0	0.99%
(934)	3	3.96%
(365)	9	12.87%
204	5	17.82%
772	7	24.75%
1,341	13	37.62%
1,910	21	58.42%
2,479	13	71.29%
3,048	15	86.14%
More	14	100.00%

Figure 267   Profit margin histogram output – high volatility world

The cumulative probability of all scenarios where a margin shortfall occurred is 10.89 *percent*. This means that using the model and the assumptions there is a *10.89 percent* chance that the airline in question will face a scenario where its operating cash flows will turn negative and it will not be in a position to completely service its debt and other obligations in the absence of hedging.

A key assumption made here is that it is a high volatility world. We want to see the impact on the margin of historically high crude oil volatility.

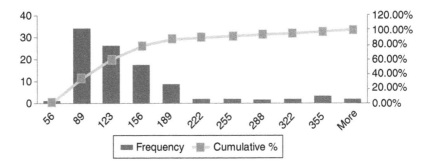

Figure 268   Crude oil price distribution in a high volatility world

The high volatility world generates the following distribution of crude oil prices.

This in turn translates into the following distribution of the airline's margins.

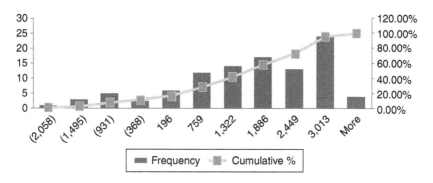

Figure 269   Distribution of profit margins in a high volatility world

The high volatility assumption is further compared against a low volatility world view with the following results.

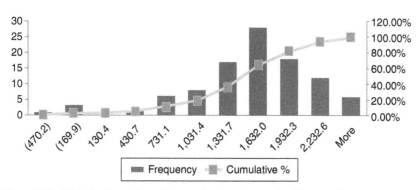

Figure 270   Distribution of profit margins in a low volatility world

The low volatility world view indicates a reduction in the probability of margin shortfall from 10.89 percent to just under 4 percent.

From a presentation point of view, the board is now more comfortable with the analysis and the reporting template and format. In terms of target accounts, a decision is made to use volatility and the probability of margin shortfall as key drivers for determining the hedging decision, as well as the amount and the percentage of aviation fuel exposure that needs to be hedged.

Bin	Frequency	Cumulative %
(470.2)	1	0.99%
(169.9)	3	3.96%
130.4	0	3.96%
430.7	2	5.94%
731.1	6	11.88%
1,031.4	8	19.80%
1,331.7	17	36.63%
1,632.0	28	64.36%
1,932.3	18	82.18%
2,232.6	12	94.06%
More	6	100.00%

Figure 271 Profit margin histogram output – low volatility world

7. Presenting the case to the client

The board has now come back to us with a few questions, and in this section our objective is to answer these questions with the data available.

a. Questions from the board

1. The first question deals with expected future volatility as well as current volatility levels. The board understands that volatility cuts both ways. It makes sense to hedge when we expect volatility to shoot up but the impact of current volatility also has a direct relationship on the cost of the hedging program, especially if we use products with built-in optionality. The board would like to know how bad volatility can get.
2. The second question deals with the impact of the hedge on the distribution of P&L. It is not sufficient to look at minimum and maximum values. The board would actually like to see how the distribution of profits shifts and moves for hedged as well as unhedged options.
3. The third question deals with the impact of volatility on these distributions.
4. The fourth question deals with the true cost of hedging when prices move against us as an airline (oil prices drop rather than rise).
5. The fifth question deals with the actual recommendation on hedge ratio. Should the airline hedge 25 percent – 50 percent – 75 percent or all of its jet fuel exposure? How does the hedge ratio impact the distribution of profits?

b. What do the numbers look like for Emirates Airline?

The first required step is to estimate fuel consumption. Take a quick look at the last public financial statement released by Emirates. Emirates consumes between 5.6 to 6.2 million metric tons of aviation fuel every year. We will use this number for our calculations.

Emirates Airline – Environmental Data					
Metric [1]	Unit	2011-12	2010-11	% change [9]	Verified [2]
Jet fuel consumption	tonnes	6,145,434	5,619,791	9.4	✓
Carbon dioxide (CO2) Emissions	tonnes	19,358,116	17,702,341	9.4	✓
Fuel efficiency	L/100PK	4.11	4.07 [4]	1.0	✓
	L/FTK	0.224	0.225	-0.3	✓
	L/TK	0.31	0.30	2.8	✓

Figure 272   Emirates financials – annual jet fuel consumption

The impact of aviation fuel price volatility in 2011–12 is apparent in its financials. Emirates profitability has declined by 70 percent as compared to the previous year.

Emirates Group				
Financial Highlights		2011-12	2010-11	% change
Revenue and other operating income [1]	AED m	67,394	57,224	17.8
Operating profit	AED m	2,606	5,943	(56.2)
Operating margin	%	3.9	10.4	(6.5) pts
Profit attributable to the Owner	AED m	2,310	5,951	(61.2)
Profit margin	%	3.4	10.4	(7.0) pts
Cash assets	AED m	17,586	16,056	9.5
Total assets [2]	AED m	84,127	71,402	17.8
Emirates				
Financial Highlights		2011-12	2010-11	% change
Revenue and results				
Revenue and other operating income	AED m	62,287	54,231	14.9
Operating profit	AED m	1,813	5,443	(66.7)
Operating margin	%	2.9	10.0	(7.1) pts
Profit attributable to the Owner	AED m	1,502	5,375	(72.1)
Profit margin	%	2.4	9.9	(7.5) pts
Return on shareholder's funds	%	7.2	28.4	(21.2) pts
Financial position and cash flow				
Total assets	AED m	77,086	65,090	18.4
Cash assets	AED m	15,587	13,973	11.6
Employee data				
Average employee strength	number	42,422	38,797	9.3

2010-11 figures have been re-classified to conform with the current year's presentation.
After eliminating inter company income/expense of AED 1,893 million in 2011-12 (2010-11 : 1,413 million).
After eliminating inter company receivables/payables of AED 78 million in 2011-12 (2010-11 : 88 million).

Figure 273   Emirates financial performance 2011–12

What does fuel volatility look like using the last five years of data? We do a quick trailing volatility plot and then run a histogram in EXCEL on the same data to get some indication of the range of price volatility. The range for daily crude oil volatility is between 0.9 and 7.5 percent. Even though this is not a perfect proxy for aviation fuel, the range does give us some indication of how much prices can jump in a 21-day period.

However, there is one big implementation challenge. Even if daily volatility hits 7.5 percent on an empirical basis, implied volatility will never rise this high.

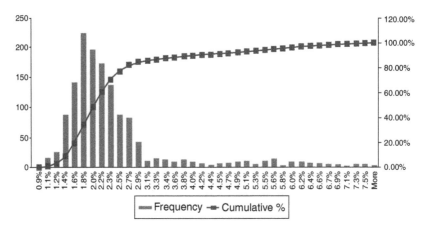

Figure 274   Crude oil price volatility distribution – 21-day moving average

We plug the numbers into our model. Emirates generates revenues of AED 62 billion growing at a rate of AED 8–9 billion a year. Projected forecast for the next 12 months is AED 72 billion. The simplistic Monte Carlo simulation model discussed above looks at a two-month revenue forecast which ties in with the average fuel purchase period (assumption). To see full year's results simply multiply the numbers below by 6.

The model also takes in assumptions that relate changes in oil prices to changes in passenger mile demand and actual consumption. It models

	ORIGINAL	HEDGED	UNHEDGED
Gross ticket proceeds	12,000	8,400	8,400
Total expenses	10,600	8,505	8,607
Margin	1,400	(105)	(207)
Fuel expense	2,745	–	–
Revised fuel expense	3,108		4,440

Figure 275   Simulation model for profitability

revenues and expenses based on expected growth, which is in turn linked to changes in oil prices. Higher oil prices lead to higher ticket prices and negative growth in demand; lower oil prices lead to lower ticket prices and positive growth in demand.

The simulation run from the model is then stored in multiple data tables and the results are used to answer questions raised earlier by the board. For example, the table below actually shows the range of margin values for hedge ratios ranging between 0 and 70 percent. It also shows the realized gains or (losses) on account of the hedge when prices move for or against us (rise or decline) in the last column.

		Margin Unhedge	Margin Hedge	Margin Difference	Hedge Gain / (Loss)
Results					
70%	Min	(2,628)	(1,640)	(1,379)	(1,826)
	Max	3,333	1,954	988	4,150
		18	26	89	44
		1,435	918	(517)	456
50%	Min	(2,641.0)	(2,608.9)	(1,086.2)	(1,435.5)
	Max	3,561.8	2,475.6	75.6	5,234.0
		12	22	94	21
		1,587	1,109	(478)	971
25%	Min	(5,200.2)	(6,554.6)	(1,354.4)	(447.5)
	Max	3,651.9	3,110.4	95.9	9,578.5
		18	28	86	7
		1,460	1,041	(419)	1,976

Figure 276 Simulation results

Note that we have assumed that the hedge product used is fuel oil future contracts traded on the NYMEX exchange. No options or structures are involved. Contracts are purchased once every two months to hedge the anticipated fuel consumption for the next 2-month period (with a time lag).

While maximum and minimum ranges are useful, what the board really wants to see are income distributions linked to hedge ratio choices. Four P&L distributions derived from the simulation engine are presented below. The P&L distribution graphs cover the following scenarios as per the board's guidelines.

1. Unhedged – High volatility world;
2. Hedged – High volatility world – 30 percent;
3. Unhedged – Low volatility world;
4. Hedged – Low volatility world – 70 percent.

Note that the high volatility world assumes a 40 to 45 percent annualized volatility in oil prices. The low volatility world assumes a 15 to 20 percent annualized volatility in oil prices. Two different hedge ratios are tried at 30 percent and 70 percent to assess the impact of changing hedge ratios.

These distributions combined with the table above give us sufficient information to answer the board's questions. The hedge vaporizes the center (as expected) and tempers the extreme ends. It also has an impact on probability of shortfall as well as the expected loss when shortfall occurs.

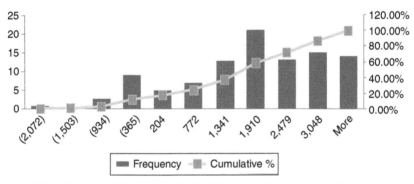

Figure 277   High volatility and unhedged strategy distribution of P&L

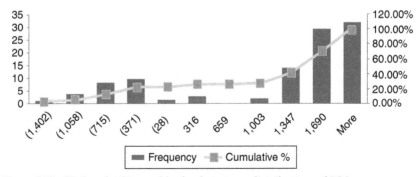

Figure 278   High volatility and hedged strategy distribution of P&L

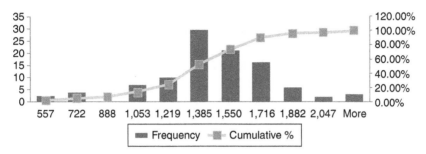

Figure 279 Low volatility and unhedged strategy distribution of P&L

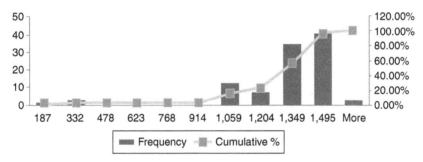

Figure 280 Low volatility and hedged strategy distribution of P&L

c. Recommended reading – Jet fuel hedging case

1. Crack Spread Gone Wrong – When correlations break down in the Jet Fuel Market – (http://www.bloomberg.com/news/2011-01-31/united-delta-profit-at-risk-from-silent-killer-in-fuel-hedges.html; Source: Bloomberg).

2. The Airline Industry – Overview – (http://seekingalpha.com/article/644991-in-depth-drilldown-of-the-airline-industry-part-1; Source: Seeking Alpha).

3. Airline Industry – A focus on Delta Airlines – (http://seekingalpha.com/article/666811-airline-industry-focus-on-delta; Source: Seeking Alpha).

4. Fuel Hedging – WTI or Brent (http://www.investmentu.com/2011/March/airline-industry-oil-prices.html).

5. Fuel Hedging at Southwest Airlines (http://www.msnbc.msn.com/id/25419436/ns/business-us_business/t/airlines-hedge-against-soaring-fuel-costs/).

6. How much does it cost to hedge Jet Fuel – The Delta experience (http://www.thestreet.com/story/11545944/1/how-delta-and-us-airways-fight-high-fuel-prices.html).

7. Jet Fuel Oil Price Trend and Data over 30 year (http://www.indexmundi .com/commodities/?commodity=jet-fuel&months=360).
8. Emirates-Financials-Disclosures (http://financetrainingcourse.com/ education/wp-content/uploads/2012/10/Emirates-Financials-Disclo sures.pdf).
9. US Airways – Fuel Hedge Case Study (http://financetrainingcourse .com/education/wp-content/uploads/2012/10/aviation-fuel-hedge-case-study-us-airways.pdf).
10. Southwest Airline Fuel Hedge Case Study (http://financetraining course.com/education/wp-content/uploads/2012/10/fuel_hedge-southwest-case-study.pdf).
11. Airline Industry Fuel Hedge Experience – Note (http://financetrain ingcourse.com/education/wp-content/uploads/2012/10/Airline-fuel-aviation-case-study-one.pdf).

3. Simulating the interest rate term structure[1]

1. CIR interest rate model

a. Simulating future short-term interest rates under the CIR model

The centered Cox–Ingersoll–Ross (CIR) model to simulate the short rate is given as:

$$dr_t = -kr_t \, dt + \sigma \sqrt{r_t + \gamma dB_t}.$$

This may be restated for the actual short rate r_t^* as:

$$\Delta r_t^* = k(\gamma - r_{t-1}^*) d_t + \sigma \sqrt{(r_{t-1}^*)\, dz_t}\ ,$$

where

r_t^*, the interest rate series, is obtained from the given benchmark yield curve;
r_t is the transformed series, such that $r_t = r_t^* \ \gamma$;
k represents the speed of adjustment (or mean reversion);
γ represents the long run mean of the short-term interest rate;
σ represents the volatility;
and dZ_t is a small random increment in the Wiener process z_t having mean 0 and variance; $dZ_t = \sqrt{dt}e_t$, where e_t are normally scaled random numbers generated in EXCEL using the function NORMSINV(RAND()).

Note: The parameters k, γ and σ are derived from market data using estimation and calibration procedures that are not included within the scope of this book.

The spreadsheet shows:

Row 1 (A1): $\Delta r_t{}^* = \kappa(\gamma - r_{t\text{-}1}{}^*)dt + \sigma{}^*sqrt(r_{t\text{-}1}{}^*){}^*dz_t$, Cox, Ingersoll and Ross Model

	A	B	C	D	E	F	G
1	$\Delta r_t{}^* = \kappa(\gamma - r_{t\text{-}1}{}^*)dt + \sigma{}^*sqrt(r_{t\text{-}1}{}^*){}^*dz_t$, Cox, Ingersoll and Ross Model						
2	κ	0.01					
3	γ	0.10%		$dr_t = k(\theta - r_t)dt + \sigma\sqrt{r_t}\,dZt$			
4	$r_0{}^*$	0.16%					
5	σ	0.74%					
6	dt	0.08					
7							
8	Random number (Z)	Time Step (t)	Scaled Random Number [dz=normsinv(rand())*sqrt(dt)]	Delta r*	Projected r*		
9	0.28	1.00		(0.17)	=$B$2*($B$3-B4)*$B$6+$B$5*SQRT(B4)*$C$9		
10	0.58	2.00		0.06	0.00%	0.16%	
11	0.76	3.00		0.20	0.01%	0.16%	
12	0.25	4.00		(0.19)	-0.01%	0.16%	
13	0.39	5.00		(0.08)	0.00%	0.15%	
14	0.33	6.00		(0.12)	0.00%	0.15%	
15	0.63	7.00		0.10	0.00%	0.15%	
16	0.27	8.00		(0.17)	-0.01%	0.15%	
17	0.62	9.00		0.09	0.00%	0.15%	
18	0.26	10.00		(0.18)	-0.01%	0.15%	
19	0.24	11.00		(0.21)	-0.01%	0.14%	
20	0.80	12.00		0.24	0.01%	0.15%	
21	0.69	13.00		0.14	0.00%	0.15%	
22	0.34	14.00		(0.12)	0.00%	0.15%	
23	0.78	15.00		0.23	0.01%	0.15%	
24	0.44	16.00		(0.05)	0.00%	0.15%	
25	0.85	17.00		0.30	0.01%	0.16%	
26	0.98	18.00		0.61	0.02%	0.18%	
27	0.06	19.00		(0.45)	-0.01%	0.16%	
28	0.94	20.00		0.46	0.01%	0.18%	
29	0.57	21.00		0.05	0.00%	0.18%	
30	0.05	22.00		(0.48)	0.02%	0.16%	

Figure 281   Short-term interest rates simulation model

For example, given that $r_0{}^* = $ current short rate $= 0.16$ percent, $dt = 1/12$ (a monthly time-step), and $dz = $ NORMSINV(RAND())$*\sqrt{dt}$ (normally scaled random number times the square root of the time-step), we get

$$\Delta r_1{}^* = k(\gamma - r_0{}^*)dt + \sigma\sqrt{(r_0{}^*)}\,dz_1 = 0.00\%$$
Projected $r_1{}^* = r_0{}^* + \Delta r_1{}^* = 0.16\% + 0.00\% = 0.16\%$.

Also as shown in the figure above:

for $r_{17}{}^* = r_{16}{}^* + \Delta r_{17}{}^* = 0.15$ percent $+ 0.01$ percent $= 0.16$ percent.

b. Modeling longer-term rates

For a short-rate, one-factor model such as CIR the assumption is that there is only one source of randomness in the yield curve, which is the short-term interest rate. This implies that longer-term rates are perfectly correlated to the short-term rate. Using this assumption, it is then possible to model the longer-term rates. One method of how this may be done is by assuming that the longer-term rates change by the same proportion as the short-term rates. Another method is to assume that the current spreads between the short rate and longer-term rate are representative of future spreads, and so on.

This assumption of perfect correlation is one of the disadvantages of using the one-factor CIR model, as empirically this is not the case. Besides the level of the yield curve (as given by the uncertainty in the short rate), the yield curve may be impacted by other significant factors such as slope (or tilt as given by the difference between yields of different maturities), twist, and so on.

Below we present two specific ways of modeling the longer-term rates once the short-term rates have been derived:

1. Long-term rates change by the same proportion as short-term rates, or
2. Current spreads between the short-term rate and longer-term rate are representative of future spreads.

Proportionate change in short-term rates

In the first case we calculate the projected long-term rate at time-step t as:

$$\text{long-term rate}_t = r_t/r_0^* \ \text{long-term rate}_0.$$

The following is a representation of the term structure of interest rates over the next five time-steps, using this proportionate method to determine long-term rates.

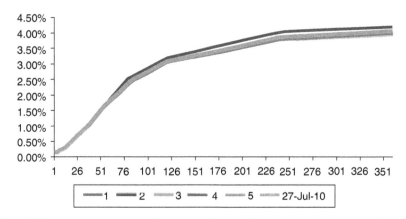

Figure 282   Longer-term rates determined using the proportionate method

Here, "27 Jul 2010" is the term structure today, "1" is the simulated term structure one month later, "2" is the simulated term structure two months down the line, and so on.

Current spreads between long- and short-term rates

In the second instance we calculate the projected long-term rate at time-step t as:

$$\text{long-term rate}_t = r_t + (\text{long-term rate}_0 - r_0).$$

The graph for the simulated term structures using a constant spread approach is given below.

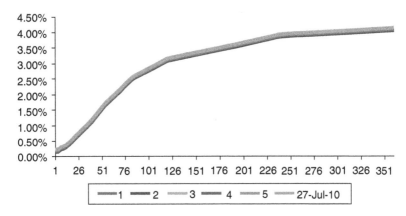

Figure 283 Longer-term rates determined using the constant spread method

Note that in both cases the long-term rates are perfectly correlated with the short-term rates.

4. Forecasting the monetary policy rate decision for Pakistan

1. Process

One way to look at the decisions on the monetary policy rate cut or rate hike is to look at simulating the rate of inflation in any economy. In order to determine what the inflation rate will be we use the underlying relationship between the Broad Money Aggregates (M2) growth rate and the inflation rate.

M2 numbers in turn are computed based on a number of elements. Our forecast model uses three primary processes to determine these elements. These involve simulation of future prices and amounts using a Monte Carlo simulator to determine:

- Crude Oil Prices,
- Exports,
- Remittances.

Why crude oil? Primarily because in most emerging and developing economies crude oil represents the biggest import and, given the volatility in oil prices over the last three years, the most significant source of economic shock to an emerging or frontier market.

We use the underlying relationship between crude oil prices and imports to determine imports and the relationship between remittances, and unilateral transfers to determine the amount of transfers.

These elements, together with balance of trade from services and net income received, which are derived based on past trends, are used to determine the current account balance or change in the net foreign asset (NFA) of the country.

The change in NFA is used as an input for determining M2. Other principle inputs for calculating the M2 number, that is, net government sector borrowing, credit to private sector and public sector enterprises, are based on past trends. M2 growth rates determine inflation rates as mentioned above, which are then used to calculate the extent of future policy rate cuts.

This process is depicted pictorially below.

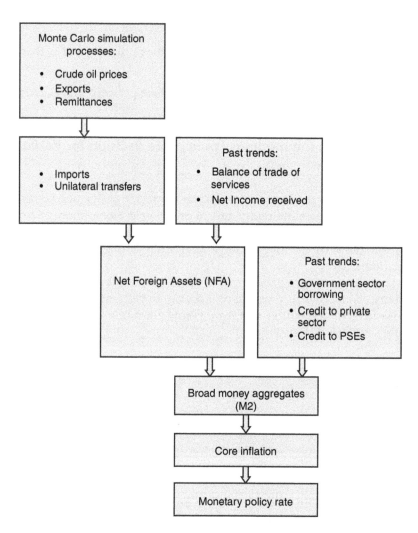

Figure 284 Process flow-forecasting the monetary policy rate

2. Results

Step 1: Simulating crude oil prices
The average crude oil prices for the months of July, August and September 2010 have been simulated using a Monte Carlo simulator.

The best- and worst-case prices (per barrel) for July 2010 are US$ 66.89 and US$ 80.05 respectively, for August 2010 they are US$ 64.12 and US$ 82.28 respectively, and for September 2010 they are US$ 62.24 and US$ 83.71 respectively.

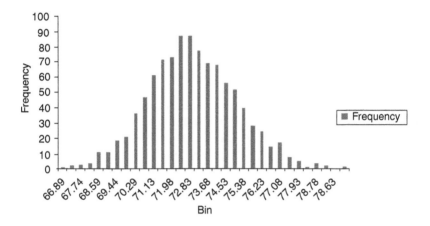

Figure 285 Simulated crude oil prices – July 2010

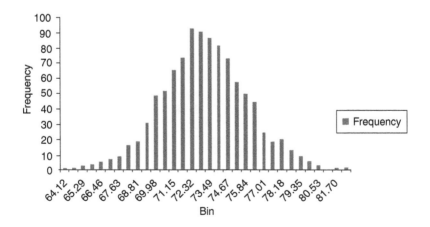

Figure 286 Simulated crude oil prices – August 2010

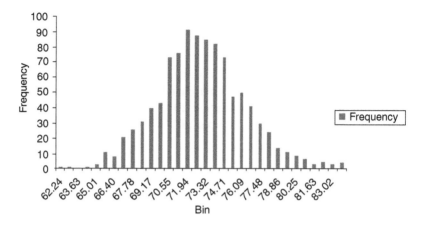

Figure 287   Simulated crude oil prices – September 2010

Step 2: Calculating imports

The historical relationship between imports and crude oil prices has been
used to derive import figures for the first quarter of fiscal year 2011.
Historically, average imports per month (over past 24 months) have been
US$ 2,624,764,000 (or US$ 7,874,293,000 for three months).

The best-case scenario under our model is US$ 6,835,517,000 of imports
while the worst-case scenario is imports of US$ 7,620,852,000.

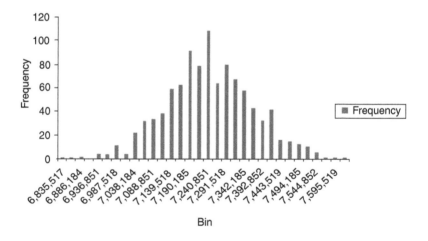

Figure 288   Simulated imports – Q1FY2011

Step 3: Simulating exports

The exports for the months of July, August and September 2010 have been
simulated using a Monte Carlo simulator.

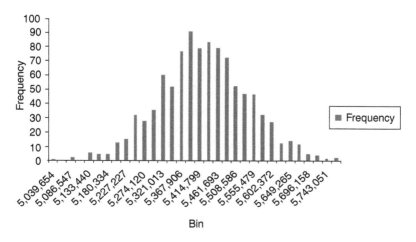

Figure 289   Simulated exports – Q1FY2011

Historically, average exports per month (over past 24 months) have been US$ 1,630,212,000 (or US$ 4,890,636,000 for three months).

The best-case scenario under our model is US$ 5,766,498,000 of exports while the worst-case scenario is exports of US$ 5,039,654,000.

Step 4: Simulating remittances
The remittances for the months of July, August and September 2010 have been simulated using a Monte Carlo simulator.

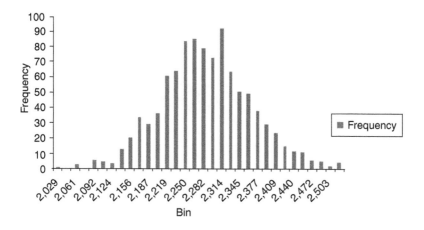

Figure 290   Simulated remittances – Q1FY2011

The best-case scenario for remittances for the first quarter of fiscal year 2011 is US$ 2,519 million whereas the worst-case scenario is US$ 2,029 million.

Step 5: Calculating the change in NFA
The change in NFA or the balance on the current account is based on the following inputs: exports, imports, unilateral transfers, trade balance for services and the net income received. Exports and imports are as derived above, unilateral transfers are based on the relationship with remittances and the latter two elements are derived based on their past trends.

The resulting increase in NFA falls in the range of US$ 128.23 million and US$ 949.57 million for the first quarter of FY 2011.

Step 6: Calculating M2 and M2 growth
The change in NFA is used to calculate NFA for the period. The other factors that are used as inputs for deriving M2 are government sector borrowing, credit to the private sector and credit to public sector enterprises, which are calculated based on their past trends.

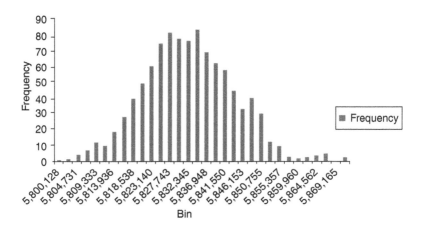

Figure 291   Simulated M2 – Q1FY2011

As at September 30, 2010, M2 aggregates are forecasted to stand between PKR 5,800 billion and PKR 5,871 billion, which accounts for an annual increase of 11.78 and 13.15 percent.

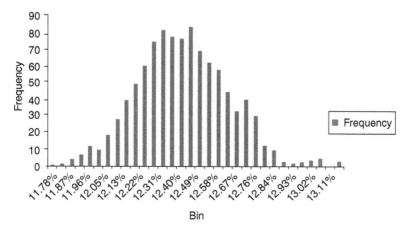

Figure 292   Simulated M2 growth – Q1FY2011

Step 7: Forecasting core inflation

Using the historical relationship between annual M2 growth rates and core inflation, the core inflation rates are derived.

Under the best-case scenario the core inflation rate is estimated to be 13.43 percent whereas under the worst-case scenario the core inflation will be 14.85 percent.

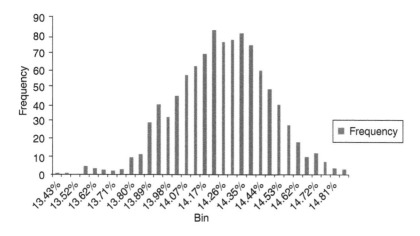

Figure 293   Simulated inflation

Step 8: Calculating the cut in the policy discount rate

There is a relationship between the core inflation rate and the policy discount rate. Generally, as inflation increases the monetary policy is tightened and the policy discount rate is increased. The opposite happens when inflation declines – the monetary policy is relaxed and the policy discount rate is cut. In Pakistan, for the prior two cuts in the policy discount in August and November 2009, a minimum difference between the policy discount rate and the core inflation rate was maintained.

In the calculation of the cut it is assumed that a minimum difference of 0 percent is maintained and that there is no attempt made to further tighten the monetary policy (that is, a policy rate increase is not on the cards).

Given the range of values for the inflation rate and the assumptions noted above, the policy rate cut is 0 percent under all scenarios for quarter one of FY 2011.[2]

Part III

Fixed Income and Commodity Markets – Dissecting Pricing Models

- A model for crude oil prices
- Investigating gold
- Crude Oil & inflation
- Commodity volatility & correlations
- Real rates

8

Identifying Drivers for Projecting Crude Oil Prices

In September 2009, we attempted to bring together opinions and views of various schools of thought regarding the possible direction that crude oil prices would take, especially in light of the historic heights and dramatic lows experienced in the second half of 2008.

Our objective was to identify drivers for crude oil price movements and, using these drivers, to build a crude oil pricing model. We wanted to see if these drivers could give directional signals rather than accurate price forecasts.

This chapter reproduces the original 2009 discussion and then compares it with what happened in the following years.

In Section 1, we revisit this discussion as is and in Section 2 we look at the actual outcome of the prices as well as considering the possible future direction that prices will take using the same spectrum of spare production capacity, excess supply, economic outlook (as indicated by the S&P 500 index) and US dollar value outlook (against Euro).

The 2009 crude oil price outlook

Given the current uncertainty in the future direction of crude oil prices, there is an interesting debate going on about where prices are likely to be in the near future.

There are two schools of thought in the market concerning the direction that crude oil prices could possibly take. The first anticipates that the prices will decline due to comparative historical trends in excess production capacity/excess supply, crude oil prices and their existing levels. The second believes that the current price trend in crude oil is being impacted not so much by the fundamental dynamics of supply and demand but rather by factors such as the weakness of the US dollar (in relation to the Euro), spreads of month on month futures contracts of crude oil and the strength of global equity markets. The latter assess that the weakened state of the dollar, growing strength of global equity markets and narrowing spread between the monthly futures contract act as floors on the falling price of crude and could possibly even lead to an increase in prices.

We present the two varying schools of thought and then provide a list of questions for investors to assess for themselves which school of thought they belong to.

Data

For the analysis, we have obtained data for OPEC's surplus capacity, world crude oil production and consumption and West Texas Intermediate crude oil prices (monthly averages) from the Energy Information Administration (EIA) website. Supply and consumption data is available from January 2001. Due to unavailability of spare capacity data for the period before January 2003, certain adjustments were made to the world crude oil total (actual and spare) production capacity to derive the excess production capacity figures for the period January 2001 to December 2002. Therefore, figures for this period represented in the graph below (left axis) may differ from actual spare capacity numbers that may be available to the reader from other sources.

The debate

School 1 – Price decline in the face of spare production capacity and excess supply

Excess production capacity and crude oil prices

Excess production capacity refers to the total production capacity for crude oil in OPEC nations less their actual production/supply at any given point in time. In the graph above we have plotted the historical trend of WTI prices (right axis) against that of excess capacity. Growth in excess capacity may indicate weak demand as production levels are cut so as to curtail a fall in price levels. This is evident in the period January 2001 to May 2004, where price levels were relatively low, whereas the crude oil production spare capacity of the OPEC nations had peaked. Steadily increasing demand for crude oil and petroleum products in the period mid-2004 to mid-2008 pushed spare capacity down to record lows as production levels rose to meet the rising demand. Before the crude oil market was hit by the global financial crisis, average prices had breached US$ 130 in June 2008.

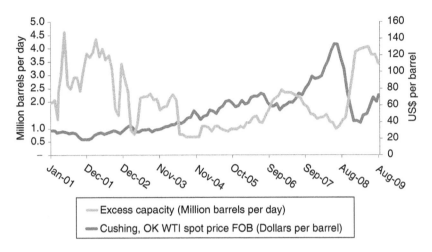

Figure 1   Excess capacity and WTI spot prices

After this, prices fell sharply as demand for crude oil declined, leading to an increase in spare capacity as production levels were cut. Currently spare capacity levels have topped at 2001–4 levels. If demand continues to remain depressed and production levels are either maintained or cut further, there is strong evidence to support the view that prices will continue to decline.

Despite the excess capacity, prices have not fallen as much as this group of analysts would have anticipated. Analysts belonging to the opposing school believe that there are a number of factors that have led to this resilience in the prices. These are addressed in the discussion of School 2.

Excess supply and crude oil prices

The graph plots the trend of WTI spot prices along with that of the excess world supply of crude oil (world production less world consumption). In general what can be seen is that as the demand for crude oil exceeds supply prices are pushed upwards. The reverse is true for excess supply.

OPEC nations have reigned in on production so as to provide support for prices at the US$ 60–75 a barrel level. However, as demand for oil remains depressed and may continue to remain so for some time to come, such production cuts may not be feasible in the long run, as these nations will be under enormous pressure to maintain revenue levels and meet budgetary requirements if prices stay at lower levels for a sustained period. As demand and trade activities stay low, economic pressures and

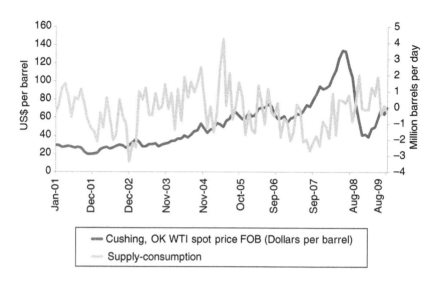

Figure 2 Excess supply and WTI spot prices

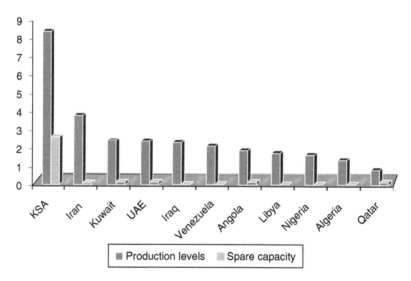

Figure 3 Production and spare capacity of OPEC nations

lower prices may lead to a rise in production quotas to meet minimum revenue thresholds.

Increased production in the light of increasingly depressed markets could lead to a selloff in prices. However, the spare capacity numbers tell a possibly different story above.

School 2 – Price will remain at current levels or increase in the face of the depreciating dollar, strengthening equity market and narrowing spreads on futures contracts

A weakening US dollar and the price of crude oil

Crude oil prices post-2001 have shown a significant negative relationship with the strength of the dollar. This can be observed in the graph above – as the dollar appreciated in value crude oil prices fell whereas when the dollar weakened the prices of crude oil increased. Some analysts believe that this is a possible result of investors moving towards the commodities market to hedge their investments against the depreciation in the value of the dollar. Despite spare capacity of OPEC nations and inventory levels of countries being at all-time highs, the price of the crude has been relatively resilient and these analysts are attributing this to the relative weakness of the US dollar, among other factors.

Other analysts hold the view that rather than the trend representing a greater move of investors towards the commodities market when the dollar value depreciates (which may be a small contributing factor to the support witnessed in crude oil prices) it is more likely just a depiction of the translation gain of this devaluation on crude oil prices which are denominated in US dollar. As the dollar value falls the price per barrel of crude oil will increase as a result of the decline in the purchasing power of the dollar.

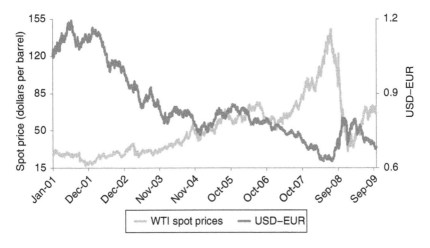

Figure 4   USD–EUR exchange rate and WTI spot prices

Equity market and the price of crude oil

In recent years, crude oil prices have been increasingly positively correlated to the growth in equity markets. This is depicted in the above graph, where we can see the price of crude oil moving in the same direction as the S&P 500

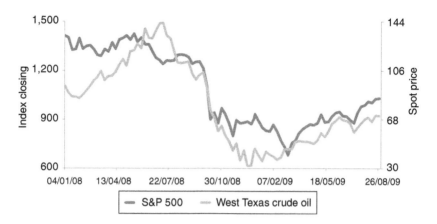

Figure 5 S&P 500 index and crude oil prices for the period January 2008–August 2009

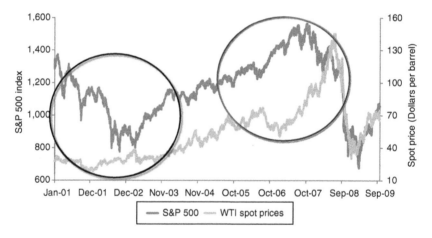

Figure 6 S&P 500 index and crude oil prices for the period January 2001–September 2009

index. Analysts in the price rise school of thought believe that this increase in the value of the index is an indication of the economic growth, increasing consumer confidence and potentially an increase in the demand for crude oil and related products with an upward tick in the global economy. With equity markets showing encouraging signs of growing strength, these analysts anticipate that crude oil prices will follow suit or at the very least prices will remain at existing levels despite the supply levels being high.

However, viewing the trend in the prices/index over the period 2001–9 (see graph below) we can see that this highly positive correlated behavior is a fairly recent phenomenon.

In fact, there are certain time periods (circled) in the duration when there appears to be a negative correlation with the equity index. This leads analysts with an opposing view to the above to believe that the recent correlation trends are coincidental and ephemeral. Some consider that the recent trends are based on increased speculative activity of commodity-based index funds and that, subjected to enough market pressure and resultant control, such correlations are more than likely to breakdown in the future.

Futures contract spreads and the price of crude oil

Spreads between futures contracts of a particular month over that of the consecutive month are a possible proxy for future demand of crude oil. In the above graph we have looked at the spread between the most current futures contract (Contract 1) and the futures contract of the month following Contract 1 (Contract 2). As can be seen, in the recent months there has been a narrowing of spreads. Analysts believe that low spreads are an indicator that the demand for crude oil will grow in the near future and potentially eat into the inventories that have built up over the past year. They believe that declining spreads are one of the factors that have dampened the recent fall in the crude oil prices. From the graph it is evident that there is a negative correlation between spreads and crude oil prices in the last twelve months or so.

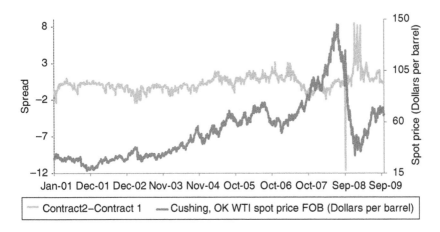

Figure 7   Contract spreads and WTI prices

Conclusion – the 2009 debate

To answer the directional question on crude oil prices one needs to form a view on the following drivers and the following countries:

- What is the outlook of the global economy? If you believe that the global economy is picking up and that there is likely to be increased economic activity leading to a potential increase in the demand for crude oil one would expect prices to rise or in the very least remain at current levels. Look no further than China to answer this question.

- What is the outlook for the US dollar? Will it appreciate, depreciate further or remain at current levels? More importantly, is this relationship true correlation at work or simply a translation adjustment?
- Does the same hold true for the correlation with the S&P 500 index?
- What is the remaining appetite of crude oil consumer's inventory build up? When the prices of crude oil fell, countries started to increase their stockpiles of oil. However, in the face of weakened demand net importers of crude may be nearing their holding thresholds. If inventory build up slows down what would be the impact on future contract spreads and support level for prices?
- What is the threshold revenue level that will force OPEC nations to review their current quotas regarding spare capacity in light of dampened demand, lower trade levels and falling or static prices? Look no further than Saudi Arabia and Iran.

Revisiting the model – 2013

Revised data

We obtained and updated data for OPEC's production and surplus capacity, world crude oil production and consumption, Brent and West Texas Intermediate crude oil prices (monthly averages) and NYMEX futures contract prices from the EIA website. The historical rates for the S&P index have been obtained from Yahoo Finance while USD–EUR rates have been downloaded from oanda.com.

Actual Outcomes and updated analysis

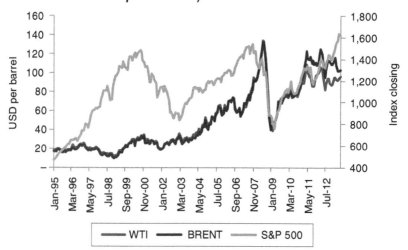

Figure 8   Crude oil prices and S&P 500 – 1995–2013

Subsequent to September 2009, crude oil prices continued to rise along with the broad market equity index (a crude but questionable proxy for the health of the US economy). In addition to this, consumption of liquid fuels have increased in non-OECD countries, rising above OECD country levels for the first time in April 2013, spurred on mainly by increasing demand in China. However, there are indications that China's growth is slowing in view of weak industrial data at the beginning of the year. This would impact prices in coming months.

From the graph below we can see that for the duration after 2009, crude oil and the S&P 500 index still appear to be closely correlated, except for the period starting January 2013.

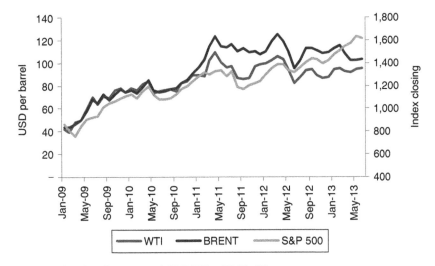

Figure 9   Crude oil prices and S&P 500 – 2009–13

In the most recent months however there appears to be a change in this relationship. This could be an indication of investors moving away from commodity markets, also evident in declining gold prices, or a revaluation of the true value of the US dollar as the US economy improves and the end nears for monetary expansion. Alternately falling or leveling out crude prices could be an indication of the slowing demand and consumption in China and other countries such as those in Europe and Japan.

The US dollar has appreciated in value on average since August 2009. Crude oil prices have also shown an increasing trend for this period for the most part, with the exception of a downturn experienced since early 2012. Prior to 2008 there was an apparent negative correlation between exchange rates and crude oil prices, but since the crisis this distinctive relation is only visible when there are jumps in the data series, that is,

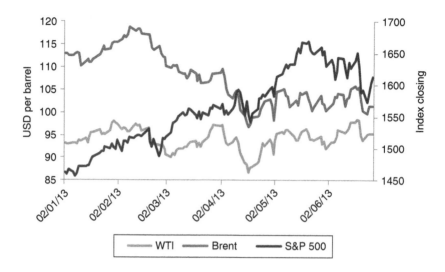

Figure 10 Crude oil prices and S&P 500 – January to June 2013

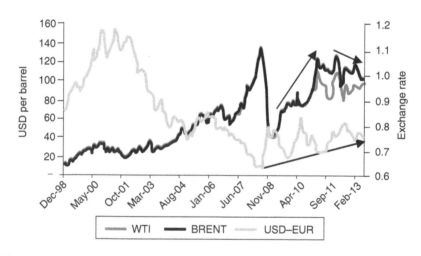

Figure 11 Crude oil prices and USD–EUR – 1998–2013

periods of increased volatilities. Given the overall positive trend in both oil prices and exchange rates since 2009, the intermittent negative relationship that we now witness could in fact be indicative of translation gains or losses. Increased volatility in exchange rates results in USD-priced crude oil to become relatively more or less expensive in terms of the US dollar's purchasing power, but as volatility dies down this relationship for the most part seems to disappear.

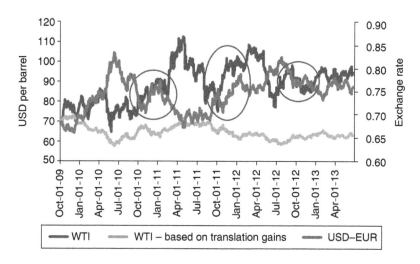

Figure 12 Crude oil prices, original series and translation adjusted, against USD–EUR

This is also evident in the graph below, which adds an exchange rate translation adjusted WTI series to the dynamics.

This series is negatively correlated with the exchange rate series, but its movements and direction do not always correspond with the original WTI price series. For example, in the areas circled, the increasing (decreasing) trend in exchange rates would suggest a declining (rising) trend in oil prices given the translation gains and losses argument, but this is not the case and prices move in the same direction as rates.

WTI started trading at discounted prices from Brent following the Arab uprising (especially Libya) in early 2011, which led to supply disruptions in crude oil in the region. Brent prices rose on account of this shortage of sweet crude oil, the preferred blend for European refineries. On the other hand, US production of crude has increased steadily over the years, due in part to successful explorations, and increased supply has led to discounted prices in relation to Brent. Shale oil fracking and the switch to natural gas has put the US on the path to self-sufficiency in fuel production, the impact of which is already evident in their significantly reduced crude oil imports over the years.

Despite supply disruptions from areas such as Syria and Yemen being forecasted to persist in the coming years, analysts believe that increased supply growth in non-OPEC countries and anticipated completion of pipeline projects in the US would likely result in a downward pressure on crude oil prices for both Brent and WTI.

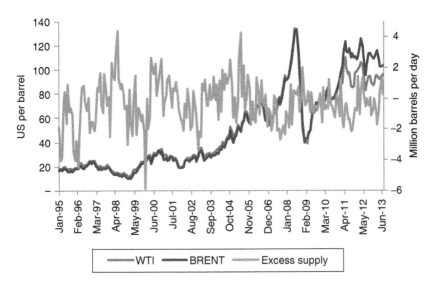

Figure 13 Crude oil prices and excess supply

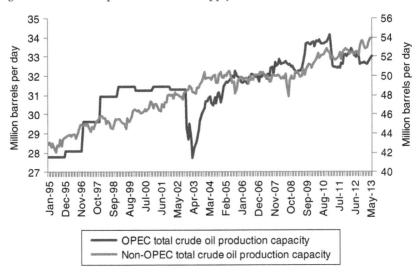

Figure 14 OPEC and non–OPEC total crude oil production capacity

The increased supply of crude oil from non-OPEC countries will mean that OPEC countries will try to curtail their own production quotas to manage price and revenue levels.

This in turn would lead to an increase in their spare production capacity. Spare production capacity has a further potential to increase in the future if Iran's current EU and US sanctioned crude capacity was brought on line. Again, the earlier question comes up regarding OPEC nations' ability to

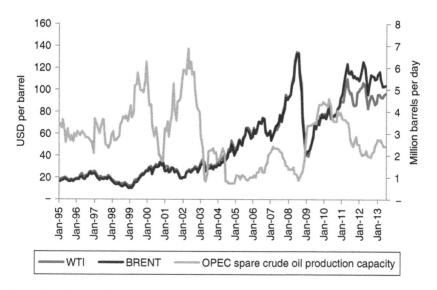

Figure 15 Crude oil prices and surplus production capacity

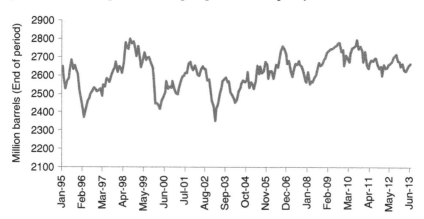

Figure 16 OECD commercial crude oil inventory

grow their own spare production capacity quotas in light of their revenue generation targets. These factors have a possibility of applying downward pressure to crude oil prices.

Analysts expect inventories to remain steady in the future.

However, a drop in inventories from an increase in the seasonal production of refined products, such as gasoline, could result in increased prices of crude. The downside risk to such a scenario would be the anticipated supply growth from non-OPEC nations, together with the deceleration in China's growth prospects, which would dampen in the longer run any rise in prices as demand for crude falters.

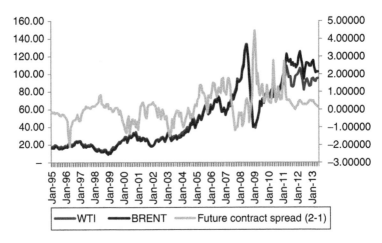

Figure 17   Crude oil prices and NYMEX futures contracts spread (contract 2 over contract 1)

Spreads between futures contracts – Contract 1 and Contract 2 – have narrowed over the past 2.5 years, indicating that demand is expected to remain strong for the coming months, which could result in a reduction in inventories. Recent reports (US Department of Energy Report – July 3, 2013) suggest just that, with US commercial inventories declining four times more than expected for the week ending June 28, 2013.

References

Short term Energy Outlook, EIA (June 11, 2013).
"Oil Price Patterns Portend Shrinking Of Excess Stockpiles", Brian Baskin of Dow Jones Newswires, Wall Street Journal (September 30, 2009).
"Energy outlook: Crude correlations and what comes next", Christine Birkner, Futures Mag.Com (October 2009).

9
Gold and the Australian Dollar

The Australian dollar is a commodity currency whose movements are dictated by movements in commodity prices, in particular coal, iron ore, copper and gold. When the prices of these commodities rise in the market then the Australian dollar tends to appreciate, when prices fall the value of the Australian dollar generally falls. However, unlike a commodity, the Australian dollar combines the benefit of a commodity driven hike with the added benefit of yield.

Given that gold is the third largest export of Australia, and Australia itself has recently become the second largest producer of the metal, there is a significant link between gold prices and the strength of the Australia dollar.

Before venturing into the correlation between the Australian dollar and gold it would be interesting to look at the various drivers of gold price in recent years. The analysis below, conducted using data for the period 2005–9, is with regard to gold price outlook for the year 2010.

Gold prices – drivers, trends and future prospects

Gold has traditionally been viewed as the ultimate asset to hold in times of financial instability. Historically its value has appreciated in stressed times and it has maintained its value against inflation.

Recent times have seen many central banks in countries such as Russia, India and China begin a steady adjustment in the composition of their FX reserves. In the past few years central banks in these countries had been building up their FX reserves in order to support export led growth strategies. Their aim was to maintain stable domestic exchange rates against the USD and protect domestic economies from the volatility in international cash flows. Because of this their reserves comprised to a relatively large extent of USD denominated asset based reserves. In the wake of the current US led economic recession, authorities in these countries started to take action to steadily reduce their dependence on the USD, and there has been a significant shift in the composition of reserves from USD denominated assets to EUR denominated assets. This move strengthened the position of the Euro against the US dollar. As the USD depreciated, more and more investors from both the private and public sectors have begun to purchase gold to diversify away from the weak dollar, which in turn has pushed gold prices up.

In 2009, signatories of the Central Bank Gold Agreement (CBGA) became net gold buyers as they reduced gold sales and built up their gold inventories. And as gold provides a means of reserve diversification, central banks of other countries, such as Russia and China, have increased their purchases of the precious metal. This has led to constraints on the supply which has supported the gold rally in past months. With a number of central banks in Asia in the process of ten-year gold buying programs, demand for gold is expected to remain high and prices are estimated to remain on average in excess of US$ 1,100 in 2010. Apart from these fundamental drivers, many investors have been viewing and speculating on the future trend in gold prices on a probability weighted basis, assuming the probability for future shortage in the supply of gold to outweigh the probability of excess supply. This has continued to push the price of gold upward. Also, future risks of rising inflation due to large levels of stimulus provided in many countries could increase demand as investors would seek to use the commodity as a hedge against potential inflation.

Key issues, or potential down risks, to gold prices remaining bullish in 2010 are:

- The USD's continued weakness,
- Need for increased liquidity and higher yielding assets,
- Gold production,
- Central banks continued stockpiling and the global demand for gold.

Recent rallies in USD against EUR due to depressed financial conditions in the Eurozone, in particular the large outstanding debt position in Greece, may dampen any further increases in gold prices.

Gold production has remained relatively flat in recent times and this has resulted in diminishing margins for gold producing countries, such as Australia and South Africa, as costs of production also rise. In order to encourage further exploration and increased mining activities gold prices would need to progressively increase. However, these activities would only be sustainable based on the future direction of demand for the product.

China has been a major player in the direction that demand for gold has taken in the past months, as it was involved in large scale restocking of the commodity. However, demand for gold from China could reduce in

2010 as domestic demand from real consumption of the physical metal as well as demand for diversifying its FX reserves could be met from domestic production and already built up stocks. Real consumption of gold has been relatively low in the rest of the world due to high costs and low physical demand for the product by end users. If China reduces demand in 2010 then overall demand for gold could decline, which in turn could make any possible global surpluses of the metal more visible and hence reverse the trend in prices.

Also, the potential for central banks in emerging countries to further increase their gold inventories would need to be weighed against their need to develop their domestic economies. If domestic expenditures were to increase, their demand for gold for stockpiling reasons would conversely decline.

Gold price and Australian dollar – relationship reviewed

There is a positive correlation between gold prices and the AUD–USD exchange rate, which can be viewed from the progression of prices and exchanges rates as well as the positive incline of the trend line in the scatter plot below.

However, when we look at correlations over time (see graph depicting 90-observation trailing correlations) we see that this relationship has not been constant. On average over the 2005–9 period the correlation stood at 0.45. However, in 2009 it has on average been at 0.79.

Figure 18   AUD–USD exchange rate and gold prices

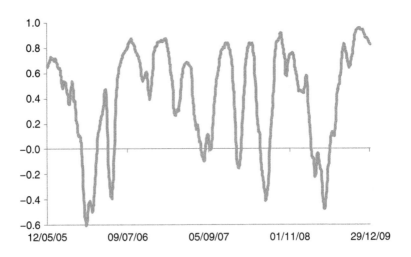

Figure 19 90-day trailing correlation between gold prices and AUD–USD exchange rates

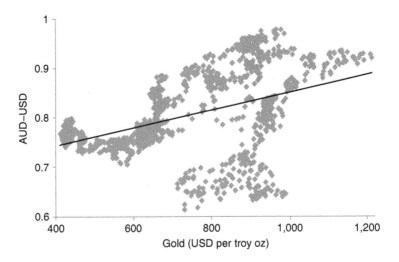

Figure 20 Scatter plot of AUD–USD exchange rate against gold prices

What is surprising is that there appears to be a much stronger relationship between the price of oil and the AUD–USD exchange rate than the price of gold and the exchange rate. This can be clearly seen in the graphs below, both in the oil price/rate trends and in the increased concentration of data points around the trend line in the scatter plot. On average over the period 2005–9 the correlation was 0.81, while it was 0.95 in 2009. Further, the trend in correlation was much more stable.

Figure 21 AUD–USD exchange rate and WTI spot prices

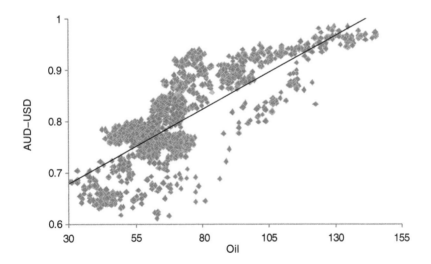

Figure 22 Scatter plot of AUD–USD exchange rate against WTI spot prices

As mentioned earlier, the weakening of the US dollar in 2009 has been a major factor for the increases that we have witnessed in the prices of gold.

Generally, as the US dollar depreciated the price of gold increased, as investors moved away from the US dollar towards this commodity, pushing up demand and hence prices. During the period 2005–9 correlation was at −0.77, meaning that when the USD appreciated against the EUR the value of gold declined 77 percent of the time and vice versa. For the year 2009 correlations stood at −0.73 on average.

Figure 23   USD–EUR exchange rate and gold prices

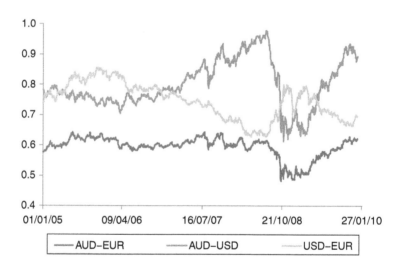

Figure 24   Exchange rates

And as the USD depreciated against the EUR, the AUD appreciated in value against both the EUR and the USD.

It is also interesting to view the relationship between gold and oil during the period of analysis and see how the ratio of gold to oil prices (both denominated in USD) relates to changes in the AUD–USD foreign exchange rate. This discussion is pertinent to the value of the Australian dollar as oil and petroleum are Australia's largest imports by value and, as mentioned earlier, gold is Australia's third largest export item. First, we look at the rate of increase in gold prices to that of oil prices as depicted in the following two graphs.

The gold/oil ratio gives the number of barrels of oil that could be purchased with 1 troy ounce of gold. We see that from December 2008 this number has increased on average to almost twice what it was in 2005. This implies that oil has become cheaper as compared to gold. Alternatively this may be viewed as Australian export items having become more expensive by comparison to its import items.

Figure 25   Gold and crude oil prices

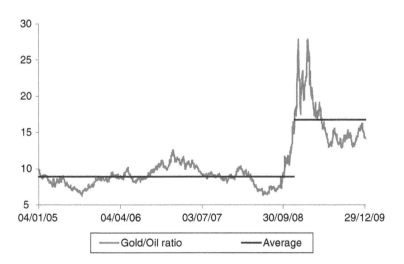

Figure 26   Ratio of gold to crude oil prices

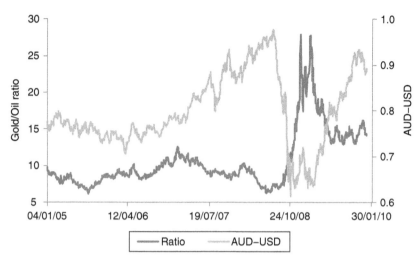

Figure 27   AUD–USD exchange rates and gold to oil ratio

Next we evaluate this ratio against the AUD–USD exchange rate, which is represented in the graph to the right. The graph shows that there is a negative correlation between the ratio and the exchange rate. However, the strength of the correlation has varied over time. On average over the period 2005–9 the correlation stood at −0.37, which is relatively low. For the year 2009 it was high by comparison at −0.80 on average. This means that when the ratio of gold to oil increased (primarily due to gold prices increasing at a faster rate in relation to oil prices) the AUD–USD exchange rate depreciated in value 80 percent of the time. It may be noted, however, that since the second half of 2009 the magnitude of (90-observation trailing) correlations has once again declined considerably and recently has even turned positive.

10
Relative Value and the Gold–Silver Ratio

To understand gold, one has to take a step back in time and look at the price series of the yellow metal over the last 10+ years.

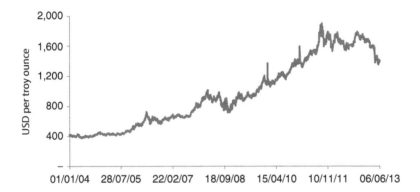

Figure 28   Gold prices – 2004–13

It is difficult to look at this chart in isolation and build a model. For context you have to add the lagged effect of two American wars (Afghanistan, Iraq) on the US dollar, a commodity spike in 2007–8, the collapse in commodity prices, the global financial meltdown, the subsequent deep recession and the run on the Euro in 2010–11. Given this context, the common explanation for the rise in the price of gold during 2002–11 is the relative value argument.

Gold captures, retains and defends long-term purchasing power of any commodity without the interference of central bank intervention and currency manipulation. Its price adjusts to reflect the loss of value in baseline currencies and goes up and down as markets reprice commodities in gold from one central bank inflationary intervention to the next. For example, between January 2005 and August 2008, the price of oil and

335

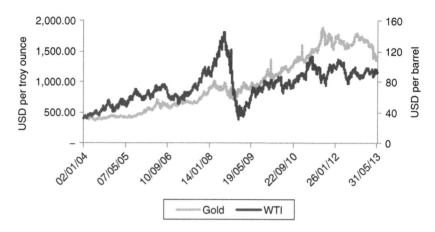

Figure 29   Gold prices vs. crude oil prices

gold in US dollar terms shared the same direction and trend – which corresponded loosely to the reduction in purchasing power of the US dollar over this time period.

As the world moved away from hiding dollars as a store of value under their mattresses post 2008 to September 2011, two things happened. The US dollar depreciated as more buyers moved away to explore alternate options when they perceived that the US dollar was no longer a guaranteed store of value (it could go down as well as up and was likely to buy less in the future compared to today). Second, the dollar value of commodities increased as markets compensated for the reduced value of the currency (for the present moment as well as in the future). Together the two drivers fed on each other to create a self-fulfilling prophecy.

As the US economy recovered and countries began to regain confidence in the dollar, we saw a reversal in the trend in gold prices and the EUR–USD exchange rate as seen below.

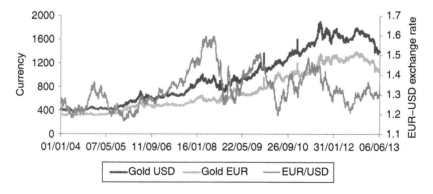

Figure 30   Gold prices in EUR and USD vs. EUR–USD exchange rate

Coming back to the graph depicting the relationship between oil and gold, we see that this relationship broke down in the last two quarters of 2008, before resuming again in early 2009 and breaking down again in between May 2011 and May 2012. In hindsight, the stabilizing trend in WTI appears to be an indication or precursor of the beginning of gold's own downward trend due to a strengthening dollar and a recovering US economy, among other reasons.

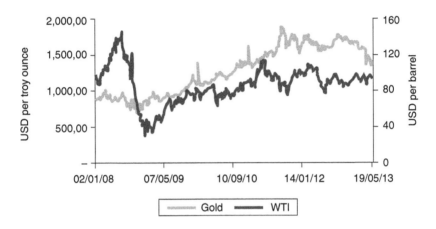

Figure 31   Gold prices vs. crude oil prices – revisited

WTI appears to be more responsive to the changes in the exchange rate as compared to gold. As the dollar has strengthened against the EUR, crude oil prices have also declined.

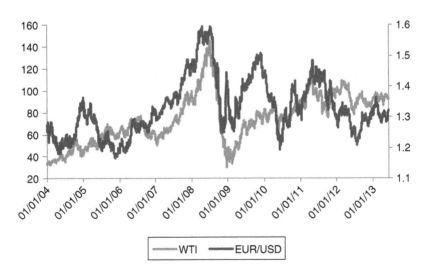

Figure 32   Crude oil prices against EUR–USD exchange rates

Relative values

An alternate and easier way of highlighting the same relationship is the gold to crude oil ratio. How many barrels of oil can a troy ounce of gold buy now? How does this compare to the historical relationship between the two commodities.

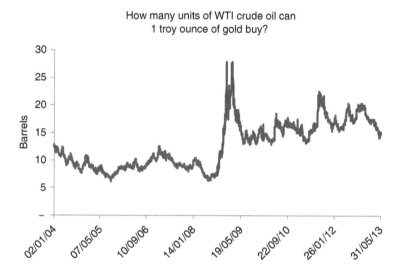

Figure 33   Ratio of gold prices to WTI prices

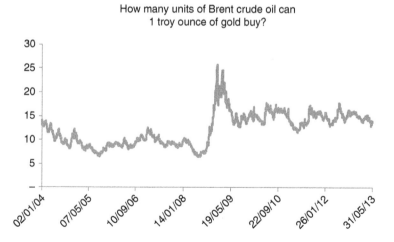

Figure 34   Ratio of gold prices to Brent prices

The graphs above show a distinct and stable trend between September 2009 and June 2013, in particular for Brent in relation to gold. However, the relationship underwent a dramatic change during the collapse of commodity prices in 2008, and hovered between 6 and 27 barrels of oil for an ounce of gold before settling down with an average ratio centered around 15 barrels of Brent and 17 barrels of WTI for an ounce of gold. In May–June 2013 the average has declined slightly to 13.81 barrels for Brent and 15 barrels for WTI. Is this downward trend linked to reversion to the existing mean/level of stability or a move towards a new normal? What are the drivers behind this recent trend?

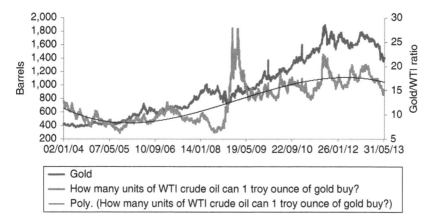

Figure 35   Ratio of gold prices to crude oil prices – fitted polynomial

A more complete graph of the same data set shows that the relationship was stable around nine barrels for 3 years before finding a higher mean reverting center in 2009. The polynomial curve fit (the thin black line) smoothes the transition from one curve to the next and highlights the mean reverting center for the two periods. Its downward slope in 2013 suggests a fall in the ratio.

Gold prices expressed in USD could continue to decline in light of the recent cut in cash rates by the Australia central bank, which led to the AUD depreciating against the US dollar. As can be seen from the graph below, and due to the fact that the AUD is a commodity driven currency, there is a relatively close relationship between the AUD–USD rate and gold and WTI spot prices. When the AUD depreciates, gold and WTI prices expressed in USD terms also decrease.

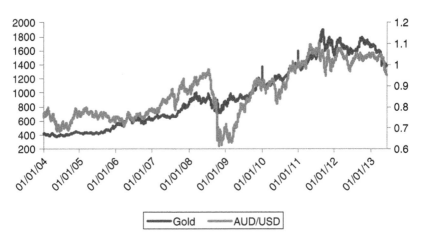

Figure 36   Gold prices against AUD–USD exchange rates

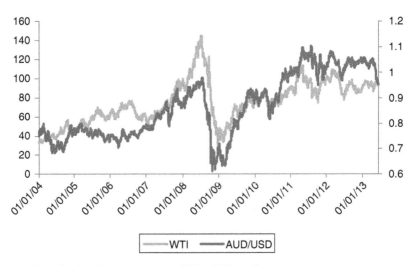

Figure 37   Crude oil prices against AUD–USD exchange rates

The final graph below completes the presentation of the relative value argument. Let us consider the period up to August 2011, before gold prices began their recent decline.

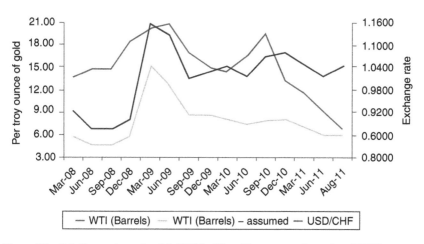

Figure 38 Relative price of gold (2008–11) – How many barrels of WTI can an ounce of gold buy?

Let us assume that compared to the US dollar, Euro and Yen, the Swiss Franc (CHF) is a relatively stable store of value. Let us also assume that in volatile markets it represents the right pricing relationships with other commodities compared to the three currencies mentioned above. The assumed WTI ratio shows what the ratio would have looked like if we held the price of gold constant at US\$ 600 an ounce. Compare this with the actual ratio & the depreciation in the value of the US dollar when compared to the Swiss Franc. Adjusting for lag, you can see that at least part of the jump in the value of oil and gold when measured in US dollar terms could be explained by the associated deprecation of the US dollar. A fall in the value of gold in US dollar terms could be associated, in like reasoning, to an appreciation in the US dollar.

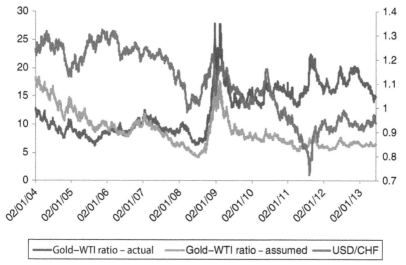

Figure 39 Relative price of gold against the USD–CHF exchange rates

The relative value argument doesn't just hold for oil and gold. It holds for a large number of commodities. We ran the same relative value analysis (how many units of the commodity in question does an ounce of gold buy?) for natural gas, aluminum, platinum, steel, corn, cotton, silver and sugar. Once again we used the USD–CHF exchange rate as a measure of depreciation and the commodity to gold ratio as a measure of relative value.

For industrial commodities (natural gas, aluminum, steel and platinum) we saw some level of long-term stability, though in the graph below you can see a rising trend for natural gas.

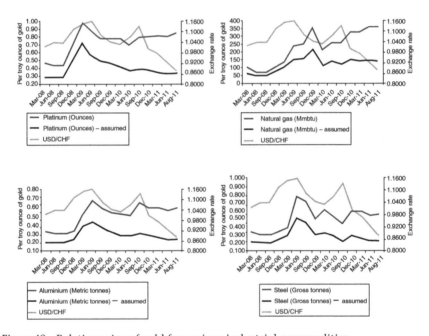

Figure 40   Relative price of gold for various industrial commodities

The most likely explanation for the above stability would be the supply side adjustment and control mechanisms that kick in when demand slacks off, and vice versa, providing an alternate buffer for decelerating price velocity compared to the price of gold. In other words, given the industrial usage of these commodities, markets do a reasonable job of providing relative price stability.

On the other hand, for sugar, corn, silver and cotton the picture is quite different, as shown in the next relative value graph. Gold as of August 2011 actually bought less corn, cotton and silver when compared to historical averages, while sugar's relative ratio was all over the place. More importantly, each commodity had its own flashpoint after which the gold commodity ratio started to decline (or in the case of sugar started to rise). Unlike the industrials, part of this may be because of the active presence of speculators in these markets or the relatively active usage of non-deliverable cash settled future contracts for these commodities compared to the industrials we saw above. Alternatively, these markets may suffer from additional external drivers or the rise in underlying prices could have indicated the formation of a price bubble which seemed to be reversing in the case of sugar and cotton.

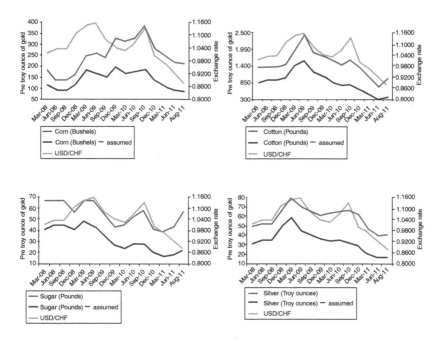

Figure 41   Relative price of gold for other commodities

In its "Handbook in Central Banking," the Bank of England notes the following motives to hold gold:

- "The 'war chest' argument – gold is seen as the ultimate asset to hold in an emergency and in the past has often appreciated in value in times of financial instability or uncertainty.
- The ultimate store of value, inflation hedge and medium of exchanges – gold has traditionally kept its value against inflation and has always been accepted as a medium of exchange between countries.

- No default risk – gold is 'nobody's liability' and so cannot be frozen, repudiated or defaulted on.
- Gold's historical role in the international monetary system as the ultimate backing for domestic paper money."

When it comes to relative value, it's the second argument that we are really interested in. "A store of value, inflation hedge and medium of exchange." A number of analysts now look at gold not as an investment but as an alternate exchange for storing and preserving "money" or "value." It reflects the original attitude towards gold before the Breton Woods agreement was discarded on August 15, 1971, replacing gold as the final exchange of value with the US dollar as the international reserve currency for the world. Interestingly enough, it was the macro economic shocks generated by the Vietnam War and the oil embargo that led to a rise in the price of gold from US$ 35 an ounce in the late 1960s to US$ 150 an ounce in 1974. Seven years later gold peaked at US$ 850 an ounce in January 1981.

Gold's value – Gold to silver ratio

It is also an interesting exercise to see how this relationship between gold and value has held over the last two thousand years as wars amongst nations destroyed the purchasing power of their currencies and fed a run on gold to preserve wealth. While we don't have price data going back two thousand years, we do have some information on gold prices as well as the gold to silver ratio courtesy of the "Measuring Worth" project at the University of Illinois at Chicago for the past 425 years.

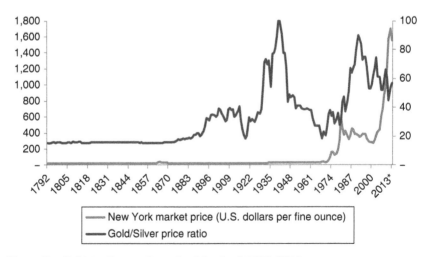

Figure 42   Gold to silver ratio and gold prices[1] 1792–2013

You can clearly see the impact of the Great Depression, the First and Second World Wars and the Vietnam war on the gold/silver price ratio and then on gold prices after the expiry of the Breton Wood agreement. For our context, it's the shift in mindset from wealth creation (gold as an investment) to wealth preservation (gold as a store or unit of value) that marks the rise in the value of yellow metal.

Weakness of reserve and safe haven currencies

While part of the volatility in commodity prices originated from real and perceived supply and demand imbalances, a large part was triggered by the weakness of the US dollar. This was not an issue before 2007, since some analysts and investors felt that any weakness on the part of the dollar would be compensated by the strength of the Euro, the Yen and some day by the Chinese Yuan. Unfortunately, with the European Central Banks PIGS (Portugal, Italy, Greece and Spain) debt crisis the Euro took a bath; the earthquake-tsunami-radioactive meltdown and resulting rise and volatility in the value of the Japanese Yen removed it from this equation, leaving the world of finance struggling to find a replacement for not one but three safe havens. While to a large extent the dollar and Yen are still used as temporary safe havens during flight to safety events, an increasingly large number of investors started using gold as their permanent store of value.

To illustrate, the two graphs below show the Euro's increasingly erratic behavior against the US dollar in the years 2008–13, reversing three prior years of steady gains, as well as the Japanese Yen's march against the US dollar till 2012.

Figure 43   Gold prices against EUR–USD exchange rates

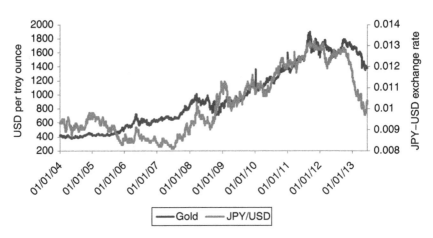

Figure 44   Gold prices against JPY–USD exchange rates

As Dr. Michael Pettis points out at China Watch, there are many costs associated with being a reserve currency and not all countries are willing to bear those costs. As the world tried to place other candidates on the reserve currency pedestal during the aftermath of the global economic crisis, it became abundantly clear that there were not many willing, fit or able candidates for this role.

In such a scenario gold had no option but to become the default currency of choice. More than investors and speculators, it was Asian and European central banks with surplus liquidity that were snapping up the yellow metal, turning them into net buyers of gold from net sellers for those years. China, Russia, Thailand, Korea, Vietnam and India acquired gold to maintain or bring their gold reserves to outstanding currency ratios closer to Western central banks.

> To gauge the size of potential gold purchases from emerging market countries, market participants often look towards gold ownership in developed nations, e.g. in the US or Germany, whose gold holdings make up more than half of their reserves. However it should be kept in mind that gold holdings in developed countries are a legacy from the gold standard and the economic objective of emerging markets is geared towards developing domestic economies, so accumulating large gold holdings may not be the best way to utilize reserves.

(Michael Pettis, China Watch Blog, July–Aug 2011)

The same central banks had been perfectly happy parking their surplus liquidity in US dollar denominated assets, however, following the US Fed's

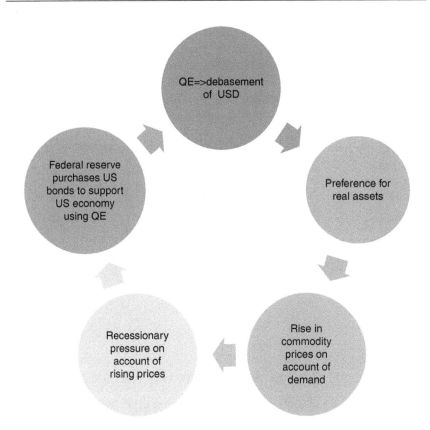

Figure 45 Shift to real assets following US Fed's QE cycles and impact on commodity prices

quantitative easing cycles and credit rating concerns they became net buyers of real assets and precious metals. While this didn't really affect the demand for US dollars and treasury bills (they were still considered the primary safe haven with sellers of real assets still parking their dollar proceeds in US treasury bills), it had a significant impact on commodity and precious metal prices, further increasing the pressure on the US dollar and the US economy. As this pressure built up, the Federal Reserve was pushed towards even more inflationary measures to jump start and support its domestic economy, further feeding the cycle.

Gold–silver ratio as trading signal?

Pre September 2011 we were asking the question "Is gold safe at current price levels?" Did this central bank buying mean that gold was safe for ordinary mortals? Could individual retail investors use it with the same sense of security that central bankers had been buying it? The answer to this question is dependent on your entry level. If you bought gold at its peak in January 1981 you would have had to wait 20 years to realize a positive return on your investment. In the high inflation years of the 1980s you would have been stuck with an investment yielding a negative carry and a 50 percent loss on your purchase cost if you bit the bullet and took an exit.

The graph below shows the annualized growth in gold price over 2013's gold price.

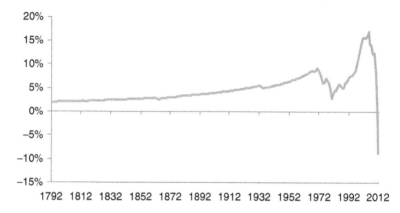

Figure 46   Annualized gold price growth rate (compared to 2013 prices)

Let us look at the gold/silver ratio graph again.

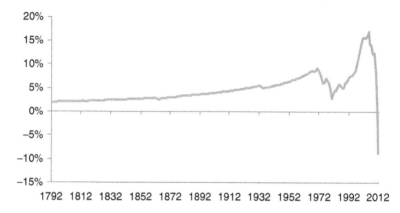

Figure 47   Gold to silver ratio – revisited

The common theme in this data set is that whenever the gold/silver ratio heads south, gold tends to follow suit, though with a significant lagged effect. The average of gold prices in 2013 indicates that this is what seems to be happening.

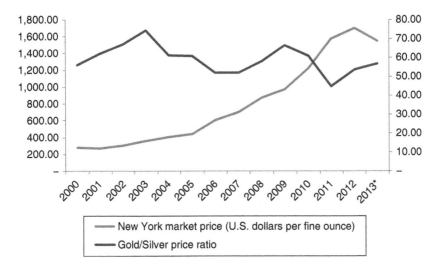

Figure 48   Gold to silver ratio – recent years

The only exception for the downward drift was from 2003–7, that should have led to a sharp decline in the value of gold but was possibly short-circuited on account of the Iraq/Afghan war and the global financial crisis that fed more uncertainty into the mix. So the question you have to answer before you continue to reduce your position in gold is what does the most recent increase in the gold/silver ratio imply? Will gold continue to head south or will it rise once again?

11
Correlations: Crude Oil and Other Commodities

Correlation describes the strength and direction of a linear relationship between two quantitative variables. In other words it is a measurement of the degree of association between two sets of numbers that describes how closely the two numbers track each other or are related to one another.

In our analysis we have assessed the linear relationships between crude oil prices and other commodities prices. Brent crude oil cash prices have been used as a proxy to crude oil. The other commodities that will be considered are as follows:

- West Texas Crude Oil
- Fuel Oil
- Diesel Fuel
- Natural Gas
- Gold

- Silver
- Platinum
- Aluminum
- Steel
- Copper

- Cotton
- Corn
- Wheat No. 2
- Wheat No. 1
- Coffee

- Sugar
- Corn Oil
- Soybean Oil
- Crude Palm Oil

Except for crude palm oil, the data used for commodities are cash prices, that is, the price of the physical commodity as opposed to prices of futures contracts of that commodity from the Wall Street Journal Asia edition website. For crude palm oil we have used the daily settlement prices on futures contracts (FCPO prices) for the spot month as available on the Bursa Malaysia website. All commodity prices except for silver and crude palm oil are denominated in US dollar. Silver prices are denominated in Sterling whereas crude palm oil prices are denominated in Malaysian Ringgit.

The correlations have principally been calculated on data for the period January 2008 to December 2009. Besides the numerical measure for correlation (the correlation coefficient or *r*), correlations have also been graphically depicted:

- First by the simple trend in the price levels over time (in general prices of Brent crude oil on the left-hand vertical axis, the other commodity's prices on the right-hand vertical axis) and,
- Second by looking at scatter plots of a given commodity's price with that of crude oil.

Scatter plots are a visual representation of the correlation between two items, in this instance Brent crude oil prices (on the horizontal axis) and the given commodity's prices (on the vertical axis). The plots are useful in assessing the form, strength and direction of the relationship between the two variables. In addition they are helpful in identifying any outliers in the data.

Form: The way that the data points lie in the scatter plot tell us of the functional form of the relationship, that is, whether a linear relationship exists or not.

Strength: A line of best fit is used in the scatter plot to assess the strength or weakness of a linear relationship. To determine how strong the relationship is we see how closely a non-horizontal straight line fits the data points of the scatter plot. The greater the dispersion of data points in the plot around the line of best fit the weaker is the correlation between these two items. A horizontal line of best fit indicates that there is no linear relationship between the prices of the two commodities. For the numerical measure this is represented by the magnitude of the value, which lies between −1 and +1; the stronger the relationship, the larger the absolute value. One way of interpreting the correlation coefficient is by using the following "Rules of Thumb" applied to the absolute value of calculated *r*:

"*r*" ranging from zero to about 0.20 indicates "no or negligible correlation,"

"*r*" ranging from about 0.20 to 0.40 indicates a "low degree of correlation,"

"*r*" ranging from about 0.40 to 0.60 indicates a "moderate degree of correlation,"

"*r*" ranging from about 0.60 to 0.80 indicates a "marked degree of correlation,"

"*r*" ranging from about 0.80 to 1.00 indicates "high correlation."

Direction: Does the scatter plot or alternatively the line of best fit slope upwards or downwards? A line sloping upwards from left to right represents positive correlation, that is, it suggests that as the price of one commodity increases the price of the other commodity tends to increase as well. A downward sloping line from left to right indicates that there is negative correlation. For the numerical measure this is represented by the sign of the correlation coefficient – a negative sign representing negative correlation, a positive sign indicating positive correlation.

Outliers: These are individual values that fall outside the overall pattern of the relationship and could lead to over- or under-inflated correlation values. They may be due to errors or anomalies or exceptions in the data.

In addition to assessing correlations over this entire period, we have also looked at how the correlation coefficients (the numerical measures) have varied over different periods. This was done to assess the degree of stability in the correlation figures and also to identify periods of time when correlations broke down or changed. Increased correlations in any period over those normally experienced could be indicative of increased systematic risk in the market. The periods considered were:

- January 2008 to December 2009
- July to December 2008
- January to December 2008
- January to June 2009
- January to December 2009
- July to December 2009
- January to June 2008

West Texas crude oil

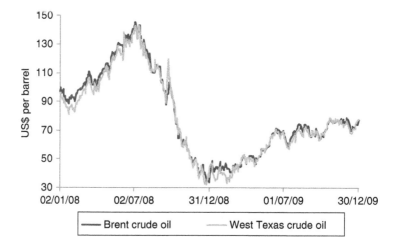

Figure 49   Brent crude oil and West Texas crude oil prices

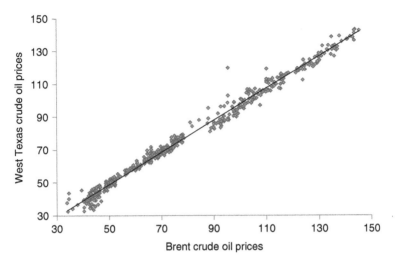

Figure 50 Scatter plot – Brent crude oil and West Texas crude oil prices

Scatter plots

- *Form:* Linear.
- *Strength:* Very clear fit of data to a non-horizontal straight line. High concentration of points around the line of best fit indicates strong relationship.
- *Direction:* Positive incline from left to right.
- *Outliers:* No significant deviations.

There is near perfect positive correlation between West Texas crude oil prices and Brent crude oil prices. As Brent crude oil prices increase, the prices of West Texas crude oil tend to increase 99 percent of the time. The relationship has remained very stable over the various durations assessed.

DURATION	CORRELATION COEFFICIENT
Jan 08–Dec 09	0.99
Jan–Jun 08	0.99
Jul–Dec 08	0.99
Jan–Jun 09	0.96
Jul–Dec 09	0.95
Jan–Dec 08	0.99
Jan–Dec 09	0.98

Figure 51 Correlations between Brent crude and West Texas crude oil prices

Fuel oil

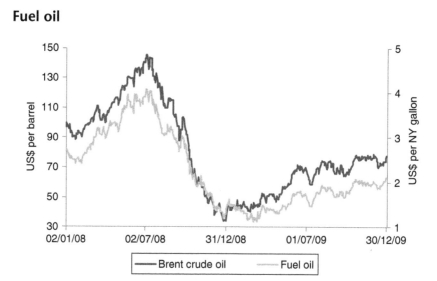

Figure 52   Brent crude oil and fuel oil prices

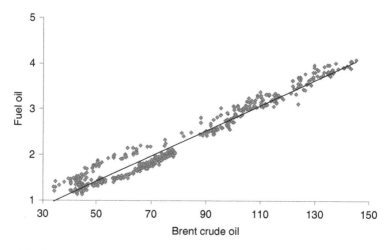

Figure 53   Scatter plot – Brent crude oil and fuel oil prices

Scatter plots

- *Form:* Linear.
- *Strength:* Clear fit of data to a non-horizontal straight line. High concentration of points around the line of best fit indicates strong relationship.
- *Direction:* Positive incline from left to right.
- *Outliers:* No significant deviations.

Once again there is near perfect positive correlation between fuel oil prices and those of Brent crude oil. It is interesting to note that the data for the period Jan–June 2009 shows a slightly lower correlation between the prices. It is still high but not a near perfect correlation as depicted in the other periods.

DURATION	CORRELATION COEFFICIENT
Jan 08–Dec 09	0.98
Jan–Jun 08	0.97
Jul–Dec 08	0.99
Jan–Jun 09	0.85
Jul–Dec 09	0.95
Jan–Dec 08	0.99
Jan–Dec 09	0.95

Figure 54 Correlations between Brent crude oil and fuel oil prices

Diesel fuel

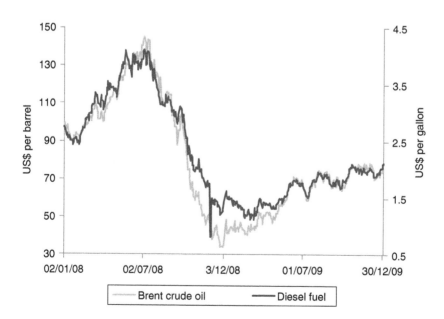

Figure 55 Brent crude oil and diesel fuel prices

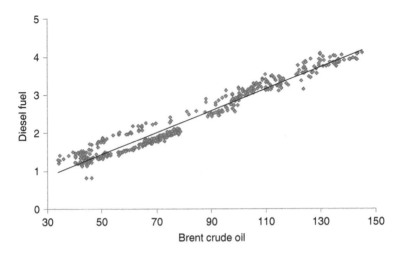

Figure 56   Scatter plot – Brent crude oil and diesel fuel prices

Scatter plots

- *Form:* Linear.
- *Strength:* Clear fit of data to a non-horizontal straight line. High concentration of points around the line of best fit indicates strong relationship.
- *Direction:* Positive incline from left to right.
- *Outliers:* No significant deviations.

There is near perfect positive correlation between diesel fuel prices and those of Brent crude oil. Once again the data for Jan–Jun 2009 shows a lower degree of correlation between the prices, though still high, as compared to the other periods assessed.

Duration	Correlation Coefficient
Jan 08–Dec 09	0.98
Jan–Jun 08	0.96
Jul–Dec 08	0.99
Jan–Jun 09	0.86
Jul–Dec 09	0.95
Jan–Dec 08	0.98
Jan–Dec 09	0.95

Figure 57   Correlations between Brent crude oil and diesel fuel prices

Natural gas

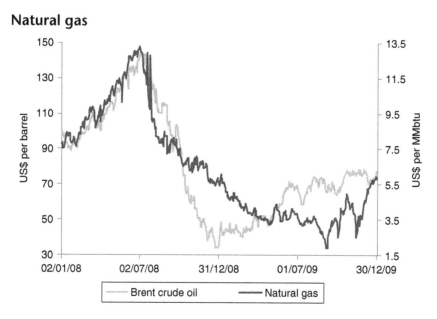

Figure 58   Brent crude oil and natural gas prices

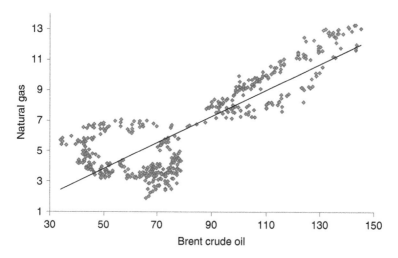

Figure 59   Scatter plot – Brent crude oil and natural gas prices

Scatter plots

- *Form:* Linear.
- *Strength:* A relatively clear fit of data to a non-horizontal straight line. Concentration of points around the line of best fit indicates a high correlation, however there are areas in the plot showing that the data points are more widely spread out as compared to the commodities discussed earlier.
- *Direction:* Positive incline from left to right.
- *Outliers:* No significant deviations.

Over the entire period of analysis the value of the correlation coefficient suggests a high positive correlation between natural gas and crude oil prices. However, we see significant variation over various subsets of the data. In general during 2008 the correlations remained fairly high throughout the year. However, in the first half of 2009 we see a low level of negative correlation between the two commodities, implying that as the prices of crude oil increased there was a 47 percent likelihood that natural gas prices would decline. The second half of 2009 shows once again a positive correlation to crude oil prices but the magnitude of this correlation remains low.

DURATION	CORRELATION COEFFICIENT
Jan 08–Dec 09	0.84
Jan–Jun 08	0.97
Jul–Dec 08	0.87
Jan–Jun 09	−0.47
Jul–Dec 09	0.44
Jan–Dec 08	0.88
Jan–Dec 09	−0.22

Figure 60   Correlations between Brent crude oil and natural gas prices

Gold

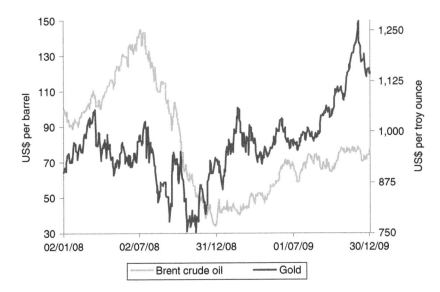

Figure 61   Brent crude oil and gold prices

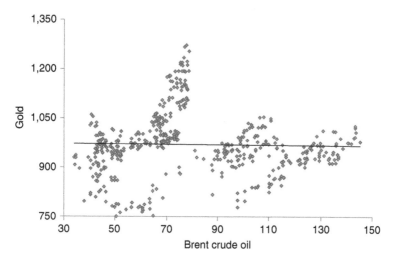

Figure 62   Scatter plot – Brent crude oil and gold prices

Scatter plots

- *Form:* No linear relationship.
- *Strength:* An almost horizontal line of best fit indicates that there is no linear relationship between the prices of the two commodities.
- *Direction:* A very slight negative incline.
- *Outliers:* No significant deviations.

Over the entire period of analysis the value of the correlation coefficient suggests no linear relationship between gold and crude oil prices. However, we see significant variation over various subsets of the data. Other than for the first half of 2008, where the data suggested a low negative correlation between prices of the two commodities, correlations have been markedly positive, indicating that as the price of crude oil increased the price of gold tended to increase as well.

DURATION	CORRELATION COEFFICIENT
Jan 08–Dec 09	−0.02
Jan–Jun 08	−0.22
Jul–Dec 08	0.62
Jan–Jun 09	0.30
Jul–Dec 09	0.67
Jan–Dec 08	0.58
Jan–Dec 09	0.69

Figure 63   Correlations between Brent crude oil and gold prices

Silver

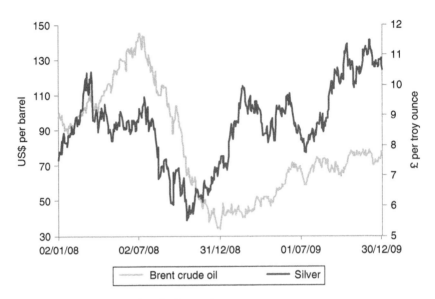

Figure 64 Brent crude oil and silver prices

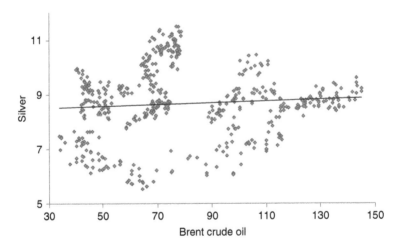

Figure 65 Scatter plot – Brent crude oil and silver prices

Scatter plots

- *Form:* No linear relationship.
- *Strength:* An almost horizontal line of best fit indicates that there is no linear relationship between the prices of the two commodities.

- *Direction:* A very slight positive incline.
- *Outliers:* No significant deviations.

Like gold, over the entire period of analysis the value of the correlation coefficient suggests no linear relationship between silver and crude oil prices. Again we see significant variation over various subsets of the data. The price data for the first halves of 2008 and 2009 suggest a negligible positive correlation whereas that of the second halves suggest moderate to marked positive correlation between silver and crude oil prices.

DURATION	CORRELATION COEFFICIENT
Jan 08–Dec 09	0.08
Jan–Jun 08	0.05
Jul–Dec 08	0.77
Jan–Jun 09	0.17
Jul–Dec 09	0.59
Jan–Dec 08	0.69
Jan–Dec 09	0.56

Figure 66   Correlations between Brent crude oil and silver prices

Platinum

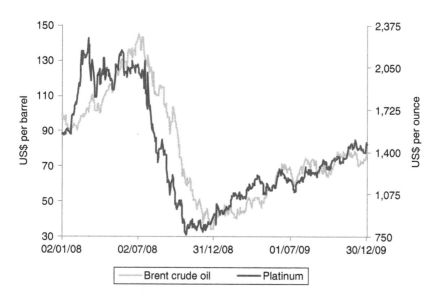

Figure 67   Brent crude oil and platinum prices

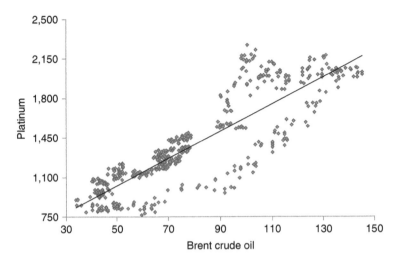

Figure 68   Scatter plot – Brent crude oil and platinum prices

Scatter plots

- *Form:* Linear.
- *Strength*: The non-horizontal line of best fit indicates that there is a linear relationship between the two commodities' prices. Concentration of points around the line of best fit indicates a relatively high correlation, however there are areas in the plot where the data points are somewhat widely dispersed.
- *Direction:* A positive incline.
- *Outliers:* No significant deviations.

The correlation coefficient over most of the periods analyzed suggest marked to very high degrees of positive correlation between the prices for platinum and crude oil. In general, as the price of crude oil increased the

Duration	Correlation Coefficient
Jan 08–Dec 09	0.86
Jan–Jun 08	0.55
Jul–Dec 08	0.94
Jan–Jun 09	0.77
Jul–Dec 09	0.74
Jan–Dec 08	0.83
Jan–Dec 09	0.88

Figure 69   Correlations between Brent crude oil and platinum prices

price of platinum tended to increase as well. The exception is the data for the period Jan–Jun 08 that suggests only a moderate level of positive correlation between the prices of the two commodities.

Aluminum

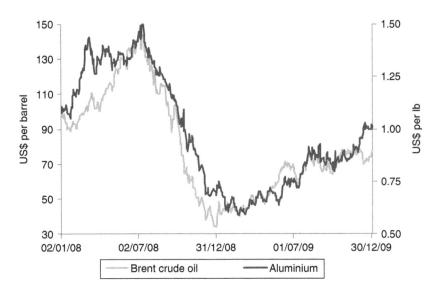

Figure 70 Brent crude oil and aluminum prices

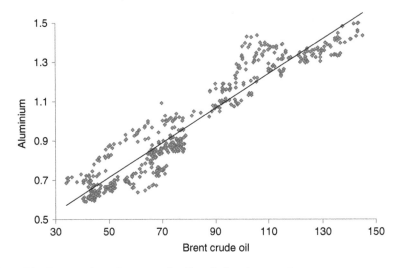

Figure 71 Scatter plot – Brent crude oil and aluminum prices

Scatter plots

- *Form:* Linear.
- *Strength:* The non-horizontal line of best fit indicates that there is a linear relationship between the two commodities' prices. Concentration of points around the line of best fit indicates a high correlation.
- *Direction:* A positive incline.
- *Outliers:* No significant deviations.

There is very high positive correlation between the prices for aluminum and those of crude oil when viewed over the period Jan 08–Dec 09. However, the correlation has not been constant over various subsets of data. We see that the correlations increased significantly in the second half of 2008 and since that time have once again declined.

Duration	Correlation Coefficient
Jan 08–Dec 09	0.95
Jan–Jun 08	0.68
Jul–Dec 08	0.99
Jan–Jun 09	0.72
Jul–Dec 09	0.65
Jan–Dec 08	0.95
Jan–Dec 09	0.87

Figure 72 Correlations between Brent crude oil and aluminum prices

Steel

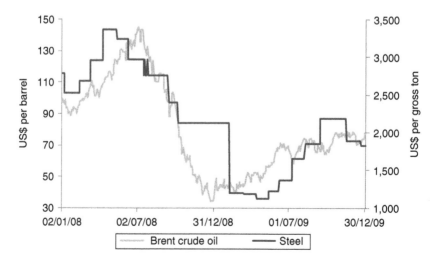

Figure 73 Brent crude oil and steel prices

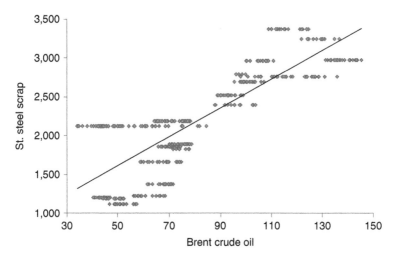

Figure 74 Scatter plot – Brent crude oil and steel prices

Scatter plots

- *Form:* Linear.
- *Strength:* The non-horizontal line of best fit indicates that there is a linear relationship between the two commodities' prices. A fairly even dispersion of points around the line of best fit indicates a relatively high degree of correlation.
- *Direction:* A positive incline.
- *Outliers:* No significant deviations.

Correlations have been relatively high in 2008, however in 2009 the correlation coefficient had declined considerably and was only moderately positive, indicating that when prices of crude oil increased in 2009 the prices of steel increased only 44 percent of the time.

DURATION	CORRELATION COEFFICIENT
Jan 08–Dec 09	0.82
Jan–Jun 08	0.70
Jul–Dec 08	0.94
Jan–Jun 09	−0.32
Jul–Dec 09	0.36
Jan–Dec 08	0.84
Jan–Dec 09	0.44

Figure 75 Correlations between Brent crude oil and steel prices

Copper

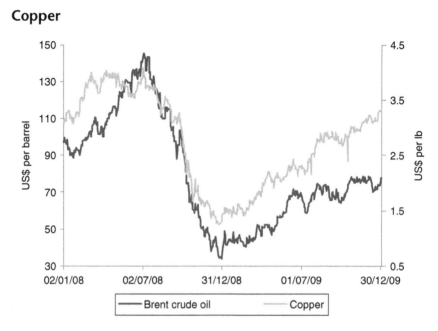

Figure 76   Brent crude oil and copper prices

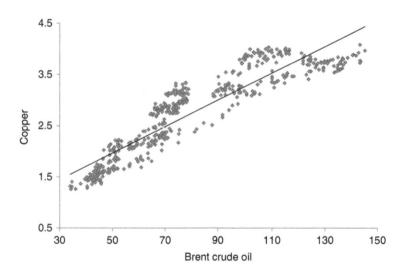

Figure 77   Scatter plot – Brent crude oil and copper prices

Scatter plots

- *Form:* Linear.
- *Strength:* The non-horizontal line of best fit indicates that there is a linear relationship between the two commodities' prices. The concen-

tration of points around the line of best fit indicates a relatively high degree of correlation.

- *Direction:* A positive incline.
- *Outliers:* No significant deviations.

In Jan–Jun 08 the correlations between the two commodities' prices were moderately positive. Since then however correlations have been high. In 2009 the data shows that when prices for crude oil increased the prices of copper also tended to increase 94 percent of the time.

DURATION	CORRELATION COEFFICIENT
Jan 08–Dec 09	0.92
Jan–Jun 08	0.48
Jul–Dec 08	0.99
Jan–Jun 09	0.89
Jul–Dec 09	0.79
Jan–Dec 08	0.92
Jan–Dec 09	0.94

Figure 78 Correlations between Brent crude oil and copper prices

Cotton

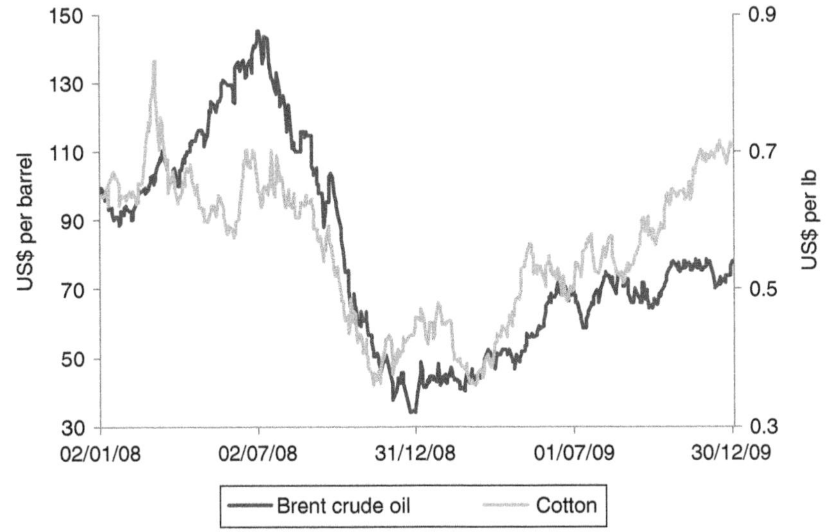

Figure 79 Brent crude oil and cotton prices

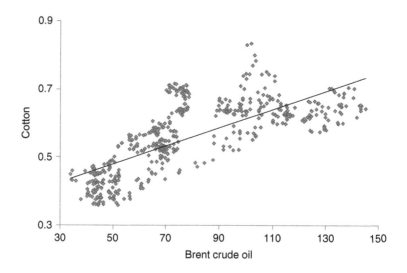

Figure 80   Scatter plot – Brent crude oil and cotton prices

Scatter plots

- *Form:* Linear.
- *Strength:* The non-horizontal line of best fit indicates that there is a linear relationship between the two commodities' prices. The data points tend to be not too concentrated around the line of best fit, but there is a definite linear pattern indicating a fairly marked degree of correlation.
- *Direction:* A positive incline.
- *Outliers:* No significant deviations.

Correlations have varied substantially from one period to the next. In particular Jan–Jun 08 saw a low negative correlation between the prices of

DURATION	CORRELATION COEFFICIENT
Jan 08–Dec 09	0.74
Jan–Jun 08	−0.20
Jul–Dec 08	0.95
Jan–Jun 09	0.70
Jul–Dec 09	0.62
Jan–Dec 08	0.79
Jan–Dec 09	0.85

Figure 81   Brent crude oil and cotton prices

the two commodities. The data for Jul–Dec 08 indicates high correlation but the data in 2009 suggest that correlations were once again declining and in the second half of 2009 correlations were marked to moderately positive.

Corn

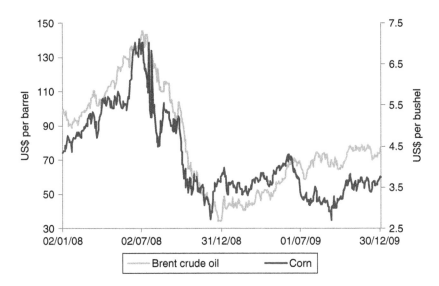

Figure 82 Brent crude oil and corn prices

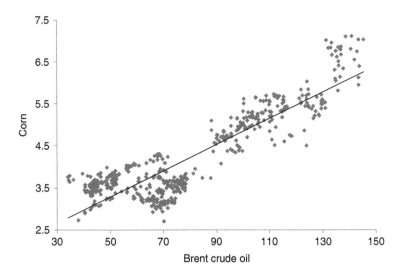

Figure 83 Scatter plot – Brent crude oil and corn prices

Scatter plots

- *Form:* Linear.
- *Strength:* The non-horizontal line of best fit indicates that there is a linear relationship between the two commodities' prices. Concentration of points around the line of best fit indicates a high degree of correlation.
- *Direction:* A positive incline.
- *Outliers:* No significant deviations.

The correlations vary by the data window used. Over the entire period of analysis and for the year 2008 correlations were high.

DURATION	CORRELATION COEFFICIENT
Jan 08–Dec 09	0.89
Jan–Jun 08	0.88
Jul–Dec 08	0.93
Jan–Jun 09	0.75
Jul–Dec 09	0.65
Jan–Dec 08	0.93
Jan–Dec 09	−0.12

Figure 84   Correlations between Brent crude oil and corn prices

Wheat No. 2

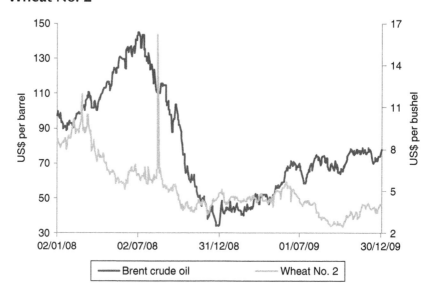

Figure 85   Brent crude oil and wheat No. 2 prices

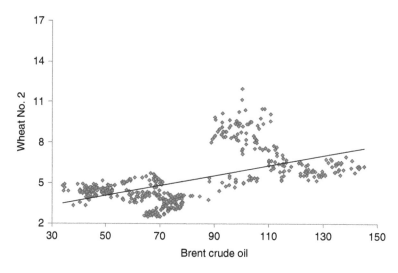

Figure 86   Scatter plot – Brent crude oil and wheat No. 2 prices

Scatter plots

- *Form:* Linear.
- *Strength:* The non-horizontal line of best fit indicates that there is a linear relationship between the two commodities' prices. The data points tend to be quite dispersed around the line of best fit.
- *Direction:* A positive incline.
- *Outliers:* One outlier on August 15, 2008 where the price of wheat increased significantly, as can also be seen in the spike in the price trend for the commodity. This price is as reported on the website of the Wall Street Journal but could be a discrepancy in the input. However, excluding this data point does not make a significant difference to the value of the correlation coefficient.

Correlations have varied substantially from one period to the next. In particular, Jan–Jun 08 saw a marked negative correlation between the

Duration	Correlation Coefficient
Jan 08–Dec 09	0.55
Jan–Jun 08	−0.78
Jul–Dec 08	0.64
Jan–Jun 09	0.63
Jul–Dec 09	0.08
Jan–Dec 08	0.39
Jan–Dec 09	−0.49

Figure 87   Correlations between Brent crude oil and wheat No. 2 prices

prices of the two commodities. Correlations became moderately positive in the next two halves, but in the last half of 2009 there was no correlation between the two commodities' prices.

Wheat No. 1

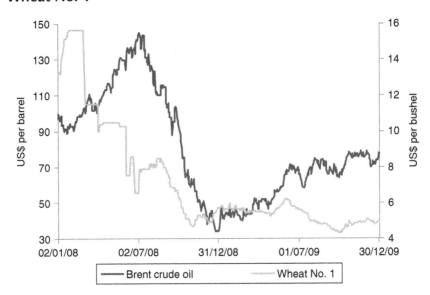

Figure 88   Brent crude oil and wheat No. 1 prices

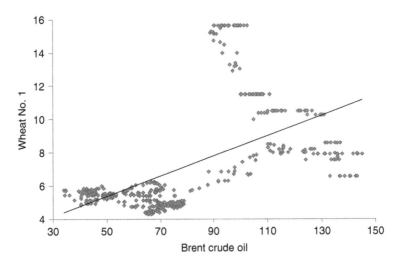

Figure 89   Scatter plot – Brent crude oil and wheat No. 1 prices

Scatter plots

- *Form:* Linear.
- *Strength:* The non-horizontal line of best fit indicates that there is a linear relationship between the two commodities' prices. The data points

tend to be widely dispersed around the line of best fit, indicating a moderate relationship.

- *Direction:* A positive incline.
- *Outliers:* No significant deviations.

Correlations have varied substantially from one period to the next. In particular, Jan–Jun 08 saw a high negative correlation between the prices of the two commodities. Correlations became highly positive in the latter half of 2008 then declined again in 2009.

Duration	Correlation Coefficient
Jan 08–Dec 09	0.57
Jan–Jun 08	−0.89
Jul–Dec 08	0.90
Jan–Jun 09	0.54
Jul–Dec 09	−0.17
Jan–Dec 08	0.34
Jan–Dec 09	−0.59

Figure 90   Correlations between Brent crude oil and wheat No. 1 prices

Coffee

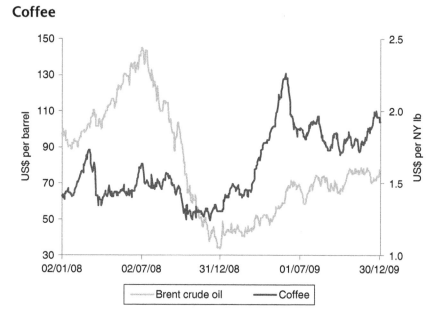

Figure 91   Brent crude oil and coffee prices

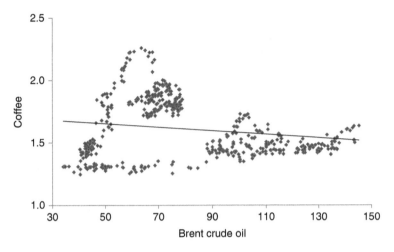

Figure 92   Scatter plot – Brent crude oil and coffee prices

Scatter plots

- *Form:* Non-linear.
- *Strength:* The almost horizontal line of best fit indicates great dispersion of data points suggesting that there is a very weak negative correlation between the two prices.
- *Direction:* A slight negative incline.
- *Outliers:* No significant deviations.

Correlations increased significantly in the second half of 2008 and first half of 2009. However, the data in the latter half of 2009 suggest that once again there appears to be no correlation between coffee prices and those of crude oil.

DURATION	CORRELATION COEFFICIENT
Jan 08–Dec 09	−0.18
Jan–Jun 08	−0.09
Jul–Dec 08	0.90
Jan–Jun 09	0.81
Jul–Dec 09	0.06
Jan–Dec 08	0.66
Jan–Dec 09	0.64

Figure 93   Correlations between Brent crude oil and coffee prices

Sugar

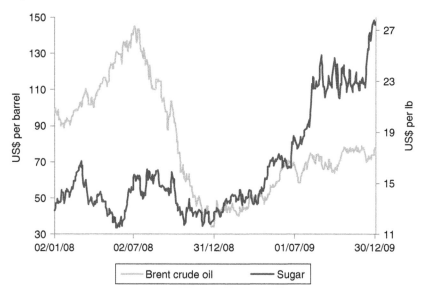

Figure 94   Brent crude oil and sugar prices

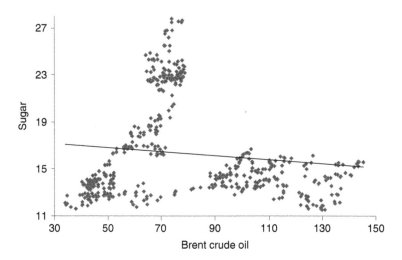

Figure 95   Scatter plot – Brent crude oil and sugar prices

Scatter plots

- *Form:* Non-linear.
- *Strength:* The almost horizontal line of best fit indicates great dispersion of data points suggesting that there is a very weak negative correlation between the two prices.
- *Direction:* A slight negative incline.
- *Outliers:* No significant deviations.

The data suggests a moderately negative correlation in the first half of 2008. Correlations increased significantly in the second half of 2008 and first half of 2009. However, the data in the latter half of 2009 suggest only a moderately positive correlation, indicating that for this period when the price of crude oil increased the price of sugar tended to increase about half of the time.

Duration	Correlation Coefficient
Jan 08–Dec 09	−0.12
Jan–Jun 08	−0.49
Jul–Dec 08	0.88
Jan–Jun 09	0.86
Jul–Dec 09	0.52
Jan–Dec 08	0.41
Jan–Dec 09	0.88

Figure 96   Correlations between Brent crude oil and sugar prices

Corn oil

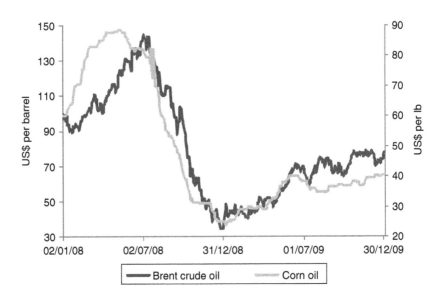

Figure 97   Brent crude oil and corn oil prices

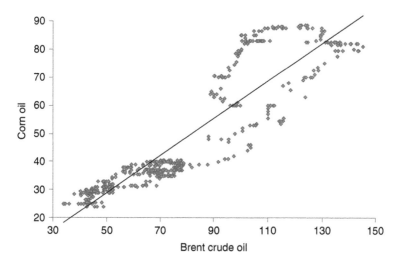

Figure 98   Scatter plot – Brent crude oil and corn oil prices

Scatter plots

- *Form:* Linear.
- *Strength:* The non-horizontal line of best fit indicates that a linear relationship exists between the two commodities. There is a greater dispersion of points at higher prices.
- *Direction:* A positive incline.
- *Outliers:* No significant deviations.

High positive correlations are suggested by the data in the latter half of 2008 and the first half of 2009. However, the data for the latter half of 2009 suggest a low positive correlation. On the whole the correlation

DURATION	CORRELATION COEFFICIENT
Jan 08–Dec 09	0.90
Jan–Jun 08	0.63
Jul–Dec 08	0.96
Jan–Jun 09	0.91
Jul–Dec 09	0.40
Jan–Dec 08	0.85
Jan–Dec 09	0.87

Figure 99   Correlations between Brent crude oil and corn oil prices

coefficient indicates that during the entire period when the price of crude oil increased, the price of corn oil tended to increase as well 90 percent of the time.

Soybean oil

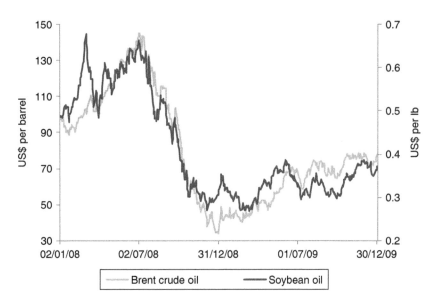

Figure 100   Brent crude oil and soybean oil prices

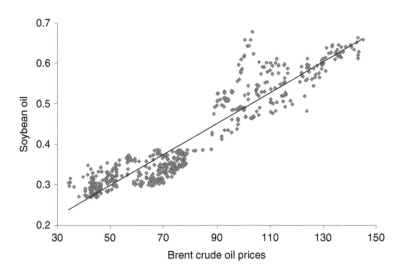

Figure 101   Scatter plot – Brent crude oil and soybean oil prices

Scatter plots

- *Form:* Linear.
- *Strength:* The non-horizontal line of best fit indicates that a linear relationship exists between the two commodities. The concentration of data points around the line of best fit suggests a high correlation.
- *Direction:* A positive incline.
- *Outliers:* No significant deviations.

The correlation between the two commodities' prices has been fairly stable ranging between marked to very high positive correlations.

DURATION	CORRELATION COEFFICIENT
Jan 08–Dec 09	0.93
Jan–Jun 08	0.71
Jul–Dec 08	0.98
Jan–Jun 09	0.74
Jul–Dec 09	0.81
Jan–Dec 08	0.93
Jan–Dec 09	0.62

Figure 102   Correlations between Brent crude oil and soybean oil prices

Crude palm oil

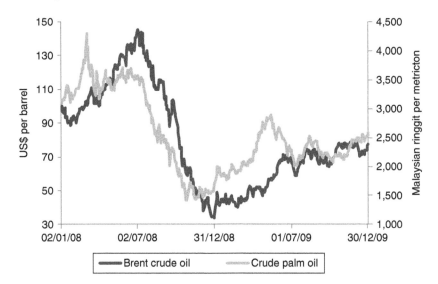

Figure 103   Brent crude oil and crude palm oil prices

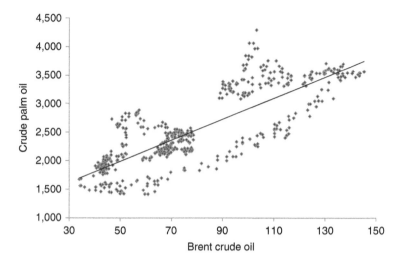

Figure 104   Scatter plot – Brent crude oil and crude palm oil prices

Scatter plots

- *Form:* Linear.
- *Strength:* The non-horizontal line of best fit indicates that a linear relationship exists between the two commodities. The concentration of data points around the line of best fit suggests a relatively high correlation.
- *Direction:* A positive incline.
- *Outliers:* No significant deviations.

Even though the correlation coefficient is high and positive over the entire period, this is mainly influenced by the increased correlation between data points in Jul–Dec 08. Other windows into this period suggest a low to moderate degree of positive correlation between crude oil and crude palm oil prices. This is particularly reflected in the year 2009.

Duration	Correlation Coefficient
Jan 08–Dec 09	0.81
Jan–Jun 08	0.35
Jul–Dec 08	0.96
Jan–Jun 09	0.63
Jul–Dec 09	0.53
Jan–Dec 08	0.81
Jan–Dec 09	0.43

Figure 105   Correlations between Brent crude oil and crude palm oil prices

12
Crude Palm Oil Futures

Data

DATA	DETAILS	SOURCE	REMARKS
FCPO	Crude palm oil futures, RM per metric ton	Bursa Malaysia	Futures settlement prices for spot month and next one-six month contracts
USD–EUR		OANDA.com	1 USD = × EUR
MYR–USD	Noon, mid exchange rate	Bank Negara Malaysia	1 MYR = ×USD
Gold	Gold: American Eagle, US$ per troy oz.	Wall Street Journal – Asia Edition	Cash prices*
West Texas	Cushing, OK WTI spot price FOB (US$ per barrel)	Energy Information Administration	Spot prices
Wheat No. 2	Wheat, No. 2 soft red, St. Louis (US$ per bushel)	Wall Street Journal – Asia Edition	Cash prices*
Corn	Corn, No. 2 yellow. Cent. Ill. Bu (US$ per Bushel)	Wall Street Journal – Asia Edition	Cash prices*

*These prices reflect buying and selling of a variety of actual or 'physical' commodities in the marketplace-separate from the futures price on an exchange, which reflects what the commodity might be worth in future months.

Figure 106   Data used in analysis

Price levels

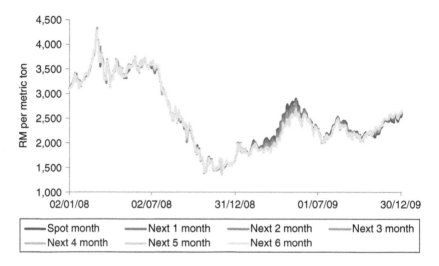

Figure 107 Crude palm oil futures contracts prices

3-SIGMA BAND	1-MONTH VOLATILITY (USING SMA VOLATILITY)	PRICE AS AT 31/12/2009	LOWER BOUND	UPPER BOUND
Spot Month	14.93%	2,578	1,423.42	3,732.58
Next One Month	15.47%	2,620	1,404.30	3,835.70
Next Two Month	15.33%	2,663	1,438.23	3,887.77
Next Three Month	15.55%	2,660	1,418.80	3,901.20
Next Four Month	15.29%	2,656	1,437.70	3,874.30
Next Five Month	16.63%	2,656	1,331.01	3,980.99
Next Six Month	15.14%	2,670	1,457.50	3,882.50

Figure 108 SMA volatility and 3-Sigma band for FCPO prices

3-SIGMA BAND	1-MONTH VOLATILITY (USING EWMA VOLATILITY)	PRICE AS AT 31/12/2009	LOWER BOUND	UPPER BOUND
Spot Month	9.16%	2,578	1,869.67	3,286.33
Next One Month	8.72%	2,620	1,934.23	3,305.77
Next Two Month	8.38%	2,663	1,993.89	3,332.11
Next Three Month	8.14%	2,660	2,010.13	3,309.87
Next Four Month	8.14%	2,656	2,007.16	3,304.84
Next Five Month	8.19%	2,656	2,003.18	3,308.82
Next Six Month	8.56%	2,670	1,984.21	3,355.79

Figure 109 EWMA volatility and 3-Sigma band for FCPO prices

Annualized volatility and 10-day holding VaR

Crude Palm Oil Futures (FCPO)	Annualized Volatility	10 Day Holding SMA VaR	10 Day Holding EWMA VaR	10 Day Holding Historical VaR
Spot Month	43.27%	20.05%	12.30%	23.27%
Next One Month	44.83%	20.77%	11.72%	23.11%
Next Two Month	44.43%	20.59%	11.25%	24.04%
Next Three Month	45.08%	20.89%	10.94%	24.35%
Next Four Month	44.31%	20.54%	20.94%	21.61%
Next Five Month	48.20%	22.33%	11.00%	24.17%
Next Six Month	43.87%	20.33%	11.50%	21.83%

Figure 110   10-Day holding VaRs

Volatility trends

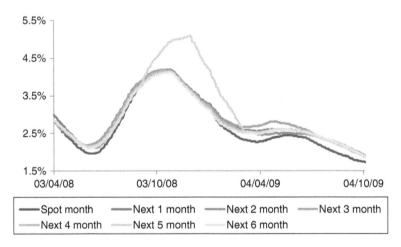

Figure 111   FCPO volatilities over time

Correlations and scatter plots

Based on Prices	Correlation* of FCPO with	Rules of Thumb	Significance
USD–EUR	−0.77	Marked	Significant
MYR–USD	0.85	High	Significant
Gold	0.15	No or negligible	Significant
West Texas Intermediate	0.79	Marked	Significant
Wheat No. 2	0.74	Marked	Significant
Corn	0.80	High	Significant

Figure 112   Correlation between FCPO and other commodity prices
Source: *for the period of January 1, 2008 to December 31, 2009

USD–EUR

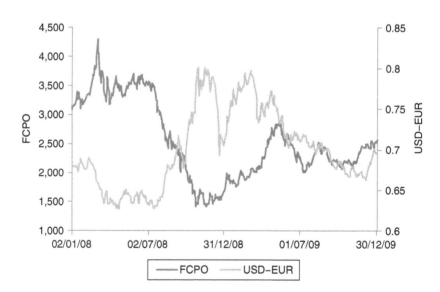

Figure 113   FCPO prices and USD–EUR exchange rates

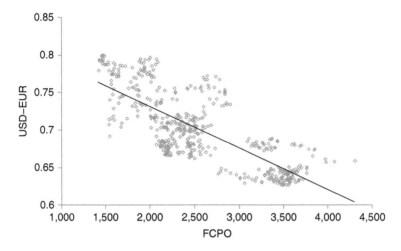

Figure 114 Scatter plot – FCPO prices and USD–EUR exchange rates

MYR–USD

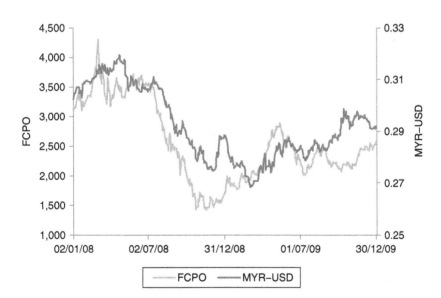

Figure 115 FCPO prices and MYR–USD exchange rates

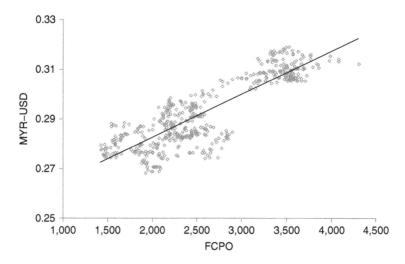

Figure 116   Scatter plot – FCPO prices and MYR–USD exchange rates

Gold

Figure 117   FCPO prices and gold prices

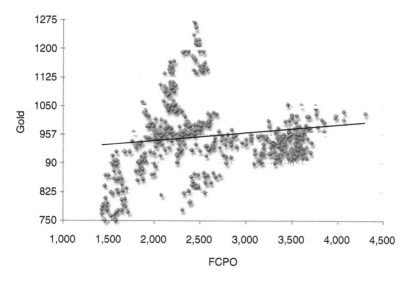

Figure 118   Scatter plot – FCPO prices and gold prices

West Texas Intermediate (WTI)

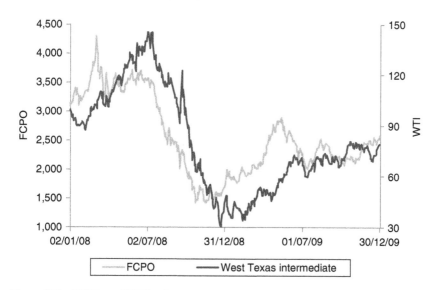

Figure 119   FCPO and WTI prices

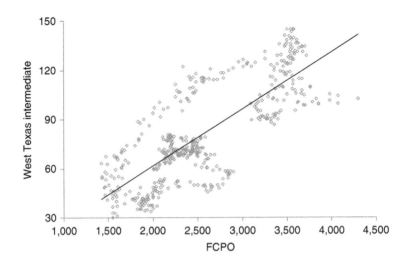

Figure 120   Scatter plot – FCPO and WTI prices

Wheat No. 2

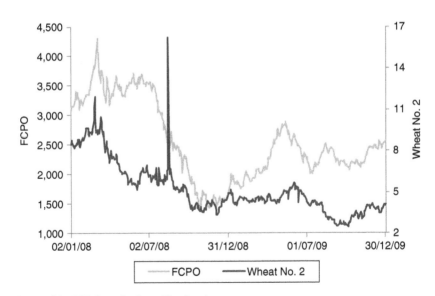

Figure 121   FCPO and wheat No. 2 prices

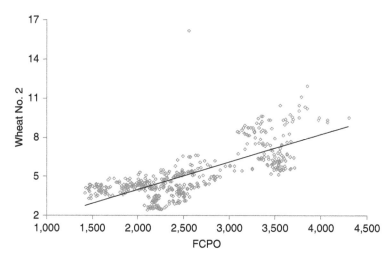

Figure 122 Scatter plot – FCPO and wheat No. 2 prices

Corn

Figure 123 FCPO and corn prices

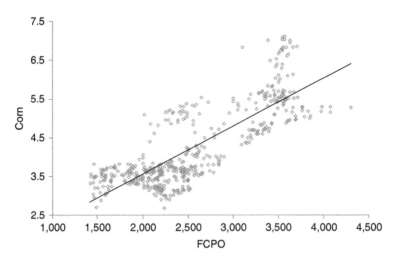

Figure 124   Scatter plot – FCPO and corn prices

13
Crude Oil and Inflation

This chapter aims to evaluate the impact of crude oil prices on inflation in Pakistan. We picked Pakistan as a developing world case study for two reasons:

1. First as an illustration of a developing world market where good data wasn't always available.
2. Second on account of its policy decision to use Fuel Oil based power generation in its IPP (Independent Power Producers) contracts, it created a strong relationship between crude oil prices & inflation. The balance of payment crisis in 2007–2008 on account of surging Fuel Oil prices, along with a host of other socio political and economic factors led to a change in government by May 2008 and an economic recession that lasted till early 2012.

We start with discussing the composition of the price indices in Pakistan and then assess the extent to which changes in crude oil prices impact indices as a whole, as well as on their various components individually.

Components of price indices

Two of the main indices used to measure inflation in Pakistan are the Consumer Price Index (CPI) and the Wholesale Price Index (WPI). The base year for both indices is 2000–1. The CPI in Pakistan covers retail prices of 374 items in 35 major cities. It reflects the changes in the cost of living of urban areas. The items are grouped into ten major commodity groups whose weights in the index are as follows.

CPI COMPONENTS	WEIGHTS
Food & beverages	40.34%
Apparel, textiles & footwear	6.10%
House rent	23.43%
Fuel & lighting	7.29%
Household, furniture & equipment, etc.	3.29%
Transport & communication	7.32%
Recreation & entertainment	0.83%
Education	3.45%
Cleaning, laundry & personal appearance	5.88%
Medicare	2.07%
General	100.00%

Figure 125   Composition of the Consumer Price Index (CPI)

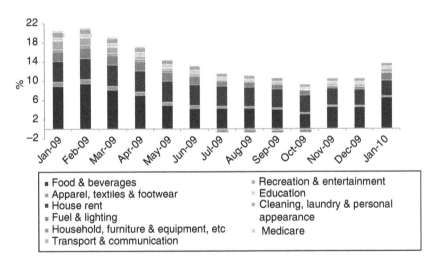

Figure 126   Impact of CPI components on inflation

Because of their weight in the composition of the index, food and beverages and house rent have the largest impact on the inflation measure. In January 2010 the cost of fuel and lighting items increased by over 20 percent on a year on year basis, which inflated the CPI General Index by 1.51 percentage points. This is principally due to the higher electricity and fuel tariffs imposed by the government at the close of 2009 in light of higher international commodity prices.

The WPI in Pakistan covers wholesale prices of 106 commodities (425 items) in 18 major cities. Commodities covered fall into five major groups, namely food, raw material, fuel, lighting and lubricants, manufacturing and building material, whose weights in the WPI are given below.

WPI COMPONENTS	WEIGHTS
Food	42.12%
Raw materials	7.99%
Fuel, lighting & lubricants	19.29%
Manufactures	25.87%
Building materials	4.73%
General	100.00%

Figure 127 Composition of the Wholesale Price Index (WPI)

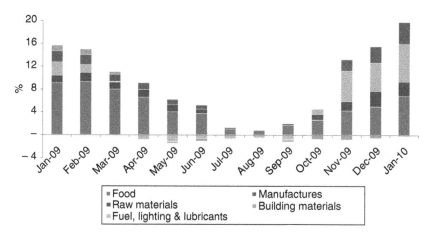

Figure 128 Impact of WPI components on inflation

As with the CPI, the food component of the WPI index has the largest impact on the WPI inflation measure. However, its impact in the past few months has been lower than in the beginning of 2009. By contrast the effect of fuel, lighting and lubricants has increased considerably and amounts to one third of the inflation measure in January 2010. This is just a bit lower than the contribution by food items for the same month, despite its weight being less than half that of food in the index, which alternatively means that the costs of fuel, lighting and lubricants more than doubled that of food costs in January 2010.

We have reviewed the trends in the general indices with West Texas Immediate (WTI) spot prices for the period July 2001 to January 2010. For the various components we have analyzed their trends against the WTI prices over the period January 2008 to January 2010.

Consumer price index

According to the trend depicted in the graph, the index has been on a steady increase since 2001. The index saw a sharper rise during 2008, which on average increased by 2 percent per month as compared to under 1 percent per month in previous durations. A similar trend was experienced in WTI prices starting in January 2007 to June 2008. This may imply that changes in oil price affect the CPI on a lagged basis, trailing by 2–6 months. However, the effect seems to be more prominent for increasing prices rather than for declining prices.

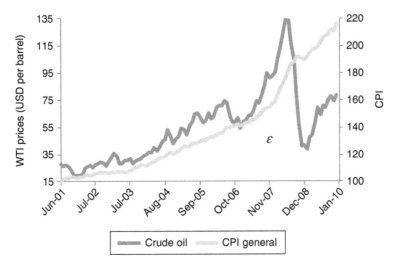

Figure 129   Crude oil prices and the Consumer Price Index

The CPI tends to be relatively persistent when prices fall, which could be the result of higher oil prices impacting the other components of the index indirectly in second and later round effects.

To assess the extent of the impact that crude oil prices may have on CPI, we have regressed the change in prices against the change in CPI over the duration, in particular:

$$\ln\left(\frac{CPI_t}{CPI_{t-1}}\right) = 0.6871\% + 0.9324\% \times \ln\left(\frac{WTI_t}{WTI_{t-1}}\right) + 1.8513\%$$

$$\times \ln\left(\frac{WTI_{t-1}}{WTI_{t-2}}\right) + 0.3464\% \times \ln\left(\frac{WTI_{t-2}}{WTI_{t-3}}\right) \mp \varepsilon$$

where ε is the error term of the regression of 1.30 percent. The change in the index in month t is explained by the change in oil prices in the months t, $t - 1$ and $t - 2$ with factors of 0.9324 percent, 1.8513 percent and 0.3464 percent respectively.

The aggregate impact over three months adds up to 3.1302 percent. The regression also indicates that 0.6871 percent of the change in CPI is not from the change in oil prices but from other components in the index. For example, if oil prices stay constant in months $t - 3$ to $t - 1$, then rise by 100 percent in month t, the change in CPI in month t would range between approximately 0.6871 percent + 100 percent $\times$ 0.9324 percent $\pm$1.3 percent, (or 0.3240 percent, 2.9151 percent). The regression also indicates that the major impact is not immediate and there is a lag of at least a month before the effect of price changes are realized in the index. The trends in the various components of CPI are depicted below in comparison to the WTI spot prices.

Two components stand out in relation to the topic being assessed, namely food and beverages and transport and communication, which depict a somewhat similar trend to the trend in crude oil prices. Again, as mentioned earlier, when prices of crude oil fell significantly in the second half of 2008, there was a less marked fall in the costs of items in these two categories. Prices of these commodities tended to persist at higher levels before increasing once again when the price of crude oil picked up again in 2009.

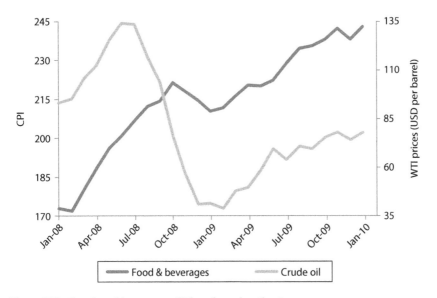

Figure 130   Food and beverages CPI and crude oil prices

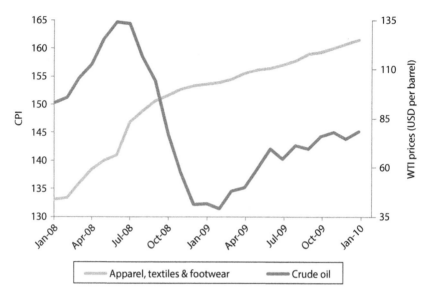

Figure 131   Apparel, textiles and footwear CPI and crude oil prices

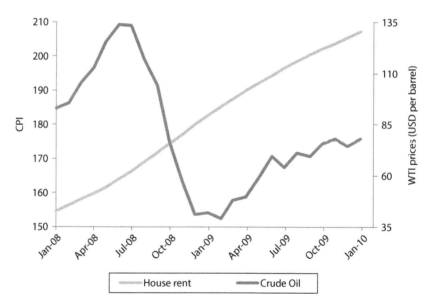

Figure 132   House rent CPI and crude oil prices

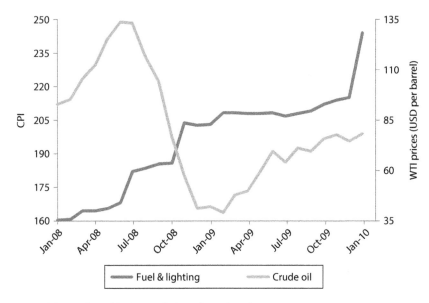

Figure 133 Fuel and lighting CPI and crude oil prices

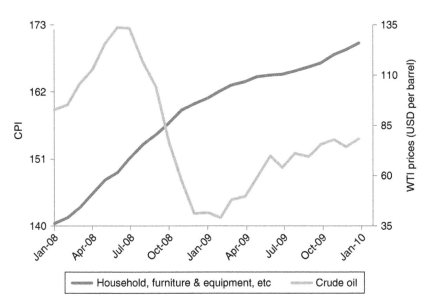

Figure 134 Household, furniture and equipment CPI and crude oil prices

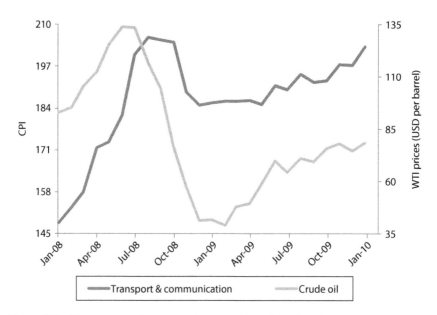

Figure 135   Transport and communication CPI and crude oil prices

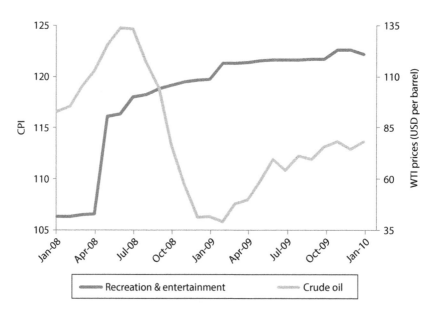

Figure 136   Recreation and entertainment CPI and crude oil prices

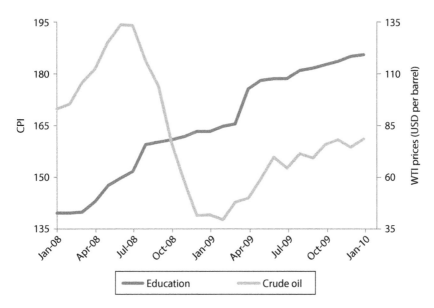

Figure 137   Education CPI and crude oil prices

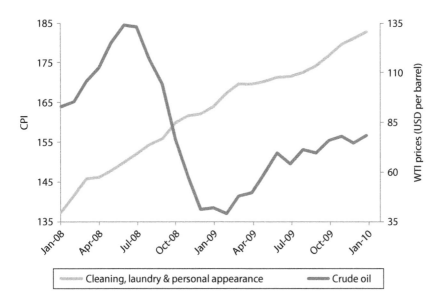

Figure 138   Cleaning, laundry and personal appearance CPI and crude oil prices

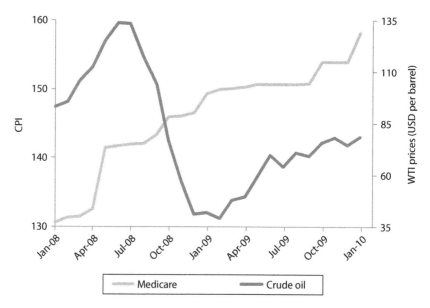

Figure 139   Medicare CPI and crude oil prices

Wholesale price index

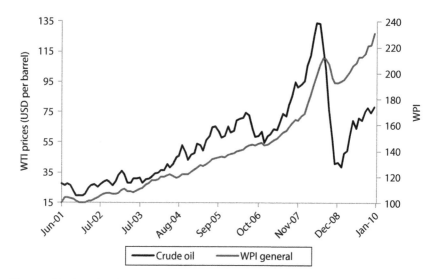

Figure 140   Crude oil prices and the WPI

The correlation between WPI and crude oil prices is marked at 0.74 for the period Jul 2001–Jan 2010, which makes it more responsive to the price changes as compared to CPI, whose correlation with crude oil prices was 0.68.

The results of a regression analysis on the changes of crude oil prices against the changes in WPI also reveal that the WPI is likely to be impacted by changes in crude oil prices more quickly than CPI.

This seems obvious given the fact that increases in the commodity prices are more likely to impact the primary production sectors first before their impact is felt in the secondary markets. The regression indicated the following relationship between the changes in WPI and WTI.

$$\ln\left(\frac{WPI_t}{WPI_{t-1}}\right) = 0.6291\% + 6.1385\% \times \ln\left(\frac{WTI_t}{WTI_{t-1}}\right) + 4.4768\%$$

$$\times \ln\left(\frac{WTI_{t-1}}{WTI_{t-2}}\right) + 1.4154\% \times \ln\left(\frac{WTI_{t-2}}{WTI_{t-3}}\right) \mp \varepsilon$$

where   is the error term of the regression of 1.77 percent. The change in the index in month t is explained by the change in oil prices in the months t, $t-1$ and $t-2$ with factors 6.1385 percent, 4.4768 percent and 1.4154 percent respectively.

The aggregate impact over three months adds up to 12.0308 percent. The regression also indicates that 0.6291 percent of the change in WPI is not from the change in oil prices but from other components in the index. For example, if oil prices stay constant in months $t-3$ to $t-1$, then rise by 100 percent in month t, the change in WPI in month t would range between approximately (5.00 percent, 8.53 percent). As compared to CPI the impact of oil price changes on WPI is 6.5 times greater in the first month and 2.42 times higher in the second, reflecting the more immediate effect of these changes on the index. The trends in the various components of WPI are depicted below in comparison to the WTI spot prices.

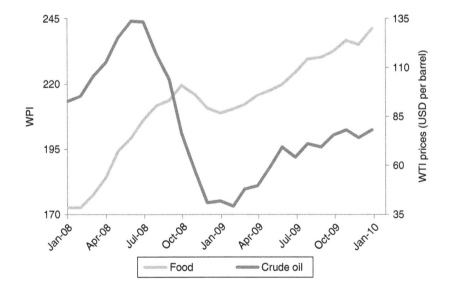

Figure 141   Food WPI and crude oil prices

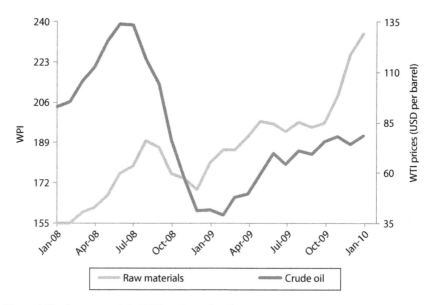

Figure 142   Raw materials WPI and crude oil prices

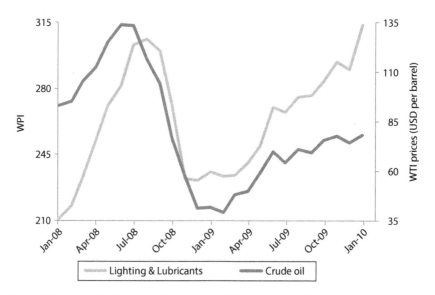

Figure 143   Fuel, lighting and lubricants WPI and crude oil prices

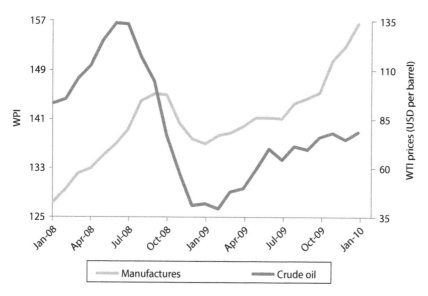

Figure 144   Manufactures WPI and crude oil prices

As compared to CPI, all the components of WPI have shown a degree of responsiveness to the movement in crude oil prices, the most defined trend of which is that of fuel, lighting and lubricants.

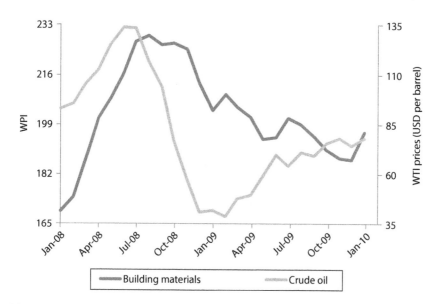

Figure 145   Building materials WPI and crude oil prices

14

Historical Spreads in Bond Yields in the Indo-Pak Sub-Continent

The Indian and Pakistani bond markets, while very different in size and volume, still share a number of common themes. They share similar food production and consumption cycles, they are net importers of crude oil and, while the manufacturing base of the Indian economy is far larger than Pakistan, when it comes to income disparity and poverty levels they share similar challenges. A comparison of the inflation and yield numbers and real rate of returns in both markets leads to some very interesting results.

We started with the following questions:

- What is the real rate of return in both markets adjusted for inflation and is there a correlation between real rates in both markets?
- Is there any correlation between bond spreads between the Indian and Pakistani markets?
- If yes, has it been stable or erratic?
- If yes, is there a lag between rate movements between India and Pakistan?

In the first section we look at the data used in the analysis. In particular we look at trends in bond yields and inflation for each country in turn. In the second section we analyze each of the above questions in turn.

Data

Historical spreads between Pakistan government bond yields and inflation have been evaluated over the period 2005–9. The bond yields (both before and after accounting for inflation) for 3, 5, 7 and 10 year bonds have also been compared against those of their Indian counterparts over the period 2008–9. A summary of data used is presented in the table below.

COUNTRY	ITEM	DETAILS
Pakistan	Inflation	CPI General year on year (YoY)
		WPI General (YoY)
	Bond yields	Pakistan government investment bond revaluation (PKRV) rates
India	Inflation	WPI – All (YoY)
		CPI for industrial workers (YoY)
	Bond yields	Indian government bond generic bid yield

Figure 146   Inflation and bond yield data for Pakistan and India

Note on inflation rates

In India the primary inflation measure is based on the Wholesale Price Index (WPI), whereas in Pakistan (as in most of the world) the primary measure is based on the Consumer Price Index (CPI). In our analysis we look at yield spreads against both of these measures in turn.

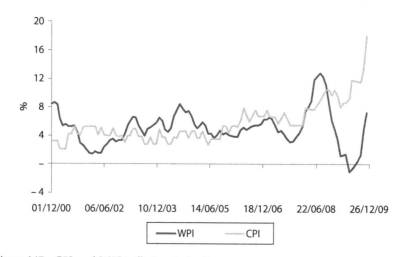

Figure 147   CPI and WPI inflation in India

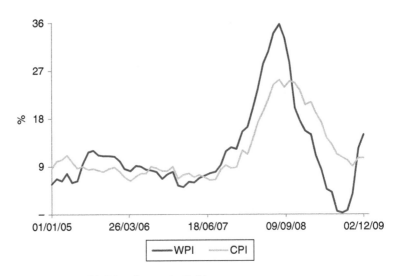

Figure 148   CPI and WPI inflation in Pakistan

Both in India and Pakistan, inflation based on WPI has a more volatile and erratic trend. In Pakistan the CPI inflation seems to be at a lag to the WPI series, though not so steeply or as inclined, whereas in India it has generally been on an upward trend since 2005.

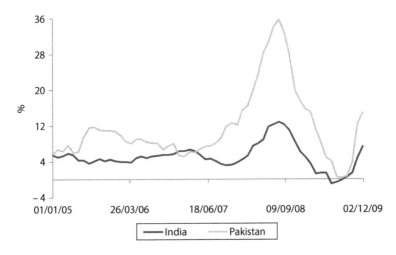

Figure 149   Inflation based on WPI in India and Pakistan

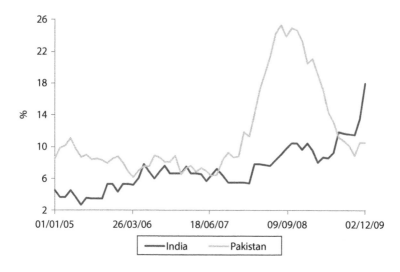

Figure 150 Inflation based on CPI in India and Pakistan

Bond yields and inflation in Pakistan – a first look at real rates

From January 2008 to the end of June 2009, bond spreads, evaluated against CPI inflation, have been negative, that is, inflation rate has exceeded the yield on these government bonds. From July 2009, there has been a slight improvement in spreads, reaching between 3.6 and 3.93 percent at the end of October 2009 before declining once again. At the end of December 2009 they stood at around 2 percent. Spreads based on the WPI series show that they had turned negative around the second week of November 2009. Given that CPI inflation is a lagged series, it is expected that the decline in CPI-based spreads will continue into early 2010 and may also possibly become negative once again, given that the inflation rate may continue to increase consequent to the government having raised power tariffs by 14 percent and gas prices by 18 percent in January 2010. Trends in spreads for 3, 5, 7 and 10 year bonds are illustrated in the following graphs.

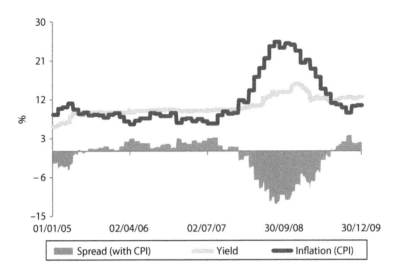

Figure 151   CPI inflation in Pakistan, 3-year bond yields and spreads

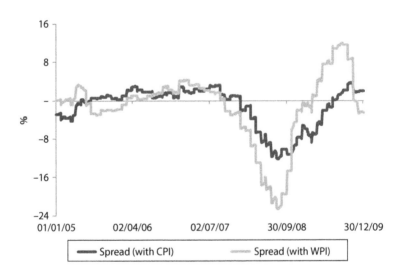

Figure 152   3-year bond yield spreads with CPI and WPI inflation in Pakistan

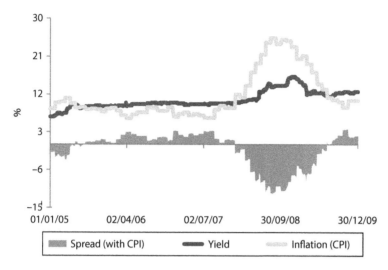

Figure 153 CPI inflation in Pakistan, 5-year bond yields and spreads

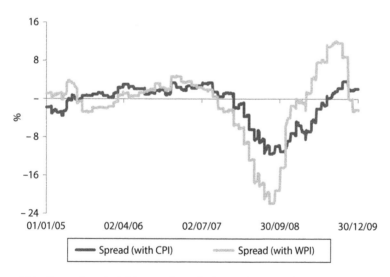

Figure 154 5-year bond yield spreads with CPI and WPI inflation in Pakistan

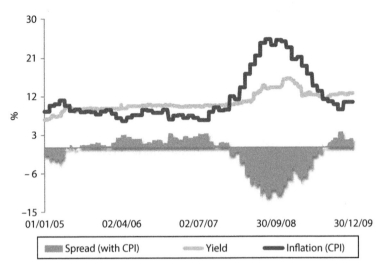

Figure 155   CPI inflation in Pakistan, 7-year bond yields and spreads

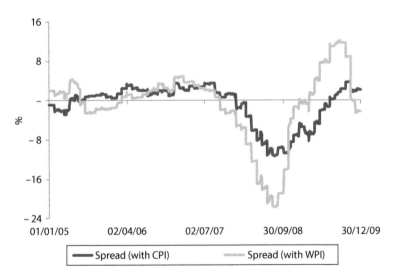

Figure 156   7-year bond yield spreads with CPI and WPI inflation in Pakistan

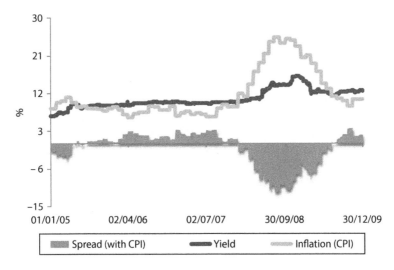

Figure 157   CPI inflation in Pakistan, 10-year bond yields and spreads

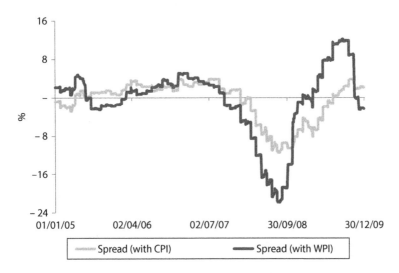

Figure 158   10-year bond yield spreads with CPI and WPI inflation in Pakistan

Bond yields and inflation in India – a first look at real rates

Unlike Pakistan, the official quote for inflation in India is based on the WPI. The WPI captures price inflation at each stage of the production process, whereas the CPI only captures it at the final stage. Because of this construct, the WPI tends to reflect price inflationary pressures immediately, whereas price increases would appear in the CPI at a time lag as increased costs gradually get passed on through the various stages of production.

India's choice of WPI as a basis for measuring inflation and related short term intervention policies is that it is the only index that is available on a weekly basis (presented with a two weeks' lag). In addition to this, while WPI is calculated on a national level, there is no unified CPI. A number of CPIs are calculated based on various consumer groups such as industrial workers, rural labor, agricultural laborers and non-manual employees.

A move to a single national level CPI has been hampered because of problems with data collection, which would require a huge data collection workforce to gather required information from the retail level. Also, some of the current CPIs (CPI for industrial workers) are used as a basis for setting dearness allowances to be paid to government employees and to industrial workers and for determining the fixation and revision of minimum wages to scheduled employments. Because of this, various workers groups have shown a resistance to the switch to a more integrated CPI. In addition to this, the existing CPI numbers are dependent on base years that have not been revised in years – some in more than two decades. The WPI base year on the other hand is revised every five years.

In order to maintain some form of consistency with the above section we have analyzed the spreads principally using a CPI (for industrial workers)-based series. This is because amongst the CPIs calculated, it has the broadest base. However, spreads with WPI inflation have also been presented below.

With respect to the graphs in the previous section we see a very different trend, especially towards the latter half of 2009. Given that the inflation (based on CPI) has been steadily increasing over the period, we see that the negative spreads which started in the last week of August 2008 continued to grow till December 2009. The WPI inflation series paints a significantly different picture for the year 2009, when spreads have been positive on the whole. However, since July 2009 these spreads have been gradually falling and now are between −0.8 and 0.3 percent.

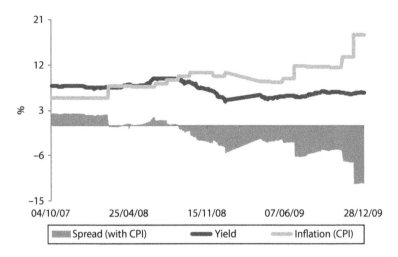

Figure 159   CPI inflation in India, 3-year bond yields and spreads

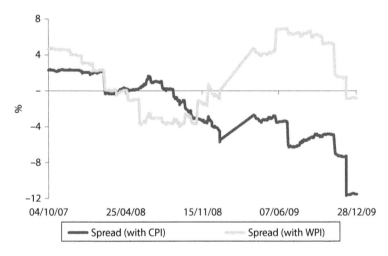

Figure 160   3-year bond yield spreads with CPI and WPI inflation in India

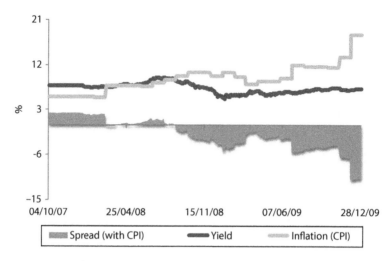

Figure 161   CPI inflation in India, 5-year bond yields and spreads

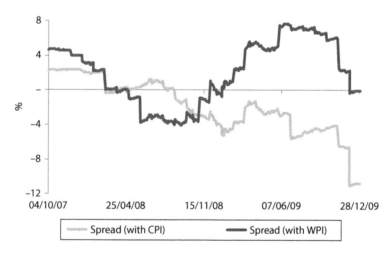

Figure 162   5-year bond yield spreads with CPI and WPI inflation in India

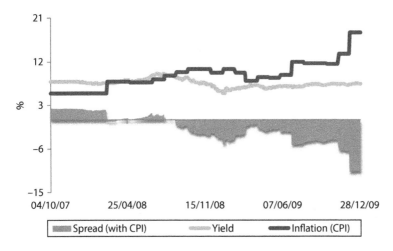

Figure 163 CPI inflation in India, 7-year bond yields and spreads

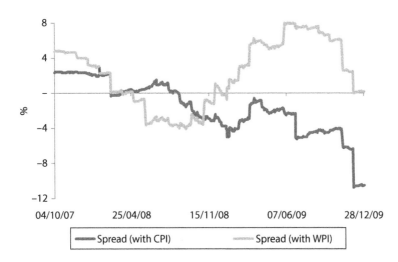

Figure 164 7-year bond yield spreads with CPI and WPI inflation in India

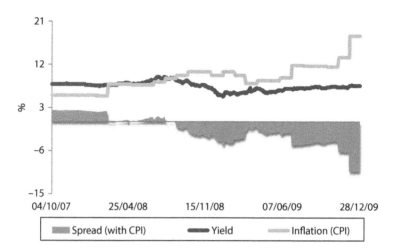

Figure 165   CPI inflation in India, 10-year bond yields and spreads

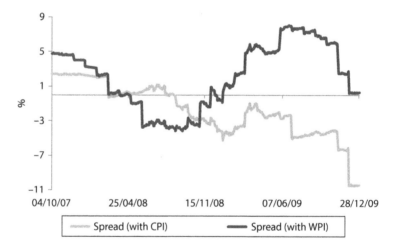

Figure 166   10-year bond yield spreads with CPI and WPI inflation in India

A comparative analysis: India and Pakistan

Is there any correlation between bond spreads in the Indian and Pakistani markets? If "yes," has it been stable or erratic?

In order to address these questions we have first looked at nominal bond yields and assessed the correlation in these yields between the Pakistani and Indian markets. Next we have assessed spreads between different tenors for these markets and determined whether or not a correlation exists between these spreads in India and Pakistan. The results are given below.

Nominal bond yields

Looking at nominal bond yields we see that for all tenors discussed, Pakistan bonds offer much higher returns as compared to their Indian counterparts for the entire period 2008–9. Spreads peaked in January 2009 and have now leveled off between 5 and 6 percent.

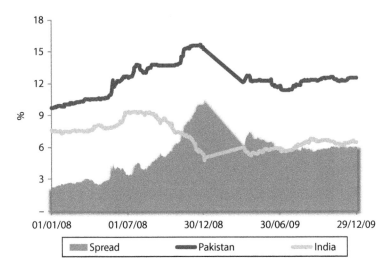

Figure 167 3-year nominal bond yields and spreads between the Indian and Pakistani markets

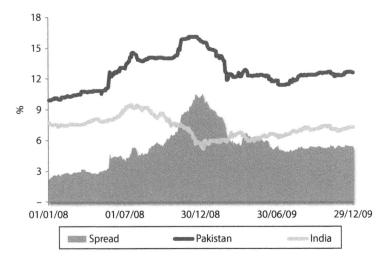

Figure 168 5-year nominal bond yields and spreads between the Indian and Pakistani markets

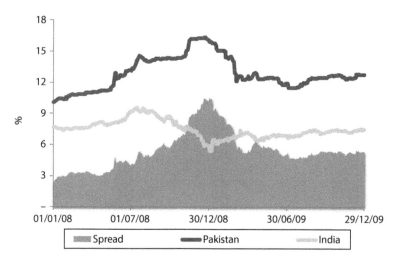

Figure 169 7-year nominal bond yields and spreads between the Indian and Pakistani markets

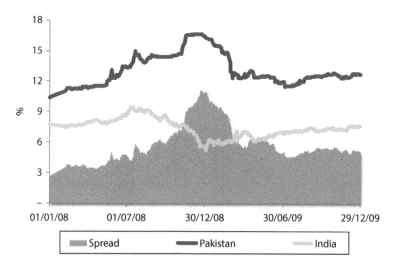

Figure 170 10-year nominal bond yields and spreads between the Indian and Pakistani markets

Correlations between nominal yields have been negligible with average correlations for the period, falling between −0.130 and 0. Correlations for spreads in bonds of varying tenors, however, reveal a slightly different picture, which is elaborated in the following paragraphs.

Spreads between tenors

Prior to January 2009, India had lower spreads between various tenors (such as the spread between the 5- and 7-year bonds) as compared to Pakistan. However, since 2009 the spreads have increased considerably. On the other hand, spreads in yields between bonds of similar tenors have declined in Pakistan. For example, the spreads (monthly averages) between 5- and 7-year bonds were as follows.

Average Spread %	Jan-08	Jan-09	Dec-09
India	0.02	0.41	0.24
Pakistan	0.30	0.19	0.13

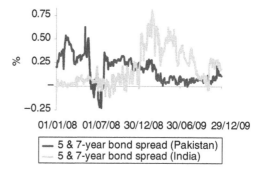

Figure 171 Spreads between 5-year and 7-year bond yields

Correlation of spreads in yields of various tenors between India and Pakistan are given below.

	Correlation Between India & Pakistan	Rule of Thumb
3 & 5-year bond spread	−0.58	Moderate
5 & 7-year bond spread	−0.30	Low
7 & 10-year bond spread	−0.13	No or negligible
3 & 10-year bond spread	−0.76	Marked

Figure 172 Correlation between India and Pakistan bond yield spreads

There appears to be a negative correlation between spreads in India and Pakistan. In general, when spreads between tenors increased in India, in Pakistan spreads declined. Viewing the magnitude of the correlations, the spread between the 3-year and 10-year bond had a marked negative correlation between India and Pakistan. On average, when the spread between these bonds increased in India, spreads between similar bonds in Pakistan declined 76 percent of the time. However, the correlation trend has not been stable, as can be seen in the graph below which shows 60-observation trailing correlations.

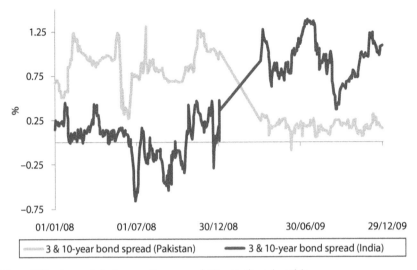

Figure 173   Spreads between 3-year and 10-year bond yields

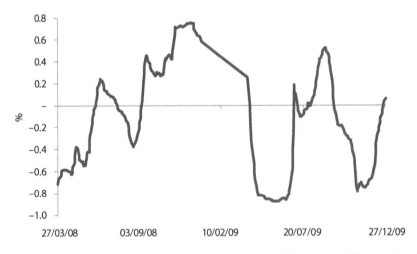

Figure 174   Correlation between India and Pakistan of 3-year and 10-year bond yield spreads

For the other pairs of bonds mentioned above the correlations have been moderate to low and seem highly erratic over time.

What is the real rate of return in both markets adjusted for inflation and once again is there a correlation between real rates in both markets? If "yes," has it been stable or erratic?
In order to answer these questions we have calculated the bonds' yields on a real rate of return basis by subtracting inflation from the nominal

bond yields. The trends in the resulting yields and the spread between Indian and Pakistani bonds have been evaluated. Then, based on the trend observed using WPI-based inflation adjusted yields, the correlations between the two countries' yields have been assessed.

Real (inflation adjusted) bond yields

On a real rate of return basis, after accounting for the impact of inflation, the bond spreads for India and Pakistan present a different picture depending on the inflation measure chosen. Based on CPI we see that there are positive spreads between the adjusted yields that have increased since May 2009.

On the other hand, when yields have been adjusted using WPI-based inflation rates we notice that even though Pakistan bond yields increased over those of India in May 2009, they began a steady decline in early September 2009 and have fallen below Indian bond yields since November 2009. This is illustrated for 5-year bonds below. It may be noted that similar trends have been experienced for bonds of other tenors as well.

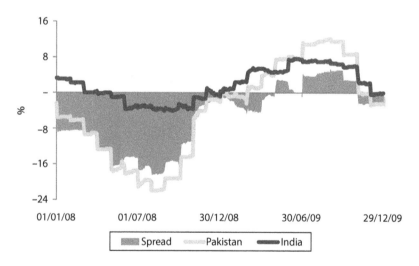

Figure 175 5-year WPI Inflation adjusted bond yields in India and Pakistan

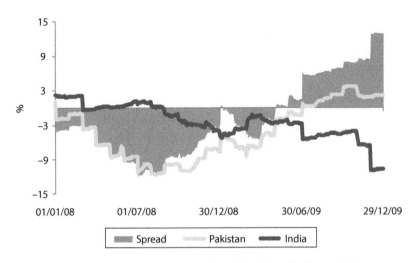

Figure 176   5-year CPI Inflation adjusted bond yields in India and Pakistan

Correlation in real bond yields of India and Pakistan

The WPI-adjusted yields between the two countries also demonstrate a high level of correlation, which is apparent in the graph above. On average correlations exceed 0.9, which tells us that when adjusted yields increased in India, adjusted yields in Pakistan also increased 90 percent of the time. The increases and decreases in the real yields seem to be in tandem and there is no apparent lag in the trend lines of either country.

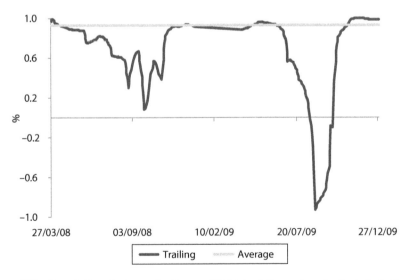

Figure 177   Correlations between Indian and Pakistani 3-year bond adjusted yields

During the period April–September 2009, however, correlations were significantly below this average, in fact demonstrating highly negative correlation. However, since November 2009 they have once again approached and leveled off around the average for the period. This is illustrated for the 3-year bond.

On the whole correlations have been fairly stable and around the period average.

If correlation existed based on the current trends, what does that say about the future rate environment in Pakistan?
In November and December 2009, India and Pakistan have both witnessed a significant increase in inflation from October levels. With increases in electricity and gas tariffs and international oil and other commodity prices inflation seems to be on an uptick in the coming months for Pakistan. Similarly, with increasing food prices India's bond yields also seem likely to be under inflationary pressure and we expect the correlation between adjusted yields to hold. We expect that in the next month or so, the bond spreads (nominal yield less inflation) will face a further decline.

15
Volatility Trends in Commodity Prices

Annualized volatilities have been calculated using data on commodity spot prices for the years 2008 to June 2013 over semi-annual periods (January–June and July–December). In addition, volatilities have been evaluated for the years July 2011–June 2012 and July 2012–June 2013 to assess the change in risk levels over these years.

Commodities

Annualized volatility

The table shows the average annualized volatilities for the years ending June 2012 and June 2013. The last column shows the change in annualized volatilities. For example we see that volatility levels for fuel oil increased by over 71 percent in 2013 as compared to 2012. In contrast the risk level for silver declined by almost 60 percent in 2013 and was 27.61 percent as compared to 50.45 percent in 2012.

Commodity	Annualized Volatility		
	Jul 2011–Jun 2012	Jul 2012–Jun 2013	Change in Volatility[1] 2012 over 2013
Brent crude oil	24.39%	20.48%	−17.48%
West Texas crude oil	33.44%	40.53%	19.23%
Fuel oil	22.00%	44.98%	71.52%
Diesel fuel	22.12%	44.38%	69.62%
Natural gas	50.66%	34.19%	−39.32%
Gold	22.73%	17.21%	−27.81%

Figure 178   Annualized volatilities in years ending June 2012 and 2013

COMMODITY	ANNUALIZED VOLATILITY		
	JUL 2011– JUN 2012	JUL 2012– JUN 2013	CHANGE IN VOLATILITY[1] 2012 OVER 2013
Silver	50.45%	27.61%	−60.29%
Platinum	22.41%	18.04%	−21.70%
Aluminium	20.48%	20.12%	−1.76%
Steel	25.51%	15.19%	−51.85%
Copper	30.60%	19.15%	−46.86%
Cotton	33.52%	24.41%	−31.73%
Corn	31.48%	25.66%	−20.44%
Wheat No. 2	44.21%	28.97%	−42.27%
Wheat No. 1	20.35%	22.25%	8.91%
Coffee	23.77%	21.77%	−8.81%
Corn oil	8.66%	12.11%	33.50%
Soybean oil	20.19%	18.98%	−6.19%

Figure 178   Continued

Trend

The following trends in volatility have been calculated by looking at price data over semi-annual periods for sectors as well as for commodities represented in those sectors in our data set.

In general we see a rise in volatility in July–December 2008 and then a decline in the following periods. For crude oil and refined products we saw a pickup in volatility levels in the second half of 2012, though they have reduced once again for the first half of 2013.

For precious metals, led by silver, 2011 was a particularly volatile year. The first half of the calendar year 2013 also shows an uptick in volatility levels for silver and gold.

Post global financial crisis, cotton prices saw increased volatilities in the second half of 2010. This continued into the first half of 2011, where volatilities almost reached the levels seen in July–December 2008. Since then volatility has once again declined.

Crude oil

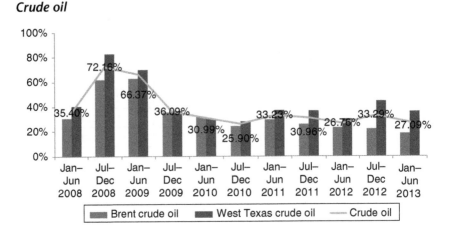

Figure 179   Crude oil volatility levels

Refined products

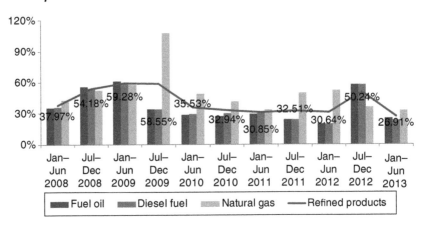

Figure 180   Refined products volatility levels

Precious metals

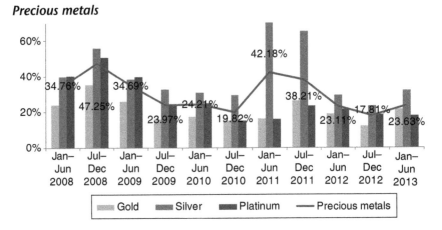

Figure 181   Precious metals volatility levels

Other metals

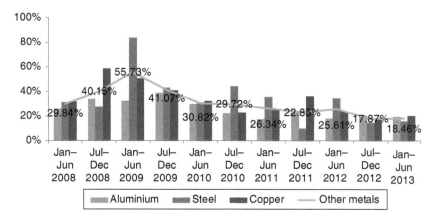

Figure 182   Other metals volatility levels

Fibers and textiles

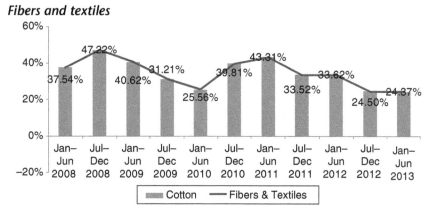

Figure 183   Fibers and textiles volatility levels

Grains and feeds

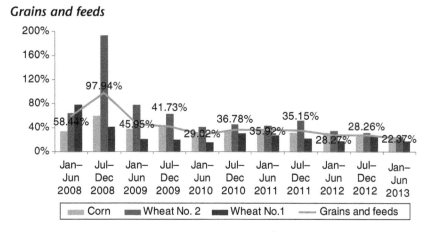

Figure 184   Grains and feeds volatility levels

Food[2]

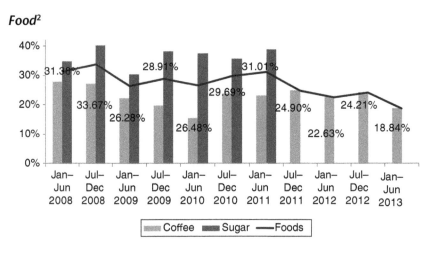

Figure 185   Food volatility levels

Fats and oils

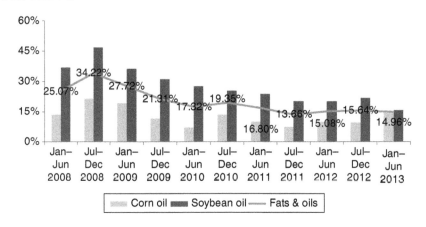

Figure 186   Fats and oils volatility levels

3-Sigma band

Using the average volatility for the latest semi-annual period, the 3-sigma band is evaluated for the coming quarter. This implicitly assumes that the average volatility for January–June 2013 will continue to persist in the third quarter of 2013 (July–September 2013). If conditions vary then the band may be breached.

The 3σ band (three sigma band) gives a range of possible prices, where the range is calculated within three standard deviations from the mean price, which in our case is taken as the final price at the end of the period of study (the price as at June 18, 2013).

Commodity	3-Month Volatility	Price as at 18/6/2013[3]	Lower Bound[4]	Upper Bound[5]
Brent crude oil	10.97%	103.87	69.69	138.05
West Texas crude oil	21.41%	98.19	35.14	161.24
Fuel oil	14.87%	2.83	1.57	4.09
Diesel fuel	13.96%	2.84	1.65	4.03
Natural gas	19.42%	3.91	1.63	6.18
Gold	12.84%	1,436.09	882.86	1,989.32
Silver	18.96%	13.96	6.02	21.90
Platinum	10.57%	1,427.00	974.61	1,879.39
Aluminium	11.64%	0.83	0.54	1.12
Steel	9.52%	1,619.00	1,156.82	2,081.18
Copper	11.94%	3.16	2.03	4.29
Cotton	14.57%	0.84	0.48	1.21
Corn	14.53%	7.07	3.99	10.14
Wheat No. 2	15.25%	6.99	3.79	10.18
Wheat No. 1	10.32%	7.77	5.36	10.17
Coffee	11.26%	1.46	0.97	1.96
Corn oil	8.60%	42.75	31.72	53.78
Soybean oil	9.28%	0.49	0.35	0.62

Figure 187   3-sigma band for commodity prices

Commodity correlations

The correlation matrices have been calculated using the *daily returns* of the following commodity sectors. The details of which commodities have been used in this sector analysis are given below.

COMMODITY	DETAILS	SECTOR
Brent crude oil	Brent crude oil spot prices	Crude oil
West Texas crude oil	Crude oil: West Texas sour, Midlands	Crude oil
Fuel oil	Fuel oil, No. 2 NY gal.	Refined products
Diesel fuel	Diesel fuel, 500 ppm S, NY harbor low sulphur	Refined products
Natural gas	Natural gas Henry Hub, $ per MMbtu	Refined products
Gold	Gold: American Eagle, troy oz.	Precious metals
Silver	Silver: London fixing, spot price, per troy oz	Precious metals
Platinum	Platinum: free market	Precious metals
Aluminum	Aluminum, LME $ per lb (1 metric ton= 2204.62 lb)	Other metals
Steel	St. steel scrap, US, $ per gross ton-D	Other metals
Copper	Copper, high grade: Comex spot price $ per lb.	Other metals
Cotton	Cotton, 1 1/16 strand lw-md Mmphs, per lb	Fibres and textiles
Corn	Corn, No. 2 yellow. Cent. Ill. Bu	Grains and feeds
Wheat No. 2	Wheat, No. 2 soft red, St. Louis, (US$ per bushel)	Grains and feeds
Wheat No. 1	Wheat, No. 1 soft white, del Portland, Ore (US$ per bushel)	Grains and feeds
Coffee	Coffee, Colombian, NY lb.	Foods
Sugar[9]	Sugar, cane, raw, world, lb. fob	Foods
Corn oil	Corn oil, crude wet/dry mill	Fats and oils
Soybean oil	Soybean oil, crude; Central Illinois lb.	Fats and oils

Figure 188   Commodity details

The first matrix shows the average correlations over the entire period of analysis, that is, January 1, 2008 to June 18, 2013.

	Crude Oil	Refined Products	Gold	Precious Metal (Excl. Gold)	Other Metals	Fibres & Textiles	Grains & Feeds	Foods	Fats & Oils
Crude oil	1.00								
Refined products	0.60	1.00							
Gold	0.27	0.21	1.00						
Precious metal (excl. gold)	0.45	0.32	0.26	1.00					
Other metals	0.26	0.66	0.33	0.17	1.00				
Fibres and textiles	0.31	0.22	0.15	0.28	0.10	1.00			
Grains & feeds	0.29	0.23	0.08	0.20	0.13	0.26	1.00		
Foods	0.03	0.08	0.15	0.02	0.11	0.04	−0.01	1.00	
Fats & oils	0.49	0.37	0.25	0.35	0.20	0.36	0.35	0.06	1.00

Figure 189 Correlation matrix (January 1, 2008 to June 18, 2013)

The following matrices show year-wise[2] average correlations.

	Crude Oil	Refined Products	Gold	Precious Metal (Excl. Gold)	Other Metals	Fibres & Textiles	Grains & Feeds	Foods	Fats & Oils
Crude oil	1.00								
Refined products	0.77	1.00							
Gold	0.35	0.34	1.00						
Precious metal (excl. gold)	0.61	0.53	0.28	1.00					
Other metals	0.39	0.65	0.59	0.31	1.00				
Fibres and textiles	0.42	0.31	0.22	0.40	0.16	1.00			
Grains & feeds	0.27	0.20	−0.02	0.25	0.02	0.22	1.00		
Foods	0.39	0.36	0.33	0.38	0.35	0.33	0.13	1.00	
Fats & oils	0.60	0.53	0.38	0.54	0.35	0.45	0.25	0.41	1.00

Figure 190 Correlation matrix (2008)

	Crude Oil	Refined Products	Gold	Precious Metal (Excl. Gold)	Other Metals	Fibres & Textiles	Grains & Feeds	Foods	Fats & Oils
Crude oil	1.00								
Refined products	0.60	1.00							
Gold	0.15	0.15	1.00						
Precious metal (excl. gold)	0.38	0.30	0.12	1.00					
Other metals	0.21	0.74	0.25	0.16	1.00				
Fibres and textiles	0.33	0.30	0.08	0.32	0.16	1.00			
Grains & feeds	0.41	0.34	0.15	0.22	0.24	0.34	1.00		
Foods	0.26	0.16	0.10	0.10	0.02	0.21	0.18	1.00	
Fats & oils	0.53	0.45	0.11	0.30	0.17	0.41	0.44	0.24	1.00

Figure 191   Correlation matrix (2009)

	Crude Oil	Refined Products	Gold	Precious Metal (Excl. Gold)	Other Metals	Fibres & Textiles	Grains & Feeds	Foods	Fats & Oils
Crude oil	1.00								
Refined products	0.66	1.00							
Gold	0.44	0.39	1.00						
Precious metal (excl. gold)	0.43	0.30	0.41	1.00					
Other metals	0.19	0.70	0.30	0.08	1.00				
Fibres and textiles	0.25	0.12	0.23	0.20	−0.02	1.00			
Grains & feeds	0.22	0.21	0.14	0.13	0.12	0.27	1.00		
Foods	0.14	0.12	0.13	0.17	0.11	0.21	0.19	1.00	
Fats & oils	0.32	0.26	0.28	0.24	0.10	0.31	0.35	0.17	1.00

Figure 192   Correlation matrix (2010)

	CRUDE OIL	REFINED PRODUCTS	GOLD	PRECIOUS METAL (EXCL. GOLD)	OTHER METALS	FIBRES & TEXTILES	GRAINS & FEEDS	FOODS	FATS & OILS
Crude oil	1.00								
Refined products	0.71	1.00							
Gold	0.21	0.17	1.00						
Precious metal (excl. gold)	0.40	0.30	0.25	1.00					
Other metals	0.33	0.70	0.31	0.18	1.00				
Fibres and textiles	0.25	0.24	0.06	0.17	0.11	1.00			
Grains & feeds	0.35	0.33	0.12	0.17	0.20	0.39	1.00		
Foods	0.11	0.10	0.24	0.15	0.14	0.09	0.04	1.00	
Fats & oils	0.40	0.36	0.14	0.24	0.19	0.40	0.57	0.10	1.00

Figure 193   Correlation matrix (2011)

	CRUDE OIL	REFINED PRODUCTS	GOLD	PRECIOUS METAL (EXCL. GOLD)	OTHER METALS	FIBRES & TEXTILES	GRAINS & FEEDS	FOODS	FATS & OILS
Crude oil	1.00								
Refined products	0.24	1.00							
Gold	0.34	0.09	1.00						
Precious metal (excl. gold)	0.33	0.10	0.47	1.00					
Other metals	0.20	0.47	0.18	0.10	1.00				
Fibres and textiles	0.25	0.09	0.24	0.25	0.00	1.00			
Grains & feeds	0.23	0.13	0.19	0.16	0.15	0.12	1.00		
Foods	−0.06	0.06	−0.00	0.02	0.04	−0.06	0.00	1.00	
Fats & oils	0.28	0.06	0.27	0.24	0.12	0.19	0.44	−0.04	1.00

Figure 194   Correlation matrix (2012)

	Crude Oil	Refined Products	Gold	Precious Metal (Excl. Gold)	Other Metals	Fibres & Textiles	Grains & Feeds	Foods	Fats & Oils
Crude oil	1.00								
Refined products	0.15	1.00							
Gold	0.26	0.09	1.00						
Precious metal (excl. gold)	0.31	0.01	0.54	1.00					
Other metals	0.02	0.47	0.42	−0.03	1.00				
Fibres and textiles	0.19	0.03	0.15	0.10	0.01	1.00			
Grains & feeds	−0.01	−0.06	0.12	0.06	0.18	0.08	1.00		
Foods	0.04	0.03	0.11	0.12	0.07	0.11	0.05	1.00	
Fats & oils	0.21	0.08	0.27	0.30	0.08	−0.05	0.10	0.18	1.00

Figure 195   Correlation matrix (2013)

Over the five and a half years, average correlations have reduced in general. For example, consider the trend in correlations with refined products:

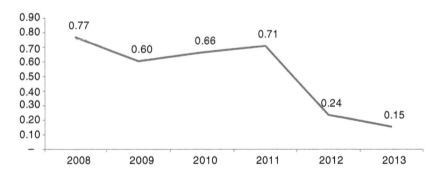

Figure 196   Correlation trend – refined products with crude oil

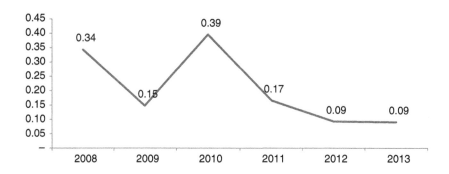

Figure 197 Correlation trend – refined products with gold

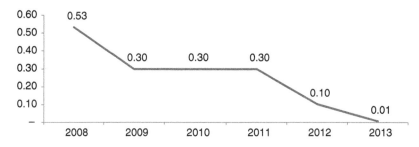

Figure 198 Correlation trend – refined products with precious metals (excluding gold)

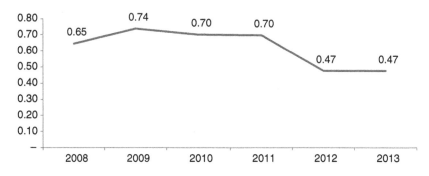

Figure 199 Correlation trend – refined products with other (non-precious) metals

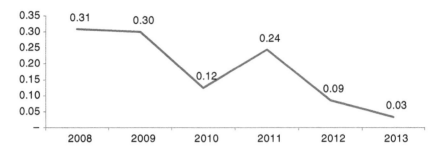

Figure 200   Correlation trend – refined products with fibers and textiles

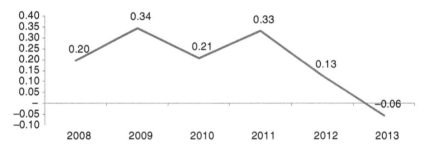

Figure 201   Correlation trend – refined products with grains and feeds

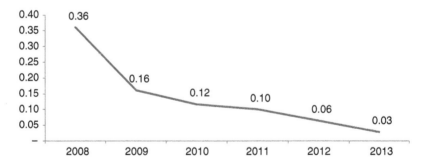

Figure 202   Correlation trend – refined products with crude oil

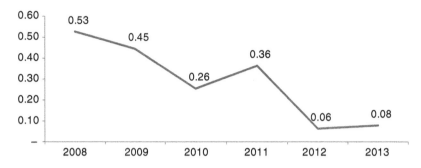

Figure 203 Correlation trend – refined products with fats and oils

One exception is the correlation of gold with other precious metals, which has increased in recent years:

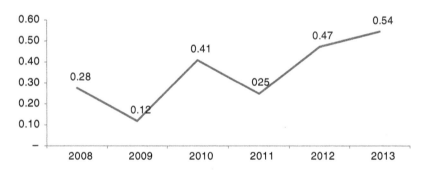

Figure 204 Correlation trend – gold with other precious metal

16
Energy Insights

The primary objective of global energy insights is to provide an overview of the history and current landscape of key energy commodities. The need for the section came about when the regional growth story hit a major roadblock, primarily on account of energy and commodity price supply shocks.

The right way to predict future supply shocks and understand their impact on a region is to understand energy consumption in the US, China and India and then translate the impact to a local setting. That is the goal we have set out to achieve with Energy Insights.

This chapter focuses on products, contracts and consumption patterns in the US market, supplemented by the supporting data for markets in India, China and Pakistan.

Overview – US

The energy industry as we know it today is fast evolving due to advances in renewable energy sources such as solar, wind, hydro and geothermal heat – all of which can be naturally replenished and are considered eco-friendly. As the global debate on reducing the dependence on oil and migrating to these renewable sources heats up, however, the world continues to remain (and will do so for the foreseeable future) heavily dependent on fossil fuels such as crude oil and natural gas.

Following is an overview of each of the major fuel types and the respective price and inventory levels as of year end 2009.

1. Natural gas

Natural gas is a non-renewable source of energy used primarily for heating and generating electricity. The main ingredient in natural gas is methane, a gas composed of four hydrogen atoms and one carbon atom. The US procures natural gas from wells within the US and through imports from abroad. The US imports natural gas from Canada and Mexico via pipelines, and in the form of "Liquefied Natural Gas" (or LNG) from countries such as Qatar, Trinidad and Tobago, and Algeria. Natural gas is super cooled and transported as a liquid on tankers before being warmed up and turned into a gas upon arrival in the US.

The US natural gas industry is dynamic and continuously evolving. Comprised of two primary segments – exploration and production, and distribution and sales – the industry went through a gradual deregulation in the 1980s and early 1990s. This deregulation process was completed with the passage of the FERC order 636 requiring open access to the pipeline system used to transport natural gas.

To understand the significance of natural gas as a fuel source, all one needs to do is take a look at the energy plan proposed by oil tycoon, T Boone Pickens. In his energy plan, Pickens is bullish about natural gas becoming the primary fuel in the US and has spent a considerable portion of his wealth promoting the idea of natural gas powered vehicles. Once fuel cell powered vehicles become practical, aided by government encouragement and subsidies, natural gas is likely to be the first fuel used to power fuel cell vehicles. The likelihood of this idea being successful is further bolstered by advances in fractioning techniques and the discovery of new gas fields in the US.

Today, industrial consumers consume approximately 36 percent of natural gas, while 21 percent is consumed by residential customers, 14 percent is used by commercial customers, and 26 percent is used for electricity generation. Transactions in the natural gas physical markets are conducted on a daily or monthly basis. The majority of the transactions take place during bid-week, the last week of the month preceding the contract month.

The natural gas market is comprised of a collection of locations, with Henry Hub in Louisiana and Waha Hub in Texas serving as major trading hubs. The natural gas futures contract developed by the NYMEX Division is widely used as a national benchmark price. The futures contract trades in units of 10,000 million British thermal units (MMBtu). The price of the NYMEX futures contract is based on delivery at the Henry Hub in Louisiana, the nexus of 16 intra- and inter-state natural gas pipeline systems that draw supplies from the region's prolific gas deposits. The pipelines serve markets throughout the US East Coast, the Gulf Coast, the Midwest, and up to the Canadian border. As a result of the volatility in natural gas prices, a vigorous basis market has also emerged in the pricing relationships between Henry Hub and other primary natural gas market locations in the US and Canada. The NYMEX Exchange makes available for trading a series of basis swap futures contracts that are quoted as price differentials between approximately 30 natural gas pricing points and Henry Hub.

The price of natural gas was in the US$5.81/MMBtu range at year end 2009, significantly lower than the price of natural gas at the end of June 2008 of US$13.16 /MMBtu, but up again from a low of US$1.92/MMBtu in September 2009.

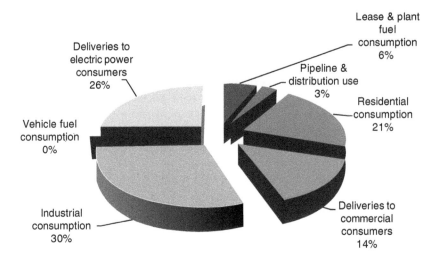

Figure 205   Natural gas consumption by end use in USA

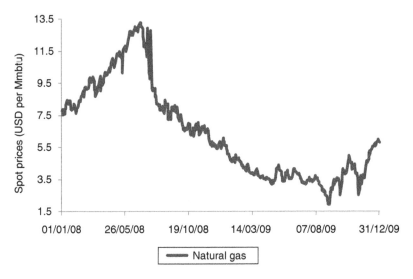

Figure 206   Natural gas prices

Natural gas inventory levels as recorded by the EIA were 3,118 billion cubic feet (Bcf) at year end 2009 as compared to 2,830 Bcf from one year before.

The downward correction in the price of natural gas was caused by low demand due to the global financial crisis and excess supply as illustrated by the inventory levels.

New fields have been discovered in Texas, Arkansas and Pennsylvania. These discoveries have come as oil has become harder to find and more expensive to produce, making natural gas a viable option for achieving long-term goals such as easing the impact of energy-price spikes, reducing dependence on crude oil, lowering emissions and speeding the transition to renewable fuels.

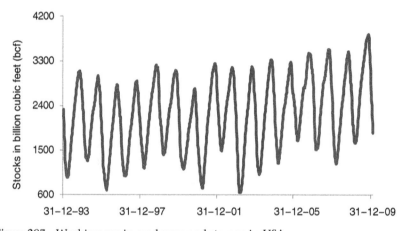

Figure 207 Working gas in underground storage in USA

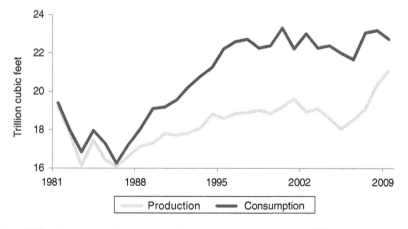

Figure 208 Dry natural gas production and consumption in USA

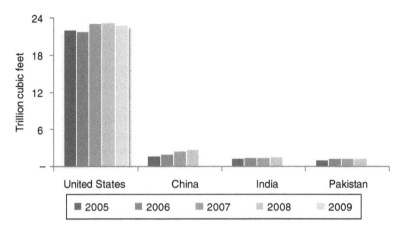

Figure 209   Dry natural gas consumption in USA, China, India and Pakistan

2. Crude oil

Crude oil is a naturally occurring, flammable liquid found in rock formations. The commodity comes in a wide variety of grades, classified by its gravity and sulfur content. The global benchmark for crude oil is Brent crude oil while the US benchmark is West Texas Intermediate (WTI) crude oil. New York Mercantile Exchange (NYMEX) and Inter Continental Exchange (ICE) are two major exchanges where WTI and Brent crude oil are traded respectively.

Crude oil is regarded as the world's most actively traded commodity. The NYMEX Exchange light, sweet crude oil futures contract is the world's most liquid instrument for trading crude oil, and the world's largest-volume futures contract trading on a physical commodity. Because of its excellent liquidity and price transparency, the contract is used as a principal international pricing benchmark. The contract trades in units of 1,000 barrels and provides for delivery of several grades of domestic and internationally traded foreign crudes, and serves the diverse needs of the physical market.

In July 2008, we witnessed the price of crude oil soar to an all-time high of US$145.31a barrel and then subsequently drop to a five year low of US$30.28 a barrel in December 2008. Reduction in crude oil production by members of the Organization of the Petroleum Exporting Countries (OPEC) lowered world petroleum supplies and substantially offset the decline in oil demand caused by the global economic recession.

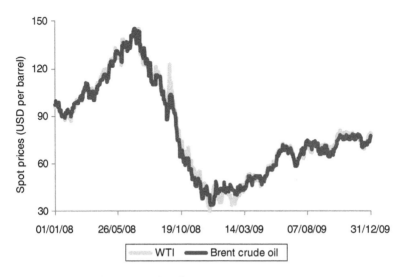

Figure 210   WTI and Brent crude oil prices

And in December 2009 the prices were just under the US$80 a barrel mark, a recovery of over 160 percent as compared to oil prices the previous year.

The crude oil market traded in deep contango for the most of 2009. In contango markets, oil companies tend to store more oil to sell it at higher prices in the future, which exerts pressure on near month oil contracts. Since December 2009 some of the unloading of inventories began, though not at the massive scale predicted by analysts.

OPEC crude oil production was 29.14 million bbl/day in December 2009. OPEC cut its crude oil production by 2.2 million bbl/day in 2009, one reason why WTI crude oil prices stabilized between US$70 and US$80 per barrel, since the middle of the preceding year. This range was consistent with the "fair price" range for crude oil proposed by King Abdullah of Saudi Arabia at the beginning of 2009.

EIA expects annual OPEC crude oil production will increase by an average of 0.4 million bbl/day in 2010, and again in 2011, as global oil demand recovers. Substantial surplus production capacity, located mostly in Saudi Arabia, should help moderate upward price pressure until higher demand begins to erode the global supply cushion. Non-OPEC supply increased by 560,000 bbl/day in 2009 and EIA projects it to increase by 430,000 bbl/ day in 2010.

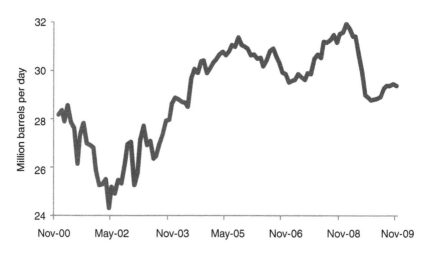

Figure 211   OPEC crude oil supply

US crude oil demand and supply drivers

The near term outlook of energy markets is directly connected to the depth of the economic downturn. In 2008, sharp decline in the global economy had a significant impact on demand for crude oil, leading to considerable downward pressure on the price of the commodity.

In addition to the basic demand supply fundamentals, the oil market is influenced by geopolitical tensions, weather patterns, movement in the US dollar, weekly inventory data and production decisions taken by OPEC. Crude oil prices have a negative correlation with the dollar and therefore a strong dollar can put a downward pressure on oil prices.

US gasoline prices

The decline in crude oil prices was followed by a considerable drop in the price of gasoline by December 2008. This rapid decline in retail fuel prices from the all-time highs in July 2008 to the lowest point in December 2008 was driven primarily by concerns of a prolonged and deep recession.

Post December 2008, prices of gasoline began to rise, even though global supply of crude oil significantly exceeded demand. This occurred largely as the factors attributed to the weakening of crude oil prices began to diminish. OPEC began to actively coordinate actions to cut output and trim global supply and the US dollar's upward rally began to show signs of weakness. At the same time, institutions with available storage capacity began to speculatively purchase crude oil. These speculators began to buy into the markets as the tide began to change on hopes that oil would be more valuable by mid to late 2009. It was this institutional buying in conjunction with improved fundamental data that resulted in an increase in the crude oil's price level and subsequently that of gasoline prices.

Gasoline prices were US$2.67 per gallon at the end of the year and are expected to be around US$2.84 in 2010, principally because of the crude oil forecasts. As the summer demand increases and output levels continue to remain stable, we anticipate the price of crude oil to continue to remain between US$60–80 a barrel.

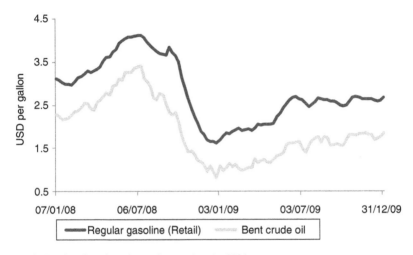

Figure 212   Crude oil and gasoline prices in USA

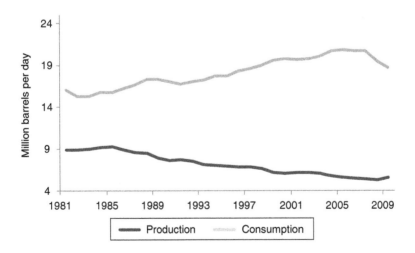

Figure 213   Crude oil production and consumption in USA

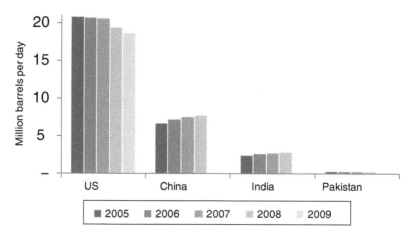

Figure 214   Petroleum consumption in USA, China, India and Pakistan

3. Relationship between crude oil and natural gas prices

Source: EIA Short-term Energy Outlook (July 2009)

Historically, oil prices have served as a barometer for the price of natural gas in the US. Substitutability between oil and natural gas in the industrial and electric power sectors meant that natural gas prices were bound, to a certain extent, on the high side by the prices of distillate fuel, typically priced at a premium to crude, and on the low side by residual fuel, typically priced at a significant discount to crude. In such an environment, changes in the price of crude oil, reflected in both distillate fuel and residual fuel oil prices, were generally accompanied by a parallel movement in natural gas prices. From 2000 through 2005, the ratio of the crude oil price in dollars per barrel to the US natural gas price in dollars per MMBtu averaged about 7:1.

Starting in 2006, however, the relationship between oil and natural gas prices began to change. At that time, the price for crude oil began to increase, pushing residual fuel oil prices higher, but the price of US natural gas didn't rise with it. If end users had the capability to switch from residual fuel oil to natural gas, they did it then. For example, switching was documented in electricity generation in the Northeast and in Florida. But instead of prices moving back into alignment as natural gas consumption expanded, with the exception of a brief period in late-2006, the spread persisted. As natural gas supply increased from 2006 through the first half of 2009, lower natural gas prices meant that oil-to-gas fuel-switching opportunities were fully utilized. With natural gas supply

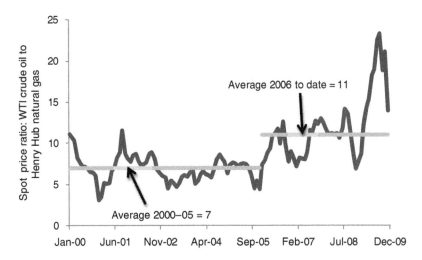

Figure 215   Spot price ratio: WTI crude oil to Henry Hub natural gas

continuing to grow, the crude oil to natural gas price ratio jumped to an average of nearly 11:1. In September 2009, the ratio was a whopping 23:1. Lower natural gas prices means that efficient natural gas generation can now compete effectively for economic dispatch against coal-fired generation even though natural gas generally remains somewhat more expensive than coal on a Btu basis. The shift in focus from fuel-switching on the margin between natural gas and oil to fuel-switching on the margin between natural gas and coal illustrates a major market shift.

Of course, both historically and in today's market, deliverability and storage constraints generated intermittent episodes of extreme movement in the ratio of oil prices to natural gas prices (see graph below). The ratio increased considerably in the third quarter of 2009 but since then has returned to the 2006 average of 11:1.

It is increasingly apparent that the markets for crude oil and US natural gas are now responding to different drivers. Whereas the market for crude oil is unquestionably global in nature, the natural gas market remains highly segmented. Asian demand and OPEC supply may be key factors influencing the current crude oil market, but they have little bearing on the natural gas market in the US. Instead, in recent years, US natural gas prices have been more responsive to conditions in North America: hurricane activity along the Gulf Coast, working inventory levels, development of natural gas shale, temperature swings that boost demand for space-heating in the winter and space-cooling in the summer, and, during the recent economic downturn, a sharp decline in industrial gas demand.

After reaching extremely high levels in mid-2008, prices for both crude oil and natural gas fell sharply amid the broad economic downturn. However, while natural gas prices have remained near recent lows, the spot price of crude oil has more than doubled since touching US$30 per barrel on December 23, 2008. The crude oil to natural gas price ratio is expected to decline in 2010, but not to pre-2006 levels. Despite the expectation of rising natural gas prices relative to crude oil, the price ratio between the fuels is anticipated to hold at roughly 12:1 through 2010.

Overview – China

Despite being affected by the economic downturn in 2007, which saw China's GDP growth decline by more than half from around 13 percent in 2007 to around 6 percent in the first quarter of 2009, its demand for energy remains high. In 2006 China was the world's third largest net importer of oil, which is in stark contrast to the fact that it used to be a net exporter of this product in the 1990s. Natural gas consumption has also increased over the years, and China has sought to increase imports of this energy source via pipelines and LNG.

China remains the world's largest producer and consumer of coal, which in 2006 accounted for more than 70 percent of domestic consumption. It has tried to diversify its energy supplies into hydroelectricity, natural gas and nuclear power, but these sources still remain relatively small in its energy consumption mix.

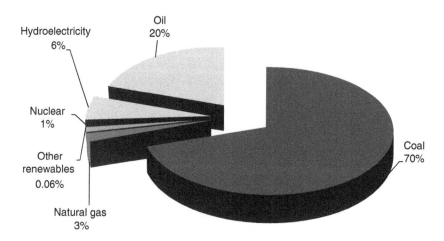

Figure 216   Total energy consumption in China

1. Oil

China is the second largest consumer of oil products in the world. Consumption for the year 2008 was 7.8 million barrels per day. It produced around 4 million barrels per day of total oil liquids while it imported approximately 3.9 million barrels per day. Most of the oil produced (96 percent) is crude oil. According to the EIA total oil consumption is expected to grow through 2010 and is expected to reach a demand level of 8.2 million barrels per day in 2010. On the other hand it is forecasted that the production levels will remain relatively unchanged. Current proven oil reserves according to the Oil and Gas Journal stand at around 16 billion barrels as of January 2009.

The government's energy policies are dictated by this ever growing demand for oil and oil products. National oil companies such as the China National Petroleum Corporation (CNPC), its publicly listed arm Petro China and China Petroleum and Chemical Corporation (Sinopec) have significant clout in the market, accounting for a major share of the total oil and gas output and revenues. Additional state-owned companies have also emerged in recent years, notably the China National Offshore Oil Corporation (CNOOC) which has become a major competitor to CNPC and Sinopec, particularly in the area of offshore exploration and production.

In December 2008, the government introduced pricing reforms in the market in the form of a fuel tax and a product pricing mechanism that would tie China's retail oil product prices more closely to that of the

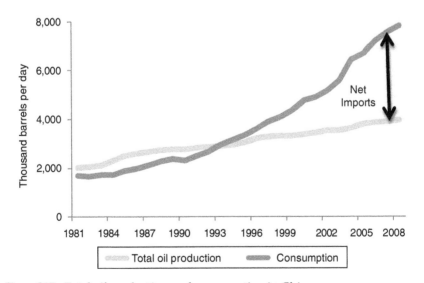

Figure 217 Total oil production and consumption in China

international crude oil market. This move also aimed to attract investment in more downstream activities such as refining and distribution, increase the revenues/maintain profit margins of the refineries and avoid supply breakdowns and subsequent financial losses to the refineries that had resulted in the past due to artificial price caps and other price distortions that were witnessed when international prices skyrocketed in mid-2008. A direct result of these reforms has been five increases in fuel prices in 2009.

China raised both gasoline and diesel prices by as much as 8 percent in November 2009 to reflect the rise in international crude oil prices and to help its refiners offset the increasing costs of raw materials. It is expected that by year end 2010 China may see a further increase of 25 percent in the fuel prices because of continued economic growth.

85 percent of China's oil production capacity is based onshore, though offshore E&P has been gaining ground at recent times, particularly in the areas of Bohai Bay and the South China Sea. Recent onshore exploration has been focused in the western interior provinces of Xinjiang, Sichuan, Gansu and Inner Mongolia. In view of its growing dependency on oil, Chinese national oil companies are also seeking interests in overseas E&P projects. They had negotiated a number of loan-for-oil deals with several countries in 2009, including Russia, Brazil, Venezuela, Kazakhstan, Ecuador and Turkmenistan, amounting to around US$ 50 million. In addition to these deals these companies are also seeking investment opportunities in Iran, Iraq, Syria and Latin America as China expands its refining capacity to accept sour and high-sulfur crude oil. Besides E&P projects, China has also negotiated a number of pipeline deals, in particular with Kazakhstan and Russia.

Middle Eastern countries, particularly Saudi Arabia, were the major source of oil imports for China. African countries, like Angola, are also significant sources.

2. Natural gas

In 2007, for the first time in 20 years, China became a net importer of natural gas. Most recently, PetroChina entered a US$ 41 billion 20-year deal with Australia to buy natural gas from them from the yet-to-be-developed Gorgon gas field off Australia's far northwest coast.

In the past natural gas did not have a prominent share in China's consumption mix, but it is anticipated that in the coming years the demand for natural gas, and hence its import of this product (principally in the form of LNG), is likely to gradually grow. EIA forecasts that by 2030 the demand for natural gas is likely to triple. This increase

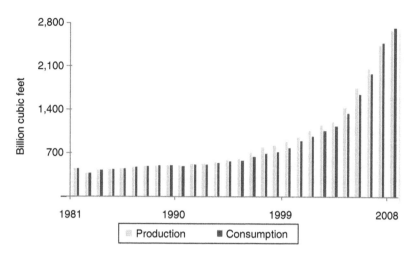

Figure 218 Dry natural gas production and consumption in China

in demand is primarily due to China's commitment to alleviate high pollution levels resulting from its high levels of coal usage. The government plans to increase total energy consumption share of natural gas up to 10 percent by 2020. Also, in contrast to the past where the main consumer was the industrial sector, consumption among the power sector and residential and commercial users has increased and is expected to continue to do so.

National oil companies CNPC, Sinopec and CNOOC are the prominent players in this market. CNPC alone accounts for 75 percent of the country's total natural gas output. China's primary gas-producing regions are the Sichuan, Shaanganing Provinces, the Xinjiang Uygur Autonomous Region and Qinghai, which produce 65 percent of China's total gas output. In addition there are many offshore natural gas fields in the Bohai Basin and South China Sea.

Natural gas prices are controlled by the government, though they tend to vary by region, industry and even user. On average they are half of international natural gas prices. However, the government, through its energy regulator, the National Energy Administration (NEA), intends to introduce price reforms as in the case of oil prices that would tie the prices to those available on the international market. Domestic natural gas prices are expected to increase by up to 30 percent in 2010. However, in increasing the prices the government would be careful not to impede the expansion of the growing demand for this product. The increase would be to the extent that it would encourage producers to expand supplies as well as encourage industries to continue usage regardless of the higher price.

3. Coal

Coal is the principal energy source in China, accounting for 70 percent of total consumption. It is both the largest producer and the largest consumer of this energy product in the world. In 2008, consumption stood at 3 billion short tons of coal, which is 40 percent of the world's total coal consumption. Consumption has been on the rise since 2000, reversing an earlier declining trend. Principal consumers are the industrial and power sectors.

Most of the production is carried out in Northern China as coal from this region is more easily accessible. Producers include large state-owned coal mines, local state-owned mines and thousands of town and village mines. The latter smaller mines account for a significant portion of the market but they are inefficiently run and cannot easily respond to market demand. China aims to consolidate the industry so as to raise output, attract more investment and new technology and improve the safety and environmental record of coal mines. It has also begun to look towards opening foreign investment to this sector, particularly in promoting newer technologies like coal liquefaction, coal bed methane (CBM) production, and slurry pipeline transportation projects.

Imports of coal by China have started to increase from 2002 primarily because imported coal prices became competitive as compared to domestic production prices and also because domestic production tends to occasionally suffer from supply disruptions. According to some projections it is expected that in the next five to ten years China could become a net importer of coal.

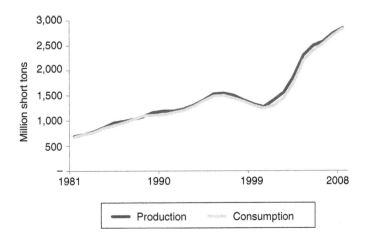

Figure 219 Coal production and consumption in China

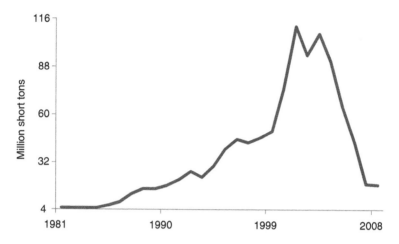

Figure 220   Net coal exports – China

Overview – India

The oil and gas history in India dates back to 1867, with the discovery of oil deposits in Makum, near Margherita, Assam. Since then the oil and gas sector in India has witnessed the birth of numerous oil and gas companies. With high rates of economic growth and over 15 percent of the world's population, India has become a significant consumer of energy resources. In 2008, India was the fourth largest oil consumer in the world. India's energy demand continues to increase. In terms of end use, energy demand in the transport sector is expected to be particularly high, as vehicle owner-ship, particularly of four-wheel vehicles, is forecast to increase rapidly once the global economic crisis abates and domestic spending levels resume.

India lacks sufficient domestic energy resources and must import much of its growing energy requirements. India is not only experiencing an electricity shortage but is also increasingly dependent on oil imports to meet demand. In addition to pursuing domestic oil and gas exploration and production projects, India is also stepping up its natural gas imports, particularly through imports of LNG. The country's ability to secure a reliable supply of energy resources at affordable prices will be one of the most important factors in shaping its future energy demand.

1. Crude oil

Several Gulf-based oil producers are considering a proposal from the Indian government to invest in creating large crude oil storage facili-ties along India's coastline. This proposal could culminate in a series of agreements, which may see India emerging as a regional hub for crude oil trade. The country is already a major exporter of refined petroleum products.

Such facilities will be developed under joint venture with national oil companies of Gulf countries, which are traditional suppliers of crude oil to India. The Gulf-based crude oil suppliers include Saudi Aramco, Kuwait Petroleum Corporation, Abu Dhabi National Oil Co and National Iranian Oil Companies. According to the proposal, India will set up several large crude oil storage facilities in its coastal areas under joint venture agreements (JVs) with companies from the Gulf region. India will offer crude oil supply contracts of 3–5 years to oil-producing countries to attract investments. At present, India's national oil companies such as IOC, BPCL and HPCL sign annual supply contracts with suppliers.

Government-run Indian Strategic Petroleum Reserves Ltd (ISPRL) and public sector Engineers India Ltd (EIL) have been assigned to chalk out strategies. The proposal says crude oil produced by the equity partners of the JVs will be stored in India and could be quickly transported to other Asian countries such as Japan on short notice. These strategic reserves will be available to oil-producing companies as well as crude oil consumers on rent.

The move is significant for a country like India, which imports over 75 percent of its crude oil requirements. India imported 109.32 million tons of oil in the nine months ended December 31, 2009, a 12 percent increase from a year earlier, according to Indian oil ministry's Petroleum Planning and Analysis Cell.

The country's current oil storage infrastructure can only meet less than 30 days' requirement, against developed countries' practice of having reserves to meet 90 days' requirement.

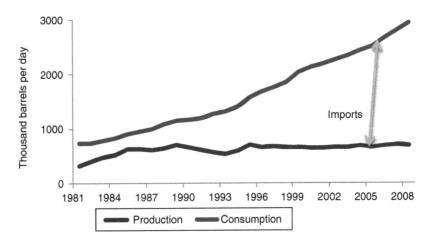

Figure 221 Production and consumption of crude oil in India

ISPRL is building three strategic crude oil storage facilities at Mangalore, Visakhapatnam and Padur (near Udupi). Given the volatility in crude prices, the storage terminals are intended as a buffer for the economy. The total capacity is, however, just 5 million tonnes, which can barely meet the country's crude oil requirements for 15 days, and would provide, together with reserves with existing oil companies, an emergency response mechanism in case of short-term supply disruptions. Construction work has begun on a strategic crude oil 1.5 million metric tonnes storage facility in the underground rock caverns of the port city of Mangalore in India's southwestern Karnataka state. The US$ 213 million project is expected to be completed in 2012.

2. Natural gas

According to Oil and Gas Journal (OGJ), India had 38 tcf of proven natural gas reserves as of January 2009. The bulk of India's natural gas production comes from the western offshore regions, especially the Mumbai High complex. The onshore fields in Assam, Andhra Pradesh, and Gujarat states are also significant sources of natural gas. The Bay of Bengal has also become an important source of natural gas for the country.

Natural gas demand is expected to grow considerably, largely driven by demand in the power sector. The power and fertilizer sectors account for nearly three-quarters of natural gas consumption in India. By 2030, EIA expects Asian demand for natural gas to more than double, and India is expected to be responsible for a sizeable part of that growth. Natural gas is expected to be an increasingly important component of energy consumption as the country pursues energy resource diversification and overall energy security.

Although India's natural gas production has consistently increased, demand has already exceeded supply and the country has been a net importer of natural gas since 2004. India's net imports reached an estimated 381 Bcf in 2008. India imports natural gas via LNG. To help meet the growing demand a number of import schemes, including both LNG and pipeline projects, have either been implemented or considered. These include the India-Pakistan-Iran (IPI) pipeline, the Trans-Afghan pipeline and a pipeline proposal with Myanmar.

In 2009 India announced that it would grant an income tax break on natural gas production after withdrawing it in the preceding year, seeking to attract overseas investment in the nation's energy exploration program. The benefit became available on earnings from oil and gas production from blocks that were awarded through auctions since April 2009, which received a lot of interest among local and foreign

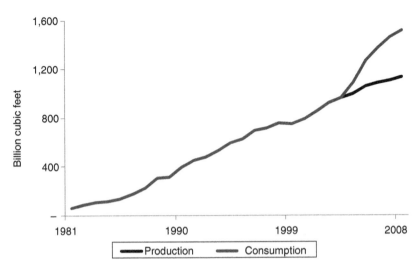

Figure 222   Natural gas production and consumption in India

companies. Controversy however still exists among companies which had purchased blocks in prior auctions and already started gas production, as they would not be able to claim the seven year income tax break – in December 2009 a proposal from the petroleum industry to bring these earlier companies into the fold of the tax holiday was rejected by India's finance ministry.

Overview – Pakistan

According to the Woodrow Wilson International Centre for Scholars, oil and natural gas supply 80 percent of Pakistan's energy needs but current energy consumption vastly exceeds the supply. Pakistan currently produces about 18 percent of the oil it consumes, fostering a dependency on imports that places considerable strain on its financial position. Pakistan's oil sector is regulated by the Ministry of Petroleum and Natural Resources. The Ministry grants oil concessions by open tender and by private negotiation. BP is currently the largest oil producer in Pakistan. Pakistan currently consumes 345,000 barrels of oil a day, ranking 34th among global consumers of oil. To address the issue, Pakistan is considering projects that would allow it to import natural gas from the Middle East and electricity from Central Asia.

Pakistan's long-term energy policy also involves a shift from a predominantly state-controlled industry to one that gives the private sector a leading role. Considerable impediments, however, prevent private enterprise

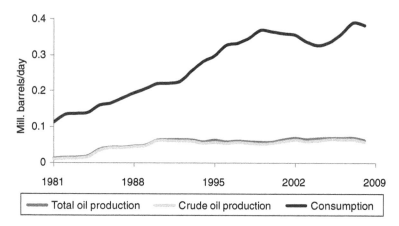

Figure 223 Total oil production and consumption in Pakistan

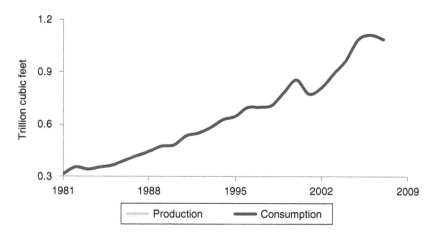

Figure 224 Dry natural gas production and consumption in Pakistan

from playing a larger role in the energy sector. These factors include the slow rate of deregulation and privatization; the political controversy and provincial disagreements associated with storage-based hydroelectric power generation projects; and overlapping responsibilities of the relevant authorities.

Pakistan is currently self-sufficient in natural gas, although this is likely to change as demand increases. According to the 2008 BP Statistical Energy Survey, Pakistan had 2007 proved natural gas reserves of 30.02 tcf, with the major gas-producing fields being Sui in Balochistan and Mari in Sindh, and annual natural gas production of 1.09 tcf.

The drop observed in prices in July was the result of Pakistan's top Supreme Court suspending a carbon tax on fuels, which forced the government to cut domestic fuel prices. The carbon tax was imposed to help meet the budget deficit target of 4.7 percent of gross domestic product in the financial year that started July 1, 2009. However, a few days later they once again revised prices upwards as a new levy was imposed on gasoline prices with effect from July 9, 2009.

Pakistan reviews domestic oil prices periodically to reflect changes in the global markets. As at year end 2009, prescribed prices for gasoline stood at Rs 53.52 per liter (ex-depot = Rs 66). Prices for diesel and high octane blending component (HOBC) were Rs 49.35 per liter (ex-depot = Rs 60.22) and Rs 62.68 per liter (ex-depot = Rs 80.52) respectively.

Pakistan's government plans to build a pipeline from Iran's massive natural gas reserves to Indian markets across Pakistani territory. Discussions are almost finalized between Iran and Pakistan on a potential gas supply deal along this proposed Iran-Pakistan-India gas pipeline. India continues to look more likely to bow out of the proposed multi-nation natural gas pipeline deal, China has indicated an interest in expanding the now-signed bilateral Iran-Pakistan project into a trans-Pakistan route that would then transit Xinjiang. Pakistan, keen on buying gas because of its own diminishing gas reserves, is looking at China to make the project a reality if India decides to pull out.

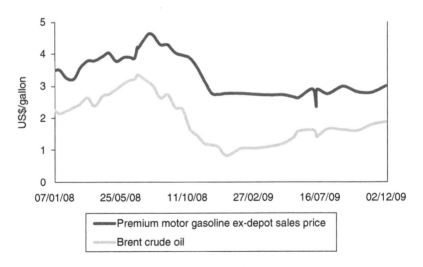

Figure 225 Crude oil and gasoline prices in Pakistan

The IPI or Peace pipeline proposes a 2,775 km pipeline to deliver natural gas from Iran to Pakistan and India. The project was envisioned in 1994 with expectations that it would benefit both India and Pakistan. According to the project proposal, the pipeline will begin from Asalouyeh and stretch over 1,100 km through Iran. In Pakistan, it will pass through Balochistan and Sindh but officials now say the route may be changed if China agrees to the project. The gas will be supplied from the South Pars gas field. The reserves in the offshore South Pars field are estimated at 450 tcf of natural gas, or about 47 percent of the total gas reserves in Iran. The initial capacity of the pipeline will be 776.84 bcf of natural gas per annum, which is expected to be later raised to 1.94 tcf. The pipeline is expected to cost US$7.5 billion and Pakistan is to receive 2.6 bcf of gas/day from Iran over the next 25 years. The Istanbul agreement sets the price of gas at 25 percent of world crude oil prices.

Pakistan's two state-owned oil exploration and production companies, Oil and Gas Development Company Limited (OGDCL) and Pakistan Petroleum Limited (PPL), are currently in discussions with Libya to seek oil exploration and production opportunities overseas. OGDCL is Pakistan's largest exploration and production company, while PPL is the country's largest gas producer. The two companies are seeking to enter overseas operations and pursue new ventures in the Middle East and Africa.

Sources of data: Wall Street Journal, Energy Information Administration and Oil and Gas Regulatory Authority (OGRA).

Part IV
Derivative Securities

- Product universe
- Binomial trees
- Exotic options
- Swaps

17
Derivatives Terminology

Think about a bottle of ice cold spring water in New York, in the Gobi Desert and in the Swiss Alps where the water was bottled.

You can assume that the bottle can be safely and cheaply beamed (as in "Beam me up Scottie") from the Alps to New York, as well as to the Gobi Desert. Would the price of the bottle be different at the three locations? Why?

The value of the bottle at each location is dependent not on itself but on an external factor. The environment! Reflected by paying capacity in New York, abundance in the Alps and heat and scarcity in the Gobi Desert.

A derivative instrument is very similar to bottled water in the Gobi Desert. Its value is determined completely by external variables. The external factor could be anything, but in general is either a financial asset or an economic variable (such as interest rates). The external factor or variable is called the underlying.

For example, a stock index is a derivative instrument. A stock index calculates its value by using the current prices of all the stocks included in that index. An Asian index would include the prices of selected Asian stocks. A technology index would include the prices of selected technology stocks. An Internet index would include the prices of selected Internet stocks. A stock index rises rise as its underlying stocks rise and falls as its underlying stocks fall. Without the underlying stocks, the index has no meaning or value.

What are the different types of derivative instruments?

The five types of derivative instruments that we will cover in this chapter are:

- Forward contracts, for example a forward contract that allows you to exchange the Euro for US dollars three months in the future.
- Futures contracts, for example a futures contract that allows you to buy silver on the New York Metal Exchange.

- Options, for example a put option on Google.
- Swaps, for example an interest rate swap that allows you to pay a fixed interest rate and receive a floating interest rate on US$ 10 million over the next three years.
- Exotics, for example a contract that allows the buyer to link what he makes to the average spread between West Texas Intermediate (WTI) crude oil, Brent and Arab Light prices in the month ended June 30, 2010.

Let's take a look at each of these contracts one by one.

Forward contracts

When you buy a Metro Card, you enter into an agreement with the Transit Authority. You agree to buy transport services in the future while the Metropolitan Transit Authority (MTA) agrees to sell you the same. The price for these future purchases is set by MTA today.

A forward contract is analogous to a Metro Card. It is an agreement between two parties to buy and sell an asset in the future for a certain price (the delivery price) set today.

If you agree to be on the buy side (you are the party purchasing the asset) you have a long position. If you agree to be on the sell side (you are the party selling the asset) you have a short position.

A forward contract is generally an agreement between institutions. It is not traded on an exchange. On the maturity or settlement date the gain or loss to a party is the difference between the delivery price and the market price.

Both parties involved are obligated to perform their side of the transaction. A forward contract is also a zero sum game. This means that if I win, you will most definitely lose.

The investment bank intern

Your first year internship in Europe with a bulge bracket investment bank will pay you GBP 10,000 net of taxes and expenses. You are worried that the British pound is overvalued right now, and by the time you take the money home it would be worth less in dollars.

You buy a forward contract from the FX desk in your bank to exchange GBP 10,000 for US$ 15,000 three months from now. The contract locks in the current exchange rate of 1.5 dollars for a pound.

Three months later, if your prediction was correct and the pound falls to a new exchange rate of US$ 1.3 dollars to a pound, you win and gain US$ 2,000 dollars [(1.5 – 1.3) * 10,000)]. If you had not used forwards you could only get US$ 13,000 for your pounds. With the forward you can get US$ 15,000, hence the gain.

On the other hand, if the pound rises to a new exchange rate of US$ 1.9 to a pound you would lose US$ 4,000 [(1.9 – 1.5) * 10,000]. You can get US$ 19,000 for your pounds but with the forward you will only get US$ 15,000, hence the loss.

In both cases you would end up with US$ 15,000 in exchange for GBP 10,000.

Futures contracts

Let's go back to our example in the previous section about forward contracts. Suppose instead of buying the contract from the FX desk, you bought it from a friend at work who disagreed with your assessment of the British pound. The two of you agree to exchange GBP 10,000 for US$ 15,000 three months later.

When the time comes to settle the account the pound is trading at US$ 1.3 to a pound. You saved two thousand dollars and feel very lucky. Then your friend calls up and tells you that he will not be able to keep his end of the bargain. He has lost everything he had on his bets on the British pound.

What can you do now? Your only option is to exchange pounds at the current rate of US$ 1.3 to a pound. Although your prediction was correct and you took timely action, you were still not able to protect yourself. This is called *Counter party or Credit risk; the risk* that the party on the other side of the transaction will not be able to keep their end of the deal.

Was there anything you could have done differently? Yes, you could have bought a futures contract. A futures contract is very similar to a forward contract except that it has very little credit risk. First, instead of dealing directly with a third party, you deal with an exchange. The exchange guarantees performance of the contract. If the party on the other side reneges, the exchange will settle with you first and then recover what it can from the third party.

To enter into a futures contract, an initial margin is posted by both parties at the exchange. This is money held on by the exchange as a performance bond. The exchange further reduces its risk by calculating the net gain and loss on a daily basis from closing market prices. Net gains and losses at the end of each trading day are posted to your margin account. If total losses on your account exceed a set percentage of the margin you have to bring the margin back to its original balance by making additional deposits. In case of gains you can take out any amounts over the initial margin. If you fail to bring the margin back to its original balance (in case of loss), your account is closed and the remaining margin is used by the exchange to recoup its losses.

A futures contract is also different from a forward contract in two other ways. First, a futures contract is a standardized contract used all over the exchange, while a forward contract is customized. Second, a futures contract has a settlement month, but no exact settlement date. A forward contract has a fixed maturity date.

Options

The problem with forwards and futures is that although you are protected against the downside, you also lose the upside. Options address this problem. They protect you against adverse outcomes, while allowing you to profit from favorable events.

Like forwards and futures, options give you the right to buy or sell a financial asset for a certain price before a certain date in the future. The price is set today and is known as the exercise price.

Unlike forwards and futures, as a buyer there is no obligation to perform. You can exercise the option if you benefit from it; if you don't you can walk away. But unlike forwards and futures you have to pay a premium to buy an option.

The two simplest (aka vanilla) options types that we will work with in this chapter are call and put option contracts. Calls give you the right to buy a financial asset for a set price in the future. You would use a call if you expected the underlying price to go up. You would exercise the call if the underlying price at maturity was greater than the exercise price. For this reason, a call is classified as a bullish instrument.

A put option is the opposite of a call option. A put option gives you the right to sell a security at a set price at a set date in the future. You would use a put if you expected the underlying price to go down. You would exercise the put if the underlying price at maturity was less than the exercise price. For this reason, puts are classified as bearish instruments.

Maturities and exercise date

Options generally come with exercise choices. Options that can be exercised at any time prior to maturity are known as American options. Options that can only be exercised at maturity are known as European options. Other configurations are also possible and include Bermudan or Mid-Atlantic (exercisable on multiple pre-set dates before expiry) and Asian (based on an average of prices that replaces the exercise price of the option or the price of the underlying at maturity.)

Payoff profiles

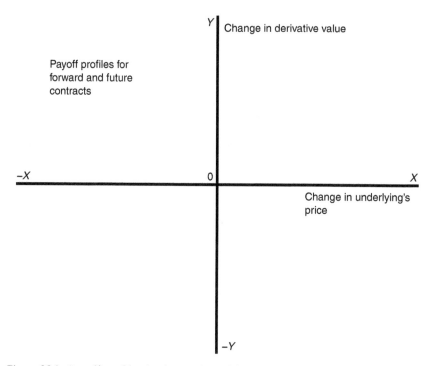

Figure 226 Payoff profiles for forwards and futures contracts

A payoff profile shows the scenarios under which a trade will make money and the scenarios under which a trade will lose money.

In the most common case it is a simple graph that plots the change in price of the underlying security on the horizontal axis and the change in price of the derivative security on the vertical axis.

Depending on the type of the instrument, the changes in value may be linear or non linear. In our case the horizontal and vertical axis have the same units, implying that the change in value is linear. "O," or origin, represents the current underlying price and the change in the underlying, as well as the derivative instrument, is marked in a single unit (+1, +2, +3).

For most contract types, this simple tool can be used to highlight the cash flow profile of a transaction type. We use the same tool for forwards, futures, interest rate swaps and options as well as to dissect exotic products into more basic forms.

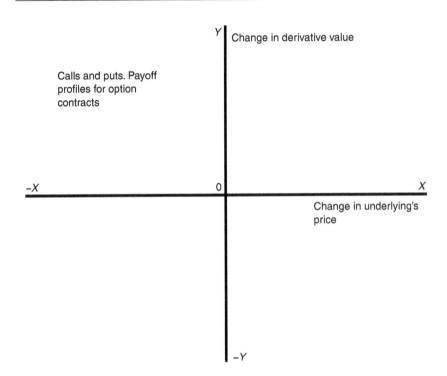

Figure 227   Payoff profiles for option contracts

The payoff profile for a forward contract

A long position (you are a buyer) forward contract is used when you wish to hedge yourself against the risk of rising prices in the future. A short position (you are a seller) is used when you wish to hedge yourself against the risk of falling prices in the future. The next four figures walk through the calculation of payoff profiles for a long forward contract.

There are four quadrants, I, II, III, IV, rotating clockwise through the grid on the right:

Quadrant I – Underlying prices fall, derivative value increases
Quadrant II – Underlying prices rise, derivative value rises
Quadrant III – Underlying prices rise, derivative value falls
Quadrant IV – Underlying prices fall, derivative value falls.

In the case of a forward contract, the resulting payoff profile across all four quadrants is the same as if you actually own and hold the security. The value of your portfolio increases as the underlying prices rise and decreases as the underlying prices fall.

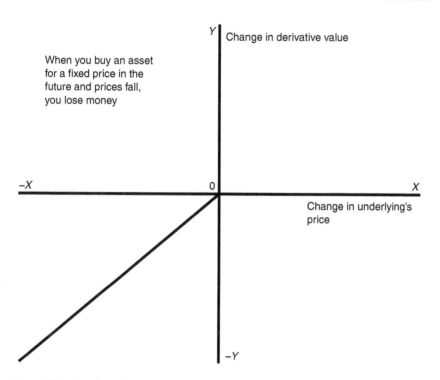

Figure 228   Quadrant IV – payoff profiles for a long forward contract

Figure 229   Payoff profile for a long forward contract

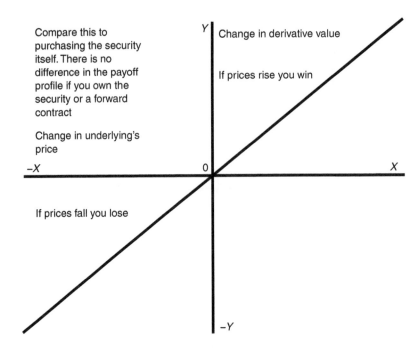

Figure 230   Payoff profile for underlying security

Payoff profiles for calls and puts

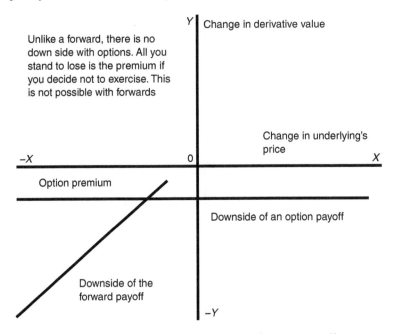

Figure 231   Comparative downsides of forward and option payoffs

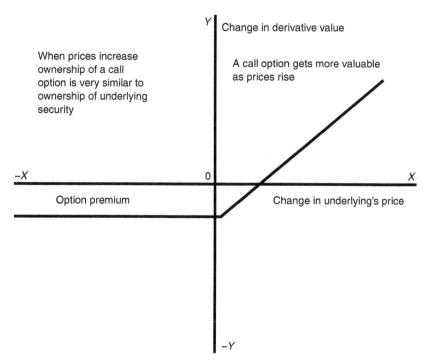

Figure 232 Payoff profile for the holder of a call option

Compare this to an option.

Unlike a forward, there is only a limited downside with option contracts. An option gives its owner the right to exercise but not the obligation to perform if the exercise would result in a loss. For that additional protection there is a price, and it is charged upfront as a premium.

Once again, a call option gives its owner the right to buy the underlying at a price and time agreed upon on the date of purchase of the option contract.

A put option gives its owner the right to sell the underlying at a price and time agreed upon on the date of purchase of the option contract.

A call option is a bullish instrument, which is purchased when you expect prices to rise and want to benefit from that rise. As you can see in the payoff diagram above, the value of a call option increases when prices rise, but the downside when prices fall is limited to the premium lost when the option is not exercised.

Unlike the buyer of a call, the seller of a call is obligated to perform. His upside is the premium that he retains when the call option is not exercised; his downside is the direct inverse of the payoff profile of the buyer of the call.

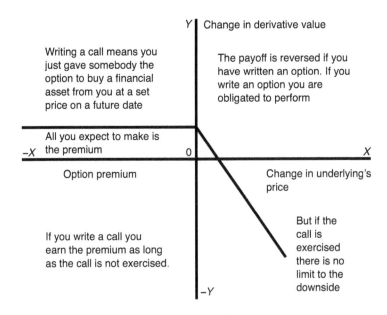

Figure 233   Payoff profile for the writer of a call option

The same rules hold true for the buyer and seller of the put option as shown in the next two diagrams.

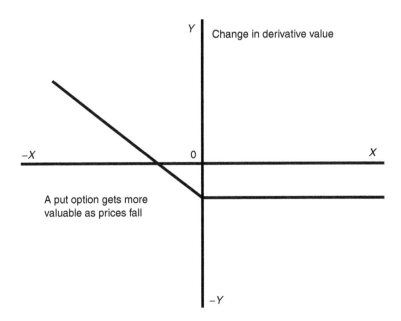

Figure 234   Payoff profile for the holder of a put option

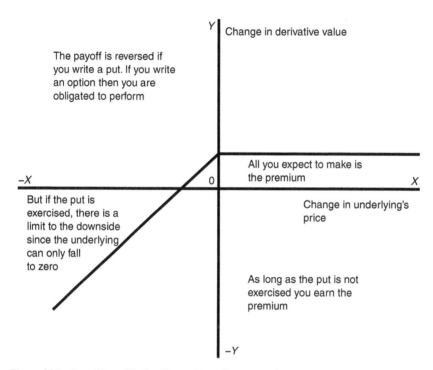

The payoff is reversed if you write a put. If you write an option then you are obligated to perform

Y

Change in derivative value

All you expect to make is the premium

−X

0

X

But if the put is exercised, there is a limit to the downside since the underlying can only fall to zero

Change in underlying's price

As long as the put is not exercised you earn the premium

−Y

Figure 235 Payoff profile for the writer of a put option

Building blocks and synthetic configurations

The basic building blocks in the derivative world are the three contract types that we have just discussed. It is possible to combine any number of them in a configuration that has a desired payoff profile.

A user can combine any two of the three products to synthetically create the third. For example, we can combine calls and puts to synthetically create both long and short forward contracts.

Product	Position	Direction
Call	Long	Bullish
Call	Short	Bearish
Put	Long	Bearish
Put	Short	Bullish
Forward	Long	Bullish
Forward	Short	Bearish

Figure 236 Building blocks for synthetic configurations

Product A	Product B	= Product Three
Long call	Short put	Long forward
Long put	Short call	Short forward

Figure 237   Synthetic forward contract creations

The concept in the above table is illustrated in the following two diagrams.

Comparing a call with a forward contract

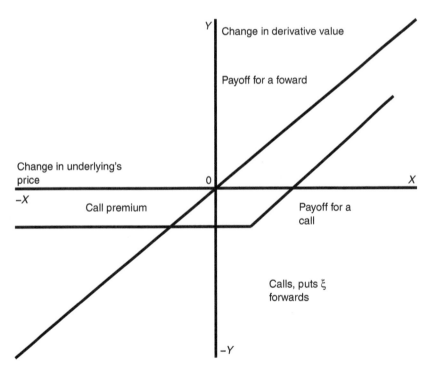

Figure 238   Comparative payoff profiles for calls and forwards

Comparing a call and a put with a forward contract

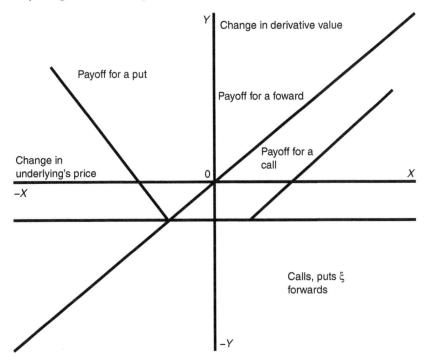

Figure 239   Comparative payoff profiles for calls, puts and forwards

18
Products and Pricing

A typical derivative deal comes with a long list of qualifications that are presented and shared with customers in the form of a term sheet. A term sheet is generally executed as a legally binding document with a number of clauses and warning labels, such as:

- Not all derivative contracts are appropriate for every investor. Some instruments are extremely complex and involve significant risks, therefore investors in derivative products should use these instruments only if they fully understand both the instrument and the overall transaction, and are able to bear the risks associated with each instrument and transaction.
- Each derivative instrument is unique and the range of their possible uses is wide, which in turn means that there are many factors that could potentially affect their performance. Over-the-counter (OTC) instruments may be highly customized to meet investor needs such as hedging, tax, credit and other needs. It is important to remember that as the complexity and customization of the instrument increases, the risks it may be exposed to may also increase, including its tradability.
- Generally, derivative transactions involve risks which include (among others) the risk of adverse or unanticipated market, financial, or political developments, risk of counterparty or issuer default and other credit and enforcement risks, and risk of illiquidity and related risks. In addition, parties may be subject to operational risks in the event that appropriate internal systems and controls to monitor the various risks are not in place.
- It is important to understand the requirements (including investment restrictions), if any, applicable that are established by regulators or

by the board of directors or other governing body. The legal, tax and accounting implications of entering into any derivative transaction need to be considered.

- Investors should take steps to understand the assumptions underlying the instrument involved in the particular transaction.
- As mentioned above swap and OTC option transactions permit precise customization to accomplish particular financial and risk management objectives that might otherwise be unachievable. Customization can, because of the individualized nature of such transactions, introduce significant liquidity risk and other risk factors of a complex character. Dealers may not always be willing to make markets in these transactions or terminate early existing positions.
- Cash settled OTC options and swaps may present certain enforceability risks due to local gaming and bucket shop laws, although certain exemptions from such laws may be available depending upon the terms of the instrument. Options that are not automatically exercisable involve monitoring requirements and may involve communication risk.
- Before entering into a derivative contract, the parties to the deal need to make an assessment of various factors involved in the transaction.

A template for making this assessment is given in the section below. At a minimum this includes evaluating the payoff formula, the maximum risks for the buyer and seller of the contract, the degree of complexity of the instruments and the variables that influence the value of the instrument.

1. Standard template for evaluating derivatives

Here is a typical template that an investment banking team would use to review a transaction or a product for risk and suitability for a client. This template is based on a slightly dated derivative product manual from Salomon Smith Barney (SSB).

There are four major categories of derivative instruments – options, forwards, futures and swaps. A quick comparison of their characteristics is given in the table below.

Each category is described in more detail below.

Factor	Details
High level review	The instrument and the risks and return (economic exposure) that the pares will be exposed to.
Motivation	The motivation behind entering the transaction from the buyer's and seller's perspecve.
Mechanics	The mechanics of the instrument including: • The payoff formula applicable and • The nature and frequency of payments that are to be made on the trade day (i.e. the day when the contract was issued) • The nature and frequency of payments that are to be made on or before the expiraon date. Additional mechanics of the derivave, for example for a swapon this includes the exercise day, which is day when the buyer and sell enter into a swap contract. For a forward start call option this could include the payment date when the buyer would pay the call option price and the nature of that payment.
Key concepts	Based on the specific instrument this will include (but is not limited to), where applicable: • Exercise style, e.g. American or European • Total/ price return, i.e. the basis on which payments are to be made • Notional amount, i.e. the notional used in the calculations of the payment as well as the actual payment calculation methodology • Resets, i.e. their nature and frequency • Underlying index (such as LIBOR) used in the calculation • Currency risk, in particular how the payments expose the party to this risk • Credit risk, in particular how exposure to the underlying exposes the party involved in the transaction • Volatility of the underlying instruments and factors that affect the value of the derivative • Breakeven point i.e. that is the minimum move in the underlying that is needed to make the payout equal the initial cost • Average, i.e. for certain options such as Asian options where the payout is based on an average value of prices, the periods and frequencies used in the calculation of the average will be specified • Path dependent, i.e. whether the value of the derivative is based on the exact path taken by the underlying
Market risks	The nature and extent of the upside and down side exposure to this risk for the buyer and the seller of the contract.
Sensitivities	The Greeks as well as various other factors (such as currency, correlation, time, etc) that impact the value of the derivative and the payouts.
Complexity	The complexity of the financial instrument is rated on a scale of one to five, one being the least complex and five the most complex.

Figure 240 Template for evaluating derivatives

	OPTION	FORWARD	FUTURE	SWAP
Downside	✓	✓	✓	✓
Upside potential	✓			
Initial cost	✓			
Credit risk	✓	✓		✓
Customizable	✓	✓		✓
Exchange traded			✓	

Figure 241   Comparative look at derivatives

2. Options

An option is a contract between the buyer/holder of the option and the seller/ writer of the option that grants the buyer the *right* to purchase from, or sell to, the option seller a designated asset at a specified price (*exercise/strike price*) within a specified period of time. The buyer of the option pays the contract seller an option price or *option premium* for this right. Options are used for (1) speculation or investment and (2) hedging or risk management.

The *maturity date*, or *expiration date*, is the date after which the option is no longer valid. *American options* are options that can be exercised at any time up to and including the expiration date. *European options* are options that can only be exercised on the maturity date.

A *call* option is one that gives the buyer the right to buy the instrument from the option seller at a specified price within a specified period of time. A *put* option is one that gives the buyer the right to sell the instrument to the option seller at a specified price within a specified period of time.

While the buyer has the right to exercise the option, the seller of the option has the *obligation* to perform on the contract. This characteristic means that the buyer will only exercise the option when it is advantageous to him and will let it expire if conditions are not in his favor. However, the seller must deliver or receive the asset, whenever the option is exercised, even if this means he will make a substantial loss. This makes the risk/ reward relationship one sided or asymmetrical where the payoff in the contract tends to favor the option buyer.

In other words, the most the option buyer (the *long position*) can lose is the option premium in the event that he never exercises the option. However, if price of the underlying instrument moves in his favor, he has all the upside potential where his gains will only be reduced by the premium that he paid when he purchased the contract.

On the other hand, the maximum amount that the contract seller (the short position) can realize is the price he receives for the option contract. However, he is exposed to substantial downside risk as the option will only be exercised to the advantage of the option buyer or conversely the disadvantage of the contract seller.

This is illustrated below for a call option:

Designated asset: 100 shares of XYZ Company
Exercise price: 50 per share
Option price: 2 per share.

If the price of the shares rises to 55 and the buyer exercises his right, he will realize a profit of 300 [= (55–50–2) × 100]. The seller of the option will only receive 5,000 for shares worth 5,500 in the market. His total loss will be 300 [= (50–55+2) × 100].

On the other hand if the share price falls to 46, the buyer of the option will not exercise the option. The most that he will lose is 200 (the option price). The seller of the option will only realize 200.

Per share payoff to the buyer and seller of the call option is depicted below.

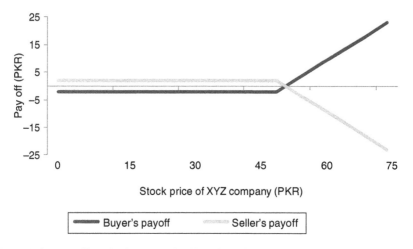

Figure 242   Payoff to the buyer and seller of a call option

Payoffs for the put option are illustrated below:

Designated asset: 100 shares of ABC Company
Exercise price: 50 per share
Option price: 2 per share.

If the price of the shares falls to 45 and the buyer exercises his right, he will realize a profit of 300 [= (50–45–2) × 100]. The seller of the option will be purchasing shares for 5,000 whereas if he were to go to the market for them he would have only to pay 4,500 in the market. Therefore his total loss will be 300 [= (45–50–2) × 100].

On the other hand, if the share price rises to 56, the buyer of the option will not exercise the option. The most that he will lose is 200 (the option price). The seller of the option will only realize 200.

Per share payoff to the buyer and seller of the put option is depicted below.

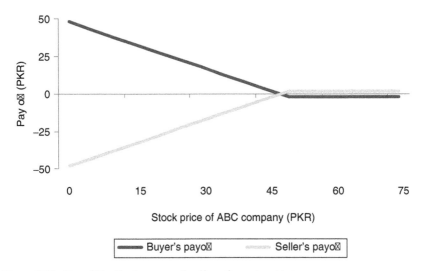

Figure 243 Payoff to the buyer and seller of a put option

Options contracts have two values that have that we have to consider.

One is the option price already mentioned above and elaborated in more detail below. The other is the *intrinsic value* of the option. This can be thought of as the price an investor would pay if the option were to be exercised immediately. Using the call example given above, when the price of XYZ share falls to 46, the option becomes worthless to the contract buyer as he could get a better deal by buying the shares directly from the market. The intrinsic value is therefore 0. However when the share price rises to 55, the shares are more expensive in the market by comparison. The intrinsic value is 5 (=55–50).

When the intrinsic value is positive the option is said to be *in-the-money*, when it is zero it is said to be *out-of-the-money*. When the market price of the designated asset is equal to the exercise price of the option, the option is said to be *at-the-money*.

Option price

The price of the option depends on the following:

- *Asset Price:* For an American or European call option, the higher the asset price the higher will be the option price, all other things unchanged. On the other hand, for a put option, the lower the asset price the higher will be the option price, all other things being held constant.
- *Exercise Price:* For an American and European call option, the higher the exercise price the lower will be the value of the option, all other things being held constant. The opposite is true for the put option,

where the higher the value of the exercise price, the higher will be the value of the option, all other things unchanged.

- *Interest Rates:* An increase in interest rates lowers the present value of the exercise price. For an American or European call option this means the cash outflow is lower in discounted terms, which in turn makes the option more valuable to the buyer of the option, other things being equal. The opposite is true for a put option as the cash inflow is lower in discounted terms when interest rates increase, making the option less valuable to the buyer of the option, other things remaining unchanged.

- *Volatility of the Asset Price:* Volatility is a friend for option contracts. When expected volatility is high there is a greater likelihood that the option price will rise (or fall) in relation to the exercise price, hence increasing the value of the American or European call (or put) option, other things kept constant.

- *Time to Expiration:* When the time to maturity is farther away in the future the American or European option prices will be higher in general. This is because:

  (a) There is greater likelihood that the prices will move sufficiently to breach the exercise price and provide value to the option buyer.

  (b) For call options, the cash outflows (from the exercise price) are discounted over a longer time, making them lower and thus more valuable to the buyer. For American put options, even though this means lower cash inflows in discounted terms the benefit from (a) usually tends to outweigh the disadvantage of discounting and, if this is not the case, contract holders have the option of exercising the option earlier than the maturity date.

  (c) For European put options, a longer time to maturity can go either way depending on whether volatility or discounting has a greater impact.

- *Cash Distributions:* This is relevant if the asset is a common stock that pays cash dividends. When a cash dividend is paid the stock price falls. For a call option this means that the value of the option will decline, all other things being equal. For a put option the opposite is true.

European option price

The option prices calculated using Black Scholes formulas are as follows:

Call option price (c)
$$C = S_0 e^{-qT} N(d_1)^{-qT} - K_0 e^{-rT} N(d_2)^{-qT}$$
Put option price (p)
$$p = Ke^{-rT} N(-d_2) - S_0 e^{-qT} N(-d_1),$$

where

$N(x)$ is the cumulative probability distribution function (pdf) for a standardized normal distribution;

S_0 is the price of the underlying asset at time zero;

K is the strike or exercise price;

r is the continuously compounded risk free rate;

σ is the volatility of the asset price;

T is the time to maturity of the option;

q is the yield rate on the underlying asset.

Alternatively, if the asset provides cash income, instead of a yield, q will be set to zero in the formula and the present value of the cash income during the life of the option will be subtracted from S_0:

$$d_1 = \frac{\ln(S_0/K) + (r - q + \sigma^2/2)T}{\sigma\sqrt{T}},$$

$$d_2 = \frac{\ln(S_0/K) + (r - q - \sigma^2/2)T}{\sigma\sqrt{T}} = d_1 - \sigma\sqrt{T}.$$

Greeks

Delta: Measures the sensitivity of the option to the underlying asset:

CALL OPTION	PUT OPTION
$e^{-qT}N(d_1)$	$e^{-qT}\left[N(d_1) - 1\right]$

Gamma: Measures the sensitivity of delta to the underlying asset:

CALL OPTION	PUT OPTION
$\dfrac{N'(d_1)e^{-qT}}{S_0\sigma\sqrt{T}}$	$\dfrac{N'(d_1)e^{-qT}}{S_0\sigma\sqrt{T}}$

where $N'(x) = \dfrac{1}{\sqrt{2\pi}}e^{-x^2/2}$ is the standard normal density function.

Theta (per year): Measures the sensitivity of the option price to time:

CALL OPTION
$-S_0 N'(d_1) s e^{-qT} / (2\sqrt{T}) + q S_0 N(d_1) e^{-qT} - r K e^{-rt} N(d_2)$
PUT OPTION
$-S_0 N'(d_1) s e^{-qT} / (2\sqrt{T}) - q S_0 N(-d_1) e^{-qT} - r K e^{-rt} N(-d_2)$

Vega (per %): Measures the sensitivity of the option price to volatility of the asset price:

CALL OPTION	PUT OPTION
$\dfrac{S_0 \sqrt{T} N'(d_1) e^{-qT}}{100}$	$\dfrac{S_0 \sqrt{T} N'(d_1) e^{-qT}}{100}$

Rho (per %): Measures the sensitivity of the option price to the interest rate:

CALL OPTION	PUT OPTION
$\dfrac{K T e^{-rt} N(d_2)}{100}$	$-\dfrac{K T e^{-rt} N(-d_2)}{100}$

American option price

The American option price will be determined using a binomial tree. The steps in the calculation are as follows:

Step 1: Divide the specified time period of the option into n time steps with each step having length Δt. For example, if the life of the option is 30 days and the number of time steps is 5, $\Delta t = (30 \div 5) \div 365 = 0.016438$.

Step 2: Calculate the price at each node of the tree. At the node suppose the price is S. At the end of a time step the price will move up to Su with probability p and down to Sd with probability $1 - p$, where,

$$u = e^{\sigma \sqrt{\Delta t}},$$

$$d = \frac{1}{u},$$

$$p = \frac{e^{(r-q)\sigma\sqrt{t}} - d}{u - d}$$

In our example, we have considered a call option with a strike of 100. The initial price is 100, the risk free rate is 10 percent and the dividend yield is 8 percent, the volatility is 20 percent, $u = e^{0.20\times\sqrt{0.016438}} = 1.0260$, $Su = 100 \times 1.0260 = 102.60$, $Sd = 100/1.0260 = 97.47$ and $p = \dfrac{e^{(0.10-0.08)0.016438} - 0.9747}{1.0260 - 0.9747} =$ 0.5. The discounting factor is $x = e^{-r\Delta t} = e^{-0.1\times0.016438} = 0.998358$.

The prices at all the nodes will be as follows.

					113.68
				110.80	
			108.00		108.00
		105.26		105.26	
	102.60		102.60		102.60
100.00		100.00			
	97.47		97.47		97.47
		95.00		95.00	
			92.60		92.60
				90.25	
					87.97

| Node Time: 0 | 0.01644 | 0.0329 | 0.0493 | 0.0658 | 0.0822 |

Figure 244 Binomial tree – prices of the underlying asset

Step 3: Starting with the final node we work backwards to determine the option price or value at time 0. The option prices at the final nodes of the tree are the intrinsic values of the option.

At earlier nodes we will first need to calculate a value assuming that the option is held for a further time step. We compare this value with the value if the option is exercised early. If the former value exceeds the latter, the earlier exercise is not optimal. If the opposite is true the early exercise value will be selected for further stages in the calculation.

This is illustrated for our example below.

					B 13.68 [113.68]
				A 10.80 [110.80]	
			D 8.00 [108.00]	10.82	C 8.00 [108.00]
		5.26 [105.26]	8.04	5.26 [105.26]	
	2.60 [102.60]	5.65	2.60 [102.60]	5.29	2.60 [102.60]
0.00 [100.00]	3.80	0.00 [100.00]	3.29	0.00 [100.00]	
2.47	0.00 [97.47]	1.96	0.00 [97.47]	1.30	0.00 [97.47]
	1.14	0.00 [95.00]	0.65	0.00 [95.00]	
		0.32	0.00 [92.60]	0.00	0.00 [92.60]
			0.00	0.00 [90.25]	
				0.00	0.00 [87.97]
Node Time: 0	**0.01644**	**0.0329**	**0.0493**	**0.0658**	**0.0822**

Figure 245   Using a binomial tree to calculate the price of an American call option

The numbers above the prices (given in the boxes) are the value of the call option, that is, max [Price – Exercise Price, 0]; let's call this O_1. For nodes 0 to 4 the values at the bottom represent the value of holding the option for a further time step; let's call this O_2. O_2 at A is $(13.68 * p + 8*(1-p)) * x$. The The option value at the particular nodes will be the maximum of O_1 and O_2. At A this is 10.82. O_2 at D is $(10.82 * p + 5.29 * (1-p)) * x$ and so on. Following this process the price of the call option is 2.47.

3. Forward contracts

These are contracts where the buyer/holder of the contract agrees to purchase while the seller/writer of the contract agrees to deliver a specified asset at some future specified time (the maturity date) for an exercise/delivery price that is fixed today. Both parties to the contract are obligated to perform on the transaction.

These are not standardized contracts and are not traded on exchanges. They are OTC contracts that can be customized to the specific needs of the parties involved. These parties are generally institutions.

Unlike the option contract, however, the buyer of the forward contract is not protected when the price of the underlying moves against his position. As he is obligated to perform on his transaction, the payoffs for buyer and seller of the contract are symmetrical, that is, when the value of underlying assets changes in favor of one party to the contract the other party suffers and vice versa. Thus, is it is a "zero sum" game.

Forward contracts are exposed to credit risk as either party can default on their obligation.

The payoffs are illustrated below:

Designated asset: 1 share of ABC company

Exercise price: 50 per share.

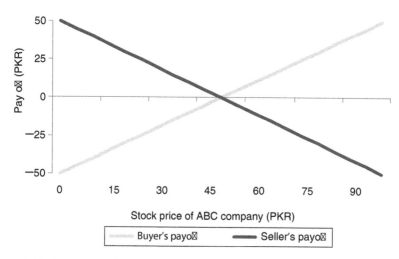

Figure 246 Payoffs for the buyer and seller of a forward contract

In effect, the seller of the contract "holds" the asset on behalf of the buyer during the period of the forward contract. This means that the buyer benefits from not having his money tied up in the asset so that he can invest it elsewhere. Additionally, he does not have to incur storage cost (for physical goods). On the other hand, by not holding the asset he may lose out on some of the cash payouts on the underlying assets (for example, cash dividend on stock) during the period of the contract and on convenience yields. Convenience yields are the value associated with holding the actual asset and therefore being able to bring it to use whenever the need arises, such as holding crude oil inventories that can be used in times of supply disruptions. Together these are known as the asset's *carrying cost*.

Forward price

At the inception of the forward contract the exercise/delivery price is equal to the forward price and hence the initial value of the forward contract is zero. As the contract approaches maturity, the delivery price remains unchanged but the forward price changes as the time to maturity shortens.

Forward price of a security with no income:

$$S_0 e^{rT},$$

where
  S_0 is the spot price of the asset today;
  T is the time to maturity (in years);
  r is the annual risk free rate of interest.

Forward price of a security with known cash income

(securities such as stocks paying known dividends or coupon bearing bonds)

$$(S_0 - I) e^{rT},$$

where I is the present value of the cash income during the tenor of the contract discounted at the risk free rate.

Forward price of a security with known dividend yield

(securities such as currencies and stock indices)

$$S_0 e^{(r-q)T},$$

where q is the dividend yield rate. For a foreign currency q will be the foreign risk free rate.

4. Futures contracts

These are contracts where the buyer/holder of the contract agrees to purchase while the seller/writer of the contract agrees to deliver a specified asset at some future specified time (the exact delivery date is not specified, only the delivery month) for a predetermined delivery price. As in the case of forward contracts, both parties to the contract are obligated to perform on the transaction.

These contracts are standardized and tradable on organized exchanges. Also, they are subject to daily settlements (marked to market) and margin requirements that help to minimize the contract's exposure to credit risk.

Margins are amounts that are deposited with the broker by both parties. There is an *initial margin* that is kept with the broker at the origination of the contract and a *maintenance margin*, which is lower than the initial margin. If this latter margin is breached, a *margin call* is generated that requires the given party to deposit additional margin (known as the *variation margin*) to restore it to the initial level. If the party does not comply, his position in the contract and account with the broker could be terminated. All gains and losses to the account are charged to the parties' margin accounts on a daily basis, which in effect is the daily *settlement* or marked to market process of the contract.

Futures contracts are usually used to hedge a company's exposure to the price of an asset.

Futures price

The price on a futures contract is equal to the price on a forward contract if the risk free rate is constant and the same for all maturities and both contracts have the same delivery date.

In theory, when interest rates fluctuate a lot this relationship breaks down. For example, if the underlying asset is positively correlated with interest rates, a forward contract would be unaffected by any short term fluctuations in interest rates since there is no daily settlement. However, a long futures contract would move with the interest rates (rates go up, asset goes up, the resulting daily gains will be invested at a higher interest rate hence the value of the futures contract goes up and vice versa). As a result, when the price of the underlying asset is positively correlated with interest rates, futures prices are higher than forward prices. When the price of the underlying asset is negatively correlated with interest rates, futures prices are lower than forward prices.

In practice, differences between the two prices arise because of taxes, transaction costs, margin treatment, varying degrees of counterparty default risk, liquidity and marketability of the contract, and so on.

5. Swaps

This is an agreement between two parties, usually institutions, to exchange cash flows according to a predefined calculation at specified periodic intervals in the future. The calculation may be based on the future value of interest rates, foreign exchange rates or some other market variable. Like forward and futures contracts, both parties to the contract are obligated to perform their end of the deal. Also like forward and futures contracts, swaps are priced to have a value of zero at inception.

Interest rate swap (IRS)

In a standard (*plain vanilla*) IRS, the buyer of the contract, usually a company, pays a predetermined fixed rate (F) payment leg and receives a floating rate (R) payment leg which is usually linked to some index (such as LIBOR).

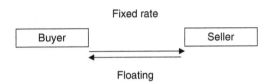

Figure 247   Plain vanilla interest rate swap

Both payments are based on the same notional amount (Q) and period of time. The principal amount is not exchanged in an IRS. Usually there is a *difference check* at each payment point and the party that is obligated to pay more will make the payment of the difference between the two cash flows.

The net cash flow for the buyer of the contract at each payment date is:

Cash flow$_t$ = $Q \times (Rt{-}1{-}F) \times$ days, where $t{-}1$ is the payment date on which the floating rate interest was observed and is one payment date prior to the payment date on which the net cash flow is paid; "days" are the period of time in the interest rate period (in years) based on the appropriate day count convention.

The fixed rate in the IRS that makes the value of the IRS zero at inception is known as the *swap rate*.

Currency swap

A currency swap exchanges the principal and interest payments in one currency with the principal and interest payments in another currency. The principals will be exchanged at commencement and expiration of the contract. At the initial stage the principals are usually equivalent based on the prevailing exchange rates at that point in time. However at the expiration date, even though the principal amounts will not change, their actual values could be significantly different based on how the two currencies have moved in relation to each other.

19
Variations

1. Options

Stock options

The contract gives the holder the right to buy or sell a given number of shares at the exercise price.

Foreign currency options

These contracts give the holder the right to buy or sell a foreign currency denominated amount. They are usually traded on the over-the-counter (OTC) market.

A call option would give the holder the right to buy a specified amount of foreign currency at a predetermined exchange rate expressed as local currency per unit of foreign currency.

For example, the holder may have the right to buy EUR 100,000 for EUR 1.34 per USD. If the exchange rate rose to 1.35 and if the holder exercised the option, the payoff (before accounting for the upfront cost of the option) would be US\$ $1,000 = 100,000 \times (1.35 - 1.34)$.

Index options

The contract gives the holder the right to buy or sell a multiple (M) of the index value at the exercise price. The index value used is the one at the end of the day in which the option is exercised. This is a cash settlement contract and it does not require delivery of the portfolio underlying the index on the exercise date. Usually these are exchange traded.

When a call option is exercised the holder will receive $(S - K) \times M$ in cash, where S is the value of the index, K is the strike price and M is a multiple of the index.

When a put option is exercised the holder will receive $(K - S) \times M$ in cash.

Futures options

This is an option on a futures contract. It gives the holder the right to enter into a futures contract at a specified futures price by a certain date. Futures options tend to be American options.

A call option gives the holder the right to a long position in the underlying futures contract plus a payoff equal to the difference between the futures price and the strike price. A put option gives the holder the right to a short position in the underlying futures contract plus a payoff equal to the difference between the strike price and the futures price.

The expiration date mentioned in a futures option pertains to the delivery date of the underlying futures contract. The option will expire on this date or may be a few days before this date.

Most common futures options are options on Treasury bond futures, Treasury note futures and Euro dollar futures.

Warrants

This is an option issued by a company that permits the owner to purchase a certain number of common stock for a specified price. Warrants are usually issued when the company issues bonds to encourage investors to purchase the bonds. They tend to have a long time to maturity and some may even be perpetual. The exercise price of the warrant is usually set higher than the market price at the time it is issued and tends to increase with time. Some warrants are *detachable* from the underlying instrument and can be traded on organized exchanges. Others can only be exercised by the bond holder and are called non-detachable warrants.

Employee stock options

These are call options offered to company employees, primarily its executives, as an incentive to work for the interests of the company. Other features include:

- The strike price usually equals the market price at issue, that is, the options are at-the-money when they are issued.
- Long tenors, between 10–15 years.
- Vesting period during which options cannot be exercised. Also, if the employee leaves the job during this time he will not be able to exercise the option in future.

- The options cannot be sold. Therefore the only way that employees can realize a cash benefit is to exercise the option and then sell the shares.
- When the option is exercised the company issues new shares which are then sold to the employee at the strike price.

Convertibles

The holder of a convertible bond has the right to convert the bond to equity (common stock) of the issuer at predetermined dates and for a predefined conversion ratio.

Interest rate options

The payoffs under these options are dependent on the level of interest rates.

Bond options

This is an option to buy/sell a specified bond for a predetermined price within a specified period of time. Most bond options tend to be European.

Embedded bond options

Callable bonds give the issuer of the bond the right to buy back the bond for a predetermined price at a specified time or times in the future. Other features of callable bonds are:

- The issuer usually cannot call the bond in the initial years of the bond.
- The call or strike price decreases with time.
- Callable bonds tend to have higher yields as compared to those which do not have any call option features.

Puttable bonds give the buyer of the bond the right to redeem the bond at certain specified times before the maturity date for a predetermined price. Other features include:

- Lower bond yields as compared to bonds without put option features.

Interest rate caps/floors/collars

An *interest rate cap* provides a payoff when the interest rate at reset on the underlying floating rate note exceeds a specified maximum known as the *cap rate*. The payoff is the difference between the actual interest rate payment at reset and the interest rate payment based on the cap rate adjusted for the appropriate day count convention. This payoff is not made on the reset date when this excess interest rate was observed, but at the end of the following tenor (reset period).

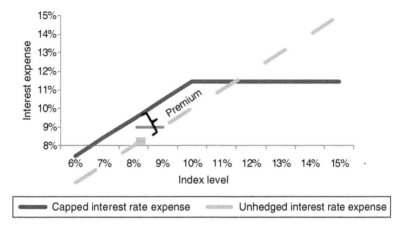

Figure 248 Interest rate cap

The following graph depicts how an interest rate cap caps the interest expense of an institution that purchases this derivative to hedge their LIBOR-indexed liabilities.

An *interest rate floor* provides a payoff when the interest rate at reset on the underlying floating rate note is below a specified minimum.

The following graph depicts how the interest rate floor is used by an institution to protect the return on its floating rate assets.

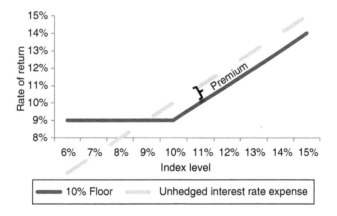

Figure 249 Interest rate floor

An *interest rate collar or floor-ceiling agreement* provides a payoff when the interest rate at reset on the underlying floating rate note is either below or above a specified range. It can be considered as having a long position in an interest rate cap and a short position in an interest rate floor. If the cost of the cap equals that of the floor the net cost of the collar will be zero.

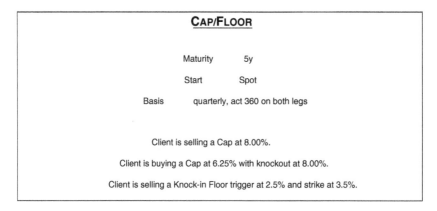

Figure 250   Sample trade ticket for a cap/floor

European swap options

This is an option on an interest rate swap, also known as a *swaption*. The contract buyer has the right to enter into an interest rate swap at a pre-determined time in the future. This is usually done to ensure that the fixed rate payments, which they will commence making in the future in exchange for receiving floating rate payments, will not exceed a certain level. They will not exercise their right if they can enter a more favorable interest rate swap that allows them to make payments at a lower fixed rate as compared to that mentioned in the swaption.

Exotic options

Exotic options can be path dependent or correlation based. Path-dependent options are dependent on the price of the underlying asset throughout the life of the option, not just at maturity.

Bermuda option

This is a blend between an American and European option, where the right to exercise the option early is restricted to certain predetermined dates.

Quanto option

Payoff is in a currency other than the currency of the underlying asset (or basket of assets) at a predetermined fixed exchange rate. The purpose is to hedge exposure to the asset without being exposed to the currency risk associated with it.

Composite option

This option gives the contract buyer the right to participate in the upside/downside of both the *foreign* asset and the *related* currency that the asset is denominated in. It is a combination of two options:

- A call (or put) on the underlying asset
- A call option on the currency of the underlying asset.

The payoff is dependent on changes in FX and changes in the price of the underlying foreign currency.

Digital or binary or "all or nothing" options

There are two main types:

- *Cash or nothing option:* If the underlying asset price exceeds the exercise price, the holder will receive a fixed amount from the contract seller. Otherwise he will receive nothing.
- *Asset or nothing option:* If the underlying asset price exceeds the exercise price, the contract holder will receive the asset from the writer. Otherwise he will receive nothing. Unlike a regular call option, the contract holder does not have to pay the strike price.

Barrier options

The payoff depends on whether the underlying asset's price crosses some predetermined barrier during a certain period of time. There are a number of types of barrier options including:

- *Knock out options* that "die" when the underlying asset's price crosses the barrier
- *Knock in options* that come into existence when the asset's price crosses the barrier.

A sample term sheet for a double barrier is given below.

USD/MXN Double Knock-out Note	
Principal Amount	USD 10 million
Issuer	XXX
Maturity	6 months from Trade Date
Issue Price	100%
Coupon	If the USD/MXN spot exchange rate trades above the Upper Barrier or below the Low Barrier at any time during the term of the Note: Zero Otherwise: 400%*max[0,(8.25-FX)/FX} Where FX is the USD//MXN spot exchange rate at maturity
Redemption Amount	100%
Upper Barrier Level	8.25
Lower Barrier Level	7.45

Figure 251 Sample term sheet for a double barrier

Asian options

Payoff depends on the average of the asset prices.

Average strike options

Unlike Asian options, instead of using the average of asset prices as the final stock price, this average is used as the strike price when the option is exercised.

Look back options

These are path-dependent options whose payouts are dependent on the minimum or maximum price experienced by the underlying asset during the life of the option. Usually these are European options, as it is beneficial to the buyer to wait until the maturity of the contract before he exercises his right.

- For floating look back call, the strike price is the minimum price of the underlying asset in the life of option.
- For floating look back put, the strike price is the maximum price of the underlying asset in the life of option.
- For fixed look back call, the final asset price is replaced with the maximum price of the underlying asset in the life of option.

- For fixed look back put, the final asset price is replaced with the minimum price of the underlying asset in the life of option.

Look backs are used in environments of high volatility.
A sample term sheet for a look back swap is given below.

Usd/Dem Look Back Swap	
Counterparties	**Counterparty A** **The Customer**
Notional Amount	USD 50 millions
Settlement Date	Two days after Trade Date
Maturity Date	Two days after Trade Date
Payments made by Customer	USD 6m LIBOR + 190 bps paid semiannually, A/360
Payments made by Counterparty A	In USD on Maturity date Notional*{(FX$_{max}$ − Strike)/FX$_{maturity}$ -1}
FX$_{max}$	The highest daily official USD/DEM Fixing from Settlement Date until Maturity Date
FX$_{maturity}$	The USD/DEM Fixing on Maturity Date
Strike	1.7180
Fixing	The daily USD/DEM FX exchange rate as seen on Telerate page SAFE1 at noon, New York time
USD 6m LIBOR	The USD 6m LIBOR rate as seen on Telerate page 3750 at noon, London time, on each Fixing Date
Documentation	ISDA
Governing Law	English

Figure 252   Sample term sheet for a look back swap

Compound options

This option gives the contract holder the right to buy (or sell) an option, such as a call on call, put on call, call on put, put on put. There are therefore two strike prices and two exercise dates. The call on call contract holder may exercise the option on the first exercise date at the first strike price and receive the call option. Then, the contract holder may exercise his right on the second exercise date at the second strike price to receive the underlying asset.

Chooser (as you like it) options

This option commences at time 0 and matures at *T*2. At an intermediary time, *T*1 (0 < *T*1 < *T*2) the contract buyer is able to choose whether to treat the option as a put option or call option.

Exchange options

This option allows the holder to exchange one asset (*A*) for another asset (*B*). The payoff is max[0, $A_T - B_T$].

Forward start options

The option does not commence immediately but at a future point in time, *T*1. The strike price is usually set equal to the asset price at *T*1. The most common application is in employee stock option plans.

Basket options

This is an option to buy or sell a portfolio of assets.

A sample term sheet for a basket option with three underlyings is given below.

"LA TRICOLORE" CAPITAL GUARANTEED NOTE	
Issuer	XXXX
Principal Amount	FRF 100 million
Issue Price	98.75%
Maturity Date	12 months after Issue Date
Coupon	Zero
Redemption Amount	If at least two of the following three appreciation indices, namely: (USD/FRF − 6.0750)/6.0750; (GBP/FRF-10.2)/10.2; (JPY/FRF − 0.0512)/0.0512 are positive at Maturity, the Note will redeem in that currency whose appreciate index is the second highest of the three; in all other circumstances the Note will redeem at Par in FRF. If the Note redeems in a currency other than FRF, the amount of that currency will be calculated by dividing the FRF principal amount by the spot currency/FRF exchange rate prevailing on the Issue date.

Figure 253 Sample term sheet for a basket option

Shout options

The payoff under this European option is the maximum of the payoff at the expiration of the contract or the payoff based on the intrinsic value of the option at the time of a "shout," which is one opportunity that the contract holder has to indicate a favorable price movement of the underlying asset to the writer during the life of the contract.

2. Forwards

Synthetic forward contract

A forward contract can synthetically be created by writing/selling a put contract and holding/buying a call contract. The call and put are structured in such a way that the net cost is zero, where the net cost is the put option price less the call option price. The payoffs for the synthetic forward contract are given below:

Designated asset: 1 share of ABC company
Exercise price for call option: 50 per share
Exercise price for put option: 54 per share
Call and put option price: 2 per share.

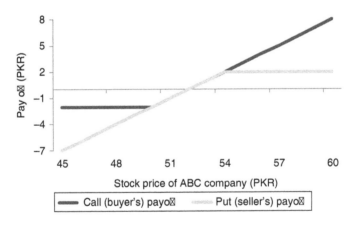

Figure 254   Payoffs for the buyer of a call and seller of a put (of a synthetic forward contract)

Forward rate agreement (FRA)

This is an OTC agreement whereby the interest amount that is paid (or received) during a specified *future* time period, on a principal amount borrowed (lent), is based on a predetermined interest rate. The FRA is generally settled at the beginning of the specified future time period, by discounting the present value of the settlement amount to the beginning of the period.

3. Futures

Stock index futures

These futures are used to offset the exposure to a well-diversified equity portfolio, in particular the systemic risk associated with the portfolio.
The futures price of stock indices with known yield is

$$F_0 = S_0 e^{(r-q)T}.$$

Futures contracts on currencies

The futures price is

$$F_0 = S_0 e^{(r-r_f)T},$$

where
F_0 is the futures price in local currency of one unit of foreign currency;
S_0 is the current spot price in local currency of one unit of foreign currency;
r is the domestic risk free rate;
r_f is the foreign risk free rate.

Futures contracts on commodities

The futures price of a commodity with no storage cost or income is

$$F_0 = S_0 e^{rT}.$$

The futures price of a commodity with storage cost and income is

$$F_0 = (S_0 - I)e^{rT},$$

where U is the discounted value of the storage costs net of income during the life of the futures contract.

Interest rate futures

Treasury bond futures

The US government bonds delivered under this futures contract should have more than 15 years to maturity on the first day of the delivery month and should not be callable for 15 years from this date, with par value of US$ 100,000.

Treasury note futures

The US government bonds/notes delivered under this futures contract should have between 6.5 and 10 years to maturity with par value of US$ 100,000.

5-year Treasury note futures

The US government bonds/notes delivered under this futures contract should have between 4 and 5 years to maturity with par value of US$ 100,000.

Treasury bill futures

The US government Treasury bills delivered under this futures contract have three months left to maturity with a face value of US$ 1 million.

Futures price for Treasury bond futures contracts

The price is given by

$$(S_o - I)e^{rT},$$

where I is the present value of the coupons during the life of the contract discounted at the risk free rate.

Eurodollar futures

The underlying instrument on these contracts is the 3-month Eurodollar Certificate of Deposit, which earns a fixed interest rate related to the US LIBOR. The face value of the contract is US$ 1 million. These futures allow the investor to lock into an interest rate for a future period. Unlike the other future contracts mentioned above, the settlement doesn't involve delivery of the underlying instrument but cash. Also unlike FRAs, the Eurodollar contract is settled daily and the settlement amount reflecting the observed interest rate is made at the beginning of the period, but without discounting.

4. Swaps

Fixed for fixed currency swap

The interest payments for both currencies are based on fixed rates.

Floating for floating currency swap

The interest payments for both currencies are based on floating rates.

Cross-currency interest rate swap

The floating interest payments in one currency are exchanged for the fixed interest payments of the other currency.

Step-up swaps

The notional principal on which the interest rate payments are determined is increased at certain predetermined times in the future.

Amortizing swaps

The notional principal on which the interest rate payments are determined is decreased at certain predetermined times in the future.

A sample term sheet for an amortizing swap is given on the next page.

Basis rate swap

In the swap agreement both interest rates in the swap are floating rates. Parties involved in the agreement pay cash flows based on one floating rate and receive cash flows based on another floating rate.

Forward or deferred swaps

These swaps obligate the holder to enter into an interest rate swap at a predetermined time in the future.

Compounding swaps

Usually there is only one payment/settlement date specified for these contracts. Therefore, besides specifying the interest rates at which the periodic interest amounts will be determined, the contract also specifies the annual compounding rate and period of compounding at which these interest amounts will be accrued forward over the life of the contract. At expiration of the swap the total accrued interest amounts will be exchanged.

LIBOR-in-arrears swap

As mentioned before, in a standard swap of fixed for floating the net cash flow determined on a payment date is based on the floating interest rate observed on the prior payment date. In this swap the two dates are the same, that is, the net cash flow paid on a given payment date is based on the floating interest rate observed on that date.

USD INDEX AMORTIZING SWAP	
Counterparties	Counterparty A The customer
Notional Amount	USD 50 millions subject to the Amortization Schedule
Settlement Date	Two days after the Trade Date
Maximum Maturity Date	Five years after the Trade Date
Early Maturity Date	On any Fixing Date leading to a Notional Amount equal to 0
Payments made by customer	USD 6m LIBOR paid semiannually, A/360
Payments made by Counterparty A	In USD X% p.a. paid semiannually, 30/360
Index Rate	USD 6m LIBOR
Base Rate	[]%
Amortization Schedule (after 1st coupon)	<table><tr><td>USD 6m LIBOR- Base Rate</td><td>Amortization</td></tr><tr><td>−3%</td><td>−[]%</td></tr><tr><td>−2%</td><td>−[]%</td></tr><tr><td>−1%</td><td>−[]%</td></tr><tr><td>0%</td><td>−[]%</td></tr><tr><td>1%</td><td>0%</td></tr><tr><td>2%</td><td>0%</td></tr></table> If the observed difference falls between two entries of this schedule, the amortization amount is interpolated
Fixing Dates	2 business days before each coupon period
USD 6m LIBOR	The USD 6m LIBOR rate as seen on Telerate page 3750 at noon, London time, on each Fixing Date
Documentation	ISDA
Governing Law	English

Figure 255   Sample term sheet for an amortizing swap

Constant maturity swap

The floating rate used in the swap is based on the *swap rate* applicable to a swap with a certain maturity.

Constant maturity treasury swap

The floating rate used in the swap is based on the *yield* applicable to a Treasury bond with a certain maturity.

Differential swap or quanto

The floating rate used in the swap is observed in one currency but is applied to the principal of another currency.

Variance or volatility swap

The variance or volatility realized during the period is exchanged for a fixed volatility or variance. Payoffs are based on the same notional principal for both legs.

A sample term sheet for a typical variance swap is given below.

REALIZED VARIANCE SWAP	
Counterparties	Counterparty A The Customer
Reference Index	S&P 500
Settlement date	Two dates after the Trade Date
Effective Date	Xxxx
Maturity Date	Six months after the Trade Date
Notional Amount	US 1 million
Payments made by counterparty A	In USD on Maturity Date National Amount *(Realized Volatility ^2-Fixed Volatility ^2)
Realized Volatility	$\sqrt{252} \times \sqrt{\frac{1}{N} \sum_{i=1}^{N} \left(\ln\left(\frac{S_i}{S_{i-1}} \right) \right)^2}$ S_i = SPX closing price on the ith day N = Number of business days from and including Effective Date and Maturity Date
Fixed Volatility	0.176
Documentation	ISDA
Governing Law	English

Figure 256 Sample term sheet for a variance swap

Equity swap

Under this contract, the payments based on the return realized on an equity index or equity portfolio are exchanged for fixed or floating interest rate payments.

Commodity swap

Under this contract one leg pays the other leg an amount based on a fixed commodity price and receives cash flows based on the market commodity price. The prices are applicable to a specified number of units of the commodity that is the same for both legs.

Asset swap

One leg to the swap pays the coupon on a bond, the other side makes payments based on a floating interest rate with spread.

Accrual swap

The interest payments on one of the legs are based on an interest rate that only accrues on those days when the floating interest rate is within a specified range. Days when the floating rate is not within this specified range will not be taken into account when determining the interest rate payment.

Cancellable swap

This is an option that allows the holder to terminate the swap at specified dates prior to maturity.

Extendable swap

This is an option that allows the holder to extend the life of the swap at specified dates.

20
Derivative Pricing

Relative pricing and risk neutral probabilities

Derivatives[1] are instruments whose payoffs depend on the movement of underlying assets. The price or value of the derivative instrument can therefore be evaluated by creating and valuing a portfolio of assets whose prices are easily observed in the market and whose cash flows replicate those of the option.

By the law of one price it then follows that in order to avoid arbitrage or riskless profits, the value of the replicating portfolio and that of the derivative instrument should be equal. Alternatively, this means that regardless of the investors' risk preferences, the same hedge portfolio would be constructed to replicate the option's cash flows.

This implies that the discount rate and the probabilities used in deriving the expected present value of the future cash flows of the security, or alternatively the value of option, do not depend on the true probabilities linked to the likelihood of payoffs or the degree of risk aversion of the investor. In arriving at the value of the derivative, risk neutral probabilities will be used to compute the expected present value of the future cash flows. Risk neutral probabilities are probabilities that make the expected rate of return of the asset equal to the risk free rate.

Binomial option pricing

In a previous chapter we saw that the European calls and puts can be priced using Black Scholes formulas. However, closed form solutions are not always available for pricing other types of options such as American options and exotic options such as barriers, capped, and so on. The prices of these options are derived using numerical methods such as the binomial trees and Monte Carlo simulation. This chapter focuses on an alternative method of implementing a two-dimensional binomial tree compared to that given earlier for pricing American options.

In particular, we will focus on implementing this method starting with European calls and puts, despite there being a convenient closed form solution for these options. This is done to illustrate the basic concepts of the methodology as well as its limitations. After this we illustrate how the concepts can be extended to price American options and exotics (in particular capped calls with automatic exercise, down-and-out and down-and-in calls). Adjustments to the basic model can be made to price other exotics but it must be noted that this may not always be possible due to the complexity and nature of the payoffs.

Before we discuss the alternative way of implementing a binomial method let us look at how the binomial tree is used to price a European call option.

Let S_0 be the price of the underlying asset at the current time. Assume that the call option will expire one period later, at time Δt; uS_0 is the price of the option one period later if the price rises with risk neutral probability of p; dS_0 is the price of the option one period later if the price falls with risk neutral probability of $1 - p$. This can be depicted in the following way.

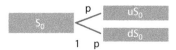

Figure 257   Binomial tree of the underlying assets prices

The above is a one-node binomial tree; p is the risk neutral probability of the asset price going up one period later and is calculated by the following formula:

$$p = \frac{e^{r\Delta t} - d}{u - d} .$$

(1)

In the above formula, r is the risk free rate, u is the proportion by which the price rises in one period and d is the proportion by which the price declines in one period, where $u = e^{\sigma\sqrt{\Delta t}}$ and $d = \frac{1}{u}$. Based on the movements in the underlying asset's price modeled above, the binomial tree for the European call option with strike K can be depicted as follows.

Figure 258 Binomial tree for the option

Where for the European call option $C_u = \max(uS_0 - K, 0)$ and $C_d = \max(dS_0 - K, 0)$.

As this is a one-node tree, the nodes at the end of time Δt are known as the terminal nodes, and C_u and C_d represent the payoffs of the option. The price of the option, or its value at time 0, the current time, is the expected present value of these payoffs and is given by the following formula:

$$C = e^{-r\Delta t}\{pC_u + (1 - p)C_d\}. \tag{2}$$

The above formula is also the generic formula of the option value at a particular node of a binomial tree. It is a function of the option values present at two successor nodes.

Let us now consider a simple example.

Assume that the European call option is due to expire at time $T = 0.04$. We will divide this period into $n = 2$ time steps, that is, the binomial tree will have two nodes. The length of a time step will be $\Delta t = T/2 = 0.02$.

The option has a strike of 45 and the initial price of the underlying asset is 44. The risk free rate is 5 percent and the volatility of the underlying asset price return, σ, is 20 percent. Using the formulas for p, u and d above, and working from left to right, the binomial tree for the underlying asset works out as follows.

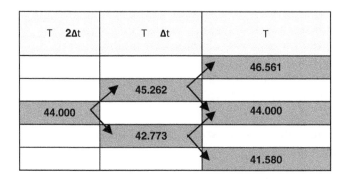

Figure 259 Binomial tree of underlying asset's prices with two time steps

The corresponding tree for the European call option will be as follows. The tree is computed starting at the terminal nodes and working backwards from right to left.

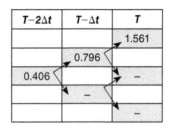

T−2Δt	T−Δt	T
		1.561
	0.796	
0.406		−
	−	
		−

Figure 260 Binomial tree of a European call option with two time steps

Note that at time T the nodes are the terminal nodes, and the option values at these nodes are the terminal payoffs as given above, that is, max $(S_T − K, 0)$ where S_T is the price of the underlying asset at time T. For example, the top most node is computed as max$(46.561 − 45, 0) = 1.561$.

The option values at the earlier nodes, the non-terminal nodes, are the expected present values of the option values at the two successor nodes as given by formula (2) above. For example, at $T − \Delta t$ the top most node is calculated as $e^{-0.05} \times 0.02 \{p(1.56) + (1 − p)()\}$. Working backwards, the call option price works out to 0.406.

The exact value of the call option using the Black Scholes formula is 0.3452.

The difference arises because the Black Scholes formula assumes continuous hedging and rebalancing of the portfolio whereas with the binomial tree we are only looking at a discrete number of asset prices as given by the nodes of the tree. As the number of nodes increase, that is, as the time steps get smaller, the option price derived by the binomial pricing method will approach the true value of the option.

The number of time steps needs to be sufficiently large. This tends to make the traditional construction of the binomial tree tedious. An alternative method of constructing this tree, based on the methodology proposed by Mark Broadie and Paul Glasserman, which simplifies the process is given in the section below.

Spreadsheet implementation of two-dimensional binomial tree[2]

The problem with the traditional method of constructing the binomial tree is that extra care must be taken to ensure that the right cells are picked up in the calculation. With the alternative method, intermediate cells that would normally be left blank in the traditional method are also filled in.

This makes it easier to work with on a spreadsheet as the relevant cells do not have to be selectively chosen in the calculation. The entire column of formulas can easily be copied to the next column without having to truncate or expand the selection or modify the formulas. This does not affect the result obtained from the binomial option pricing method, but eases the calculation, especially for a larger number of time steps as the relevant column can simply be copied and pasted repeatedly to achieve the desired number of time steps.

This is illustrated in detail for the European call option below. The parameters used for the European call are the same as given in the examples above. Additional examples for European put, American call and put, barriers and other exotics are also given to illustrate how adjustments to the basic model are made.

European call option

Step 1: Determine the prices of the underlying asset at expiry. For a time step of $n = 2$ this works out to five $(2n + 1)$ possible outcomes as compared to the three prices under the traditional method.

	S_T
1	$u^2S_0 = 46.561$
2	$u^2S_0 = 45.262$
3	$S_0 = 44.000$
4	$dS_0 = 42.773$
5	$d^2S_0 = 41.580$

Figure 261   Prices of the underlying asset at expiry

Step 2: Determine the terminal payoffs at the end of time T.

	$C_T = Max(S_T - K, 0)$
1	1.561
2	0.262
3	0
4	0
5	0

Figure 262   Terminal payoffs of the European call option

Step 3: Calculate the expected present values of the option values at the time steps prior to expiry. The following table also illustrates how the formulas will be applied in the spreadsheet for $n=2$.

COLUMN	A	B	C	D
Row	S_r	C_r	$T - 1\Delta t$	$T - 2\Delta t$
1	$= u^2 S_0$	$= \max(A1-K, 0)$	$= \exp(-r\Delta t)^*\{p^*B1 + (1 - p)^*B2\}$	$= \exp(-r\Delta t)^*\{p^*C1 + (1 - p)^*C2\}$
2	$= A1^*d$	$= \max(A2-K, 0)$	$= \exp(-r\Delta t)^*\{p^*B1 + (1 - p)^*B3\}$	$= \exp(-r\Delta t)^*\{p^*C1 + (1 - p)^*C3\}$
3	$= A2^*d$	$= \max(A3-K, 0)$	$= \exp(-r\Delta t)^*\{p^*B2 + (1 - p)^*B4\}$	$= \exp(-r\Delta t)^*\{p^*C2 + (1 - p)^*C4\}$
4	$= A3^*d$	$= \max(A4-K, 0)$	$= \exp(-r\Delta t)^*\{p^*B3 + (1 - p)^*B5\}$	$= \exp(-r\Delta t)^*\{p^*C3 + (1 - p)^*C5\}$
5	$= A4^*d$	$= \max(A5-K, 0)$	$= \exp(-r\Delta t)^*\{p^*B4 + (1 - p)^*B5\}$	$= \exp(-r\Delta t)^*\{p^*C4 + (1 - p)^*C5\}$

Figure 263 Formulas for spreadsheet implementation of binomial tree for a European call option

There are two things to note about Column C.

First, the formulas for the first and last cells differ from those in the middle rows. This is because there is no cell prior to row 1 for which there is a payoff in Column B and there is no cell after row 5 for which there is a payoff in Column B. This is a necessary adjustment that has to be made in the spreadsheet.

Second, Column D is a replica of C except that it refers to cells in Column C instead of B. This is evidence of the fact that once formulas for columns A, B and C are determined, later columns are simply a function of copying the Column C formulas and pasting it forward, which simplifies the binomial tree construction process for larger time steps.

The numerical results are given below.

COLUMN	A	B	C	D
Row	S_r	C_r	$T - 1\Delta t$	$T - 2\Delta t$
1	46.561	1.561	0.924	0.861
2	45.262	0.262	0.796	0.537
3	44.000	–	0.134	0.406
4	42.773	–	–	0.068
5	41.580	–	–	–

Figure 264 Spreadsheet for European call option example

Step 4: Determine the option price. This is the value in the $n + 1$th cell in the last column of the spreadsheet. For $n = 2$, this is the third entry at time $T - 2\Delta t$, that is, the entry in cell D3 above or 0.406. As we can see, this is the same value that we have obtained using the traditional binomial tree construction method.

By increasing the time steps, which means recalculating Δt, u, d and p and simply adding on rows below and columns to the right above, greater accuracy in the option price can be obtained. For time steps $n = 200$, the option price works out to 0.3445, which underestimates the price by 0.0007 as compared to overestimating it by 0.0609 when only two time steps were used.

It must be noted the progression towards the exact price given by the Black Scholes formula as time steps are increased is fairly erratic – at times very close to the value and then oscillating away from it. In general, though, as the time steps increase the precision increases. However, employing more steps does not necessarily lead to greater accuracy for other options such as barriers. In these cases it is more a question of selecting an appropriate value for n. This will be elaborated in more detail later.

European put option

The procedure to be followed is the same except that in Step 2 the payoffs calculated in Column B will be $C_T = \text{Max}(K - S_T, 0)$.

For a put with a strike and initial price of underlying of 45 the following would be the output for $n = 2$. All other parameters are the same as for the call.

COLUMN	A	B	C	D
Row	S_T	C_T	$T - 1\Delta t$	$T - 2\Delta t$
1	47.619	–	–	0.000
2	46.291	–	0.000	0.300
3	45.000	0.000	0.614	0.592
4	43.745	1.255	1.210	1.218
5	42.525	2.475	1.850	1.522

Figure 265 Spreadsheet for European put option example

The price of the put option is 0.592.

American call option

Assume the same parameters as for the European call. The adjustment will be made in Step 3 in Column C and then copied to Column D and later columns.

At non-terminal nodes the option will only be exercised early if its intrinsic value at that point in time, $S - K$, exceeds the expected present value of the option values at the successor nodes. That is, the formula at these non-terminal nodes will be $\max[S - K, \ C = e^{-r\Delta t}\{pC_u + (1-p)C_d\}]$ where S is the price of the underlying at that node. In terms of the spreadsheet, Column C will read as follows for $n = 2$.

COLUMN	A	B	C	D
Row	S_T	C_T	$T - 1\Delta t$	$T - 2\Delta t$
1	$= u^2 S_0$	$= \max(A1-K, 0)$	$= \max[A1-K, \exp(-r\Delta t)^*\{p^*B1+(1-p)^*B2\}]$	$= \max[A1-K, \exp(-r\Delta t)^*\{p^*C1+(1-p)^*C2\}]$
2	$= A1^*d$	$= \max(A2-K, 0)$	$= \max[A2-K, \exp(-r\Delta t)^*\{p^*B1+(1-p)^*B3\}]$	$= \max[A2-K, \exp(-r\Delta t)^*\{p^*C1+(1-p)^*C3\}]$
3	$= A2^*d$	$= \max(A3-K, 0)$	$= \max[A3-K, \exp(-r\Delta t)^*\{p^*B2+(1-p)^*B4\}]$	$= \max[A3-K, \exp(-r\Delta t)^*\{p^*C2+(1-p)^*C4\}]$
4	$= A3^*d$	$= \max(A4-K, 0)$	$= \max[A4-K, \exp(-r\Delta t)^*\{p^*B3+(1-p)^*B5\}]$	$= \max[A4-K, \exp(-r\Delta t)^*\{p^*C3+(1-p)^*C5\}]$
5	$= A4^*d$	$= \max(A5-K, 0)$	$= \max[A5-K, \exp(-r\Delta t)^*\{p^*B4+(1-p)^*B5\}]$	$= \max[A5-K, \exp(-r\Delta t)^*\{p^*C4+(1-p)^*C5\}]$

Figure 266 Formulas for spreadsheet implementation of binomial tree for an American call option

And the numerical values will be:

COLUMN	A	B	C	D
Row	S_T	C_T	$T - 1\Delta t$	$T - 2\Delta t$
1	46.561	1.561	1.561	1.561
2	45.262	0.262	0.796	0.862
3	44.000		0.134	0.406
4	42.773	-	-	0.068
5	41.580	-	-	-

Figure 267 Spreadsheet for American call option example

The American call option price is equal to 0.406.

American put option

Assume the same parameters as for the European put. The adjustment will be made in Step 3 in Column C and then copied to Column D and later columns.

At non-terminal nodes the option will only be exercised early if its intrinsic value at that point in time, $K - S$, exceeds the expected present value of the option values at the successor nodes. That is, the formula at these non-terminal nodes will be $\max[K - S, C = e^{-r\Delta t}\{pC_u + (1-p)C_d\}]$ where S is the price of the underlying at that node. In terms of the spreadsheet, Column C will read as follows for $n = 2$.

COLUMN	A	B	C	D
Row	S_T	C_T	$T-1\Delta t$	$T-2\Delta t$
1	$= u^2S_0$	$= \max(K-A1, 0)$	$=\max[K-A1, \exp(-r\Delta t)^*$ $\{p^*B1+(1-p)^*B2\}]$	$=\max[K-A1, \exp(-r\Delta t)^*$ $\{p^*C1+(1-p)^*C2\}]$
2	$= A1^*d$	$= \max(K-A2, 0)$	$=\max[K-A2, \exp(-r\Delta t)^*$ $\{p^*B1+(1-p)^*B3\}]$	$=\max[K-A2, \exp(-r\Delta t)^*$ $\{p^*C1+(1-p)^*C3\}]$
3	$=$ $A2^*d$	$= \max(K-A3, 0)$	$=\max[K-A3, \exp(-r\Delta t)^*$ $\{p^*B2+(1-p)^*B4\}]$	$=\max[K-A3, \exp(-r\Delta t)^*$ $\{p^*C2+(1-p)^*C4\}]$
4	$= A3^*d$	$= \max(K-A4, 0)$	$=\max[K-A4, \exp(-r\Delta t)^*$ $\{p^*B3+(1-p)^*B5\}]$	$=\max[K-A4, \exp(-r\Delta t)^*$ $\{p^*C3+(1-p)^*C5\}]$
5	$= A4^*d$	$= \max(K-A5, 0)$	$=\max[K-A5,\exp(-r\Delta t)^*$ $\{p^*B4+(1-p)^*B5\}]$	$=\max[K-A5,\exp(-r\Delta t)^*$ $\{p^*C4+(1-p)^*C5\}]$

Figure 268 Formulas for spreadsheet implementation of binomial tree for an American put option

And the numerical values will be:

COLUMN	A	B	C	D
Row	S_T	C_T	$T - 1\Delta t$	$T - 2\Delta t$
1	47.619	–	–	0.000
2	46.291	–	0.000	0.300
3	45.000	0.000	0.614	0.614
4	43.745	1.255	1.255	1.523
5	42.525	2.475	2.475	2.475

Figure 269 Spreadsheet for American put option example

The American put option price is equal to 0.614.

Pricing European call options using Monte Carlo simulation

The price of the European call option may be derived using the closed form Black Scholes formula. However, for the purpose of understanding the difference between results derived using Monte Carlo simulations and Black Scholes and the convergence to actual results we present a step by step procedure for constructing a Monte Carlo simulator in order to derive the value of a European call option.

Parameters	Explanation	Inputs
Equity	Google	
S_0	Spot price at time 0	677.14
K	Strike or exercise price	650.00
R	Risk free rate	0.14%
Q	Dividend yield rate	0.00%
Σ	Annualized volatility in stock price	25.00%
T	T/N = Time step (in years)	0.05
e^{-rT}	Discount Factor	1.00
N	Number of time steps	10.00
T	Tenor (year)	0.50

Figure 270   Inputs for determining a European call option

Using the Black Scholes call option price formula the call premium works out to US\$ 61.80.

Step 1: Construct a Monte Carlo Simulator for prices of the underlying
Using the methodology already described, construct a Monte Carlo simulator for determining the terminal price of the underlying security, in this case Google stock. We have used the terminal price formula from Chapter 6, to derive the values below.

$$S_t = S_0 e^{\left(\mu - \frac{1}{2}\sigma^2\right)t + \sigma\sqrt{t}z_t}.$$

Figure 271   Generation of terminal prices using the Monte Carlo simulation

Step 2: Run scenarios

Next run a number of scenarios and store the resulting terminal prices using EXCEL's data table functionality. This is shown for 25 simulated runs below.

Scenario	Terminal Price (S_T)
1	846.51
2	682.64
3	655.83
4	461.79
5	517.08
6	653.98
7	644.33
8	771.71
9	631.30
10	667.40
11	511.25
12	765.34
13	597.17
14	530.64
15	525.84
16	662.50
17	591.02
18	739.25
19	648.14
20	856.94
21	797.46
22	697.14
23	527.25
24	829.51
25	893.20

Figure 272 Terminal prices from 25 simulated runs

Step 3: Calculate the intrinsic value or payoffs
For each of the simulated runs calculate the payoff of the European call
option using the terminal price and the strike value, that is, Payoff =
Maximum of (Terminal Price – Strike, 0). The payoffs corresponding to
the 25 terminal prices are given below.

Scenario	Terminal Price (S_T)	Payoff
1	846.51	196.51
2	682.64	32.64
3	655.83	5.83
4	461.79	–
5	517.08	–
6	653.98	3.98
7	644.33	–
8	771.71	121.71
9	631.3	–
10	667.4	17.40
11	511.25	–
12	765.34	115.34
13	597.17	–
14	530.64	–
15	525.84	–
16	662.5	12.50
17	591.02	–
18	739.25	89.25
19	648.14	–
20	856.94	206.94
21	797.46	147.46
22	697.14	47.14
23	527.25	–
24	829.51	179.51
25	893.2	243.20

Figure 273   Payoffs for 25 simulated runs

Step 4: Calculate discount values of payoffs (prices)
For each simulated run calculate the discounted values of the payoff as
follows:

Payoff * e^{-rT},

where *r* is the risk free rate and *T* is the tenor of the option, that is, 0.5 years. The results are shown below.

Scenario	Payoff	Discount Value
1	196.51	196.37
2	32.64	32.62
3	5.83	5.83
4	-	-
5	-	-
6	3.98	3.98
7	-	-
8	121.71	121.62
9	-	-
10	17.40	17.39
11	-	-
12	115.34	115.26
13	-	-
14	-	-
15	-	-
16	12.50	12.49
17	-	-
18	89.25	89.19
19	-	-
20	206.94	206.80
21	147.46	147.36
22	47.14	47.11
23	-	-
24	179.51	179.38
25	243.20	243.03

Figure 274   Discount value of payoffs for 25 simulated runs

Step 5: Determine the call premium

Finally take the average of the discounted payoffs across all simulated runs to determine the call premium. Alternatively, take the average of all the payoffs across simulated runs and discount this average payoff using the discount factor, e^{-rT}, to determine the value of the European call option. In our example and for the 25 simulated runs illustrated above the result is USD 56.74.

There is a difference of around USD 5 between the result obtained using the Black Scholes formula and that obtained using the Monte Carlo simulator.

Pricing exotic options using Monte Carlo simulation

Picking up on where we left off in our introduction to Monte Carlo simulation, we now revisit the usage of Monte Carlo simulation for exotic option pricing. We will focus solely on the intermediate value section (that is, Section 3 from Chapter 6 on Monte Carlo Simulation) where we estimate the payoff values for vanilla options, Asian, barrier, look back and chooser options. As discussed earlier, the Monte Carlo simulation process is as follows:

- Simulate a price series;
- Evaluate intermediate values;
- Calculate option payoffs;
- Store the payoff results for a single iteration in an EXCEL data table; and
- Calculate the average across all iterations (simulations runs) to estimate the true value of the option in question.

F	G
Intermediate Values	
Regular	
Call_9_mth	0.84
Put_9_mth	-
3_mth_pick	0.84
Chooser_prem	0.84
3_Mth_Spot	95.351067
ST_Normal	100.85
Call Prem	0.84
Put Prem	-
Max	100.85
Min	95.35
Avg	98.31
Asian Call	-
Asian Put	1.67
Lookback Call	0.84
Up Barrier	-
Down Barrier	-
Ladder 1	0
Ladder 2	0
Barrier Call	-
Ladder Call	0.84
Call Out of M	-
Put Out of M	-

Figure 275   Monte Carlo simulator – intermediate values

Within the intermediate value section, some of the options discussed here will only need single-step calculations. Others such as barriers and choosers will require a multi-step calculation. The multi-step logic has already been covered so over here we will only share the marked up EXCEL snapshots from the Monte Carlo simulator to show how the same principals used for pricing vanilla call options can be applied to price more exotic option contracts.

In this section we have a column for regular and antithetic values. Note as mentioned earlier in this text we use the antithetic technique to speed up convergence.

Vanilla call, put options and exotic Asian and look back cousins

Our first step is to price a vanilla European call or put option based on the simulated terminal price at the end of a single iteration.

	LEFT	▾	× ✓ ƒx	=C26*MAX(Strike-G10,0)				
	A	B	C	D	E	F	G	H
9		Inputs & Assumptions						
10		Primary				ST_Normal	100.85	ST_A
11	S	Spot	100			Call Prem	0.84	Call
12	X	Strike	100			Put Prem	=C26*MAX(Strike-G10,0)	
13	sigma	Sigma	7.5%			Max	100.85	Max
14	T	Time	1			Min	95.35	Min
15	N	Steps	12			Avg	98.31	Avg
16	D_T	Delta_T	0.08333			Asian Call	-	Asia
17	risk_free	RiskFreeRate	1%			Asian Put	1.67	Asia
18						Lookback Call	0.84	Look
19		Out of Money Strike - Call	120			Up Barrier	-	Up B
20		Out of Money Strike - Put	89			Down Barrier	-	Dow
21		Exotic				Ladder 1	0	Ladd
22		Up and In Barrier	120			Ladder 2	0	Ladd
23		Down and out Barrier	89			Barrier Call	-	Barr
24		Ladder 1	110			Ladder Call	0.84	Ladd
25		Ladder 2	125			Call Out of M	-	Call
26		PV @ T	0.99005			Put Out of M	-	Put

Figure 276 Intermediate values – vanilla put option

We repeat more or less the same process for Asian and look back options, with one difference. For *Asian options*, the only thing that changes in the above model is that the terminal price is replaced by the average of the path simulated in that iteration.

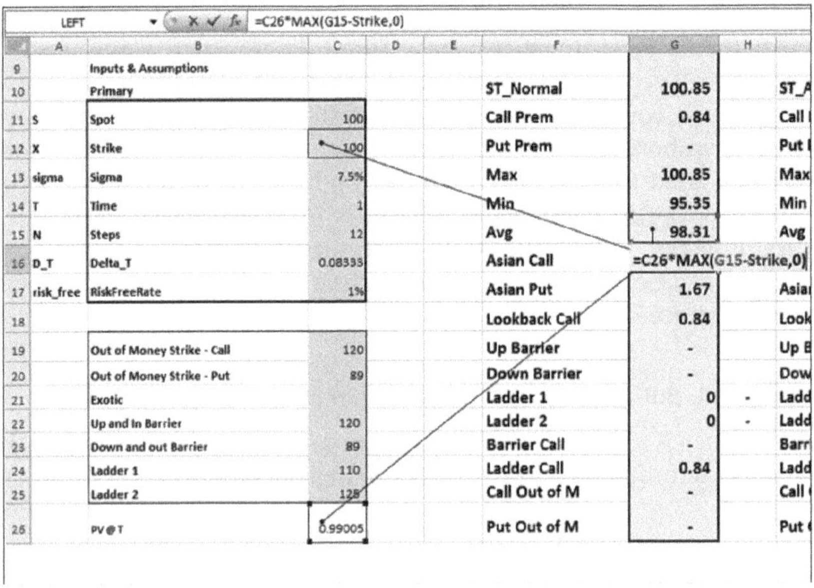

Figure 277 Intermediate values – Asian call option

For *look back* options, the average is replaced by the maximum value touched by the path during the life of the option.

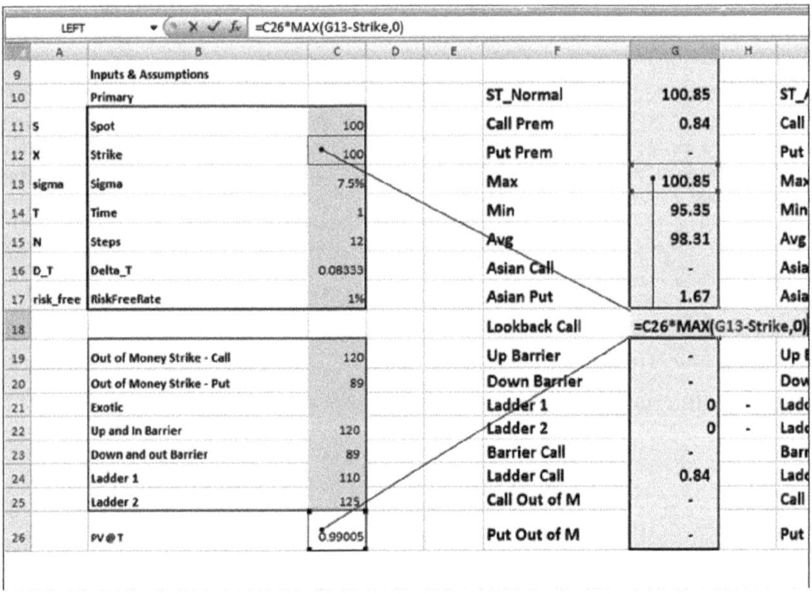

Figure 278 Intermediate values – look back call option

Pricing barrier and chooser options

A *barrier* option (sudden death, knock in, knock out, single or double touch option) is a little more involved. We actually need to create and track a flag that gets turned on or off depending on whether the barrier has been touched during the life of the option. We then multiply the flag with the value of the regular call option. When we calculate the average across all iterations the correct expected value is generated. You would need a single flag for single touch and two for a double touch barrier option.

	LEFT		▼ ● ✕ ✓ *fx*	=G19*G11*(1-G20)	
	D	E	F	G	H
7			Chooser_prem	2.90	3.70
8			3_Mth_Spot	101.24171	
9					
10			ST_Normal	97.07	
11			Call Prem	-	
12			Put Prem	2.90	
13			Max	102.12	
14			Min	97.07	
15			Avg	99.41	
16			Asian Call	-	
17			Asian Put	0.59	
18			Lookback Call	2.09	
19			Up Barrier	-	
20			Down Barrier	-	
21			Ladder 1	0	-
22			Ladder 2	0	-
23			Barrier Call	=G19*G11*(1-G20)	
24			Ladder Call	-	
25			Call Out of M	-	
26			Put Out of M	-	

Figure 279 Intermediate values – barrier call option

Chooser and compound options are even more involved than a barrier. Here is the sequence of steps needed for calculating the price of a chooser option:

- Create a secondary model on the side to price options at the point of exercise. In this case we have used the Black Scholes option pricing formula. The 3-month spot price for the secondary model comes from the primary simulator.

	NORMAL	ANTI
Spot	101.49	100.57
Strike	100	100
Sigma	0.075	0.075
Time	0.75	0.75
RiskFreeRate	0.01	0.01
PVF	0.993	0.993
d_1	0.376	0.235
d_2	0.311	0.170
Call Prem	3.871	3.298
Put Call Prem	1.633	1.985

Figure 280   Intermediate values – secondary pricing model for determining call/put option price at chooser option exercise

- Plug in the values in Column H from the second pricing model at the point of exercise.

H5				f_x	=Secondary!C13	
	D	E	F		G	H
1			**Intermediate Values**			
2						
3			**Regular**			
4			Call_9_mth		0.87	3.871
5			Put_9_mth		-	1.633
6			3_mth_pick		0.87	3.87
7			Chooser_prem		0.87	3.86
8			3_Mth_Spot		101.48998	

Figure 281   Intermediate values – using outputs of secondary model as primary model inputs for determining chooser option price

- Use the secondary values to price the chooser option. We do this by first picking up the maximum of the two premium choices determined using the secondary model (rational choice), discounting this result (payoff) to time 0, storing the results across iterations and then taking the average.

Pricing ladder options

Ladder options are options where the strike is reset whenever the price of the underlying asset reaches certain trigger levels or rungs during the tenor of the option. When the next strike or rung of the ladder option is triggered, the profit between the old and new rungs/strike prices are locked in. The rungs of a ladder option can be structured in one or both directions to allow for greater flexibility in the option design.

For a call option, assuming that all the rungs are in one direction (that is, all long calls), on maturity the payoff will be the maximum of the underlying asset's price at maturity and the rungs reached, less the original strike. In effect this means that the payoff will be the maximum of

(a) the terminal price less the original strike, or
(b) the highest rung reached less the original strike.

The payoff will be floored at zero.

In a similar manner, the payoff for a put option with all rungs structured in the same direction (that is, all long pulls) will be the original strike price less the minimum of the terminal price and the rungs reached. In other words the payoff will be the maximum of

(a) the original strike less the terminal price or
(b) the original strike price less the lowest reset strike/rung reached.

The payoff will be floored at zero. Let us now consider the following examples. Note that we will be using a ten time step Monte Carlo simulator to simulate the future prices of the underlying asset. Let us assume that you are bullish on the stock of McDonald's Corporation (MCD). You therefore buy a one year ladder European call option on MCD's stocks that can be exercised only on maturity. The current price of MCD stock is 90 and the original strike is set at 92. The ladder for strike resets are at 97, 99 and 109. The volatility in MCD is 30 percent. The risk free rate is 2 percent and there are no dividends on the stock.

Equity	MCD	
Parameters	Explanation	Inputs
S_0	Spot price at time 0	90
r	Risk free rate	2.00%
q	Dividend yield rate	0.00%
σ	Annualized volatility in stock price	30%
T	Tenor of option (in years)	1.00
PV	Discount Factor $= e^{-rT}$	0.9802
N	Number of Time Steps	10.00
t (Delta_T)	Length of time step (in years) = T/N	0.1

Figure 282   Monte Caro model parameters

Every time the stock price reaches a particular rung the strike will be reset to the price at that rung and a profit/payoff equal to the difference between the new strike and the old strike will be locked in. For example, consider the following path of prices generated using the Monte Carlo simulator.

Time Step	Simulated Stock Price; S_t
1	106.90
2	106.79
3	122.73
4	110.45
5	107.17
6	97.32
7	89.20
8	86.68
9	93.41
10	**88.71**

Figure 283   Monte Carlo simulator generated price path

At time step 1, the stock price is 106.90. This means that the option has reached the second rung price of 99. Therefore the payoff of 99−92 = 7 will be locked in. At time step 3, the option has now reached the third rung price of 109 as the underlying asset's price is now 122.73. An additional profit of 10 (= 109−99) will be locked it. So, the total profit locked in is 17 (= +10).

In this scenario, the terminal price of the option at expiry is 88.71, which is below the original strike price of 92. In a regular vanilla European call option this would have resulted in no payoff as the Max (Terminal Price – Strike Price, 0) is zero. However, in the case of the ladder option the payoff, despite the terminal price being below the original strike price, will be that already locked in: that is 17.

To arrive at the result in another way, consider that the maximum price in the price path series is the price at time step 3 of 122.73, which means that the highest rung price reached was the third reset of 109. As mentioned earlier, the payoff is the maximum of (Highest Rung Reached – Original Strike, Terminal Price – Original Strike, 0) or, stated in another way, maximum of (Highest Rung Reached, Terminal Price) – Original Strike, floored at zero. That is,

Payoff = max(109 – 92, 88.71 – 92, 0) = max(max(109, 88.71) – 92,0),
Payoff = max(17, –3.29, 0) = max(109 – 92,0) = 17.

The ladder call option premium is then simply the discounted value of the payoff = Payoff $\times e^{-rT}$ Ladder Call Premium = $17e^{-0.02 \times 1}$ = 16.66.

Using the data table functionality we simulate results for 100 scenarios as follows.

SCENARIO	TERMINAL PRICE	MAXIMUM PATH PRICE	HIGHEST RUNG REACHED	PAYOFF	CALL PREMIUM
1	95.09	102.33	99.00	7.00	6.86
2	142.59	162.03	109.00	50.59	49.59
3	67.37	83.52	–	–	–
–	–	–	–	–	–
–	–	–	–	–	–
–	–	–	–	–	–
99	94.39	97.11	97.00	5.00	4.90
100	155.06	175.73	109.00	63.06	61.81

Figure 284 Results across 100 simulated runs

The average of all the results in the call premium column is the price of the ladder option obtained using the Monte Carlo simulation approach. Based on 100 scenarios, this price falls in the range between 9.5 and 19.5. One view of the distribution of the results across these 100 scenarios is given in the following graph.

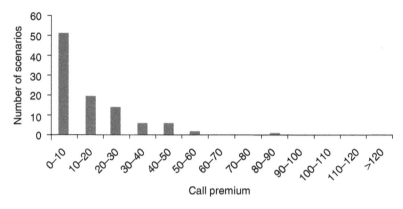

Figure 285 Graphical representation of distribution of results

To get a more stable and accurate value, or a more narrow range of results, for the ladder call premium, the number of scenarios may be increased or convergence and variance reduction techniques may be used.

21
Advanced Fixed Income Securities

Cash flows

The key to pricing or valuing any instrument is to estimate the cash flows of the instrument and discount each cash flow using an appropriate rate of interest.

Cash flow is simply the cash that is expected to be received each period from an investment. For a bond this includes coupon and principal payments; for an interest rate swap this would include fixed or floating rate coupon payments, and so on. In order to price an instrument is it important to project the amount and timing of cash flows. For non-callable Treasury bonds, the timing and amount of the cash flows are known in advance. For other instruments there may be greater difficulty in projecting cash flows. Some of the reasons for this difficulty include:

- The buyer or seller of the instrument may have the option to change the contractual due date(s) of the payments.
- The coupon payment may be based on a floating rate that is reset periodically based on some reference rate such as the LIBOR.

A key factor in determining the projected cash flows is the level of interest rates in the future. It will be discerned in relation to the instrument's coupon rate to determine whether the buyer or seller will exercise the option to change contractual payment dates. It will also be used to discern what the coupon payment will be for floating rate instruments whose payments are dependent on the level of some reference rate.

Discounting cash flows

Once the cash flow is estimated, it is then important to determine the appropriate interest rate to use to discount the cash flows in order to value or price the instrument. The value of the instrument is the sum of the present values (PV) of each of its cash flows.

Spot rates

A *t*-period spot rate is the per period rate of interest that can be earned on an investment made today (time 0) which would be repaid with interest on a specified date in the future (time *t*). Another name used for a spot rate is a zero coupon rate.

Forward rates

Assume you are choosing between buying a 6-month zero coupon bond and then reinvesting the money in another 6-month zero coupon bond *or* buying a 1-year zero coupon bond. Today you know the rates on the 6-month and 1-year bonds, but you are uncertain about the future 6-month rate.

The forward rate is the rate on the future 6-month bond that would make you indifferent between the two options. It is the rate of interest that would be applicable from one point in time in the future to another point in time in the future. These rates are implicit in the current quoted spot rates. Typically, forward interest rates are expressed as single period rates but they could also be applied to several time periods. The rates are inferred from available data.

The difference between spot (s_t) and forward rates ($f_{t-1,t}$) is illustrated in the time line below.

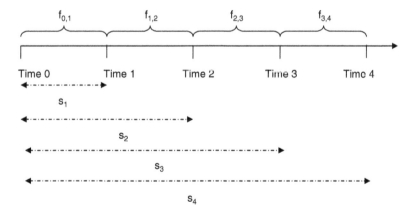

Figure 286 Forward and spot rates

The line segments appearing below the time line in the illustration above represent the lengths of time over which the various spot rates, s_t, are applicable. The spot rates of interest always refer to a time interval beginning now, at time 0. The lengths of time appearing above the time line indicate the lengths of time over which the forward rates are applicable. As can be seen above, and as mentioned earlier, forward rates are single period rates.

The following formulas summarize the relationship between the spot and forward rates of interest:

$$f_{t-1,t} = (1 + s_t)^t \div (1 + s_{t-1})^{t-1} - 1$$

or alternatively

$$s_t = \sqrt[t]{(1 + f_{0,1})(1 + f_{1,2}) \ldots (1 + f_{t-1,t})} - 1.$$

As can be seen above, the spot rates are geometric averages of the forward rates of interest.

Forward rates do not generally do a good job of actually predicting the future rate, but they do allow the investor to hedge. Take our earlier example of choosing between buying a 6-month zero coupon bond and then reinvesting the money in another 6-month zero coupon bond *or* buying a 1-year zero coupon bond. If the investor's expectation of the future rate is less than the forward rate they are better off investing for the entire year and locking in the 6-month forward rate over the last six months now by buying a 1-year zero coupon bond.

Short rates

These are single period future short term rates of interest that may arise over time. The difference between short rates and forward rates is that forward rates are implicit in the spot rates applying to different lengths of time, and that for each future time period there exists at time 0 one and only one applicable vector of forward rates. However, the future short term rate that may unfold one period later may or may not be equal to the forward rate that was calculated when we were at time 0. In fact there could be several possibilities of short rates for each future point in time, and each possibility has a different probability of occurrence attached to it. These probabilities are consistent with the term structure of spot and forward rates that exist at time 0.

Yield to maturity

The yield to maturity (YTM) is another type of interest rate. For zero coupon bonds, which are bonds that have only a single cash flow, the YTM will equal the spot rate. For coupon bearing bonds on the other hand, which may have several payments during their term, the YTM will depend on the spot rates that are associated with each individual cash flow. Alternatively, a coupon bearing bond may be thought of as a collection of zero coupon bonds with each cash flow valued as a separate zero coupon bond using a different spot rate of interest (depending on the tenor of the cash flow). The YTM will depend on the entire collection of spot rates used to value all the cash flows of the bond.

The YTM may be thought of as a complex weighted average of the spot rates on interest, where the weights depend on the pattern of cash flows that are due on the bond over its life.

To solve for YTM we are solving for the interest rate (r) in the bond valuation formula:

$$V_{Bond} = \left[\sum_{t=1}^{n} \frac{CP_t}{(1+r)^t} \right] + \frac{MV}{(1+r)^n},$$

where CP_t is the coupon payment at time t and MV is the maturity value at time n (that is, at maturity).

We cannot solve for r algebraically, only by trial and error or by using a financial calculator or EXCEL.

Term structure of interest rates

The term structure of interest rates illustrates the level of interest rates by maturity on instruments of a similar credit risk.

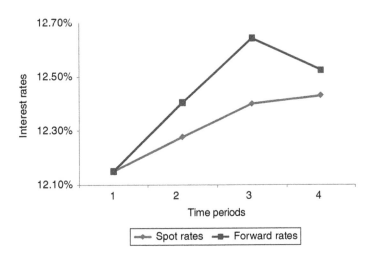

Figure 287 Term structure of interest rates

The most commonly investigated and used term structure is the Treasury yield curve. Treasuries are used since they are:

- Considered free of default, and therefore differ only in maturity;
- The benchmark used to set base rates;
- Extremely liquid.

Forward rate agreements (FRA)

This is an over-the-counter agreement whereby the interest amount that is paid (or received) during a specified future time period on a principal amount borrowed (or lent) is based on a predetermined interest rate. For example, let us assume that X has agreed to enter into an FRA with Y whereby X will receive from Y interest on the principal (L) between T_1 and T_2 at the fixed rate of R_K, and pay interest at the realized rate of R_M (which is the actual benchmark or floating rate (usually LIBOR interest rate) observed in the market between times T_1 and T_2).

Assuming that the forward rates are realized, we have $R_M = R_F$, where R_F is the forward interest rate for the period of time between times T_1 and T_2. For X, the value of the FRA at time 0, V_{FRA}, will be

$$V_{FRA} = \frac{L(R_K - R_F)(T_2 - T_1)}{(1 + R_2)^{T_2}},$$

where R_2 is the zero coupon rate for a maturity of T_2 if R_2 is calculated on a discrete basis or

$$V_{FRA} = L(R_k - R_F)(T_2 - T_1)e^{-R_2 T_2},$$

if R_2 is calculated on a continuous basis.

Forward contracts

A forward contract is an over-the-counter agreement to buy or sell an asset at some specified future date for a specified price (the delivery price). A long position to the contract agrees to buy the underlying asset on a specified future date for a certain specified price. The short position agrees to sell the asset on that date and for that price.

When a forward contract is first entered into its value will be zero, as the delivery price will equal the forward price. But as time passes the forward price, F_0, which is dependent on the spot price, S_0, at that given time, the remaining time to maturity, T, and the risk free rate, r, will change, but the delivery price K, which is set in the contract, will remain unchanged.

Hence the value of the contract at that point in time could be either positive or negative. The value of the long forward contract therefore is:

$$f = (F_0 - K)e^{-rT}.$$

where $F_0 = S_0 e^{rT}$ is the forward price.

Substituting the forward price in the equation for the value of the long forward we get

$$f = S_0 - Ke^{-rT}.$$

Using discrete compounding instead of continuous compounding,

$$f = \frac{(F_0 - K)}{(1+r)^T} \, d \, F_0 = S_0 (1+r)^T$$

so that f in terms of the spot price is $f = S_0 - K(1 + r)^T$.

Assuming that the investment assets provides a known income with a PV (present value) of I, the value of the long forward would be

$$f = S_0 - I - Ke^{rT}.$$

Assuming that the underlying asset provides a known yield at rate q instead of the income, the value of the long forward would be

$$f = S_0 e^{-qT} - Ke^{-rT}.$$

The value of a forward foreign currency contract would be

$$f = S_0 e^{-r_f T} - Ke^{-rT},$$

where r_f is the value of the foreign risk free interest rate when the money is invested for time T.

Swaps

This is an agreement between two parties, usually institutions, to exchange cash flows according to a predefined calculation at specified periodic intervals in the future. The calculation may be based on the future value of interest rates, foreign exchange rates or some other market variable.

Pricing interest rate swaps

The interest rate swap (IRS) will be valued as a portfolio of FRAs. The zero curve will be used to calculate the forward rates for each of the floating rates that will determine the swap cash flows, which will then be discounted using the zero curve to obtain the swap value. In particular, the following process will be followed when determining the value or price of an IRS.

Firstly, a default par term structure will be defined. This consists of selecting an appropriate par term structure based on the terms of the IRS, in particular the coupon rate payments and the frequency of the payments. As given, par structures may only be available for specified tenors; if the tenors required for the swap exceed the maximum tenor available in the chosen term structure, rates from another term structure may be chosen. A spread may be added to these rates to reflect the differential between these two par term structures. For cases where the payment frequency is semi-annual or quarterly, and so on, par rates may not be available for all tenors. These rates will have to be determined by interpolating the available rates.

After the par term structure has been determined, the zero coupon rates are derived using the bootstrapping methodology. This consists of stripping each coupon bearing instrument represented in the par term structure into individual cash flows, iteratively working through each tenor of the par term structure starting with the smallest, discounting cash flows, substituting the derived discount rates to determine the entire zero curve. The zero curve is then used to derive forward rates for each successive interest rate period, again using a bootstrapping methodology.

Once we have the zero curve we are ready to start with the pricing of the IRSs. We strip each coupon from the structure and determine the time to maturity or tenor for each from the date of valuation to the date when the payment is due. Using the calculated tenors and the zero coupon rates derived earlier, interpolated zero coupon rates for the specific IRS instrument being priced will be determined. These interpolated zero coupon rates will be used to a) discount the cash flows and b) derive the forward rates which will serve as the basis for the future coupon rates of the floating leg(s) of the transaction.

Forward rates will be calculated by applying the bootstrapping formula to the interpolated zero coupon rates to determine the rate applicable to each successive interest rate period. The floating rate will be the forward rate so determined plus a spread if applicable.

Cash flows for the fixed payment leg will be simply the fixed rate times the notional amount. For the floating leg the cash flows will be the forward rate (plus spread) times the notional amount. These cash flows will be discounted using the interpolated zero rates over the term between the due date and the pricing date. The total PVs will be sum of these discount cash flows, and the price of the instrument is the difference between the total PVs of the receiving leg and the paying leg.

The flow chart below summarizes the process. This is then followed by a detailed step-by-step write up on the process, together with numerical examples.

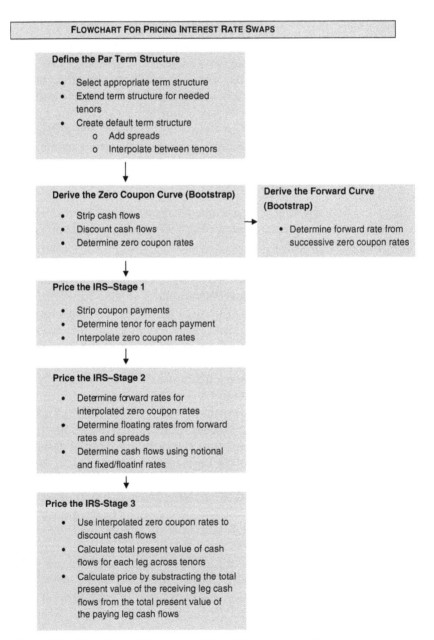

Figure 288   Flowchart of the process for pricing interest rate swaps

Defining the par term structure

Step 1: Select an appropriate term structure

Based on the IRS being priced, an appropriate term structure or structures will be chosen. This is an important process because both the zero curve and the forward curves are derived from it, and are in turn used to discount the cash flows and calculate the future coupon rates for the floating legs of the transaction.

Let us assume that we select the interbank offer rates as our par term structure. The interbank offer rate structure that we have chosen has quoted rates for terms of three months, six months, one year, two years and three years as follows.

INTERBANK OFFER RATES	BID	OFFER	AVERAGE
3m	11.87%	12.12%	12.00%
6m	11.99%	12.24%	12.12%
1yr	12.15%	12.65%	12.40%
2yr	12.27%	12.77%	12.52%
3yr	12.38%	12.88%	12.63%

Figure 289   Interbank offer rates

Step 2: Extending the term structure

If the term of the IRS is greater than the maximum tenor of the selected par term structure then rates from another available term structure having longer tenors may be used as a proxy to the selected par term structure to supplement it. For example, a Treasury term structure that extends to longer tenors such as 20 years and 30 years may be used.

TENOR	TREASURY RATE
1yr	12.21%
2yr	12.32%
3yr	12.36%
4yr	12.41%
5yr	12.45%
6yr	12.51%
7yr	12.56%
8yr	12.61%
9yr	12.60%
10yr	12.61%
15yr	12.85%
20yr	13.07%
30yr	13.21%

Figure 290   Treasury rates

Step 3: Creating a default term structure

Adding a spread

The rates quoted for respective term structures are based on the underlying instruments. Treasury term structures are based on Treasury instruments that are usually compounded on a semi-annual basis. Interbank offer rates, on the other hand, tend to be based on corporates that are compounded on a quarterly basis. These rates, presented on an annualized basis, are therefore usually nominal rates compounded based on the payment frequency of the underlying instruments.

Depending on the IRS to be priced, spreads (positive or negative) may need to be added to the rates to account for the differentials between quoting basis and the payment frequency of the IRS. The resulting rates would then be considered as having been quoted on the appropriate basis.

For illustration purposes we assume that no spreads are added to any of the rates in the term structure. The default term structure in our example consists of 1-year, 2-year, 3-year and 4-year tenors. As mentioned above, our primary term structure is the interbank term structure with rates for tenors exceeding the maximum tenor being taken from the Treasury term structure.

The resulting default term structure is as follows.

TENOR (IN YEARS)	DEFAULT TERM STRUCTURE
1	12.15%
2	12.27%
3	12.38%
4	12.41%

Figure 291   Default term structure

Interpolating par rates for intermediate tenors

Depending on the payment frequency of the IRS, par rates for intermediate tenors may need to be calculated. For example, if the payment frequency was semi-annual then a rate for tenor 1.5 years would be required. However, this is not readily available in the default term structure. The rate would be interpolated from the rates of the adjacent tenors, that is, the 1-year and 2-year rates as follows:

T = intermediate tenor =1.5 years

T_1 = 1 year

T_2 = 2 years

$$Rate_{1.5\ years} = \frac{(T_2 - T) \times Rate_{1\ year} + (T - T_1) \times Rate_{2\ year}}{(T_2 - T_1)}.$$

If the payment frequency was quarterly then the rates for tenors 1.25 years, 1.5 years and 1.75 years would also be required for the period 1 to 2 years. The rate for 1.25 years would be calculated from the available 1-year and 2-year rates using interpolation as follows:

T = intermediate tenor =1.25 years;
T_1 = 1 year;
T_2 = 2 years.

$$Rate_{1.5\,years} = \frac{(T_2 - T) \times Rate_{1\,year} + (T - T_1) \times Rate_{2\,year}}{(T_2 - T_1)}.$$

In our example, however, we assume that the underlying payment frequency for the IRS is annual. Therefore our default par term structure is as given below:

TENOR (IN YEARS)	DEFAULT TERM STRUCTURE
1	12.15%
2	12.27%
3	12.38%
4	12.41%

Figure 292   Default term structure

Deriving the zero curve

We use the bootstrapping method for deriving the zero curve from the par term structure. This is an iterative process that allows us to derive a zero coupon yield curve from the rates/prices of coupon bearing instruments. The step-by-step procedure employed is given below.

Step 4: Develop the cash flows matrix

Given the default par term structure above we calculate the cash flows for coupon bearing instruments for each tenor. The par value for each instrument is assumed to be 100. The instruments are assumed to be at par, meaning that the coupon rate is equal to the par rate. An instrument with 1-year tenor means a cash flow at maturity of the face value, 100 plus a coupon of par rate * face value = 12.15% * 100 = 12.15 or a total of 112.15. An instrument with a tenor of two years will have a coupon payment at the end of year 1 and a payment of the face value + coupon at the end of year 2, and so on. Further details of the cash flows are given in the matrix below.

Coupon	12.15%	12.27%	12.38%	12.41%
Tenor/Duration	1	2	3	4
1	112.15	12.27	12.38	12.41
2		112.27	12.38	12.41
3			112.38	12.41
4				112.41

Figure 293   Cash flow matrix

The columns pertain to a particular tenor; the rows pertain to the duration when a payment is due within the tenor.

Step 5: Developing the discounted value of cash flows matrix and the zero curve

As mentioned above, as the instruments are assumed to be priced at par the total PV of the future cash flows must equal the face value of the instrument, that is, 100. In order to derive the discounted cash flows and the zero coupon rates we start with the shortest tenor and work our way to the larger tenors. This is illustrated for the first two tenors below using timelines to help in understanding the process more clearly.

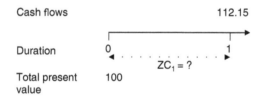

Figure 294   Determination of zero coupon rates – 1

As mentioned above, the total PV of cash flows is equal to the face value. For the coupon bearing instrument with tenor 1 the cash flows are due at duration 1 amounting to 112.15. We know that the discount value of this total cash flow is 100. The zero coupon rate would therefore be the rate that discounts the cash flows to this value:

$$112.15 \div (1+ZC_1) = 100.$$

Therefore $ZC_1 = [112.15 \div 100] - 1 = 12.15\%$.

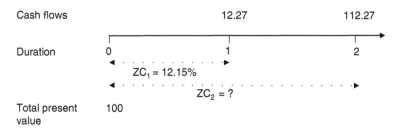

Figure 295   Determination of zero coupon rates – 2

The cash flow at duration 1 will be discounted using the zero coupon rate determined earlier, that is, $ZC_1 = 12.15\%$. The cash flow at duration 2 will be discounted at ZC_2 (annually compounded rate) which is an unknown at this point in time. Using the fact that the total PV is equal to the face value, we determine ZC_2 by solving the following equation:

$$100 = [12.27 \div (1+ZC_1)] + [112.27 \div (1+ZC_2)^2]$$

$$(1+ZC_2)^2 = 112.27 \div \{100 - [12.27 \div (1+12.15\%)]\} = 1.2606021$$

$$ZC_2 = (\sqrt{1.2606021})-1 = 12.277\%.$$

The same iterative and substitution process will be used to determine the zero coupon rates for the other tenors. The matrix of discounted cash flows is given below.

TENOR/DURATION	1	2	3	4
1	100	10.9407	11.03879	11.06554
2		89.0593	9.820558	9.844356
3			79.14065	8.739416
4				70.35069
Total PV	100	100	100	100

Figure 296   Discounted cash flows matrix

And the zero curve is as follows.

T	ZC_r
1	12.150%
2	12.277%
3	12.399%
4	12.431%

Figure 297   Zero curve

Deriving the forward curve

Step 6: Deriving forward rates

In order to derive forward rates from the zero coupon rates for successive interest rate periods the bootstrapping methodology has been employed. In particular, the following formula has been used:

$$FC_{t-1,t} = \frac{(1+ZC_t)^t}{(1+ZC_{t-1})^{t-1}} - 1,$$

where t is the tenor in years, ZC_t is the zero coupon rate for a tenor of t years and $FC_{t-1,t}$ is the forward rate for the period $(t-1,t)$.

For example, the forward rate for the interest rate period three years to four years using zero coupon rates is

$$FC_{3,4} = \frac{(1+12.431\%)^4}{(1+12.399\%)^3} - 1 = 12.525\%.$$

The forward rates are as follows in our example.

T	$FC_{t-1,t}$
1	12.150%
2	12.405%
3	12.643%
4	12.525%

Figure 298 Forward rates

Pricing coupon swaps or fixed for floating swaps

Term sheet

COUPON SWAP (FIXED FOR FLOATING)	
Notional	100,000
Fixed rate (Paying leg)	12.00%
Floating rate (Receiving leg)	Interbank offer rate + spread
Spread	0.50%
Payment	Annual
Fixed rate payment dates	1st Day of the year starting January 2011 and ending on the maturity date
Floating rate	same as fixed
Valuation date	27/05/2010
Maturity date	01/01/2014
Day count convention	Actual/365 for both legs

Figure 299 Term sheet coupon swap

Step 7: Determine the coupon paying/receiving periods

For each coupon that is due to be paid or received we determine the length of the period and the duration between the due date and the valuation or pricing date. For the IRS given above:

Period Start	Period End	Days to Coupon	Days in Period	Ten or (in Years) (Basis = Actual/365)
01/01/2010	01/01/2011	219	365	0.60
01/01/2011	01/01/2012	584	365	1.60
01/01/2012	01/01/2013	950	366	2.60
01/01/2013	01/01/2014	1315	365	3.60

Figure 300   Duration to next coupon date

Period Start = start of the period for which coupon is assessed

Period End = date on which the payments are to be made

Days to coupon = number of days between the date when coupon will be paid and the valuation date = Period End − Valuation Date

Days in period = number of days in the coupon paying period = Period End − Period Start

Tenor (in years) = duration between when the coupon will be paid and the valuation date in years (depending on the day count convention) = Days to Coupon/365.

Step 8: Determine the zero coupon rates applicable

Based on the duration between the valuation date and the coupon payment date the zero coupon rates are determined by interpolating between the zero coupon rates derived earlier. For tenors less than one year we will use the zero coupon rates for tenor = one year. These rates will be used to discount the cash flows as well as to determine forward rates, which will be used to calculate the future coupon payments under the floating leg of the IRS.

For example, for tenor 3.6 years the zero coupon rate is determined by interpolating the rates for three years and four years as follows:

$$Interpolated\,Zero\,Coupon\,Rate_{3.6\,years} = \frac{(4-3.6)\times12.399\% + (3.6-3)\times12.431\%}{(4-3)} = 12.418\%$$

The interpolated zero coupon rates applicable for the pricing of this sample IRS product are as follows.

Period End	Tenor	Interpolated Zero Coupon Rates
01/01/2011	0.60	12.150%
01/01/2012	1.60	12.226%
01/01/2013	2.60	12.351%
01/01/2014	3.60	12.418%

Figure 301   Interpolated zero coupon rates

Step 9: Determine the forward rates applicable

From the interpolated rates calculated above, the forward rates will be determined using the formula presented earlier. These rates will be used to calculate the coupon payments to be made under the floating leg of the swap transaction. For example, the forward rate for the period Jan 1, 2011 and Jan 1, 2012 will be calculated by using the zero coupon rate for tenors 0.6 and 1.6:

$$FC_{0.6,1.6} = \frac{(1+12.226\%)^{1.6}}{(1+12.150\%)^{0.6}} - 1 = 12.272\%$$

The interpolated forward rates are as follows.

Period Start	Period End	Interpolated Forward Rates
01/01/2010	01/01/2011	12.150%
01/01/2011	01/01/2012	12.272%
01/01/2012	01/01/2013	12.586%
01/01/2013	01/01/2014	12.593%

Figure 302   Interpolated forward rates

Step 10: Determine the cash flows

The cash flows for the receiving and paying legs are as follows.

	Fixed Leg Payment		Floating Leg Payment	
Period End	Rate	Cash flow	Rate	Cash flow
01/01/2011	12.00%	7,200.00	12.65%	7,590.00
01/01/2012	12.00%	12,000	12.77%	12,772.30
01/01/2013	12.00%	12,000	13.09%	13,085.98
01/01/2014	12.00%	12,000	13.09%	13,093.33

Figure 303   Determination of cash flows for the receiving and paying legs

The fixed leg payments are straightforward, simply the fixed rate * notional amount, that is, 12% * 100,000 = 12,000. For the first duration, because of the fractional period, the cash flow will be adjusted as follows: fixed rate * tenor * notional amount = 12% * 0.6 * 100,000 = 7,200.

The floating leg payments are based on interbank rate + spread, where spread is given as 50 basis points. Interbank rate will be the forward rate derived. Therefore the floating rate above is the forward rate + spread and the cash flow is (forward rate + spread) * notional amount. For the second payment due this is (12.272% + 0.50%) * 100,000 = 12,772.30. As in the case with fixed rate payments, the first payment has to be adjusted because it is only for a fractional period. The cash flow will equal (12.15% + 0.50%) * 0.60 * 100,000 = 7,590.

Step 11: Discount the cash flows

The next step is to discount the cash flows using the interpolated zero coupon rates. The resulting PVs for the sample IRS are given below.

Period End	PV of Fixed Leg	PV of Floating Leg
01/01/2011	6,721.29	7,085.36
01/01/2012	9,977.67	10,619.81
01/01/2013	8,862.27	9,664.28
01/01/2014	7,871.04	8,588.18
Total	33,432.2680	35,957.6383

Figure 304   Present value of cash flows

For example for the period ending 1 Jan 2010, the discount cash flows for the fixed leg are calculated as follows:

PV of fixed leg = 12000 ÷ (1+12.226%)1.6 = 9,977.67.

Step 12: Calculating the price of the IRS

The price of the IRS is the net PV of cash flows, that is, the total PV of the receiving leg less the total PV of the paying leg.

In our example this is the total PV of floating leg – total PV of fixed leg

= 35,957.64 − 33,432.27 = 2,525.37.

Pricing basis swaps or floating for floating swaps

The same methodology will be used to price floating for floating or basis swaps, except that zero curves and forward rates will be derived for both legs of the swap accordingly.

The following basis swap has been priced below:

Term sheet

BASIS SWAP (FLOATING FOR FLOATING)	
Notional	100,000
Floating rate 1 (paying leg)	Treasury Rate
Floating rate 2 (receiving leg)	Interbank Offer Rate + spread
Spread	0.50%
Payment	Annual
Fixed rate payment dates	1st Day of the year starting January 2011 and ending on the Maturity Date
Floating Rate	same as Fixed
Valuation Date	27/05/2010
Maturity Date	01/01/2014
Day count convention	A/360 for Leg 1 & A/365 for leg 2

Figure 305   Term sheet for a basis swap

Pricing

	TREASURY		INTERBANK		PAYING LEG		RECEIVING LEG PAYMENT			
PERIOD END	ZC	FC	ZC	FC	RATE	CASH FLOW	RATE	CASH FLOW	PV PAYING LEG	PV RECEIVING LEG
01/01/11	12.21%	12.21%	12.15%	12.15%	12.21%	7,326	12.65%	7,590	6,830	7,085
01/01/12	12.28%	12.33%	12.23%	12.27%	12.33%	12,326	12.77%	12,772	10,214	10,620
01/01/13	12.35%	12.50%	12.35%	12.59%	12.50%	12,505	13.09%	13,086	9,195	9,664
01/01/14	12.41%	12.55%	12.42%	12.59%	12.55%	12,546	13.09%	13,093	8,184	8,588
							Total PV		34,424	35,958
							Price		1,533.73	

Figure 306   Pricing of a basis swap

Pricing cross currency swaps

Fixed for fixed currency swap

The fixed for fixed cross currency swap will be priced as a portfolio of forward foreign exchange contracts, where each exchange of payments is a forward foreign exchange contract. The assumption is that the forward exchange rates will be realized. The forward exchange rates will be calculated using the following equation:

$$F_0 = S_0 e^{(r-r_f)T},$$

where r and r_f are compounded continuously, or

$$F_0 = S_0 \left(\frac{1+r}{1+r_f} \right)^T,$$

if the interest rates were compounded on a discrete basis.

In our example below we will assume discrete compounding. We assume that the financial institution makes fixed USD payments and in return receives fixed Yen payments. Also we assume that the principal is exchanged at the beginning and end of the trade.

The payments in the swap will be as follows.

Stage 1: Principal exchange
The principals/notional amounts will be exchanged at the current exchange rate. The principal amounts in the two currencies are US$ 10 million or 910 million Yen calculated at the current exchange of US$ 1 = 91 Yen. The financial institution will pay the Yen notional and receive the USD principal amount from the counterparty.

Stage 2: Interest flows
The currency swap that the financial institution has entered has the following terms regarding interest payments. It will receive 6 percent of the notional amount per annum in Yen and pay 5 percent per annum in dollars on an annual basis.

Stage 3: Principal exchange
At maturity, it will receive the Yen notional and pay the USD notional amount.

The other terms of the contract will be as follows:

- The payments are to be made on the first day of the year starting 1 Jan 2011 and ending on the maturity date
- The maturity date is 1 Jan 2014
- The valuation or pricing date is 31 May 2010
- The day count convention used in calculating the interest rate payments for both legs is Actual/365.

The LIBOR/SWAP zero curve rates for USD and JPY (Yen) are assumed to have been calculated as follows.

	LIBOR/ SWAP ZERO RATES	
TENOR (IN YEARS)	USD	JPY
1	1.200%	0.670%
2	1.230%	0.490%
3	1.502%	0.594%
4	1.776%	0.699%

Figure 307   LIBOR/SWAP zero rates

The results are given in the spreadsheet below. Just a few notes on the worksheet:

- Forward exchange rate is calculated using the formula given above:
  $F_0 = S_0 \left(\dfrac{1+r}{1+r_f} \right)^T$. For example, for the period ended 1 Jan 2012, the forward exchange rate = (1/91) * (1.0122/1.0056)^1.59 = 0.01110.
- The dollar value of Yen cash flow is calculated using this forward exchange rate to convert the Yen cash flow into dollar. For example, for period ended 1 Jan 2012, the dollar value of Yen cash flow = fixed rate applicable to Yen * Yen notional amount * forward exchange rate = 6%*910,000,000*0.011,10=US$ 606,213.
- Net cash flow = dollar value of Yen cash flow (receiving leg) – USD cash flow (paying leg) = 606,213–500,000 = US$ 106,213.
- PV of net cash flow is the net cash flow discounted to the valuation date using the USD zero curve interpolated rates. For example, for the period ended 1 Jan 2012 the PV = 106,213/(1.0122)^1.59 = US$ 104,190.
- The price or value of the fixed for fixed currency swap is the sum of the PVs of each future net cash flow payment.

Period End	Tenor (in Years)	Interpolated Zero Coupon Rate-USD	Interpolated Zero Coupon Rate-JPY	Forward Exchange Rate	Paying Leg – USD		Receiving Leg – JPY		Dollar Value of Yen Cash Flow	Net Cash Flow	Present Value of Net Cash Flow
					Rate	Cash Flow	Rate	Cash Flow			
01/01/2011	0.59	1.20%	0.67%	0.01102	5.00%	294,521	6.00%	32,161,644	354,519	59,999	59,579
01/01/2012	1.59	1.22%	0.56%	0.01110	5.00%	500,000	6.00%	54,600,000	606,213	106,213	104,190
01/01/2013	2.59	1.39%	0.55%	0.01123	5.00%	500,000	6.00%	54,600,000	613,069	113,069	109,093
01/01/2014	3.59	1.66%	0.66%	0.01139	5.00%	10,500,000	6.00%	964,600,000	10,986,229	486,229	458,245
										Price	731,107

Figure 308 Pricing fixed for fixed currency swap

Floating for floating currency swap

For our pricing example, most of the assumptions will be the same as those used in the example for fixed for fixed currency swap above except for the interest rates used to calculate the floating rate payments. Let us assume that the floating interest rate payments for the USD leg are based on the US LIBOR and the floating interest rate payments for the Yen leg are based on the JPY LIBOR plus a spread of 80 basis points. As in the case of floating for floating IRSs discussed earlier, the swap will be valued assuming that the forward rates implicit in the zero curve on the valuation date will be realized.

The results are given in the worksheet below. Just a few notes on the results:

- The forward rates that are used in the floating rates payments (*FC*) are derived from the interpolated zero coupon rates (*ZC*) using the applicable formula. For example, for the period ended Jan 1, 2012, the forward rate for USD was calculated as follows:

$$FC_{0.59,1.59} = \frac{(1+1.22\%)^{1.59}}{(1+1.20\%)^{0.59}} - 1 = 1.23\%.$$

- The floating leg payments will be equal to the forward rate (+ spread if applicable) * notional amount. For example, for the period ended Jan 1, 2012, the Yen cash flow is calculated as (0.501% + 0.80%) * 910,000,000 = 11,840,543 Yen. The dollar value will be this amount * the forward exchange rate = 11,840,543 * 0.011,10 = US$ 131,463.

PERIOD END	TENOR (IN YEARS)	USD		JPY		PAYING LEG – USD			RECEIVING LEG – JPY		DOLLAR VALUE OF YEN CASH FLOW	NET CASH FLOW	PRESENT VALUE OF NET CASH FLOW
		ZC	FC	ZC	FC	FORWARD EXCHANGE RATE	RATE	CASH FLOW	RATE	CASH FLOW			
01/01/11	0.59	1.20%	1.20%	0.67%	0.67%	0.01102	1.20%	70,685	1.47%	7,879,603	86,857	16,172	16,059
01/01/12	1.59	1.22%	1.23%	0.56%	0.50%	0.01110	1.23%	122,825	1.30%	11,840,543	131,463	8,638	8,473
01/01/13	2.59	1.39%	1.67%	0.55%	0.53%	0.01123	1.67%	167,034	1.33%	12,132,842	136,232	−30,802	−29,719
01/01/14	3.59	1.66%	2.38%	0.66%	0.93%	0.01139	2.38%	10,237,532	1.73%	925,723,103	10,543,444	305,912	288,306
												Price	283,120

Figure 309   Pricing floating for floating currency swap

Amortizing floating for floating currency swap

In an amortizing swap, the principal reduces in a predetermined way. For our illustration we assume that the principal reduces by 25 percent in each period. The rest of the parameters and assumptions are the same as for the floating for floating currency swap given above.

The amortization schedule is as follows:

PERIOD	USD	JPY
1	10,000,000	910,000,000
2	7,500,000	682,500,000
3	5,000,000	455,000,000
4	2,500,000	227,500,000

Figure 310 Amortization schedule for amortizing floating for floating currency swap

The results are as follows:

PERIOD END	NOTIONAL	REDEEMED	RATE	CASH FLOW (INTEREST + REDEMPTION)	NOTIONAL	REDEEMED	RATE	CASH FLOW (INTEREST + REDEMPTION)	DOLLAR VALUE OF YEN CASH FLOW
	PAYING LEG – USD				RECEIVING LEG – JPY				
01/01/11	10,000,000	2,500,000	1.20%	2,570,685	910,000,000	227,500,000	1.47%	235,379,603	2,594,602
01/01/12	7,500,000	2,500,000	1.23%	2,592,119	682,500,000	227,500,000	1.30%	236,380,407	2,624,485
01/01/13	5,000,000	2,500,000	1.67%	2,583,517	455,000,000	227,500,000	1.33%	233,566,421	2,622,572
01/01/14	2,500,000	2,500,000	2.38%	2,559,383	227,500,000	227,500,000	1.73%	231,430,776	2,635,861

PERIOD END	NET CASH FLOW	PRESENT VALUE OF NET CASH FLOW
01/01/11	23,917	23,749
01/01/12	32,366	31,749
01/01/13	39,055	37,681
01/01/14	76,478	72,077
	Price	**165,256**

Figure 311 Pricing an amortizing floating for floating currency swap

The cash flow for the period comprises of the interest payment plus the redemption amount. The interest payment is based on the outstanding notional amount at the beginning of the period, prior to principal redemption for the period. For example, for the period ended 1 Jan 2012 the cash flow for the USD leg is 1.23% * 7,500,000 + 2,500,000 = US$ 2,592,119.

Caps and floors

The most commonly used options in the swaps market are caps and floors. A cap is a call on the rates where the payoff depends on Max(LIBOR – Strike, 0). A floor is a put on the rates where the payoff depends on Max(Strike – LIBOR, 0).

Cap

A cap may be considered as a portfolio of caplets on the underlying asset, which is the LIBOR. The value of the caplet may be derived using *Black's formula*. The value of a caplet which resets at time t_i and payoffs at time t_{i+1} is:

$$\frac{\text{Notional}}{\left(1 + ZC_{t_{i+1}}\right)^{t_{i+1}}} \times \left[F_i N(d_1) - XN(d_2) \right],$$

where $\left[F_i N(d_1) - XN(d_2) \right]$ is known as the forward premium per unit of notional amount, X is the strike, F_i is the forward rate at time 0 for the period between t_i and t_{i+1} and σ_{t_i} is the volatility of this forward interest rate:

$$d_1 = \frac{\ln(F_i / X) + \sigma_{t_i}^2 t_i / 2}{\sigma_{t_i} \sqrt{t_i}},$$

$$d_2 = d_1 - \sigma_{t_i} \sqrt{t_i}.$$

This is illustrated below for a 4-year cap on a 1-year interbank offer rate with a strike of 12.5 percent. The annualized constant volatility is 3.13

PERIOD START (*i*)	PERIOD END (*i*+1)	t_i	t_{i+1}	ZCt_{i+1}	F_i	d_1	d_2	FORWARD PREMIUM	VALUE OF CAPLET
01/01/10	01/01/11	n/a	0.59	12.150%	12.150%	n/a	n/a	-	-
01/01/11	01/01/12	0.59	1.59	12.225%	12.269%	−0.76	−0.79	37.26	31.02
01/01/12	01/01/13	1.59	2.59	12.349%	12.583%	0.19	0.15	241.75	178.77
01/01/13	01/01/14	2.59	3.59	12.418%	12.595%	0.18	0.12	302.29	198.53
								Price of cap	408.33

Figure 312 Pricing a cap in the swap market

percent. The valuation date is May 31, 2010 and the payment frequency is annual. The notional amount is 100,000.

The calculations of d_1 and d_2 are based on the duration at the start of the period, that is, t_i. Therefore, for the first row we see that these values cannot be calculated. The forward premium in this case is simply equal to the payoff, that is, $\text{Max}(F_i - X, 0) * \text{Notional} * \Delta t/365 = \max(12.15\%-12.5\%, 0) * 100,000 * 0.59 = 0$

For the other rows, as d_1 and d_2 can be calculated the forward premium from Black's formula will be used.

The price of the cap is the sum of the values of the caplets, which are the PVs of the forward premiums.

Floor

A floor may be considered as a portfolio of floorlets on the underlying asset, which is the LIBOR. The value of the floorlet may be derived using *Black's formula*. The value of a floorlet which resets at time t_i and payoffs at time t_{i+1} is:

$$\frac{\text{Notional}}{\left(1 + ZC_{t_{i+1}}\right)^{t_{i+1}}} \times \left[XN(-d_2) - F_i N(-d_1)\right],$$

PERIOD START (*i*)	PERIOD END (*i*+1)	t_i	t_{i+1}	ZCt_{i+1}	F_i	d_1	d_2	FORWARD PREMIUM	VALUE OF FLOORLET
01/01/2010	01/01/2011	n/a	0.59	12.150%	12.150%	n/a	n/a	206.16	192.70
01/01/2011	01/01/2012	0.59	1.59	12.225%	12.269%	−0.76	−0.79	268.02	223.14
01/01/2012	01/01/2013	1.59	2.59	12.349%	12.583%	0.19	0.15	158.39	117.12
01/01/2013	01/01/2014	2.59	3.59	12.418%	12.595%	0.18	0.12	207.47	136.26
								Price of Floor	669.22

Figure 313 Pricing a floor in the swap market

where $\left[XN(-d_2) - F_i N(-d_1)\right]$ is the forward premium per unit of notional amount, d_1 and d_2 are as given above. The value of a 4-year floor with strike, constant volatility, notional, maturity and payment frequency the same as for the cap above is illustrated below.

Again it may be noted that the calculation of d_1 and d_2 are based on the duration at the start of the period, t_i. Therefore, for the first row we see that these values cannot be calculated. The forward premium in this case is simply equal to the payoff: $\text{Max}(X - F_i, 0) * \text{Notional} * \Delta t/365 = \max(12.5\%-12.15\%, 0) * 100,000 * 0.59 = 206.16$

For the other rows, as d_1 and d_2 can be calculated the forward premium from Black's formula will be used.

The price of the floor is the sum of the values of the floorlets, which are the PVs of the forward premiums.

Cap–floor parity

The cap–floor parity says that being long a cap and short a floor with the same strike is equivalent to paying the fixed leg in the swap, where the fixed rate is equal to the strike rate.

In other words, *Cap – Floor = Swap.*
From the above two examples on caps and floors we see that this value is: $408.33 - 669.22 = -260.89$.
Calculating an IRS with

- fixed rate equal to the strike of 12.5 percent,
- notional = 100,000,
- payment frequency = annual, and
- payment dates similar to that of the cap and floor above,

Swap					Fixed		Floating			
Period Start	Period End	t_{i+1}	ZCt_{i+1} %	F_i	Rate %	Cash Flow	Rate %	Cash Flow	PV of Fixed Leg	PV of Floating Leg
01/01/10	01/01/11	0.59	12.150	12.150	12.5	7,363.01	12.15%	7,156.85	6,882.11	6,689.41
01/01/11	01/01/12	1.59	12.225	12.269	12.5	12,500.00	12.27%	12,269.24	10,406.76	10,214.64
01/01/12	01/01/13	2.59	12.349	12.583	12.5	12,500.00	12.58%	12,583.37	9,243.60	9,305.25
01/01/13	01/01/14	3.59	12.418	12.595	12.5	12,500.00	12.59%	12,594.82	8,209.61	8,271.89
								Total	34,742.08	34,481.20
								Price		2260.89

Figure 314 Pricing an interest rate swap – cap–floor parity

we see that the value of the swap is as follows.

As we can see, the value of the IRS is equal to the value of the cap minus the value of the floor.

Accrual swaps

In an accrual swap, the interest for one leg accrues only when the floating reference rate is within a specified range. This range may remain the same for the life of the swap or may be reset periodically.

We illustrate the pricing of an accrual swap with a simple example. The fixed rate, 12 percent per annum, is exchanged for the interbank rate once every year and the fixed rate only accrues if the interbank rate is below the cutoff rate of 12.3 percent per annum on the payment date. The principal is 100,000. The day count convention is Actual/365.

Method 1

From a fixed rate payer's position, there is increased value in this swap as he will save on interest payments for those days when the interbank rate is above 12.3 percent.

The fixed rate payer's position can therefore be considered equal to the value of a regular swap plus the value of a series of binary call options as he receives added value if the interbank rate is higher than 12.3 percent.

The value of a binary call option paying fixed rate * notional = fixed rate * notional * $N(d_2)/(1+zct_{i+1})^{\wedge} t_{i+1}$, where $N(d_2)$ is the probability that the interbank rate will exceed the cutoff rate and

$$d_2 = \frac{\ln(F_i/X) - \sigma_{t_i}^2 t_i/2}{\sigma_{t_i}\sqrt{t_i}},$$

where F_i is the forward value of the interbank rate, X is the cut off rate, σ is the volatility of F_i (we have assumed a constant volatility of 4 percent) and t_i is the time from the valuation date to time i.

Method 2

Alternatively, the fixed rate cash flows may be calculated assuming that they are binary put options which pay the fixed rate only if the interbank rate is below the cut off date. The value of a binary put option will be fixed rate * notional $\times N(-d_2)/(1+zct_{i+1})^{\wedge} t_{i+1}$. The sum of the values of the series of binary put options here represents the paying leg. The receiving leg will be calculated as in the case of a normal swap. The difference

PERIOD START (i)	PERIOD END (i+1)	t_i	t_{i+1}	ZCt_{i+1}	F_i	FIXED LEG PAYMENT RATE	FIXED LEG PAYMENT CASH FLOW	FLOATING LEG PAYMENT RATE	FLOATING LEG PAYMENT CASH FLOW	PV OF FIXED (PAYING) LEG	PV OF FLOATING (RECEIVING) LEG
01/01/10	01/01/11	n/a	0.59	12.150%	12.150%	12.0%	7,035.62	12.15%	7,123.56	6,578.17	6,660.39
01/01/11	01/01/12	0.59	1.59	12.225%	12.268%	12.0%	12,000	12.27%	12,268.48	9,993.69	10,217.29
01/01/12	01/01/13	1.59	2.59	12.349%	12.583%	12.0%	12,000	12.58%	12,582.71	8,876.76	9,307.81
01/01/13	01/01/14	2.59	3.59	12.418%	12.595%	12.0%	12,000	12.60%	12,595.19	7,883.78	8,274.81
									Total PV	33,332.39	34,460.30
									Price		1,127.91

Figure 315 Value of a regular swap

between the total PV of the receiving leg and the total PV of the paying leg will equal the price of the accrual swap.

Given that the valuation date is Jun 1, 2010, the first payment is due on Jan 1, 2011 and the maturity date is Jan 1, 2014, the results are as follows.

PERIOD END	d_2	$N(d_2)$	CASH FLOW	VALUE OF BINARY CALL
01/01/2011	n/a	n/a	0	-
01/01/2012	−0.10	0.460538002	5,526.46	4,602.48
01/01/2013	0.43	0.664903511	7,978.84	5,902.19
01/01/2014	0.34	0.631676584	7,580.12	4,980.00
			Sum	15,484.66

Figure 316   Value of binary calls

Value of regular swap

Method 1: Additional value to fixed rate payer, that is, sum of values of series of binary call options

As mentioned above, this method gives the value of the regular swap plus the value of a series of binary call options where the strike is the cutoff rate. The value of the series of binary call options is given below.

In the first row, the value of d_2 and subsequently $N(d_2)$ is given as n/a because the input of t_i is not available as the period start date is prior to the valuation date. On this date we already know the forward value of the interbank rate, which is 12.15 percent. For the binary call option payment will only be made if it is greater than the cutoff rate of 12.3 percent. As this is not the case, the cash flow is 0 and the subsequent PV is also zero.

For the other rows the value of d_2 is calculated using the formula given above and the probability of the forward rate exceeding the cutoff rate is calculated using $N(d_2)$. The cash flow is then equal to fixed rate * notional * $N(d_2)$. The value of the binary call is the cash flow discounted at the applicable ZC rate for the applicable duration (t_{i+1}). For example, for the period ended Jan 1, 2012 the value of the binary call = 5526.46/ (1+12.225%)^1.59 = 4602.48.

The value of the accrual swap in this example = value of regular swap + sum of values of binary calls = 1127.91 + 15,484.66 = 16,612.57.

Period End	d_2	$N(-d_2)$	Cash Flow	Value of Binary Put = PV of Paying Leg
01/01/2011	n/a	n/a	7,035.62	6,578.17
01/01/2012	−0.10	0.5395	6,473.54	5,391.22
01/01/2013	0.43	0.3351	4,021.16	2,974.57
01/01/2014	0.34	0.3683	4,419.88	2,903.78
			Total PV of paying leg	**17,847.73**

Figure 317   Value of binary puts

Method 2: PV of fixed (paying) leg is the value of a series of binary put options

In the second method we assume that the fixed paying leg is made up of a series of binary put options where the payment of interest is only made if the interbank rate is below the cutoff rate. The values of the binary put options are given below.

As in the case above, in the first row the value of d_2 and subsequently $N(-d_2)$ is given as n/a because the input of t_i is not available as the period start date is prior to the valuation date. On this date we already know the forward value of the interbank rate, which is 12.15 percent. For the binary put option payment will only be made if it is less than the cutoff rate of 12.3 percent. As this is the case, the cash flow is 12% * 100,000 * 0.59 = 7035.62 and the subsequent PV is 6578.17 discounting at the applicable ZC rate over the applicable duration (payment date to valuation date).

For the other rows the value of d_2 is calculated using the formula given above and the probability of the forward rate being less than the cutoff rate is calculated using $N(-d_2)$. The cash flow is then equal to fixed rate * notional * $N(-d_2)$. The value of the binary put is the cash flow discounted at the applicable ZC rate for the applicable duration (t_{i+1}). For example, for the period ended Jan 1, 2012 the value of the binary put = 6473.54 / (1+12.225%) ^ 1.59 = 5391.22.

The value of the accrual swap in this example = total PV of the receiving leg of the regular swap − sum of values of binary puts (total PV of the paying leg) = 34,460.30 − 17,847.73 = 16,612.57.

Hence the result from Method 1 is equal to the result from Method 2.

Range accrual note

Range accruals are a form of interest accrual in which the payment is only earned on days when a specified benchmark rate falls within a specified range.

As the payment is conditional on the rate falling within a certain range, the cash flow is multiplied by the probability of such an event occurring. The probability is calculated as the probability that the rate will exceed the lower bound less the probability of it exceeding the upper bound of the range.

The probability that the rate, F_i, will exceed a given rate, X, is given by $N(d_2)$ where

ITEM	TERMS AND CONDITIONS
Notional	100,000
Binary rate	12.00%
Payment	Annual
Payment dates	1st Day of the year starting January 2011 and ending on the maturity date
Valuation date	01/06/2010
Maturity date	01/01/2014
Day count convention	A/365
Lower bound	12.00%
Upper bound	12.20%
Sigma (Volatility of F_i)	4.00%

Figure 318   Term sheet for a range accrual note

$$d_2 = \frac{\ln\left(F_i / X\right) - \sigma_{t_i}^2 t_i / 2}{\sigma_{t_i} \sqrt{t_i}} \, ,$$

PERIOD START (i)	PERIOD END (i+1)	t_i	t_{i+1}	ZCt_{i+1}	F_i	d_2-LOWER BOUND	d_2-UPPER BOUND	$N(d_2)$- LOWER BOUND	$N(d_2)$- UPPER BOUND
01/01/2010	01/01/2011	n/a	0.59	12.150%	12.150%	n/a	n/a	n/a	n/a
01/01/2011	01/01/2012	0.59	1.59	12.225%	12.268%	0.71	0.17	0.7603	0.5665
01/01/2012	01/01/2013	1.59	2.59	12.349%	12.583%	0.92	0.59	0.8202	0.7217
01/01/2013	01/01/2014	2.59	3.59	12.418%	12.595%	0.72	0.46	0.7642	0.6784

Figure 319   Pricing a range accrual swap – 1

$N(.)$ is the cumulative standard normal distribution and σ is the volatility of F_i. To illustrate, we have the following term sheet for a range accrual note.

PERIOD START (i)	PERIOD END (i+1)	PROBABILITY OF BEING WITHIN RANGE	CASH FLOW	PV OF CASH FLOW	PV OF LIBOR
01/01/2010	01/01/2011	1	7,035.62	6,578.17	6,660.39
01/01/2011	01/01/2012	0.193764156	12,000.00	1,936.42	10,217.29
01/01/2012	01/01/2013	0.098463897	12,000.00	874.04	9,307.81
01/01/2013	01/01/2014	0.08585694	12,000.00	676.88	8,274.81
			Price	**10,065.50**	**34,460.30**

Figure 320 Pricing an accrual swap – 2

The instrument pays 12 percent annually if the benchmark rate falls with the range of (12 percent, 12.2 percent).

The results will be as follows.

The "d_2-Lower Bound" uses the lower bound rate of 12.00 percent as X in the formula, whereas "d_2-Upper Bound" uses the upper bound rate of 12.20 percent as X in the formula. In the first row the d_2 values are n/a because the period start date falls before the valuation date.

The probability that the rate will fall within the range is equal to "$N(d_2)$ – lower bound" minus "$N(d_2)$ – upper bound." For the first row the probability will be 1 if F_i lies within the range and 0 otherwise.

The cash flow column is equal to the binary rate (that is, the rate at which payments are to be made) * notional. For the first period, since it is fractional, the cash flow will be multiplied by the remaining tenor in that period to determine the payment: 12% * 100,000 * 0.59.

The PV of cash flow = (cash flow * probability) / ((1+zct_i+1) ^ t_{i+1}). For comparison purposes we show the PV of the actual LIBOR payment = (F_i * Notional)/((1+zct_i+1)^ t_{i+1}). Again for the first period the payment is adjusted for the fractional period.

The price is the sum across PVs.

Commodity linked note

These are similar to the accrual range note in that their payment is tied to the performance of a specific physical commodity or commodity index. The procedure followed is similar to that given above, expect that F_i now represents the future commodity price. This is calculated using the following formula:

$$F_0 = S_0 e^{(r-q)T},$$

where S_0 is the spot price of the commodity today, r is the risk free rate (of the currency in which the price is denominated), q is the convenience yield of the commodity, *T* is the duration between the payment date and

TERMS AND CONDITIONS	
Notional	100,000
Binary rate	12.00%
Payment	Annual
Payment dates	1st Day of the year starting January 2011 and ending on the maturity date
Valuation date	01/06/2010
Maturity date	01/01/2014
Day count convention	A/365
Lower bound	USD 73.00
Upper bound	USD 74.00

Figure 321   Term sheet for a commodity linked note

the valuation date.

For instance let us assume the note ties the payment to the performance of Brent crude oil prices.

PERIOD START (*i*)	PERIOD END (*i*+1)	t_{i+1}	F_i
01/01/2010	01/01/2011	0.59	73.56
01/01/2011	01/01/2012	1.59	71.84
01/01/2012	01/01/2013	2.59	73.26
01/01/2013	01/01/2014	3.59	76.99

Figure 322   Forward prices of the commodity

On the valuation date the price of Brent is US\$ 73.47 per barrel. The

PERIOD START (*i*)	PERIOD END (*i*+1)	t_i	t_{i+1}	ZCt_{i+1}	d_2-LOWER BOUND	d_2-UPPER BOUND	$N(d_2)$- LOWER BOUND	$N(d_2)$- UPPER BOUND
01/01/2010	01/01/2011	n/a	0.59	12.150%	n/a	n/a	n/a	n/a
01/01/2011	01/01/2012	0.59	1.59	12.225%	−1.05	−1.94	0.14662	0.02622
01/01/2012	01/01/2013	1.59	2.59	12.349%	0.13	−0.41	0.55106	0.34024
01/01/2013	01/01/2014	2.59	3.59	12.418%	1.64	1.21	0.94922	0.88773

Figure 323   Pricing a commodity linked note – 1

base volatility of the forward prices is assumed to be 2 percent. The USD risk free rate is 0.2 percent and the convenience yield is assumed to be 0 percent.

The terms for the note are as follows.

PERIOD START (i)	PERIOD END (i+1)	PROBABILITY OF BEING WITHIN RANGE	CASH FLOW	PV OF CASH FLOW
01/01/2010	01/01/2011	1.00000	7,035.62	6,578.17
01/01/2011	01/01/2012	0.12040	12,000.00	1,203.23
01/01/2012	01/01/2013	0.21081	12,000.00	1,871.33
01/01/2013	01/01/2014	0.06149	12,000.00	484.75
			Price	10,137.47

Figure 324   Pricing a commodity linked note – 2

The instrument pays 12 percent annually if the price falls with the range of (73, 74). Using the forward price formula above, the forward prices at each future payment date are as follows.

And the results of the calculation are as follows.

The "d_2-Lower Bound" uses the lower bound price of 73 as X in the formula, whereas "d_2-Upper Bound" uses the upper bound rate of 74 as X in the formula. In the first row, the d_2 values are n/a because the period start date falls before the valuation date.

The probability that the price will fall within the range is equal to "$N(d_2)$ – lower bound" minus "$N(d_2)$ – upper bound." For the first row the probability will be 1 if F_i lies within the range and 0 otherwise.

The cash flow column is equal to the binary rate (that is, the rate at which payments are to be made) * notional. For the first period, since it is fractional, the cash flow will be multiplied by the remaining tenor in that period to determine the payment, i.e. 12% * 100,000 * 0.59.

The PV of cash flow = (cash flow * probability)/((1+zct_{i+1})^ t_{i+1}).

The price is the sum across all PVs.

Annexure 1 – How to determine spot rates and forward rates and yield to maturity

How to determine forward rates from spot rates

The relationship between spot and forward rates is given by the following equation:

$$f_{t-1,1} = (1+s_t)^t \div (1+s_{t-1})^{t-1} - 1$$

	A	B	C
1			
2	**How to determine forward rates from spot rates**		
3			
4	$f_{t-1,t}$ = forward rate applicable for the period (t-1,t)	= $(1+s_t)^t \div (1+s_{t-1})^{t-1}$ -1	
5	s_t is the t-period spot rate		
6		Spot Rate	Tenor (in years)
7		s_1 11.67%	1
8		s_2 12.00%	2
9		=(((1+B8)^C8)/((1+B7)^C7))-1	

8	s_2	12.00%
9	$f_{1,2}$	12.33%
10		

where
S_t is the *t*-period spot rate,
$f_{t-1,t}$ is the forward rate applicable for the period (*t*–1,*t*).

If the 1-year spot rate is 11.67 percent and the 2-year spot rate is 12 percent then the forward rate applicable for the period one year to two years will be:

$$f_{1,2} = (1+12\%)^2 \div (1+11.67\%)^{1-1} = 12.33\%.$$

You may calculate this in EXCEL in the following manner.

How to determine spot rates from forward rates

Alternatively (and equivalently) the relationship between spot rates and forward rates may be given by the following equation:

$$S_t = \sqrt{(1+f_{0,1})(1+f_{1,2})...(1+f_{t-1,t})} - 1.$$

For example, you have been given forward rates as follows:

$f_{0,1} = 11.67\%$
$f_{1,2} = 12.33\%$

	A	B	C	D
12				
13	s_t is the t-period spot rate	$s_t = \sqrt[t]{(1+f_{0,1})(1+f_{1,2})\dots(1+f_{t-1,t})} - 1$		
14				
15	Method 1			
16		$f_{0,1} =$	11.67%		
17		$f_{1,2} =$	12.33%		
18		$f_{2,3} =$	12.55%		
19		$f_{3,4} =$	12.89%		
20		$f_{4,5} =$	13.00%		
21					
22		$s_5 =$	=((1+B16)*(1+B17)*(1+B18)*(1+B19)*(1+B20))^(1/B23)-1		
23		Tenor (in years)=	5		

$f_{2,3} = 12.55\%$
$f_{3,4} = 12.89\%$

	A	B	C
22		$s_5 =$	12.49%	
23		Tenor (in years)=	5	
24				
25	Method 2		Accumulation Factor
26		$f_{0,1} =$	11.67%	111.67%
27		$f_{1,2} =$	12.33%	=1+B27
28		$f_{2,3} =$	12.55%	112.55%

$f_{4,5} = 13.00\%$.

	A	B	C
24				
25	Method 2		Accumulation Factor
26		$f_{0,1} =$	11.67%	111.67%
27		$f_{1,2} =$	12.33%	112.33%
28		$f_{2,3} =$	12.55%	112.55%
29		$f_{3,4} =$	12.89%	112.89%
30		$f_{4,5} =$	13.00%	113.00%
31				
32		$s_5 =$	=PRODUCT(C26:C30)^(1/B33)-1	
33		Tenor (in years)=	5	

30			Tenor (in years)
31		$s_5 =$	12.49%	5
32				

The 5-year spot rate, s_5, will be:

$$[(1+11.67\%)\times(1+12.33\%)\times(1+12.55\%)\times(1+12.89\%)\times(1+13.00\%)]^{1/5}$$
$$-1 = 12.49\%$$

You may calculate this in EXCEL in the following manner:
Alternatively you may first calculate accumulation factors, $1+f$, for each forward rate as follows:
And then calculate the spot rate as follows:

How to calculate the YTM of a bond

The equation below gives the value of a bond at time 0. The cash flows of the bond, coupon payments (CP) and Maturity Value (MV = principal amount + coupon payment) have been discounted at the YTM rate, r, in order to determine the PV of cash flows or alternatively the price or value of the bond (V_{Bond}):

$$V_{Bond} = \left[\sum_{t=1}^{n} \frac{CP_t}{(1+r)^t}\right] + \frac{MV}{(1+r)^n}.$$

For example, you have a 2-year bond with face value (or principal amount) of 100 which will be paid at maturity (the end of the tenor of the bond). The bond pays an annual coupon of 10 at the end of each year. The value of the bond at time 0 is given as 95. Putting these values into the equation above we have:

CP = 10,
MV = Face Value + CP = 100 +10 = 110,
V_{Bond} = 95 = 10/(1+r) +110/(1+r)^2.

This may be solved using a trial and error process or the equation may be solved for in EXCEL using the GOAL SEEK functionality.

Trial and error process for calculating YTM of a bond

1. Start with two points r = 0% and r = 15%.
   When r = 0%, V_{Bond}–Discounted Value = Net PV (NPV) = –25.00.
   When r = 15%, NPV = 3.00.
   Since one value is positive and the other negative the solution lies in the range 0% to 15%.
2. Half the interval. Consider r = 7.5% and r = 15%.
   When r = 7.5%, NPV = –9.49
   When r = 15%, NPV = 3.00.

Again, since one value is positive and the other negative the solution lies in the range 7.5% to 15%.

3. Again half the interval. Consider $r = 11.25\%$ and $r = 15\%$.
When $r = 11.25\%$, NPV = -2.87
When $r = 15\%$, NPV = 3.00.
Again since one value is positive and the other negative the solution lies in the range 11.25% to 15%.

4. Again half the interval. Consider $r = 13.125\%$ and $r = 15\%$.

RANGE		V_{BOND}	DISCOUNT VALUE LOWER Bound	DISCOUNT VALUE UPPER BOUND	$NPV_{Lower\ Bound}$	$NPV_{UPPER\ BOUND}$
0.00000%	15.00000%	95	120.00	91.87	(25.00)	3.13
7.50000%	15.00000%	95	104.49	91.87	(9.49)	3.13
11.25000%	15.00000%	95	97.87	91.87	(2.87)	3.13
13.12500%	15.00000%	95	94.80	91.87	0.20	3.13
11.25000%	13.12500%	95	97.87	94.80	(2.87)	0.20
12.18750%	13.12500%	95	96.31	94.80	(1.31)	0.20
12.65625%	13.12500%	95	95.55	94.80	(0.55)	0.20
12.89063%	13.12500%	95	95.17	94.80	(0.17)	0.20
13.00781%	13.12500%	95	94.98	94.80	0.02	0.20
12.89063%	13.00781%	95	95.17	94.98	(0.17)	0.02
12.94922%	13.00781%	95	95.08	94.98	(0.08)	0.02
12.97852%	13.00781%	95	95.03	94.98	(0.03)	0.02
12.99316%	13.00781%	95	95.01	94.98	(0.01)	0.02
13.00049%	13.00781%	95	94.99	94.98	0.01	0.02
12.99316%	13.00049%	95	95.01	94.99	(0.01)	0.01
12.99683%	13.00049%	95	95.00	94.99	(0.00)	0.01
12.99866%	13.00049%	95	95.00	94.99	0.00	0.01
12.99683%	12.99866%	95	95.00	95.00	(0.00)	0.00
12.99774%	12.99866%	95	95.00	95.00	0.00	0.00
12.99683%	12.99774%	95	95.00	95.00	(0.00)	0.00
12.99728%	12.99774%	95	95.00	95.00	(0.00)	0.00
12.99751%	12.99774%	95	95.00	95.00	0.00	0.00
12.99728%	12.99751%	95	95.00	95.00	(0.00)	0.00
12.99740%	12.99751%	95	95.00	95.00	0.00	0.00
12.99728%	12.99740%	95	95.00	95.00	(0.00)	0.00
12.99734%	12.99740%	95	95.00	95.00	0.00	0.00
12.99728%	12.99734%	95	95.00	95.00	(0.00)	0.00
12.99731%	12.99734%	95	95.00	95.00	(0.00)	0.00
12.99733%	12.99734%	95	95.00	95.00	0.00	0.00
12.99731%	12.99733%	95	95.00	95.00	(0.00)	0.00
12.99732%	12.99733%	95	95.00	95.00	0.00	0.00

RANGE		V_{BOND}	DISCOUNT VALUE LOWER Bound	DISCOUNT VALUE UPPER BOUND	$NPV_{LOWER Bound}$	$NPV_{UPPER BOUND}$
12.99731%	12.99732%	95	95.00	95.00	(0.00)	0.00
12.99732%	12.99732%	95	95.00	95.00	0.00	0.00
12.99731%	12.99732%	95	95.00	95.00	(0.00)	0.00
12.99731%	12.99732%	95	95.00	95.00	0.00	0.00
12.99731%	12.99731%	95	95.00	95.00	(0.00)	0.00

When r = 13.125%, NPV = 0.20.
When r = 15%, NPV = 3.00.
Since both values are positive, the solution lies in the range 11.25% to 13.125% and not 13.125% to 15%.

5. Half the interval between 11.25% and 13.125%. Consider r = 12.1875% and r = 13.125%.
When r = 12.1875%, NPV = −1.31.
When r = 13.125%, NPV = 0.20.

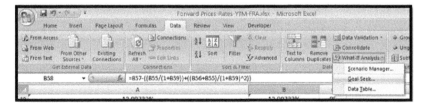

Again, since one value is positive and the other negative the solution lies in the range 12.1875% to 13.125%.

And so on till we arrive at the solution of r = 12.99731%. The complete list of iterations is given in the table below:

A	B	C	D
52			
53		Goal Seek	
54 **Method 2**		Set cell: $B$58	
55 CP are the coupon payments	10.00	To value: 0	
56 MV is the maturity value (Principal Amount + Coupon Payments)	100.00	By changing cell: $B$59	
57 V_{bond} is the price or value of the bond at time 0	95.00	OK Cancel	
58 NPV is the Net Present Value = V_{Bond} -Discount Value of bond cash flows	(1.62)		
59 r is the yield to maturity (YTM)	12%		

EXCEL's goal seek method for calculating YTM of a bond

7 V_{bond} is the price or value of the bond at time 0	95.00
8 NPV is the Net Present Value = V_{Bond} -Discount Value of bond cash flows	(0.0000000)
9 **r is the yield to maturity (YTM)**	**12.99731%**

First set up the input and output cells on the worksheet as follows:

Note that the value of *r* (the YTM) is initially a dummy value.

Next, set up the goal seek functionality. In the data tab, go to the "What-if Analysis" menu and click on "Goal Seek":

Then enter the values in the Goal Seek pop up window as follows:

- Set cell = NPV
- To Value = 0
- By changing cell = YTM.

Click OK to solve for the YTM. The result is as follows:

As you can see Method 2 yields the same results as Method 1 (up to 7 decimal places) and is less cumbersome.

22
The Treasury Function

Trade flows (FX desk)

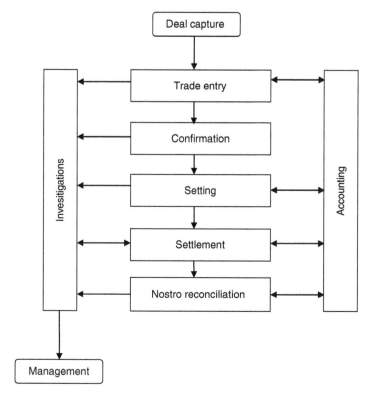

Figure 325   Flow chart for treasury function

The Treasury function operations

There has to be effective segregation of duties between operations personnel (middle and back office) and sales and trading personnel (front office). The front office should enter into transactions while the back office should confirm and settle transactions. Each function should be maintained separately, as without this basic segregation the risk of fraud arises.

Reporting lines for each function should be independent. Other basic segregation controls include separate computer logical access controls to ensure that front office personnel cannot access settlements systems and back office personnel cannot access deal capture systems. Confirmations should be sent directly, to and from, back office staff, and so on.

Front office function

The front office in any treasury is primarily responsible for the trade execution and liquidity management of the bank. A treasury in a bank normally has a Money Market (MM) desk, a Foreign Exchange (FX) desk, a Capital Market (CM) desk and a Derivative desk, characterized by product types. Each desk has multiple dealers; each is designated a different level of authority, based on roles. The major roles that can be defined for the users of a treasury system are:

User roles
1. Treasurer
2. Chief dealer
3. FX dealer
4. MM dealer
5. CM dealer
6. Derivative dealer.

MM desk activities
1. The MM dealer needs a blotter updated with the banks liquidity position at the start of the day.
2. For any transaction to take place, the dealer asks for quotes from the broker or dealing system.
3. He then records the deal information.
4. The limits applicable to the trade must be checked and their availability verified.

5. If none of the limits are breached, the transaction is validated and confirmed.
6. If any of the limits are breached, the deal can either be terminated or sent to the risk management group (or middle office) for re-assignment of limits.
7. If the limits are re-assigned, the transaction is validated and confirmed.
8. The trade impacts the blotter.
9. The cash reserve ratio (CRR) and statutory liquidity ratio (SLR) requirements are actively updated and can be monitored at all times.

FX desk activities

1. For any transaction to take place, the dealer asks for the quotes from the broker or Reuters.
2. He then negotiates FX deals – spot, forward and swap.
3. He then records the deal information.
4. The limits applicable to the trade must be checked and their availability verified.
5. If none of the limits are breached, the transaction is validated and confirmed.
6. If any of the limits are breached, the deal can either be terminated or sent to the risk management group (or middle office) for re-assignment of limits.
7. If the limits are re-assigned, the transaction is validated and confirmed.
8. The trade impacts the FX blotter.
9. In case of transactions involving inflow or outflow of domestic currency, the impact on the MM blotter is also reflected simultaneously.

CM desk activities

1. For any transaction to take place, the dealer asks for quotes from the broker or dealing system.
2. He buys/sells the security at the given rates and records the information.
3. If the deal is executed at that rate, the deal is recorded on the equity blotter.
4. Checks transaction limits (individual equity limits and overall equity exposure limits).
5. Checks the dealer limits, VaR limits, and so on.
6. If limits are breached, takes appropriate action to bring the exposure in line with the limits.
7. At the end of the day, generates a single deal ticket for all buy transactions and generates another deal ticket for all sell transactions.

Middle office function

The middle office is responsible for ensuring adherence to the various tolerance limits specified by the bank management. These limits include net open position (NOP), exposure, counterparty, dealer, product, VaR, stop Loss, currency, broker, and so on. The middle office is also responsible for the proper valuation of the entire portfolio. It also monitors the overall performance of the treasury function at the bank.

User roles

1. Middle office administrator
2. Risk/hedging manager

Activities

1. Monitors and controls limit utilization and excesses
   a. Limits
      - Defines limit
      - Applies limits to transactions
   b. Limit utilization and notification of excesses
2. Conducts risk monitoring and regulatory compliance
3. Undertakes hedging
   a. Hedge policies
      - Identifies the exposure sources, that is, the items that need to be hedged
      - Identifies hedge instruments
   b. Hedge strategies
      - Defines the reasons for hedging the exposures
   c. Monitors hedge success and decides whether to create additional hedges or terminate the existing ones
   d. Reclassifies hedges
      - Based on effectiveness criteria, as per IAS 39
4. Undertakes regulatory and management reporting.

Back office function

The back office is responsible for settling the deal executed by the front office. Once a deal is executed by the dealers, the back offices of the counterparties involved in the transaction confirm the details of the transaction with each other. On the settlement date the transaction is settled by the exchange of funds and/or securities. Further, General Ledger (GL) entries are passed for trades executed and confirmed and the Treasury GL is reconciled with the bank's GL.

In the absence of an active middle office, the back office would also perform the task of limit monitoring.

User roles

1. Cash manager
2. Back office administrator
3. Settlement manager

Activities

The process of trade confirmation and settlement works as follows:

1. Validation of the deal transaction is carried out once the process of confirmation with the counterparty or broker has been completed.
2. If the back office traces any errors during the process of confirmation, the deal ticket is sent back to the concerned dealer for amendment. Once the dealer edits the transaction, the validation process is repeated and the trade re-sent to the back office for confirmation.
3. A confirmation may be generated for supervised deals only.
4. Creation of adjustments to settle tax and brokerage fees.
5. Generation of any documentation necessary, for example SGLA advice.
6. Generation of payment instructions.
7. Creation of journal entries and the posting of such transactions to ledger.

Basic treasury administrator functions

1. Defines all setup information for:
   - Counterparties
   - Brokers
   - Dealers
   - Instruments
   - Products
   - Nostro details of bank and counterparties
   - Central bank account details of bank and interbank counterparties
   - Other account details for DFIs and NBFIs.
2. Sets up limit structure
   - Dealer limits
   - Product limits
   - Counterparty lines and limits
   - Broker limits
   - Currency limits
   - CFS limits
   - Equity trade limits.

3. Maintains daily rates history
   - Revaluation rates of government bonds
   - Interbank offer rates
   - Currency spot and revaluation rates
   - Foreign currency yield curves
   - Equity rates.
4. Maintains schedules
   - Tax
   - Brokerage
   - Currency-wise holiday calendars.

Related terminologies

Four eyes

The ticket workflow is implemented on the four eye principle. All tickets *created* need to pass through a confirmation cycle of *approval, verification* and *authorization*. The creation and approval are conducted by the front office personnel, whereas the remaining two confirmations, verification and authorization, are performed by the back office.

Ticket approval

Once the deal ticket has been created, it needs to be approved by another user residing in the front office. For approval purposes, each user has been provided with a financial limit. If the ticket amount is more than the limit assigned to that user, then the user is not able to approve that ticket.

Ticket verification

Once the deal ticket has been approved, it needs to be verified by another user. The verification is done by a user residing in the back office.

Ticket authorization

Once the deal ticket has been approved and verified, it needs to be authorized by an independent user, once again, residing in the back office. For authorization purposes, each user has been provided with a financial limit. If the ticket amount is more than the limit assigned to that user, then the user is not able to authorize that ticket.

At any stage during the confirmation process the ticket may be returned to the original dealer who created the ticket either for cancellation or for corrections/editing. The edited ticket will be go through the confirmation cycle again: approval, verification and finally authorization.

Confirmation

Whenever a deal is complete, a confirmation letter setting forth the terms and conditions of the deal is sent to the counterparty. A confirmation is then required from the counterparty which usually arrives the same day. The confirmation provides a necessary final check against dealing errors. It should be independent of the trading room (front office) and be performed entirely by operations (back office). Using the data from the settlements and payments systems, the confirmations provide a check to ensure that the operations areas of each party to the deal have recorded the same details for each of the transactions carried out.

The confirmation should contain (at a minimum) details of the counterparties and location, brokerage, transaction date, value/settlement date, settlement instructions, currency amounts and exchange rates (for FX deals), and so on.

The treasury system tracks the confirmation status of all deals including the monitoring of all unconfirmed transactions. There are dour ways of receiving a deal confirmation from the counterparty:

- SWIFT
- Manual confirmation
- System generated confirmation
- Others.

In the event that there are delays or where confirmations are not received there should be an established escalation procedure to follow up on missing confirmations. In addition to this, management also needs to be informed.

Risk in the confirmation process arises either when discrepancies are missed or when trades are not confirmed. Failure by the counterparty to send confirmations could be the first sign that the counterparty is facing impending financial failure.

Society for Worldwide Interbank Financial Telecommunications (SWIFT)

Financial services organizations worldwide face increasingly complex and diverse messaging requirements. These include connecting to market infrastructures, communication with commercial correspondents and servicing clients. SWIFTNet is SWIFT's advanced Internet protocol-based messaging platform. It provides a single window that caters for all these messaging needs.

Settlement

Settlement entails carrying out a series of duties in respect of all transactions emanating from the front office effectively leading to making an actual payment.

Settlement risk is the risk that after having sent the payment instructions, there is a delay in receiving the payment or the payment is not made at all, that is, there is a default.

Price discovery

Price discovery is the process by which buyers and sellers interact to determine the fair market price of an asset. Trading in the financial markets is about obtaining prices. In efficient financial markets prices reflect the future risk and return associated with a security. But trading decisions also impact how prices will move and trading activities continuously feed new information into market prices.

Proprietary trading

Proprietary (or prop) trading is the means by which the bank trades stocks, bonds, options, commodities, derivatives or other financial instruments for its own account, that is, for its own profit rather than trading on behalf of its customers. It involves active position taking with a view to capital gain. Banks involved in this form of trading believe that they have a competitive advantage that will allow then to earn excess returns. Their aim therefore is to directly benefit from the market rather than through the commissions they could earn from processing trades on behalf of their customers. Due to the volatility in the markets, earnings from proprietary trading tend to be more volatile as compared to the bank's earnings from processing client trades.

Banks engaged in proprietary trading usually have separate desks that are solely devoted to prop trade. These desks work in isolation from those processing trades on behalf of the bank's clients. The objective of these desks is to earn profits that are above those that could be earned in their normal market-making trades. Another reason why the trading desk is kept separate from the other desks is to avoid conflicts of interest or situations where the prop desk's trades could harm the bank's customers' interests. One such activity is *fronting running* a customer's order, where the prop desk knowingly purchases shares ahead of the customers' trades so as to benefit from the price increases that could result when the customers' deals are processed. This results in profits for the prop desk at the cost of the banks customers, who end up paying higher prices on their trades.

Operational risk

The following are some of the operational risks that a Treasury function may face.

Transaction risk: Execution error, product complexity, booking error, settlement error, commodity delivery risk, documentary/contract risk.

Operational control risk: Exceeding limit, rogue trading, money laundering, security risk, key personnel risk, processing risk.

Systems risk: Programming error, model/methodology error, IT systems failure, telecommunications failure.

Business events risk: Currency convertibility risk, shift in credit rating, reputation risk, legal risk, taxation risk, disaster risk, wars, collapse/suspension of market.

Regulatory risk: Breaching capital requirements, regulatory changes.

23
Advanced Products

Structured products

Cross currency swaps

A swap is an agreement between two companies to exchange cash flows in the future. It is different from a forward contract in that a forward contract requires settlement of cash flows on just one future date, whereas a swap leads to cash flow exchanges taking place on several future dates. A cross currency swap (CCS) specifically involves an exchange of a stream of principal and interest payments in one currency for a stream of principal and interest payments in another currency over multiple specified interest periods. As well as the exchange of interest payments, there is also an exchange of the principals (in two different currencies) at the beginning of the contract and at the end.

The principal amount to be swapped is established in one currency. The prevailing spot exchange rate is used to establish the amount in the other currency. The legs of the swap are in different currencies and the interest rates of the two legs can be both fixed-rate, both floating-rate or one fixed-rate and one floating-rate. The interest flows are swapped at the end of each interest period. The exchange rate is set at the beginning of the transaction and is fixed for the entire life of the CCS.

Currency swap is an off-balance sheet item and is economically equivalent to a portfolio of forward currency contracts.

Participating forwards

The participating forward is a hybrid of a forward contract and an option contract. The basic participating forward requires the simultaneous purchase of a forward contract and call option to hedge a foreign currency payable, or the sale of a forward contract and the purchase of a put option to hedge a foreign currency receivable. Forwards and options can be used in any ratio adding up to 100 percent coverage. Changing the ratio of the forward contracts to the foreign currency options changes the participation level. While providing full downside protection, the ratio allows for partial participation in favorable moves of the exchange rate.

They are usually structured so that there is no upfront premium.

Example of how a participating forward contract works
The buyer protects against a strengthening Euro by executing a participating forward contract with a 1.30 cap and a 50 percent participation level expiring June 29. If at expiry the EUR spot is:

- Above 1.30, the buyer can purchase 100 percent of EUR at 1.30,
- Below 1.30 (for example, 1.20), the buyer can purchase 50 percent of EUR at 1.30 and the balance at 1.20, creating a blended rate of 1.25.

Equity linked notes

These are instruments whose returns are determined by the performance of a single equity security, a basket of equity securities or an equity index. A sample term sheet for an equity linked note is given below:

XYZ Bank	
5-Year Equity-Linked Structured Deposit (Bullish Equity Index – Bearish Bond Index)	
Term Sheet	
This 5-year SGD Equity-Linked Structured Deposit ("SD") offers depositors an opportunity to have yield enhancement linked to the relative performance of an equity index and a bond index. An Interest Rate of 4.00% per annum* is payable if the return of the equity index is greater than or equal to the return of the bond index, otherwise, no interest will be payable for the relevant 6-month period. In addition, the SD can be terminated early upon the occurrence of a Trigger Event, when the return of the equity index outperforms the bond index by 15% or more on any 6-monthly valuation dates. Upon Early Termination, depositors will be repaid with 100% of the principal amount plus the applicable accrued interest. The SD is 100% principal protected when it is held to maturity **.	
Principal Amount	Minimum of SGD 5,000 and in subsequent multiples of SGD 1,000.
Deposit Taker	XYZ Bank ("the Bank")
Deposit Start Date	5 December 2005
Maturity Date	6 December 2010 (subject to Early Termination Provision as stated below)
Interest Period	Every 6 months, ending on but excluding every 5th of June and December of each year, commencing from the Deposit Start Date to but excluding the Maturity Date.

Figure 326 Term sheet for an equity linked note

Interest Payment Dates	Semi-annually on every 5th of June and December, commencing on 5th June 2006, to and including the Maturity Date, subject to adjustment in accordance with the Following Business Day Convention.
Interest Rate Formula	The Interest Rate (t) for each 6-month period is determined as either: A. 4.00% per annum – if the Equity Return (t) is greater than or equal to the Bond Return (t) on the Valuation Date (t), or B. 0% per annum – if the Equity Return (t) is less than the Bond Return (t) on the Valuation Date (t)
Interest Amount	= Principal Amount × Interest Rate × Actual Number of Days in the Interest Period/365
Equity Return (t)	The ratio of the Equity Index Level (t) for period (t) over the initial Equity Index Level (0).
Equity Index Level (t)	The Official Closing Level of the Equity Index on Valuation Date (t).
Equity Index Level (0)	The Official Closing Level of the Equity Index on the Initial Valuation Date.
Bond Return (t)	The ratio of the Bond Index Level (t) for period (t) over the initial Bond Index Level (0).
Bond Index Level (t)	The Official Closing Level of the Bond Index on Valuation Date (t).
Bond Index Level (0)	The Official Closing Level of the Bond Index on the Initial Valuation Date.
Initial Valuation Date	1 December 2005 (or the first day thereafter that is a Scheduled Trading Day if 1 December 2005 is not a Scheduled Trading Day).
Valuation Date (t)	The Valuation Date for a relevant 6-month period shall be the date which is 5 Business Days prior to the Interest Payment Dates.
Trigger Event	A Trigger Event shall deem to have occurred if the rate differential, measured as the Equity Return minus the Bond Return, is greater than or equal to 15% on any Valuation Date (t).
Early Termination Provision	Upon the occurrence of the Trigger Event, the Depositor will be repaid with an Early Termination Amount on the Early Termination Payment Date.
Early Termination Amount	100% of the Principal Amount plus applicable Interest Amount.
Early Termination Payment Date	The immediate Interest Payment Date following the occurrence of the Trigger Event.

Figure 326 Continued

Pre-Mature Withdrawal Fee	The full tenor of this deposit is 5 years and Depositor should keep the Deposit until maturity unless the Early Termination Provision applies. If a Depositor wants to pre-maturely withdraw the Deposit, it can only be done on a monthly basis (middle of the month) and the Depositor must pay a Pre- Mature Withdrawal Fee, derived as the cost of replacing the above Deposit at market rates for such tenor. A minimum of 1% will be imposed if such pre-mature withdrawal is made within the first 6 months.

Notes:
* Under the worst case scenario where the Equity Return is less than the Bond Return on every Valuation Date till maturity, the effective rate of return is 0.00% p.a.
** Full amount (100%) of the Principal Amount will be protected provided that there is no pre-mature withdrawal of the deposit by the depositor before the Maturity Date. Should depositor choose to early terminate the deposit, charges will be incurred and the Principal Amount may be subject to deduction. The charges will be calculated based on the replacement cost of such deposit at the then prevailing market rates and any administrative costs that may be incurred by the Bank.

Figure 326   Continued

Capital protected/capital guaranteed notes

Under the capital protected note (CPN) the principal investment of the buyer is protected and is the minimum amount returned at maturity. In addition to this, the purchaser also has the opportunity to participate in specific markets/segments and enjoy the benefit of exposure to a selected asset class. Returns are linked to the performance of the underlying asset or combination of assets such as stock market indices, interest rates, foreign exchange or commodity markets.

Key elements of a CPN term sheet are given below.

Capital protection	This is the minimum amount of your capital that the Issuer agrees to return to you at maturity. It may not necessarily be 100% and the capital protection offered at redemption will be set out clearly for each CPN Issue.
Asset linkage	Each CPN Issue is linked to an underlying asset or combination of assets.
Participation rate	This measures how much you will participate in any movements to the underlying assets that the CPN is tracking.
Issuer and credit rating	The Issuer(s) of each CPN and their credit rating, as quoted by Standard &Poors, Moody's and/or Fitch.
Currency	A CPN may be issued in any of the major currencies, for example, AUD, EUR, GBP, JPY, SGD, USD.

Figure 327   Key elements of a capital protected note term sheet

Minimum investment	The minimum initial amount required from you to purchase a new CPN Issue.
Denomination	The minimum currency value of an individual CPN Issue which is also referred to as the nominal value.
Term	The life span of the CPN Issue from settlement date to maturity.
Subscription period	The time period during which you can subscribe to a specific CPN Issue.
Call feature (callable/ non-callable)	The Issuer of a callable CPN reserves the right to call back the CPN at a certain stage in the CPN's life and guarantees a fixed level of redemption. A non-callable CPN cannot be called by the issuer prior to maturity.

Figure 327   Continued

Commodity linked notes

These are instruments whose returns are tied to the performance of a specific physical commodity or commodity index. A sample term sheet for a commodity linked note is given below.

Term Sheet (To Prospectus dated April 20, 2009, Series L Prospectus Supplement dated April 21, 2009, and Product Supplement CLN-2 dated December 29, 2009) April 30, 2010 Commodity-Linked Notes Linked to the Dow Jones-UBS Commodity Index^{SM} 2 Month Forward Total Return, due June 7, 2011	
Issuer:	Bank of America Corporation
Pricing Date:	April 30, 2010
Issue Date:	May 7, 2010
Stated Maturity Date:	June 7, 2011
Aggregate Principal Amount:	$8,000,000
Underlying Index:	The Dow Jones-UBS Commodity Index^{SM} 2 Month Forward Total Return (Bloomberg symbol: "DJUBSF2T")
Starting Value:	TBD

Figure 328   Term sheet for a commodity linked note

Ending Value:	The closing level of the Underlying Index on the Valuation Date. If it is determined that the scheduled Valuation Date is not a business day, or if a Market Disruption Event occurs on the scheduled Valuation Date, the Ending Value will be determined as more fully described in product supplement CLN-2.
Leverage Factor:	3
Investor Fee:	The greater of (a) the fixed percentage of 0.00% and (b) a percentage equal to 0.42% per annum, as described in product supplement CLN-2 under "Description of the Notes – Payment at Maturity."
Treasury Rate Charge:	Applicable
Interest Rate Basis:	LIBOR
Designated Maturity:	One Month
Interest Reset Dates:	The 7th of each calendar month, commencing on June 7, 2010.
Interest Payment Dates:	Unless the Notes are redeemed on an earlier date, interest will be payable only at maturity.
Spread:	Minus 10 basis points
Initial Optional Redemption Date:	May 7, 2010
Upper Mandatory Redemption Trigger Level	Not Applicable
Lower Mandatory Redemption Trigger Level	85% of the Starting Value
NPV Factor	Not Applicable
Bear Note	No
Calculation Agent	Merrill Lynch Commodities, Inc.
Listing	No listing on any securities exchange.

Figure 328 Continued

Range accruals

Range accruals are a form of interest accrual in which the coupon rate is only earned on days when another rate from which the coupon is derived falls within a specified range. Applied to FX rates, the payoff on the contract at expiration is dependent on how long an exchange rate has been within a specified range. The usual payoff is an amount proportional to the fraction of time the exchange rate has been within the range. For a typical contract this proportion would be number of days in range/ number of days in period.

A sample term sheet is given below.

6 Month In-Out Range Accrual Option in **MXN/USD FX Rate**	
Settlement Date	One week from Trade Date
Maturity Date	6 months from Trade Date
Option Premium	USD 50,000
Option Type	IN minus OUT Range Accrual on MXN/USD FX rate
Option payment date	2 business days after Maturity Date
Option Payout	USD 125000*Index
Where Index equals	(FX daily IN minus FX daily Out)/Total Business Day
FX daily IN	The number of business days Spot MXN/USD exchange rate is within Range
FX daily OUT	The number of business days Spot MXN/USD exchange rate is outside Range
Range	MXN/USD 7.7200–8.1300
Spot MXN/USD Exchange Rate	Official Spot exchange rate as determined by the Bank of Mexico as appearing on Reuters page "BNMX" at approximately 3:00 pm New York time
Current Spot MXN/USD	7.7800

Figure 329   Term sheet for a range accrual option

Switchable

Switchable 1

Currency   AED
Maturity   5Y
Start   Spot
Client pays   2.95%
Client receives   (3M Ebor) *n/N Subject to range: 3M Ebor [0–5%]
Client has the right after 3Y and quarterly thereafter to cancel the swap and receive 0.30% quarterly

Alternative level

Client pays   3.55%
Client receives   (3M Ebor) *n/N Subject to range: 3M Ebor [0–5.75%]
Client has the right after 3Y and quarterly thereafter to cancel the swap and receive 0.30% quarterly

Figure 330   Sample trade tickets for switchables

Interest rate differential (IRD) trades

Swap Basis

	Cras	Floating Cras	Cras	Cras
	5y	5y	10y	5y
Settlement	11-Aug-2008	11-Aug-2008	11-Aug-2008	11-Aug-2008
Maturity	11-Aug-2013	11-Aug-2013	11-Aug-2018	11-Aug-2013
Currency	AED	AED	AED	Sibor
Index	3m Eibor	3m Eibor	3m Eibor	3m Sibor
Range	0% - 7%	0% - 7%	0% - 8%	0% - 7.20%
Coupon	7.20%	3M Eibor + 2.5%	7.90%	7.00%
Call Feature	Nc3M 3M	Nc3M 3M	Nc3M 3M	Nc3M 3M
Coupon Basis	Quarterly,Modified Following A360 on both legs	Quarterly,Modified Following A360 on both legs	Quarterly,Modified Following A360 on both legs	Quarterly,Modified Following A360 on both legs

Figure 331   Sample trade ticket for an IRD swap

Note basis

	Cras	Cras
	5y	10y
Settlement	4 weeks	4 weeks
Maturity	4-Sep-2013	4-Sep-2018
Issuer	Hsbc Plc	Hsbc Plc
Currency	AED	AED
Index	3m Eibor	3m Eibor
Range	0% - 6.5%	0% - 7.25%
Coupon	6.00%	7.25%
Call Feature	Nc3M 3M	Nc3M 3M
Coupon Basis	Quarterly,Modified Following A360 on both legs	Quarterly,Modified Following A360 on both legs
Offer Price	98.50%	99.50%

Figure 332   Sample trade ticket for an IRD note

Quanto

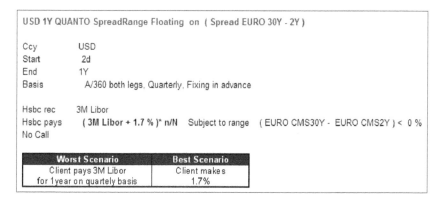

Figure 333   Sample trade ticket for a quanto

Cumulative cap

Start Date	1w
Maturity	Start Date +10 years
Client pays	3mLIBOR + Top Up (Q, A/360,MF) Q1-4 Top Up= 0 Q5- Q40 Previous Top Up + Max { Index - Strike ,0%}
Client receives	3mLIBOR + Carry (Q, A/360,MF)

Index	Strike	Carry
10Y CMS fixing in arrears	7.55%	1.5%
3m Libor fixing in arrears	7.4%	1.5%

Reference Information	3m Libor 2.802% 10Y Swap 4.764%

Historical Data for 3m Libor and 10Y CMS

	USD spot-into-10 year swap rate				USD spot-into-3M swap rate		
	Statistics from 01-Jan-1991 to 26-Jul-2008				**Statistics from 01-Jan-1991 to 25-Jul-2008**		
Current (bp)	4.71	Avg (bp)	6.13	10 chg (bp)	-7.2		
High (bp)	8.15	StdDev	1.22	1W chg (bp)	-6.8		
Low (bp)	3.44	Z-score	-1.16	1M chg (bp)	-10.2		

The historical back-testing case here is clearly not as strong as the Top Up floors. However 3m Libor has not fixed above the barrier in the last 17 odd years and in the last two cycles when the 10Y CMS fixed above the barrier, the short term rates were more than 3% higher than what they are today.

Also the fact that the USD inflation curve is inverted might lead some observers to believe that the high inflation threat is relevant only for the near future. Attached below is the USD Zero Coupon Inflation Swap Curve and its worth pointing out that the curve looks like this despite the fact that the last CPI YOY reading was 5.0%. If your view is that inflation is a short term threat only, then one of the biggest drivers for higher rates is taken out of consideration.

	1Y	2Y	3Y	4Y	5Y	6Y	7Y	8Y	9Y	10Y	15Y	20Y	30Y
Spot	3.01	2.85	2.86	2.88	2.91	2.93	2.90	2.91	2.92	2.89	2.86	2.85	2.86

MTM Sensitivity

Assumptions

1) The analysis is done assuming that the shifts happen immediately after the trade date and for a notional of 10 mio USD

2) The rate and volatility sensitivity is calculated by shifting the rate and volatility curve in parallel

Figure 334   Sample term sheet for a cumulative cap

3) Positive numbers refer to the MTM sensitivity in favour of the client and negative(red) numbers are against the client

10Y Underlying trade MTM analysis

Structure Sensitivity

Shift	Vols Unchanged	Vols 1% Lower	Vols 2% Lower
+ 25bps	547,105	448,498	222,675
+ 50bps	1,293,079	738,591	283,396
+ 100bps	2,888,762	2,278,891	1,728,257

Shift	Vols Unchanged	Vols 1% Higher	Vols 2% Higher
- 25bps	442,671	132,689	-291,776
- 50bps	884,762	548,420	272,158
- 100bps	1,294,077	1,135,678	987,480

3m Underlying trade MTM analysis

Structure Sensitivity

Shift	Vols Unchanged	Vols 1% Lower	Vols 2% Lower
+ 25bps	467,678	175,973	92,679
+ 50bps	1,011,590	684,037	383,103
+ 100bps	2,322,795	1,833,707	1,547,947

Shift	Vols Unchanged	Vols 1% Higher	Vols 2% Higher
- 25bps	481,912	171,531	-72,878
- 50bps	734,840	538,317	338,487
- 100bps	1,321,322	1,098,444	851,575

USD CUMULATIVE CAP

It's a simple variation of the TOP Up. Here instead of client selling us cumulative floors on strikes of 3.00% or below on USD 10Y CMS, the client sells us cumulative caps on strikes of 7.35% or above on USD 3m Libor/10Y CMS. Please note that this is a leveraged trade and we have thus attached the MTM sensitivity of the trade below.

Figure 334 Continued

Steepener/flattener note

A steepener/flattener note takes advantage of how the yields on shorter term issues move in relation to the yields on longer term issues when interest rates change.

Definition: flatteners and steepeners
A flattener takes place when:

- The yield on longer dated issues moves up at a slower pace than the yield on shorter dated issues while interest rates are moving up.
- A decline in interest rates results in the yield on the longer dated issue decreasing at a faster pace than the yield on the shorter dated issue.
- The yield on the shorter dated issue is increasing while the yield on the longer dated issue is falling.

In general, a flattener is said to occur if the movement of yields between the longer dated issue and the shorter dated issue results in a *narrowing* or *flattening* of the spread between them.

A steepener takes place when there is a *widening* of the spread between the longer dated issue and the shorter dated issue.

5y HSBC EUR Steepener Note		10y HSBC EUR Steepener Note	
Currency	EUR	Currency	EUR
Start	3w	Start	3w
Maturity	5y	Maturity	10y
	q. 30/360		q. 30/360
Coupon	8*(1.25% + Index),	Coupon	8*(1.25% + Index),
	floor 0%, and cap 8%		floor 0%, and cap 8%
Index	EUR CMS(30-2)y, in arrears	Index	EUR CMS(30-2)y, in arrears
NC3m3m		NC3m3m	
Price	99.90%	Price	99.50%

Figure 335   Sample trade tickets for steepener notes

Inverted curve instrument

These products are used to take advantage of the inversion of a particular yield curve.

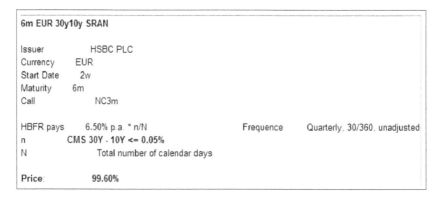

Figure 336   Sample trade ticket for an inverted curve instrument

Ranges

```
5y Libor single range step-up

Start Date      3w
Maturity         5y
Currency     USD
Call                    NC3m3m
Issuer              HSBC PLC
Coupon       6.50% * n/N
n                    Y1-2: 0% < 3m Libor < 5.00%
                         Y3-5: 0% < 3m Libor < 6.00%

N                      Total number of calendar days
Basis              quarterly, 30/360 unadjusted

Price                 99.20%
```

Figure 337 Sample trade ticket for a single range step up

```
5y CMS tiered range

Start Date      3w
Maturity         5y
Currency     USD
Call                    NC3m3m
Issuer              HSBC PLC
Coupon       3.60% * n1/N + 3.60% * n2/N
n1                      0% < CMS 10y < 5.50%
n2                      0% < CMS 10y < 7.00%

N                      Total number of calendar days
Basis              quarterly, 30/360 unadjusted

Price                 99.50%
```

Figure 338 Sample trade ticket for a tiered range

```
┌─────────────────────────────────────────────────────┐
│ 5y RMS range                                         │
│                                                      │
│ Start Date        3w                                 │
│ Maturity          5y                                 │
│ Currency        USD                                  │
│ Call                     NC3m3m                      │
│ Issuer                 HSBC PLC                       │
│ Coupon         7.00% * n/N                           │
│ n                   Y1:    0 < CMS 5Y < 6.0 %         │
│                                                      │
│                     ...                              │
│                   Y5:    0 < CMS 1Y < 6.0 %          │
│ N                  Total number of calendar days     │
│ Basis             quarterly, 30/360 unadjusted       │
│                                                      │
│ Price               99.15%                           │
└─────────────────────────────────────────────────────┘
```

Figure 339   Sample trade ticket for a range note

Credit products

Credit default swaps

This swap transfers the credit risk of fixed income products, such as municipal bonds, mortgage backed securities and corporate debt between two parties. The buyer of the credit swap receives credit protection against default, a credit rating downgrade or any other negative credit event. The seller of the product assumes the risk and in return receives a periodic payment. The contract references an underlying fixed income instrument which is known as a 'reference entity'. In the event that the negative credit event occurs, the seller will be obligated to deliver either the current cash value of the referenced bonds or the actual bonds to the buyer, depending on the terms of the contract.

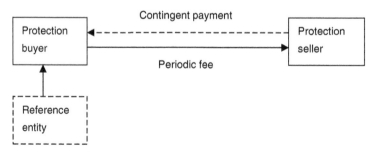

Figure 340   Structure of a credit default swap

SAMPLE TERM SHEET FOR A CREDIT DEFAULT SWAP TRADED BY XYZ BANK PLC	
DRAFT TERMS – CREDIT DEFAULT SWAP	
1. General Terms	
Trade Date	Aug 5, 2003
Effective Date	Aug 6, 2003
Scheduled Termination Date	Jul 30, 2005
Floating Rate Payer ('Seller')	XYZ Bank plc, London branch
Fixed Rate Payer ('Buyer')	ABC Investment Bank plc
Calculation Agent	Seller
Calculation Agent City	New York
Business Day	New York
Business Day Convention	Following
Reference Entity	Jackfruit Records Corporation
Reference Obligation	Primary Obligor: Jackfruit Records
Maturity	Jun 30, 2020
Coupon	0%
CUSIP/ISIN	xxxxx
Original Issue Amount	USD 100,000,000
Reference Price	100%
All Guarantees	Not Applicable
2. Fixed Payments	
Fixed Rate Payer	
Calculation Amount	USD 7,000,000
Fixed Rate	0.3% per annum
Fixed Rate Payer Payment Date(s)	Oct 30, Jan 30, Apr 30, Jul 30, starting Oct 30, 2003
Fixed Rate Day Count Fraction	Actual/360
3. Floating Payments	
Floating Rate Payer	
Calculation Amount	USD 7,000,000
Conditions to Payment	Credit Event Notice (Notifying Parties: Buyer or Seller) Notice of Publicly Available Information: Applicable (Public Source: Standard Public Sources. Specified Number: Two)
Credit Events	Bankruptcy, Failure to Pay (Grace Period Extension: Not Applicable. Payment Requirement: $1,000,000)
Obligation(s)	Borrowed Money

Figure 341 Sample term sheet for a credit default swap

4. Settlement Terms	
Settlement Method	Physical Settlement
Settlement Currency	The currency in which the Floating Rate Payer Calculation Amount is denominated
Terms Relating to Physical Settlement	
Physical Settlement Period	The longest of the number of business days for settlement in accordance with the then-current market practice of any Deliverable Obligation being Delivered in the Portfolio, as determined by the Calculation Agent, after consultation with the parties, but in no event shall be more than 30 days
Portfolio	Exclude Accrued Interest
Deliverable Obligations	Bond or Loan
Deliverable Obligation Characteristics	Not Subordinated Specified Currency – Standard Specified Currencies Maximum Maturity: 30 years Not Contingent Not Bearer Transferable Assignable Loan Consent Required Loan
Restructuring Maturity Limitation	Not Applicable
Partial Cash Settlement of Loans	Not Applicable
Partial Cash Settlement of Assignable Loans	Not Applicable
Escrow	Applicable

5. Documentation

Confirmation to be prepared by the Seller and agreed to by the Buyer. The definitions and provisions contained in the 2003 ISDA Credit Derivatives Definitions, as published by the International Swaps and Derivatives Association, Inc., as supplemented by the May 2003 Supplement, to the 2003 ISDA Credit Derivatives Definitions (together, the 'Credit Derivatives Definitions'), are incorporated into the Confirmation

6. Notice and Account Details

Telephone, Telex and/or Buyer:
Facsimile Numbers and Phone:
Contact Details for Notices Fax:
Seller: A.N. Other
Phone: +1 212-xxx-xxxx
Fax: +1 212-xxx-xxxx
Account Details of Seller 84-7512562-85

Figure 341 Continued

> **Risks and Characteristics**
> *Credit Risk.* An investor's ability to collect any premium will depend on the ability of XYZ Bank plc to pay.
> *Non-Marketability.* Swaps are not registered instruments and they do not trade on any exchange. It may be impossible for the transactor in a swap to transfer the obligations under the swap to another holder. Swaps are customised instruments and there is no central source to obtain prices from other dealers.

Figure 341 Continued

Total return swaps

This is a swap agreement in which one party makes payments based on a set rate, either fixed or floating, while the other party makes payments based on the return of an underlying asset, which includes both the income it generates and any capital gains. In total return swaps, the underlying asset, referred to as the reference asset, is usually an equity index, loans, or bonds.

The total return swap allows the user to accept the economic benefits of asset ownership without utilizing the balance sheet. The other leg of the swap, usually LIBOR, is spread to reflect the non-balance sheet nature of the product. A total return swap can be designed with any underlying asset agreed between two parties. No notional amounts are exchanged with the swap. The total return payer is the legal owner of the reference asset.

The total return receiver may also be required to post initial collateral as well as marginal collateral in the event that the market price of the collateral declines.

A key element of a total return swap is that both the market risk and the credit risk of the underlying asset are transferred.

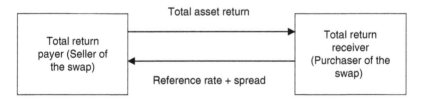

Figure 342 Structure of a total return swap

Reference Asset Details	
Reference Party	Sinclair Broadcast Group
Facility Type	Bond
Notional Amount	USD 10 million
Facility Maturity Date	15th July 2007
Coupon Rate	9%
Swap Details	
Initial Price of Reference Asset	102%
Swap Counterparty	Bank ABC
Trade Date	5th August 2002
Swap Termination Date	8th August 2005
Swap Amount	USD 10 million
Settlements	Semi-Annual
Reference Rate	6-month LIBOR
Deal Spread	0.85%
Initial Collateral	An amount of cash equal to 10% of the swap funded amount
Marginal Collateral	Cash collateral by the swap receiver to the swap payer. Greater of Reference Asset Initial Price minus the Market Price, and zero

Figure 343   Sample term sheet of a total return swap

Collateralized debt obligation (CDO)

A collateralized debt obligation (CDO) is a debt security collateralized by a variety of debt obligations including bonds and loans of different maturities and credit quality. It is designed to give protection against losses in a portfolio. Returns on the CDOs are paid in tranches. Each tranche has a different maturity and risk associated with it. The higher the risk, the more the CDO will pay the protection buyer.

There are two types of cash flows in this instrument. Periodic premiums are paid by the protection buyer to the seller. There may also be an upfront premium. In return the buyer will receive the amount of loss suffered by the tranche that he has acquired.

Notes

Chapter 1

1. We use the term trader to denote a price trader – an individual who makes a living by buying or selling securities, commodities, currencies, bonds, or any combination of the above.
2. See Occam's Razor, also Ockham's Razor.
3. See Annexure 2 of this chapter for details on how to calculate returns, volatility and rolling volatility.
4. *Source:* Emirates Group Financial Statement & Disclosures, 2011–12–13.

Chapter 3

1. See http://www.derivativesstrategy.com/magazine/archive/1997/0497 fea2.asp and http://www.derivativesstrategy.com/magazine/archive/1997/1296qa.asp for the original VaR debate between Taleb and Jorion.
2. For formulas of duration and convexity, see Annexure 2: Risk Metrics.
3. For a more detailed review of value at risk the reader is referred to.

Chapter 4

1. See http://baselinescenario.com/2013/02/09/the-importance-of-excel/ and https://news.ycombinator.com/item?id=5198187.
2. http://files.shareholder.com/downloads/ONE/2272984969x0x628656/4cb574a0-0bf5-4728-9582-625e4519b5ab/Task_Force_Report.pdf.
3. Request for proposal

Chapter 5

1. See Antifragile, Nicholas Nassim Taleb.
2. See *Determination of the risk of ruin* by Joseph De Vinso, Working paper 18–76a, University of Pennsylvania.
3. Please see Integrating Corporate Risk Management, 1st Edition, Prakash Shimpi, Jan 2001, TextRe Publications.
4. http://www.bis.org/publ/bcbs188.pdf
5. http://www.bis.org/publ/bcbs144.pdf
6. See *The End of Wall Street*, Roger Lowenstein, March 2011, Penguin for an insightful and detailed timeline of the 2008 financial crisis.

Chapter 6

1. See the following video for the accompanying video lecture for this section. https://www.youtube.com/watch?v=E0TdEUr9tAc.
2. Also see Derivation and interpretation of Black Scholes Model – Teaching Note, Don Chance, Louisiana State University Business School, at http://www.bus.lsu.edu/academics/finance/faculty/dchance/Instructional/TN99-02.pdf
3. See, Fooled by Randomness, Nicholas Nassim Taleb, Penguin Books, 2001.
4. See http://www.ltnielsen.com/wp-content/uploads/Understanding.pdf

Chapter 7

1. For background reading see the following two papers:
   Forecasting the term structure of government bond yields, Francis X Diebold and Canlin Li, Wharton Financial Institution Center, Working Paper series, Aug 2002 http://fic.wharton.upenn.edu/fic/papers/02/0234.pdf and
   The Volatility of Short-Term Interest Rates: An Empirical Comparison of Alternative Models of the Term Structure of Interest rates by K.C. Chan, G. Andrew Karyoli, Francis A. Longstaff and Anthony B. Sanders (1992) at http://financetrainingcourse.com/wp-content/uploads/2010/08/CKLS-Chan-Paper.pdf
2. State Bank of Pakistan increased the policy rate by 50 basis points to 13 percent on August 2, 2010 and again by another 50 basis points to 13.5 percent on September 30, 2010. In hindsight, had the assumption of the impossibility of further tightening not been included in our model and based on the assumption that the minimum difference between the policy discount rate and core inflation was 0 percent, our projections would have indicated a rise in policy rates to 13.43 percent for FY 2011 under the best-case scenario.

Chapter 10

1. Average of 2013 spot prices to date (till June 7, 2013).

Chapter 13

1. Data from Monthly Review on Price Indices published by the Federal Bureau of Statistics (Pakistan) on their website (www.statpak.gov.pk).
2. West Texas Intermediate Spot Prices, Cushing OK, available on the Energy Information Administration (EIA) website.

Chapter 15

1. $\ln\left(\dfrac{\text{volatility}_{jul\,2012-jun\,2013}}{\text{volatility}_{jul\,2011-jun\,2012}}\right)$

2. Sugar cash prices were no longer available on the Wall Street Journal website after June 30, 2011. Hence they were not considered in the calculations and analysis for periods falling after this date.
3. All commodity prices except Silver are denominated in USD. Silver prices are denominated in Sterling.
4. Lower Bound = Price * (1 − 3 * volatility), floored at zero
5. Upper Bound = Price * (1 + 3 * volatility)
6. For 2013 the calculations are for the period Jan 1, 2013 to June 18, 2013.
7. Sugar cash prices were only available on the Wall Street Journal website till June 30, 2011. Sugar therefore will not be included in calculations for any period which includes dates that fall after this date.

Chapter 19

The outline of this chapter is based on John C Hull's description of the option products universe in Options, Futures & Other derivatives. For a more detailed treatment of the product universe please see Options, Futures & Other Derivatives, 7th Edition, John C. Hull, Prentice Hall, 2009 and Paul Wilmott on Quantitative Finance, 2nd Edition, Volume 1, 2 & 3, John Wiley & Sons, 2006.

Chapter 20

1. In this chapter we have focused on pricing options. Hence the terms 'derivative' or 'option' have been used interchangeably.
2. The material in this section is based on the teaching notes of Professor Mark Broadie from the Security Pricing Class at Columbia Business School. For a more detailed and comprehensive treatment please see Hedging with Trees. Advances in Pricing and Risk Managing Derivatives, Mark Broadie, Paul Glasserman, Risk Books, 1998 and Monte Carlo Methods in Financial Engineering, by Paul Galsserman, Springer 2004.

Chapter 21

1. The material in this chapter is based on the teaching notes of the Advance Derivatives class of Professor Howard Corb at Columbia Business School. For a more detailed and comprehensive treatment of the same topic please see Interest Rate Swaps and other Derivatives, Howard Corb, Columbia Business School Publishing, 2012.

Bibliography

Part I   What Is Risk?

1. *Fooled by Randomness*, Nicholas Nassim Taleb, Random House Trade, 2005.
2. *The Black Swan: The Impact of the Highly Improbable*, Nassim Nicholas Taleb, Random House, 2008.
3. *Antifragile: Things that Gain from Disorder*, Taleb, Nassim Nicholas, Random House publishers, 2012.
4. *Quantitative Finance*, Paul Wilmott, 2nd Edition, John Wiley & Sons, Ltd., 2006.
5. *Beyond Value at Risk, The New Science of Risk Management*, Kevin Dowd, John Wiley & Sons, 1999.
6. *VaR Applications: Setting VaR-based Limits*, Carlos Blanco and Sally Blomstrom, Financial Engineering Associates, Inc., May 1999.
7. *Investments*, Zvi Bodie, Alex Kane, Alan J. Marcus, 4th Edition, Irwin McGraw-Hill, 1999.
8. *Comparative Analyses of Expected Shortfall and Value-at-risk under Market Stress*, Yasuhiro Yamai and Toshinao Yoshiba, Bank of Japan, 2002.
9. *Capital Shortfall: A New Approach to Ranking and Regulating Systemic Risks*, Viral Acharya, Robert Engle, Matthew Richardson, March 14, 2012.
10. *Liquidity Risk Management*, Leonard M. Martz, Sheshunoff & Co., 2005.
11. *Risk Management and Financial Institutions*, John C. Hull, Low Price Edition, Pearson Education, Inc., 2007.
12. *Understanding Market, Credit and Operational Risk: The Value at Risk Approach*, Linda Allen, Jacob Boudoukh and Anthony Saunders, Blackwell Publishing, 2004.
13. *Mind on Statistics*, Utts and Heckard, 3rd Edition, Cengage Learning, 2006.
14. *Risk Management and Capital Allocation*, Reto Gallati, McGraw Hill, 2003.
15. *Integrating Corporate Risk Management*, Prakash A. Shimpi, 1st Edition, Texere, 2001.
16. *Modern Portfolio Theory and Investment Analysis*, Edwin J. Elton, Martin J. Gruber, 5th Edition, John Wiley & Sons, Inc., 1998.

17. *Back Office and Beyond: A Guide to Procedures, Settlements and Risk in Financial Markets*, Mervin J. King, Harriman House Ltd., GDP Publishers, 1999.
18. *Financial Risk Manager Handbook*, Phillipe Jorian, 5th Edition, John Wiley & Sons, 2009.
19. *Expected Shortfall: A Natural Coherent Alternative to Value at Risk* – Carlo Acerbi, Di.rk Tasche – May 9, 2001.
20. *Contemporary Financial Intermediation*, Greenbaum & Thakor, Dryden Press, 1997.
21. *Managing Financial Institutions*, Gardner, Mills, Cooperman, 5th Edition, Thomson South Western, 2004.
22. *The End of Wall Street*, Roger Lowenstein, Reprint edition, Penguin Books, 2011.
23. *The Big Short: Inside the Doomsday Machine*, Michael Lewis, W. W. Norton & Company, 2011.
24. *Boomerang*, Michael Lewis, W. W. Norton & Company, 2012.
25. *Models Behaving Badly*, Emanuel Derman, Free Press, 2011.
26. *Bull By the Horns*, Sheila Blair, Simon & Schuster, 2013.
27. *Asset & Risk Management*, Louis Esch, Robert Kieffer, Thierry Lopez, Wiley Finance, 2005.
28. *Modern Portfolio Theory & Investment Analysis*, Elton & Gruber, 8th Edition, John Wiley, 2009.
29. *Managing Credit Risk: The Great Challenge for Global Financial Markets*, John B. Caouette, Edward I. Altman, Paul Narayanan & Robert Nimmo, 2nd Edition, Wiley Finance, 2008.
30. *The Professional Risk Manager's Guide to Energy Markets*, Peter Fusaro, McGraw Hill, 2007.
31. *Value Added Risk Management*, David P. Belmot, 1st Edition, Wiley Finance, 2004.
32. *Internal Credit Risk Models: Capital Allocation and Performance Measurement*, Michael K. Ong, Risk Books, 1999.
33. *Case Problems in Finance*, Kester, Fruhan, Piper, Ruback, 11th Edition, Irwin/McGraw-Hill, 1997.
34. *The Handbook of Fixed Income Securities*, Frank J. Fabozzi, 7th Edition, McGraw-Hill, 2005.
35. Basel III: International Framework for Liquidity Risk Measurement, Standards and Monitoring – Basel Committee on Banking Supervision – December 2010. (http://www.bis.org/publ/bcbs188.pdf)
36. Principles for Sound Liquidity Risk Management and Supervision – Basel Committee on Banking Supervision – September 2008. (http://www.bis.org/publ/bcbs144.pdf)

37. Commonly Used Market Risk Limits, Guidelines on Risk Management of Derivatives and Other Traded Instruments, Annex D.

38. Establishing Exposure Limits for a Credit Portfolio, James V. Lentino, *The RMA Journal*, vol. 87, no. 10, 48–53, 6 pages, Jul/Aug 2005.

Part II   Monte Carlo Simulation

39. *The New Corporate Finance*, Donald H. Chew, McGraw Hill, 2001.

40. *Practical Methods of Optimization*, R. Fletcher, 2nd Edition, John Wiley & Sons, 2006.

41. *Monte Carlo Methods in Financial Engineering*, Paul Glasserman, Springer-Verlag New York, Inc., 2003.

42. Understanding $N(d_1)$ and $N(d_2)$: Risk-Adjusted Probabilities in the Black-Scholes Model, Lars Tyge Neilsen, 1992. (http://www.ltnielsen.com/wp-content/uploads/Understanding.pdf)

43. Higher-Order Simulations: Strategic Investment Under Model-Induced Price Patterns, Gilbert Peffer and Barbara Llacay, Journal of Artificial Societies and Social Simulation, vol. 10, no. 2, 6, 2007. (http://jasss.soc.surrey.ac.uk/10/2/6.html)

44. Quasi Monte Carlo Methods in Numerical Finance – Corwin Joy, Phelim P. Boyle and Ken Seng Tan, 1999. (Monographs – www.soa.org)

45. Quasi Monte Carlo Simulation, Marco Antonio Guimaraes Dias (http://www.puc-rio.br/marco.ind/quasi_mc.html).

46. Ladder Options, Benhamou Eric, Swaps Strategy, London, FICC, Goldman Sachs International (www.ericbenhamou.net/documents/Encyclo/Ladder%20option.pdf).

47. Valuation of Interest Sensitive Financial Instruments – SOA Monograph M-FI96-1 by David F. Babbel, Craig B. Merrill, 1996.

Part III   Dissecting Risk Models

48. Commodities: 2010 Outlook, Goldman Sachs, December 18, 2009.

49. Weekly Comment: Things to Ponder Over the Christmas Break, Economics, Goldman Sachs, December 18, 2009.

50. Global Oil & Gas Daily, J. P Morgan, December 24, 2009.

51. Global Metals & Mining Weekly Wrap-Up, J. P Morgan, December 18, 2009.

52. Gold & Precious Metals, J. P Morgan, December 18, 2009.

53. Precious metals as alternative FX reserve diversifiers, Global Metals Weekly, Bank of America Merrill Lynch, December 18, 2009.

54. 8 Reasons to Own Gold, Tony Daltorio.

55. A Forex Trader's View of the Aussie/Gold Relationship, Richard Lee.

56. Commodity Prices and Currency Movements, Kathy Lien.

57. Oil Price Patterns Portend Shrinking of Excess Stockpiles, Brian Baskin of Dow Jones Newswires, *Wall Street Journal*, September 30, 2009.

58. Energy Outlook: Crude Correlations and What Comes Next, Christine Birkner, Futures Mag.Com, October 2009.

59. Monthly Review on Price Indices, Statistics Division, Federal Bureau of Statistics, Government of Pakistan, December 2009 & January 2010.

60. Understanding Commodities Risk, 1st Edition, Jawwad A. Farid, Alchemy Publications, March 2010.

61. Risk Frameworks and Applications, 2nd Edition, Jawwad A. Farid, 2011.

62. Oil Prices and Inflation: Learning the Arithmetic Anew, Dr Benjarong Suwankiri and Dr Sutapa Amornvivat, Bangkok Post Business, February 2010.

63. Pakistan Risk Review, Volume 01, January 2010, Jawwad A. Farid, Alchemy Publications.

64. Pakistan Risk Review, Volume 04, September 2009, Jawwad A. Farid, Alchemy Publications.

65. Pakistan Risk Review, Volume 03, July 2009, Jawwad A. Farid, Alchemy Publications.

66. Pakistan Risk Review, Volume 02, May 2009, Jawwad A. Farid, Alchemy Publications.

67. Pakistan Risk Review, Volume 01, April 2009, Jawwad A. Farid, Alchemy Publications.

68. Short-term Energy Outlook – EIA – June 11, 2013.

Part IV   Derivative Pricing

69. *Interest Rate Swaps and Other Derivatives*, Howard Corb, Columbia University Press , 2012.

70. *Refresher in Option Pricing*, Howard Corb, Columbia University Press, 2012.

71. *Options, Futures and Other Derivatives*, John C. Hull, 7th Edition, Prentice Hall, 2009.

72. *Exotic Equity Derivatives Manual*, Salomon Smith Barney, August 1998.

73. *Dynamic Hedging, Managing Vanilla and Exotic Options*, Nassim Taleb, John Wiley & Sons, Inc., 1997.

74. *Currency Derivatives*, Edited by David F. DeRosa, John Wiley & Sons, Inc., 1998.

75. *Interest Rate Modelling*, Jessica James and Nick Webber, John Wiley & Sons Ltd, 2000.

76. *Fixed Income Securities*, Bruce Tuckman, 2nd Edition, John Wiley & Sons, Inc., 2002.
77. *Modelling Fixed-Income Securities and Interest Rate Options*, 2nd Edition, Robert A. Jarrow, Stanford Economics and Finance, 2002.
78. *Swaps/Financial Derivatives*, Volumes 1–4, Satiyajat Das, 3rd Edition, John Wiley & Sons, 2004.
79. *Risk Management & Derivatives*, Rene Stultz, 1st Edition, Thomson South-Western Publisher, 2003.
80. *Financial Modeling*, Simon Benninga, 3rd Edition, MIT Press, 2008.
81. *Financial Risk Management in Banking: The Theory of Application of Asset Liability Management*, Dennis G. Uyemura & Donald R. Van Deventer, BankLine Publication, 1993.
82. *Advance Modelling in Finance using Excel and VBA*, Mary Jackson & Mike Staunton, John Wiley & Sons, 2001.
83. *Fixed Income Securities and Derivates Handbook*, Moorad Choudry, Bloomberg Press, 2005.
84. Numerical Option Pricing, Mark Broadie and Paul Glasserman, Columbia University. (http://www4.gsb.columbia.edu/cbs-directory/detail/494921/Mark%20Broadie)
85. The Principles and Practices of Verifying Derivative Prices, Emanuel Derman, Goldman Sachs & Co. (http://www.emanuelderman.com/media/risk-price_verification.pdf)
86. TN 96-02. Risk Neutral Pricing in Discrete Time, D. M. Chance. (http://www.bus.lsu.edu/academics/finance/faculty/dchance/instructional/tn96-02.pdf)
87. The Boy's Guide to Pricing and Hedging, Emmanuel Derman, Columbia University. (http://www.emanuelderman.com/media/risk-the_boys_guide.pdf)

Index

Printed and bound by CPI Group (UK) Ltd, Croydon, CR0 4YY